636 COO

9 4575 00092614 8

W9-DBP-191

The Complete Beginner's Guide to Raising Small Animals

Everything You Ne
About Raising Cows, S
Ducks, Rabbits,

DATE DUE

JAN 2 6 2013	
MAR 1 8 201	
MAR 1 5 2013	
MAY 1 3 2013	
JUN 2 1 2013	
JUL 3 0 2013	
SEP 0 6 2014	
FEB 1 7 2015	
AUG 1 1 2016	
MAY 1 0 2019	

BRODART, CO.   Cat. No. 23-221

Carlotta Coo[

THE COMPLETE BEGINNER'S GUIDE TO RAISING SMALL ANIMALS: EVERYTHING YOU NEED TO KNOW ABOUT RAISING COWS, SHEEP, CHICKENS, DUCKS, RABBITS, AND MORE

Copyright © 2012 Atlantic Publishing Group, Inc.
1405 SW 6th Avenue • Ocala, Florida 34471 • Phone 800-814-1132 • Fax 352-622-1875
Web site: www.atlantic-pub.com • E-mail: sales@atlantic-pub.com
SAN Number: 268-1250

No part of this publication may be reproduced, stored in a retrieval system, or transmitted in any form or by any means, electronic, mechanical, photocopying, recording, scanning, or otherwise, except as permitted under Section 107 or 108 of the 1976 United States Copyright Act, without the prior written permission of the Publisher. Requests to the Publisher for permission should be sent to Atlantic Publishing Group, Inc., 1405 SW 6th Avenue, Ocala, Florida 34471.

Library of Congress Cataloging-in-Publication Data

Cooper, Carlotta, 1962-
  The complete beginner's guide to raising small animals : everything you need to know about raising cows, sheep, chickens, ducks, rabbits, and more / by: Carlotta Cooper.
     p. cm.
  ISBN-13: 978-1-60138-376-1 (alk. paper)
  ISBN-10: 1-60138-376-2 (alk. paper)
  1. Small animal culture. 2. Domestic animals. 3. Livestock. I. Title.
  SF65.2.C66 2011
  636--dc23
                    2011025762

LIMIT OF LIABILITY/DISCLAIMER OF WARRANTY: The publisher and the author make no representations or warranties with respect to the accuracy or completeness of the contents of this work and specifically disclaim all warranties, including without limitation warranties of fitness for a particular purpose. No warranty may be created or extended by sales or promotional materials. The advice and strategies contained herein may not be suitable for every situation. This work is sold with the understanding that the publisher is not engaged in rendering legal, accounting, or other professional services. If professional assistance is required, the services of a competent professional should be sought. Neither the publisher nor the author shall be liable for damages arising herefrom. The fact that an organization or Web site is referred to in this work as a citation and/or a potential source of further information does not mean that the author or the publisher endorses the information the organization or Web site may provide or recommendations it may make. Further, readers should be aware that Internet Web sites listed in this work may have changed or disappeared between when this work was written and when it is read.

TRADEMARK DISCLAIMER: All trademarks, trade names, or logos mentioned or used are the property of their respective owners and are used only to directly describe the products being provided. Every effort has been made to properly capitalize, punctuate, identify, and attribute trademarks and trade names to their respective owners, including the use of ® and ™ wherever possible and practical. Atlantic Publishing Group, Inc. is not a partner, affiliate, or licensee with the holders of said trademarks.

Printed in the United States

PROJECT MANAGER: Gretchen Pressley • gpressley@atlantic-pub.com
INTERIOR LAYOUT: Antoinette D'Amore • addesign@videotron.ca
COVER DESIGN: Meg Buchner • meg@megbuchner.com
COLOR INSERT & BACK COVER DESIGN: Jackie Miller • millerjackiej@gmail.com

Printed on Recycled Paper

A few years back we lost our beloved pet dog Bear, who was not only our best and dearest friend but also the "Vice President of Sunshine" here at Atlantic Publishing. He did not receive a salary but worked tirelessly 24 hours a day to please his parents.

Bear was a rescue dog who turned around and showered myself, my wife, Sherri, his grandparents Jean, Bob, and Nancy, and every person and animal he met (well, maybe not rabbits) with friendship and love. He made a lot of people smile every day.

We wanted you to know a portion of the profits of this book will be donated in Bear's memory to local animal shelters, parks, conservation organizations, and other individuals and nonprofit organizations in need of assistance.

– Douglas & Sherri Brown

PS: We have since adopted two more rescue dogs: first Scout, and the following year, Ginger. They were both mixed golden retrievers who needed a home.

Want to help animals and the world? Here are a dozen easy suggestions you and your family can implement today:

- *Adopt and rescue a pet from a local shelter.*
- *Support local and no-kill animal shelters.*
- *Plant a tree to honor someone you love.*
- *Be a developer — put up some birdhouses.*
- *Buy live, potted Christmas trees and replant them.*
- *Make sure you spend time with your animals each day.*
- *Save natural resources by recycling and buying recycled products.*
- *Drink tap water, or filter your own water at home.*
- *Whenever possible, limit your use of or do not use pesticides.*
- *If you eat seafood, make sustainable choices.*
- *Support your local farmers market.*
- *Get outside. Visit a park, volunteer, walk your dog, or ride your bike.*

Five years ago, Atlantic Publishing signed the Green Press Initiative. These guidelines promote environmentally friendly practices, such as using recycled stock and vegetable-based inks, avoiding waste, choosing energy-efficient resources, and promoting a no-pulping policy. We now use 100-percent recycled stock on all our books. The results: in one year, switching to post-consumer recycled stock saved 24 mature trees, 5,000 gallons of water, the equivalent of the total energy used for one home in a year, and the equivalent of the greenhouse gases from one car driven for a year.

Dedication

This book is dedicated to my own animals,
who always give me a reason to get up in the morning,
like it or not.

Acknowledgment

I would like to thank several people for their help while I worked on this book. My thanks to James Weaver for his patience and kindness. Thanks to editors Amy Moczynski and Gretchen Pressley for all of their hard work and encouragement. Thanks to the Greeneville/Greene County Public Library in Greeneville, Tennessee, and to their staff for their help. And, thanks once again to my friend Donna Fefee for allowing me to discuss livestock and agriculture with her, as well as for being a supportive friend.

Table of Contents

Introduction

By most estimates, the concept of human civilization really begins when people transitioned from a nomadic hunter-gatherer lifestyle to that of a more settled way of living in one place. This was made possible by the growth of crops and the domestication of many of the animals we still use on farms today. Early agriculture and the domestication of animals are dated to around 10,000 to 12,000 years ago in Mesopotamia, part of the "Fertile Crescent" of the Middle East. The agricultural way of life and the domestication of animals soon spread to Egypt and India. Agriculture and the domestication of animals are believed to have developed independently at similar times in parts of China, Africa, and places on the American continent. Early crops included wheat, barley, and rice in different places.

The first animal domesticated was probably the dog because it was useful as a hunting companion, a livestock guardian, and a protector, among other things, but other animals soon followed. With humans living in settlements, it became possible to keep herds of animals or contain them in pens. Humans were able to begin practicing selective breeding in order to develop animals that were most helpful to them. A wide range of animal traits was possible, depending on where people lived and what specialties they required. For instance, they could breed larger versions of cows so they would have more meat or breed sheep with more wool so they would have more fiber to spin and sell.

The development of agriculture and the domestication of animals were key to developing human economies because people were able to trade or barter for animals or the products produced from them. Milk, meat, cheese, wool, and other staples commonly were bought and sold at markets. Vegetables and grain crops also could be sold. Agriculture required people to create new inventions such as the plow to make working easier and more productive. Farming and agriculture are even more important today than they were thousands of years ago, and our domestic farm animals still play a vital role in producing the food and products we need. The agricultural revolution that began some 12,000 years ago, which included raising domestic farm animals, lasted for thousands of years, and it continues today as farmers study genetics, chemistry, and the environment and look for new solutions to feed the world.

Types of Animals Covered in This Book

In *The Complete Beginner's Guide To Raising Small Animals*, we will cover all of the animals you might be interested in raising on a farm, from keeping a few rabbits or chickens to taking on some cattle to raise for their meat or milk. It is possible to keep some of these animals in your backyard as long as your local zoning and laws allow you to do so. However, some of the animals will be too large and require too much pasture to live in a suburban setting. It is best to consider how much room animals require and the other things they need before you start your venture.

We will cover in detail rabbits, chickens, ducks and geese, pigs, goats, sheep, and cattle. Some of these animals have multiple uses such as producing milk, meat, and fiber. All of them can be eaten for meat, and their meat can be sold for profit, although there is a bigger demand for some kinds of meat than others. For instance, there may not be a big demand if you intend to sell geese for their meat because goose is not commonly served in the U.S. However, you may be able to find a niche market for your geese.

Some of these animals produce eggs. Chicken eggs can be sold to bring in additional income, but there might not be much demand for duck and especially geese eggs because of their large size. These eggs have a different flavor from chicken eggs and few recipes that call for them. Again, these are things to consider before you purchase your animals.

Several animals also produce milk: goats, sheep, and cows. We will discuss milking your animals and selling their milk. Selling raw milk is a hot button issue in many areas, and we will go into this issue. You also can make other dairy products from the milk, such as cheese, yogurt, ice cream, and even soap from goat's milk.

Goats and sheep can provide fiber, especially if you choose breeds that produce desirable fibers for wool. You will need to learn to shear your animals and find outlets to sell the material.

We will cover these topics in this book to help you select your animals wisely and know what to do with them after you bring them home.

A Few Things to Expect When Starting Out

When you are first starting out, you can expect to make some mistakes. Everyone does. You may get too many animals or wish you had bought more. You may not like the breed you start with. You may hate your housing. Your animals may laugh at your fences. There likely will be a few things you will wish to change or improve after you start, and that is perfectly normal. It is part of farming to make changes from season to season or year to year. The important thing is for you to learn and grow from everything you do with your animals. You may consider something a mistake but what you are really gaining is valuable farming experience. There is no farmer anywhere who has not made mistakes. That is how we learn and how experience is gained.

Warnings About Raising Small Animals

If this is your first encounter with farm animals, you might be in for some surprises. Animals are not usually the way they are portrayed in films. You may not even get a good idea about them from books or other sources. There is no substitute for real, hands-on work with animals. Whether you think animals are cute, or you see them as a way to supplement your income, they are real, living, breathing creatures, just like people. This is not to say they are the same as humans — they are not — but each one is different. They have likes and dislikes. They do interesting things. There is usually a reason why an animal does something. In order to understand why animals do things, you need to consider things from the animal's point of view.

It is a mistake to assume your animals see things or feel things the same way that humans do. Cattle see the world in cattle terms. Rabbits see the world in rabbit terms. There is nothing wrong with that. You should always treat your animals with respect and dignity. Treat them well, but remember that they are animals and not people. Thinking of the animals as though they are human is only likely to confuse them and make them unhappy.

No matter how well you treat your animals, there always will be some people and some groups who will try to find fault with you and with animal agriculture in general. Treat your animals well. Follow the laws as they apply to you, and your animals and you can go to bed at night with a clear conscience.

Benefits of Raising Small Animals

There are many benefits of raising small animals. There are the obvious financial benefits than can come from raising animals for profit, whether you are raising them for meat, milk, or fiber production. There is the also great benefit that comes from being able to raise your own animals for personal consumption and knowing exactly where your meat and milk come from and how they were produced. Living a life with animals can be deeply satisfying. Most people today do not know the joy that comes from assisting an animal to bring a newborn into the world. They do not know the pleasure that comes from watching young animals grow and mature while knowing you may have their parents and even grandparents living with you. You know that these young animals are the link to the next generation. There is a deep sense of continuity that comes from raising generations of animals. You can feel connected to the animals and to the land in a way that most people have forgotten. You know where food comes from. You have worked to produce it. You can be grateful to the animals. These are important things to know and to appreciate. That is one of the most important benefits that comes from raising animals. It is good for your soul. It makes you a better person.

Chapter 1

Raising Small Animals 101

hether you intend to have a few chickens in your backyard or you are thinking of opening a dairy farm, there are some basic things to know about raising animals. You need to be prepared before you go out and buy any.

About Small Animals

No matter what kind of animal interests you, all animals require shelter, containment, and feed. Without these basics, your animals will be in trouble. Take time to make sure you have these requirements in place before bringing home any animals. This book describes housing, pens and fences, and feeding for all of the animals, so do your homework before you start.

You will need to know the laws as they apply to keeping animals in your situation. Laws vary widely by location and by animal. You will find some laws described in this book for each animal but laws change rapidly, especially at the local level. For example, a town council can meet in just two or three sessions and change the law about whether you can keep chickens in your town. You will need to check carefully to make sure you are able to keep the kind of animals you are considering where you live.

Talk to your neighbors. This is a key piece of advice that can spare you a lot of trouble later. Although you may find your honking geese fascinating or think that your pigs are adorable, your neighbors may not share your views. Even if your neighbors are normally animal lovers, they may change their mind if there is a manure pile within sight of their front door or runoff from your farm into their stream. Take time to talk to them, and go over your plans. Work out any difficulties before you bring animals to your property. You may want to offer your neighbors something to make them more agreeable to your plans such as a share of your meat, a supply of eggs, or cheese that you plan to make. Consider your neighbors when you lay out your pens and buildings so they will not be subject to runoff or things that are too unsightly.

Raising Small Animals as Pets

Raising animals as pets can be fun for you and for your entire family. You do not need to make a large investment or buy a lot of animals. In most cases, you simply need a breeding pair. In some cases, you only need a young female animal, and you can contract for stud service. Rabbits, chickens, ducks, and even pigs and goats often are kept as pets. Pigs and goats have pygmy varieties, if you are interested in keeping a smaller version of these animals.

You will need to care for animals as pets in much the same way that you would care for them if they were being raised for consumption. They have the same requirements of shelter, containment, and feed. However, in some cases, people prefer to keep pets indoors at least part of the time. Rabbits often are allowed free run of the home, or they are caged indoors. There are diapers for chickens kept indoors. Pigs are highly intelligent and can be house trained as easily as dogs.

You will need to socialize your animals and teach them some manners animals kept for consumption do not usually learn. "Manners" may mean some house training lessons and social training that will result in them allowing you to pick them up and pet them, eating and drinking from their own special dishes, sleeping in an area set aside for them in the house or yard, and so on. They also will need to learn to get along with, or be protected from, other household pets, such as dogs and cats. Rabbits, chickens, and ducks will be at particular risk from cats and dogs, so they should be raised with other pets starting when the other animals are young so there is less chance of them being injured.

Many of these animals can be taught to walk on a leash and learn other commands. Even chickens can be trained.

Raising Small Animals for Profit

Space and budget considerations are usually important if you are considering raising animals for profit. You will need to know how much room you have so you can know how many animals you can keep. This will affect all of the other decisions you make, such as what breed you get and how you raise the animals. Will you buy young animals and raise them to maturity? Will you buy several adults and breed them? Once you know how much space you have, you can start making your decisions.

Raising animals for profit usually involves a financial investment beyond buying the animals. You will need housing for them and fencing or pens; you will need to arrange for feed or good pasture; and you may need to purchase or rent tools so you can put up housing or fencing. Planning is important. You need to keep track of expenditures because you will be trying to produce enough meat, milk, and/or fiber to cover your expenses. You may not break even in the beginning. If you are operating your farm as a business, talk to an accountant about how to make these investments in farm equipment work for you on your taxes.

If you are raising animals for profit, you do need to report your income to the government. Even if you operate at a loss, you need to file your taxes. There is a special tax form for people engaged in farming. Get Publication 225 from the IRS for more detailed information: **www.irs.gov/publications/p225/ar01.html**. It is a good idea to talk to an accountant about reporting your taxes as a farmer, especially if you have not filled out this kind of form before. Without professional assistance, you might miss deductions.

Raising Small Animals for Personal Use

Raising animals for personal use is becoming increasingly popular in the U.S. as more and more people become concerned about their health and the source of their food. They may want to have fresh eggs from their own chickens. They may want to have their own meat from animals carefully raised under conditions they can control and fed the way they want the animals to be fed. When you raise your own animals, you know with a great degree of certainty what the animal eats and how the animal is treated. You know the animal has not been fed antibiotics or growth hormones you may find objectionable. Raising your own animals for personal use can provide you with peace of mind as well as healthy food.

When you raise animals for your personal use, you also can have the pleasure of spending time with them. Many people enjoy farming on this small scale. Perhaps you want to keep a few animals to find out if you would like to become more deeply involved in farming. Or perhaps you are content to have just a few animals and raise them for your own table. You can sell or barter extra meat, eggs, or milk if you have more than you can use. If you are raising animals for their meat, it helps to have a large freezer so you can freeze meat for the months ahead when you might not have any animals to harvest.

Most people who raise animals genuinely like the animals, so it can be hard to reconcile yourself to the knowledge you will be harvesting some of them for meat. It is easy to become attached to pigs, beef cattle, and other animals usually sent to the butcher, and it can be hard to say goodbye. However, animals such as cattle, pigs, and sheep were domesticated to be raised as a source of food for humans. Remember that much of the world's food supply depends on harvesting animals, and it is normal to use these animals for meat. Most people discover the advantages of raising their own animals far outweigh the sadness of sending their animals to the butcher.

If you are raising chickens for eggs, or cows, goats, or even sheep for milk or other dairy products, your job will be different. Collecting eggs and milking animals on a daily basis often will require more daily work than is needed with animals being raised for meat. Meat animals often can be pasture raised or only minimally supplemented with grain. They do not need much daily tending beyond making sure they have food and water and that manure is picked up. Animals that produce eggs or milk and other dairy products, however, will need daily attention if you plan to keep things running smoothly.

Raising animals for personal use is a wonderful way to find out if farming is something you would like to pursue. You can learn a great deal about farming from this approach, as well as enjoy excellent meat, eggs, and dairy products, not to mention being able to produce your own wool from sheep and goats. You can start with just one or two animals and see how you like it. Who knows? You may end up farming for the rest of your life.

Chapter 2

Rabbits

RABBIT GLOSSARY	
Buck: An adult male rabbit	**Kindle (kindling):** Term used to for rabbits giving birth
Coprophagia: An act in which an animal eats its own fecal matter. Rabbits need to do this to acquire needed nutrients.	**Kit:** A newborn or very young rabbit
	Nest box: A box used to give a doe privacy and security when she gives birth
Doe: An adult female rabbit	
Fryer: A young rabbit about 8 to 12 weeks old and 4 ½ pounds that is ready to be butchered	**Pelt:** The skin of an animal with the hair or fur still attached

R aising rabbits can be a fun way to introduce mammals to a small-scale farm. As most people know, rabbits can multiply quickly, but as with any animal, improper management can lead to loss due to sick animals, predation, and poor reproductive performance. Starting out with a small colony can expose you to the day-to-day management of rabbits to see if you really do have the stick-to-it attitude needed for rabbit production.

History of Rabbits and People

The domestic rabbits we have today are all descendants of the wild European rabbit. The wild European rabbit (Oryctolagus) began developing some 6.5 million years ago and developed in Europe's Iberian Peninsula. By 12,000 years ago, humans were hunting rabbits as a source of food. The Phoenicians referred to rabbits in the Iberian Peninsula about 1000 BC. Rabbit domestication is said to have begun at this time.

Rabbits were raised in ancient Rome for meat and pelts. The Romans also are thought to have selectively bred an Angora rabbit for its long hair to be used for yarn. During the Middle Ages, French monks practiced selective breeding in rabbits to maximize the desirable traits such as size and coat color. Rabbit pelts and meat were a valuable food and clothing source in monasteries. From this start, different breeds were developed slowly until the 18th and 19th centuries, when breed development took off to the point that there are currently more than 100 breeds of rabbits worldwide.

The European wild rabbit is the only species of rabbit that has been domesticated. In some parts of the world, the European wild rabbit is still a pest. Twenty-four such rabbits introduced into Australia in 1859 grew to 600 million rabbits in the course of a century and became destructive pests in the country. All breeds of rabbits kept today as pets, raised for fur, and kept for meat are the result of careful selective breeding of the European wild rabbit.

Domesticated rabbits are typically much larger than the original European wild rabbit. The European wild rabbit is usually a small animal, about 13 to 18 inches long and weighing just 3 to 5 pounds. They are gray-brown color. Domesticated rabbits today have been bred selectively to be much larger in most cases. They come in many colors and color combinations. Where the European wild rabbit has long ears that stand straight up, domestic rabbit breeds might have pendulous or "lop" ears that hang down beside their faces, or they may have long ears that stand straight up.

Despite their legendary reproductive abilities, the European wild rabbit has a precarious existence in some places in Europe due to predators and urbanization. As a species, they are "near threatened" in Portugal," one of the places where they originated, and "vulnerable" in Spain. Because of their declines in population, the World Conservation Union has labeled the European wild rabbit as "near threatened" in its native area.

Today, Italy and France maintain a relatively high demand for rabbit meat and lead the world in rabbit production.

Domesticated Rabbits in the United States

In the U.S. today, rabbits are raised as pets, for commercial purposes (food, fur), and for use as laboratory animals. Some people enjoy raising rabbits as a hobby. They may raise rabbits for rabbit shows, to eat at home, to sell as pets, or to provide them as 4-H and FFA project animals. Per capita U.S. meat consumption of rabbit meat was .02 pounds in 2000. In the U.S., people usually have purchased rabbit meat at retail grocery stores or at fancier restaurants but that may be changing as rabbit meat becomes more available at farmers markets and ethnic grocery stores. Most rabbit growers do not have industry groups or national representatives, so rabbit production is often hard to gauge and track.

Hobby rabbit breeders raise and sell rabbits for the same reasons as other rabbit growers. They raise and sell rabbits for showing, home meat consumption, direct pet sales, and fur production. The American Rabbit Breeders Association (ARBA) sponsors 4,000 rabbit shows per year. An annual, national show, with entries from around the country, can draw as many as 20,000 rabbits and their owners. Show breeders travel to show, spend money on hotels and restaurants, sell rabbits to other enthusiasts and to pet rabbit owners, breed their rabbits, consume their own meat rabbits, and harvest the wool from long-haired rabbit breeds. Commercial rabbit breeders sometimes keep small rabbit herds for show purposes but, in general, industry groups advocate maintaining a separation between breeding for fancy show rabbits and commercial rabbits.

The exact number of rabbits kept in the U.S for various purposes is unknown, according to the United States Department of Agriculture. They track some rabbit industry populations as they impact meat inspections and sales, but they

estimate that they inspect only about a quarter of the rabbit meat that is slaughtered in the U.S. The rest is slaughtered for personal consumption. In 2001, the USDA estimated that about 2 million rabbits were slaughtered. They further estimated that 2.2 million households owned 5 million pet rabbits. There were more than 250,000 rabbits involved in laboratory research. 4-H and FFA (Future Farmers of America) programs had one million rabbits involved in their projects. Hobby rabbit breeders, represented by the ARBA, raised and showed nearly one million rabbits per year. The USDA concluded that the total domestic rabbit population in the U.S. in 2000 was about 9 million rabbits.

According to the American Pet Products Association in their 2009/2010 National Pet Owners Survey, 5.3 million U.S. households owned 15.9 million "small animals." The survey does not distinguish among rabbits, gerbils, hamsters, and other small animals, however. The American Veterinary Medical Association estimates that 1.8 million U.S. households own 6.1 million pet rabbits, as per their 2007 U.S Pet Ownership & Demographics Sourcebook. Rabbits are considered an "exotic" animal.

Compared to the cattle industry, or the poultry industry, the value of the rabbit industry in the U.S. is very small. In 2000, cattle were marketed for $41 billion. Meat rabbits were marketed for between $7 and 8 million. Retail sales of rabbit meat sold for between $16 and 20 million. Sales of rabbits as pets are more valuable. In 2000, rabbits sold as pets accounted for $612 million. Pet owners spent $75 billion on pet supplies that year, according to the American Pet Products Manufacturers' Association. Even sales of rabbit fur and wool are relatively modest. Total value for rabbit industry products in 2000 to 2001 was between $745 million and $831 million.

Purebred rabbits can be used as breeding stock to establish a small-scale young rabbit selling operation. Another business to explore is selling rabbit meat to specialty markets or gourmet restaurants. Rabbit meat producers find that having 40 does will give them a good return on their investment. Rabbit manure also can be used as a fertilizer. Pelts can be sold or used for high-end fashions. A requirement for any small-scale farming business is to generate a reliable, healthy flow of rabbits. This can be accomplished by purchasing healthy stock, choosing the right breed of rabbits, keeping a breeding schedule, and maintaining your rabbits in the best health possible. To begin, you will need to decide which breed will fit best with your plans.

Breeds

There are more than 100 recognized breeds of rabbits. Rabbits range in size from the mini, which weigh as little as 2 pounds as adults, up to the giant breeds, which can weigh more than 20 pounds. Following is a listing of some of the more common breeds of rabbits that you should be able to obtain easily to start a small-scale rabbit-raising operation:

Pet breeds

Dutch: The Dutch rabbit is an old breed developed in England. It comes in six colors: gray, tortoiseshell, steel, chocolate, brown, and black. All colors have a band of white around the chest, a wedge-shaped patch of white on the face, and white on the tips of the hind feet. The Dutch rabbit weighs about 4 pounds when mature. They make good pet rabbits.

Flemish Giant: This is the largest breed of rabbit. When mature, it will weigh more than 14 pounds; some rabbits are more than 22 pounds when full grown. It is a popular pet rabbit and comes in a variety of colors.

Netherland Dwarf: The Netherland Dwarf is the smallest breed of rabbit, weighing in at only 2 pounds when full grown. It comes in a vast variety of colors. The Netherland Dwarf is primarily a pet rabbit due to its small size and its baby bunny-like appearance. Males can become dominant over much larger rabbits, but they can become tame for people.

Meat breeds

American Sable: The American Sable is a beautiful, dark brown rabbit with darker coloring around the legs, ears, face, and tail. It weighs about 9 pounds when mature. The Sable makes a good meat and pelt production rabbit.

Californian: The Californian rabbit is a large rabbit weighing 9 pounds when mature. It has white fur, and its tail, feet, ears, and nose are black. It is a good meat production rabbit.

New Zealand: The New Zealand is a large, albino rabbit weighing about 10 pounds when mature. Its name is misleading as it was developed in the United States. It is a common rabbit used for meat and fur. It is also a popular animal used for scientific research purposes. The visibility of the peripheral vasculature, or veins and arteries, in albino rabbits is advantageous for the biomedical use of this rabbit. This rabbit has red, black, or white fur.

Fur breeds

Angora: The Angora breed has actually four different sub-breeds of rabbits: the English Angora, Satin Angora, the French Angora, and the Giant Angora. The English Angora, despite its name, originated in Turkey. It comes in many colors and weighs about 6 pounds when mature. The Satin Angora has a silkier coat than the other types and weighs 7 pounds at maturity. The French Angora is similar to the English Angora in color but is heavier. The Giant Angora has the most fur of the Angoras. It weighs about 9 pounds when mature. All of these breeds have been valued for their fine fur production.

Satin: This rabbit has a soft and shiny fur coat. It comes in many different colors. The Satin weighs about 9 pounds when mature. In addition to having a great pelt, they make good meat production rabbits.

Whichever breed you chose, you should purchase your rabbits carefully from a reputable breeder. You can find a listing of these breeders from state or regional rabbit associations or by attending rabbit shows and asking exhibitors for advice. The breeder should have careful records on each rabbit that show its pedigree and its mother's and father's production records.

Rabbit Husbandry

If you are raising rabbits for meat or for their pelts, the cuteness and cuddliness of rabbits might work against you when it comes time to sell or butcher the offspring of your breeding rabbits. Before you begin, you will want to do some market research to make sure you will be able to sell your stock at a profit — you would not want to invest the time and effort raising rabbits if there are not people ready to buy the meat or live rabbits. There may be a rabbit association in your state or region that can give you an idea of the demand. Your county extension agent will be able to direct you to the right group. Once you link up with an association, ask them what breed of rabbit sells the best in your area. You should also ask if there is a nearby rabbit raiser who would let you tour their operation. They will be a good source to inquire about new or used equipment dealers. Finding a market for your rabbits can be difficult, so start early, and look hard for a reliable, steady sales outlook.

A few things about rabbits might surprise you. Most people are familiar with rabbit pellets — the rabbit's normal round stool. However, rabbits also pass a soft stool, called a cecotrope, which is produced in the rabbit's cecum. The rabbit will eat the cecotrope — which is full of needed nutrients — and most rabbit owners may not even see this stool in the pen. This is a natural function and should not be confused with diarrhea.

Also, rabbits' hind legs are very powerful, giving this prey animal a powerful spurt of speed to outrun predators. Rabbits on open ground can reach speeds of 25 miles per hour when being pursued. Their front legs are adapted for digging, either to dig a hole to hide from predators or to dig burrows to live in. In the wild, rabbits live in groups in a collection of burrows, or a warren. Rabbits are social animals, but they need to bond before they can live peacefully with other rabbits. It can sometimes take several weeks or even months for two rabbits to bond. They will fight over territory or mating, a trait that can make introducing new rabbits into an established group difficult. The easiest way for rabbits to bond is

when they are raised together from a young age. You can also help rabbits bond by placing them together in a neutral place to reduce territorial feelings. You can place the rabbits together in the neutral area for a short time each day until the rabbits begin accepting each other. You should watch the rabbits and be ready to intervene if there is any fighting. Once the rabbits accept each other, you can place them in a normal cage or hutch.

Buying Rabbits

You can buy rabbits from a number of sources: pet stores, newspaper ads, Craigslist (**www.craigslist.org**), and flea markets, for example. However, if you are serious about breeding rabbits, whether as pets or for meat or their pelts, it is usually best to purchase your rabbits directly from another breeder. You can find rabbit breeders by checking the Internet on sites such as The Nature Trail Rabbitry (**www.thenaturetrail.com/Local-Rabbit-Breeder.htm**), Raising-Rabbits.com (**www.raising-rabbits.com/rabbits-for-sale.html**), and the American Rabbit Breeders Association (**www.arba.net/ Breeders.php**). You will have access to better quality rabbits this way. You will be able to find a wider variety of breeds from which to choose, and you can select exactly the kind of rabbits that suit your needs. Buying from a good breeder will put you in touch with someone knowledgeable about rabbits. The breeder can provide you with information about how to raise and care for rabbits, and the breeder can answer specific questions about the breed that interests you. Let the breeder know that you are looking for breeding quality rabbits. He or she can be a good contact for you in the future.

When purchasing rabbits, make sure you buy healthy stock. Check to make sure the rabbit's eyes and nose are free of any discharge that could indicate illness. The ears should be clean and free of wax or any crusting from fleas or mites. The rabbit's front paws should be clean. Rabbits use their paws to clean themselves. If the paws are dirty with any discharge, it could indicate that the animal has been sick. The rabbit's stomach and tail should be free of any fecal matter, which could indicate gastrointestinal stasis or other stomach problems. Check the rabbit's teeth to make sure there is no malocclusion or ulcers. The rabbit's coat should appear healthy. Even if the rabbit has been shedding, the fur should be clean, and there should not be any parasites.

Handling Rabbits

You should never pick a rabbit up by the ears. This can hurt their ears, and they will kick, potentially injuring their backs, which may lead to paralysis or death. Instead, gently slide one hand under its chest and the other underneath its rump. Lift the rabbit using the hand under the chest while scooping with the hand under the rump. Pull the rabbit toward your body and slide the rabbit along the arm supporting his chest. Gently press the rabbit against your body, much like a football is held, with the arm supporting the body and the head tucked under the elbow. Try to handle your rabbits frequently, at least two to three times a week, so they get used to being held and so you can check their health. Their back feet are powerful, and if they feel frightened or insecure in your grasp, they will kick.

Housing and Feeding Rabbits

Rabbits typically are raised in cages as opposed to pens or loose in buildings. The cages can be either single tier or double tier. Single-tier cages make cleaning and observation easier. Double-tier cages are more economical as you can keep twice as many rabbits under one roof. Cages should be constructed of 14-gauge welded wire with ½- by 1-inch mesh. Any mesh smaller than that will make cleaning difficult, as manure will not be able to fall through. If you have a double-tier cage, the upper tier of cages will need a sided-catch pan of stainless steel to catch manure.

SUGGESTED CAGE SIZES	
Small breed	2 ½ x 2 ½ ft.
Medium breed	2 ½ x 3 ft.
Large breed	2 ½ x 4 ft.

Cages should be placed in a well-ventilated building on ground with good drainage. They can be suspended from the ceiling, but supporting legs will make the cages more stable. The roof of the cage should be insulated to reduce heat absorption in the summer and condensation in the winter. Heat is not usually needed in the winter unless rabbits **kindle** (give birth) during subzero weather. If you plan to have cages facing each other, have an aisle with a minimum width of 3 feet. Allow a generous space at the end of the aisle to be able to turn around a wheelbarrow or cart, which you will need to clean the rabbit manure. Lighting should be provided for 16 hours a day to help prevent breeding problems in the fall and winter — 25-watt lights are sufficient.

Feeding

Many styles and varieties of waterers and feeders are available for rabbits. A bottle waterer that attaches to the outside of the cage along with a metal feeder with an outside feed chute makes feeding and watering easy, as individual cage doors do not need to be opened. After rabbits are 3 months old, they should be segregated by sex, two to a cage. After age 5 months, each rabbit should have its own cage. This will prevent fighting and give each rabbit its own private area.

The best food for rabbits is a commercial rabbit pellet. This food is a complete feed, so using supplemental salt or other feeds is not needed with pellets. Try to purchase only enough pellets for one month of feeding, and check the bags for a recent production date when you purchase the pellets. This way you will keep your feed supply as fresh as possible because certain vitamins and some fats can deteriorate quickly after production.

Rabbits prefer to eat at night, so a good time to feed your rabbits is in the evening. Check the feeders daily for any wet or moldy feed. Empty as needed before refilling the feeders. The biggest health problem a rabbit has is overfeeding. Large-breed rabbits need 4 to 6 ounces of pellets once a day. Small rabbits (dwarf type) need only 2 ounces of pellets a day.

Rabbits should have access to good, leafy alfalfa hay at all times. The hay should be checked often to make sure it does not become moldy. A pregnant or lactating **doe** (female rabbit) should have all the feed she wants. While her young are still with her (up to 8 weeks), they all should have **free-choice feed** (feed that is available at all times) along with plenty of water. If young bucks or does are being raised as breeding rabbits, they should be fed 1 ounce of feed daily for each pound of body weight.

Rabbit health

Good nutrition; sound breeding stock; regular cleaning and disinfecting of cages, feeders, and waterers; and weekly manure removal will go a long way toward ensuring your rabbits will remain in optimal health. Keeping your rabbit housing well ventilated and in good repair are part of keeping rabbits as healthy as they can be. The building and feed supply should be rodent, predator, and bird proof. Cages and feeding and watering equipment should be disinfected on a regular basis. **Nest boxes**, or a box in a cage where an expectant doe prepares to give birth and raises her offspring for several weeks, should be disinfected after each litter and before placing the expectant does in the cage. All manure and debris should be scraped from the item being disinfected before being scrubbed with a disinfecting solution. Bleach water, vinegar, or a commercial disinfectant can be used. After disinfecting, the item should be allowed to dry thoroughly before being placed into use. Letting the item dry in the sunlight lends an additional level of sanitation.

Despite all this attention, occasionally some health problems may crop up in your rabbits. To minimize losses, observe all your rabbits every day. Are they eating their feed and drinking their water? Does the manure under the pen appear normal? Are their eyes clear and noses free from discharge? Do they act interested in your presence at the front of their cage? Many diseases are hard to detect with just a brief visual observation. You should examine your rabbits closely at least once a week by handling them and checking their ears, toenails, and teeth. The ears should be clean and dry. The toenails should not be overly long. The teeth should not be long or cutting into the roof of the mouth.

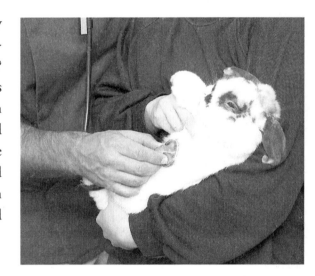

Common Rabbit Illnesses

Common health problems include ear mange, coccidiosis, and pasteurellosis. Many diseases are spread by introducing new animals into an established herd. New animals should be quarantined from the main herd for 14 days and observed for any sign of disease during this time. If you do find a sick animal, either a new arrival or one from your established herd, the sick rabbit should be isolated from the rest of the rabbits, preferably in a different building. The sick animal should be cared for only after you have taken care of the healthy rabbits. Wash your hands and disinfect your shoes after caring for the sick animals. If the rabbit dies, its carcass should be burned or buried to stop the spread of diseases. Any pens and equipment used for caring for the sick rabbit should be cleaned and disinfected before being reused.

Coccidiosis: This disease is caused by a protozoa parasite. Coccidiosis affects the liver and intestine of rabbits and causes diarrhea, loss of appetite, and weight loss. Occasionally a rabbit will die from coccidiosis. It is spread through fecal contamination of cages, waterers, and feeders, so daily cleaning of these items will help reduce the incidence of coccidiosis. Treatment is through feeding a medicated feed for two to three weeks to reduce the number of parasites.

Conjunctivitis (pink eye): Young rabbits are commonly affected by conjunctivitis, especially those that are raised in crowded conditions. Bacteria invade the conjunctiva (the red lining around the eye) and cause infection. The eye then becomes red and swollen. A thick discharge collects around the eye frequently, pasting the eye shut. One or both eyes may be affected. You can treat the affected area by gently washing the eyelid with a warm washcloth to remove the discharge, flushing the eye with sterile saline, and treating the eyes with an eye antibiotic ointment.

Ear mites: Ear mites are the most common external parasite of rabbits. Mites invade the ear and thick, brown crusts of serum accumulate inside the ear. The rabbit shakes its head and scratches its ears due to the intense itching. When the rabbit tries to scratch the itch, the toenails on the hind feet cause scratches to the outside of the ear, as well. Serious infections can cause weight loss, nerve damage, and ear infection due to bacterial invasion. Even if only one rabbit in your herd is showing signs of an ear mite infection, all rabbits should be treated because it is so easy for the mites to pass from rabbit to rabbit. If there is a lot of debris built up in the ear, mineral oil should be placed in the ear to soften the debris. The material should then be wiped out with a cotton ball. Medication is readily available in the form of eardrops, which you can pick up at your local veterinarian's office. Each ear should be treated and the base of the ear massaged after applying the drug.

Enterotoxemia: This disease is characterized by an explosive diarrhea. It usually occurs in young rabbits 1 to 2 months old. The rabbits may be normal one day, and then found dead the next. It is caused by a bacterium, *Clostridium spiroforme*, which releases a deadly toxin causing death in one to two days after infection. How the rabbits are infected with these bacteria is not entirely known, but it is thought that giving rabbits extra fiber such as supplemental hay will help reduce the disease occurrence. Giving rabbits penicillin will also cause enterotoxemia.

External parasites (fleas, mites): Rabbits generally have mites on their skin, which usually does not become a problem unless the animal becomes unhealthy. Then the mites can flourish, causing intense itching, hair loss, and sores. To treat external parasites, apply a cat flea powder weekly. This treatment is also effective against the rabbit flea, a seldom-encountered parasite in domestic rabbits. If your rabbit does have fleas, its environment will need to be treated with an insecticide to destroy flea eggs and larva.

Fungal infections: Rabbits can harbor fungus that cause skin lesions. These fungi also can be transmitted by and to humans. A rabbit with a fungal infection will have patchy hair loss, usually around the nose, eyelids, ears, and face. The affected skin may also become thick and have yellow crusts. Usually, a young rabbit will show more severe hair loss and skin changes. Treatment consists of spot treatment of affected areas with an antifungal ointment. If many rabbits are affected, oral medication can be given.

Hutch burn: This condition is caused by rabbits being subjected to wet and dirty floors. The anus and genital region of the rabbit become chapped and red. The damp condition irritates these delicate membranes, and soon, they become infected with a secondary bacterial infection. There is no reason for this condition to occur if you keep your pens clean and dry. You can treat this ailment by cleaning and drying the pen and applying antibiotic ointment to the affected areas.

Malocclusion: A rabbit's teeth continuously grow throughout its lifetime, and they should be straight and meet evenly. If the teeth do not meet properly, this condition is called malocclusion. This can become a serious issue, as overgrown teeth will lead to the rabbit not being able to eat properly or to mouth and jaw problems. A rabbit with this condition will need to have its teeth regularly trimmed by a veterinarian. Ordinarily, rabbits with normal teeth do not need to have them trimmed. Hay in the diet seems to help lessen the occurrence of teeth overgrowing.

Pasteurellosis: This disease is caused by the bacterium *Pasteurella multocida.* Pasteurellosis causes many different types of infections including snuffles (rhinitis), abscesses, pneumonia, pyometra (uterine infection), ear infections, and eye infections. This is a common disease of the nasal sinuses. The rabbit has trouble breathing due to a thick discharge from the nose and makes a characteristic nasal sound when trying to breathe. The front paws may become wet with the discharge as it tries to clean its nose. The rabbit can spread the disease through sneezing, and objects used in its cage become loaded with the microorganism. It is difficult to eradicate the bacteria from the infected rabbits, although antibiotics can be used in pet or show animals. If the rabbits are used for meat, it is not advisable to give them antibiotics as it can remain in the meat for some time after administration; this is an illegal practice in most states. Penicillin is *not* to be used in rabbits, as it can cause a fatal toxemia in this species. Rabbits affected with pasteurellosis in a commercial enterprise should be culled and their carcasses burned or buried to prevent the spread of the disease. All equipment and cages the sick rabbit contacted should be thoroughly disinfected.

Pododermatitis: This condition comes with ulcers or sores on the feet or footpads. It is usually associated with rabbits kept on wire-floored cages. To treat, place a flat piece of wood on the floor of the cage, and clean it frequently if it becomes dirty. Using straw bedding can help alleviate the condition as well. Sores or ulcers can be treated with protective ointments you can obtain from your local veterinarian's office.

Torticollis (wry neck): Wry neck occurs when otitis media (inflammation of the middle ear) spreads to the inner ear. The inner ear regulates an animal's equilibrium, so when it is infected or damaged it causes the head to tilt. An inner ear infection is hard to treat as antibiotics have difficulty penetrating this area of the body. Rabbits that do recover from an inner ear infection may have a permanent head tilt.

Urolithiasis: Rabbits excrete calcium in their urine, which gives the urine a cloudy appearance. Because of this excretion, they are prone to urine calcium sludge or stone formation. Feeding rabbits an excessive amount of calcium (as can be found in alfalfa hay) or genetics can predispose a rabbit to this disease. A rabbit affected by urolithiasis will strain when trying to urinate, will go off feed (meaning they will refuse to eat), have a painful abdomen, and bloody urine. To prevent this from occurring, feed your rabbits grass hay and make sure they have plenty of water at all time.

Rabbit Breeding

Rabbits reach sexual maturity at different ages depending on their size. A small breed, such as a Netherland Dwarf, will be able to breed at 4 months old. A medium-sized rabbit like the Angoras will be able to be first bred at 5 to 6 months, and large breeds such as the Flemish Giant can be bred from 9 to 12 months of age. Most rabbits are bred through the natural breeding method.

A doe does not have regular heat periods or an estrus cycle. Instead, she will ovulate after mating. A doe can breed any time of the year, but she does have variable times where she will not accept mating. You should watch the doe for signs she is ready to be mated. These signs include:

- Restlessness and nervousness
- A deep red coloration of the vulva
- Rubbing her chin on equipment
- A desire to join other rabbits

To determine the sex of a rabbit, you need to turn the rabbit on its back. For small rabbits, they can be turned on their back using the crook of your arm to hold them. For larger rabbits, sit down and turn them on their back in your lap. If the rabbit struggles, hold it securely until it stays still. Use one hand to hold the rabbit's chest and with the other take your thumb and forefinger to part the hair near the tail to expose its genitals — the opening nearest the belly. The anus is closest to the tail. Adult males older than 20 weeks will have flesh-colored testicles lying near the genital openings. These may be covered by fur so you may have to part the fur to find the testicles. If you do not see the testicles, you will need to place your thumb and your index finger on either side of the genital opening. Apply gentle pressure to expose the genitals. If you see a tube-like structure with a small opening, this is the penis. Females will have a somewhat prominent structure, but instead of a small opening, there will be a slit-like opening.

You will want to keep two bucks for every ten to 20 does. If you have less than ten does, it is also wise to keep two bucks in case one buck fails to inseminate the does. Good bucks will have a productive mating life of two to four years. Bucks will **molt** (shed part of the fur coat) once a year for about a month and may not breed during this time. The productive reproduction schedule of a doe is two to three years. Do not breed closely related bucks and does such as siblings or half-siblings as inbreeding will increase the chance of genetic defects. When you obtain rabbits, you should make sure you know whether your rabbits are closely related to each other. If they are purebred or pedigree rabbits, they should come with paperwork that shows their parentage.

When to breed

The doe always should be brought to the buck's cage for mating; otherwise, she may fight him. When the mating is over, the doe should be removed from the buck's cage and returned to her cage. You will know the mating has been completed when the buck falls away to the side from the doe. If you do not see this motion, take the doe out of the pen and place her with another buck. The doe will ovulate about 12 hours after this first mating. The doe can be taken back for a second mating with the same buck at this time to help conception rates. If the doe tries to fight the buck, take her out right away and wait a few days before trying to mate her again. Once in while, you will encounter a female that is showing all the signs of being ready to mate but will not allow the buck to mate her. This doe will need to be restrained so the buck can mount her. However, this trait can be inherited, so it is best to get rid of these does so this trait is not passed on to her female progeny.

If you are breeding the rabbits for commercial meat production, a good breeding program to follow is to breed the does 42 days after **kindling** (giving birth). This will let each doe produce five litters a year. With an average litter size of eight **kits** (newborn rabbits), this means each doe will produce 40 young rabbits each year. Keep records for each doe and buck during the breeding, including the pairs mated, date, and number of young kindled and weaned. This will help you keep track of productivity of each animal, and help you decide which rabbits to **cull** (get rid off) according to poor performance — fewer than seven young kindled per doe or if bucks fail to service the does — or you can keep the young of those breeding pairs who perform exceptionally well.

Nest boxes

Nest boxes are necessary for the doe to kindle in so she has privacy and so the young are not born onto metal wire, which is too cold and can kill the newborns. These boxes can be built of any type of lumber, but a common box is built of plywood. The edges of the wood should be lined with galvanized metal, as the does will chew on the wood. A good box for a medium-sized rabbit is 18 by 10 by 8 inches. The top can be covered to provide extra privacy for the doe. You should place clean, dry bedding in the nest box, even though the doe will pluck her own fur to make a nest. This is especially important if the doe is kindling during cold weather. Soft grass, hay, wood shavings, or straw can all be used. The doe may eat some of the bedding, so replenish often. Place nest boxes into the pregnant doe's cage 27 days after mating so she can get used to it.

Kindling (Birth)

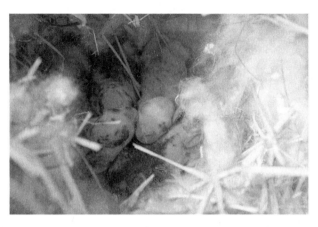

A doe will kindle about 31 days after she is bred. It is important not to disturb a doe giving birth because she might kill the young and eat them. You do want to observe her quietly from a distance to make sure she is giving birth. The day after kindling, you can check the nest box for any dead kits and take them away. Newborn rabbits are born with closed eyes and ears and are furless. The kits eyes will open at about 10 days old, and at 3 weeks they will begin to venture out of the nest box. They will begin to nibble on pellets and start to sip water, so keep feeders and waterers full of fresh material at all times. Young rabbits will be ready to wean at 8 weeks old, which is also the time they can be marketed as live young or fryers. **Live young** means the young rabbits can be sold as potential breeding rabbits, as pets, or to be raised to a larger size for meat. Young rabbits sold as **fryers** produce a tender meat.

If find the kits are born outside of the nest box, place them inside the box, and cover them with the fur the doe has lined the nest with. Wait a couple of hours, and if the doe has not joined them inside the box, place her inside with them. Hold her inside until the kits start to nurse. Kits nurse once or twice a day for only two to four minutes. If a doe has more than eight kits, you can transfer some of the kits to another mother with fewer kits as long as the young are around the same age. This will make sure there is enough milk to go around. Most does will accept the young of another mother without any problem.

Pregnancy-related problems

Mastitis: Does can acquire mastitis, or an infection of the mammary glands, while producing milk. The glands become swollen, hot, reddened, or bluish, and milk production may cease. Bacteria enter the mammary glands and invade the tissues. The most common bacteria causing mastitis is *Staphylococcus aureus*, a bacterium found in the nasal passages of all rabbits. The affected doe usually stops eating and may refuse to nurse her kits. The kits also can get the disease through drinking infected milk. Treatment is through use of antibiotics and good nursing care. The kits born of a doe with mastitis should be hand-fed. Do not foster them to another doe as this can spread the disease to the doe and her young.

False pregnancy: Does can sometimes exhibit a false pregnancy. This can occur due to mating with a buck that does not result in pregnancy or by being mounted by another doe. Even though the doe does not conceive, she will go through all the pregnancy-related hormonal changes. The false pregnancy will last 16 to 18 days. At the end, the doe may build a nest and may even produce milk. She eventually will return to normal and be able to breed again.

Pregnancy toxemia: Does in the last few days of pregnancy or during the first few days after birth are susceptible to this condition. It is common, but little is known about how it occurs. Does stop eating, become depressed and weak, miscarry the kits, and can die. The liver becomes infiltrated with fat and enlarges. This stops the normal functioning of the liver. One major function of the liver is to remove toxins from the blood. Treatment consists of force-feeding the doe and using steroids, which are only available from a veterinarian. Obese does or does with hairballs from nest building are most susceptible to pregnancy toxemia.

CASE STUDY:
THOSE SILLY RABBITS

Scott Marshall
Marshall Farms
9212 Neal Avenue South
Hastings, Minnesota
marshallrabbits@yahoo.com

Scott Marshall started raising rabbits at a young age. His parents were hog and grain farmers, and he received four or five pet rabbits when he was about 10. Now he raises about 150 rabbits, and it is definitely a family project. His 5-year-old daughter Rebecca helps care for the rabbits with supervision. Marshall definitely thinks rabbits are a good family project. It helps children learn a lot of life lessons: how to care for animals, how to follow the rules, and that sometimes animals die.

Marshall recommends that a person interested in raising rabbits do the homework first. Think about the worst part of the year — typically winter. A rabbit grower needs to be out every day, in all kinds of weather, to feed and water the rabbits twice a day. Another useful piece of advice is to find a market and local processor if you do not want to process them yourself.

Marshall spends five hours a day on the weekdays and four to eight hours a day on weekends caring for his rabbits. Much of his time is spent on his three tasks: cleaning the barn and cages, butchering and packaging rabbit meat, and feeding and watering the rabbits. Cold winter weather makes his work more difficult when he has to thaw out water cups and tackle frozen manure. Predators can be a real problem as well: Stray dogs, raccoons, possums, cats, and coyotes can kill adult rabbits. Rats can kill young bunnies. Bees and wasp stings also can kill a rabbit. Marshall counters these dangers by having a barn with a strong door and a lock.

As for health problems, Marshall has some great advice for the beginning farmer: "Clean, clean, clean, and protect," he said. "What I mean is clean water, clean feed, clean housing and nest boxes, and protect from weather and predators. That will take care of most of the health issues. In my 30 years raising rabbits, I have been lucky not to have had any major issues."

Marshall also had to deal with sore feet, colds, and ear mites, "That was my fault for bringing in new stock and not quarantining them," he said. "Quarantining new stock is very important. Also, do not become a petting zoo. Sick people can make sick rabbits. It also stresses the rabbits. And that weed a kid pulls to feed the bunny could be poisonous."

The Marshalls take great satisfaction in knowing they provide their family and customers with healthy, quality meat, and they enjoy raising rabbits. Marshall is optimistic about the future market for rabbits. He loves the renewed interest in eating local. "It is back to the basics — the way our grandparents and their parents ate," he said.

Raising Rabbits as Pets

Rabbits are popular pets. The AVMA estimates that there are 6.1 million pet rabbits in the United States. Each household that has rabbits is estimated to have 3.4 rabbits. It seems you cannot have just one.

What to expect

There are many things to consider when choosing a pet rabbit. Ideally, you will have some idea of the personality of the individual rabbit. This is often one of the most important factors in choosing a rabbit. You also should consider how large the rabbit will be when it is fully grown. There can be a big difference between the smallest breeds and the largest ones. Keeping a male or female rabbit can also make a difference. An intact doe may be territorial when she is an adult.

Rabbits may be spayed, but if you plan to breed your rabbit, you will need to keep your females intact. Male rabbits, or bucks, usually are not aggressive, but they may spray in the house if they are allowed to be loose. You can solve this problem if you have your buck neutered but, again, if you plan to breed your rabbits, you will not want to neuter your males.

If you prefer a longhaired rabbit or one with a woolly coat, such as an Angora or a Jersey Woolly, then you will need to count on spending more time grooming your rabbit. No matter what kind of rabbit you get, you will need to devote some time to regular grooming. Not to worry though. Rabbits usually only need some basic brushing, which can be quite soothing and enjoyable for both of you.

One of the best ways to learn about the different breeds of rabbits is to attend a rabbit show. You can see many of the breeds available and talk to breeders who are knowledgeable about rabbits and rabbit husbandry. They may have young rabbits for sale as pets or even show prospects. You can learn more about rabbit shows by visiting the website for the American Rabbit Breeders Association (ARBA) **www.arba.net**. ARBA lists upcoming shows throughout the U.S. and outside the country, gives the latest news and information, provides information about breeds, and includes a membership application if you are interested in becoming more involved. Adult membership is $20 for one year; youth membership is $12; and husband and wife membership is $30. If you are interested in showing your rabbits or learning more about breeding, becoming a member of ARBA is a good way to learn more and to meet other serious rabbit breeders.

Rabbits are a prey animal; other animals often eat them, so they must be alert at all times. They are constantly scanning their environment for danger signals. They have excellent peripheral vision (from the side), though they do not see well directly in front. They also have outstanding hearing and a great sense of smell. They use their senses to detect danger. You can use a soothing voice and slow movements to let your rabbit know you are close by to avoid frightening it.

Rabbits are also territorial, and they will defend their territory against invaders. They prefer to live in groups with a social hierarchy. Groups of rabbits are called **warrens**. They can communicate with each other through body language and through some vocalizations. They will also exhibit dominance behaviors toward each other. Dominance behaviors may include mounting each other and having subordinate rabbits groom more important rabbits in the group.

Your rabbit might make the following vocalizations:

Grunting/growling: Anger or disapproval at some behavior. Your rabbit might follow this sound by biting or scratching. This means to back off or leave the rabbit alone.

Honking: This soft sound may be heard during courtship. Your rabbit may circle while making this sound. It means: "Hey, how about you and me getting together?"

Screaming: If your rabbit is screaming, it means your rabbit is terrified or in great pain.

Snorting: Snorting means your rabbit wants attention. Your rabbit is not happy about something. (Or your rabbit could be sick.) Your rabbit likely wants some petting or feels bad.

Tooth clicking or "purring": The easy grinding or clicking of teeth means that your rabbit is happy. Your rabbit is relaxed and comfortable.

Tooth grinding: Real tooth grinding means your rabbit is in pain or distress. Your rabbit needs help right away.

Whimpering, squealing, and squeaks: These sounds mean your rabbit is in pain or hurt. However, some squeaking in a pleasant situation can mean that your rabbit is pleased.

Rabbits exhibit all kinds of body language that humans can learn to read to know what their rabbit is feeling. A rabbit may race wildly through the house, which usually indicates the rabbit feels good and is playing. Rabbits can take up a boxing position, which indicates they are willing to fight. They may "chin" or rub their faces on things to mark their territory. Rabbits also chew, dig, and display other inherited behaviors. Rabbits can learn some words or at least understand what you are saying or want. It all depends on how closely you bond with your rabbit.

Selling Pet Rabbits

Rabbits are a popular pet in the U.S., so many people would like to have their own rabbit. If you are breeding rabbits as pets, you can find ways to sell young rabbits. However, it is also true that many rabbits do end up in rabbit rescues and animal shelters each year, so you should use some care about selling your rabbits.

Most people who buy rabbits as pets have not had any experience with rabbits before. You should provide them with some information about caring for rabbits and encourage them to have a cage and other equipment set up for their rabbit before they take it home. Instruct them on what to feed their rabbit and other basics. You should warn them that rabbits do chew. Let them know that rabbits are not cats or dogs, and make sure your buyers have the correct expectations about owning a rabbit.

You also should help your buyers select an appropriate rabbit for their situation. Do not sell them rabbits that are too young to take home. Sell only healthy, happy rabbits to your customers. Make sure you are being an ethical breeder and seller.

Where to sell

When it comes to selling pet rabbits, most people who are not commercial breeders sell from their own homes or farms. It is up to you if you would like to allow buyers to visit your home or farm in order to select their own rabbit. You also may be able to sell rabbits at a farmers market or flea market depending on the regulations in your state and city or county. You will need to check the laws in your area to find out if it is legal to sell rabbits in these places. You also can sell rabbits to local pet stores. There are people and organizations opposed to any stores that sell live animals, but pet stores usually are inspected by local animal control and state agencies to make sure they are treating animals properly.

However, if you sell your rabbits to pet brokers or if you sell your rabbits wholesale, you will need to become licensed as a commercial rabbit breeder. This will entail having your facilities inspected by the USDA and following Animal Welfare Act guidelines. You probably will not be able to raise your rabbits in your home, and you will need separate outdoor facilities for them. Most people who are commercial rabbit breeders raise rabbits full time and rely on this business for their income.

Pricing your rabbits

Depending on the breed, pet rabbits usually cost between $15 and $100. Lops, or rabbits with droopy ears, may cost $15 to $60. Dwarf rabbits may be $25 to $40. Mini Rex rabbits, another breed, may be $10 to $50. Rabbits with unusual colors or markings may cost more. Angoras may be $25 to $50. Flemish Giants may be $45 to $100. Lionheads may be $20 to $50. These prices will depend on how much rabbits usually cost in your area, too. If someone in your area breeds Angoras constantly, you can expect the price to be low.

When you sell purebred rabbits, provide the buyer with a copy of the rabbit's pedigree as well as a health certificate.

Rabbits for Meat

Although raising rabbits for personal consumption is often enjoyable, it does mean that you will need to harvest your rabbits, either for their meat or for their pelts, or both. You may find this difficult at first, especially if you have grown close to your rabbits and made pets of them. It helps to remember that this is often the reason why you got your rabbits in the first place. You have invested your time, money, and work in raising the rabbits so they could provide you with nutritious food and good pelts. In a sense, this is their purpose in life. Be grateful for their contributions to your way of life.

Types of meat

Rabbit meat is a good source of high-quality protein and one of the most nutritious meats available. It is fine-grained with a mild flavor. According to the USDA, the rabbit meat sold in the U.S. is usually sold one of three ways:

Fryer or **young rabbit** — the terms "fryer" or "young rabbit" refer to a rabbit weighing not less than 1 ½ pounds and rarely more than 3 ½ pounds, and less than 12 weeks of age. The flesh is tender, fine grained, and a bright pearly-pink color. These rabbits may be cooked in much the same way as young poultry.

Roaster or **mature rabbit** — the terms "roaster" or "mature rabbit" refer to a mature rabbit of any weight but usually more than 4 pounds and more than 8 months of age. The flesh is firm and coarse grained, and the muscle fiber is slightly darker in color and less tender. The fat may be a creamier color than that of a fryer or young rabbit. The meat of larger rabbits may be tougher, so the best methods of cooking are braising or stewing.

Giblets — the liver and heart

Learning to butcher

Items you may need:

- • Butcher knife
- • Sharp knife for cutting and skinning
- • Skinning knife
- • Hammer

You can find a good selection of knives for harvesting and skinning at Lem Products (**www.lemproducts.com/product/ 3939/Knives**).

If you are slaughtering rabbits for home use, there are two ways to kill the rabbit. The neck can be dislocated by firmly grasping the hind legs and head. Then it is stretched to full length and with a hard, sharp pull, the head is bent backward to dislocate the neck. The other way to butcher the rabbit is to stun it with a hard blow behind the ears with a blunt object such as a stout stick or hammer.

Using a rope attached to one of the hind legs, hang the rabbit with the head down. Use a sharp knife to remove the head and allow the blood to drain from the carcass completely. Rabbits are small, and it only takes a few minutes for all the blood to drain. The forefeet should be removed next right at the joint. Use the knife to cut the skin around the hock joint, where the thigh meets the lower leg bone. Make a cut down the legs toward the tail, and peel the hide down to the tail. Remove the tail and pull the skin down the rest of the body. Then, set the skin aside. Wash the knife to remove any blood clots or fur.

Next, make a cut starting near the anus down the abdomen to the sternum. Cut through the entire abdominal muscle, but make sure you do not cut too deep and cut into the intestinal tract. You want to avoid this to keep from contaminating the meat with fecal material. Remove the intestinal tract and lungs and discard into the garbage. The heart, kidney, and liver can be removed and saved if desired. Once the abdominal contents are removed, take the body off the rope and cut off the hind feet at the hock. The carcass should be washed with clean, running water to remove fur, blood clots, and other debris. The carcass then should be placed in sturdy freezer bags and stored either at refrigerator temperatures (35 to 40°F) or placed in the freezer if the meat is not consumed within two days.

Finding an outside butcher

Finding an outside butcher to harvest your rabbits for personal consumption is not usually difficult. You can check online, in the phone book, or with your state meat inspection agency. Your state meat inspection agency licenses most local butchers, so they should keep a listing of butchers in your area that they can pass on to you. Your local feed store also may have notices about butchers that are willing to travel to farms and butcher animals. These butchers operate mobile processing units called MPUs. They usually carry everything with them they will need to process animals, though they may need assistance from you or a few other people if you are butchering larger animals.

Rabbits are not required to be inspected under either the Federal Meat Inspection Act or the USDA Food Safety and Inspection Service. Your state may have its own meat inspection program. Ask your butcher about any licenses required for custom butchering and whether he or she has the necessary licensure.

Before choosing a butcher, it is a good idea to visit the facility and make sure it is appropriately clean and sanitary. You can ask around to find out what kind of reputation the butcher has with other farmers. You are trust the butcher with animals you intend to eat yourself, so you should be satisfied that he or she will do a good job.

Raising rabbits for profit

If your plans include slaughtering rabbits for sale to commercial businesses, such as grocery stores or restaurants, they will need to be processed according to local or state health codes. You will need to contact your local or state meat inspection agency for rules and regulations. Codes usually are enforced by state agencies. It is usually sufficient to meet state rules and slaughter rabbits with a state license but you should check with your county extension service agent or your state meat inspection agency to make sure of the rules for rabbit processing where you live.

If you are raising rabbits for profit, then the obvious places to sell rabbit meat are local restaurants and grocery stores. If local butchers who are state licensed have processed your meat, you should have no trouble meeting the standards for these establishments, or for restaurants or stores anywhere in your state. You also may be able to sell your rabbit meat at farmers markets if you have a way to keep the meat cold. It may be worth testing this niche to find out if there is a demand for rabbit meat in your area from local consumers.

Processors and slaughterhouses

Processors and slaughterhouses are where butchers work to harvest and process animals, such as rabbits. Rabbits are one of the easiest animals to process. They are said to be even easier to process than chickens. Some butchers may want you to bring live rabbits to them while other butchers may allow you to bring them rabbits you have already killed. You will need to talk to the butcher about what they prefer. In fact, you should talk to the butcher about everything, especially if you have any special requests in the way your rabbits are processed or cut up.

If your rabbits are being sold to restaurants, then they probably can be wrapped in plain butcher paper. However, if you are planning to sell your rabbits to grocery stores, they will need to be wrapped in clear plastic. Consumers like to see what they are buying in the meat counter. Talk to the butcher about your packaging options, and arrange to have the rabbits picked up or delivered where they are going after processing.

Although rabbit meat does not have to be inspected by the USDA, there is a voluntary grading system. Before being graded, the rabbit meat has to be inspected and passed by the Food Safety and Inspection Service or some other inspection service, such as a state meat inspection program. Consumer grades for rabbit meat are U.S. Grade A, U.S. Grade B, and U.S. Grade C.

Handling rabbit meat

From the USDA:

Take rabbit home immediately and refrigerate at 40 degrees F or below. Use it within 2 days or freeze at 0 degrees F. If kept frozen continuously, it will be safe indefinitely; however, quality will diminish over time. It is safe to freeze rabbit in its original packaging. For prolonged storage, overwrap as you would any food for long-term storage. For best quality, use frozen whole rabbit within a year, pieces within 9 months.

Safe thawing

There are three ways to safely defrost rabbit: in the refrigerator, in cold water, or in the microwave oven. *Never defrost at room temperature.*

> **Refrigerator:** It is best to plan for slow, safe thawing in the refrigerator. Bone-in parts or whole rabbits may take a day or longer to thaw. Once thawed, rabbit may be stored in the refrigerator for 2 days before cooking. During this time, if you decide not to use the rabbit, you can safely refreeze it without cooking it.

> **Cold Water:** To defrost rabbit in cold water, do not remove the packaging. Be sure the package is airtight or put it into a leak-proof bag. Submerge the rabbit in cold water and change the water every 30 minutes so it continues to thaw. Small packages may defrost in an hour or less; larger packages may take 2 to 3 hours. Plan to cook the rabbit immediately after thawing.

> **Microwave oven:** When defrosting rabbit in the microwave oven, plan to cook it immediately after thawing because some of the areas of the food may become warm and begin to cook.

Safe cooking

- When roasting rabbit parts, set the oven temperature no lower than 325 degrees F. A 2-pound, cut-up rabbit should take about one hour to cook.

- A whole, 2- to 2 ½-pound rabbit should take about one to one and a half hours to roast. Stuffing it will add about half an hour to the cooking time.

- Braising rabbit (cooking it in a small amount of liquid in a covered pan on the range or in the oven) also takes about an hour. Rabbit can be broiled about 15 minutes on each side.

- For safety, USDA recommends cooking rabbit to an internal temperature of at least 160 degrees F. The use of a food thermometer is recommended to make sure your rabbit is safe to eat.

- It is safe to cook frozen rabbit in the oven or on the range or grill without defrosting it first, though the cooking time may be about 50 percent longer.

- Do not cook frozen rabbit in a slow cooker; thaw first. Cut whole rabbits into smaller pieces so heat can penetrate the meat more quickly.

Safe handling of leftovers

Refrigerate leftovers within two hours after cooking. Use within three to four days or freeze.

Use frozen, cooked rabbit within four to six months for best quality.

Reheat leftovers to 165 °F.

Rabbits for Fur

Most rabbits can be harvested for their fur, as well as for meat, but some rabbits are particularly raised for their pelts. The Angora rabbit is the best-known rabbit raised for its coat, but the Rex is also known for producing a desirable fur. In many cases, rabbit fur is a byproduct of the rabbit meat industry, but the rabbits killed for meat are often young and their fur is not desirable commercially. The highest quality furs come from rabbits that are more than five months old. The fur is thicker, and the pelts are of better quality for clothing.

Removing the rabbit's pelt

If you would like to harvest your rabbit's pelt, while the carcass is hanging by one of its hind legs, you should make a cut around the hock joint to release the skin from the body. The hock joint is the rear knee joint of the animal's leg. Do this for both rear legs. You can use the same knife you are using to cut the rabbit, or you can use a skinning knife. Next, cut the skin between these hock joints on the lower part of the body. Remove the tail and pull the skin down over the body toward the animal's head. The skin of young rabbits is loose and easy to remove. It is a little more difficult to remove the skin from older rabbits, but if you work carefully, you can remove it without much trouble. Be careful to avoid cutting or tearing the skin, as this will lessen its value.

Once the skin is removed from the rabbit, turn it inside out while it is still warm and soft. Place the skin on a wire hanger or stretcher with the leg casings on one side of the hanger. You can make a shaper or hanger from a piece of No.

9 gauge galvanized wire. A shaper helps extend or expand the pelt to its full size without stretching it out of shape. You can fasten the rear legs to the wire with a clothespin or another fastener to hold them in place. Hang the pelt in a well-ventilated place so it can dry, but do not place it in direct sunlight. Once the skin is dry, you can remove the hanger.

Preparing your rabbit skins

Once you have as many rabbit skins as you want, you can move on to tanning them. There are several methods for tanning, but before tanning, you will need to prepare the skins. Preparing the skins means softening them, removing any fat or flesh remaining on them, and removing the oil from the skins. After the skin is dry, open it by making a cut along the midline or the stomach so you can stretch it out on a flat surface. Use a blunt knife to scrape off any flesh or fat still on the skin. Remove the remaining oil from the skin by working it in a fat solvent.

Soften the dried skins by soaking them in several different vats of water over a one- to three-hour period. Depending on the rabbit skin, it can take more or less time to soften. You will need to keep the soaking time to a minimum, as too much soaking will loosen the fur. Adding one ounce of borax or bicarbonate of soda to a gallon of water for soaking will help soften the skins. Putting some soap or detergent in the mix can help remove fat.

Your rabbit skins are now ready for tanning.

Salt alum tanning

One way to tan your skins is by using salt alum. Here is the recipe for this solution:

Step 1.   Dissolve 1 pound of ammonium aluminum sulfate or potassium aluminum sulfate (alum) in 1 gallon of water.

Step 2.   Dissolve 4 ounces of sodium carbonate and 8 ounces of sodium chloride (salt) in ½ gallon of water.

Step 3.   Slowly add the soda and salt solution to the alum solution and stir vigorously.

Step 4.   Mix flour with the combined solutions to form a thin paste; mix the flour with a little water first to aid in preventing lumps from forming.

After your rabbit skins are prepared and ready for tanning, they should be tacked to a flat surface. Use the paste made from this salt alum recipe to coat the skins with a layer of paste about ⅛-inch thick. Cover the skins lightly with a cloth or paper. Let the skins set for about 24 hours. Remove the paste with a cloth and apply a second coat for another 24 hours. For thick skins, another coat may be necessary. The last coating should stay on the skins for three to four days.

When you remove the last coat, you should wash the skins in a solution of borax and bicarbonate of soda (1 ounce per gallon of water). Gently squeeze out the excess solution, then rinse out the skins in plain water and squeeze out the excess water. Do not wring the skins. Stretch the skins on the hangers or stretchers again. When they are almost dry, you should work on the skin by rubbing and pulling on the skins over a table edge to soften it. This will stretch and soften the skin. If the skin is still rough, you can use a block of sandpaper to make it softer. You can add Neat's foot oil, leather conditioner, or glycerin to make the skin softer and more pliable.

The salt alum method is usually considered a better tanning method than the salt acid method, but the rabbit skin may still be slightly tough and hard when it is finished, so you may need to work more to get the skins softened. You may have to resoak the skins or repeat the rubbing procedures to make the skins softer.

You should be able to tan three or four rabbit skins with this recipe.

Salt acid tanning

You can also tan rabbit hides using this recipe:

Step 1. Dissolve 1 pound of sodium chloride (salt) in 1 gallon of water

Step 2. Add ½ ounce of concentrated sulfuric acid to the sodium chloride solution very carefully. CAUTION: Sulfuric acid is a corrosive agent and must be handled cautiously. Avoid contact with your skin or clothing. Store the acid and the finished solution in a glass or earthenware contain. Do NOT store it in a metal container. When adding the acid to the salt solution, pour it slowly, and stir constantly. If the acid of the acid mixture comes in contact with your skin, rinse immediately with a solution of bicarbonate of soda.

Step 3. Adding acid to the salt will generate heat. As soon as the mixture cools, it is ready for use.

Prepare the rabbit skins in the same way as with the salt alum tanning method. Place each skin in the salt acid solution, fully covering the skin, and allow it to stay there for one to three days, stirring periodically. Once the skin is tanned, remove it from the solution, rinse it in plain water, and then rinse again in a solution of borax or bicarbonate of soda (1 ounce per gallon of water). Finish by rinsing with plain water again. Squeeze out excess water, stretch the skin, allow the skin to almost dry, and then work with the skin (rubbing and pulling it) to soften it as it dries, as with the salt alum method.

You can obtain the chemicals and materials for tanning your rabbit skins from biological supply companies, handcraft shops, and stores that offer supplies for home butchering and tanning such as F & T's Fur Harvester's Trading Post (**www.fntpost.com/Categories/Fur+Handling/Tanning/Tanning+Kits+Supplies**). They also offer premixed tanning solutions and other tanning supplies.

Laws

Rabbits are not considered livestock, so their meat generally is not inspected by the USDA. There is a voluntary inspection system in place, and most states require meat to be inspected before it can be sold commercially. Federally, commercial rabbit breeders must comply with Animal Welfare Act regulations when raising and selling rabbits wholesale. Those regulations may be found here at **www.animallaw.info/administrative/adusawaregc.htm**. However, these regulations do not apply to rabbit breeders who sell small numbers of rabbits or who sell them directly to the public as pets.

Most laws regarding rabbits are local laws made by cities and counties. They may set limits about how many rabbits you can keep or set zoning laws regarding what kind of animals can be kept inside city limits. You will need to check with your city and county regarding local laws before you purchase any rabbits or invest in any equipment. You also may wish to talk to your local animal control officials to find out if they are aware of any local ordinances pertaining to rabbits.

Chapter 3

Chickens

CHICKEN GLOSSARY

Candle or candling: Taking an egg and holding it in front of a bright light in a dark room to see the development of the embryo inside the egg

Cape: The area of feathers between the shoulders and neck on a chicken

Capon: A castrated rooster

Chalazae: The two coils that hold the yolk in place inside of an egg

Chicks: Baby chickens hatched from fertilized eggs

Clutch: A group of eggs laid by a broody hen

Coccidiosis: A protozoal infestation causing disease and sometimes death

Cock: A male chicken after his first molt

Cockerel: A male chicken under 12 months of age

Comb: The fleshy piece of skin on top of a chicken's head. It helps to identify the breed. It comes in a variety of shapes including single, pea, V-shaped, and rose.

Coop: Housing for chickens; can be made of different material and customized to fit the needs of your flock

Crest: The feathers on top of a chicken's head

Crop: Located inside the base of a chicken's neck, right before the gizzard. Food passes through the crop where it is softened and then moves on to the gizzard.

Crumbles: Food for birds, often broken up pellets, into medium size shapes for the birds to eat

Cull: Killing sick or unwanted birds in a humane fashion

Debeak: Removing the tip of the beak from a bird. Often, it is done to birds raised in close quarters in order to prevent them from pecking at each other.

Down: The new, soft feathers on a baby chick before it grows its feathers. It is also the fluffy layer of feathers underneath the main feathers on an adult bird.

Dual-purpose breed: A breed raised to provide both meat and eggs

Dust bath: Birds "bathe" or roll around in fine dirt or sand to help remove external parasites from their bodies.

Earlobes: Skin below a chicken's ears that can vary in color and shape depending on the breed

Egg tooth: The very tip of the chick's beak that pierces the egg when the chick is ready to hatch. It falls off within the first week of hatching after it is no longer needed.

Exterior albument: The narrow fluid layer next to the shell membrane in an egg

Fertilized egg: An egg containing an embryo that will produce a baby chick

Flighty: Unstable behavior

Flock: A group of chickens

Free-range: Chickens that are not caged

Frizzled: Feathers that curl on a bird and give the appearance of a fuzzy, fluffy look

Fryer: A chicken, typically smaller, bred for meat. Another name for broiler, this is the type of chicken found mostly in grocery stores.

Germinal disk or blastoderm: The small circular spot on the surface of the yolk. It is the point where sperm enters the egg.

Gizzard: The part of the chicken's digestive system that contains the grit used to breakdown the food

Hackles: The feathers located on a chicken's back between the shoulder and neck

Heavy breed: A breed in which the female weighs more than 5 ½ pounds

Hen: A female chicken after her first molt

Hock: The joint between the thigh and shank on a chicken

Hybrid: A crossbreed

Incubation: The stage of a chicken's life cycle when the fertilized egg is in an artificial incubator or under a hen as it matures 21 days to hatch

Keel: The blade of a chicken's breastbone.

Kill cone: A cone-shaped cylinder tube, typically made out of plastic or steel, to place chickens in upside down for slaughter and to drain the blood from their bodies after they have been killed

Lacing: The markings on a chicken's feathers. This can sometimes help identify the breed. It is a contrasting color on the edge of a feather.

Layer: A hen proficient in laying eggs

Mandibles: The upper and lower part of a beak

Marek's disease: A highly contagious viral neoplastic disease in chickens

Mash: Finely ground food usually used to feed baby chicks

Newcastle's disease: Avian distemper affecting the respiratory system

Middle albumen: The thick, white layer of dense matter known as the egg white inside of an egg

Molt: The shedding of feathers on a bird. It usually takes 3 months to complete the process, and it occurs once a year. Hens do not lay eggs during this time.

Mottled: Markings on a chicken's coat. The feather's tips or spots on the feather have a contrasting color, typically black with a white tip.

Nest boxes: An area in the coop that hens can lay eggs and sit on them until they hatch if they are fertilized

Nest egg: A fake egg or egg replacement to fool a hen into thinking she has laid an egg to induce egg laying in the bird

Nucleus of pander: The plug of whitish yolk inside the yellow yolk that is purely for nutritional value

Ovum: A hen's egg cell

Pasted vent: A condition in which a chick or chicken's vent is clogged with feces; more common in baby chicks than chickens

Pecking order: The social hierarchy in a flock of chickens

Pencil: Markings on a chicken's coat

Pellet: Food for birds, compressed into a long, cylinder shape

Pinfeather: Sometimes called a "blood feather." It is a developing feather on a bird. It can be a new feather during infancy or a replacement feather during molting.

Plucker: A piece of equipment that removes feathers from a dead chicken, turkey, duck, or other poultry; can be commercial and automated or homemade

Pox: A virus in which wart-like bumps appear on the wattles and combs of chickens

Pullet: A female chicken under 12 months of age

Purebred: A breed of chicken whose parents are the same breed

Run: An area of space for chickens to run, forage, and roam

Rooster: An adult male chicken

Scalder: A piece of equipment that submerges a dead animal, typically a bird or fowl, with the intent to burn the feathers off the carcass

Sexing: The process of determining the gender of a baby chick

Spangled: A "V" marking at the tip of a feather on a chicken's coat

Splash: A term used to describe the colors and markings on chicks' and chickens' coats

Spur: A stiff, sharp spine on the leg rear of a chicken's leg

Stress: To a chicken, stress can be triggered by a number of things, including loud noises, overcrowding, children, other animals, and bright light. Stress is harmful for chickens because they are sensitive birds. Too much stress can cause illness, decreased egg production, and even death in some cases.

Thrush: A condition in a chicken that affects the upper digestive tracts

Twisted legs: A leg deformity in birds

Wattle: The fleshy pieces of skin that hang down on either side of a chicken's beak. It can be used in identifying a breed of chicken and is typically larger on males than females.

Wheaton: The color of a chicken's coat, referring to an array of browns and tans

Vent: The opening in the rear of a chicken where eggs and bodily excretions pass through

Yolk: The yellow mass of materials found in an egg that surrounds and provides nutrients to the developing embryo and consists of protein, lecithin, and cholesterol

Chickens and People

What came first: the chicken or the egg? There are several theories. Some scientists agree on the theory that chicken eggs developed as dinosaurs evolved into birds, thus reptile eggs came first. Others believe the chicken came first based on a protein found in both eggs and chickens. But whatever the case, chickens originated in India and Thailand from the single Red Junglefowl breed and evolved through the centuries into hundreds of breeds as they were carried from continent to continent.

The origin and history of chickens

It may be hard to imagine, but sketches of chickens found on shards of pottery and on cave walls suggest that during the Roman Empire, these birds were worshipped. Long before being considered a menu item, they were used as sacrifices to Roman and Greek gods. In Greek culture, the Greeks would offer chickens as sacrifices to the gods to try to appease them or in the hopes of receiving something they wanted. The Romans, who were a superstitious people, believed slaughtering a chicken could help them make decisions in battle. "The Keeper of the Sacred Chickens" was a position in the army and a title one of the soldiers held. Romans carried a cage of sacred chickens with them when they went to war. They would throw food and crumble at the bottom of the chicken cages when the troops needed assistance, such as when they should attack. If the chickens ate, it was a sign that everything was fine. If they did not eat, then something was wrong, and the soldiers were to take caution.

In one particular battle, when the Keeper of the Sacred Chickens fed the birds, they did not eat. The Roman general Publius Claudius Pulcher was headstrong and ignored the birds; he tossed their cage into the sea. He said they could drink if they did not want to eat. The Romans then lost their battle, the Battle of Drepanum.

So how did hens and roosters get from Asia and Europe to America? History suggests Christopher Columbus carried chickens with him on his ships from Italy during his second voyage to the New World. With today's ever-changing technology, scientists still search for more specific answers and are conducting DNA testing on remnants of chicken bones found in North and South America. These bones may predate Columbus, indicating the birds were there before he landed on the continent. If this is the case, a breed of chicken may have developed in the Western Hemisphere from another breed of bird, or another explorer might have brought chickens with him.

From 1500 to the 1900s, chickens were raised on small farms and in family backyards primarily for producing eggs. America's poultry industry did not come to fruition until 1923, when Celia Steele, a housewife in Sussex County, Delaware, had the foresight to see that chickens also could be sold as broilers and not just layers. A broiler chicken is raised for meat, and a layer lays eggs. She saw the profit potential and purchased 500 chicks intending to sell them for meat. At the time, poultry was a delicacy and typically was not sold for meat, so Steele's first flock sold for 62 cents per pound. Later in 1924, the birds sold for 57 cents per pound, which is the equivalent today of close to $15 per pound. Homemakers and restaurant owners discovered the versatility of preparing chicken (frying, broiling, roasting, and as stew meat), causing demand to increase.

By 1926, Steele's flock increased to 10,000, and less than ten years later, the prospering Steeles owned seven farms. Even today, Delaware, the birthplace of the broiler chicken industry, remains one of the country's biggest chicken producers; the state delivers millions of birds each year.

The 1940s saw the integration of the chicken industry. Before that time, feed mills, farms, processing operations, and hatcheries worked independently of each other, according to the National Chicken Council. The integration of these made the chicken industry more efficient and streamlined — the feed mills loaned money to the farms to buy chicks from the hatcheries. When farmers sold the flock to the processors, they used the money they received from the processors to pay back the feed mills. This practice became more common and regulated as chicken consumption increased. Refrigeration also helped the industry because it allowed consumers to store their meat longer. Factory farming produced more products for less money, and raising chickens that scratched around in the backyard became less popular and not as lucrative.

In the 1950s, production increased to meet the needs of the baby boom. Vertical integration — when one company controls all processes from marketing to production in an effort to reduce costs — helped manufacturers afford new technology, which increased sales and profits. Entrepreneurs with vertical integration systems controlled most of the chicken industry at this time. In the 1960s, marketing expanded to television and print, which made poultry brand names more recognized and popular than ever.

Automation technologies of the 1970s helped producers meet consumer demands. Regulations and laws became more focused on production as people became more educated on the poultry's nutritional values, diseases associated with chickens, and the process of speeding up chicken growth. The government and the public scrutinized the cleanliness of chicken plants, the environments the chickens lived in, and the way the birds were killed. Poultry was not the only industry with stricter regulations; the United States overall was setting higher standards and fine-tuning its food markets. Regulators' eyes were open to the potential harm of unsafe practices, and they closely monitored the progress of food production. Demand was steadily increasing, and chicken producers enhanced chicken

growth to meet these needs because faster-growing birds meant more poultry available in a shorter amount of time, which in turn meant increased profits.

In the 1980s, demand for poultry expanded further, when fast-food restaurants added chicken tenders and nuggets to their menus. Fast-food giant McDonald's, famous for its burgers, introduced Chicken McNuggets in 1983. By the end of the year, the chain was the second-largest chicken retailer in the world, second to Kentucky Fried Chicken in the fast-food market. This chicken sensation helped increase poultry sales overall. In 2003, the amount of chicken nuggets sold in all restaurants increased to more than 200 percent of the amount sold in the 1990s. McDonald's is credited with introducing the nugget into the American way of life. It was not just a fad; the chicken nugget became a staple that appeals to all age groups.

By 1992, chicken sales surpassed beef sales for the first time. In 2001, U.S. exports of poultry to other countries reached $2 billion, an all-time high. Not only were poultry broilers booming within America, they were also increasing globally.

Stricter laws developed in the past six decades to ensure the safety of the birds produced for consumption, and the U.S. Department of Agriculture (USDA) enforces these rules. These laws became necessary after animal-handling practices were deemed inhumane, and factory conditions were ruled unclean. Because of the new rules, birds are less expensive than they once were. More birds are currently available, which drives the cost down. The birds have more meat on their bones because they are given special feed to plump them up quicker. They are produced in cleaner, safer environments than they were in the past. Although debate continues over the humane treatment of these animals, government regulations aim to achieve the best possible conditions for both the workers and the birds.

Breeds

Shopping for your new feathered friends is fun but can be overwhelming with all of the choices available. To help you decide which breed is best for you, figure out your primary reason for keeping birds. Owning birds to show in competitions or for ornamental purposes is one reason. Some people own chickens primarily for eggs, some for meat only, some for both eggs and meat (these birds are referred to as dual), and some for pets. In this chapter, you will find the best breeds in each category.

First, it is helpful to know the terminology of chickens in each stage of their lives.

- A **chick** is a baby chicken.
- A **hen** is a mature, adult female chicken.
- A **rooster**, or cock, is a mature, male chicken that has not been castrated.
- A **pullet** is a female chicken under 1 year old.
- A **cockerel** is a male chicken under 1 year old.
- A **capon** is a castrated male bird.

You do not need to have a rooster for a hen to produce eggs. The eggs will not be fertilized and will not hatch into baby chicks, but your flock will be more docile without a male. Roosters can be aggressive, especially when mating with a hen. If you have a male, you can still eat eggs the rooster fertilizes as long as the embryo has not started to form. An embryo only can form under specific conditions that your refrigerator does not mimic.

Best Breeds for Exhibition

Attend county fairs or local exhibitions to take a gander at the popular breeds that participate in these events. Any purebreds can be used for show, and some shows allow for hybrids. One of the most prestigious organizations chicken owners can join is the American Poultry Association (APA) (**www.amerpoultryassn.com**), which uses a point system to classify its members. For example, if you participate in a state meet or any APA-sanctioned show with 750 to 1,499 birds, you receive ten points. The more points you receive, the higher your standing in the association. The association has various levels, including Master Exhibitor, Grand Master Exhibitor, and Hall of Fame Exhibitor. Once you reach each level, you receive an award, such as a plaque and recognition in the APA yearbook. Join the APA through their website, where you also can find more information on where meets are located and how to register.

Start with small, local shows before traveling to larger regional shows with your birds. This will give you an opportunity to learn from more experienced chicken fanciers and see how the shows operate. When you are ready to show your chickens, be sure they are in top condition. Follow the guidelines the judges give, which should be outlined for you when you register. Ask a representative if you do not receive them. Even a small detail that is not followed could disqualify your bird. To avoid disappointment on show day, be prepared ahead of time, and make sure you understand all of the rules.

Below is a list of birds that are visually impressive and are good breeds to choose should you want to show chickens.

Silkies

These birds originated in China and Japan and arrived in America in the 1800s. Their feathers do not have the barbicels that hold a normal feather together, which gives the birds the illusion they are fluffy. Their feathers are similar in texture to fur and are not like the smooth feathers other chickens have. They typically have a **topknot,** which is a poof of feathers on top of their head, or their faces can be completely covered with feathers, similar to a shaggy dog. Silkies come in a variety of colors: red, buff, white, black, splash (a chicken that is one color with a splash of another color highlighted typi-

cally on its head and back), cuckoo (barred or striped with another color such as black and white), and lavender, with blue/black skin and black bones. Their earlobes are blue or turquoise, and their eyes are brown or black.

The **comb** is the fleshy growth on top of a chicken's head. It is a thin piece of skin that comes in different shapes and is either red or purple. Some chickens have thicker combs. Silkies have walnut-shaped combs that should be wider than they are long. Some Silkies have **pea combs**, which are low combs with three ridges, or a thin **single comb** that is thin, attaches to the beak along the skull with five or six grooves, and stands up. This type of comb probably would be disqualified from a show because it is not the ideal comb for a pure breed. Whereas most chickens have four toes, silkies have five, which adds to their uniqueness.

Male bantam Silkies weigh approximately 36 ounces. A **bantam** is a miniature version of a full-sized chicken, usually about one-fourth the size. The female bantam weighs about 32 ounces. The weight of standard-sized Silkies is about 6 pounds for the male and 5 for the female. These birds are not proficient egg layers and lay only 50 to 120 eggs per year. Their eggs are a dark cream to brown color.

Silkies are a docile breed, which makes them a great choice for novices. They also make wonderful pets. Because their feathers are not webbed, they cannot fly. Silkies, like all chickens, require a protective coop to keep them safe from predators. Hens and roosters of this breed are known for their parenting skills. The roosters often call to the chicks when food is found, which, with other breeds, is usually the hen's responsibility.

Showgirls

Showgirls are a crossbreed between Silkies and the naked neck Turken. It is an ornamental breed that looks like a miniature version of an ostrich. They come in a bantam size. These little birds have both male and female genders, but both are called Showgirls, which is sometimes confusing.

They have five toes on each foot. They come in white, black, buff, blue, lavender, and splash with dark skin. A full crest of feathers sits on top of their heads, but their necks are bare. Their bodies are fluffy, and their legs are feathered. Like the Silkies, their comb is walnut-shaped.

Showgirls are gentle, friendly, and are perfect birds for new chicken owners looking for a docile breed that is easily handled. They bear confinement well, and they weigh about 3 pounds each. They do not require much space.

They have a relatively high production rate when it comes to laying eggs. Their eggs are small and range in color from creamy white to light tan. The naked neck is a dominant gene and will always come through. Mating two Showgirls lessons the quality of their feathers and immune system, so breeders usually breed Silkies to Turkens to continue to produce Showgirls.

These birds make great birds to show. Their look is unique, and their demeanor is gentle. They are a crowd-pleaser and a judge favorite.

Andalusian

This breed had its start in Spain and was further developed in the United States and England. The Andalusian lays white eggs. Colors seen in this breed are blue (which is the required color to show this breed of chickens), black, white, or black and white. The adult blue chickens have slate blue feathers with a narrow ridge of dark blue. This breed is an active forager, which will keep feed costs down during warm weather when the chicken can remain outside. However, the bird is so active that it can run very fast, which makes its capture quite the event.

Cochin

This Chinese ornamental breed is a favorite for poultry shows. They have feathered feet and come in a variety of colors. It is a heavy breed, with roosters weighing up to 11 pounds. The hen only lays medium-sized, brown eggs for a short time but makes an excellent mother. She will even become a foster mother to chicks of other breeds.

American Game

These feisty birds were originally bred for cockfighting, which is now illegal in the United States. Although they are not used for fighting, they still have a natural instinct to be territorial, so adult cocks should be separated to avoid fighting. Despite being aggressive birds, they are easily handled by humans. Today, many breed these chickens for exhibition because of their strong physical and gameness traits. The American Game is known to be a hardy bird because of their good flying and foraging skills. Hens of this breed lay medium-sized eggs that are white or cream-colored from mid-spring to late summer or fall. The American Game comes in virtually every color and can have pea, straight, triple, or a combination comb.

Clown Face, also known as Spanish, White-Faced Black Spanish, and Spanish White-Ear

Their name says it all. They are white-faced with a black body. They are fancy birds but proficient egg-layers as well. Originating in Spain, Clown Faces are the oldest of Mediterranean breeds.

They have gray skin, a clean leg (no feathers) with dark shanks, and a single comb, and their eggs are white. Clown Faces are slow to develop, and their white faces take about a year to completely develop. These birds tolerate confinement and bear the heat well; however, they are prone to frostbite, so in cold climates or in cold weather it is important to take good care of them and keep them in warm surroundings.

Males weigh about 6 pounds. Females weigh about 4 to 5 pounds. Bantams usually weigh around 2 ½ pounds. These beautiful and unique birds are good pets, as their temperament is docile, and they are good exhibition birds.

Houdan

A French ornamental bird, Houdan was developed from Polish, Crevecoeurs, and possibly Dorkings breeds. Houdans were commonly raised on small farms around the towns in Normandy, France. Considered dual-purpose birds, these birds are raised for their fine, tender, and juicy white meat with delicate bones, as well as their ability to produce an ample amount of eggs each year. They come in two varieties: mottled and white. Mottled is a blended mixture of two colors. In this case, it is typically black and white. The chicks are a fluffy ball of black and white markings with the beginnings of its trademark crest just starting to flare out. The white variety was created in America.

Houdans have a V-shaped comb. Their legs are clean, and they have five toes. Four of the toes are at the bottom of the chicken's leg, and the fifth toe is higher up on the leg. Their crest, which is a puff of feathers atop the head, is their most noted feature. As with all crested breeds, they need to be checked for mites and lice daily. The roosters weigh 8 pounds and the hens weigh 6 ½ pounds. Houdan bantams are a delicate bird at about 3 pounds. The standard hen lays medium, white eggs regularly, totaling about 100 eggs yearly. Bantam hens are sporadic and are not proficient layers.

Houdans are easy to handle as they have a gentle nature. They are a good show bird. They make good pets, too. They are available at most hatcheries or online. Even though they are flighty birds, they bear confinement well. All they need is some room to run and a roost at night to be content.

Brabanter

The Brabanter chicken is thought to have originated in the Netherlands. The breed was nearly extinct in the early 20th century but was recreated from German breeds to become the chicken we know it to be today. Brabanters are largely ornamental birds. They have a crest that is tight and pointed forward, which means it does not block their vision. Brabanters also have **muffs**, which are feathers that protrude from the sides of the chicken's face, and some have a beard.

Brabanter bantams are a cross between the bearded Polish bantam and the standard Brabanter. They weigh about 3 pounds, with the standard rooster weighing about 7 pounds and the hen weighing about 5 to 6 pounds.

There are several varieties of the Brabanter breed of chicken, including cream and the gold colored, both of which are found in the United States. Outside of the United States, there are other varieties, including self black, white, blue laced, cuckoo, golden black half moon spangled, silver black half moon spangled, yellow white half moon spangled, golden blue half moon spangled, and lavender. This breed is gentle, friendly, and would be a welcomed addition to your flock or family.

Frizzles

This bird is from Southeastern Asia and gets its name from its feathers, which curl outward. Frizzles' colors include red, black, white, blue, silver-gray, splash (spotted), and buff, and their eyes are red. Although Frizzle here refers to a breed of chicken, the term "frizzle" is also a way to describe a bird that has fuzzy-looking feathers.

Frizzles have a single comb on top of their heads and a clean leg that does not have any feathers on it. The standard weight for the rooster Frizzle is 11 pounds, the hen is about 8 ½ pounds, and the bantam for this breed is 4 to 6 pounds. Not only are they popular show birds, but they are also proficient egg layers; hens can lay more than 200 eggs per year. Their eggs are cream or tinted and of a medium size.

Frizzles have a friendly demeanor and docile temperament, which makes them excellent additions to your family. They are easy for novice chicken owners. Their feathers do not fare well in wet weather, so they need a dry coop. They do not mind being confined, so you could keep them indoors.

Polish

Also called a Padua or Poland, this chicken is most known for the tall, starburst-shaped crest that engulfs its head. Polish breeds are available in several colors and markings. Solid colors are typically white, black, blue, and cuckoo (also referred to as barred). Some birds have lace markings and are gold, silver, and chamois. The crests can sometimes cover the chickens' eyes, so they can be startled easily. Use a special waterer, such as a nipple drinker, so the crest stays dry and clean. Their comb is V-shaped or horn-shaped.

Polish roosters weigh about 6 pounds, and hens weigh 4 ½ pounds. Bantams are about 3 pounds for males and 2 pounds for females. Care for this fowl requires more work than other breeds because of their coat. They are a magnet for mites because of the thickness of their topknot, which is another term for crest. One way to prevent mites is to use a spray insect repellent, but be careful not to get it in the bird's eyes. The birds should be kept dry because their thick feathers will hold moisture longer. Polish hens are good layers and produce 150 to 200 white eggs per year. They are not good sitters, though, and have been known to abandon or destroy their eggs. You can use a hen that is broody (meaning in her fertile cycle and instinctively wants to sit on eggs) or use an incubator for the eggs this breed produces.

Yokohama

This is a striking bird with a long tail that can grow up to 2 feet long. They are white and red, saddled, or red-shouldered, meaning the feathers that cover their shoulders and upper back are a strikingly different color than their body feathers. Their skin is yellow. These are ornamental birds and are not good layers or typically used for meat because they are not fleshy, nor are they tender to eat. Their combs are single and thin or walnut-shaped and red in color.

Yokohamas require a taller coop and higher perch than most breeds because of their magnificent tail. The cock of the breed weighs about 6 ½ pounds, and the hens weigh about 5 ½ pounds. The bantam Yokohama weighs about 3 pounds for a male and 2 ½ pounds for a female. The males tend to be aggressive and dominating. This breed is not recommended for a novice, but as you gain more experience, they are an excellent ornamental breed to show.

New Hampshire Red

With its bold, red and orange body and black tail, this bird is a classic vision of a chicken. It is an American breed derived from the popular Rhode Island Red. Originally, these birds were bred for laying eggs, but their hearty bodies make them good meat providers. Their eggs are brown and typically classified as large. Their red single combs have five points, and their eyes are red. They make great show birds because of their colorful coats. This is one of the easiest breeds to raise, and they are versatile to show, to use for egg laying, or to produce meat.

New Hampshire Reds are great for beginners because of their friendly nature and tame attitude. They are not aggressive or as flighty as other breeds and are easy to handle. Roosters weigh about 8 ½ pounds, and hens weigh about 6 ½ pounds. The bantams weigh about 5 ½ pounds.

Japanese Bantam

This bird is a true bantam, meaning it does not have a large counterpart. The color varieties are white, black, black-tailed white, black-tailed buff (buff is a rusty color), barred brown red (meaning they have a red body with brown stripes), grey, and wheaten (a creamy tan). They have a single red comb, red earlobes, and black eyes. Their legs are short and clean with four toes.

The most notable feature of this bantam is its tail. The body is petite, but the tail is large and often reaches over the chicken's head. The males sometimes are disqualified from competition because their tails are **rye**, or fall to the side rather than standing erect. The females have profuse tails, but not as large as the males'.

The Japanese Bantam is not a proficient egg layer, and the eggs they lay are tiny and rare. They make good pets because they are easy to tame and gentle on landscape, and they are social birds that will interact with people.

Black or Blue Sumatras

The Black and the Blue Sumatras are beautiful, ornamental birds that have long tails. The Black Sumatras, both the hen and the cock, have chocolate brown eyes and no wattles, which are the flaps of red or purple skin under a chicken's chin. Their legs are clean, bluish in color, and have multiple spurs, or sharp protrusions. Their faces are deep purple and their black plumage has a green sheen to it.

The males have long, flowing tails that hang down. They are a beautiful breed of chicken with black skin and bones. They are bantams, with the rooster weighing 5 pounds and the hen weighing 4 pounds. Although the hens lay about 100 eggs per year, the birds themselves are used mostly as a pet or show bird and not for their egg-laying ability. Their eggs are white, and the chicks often are born yellow with splashes of black.

Black and Blue Sumatras are believed to be derived from the jungle fowl and possibly crossed with another species of bird, such as a pheasant or pheasant crossbreed. They were imported to the United States and Europe in 1847 from the island of Sumatra, which is located in the far Southeast Asia.

Although somewhat a rare breed of bird, many hatcheries have the black, blue, and a splash variety for sale. There is a White Sumatra, which is hard to find. Although this breed mostly is used as a show bird, they are beautiful birds to own and care for as pets.

Dutch

The tiniest bantam of all, the Dutch chicken, weighs only 1 pound. It is a true bantam chicken with no large counterpart. The petite bird is somewhat docile in the female gender, but the male has been compared to a snapping turtle. They are lively and active but tolerate confinement well. These little birds are perfect if you do not have much room for your flock to roam.

Dutch chickens come in several colors. They are silver, light brown, blue, black, white, bluish-light brown (called blue partridge in the UK), and many other colors. They have a clean leg, with white skin and white or blue shanks. Their earlobes are white. Dutch hens produce about 100 tiny eggs per year.

These birds were originated in Holland where they are still popular today. They were introduced to the United States shortly after WWII but did not catch on in popularity. In the 1970s, they were reintroduced once again. Dutch bantams are an exhibition favorite.

Appenzeller Spitzhauben

The Appenzeller Spitzhauben's origin is in Switzerland. This breed of chicken forages well and loves to roam the mountainside and roost in trees. It is a rare breed but a beautiful bird with crested feathers on top of its head. Spitzhauben means pointed bonnet, which is what the crest looks like. It is available in blue spangled, black spangled, gold, gold spangled, silver spangled, and barthuhner.

The rooster Appenzeller Spitzhauben weighs about 4 ½ pounds, and the hens weigh about 3 ½ pounds. Their comb is V-shaped, except in the barthuhner variety. They have a rose comb and no crest. The Appenzeller Spitzhauben has a clean, blue leg, with four toes. Their eyes are brown. Their eggs are white and medium size. They are average egg layers, laying about 155 eggs yearly.

These birds are very active and do not bear confinement well. They love to roam and forage for insects. They require little food and are easy to maintain. If you want an Appenzeller Spitzhauben, be sure you have lots of room for them to roam, and make sure their run and coop are secure. They like to take flight as best as they can. Their nature is overall friendly, docile, and calm. They are good in all climates. Their combs and wattles are relatively small, which means in cold weather there is little skin susceptible to frostbite.

Although Appenzeller Spitzhaubens are rarely found in the United States of America, they are popular in Europe. They are not recognized by the American Poultry Association, possibly because of their limited availability in the U.S.

Aseel

Aseels are a somewhat rare bird and one of the oldest breeds of chickens. They originate from India and were developed to be an aggressive, belligerent bird. The instinct to fight is a dominant gene that has been bred into them. It is said that even chicks just a few weeks old will start attacking their own mother. More than one rooster should not be in your flock. However, owners claim that these birds are docile toward people and easy to care for at home.

The Aseel's feathers are short, hard, and glossy. Aseels have strong, curved necks and short beaks, making their faces almost predator-like. Their eyes are pearl colored and set close together. The skin and legs are yellow, and they have a clean leg with 4 toes. This bird does not have a wattle or a crest. Their pea comb is small.

Aseels are kept as pets or used as an ornamental breed. They are available in black-breasted red, dark, spangled, white, and wheaton. They bear confinement well and are fine in any climate. Hens weigh 4 pounds, while roosters weigh between 5 and 6 pounds. Bantams are 2 ½ pounds. The hens are low-producing egg layers. They lay light brown eggs of a medium size.

Crevecoeur

This beautiful yet rare breed was originally meant to be a **table bird**, which is a bird meant to eat, but its striking coat and crest make it a popular ornamental bird used for show. Crevecoeurs hail from Normandy, France. Black is the only color recognized, but some variations are blue. Because their feathers are delicate, they are best suited for climates with warmer weather; cold and wet regions are hard on them. They do well in confinement but are active and need room to run during the day.

These chickens have a clean leg, with four toes on each foot. They are friendly and quiet, and the hens are seldom broody. Under all of those black feathers is white skin, and they have dark shanks. Crevecoeurs have a V-shaped comb and a long wattle. The roosters weigh about 7 to 8 pounds and hens weigh about 6 pounds.

The eggs of the mother hens are medium size and white. They lay about 2 eggs per week or about 100 eggs a year. Overall, the Crevecoeur can provide plenty of eggs, it is a good size for a table bird, friendly enough to be a pet, and it has unique features for showing and competitions. It is an endangered bird but can be found at various hatcheries online.

Sicilian Buttercup

This Mediterranean class of chicken was discovered in 1892 in Italy. It is named Buttercup because its comb is a perfect buttercup comb with 5 points. The rich colors of the roosters and hens of this breed attracted the attention of Americans who show birds. The males are a rich, orange-red bird with black spangles in their feathers. Their lustrous black tail has a green sheen to it. The female Buttercup is a deep gold or amber, and black spangles accent all of her feathers. Their shanks and toes are olive or yellow green, their skin is yellow, and their earlobes are white.

Buttercups are foragers by nature and prefer to be free-range. They do not bear confinement well, and owners claim their birds are friendly but restless. One of the most typical characteristics of this breed is that they tend to be a bit wild and do not prefer to be social with people.

The hens are seldom broody, and they have a low egg production. The eggs they do produce are small and white. Even though they do not provide an ample supply of eggs, they are attractive show birds that will surely please the crowd. They are a small bird and only weigh 4 to 5 pounds.

Pekin Bantam

The true bantam, Pekin Bantam, from China circa 1830, is an ornamental breed with an uncertain history. There are several theories surrounding this breed. One rumor is that the first Pekin Bantam was stolen from the Chinese emperor's private collection in 1860. Another theory is that the breed was brought from China to Queen Victoria as a gift and then bred with other breeds, which explains the breed that we know today.

These light birds are great for show. They are extremely gentle and make for great family pets as well. Children will delight in fact that Pekin Bantams are lively and active, yet very docile and well adjusted. They are so petite that they require little room. They love to forage for garden bugs and other pests.

Malay

The Malay chicken comes from Eastern Asia. This aggressive chicken is not recommended for novice chicken owners. The breed stands tall; some are reported to be close to 3 feet tall. The Malay is also a heavy breed, with roosters weighing 8 to 9 pounds and hens weighing about 7 pounds. Flighty and wild, Malays do not tolerate confinement. With their long legs, slanted eyes, and tight feathers, this breed looks intimidating.

Malays have a clean leg with four toes. They have a reputation for being vigorous and having a hardy constitution. They come in black, white, spangled, red pyle, black-breasted red, and wheaton for the female only. The comb is strawberry.

Malay hens are poor egg layers. On average, they lay one egg per week, and the hens are not broody. Malay chickens should have lots of room to run, roam, and forage. Cold weather does not suit this breed well because their feathers are hard and do not provide much insulation. Softer feathers, such as down, hold body heat and protect the birds from the cold. Malays are best kept as an ornamental bird.

Best Chickens for Egg Laying

A good egg layer will produce 150 to 250 eggs per year. Hens usually start to lay eggs about 4 to 6 months old and will continue to lay eggs into their teens. As a rule, good egg layers should have deep, full abdomens. Eggs come in different colors but taste the same, and a hen always will lay the same color egg. If you are a novice owner and would like to get chickens primarily for eggs, you will need only about four birds to get started, which will give you 20 to 28 eggs per week.

Araucana

Not only is this bird a good layer, but also the eggs she produces are blue-green or turquoise. Some varieties of this chicken also lay pink eggs or brown eggs with pink hues. These eggs are perfect for Easter decorating, gifts for neighbors, or just to add some variety in your egg basket. The chickens come in partridge (black stripes that meet at the middle of the feather then move outward), silver-blue partridge, yellow partridge, fawn, wheaten (creamy tans), white, black, and lavender.

The roosters of this breed weigh about 5 pounds, and hens weigh about 4 pounds. Bantams of the breed weigh 28 ounces for a male and 26 ounces for a female. Araucanas can be tailed or **rumpless,** meaning without a tail. They have a pea comb that is low to the head with three ridges, and they have a clean leg without any feathers. A unique feature of these birds is the tufts of feathers they have by their ears.

Araucanas are a good choice for novice bird owners because they have high energy, but it is okay to pen them. Their home should offer fresh green grass every day, so a mobile coop or allowing them to roam freely might be best. They will provide you with about 200 eggs per year.

Cream Legbar

The Legbar breed of chicken has three varieties: gold, silver, and cream. The gold and silver varieties are a type of Leghorn and lay cream-colored or white eggs. The Cream Legbar, though, is an **autosexing**, blue egg layer, which means you can tell the sex of the chick by the color of its feathers. Cream Legbars are very popular for their egg laying abilities. They lay green and blue eggs.

This breed is a mix of Barred Rock, Brown Leghorn, and Araucana breeds. Through much trial and many generations of mating, the Cream Legbar was developed. The process began in the 1930s. If you were to cross your own chickens of the aforementioned breeds, you mostly will not have the same result. Through the generations of breeding, the ideal hybrid was developed with the dominant genes presiding to ensure colorful eggs.

Cream Legbars have a yellow beak, a smooth, red face; red comb; and red, long and thin wattles. The comb is a single erect comb with five to seven even spikes. The comb is smaller in males than it is in females. The earlobes are pale blue on both the male and female. They have a crest on the back top portion of their head. Their skin is yellow with a clean leg. Cream Legbars have four evenly spaced toes on each foot. Their shanks are typically strong, clean, and rounded.

The roosters are muscular birds with long, feathered necks and a tail that sits at a 45-degree angle. The females are decent egg layers and produce about 180 eggs per year. The temperament of both genders is flighty. They are noisy birds with cackles that are similar to those of the Araucana. They are hearty in any climate, but do not bear confinement well. They are non-broody, but nervous. If you are looking for a bird to provide you with a colorful array of eggs and you are able to tolerate the noise, this may be the breed for you.

Ancona

Originating near Acona, Italy, this breed is black with white-tipped feathers. They are a smaller chicken that lays about five small, white eggs per week. This breed can be flighty. This trait combined with their darker color helps them avoid predators.

Holland

This often-overlooked breed has a high productivity of medium, white eggs. This breed does well in all climates, even extreme cold. However, their single comb might become frostbitten in the winter. As a calm and hardy breed that forages well, these birds are able to adapt to virtually any surrounding. They are known to be quiet, friendly, and calm chickens, and hens of this breed seldom become broody.

Sussex

These birds, which originated in Sussex County, England, are also known as Speckled Sussex in America. They are plump birds, available in white, silver, red, brown buff, and speckled. Avoid exposing this bird to excessive sunlight because their coats have a tendency to become brassy. The speckled variety gets more speckled with each molting, making it an attractive bird.

Sussex chickens have a single comb and a clean leg. They are a heavy breed weighing about 9 pounds for the male and 7 pounds for the female. The bantam variety is about 4 pounds. The earlobes and eyes are both red, and their skin is white. They are proficient egg layers, laying 240 to 260 eggs per year. They are also plump enough for meat. Their eggs are large and cream to light-brown color.

Because they are alert, curious, and docile, these chickens make great pets. They can be free-range or penned. This hearty breed will lay eggs even in the coldest part of the season, which is not typical in all breeds.

Leghorns

In America, the colors of the Leghorn range from white, black, red, Columbian (mostly white body with a black tail or black wing tips on tail), partridge (black stripes meeting at the middle of the feather then moving outward), brown, silver partridge, and black-tailed red with white skin.

Their combs are large and can be single or **rose**, which means almost flat on top and fleshy with small, round protuberances. They have red eyes and a clean leg. White earlobes are a trait of the Leghorn that indicates a good egg layer. Hens will produce about 200 white eggs each year.

Roosters are somewhat aggressive, and the breed in general can be excitable and noisy. Leghorns like to take flight. Ideally, they need large, tall coops that allow movement but which are secure. It is also a good idea to have trees with branches for the birds to perch on, as this will help satisfy their desire to fly. The bantams are calmer than their larger counterparts. The rooster weighs typically 6 pounds and the hen 4 ½ pounds. Bantams of this variety weigh about 1 pound.

Rose Comb Brown

The Rose Comb Brown is a variety of the Leghorn chicken breed. The male weighs about 6 pounds, the female weighs about 4 ½ pounds, and the bantams weigh in at about 3 pounds.

The Leghorn varieties, including Rose Comb Buff, Single Comb Silver, Single Comb White, Single Comb Black, and Single Comb Dark Brown, are all proficient egg layers. They are an economical bird to own to produce more than 200 eggs a year. The Rose Comb Brown produces white eggs. Some varieties of the Leghorn breed produce brown eggs. Most of the white eggs found in grocery stores are from Leghorns.

Their homes should be tall and large coops as they are flighty birds like Leghorns. They are easy to care for as they are independent and are good foragers. They make great pets, lay almost an egg a day, and are good for meat, too. They are a great value.

Friesian

This ancient breed of chicken originated in the Friesian Islands. Their unique and dazzling markings make this a great ornamental bird, as well as a good layer. The Friesian's feathers come in chamois penciled, silver penciled, and gold penciled coloring. Although this breed has been around for more than 1,000 years, it is relatively new to the United States and was introduced in the 1980s.

Friesians are not only known for their beauty. They lay about 230 white eggs per year. They are a small breed with roosters weighing 6 pounds, hens weighing 5 pounds, and bantams weighing between 2 ½ and 3 pounds.

The temperament of this breed is extremely nervous. These birds are flighty and not easily kept in a confined space. If you have lots of room for these chickens to forage and want an egg layer, this may be a good bird for you to own. They are beautiful and serve many purposes.

Australorp

These chickens have white skin and black and blue feathers with a beetle-green sheen that sunlight enhances. Their combs are single and bright red. The eyes, beak, and earlobes are dark. Their legs are clean and are slate blue, except for the toes and soles of the feet, which are white.

The Australorp weighs up to 10 pounds for a rooster and up to 8 pounds for a hen. The bantams weigh between 28 and 36 ounces. Their temperament is quiet and gentle, which makes them perfect for children to handle, and the neighbors will not even know they are there. They produce brown eggs, and owners should expect about 200 eggs during the laying season, which ends when the weather gets cold. Australorps do not fly and tend to stay grounded because they are heavy. Their home and run do not have to be especially secure to keep them in, just secure enough to keep predators out.

Catalana

This bird is popular in South America and Spain but is also available in North America. They are hardy birds and good egg layers. They are buff colored, and some have a black tail. They are a large breed, with males weighing 6 to 7 pounds and females weighing 4 to 6 pounds. Bantams are about 3 pounds. They have a single comb with six points, and the male's comb stands erect. They also have a clean leg and four toes. Their wattles are red, and their earlobes are white.

The hens lay medium-size eggs, which are cream-colored or sometimes tinted pink. Although these birds are not aggressive, they are active and flighty. They do not particularly like confinement and would prefer free-range living with lots of room to move. The males can be aggressive toward each other. This breed fares well in the heat and hot environments.

Hamburg

Hamburgs or Hamburghs derive from Holland. They come in silver-spangled, golden-spangled, golden-penciled, silver penciled, and black and white. This breed is typically a small bird, with the adult male weighing 5 pounds and females weighing about 4 pounds. Bantams weigh 1 ½ pounds.

They have clean legs with 4 toes, and their comb is rose. Their skin is white with slate blue shanks. The hens are proficient egg layers and lay about 200 small white eggs yearly. They fare well in the winter. Hamburgs are alert, active birds that do not do well in confinement. They fare better as free-range birds. Hamburgs tend to avoid human contact and are not as friendly as other breeds. This chicken breed is spritely, though and will not disappoint if you want an egg layer.

Fayoumi or Egyptian Fayoumi

The Egypitan Fayoumi dates back to B.C., originating in the area along the Nile River in Egypt. The roosters walk tall with an impressive posture. Their carriage is almost vertical, which gives them a long, lean look. They are flighty birds and known to be excellent escape artists if you keep them confined. Fayoumis mature quickly, and the males will try to crow as early as 5 or 6 weeks old. They continue their enthusiasm for crowing as they grow. Your nearest neighbor may not be a fan of the early morning ritual, so be sure you are prepared.

Fayoumis weigh in at 4 pounds for the male and 3 pounds for the female. The hens can start laying eggs as early as 4 months. They lay small, white eggs. Fayoumis have rose combs, white skin, and slate blue or willow green shanks. If you live in a warm climate, these hardy birds endure heat well. They are economical eaters and are inexpensive to raise.

Lakenvelder

This chicken is a sight to behold. The Lakenvelder's head and tail are a deep black color. Its body and breast are snowy white. The comb, wattle, and eyes are bright red. This breed is a classic chicken. They have a high carriage. That, combined with the striking colors of their feathers, makes them a great show bird as well as a proficient layer. Lakenvelders are a lightweight breed, too. The rooster weighs 5 pounds, and hens weigh 4 pounds.

Lakenvelders come from Germany. They are not aggressive toward other chickens. Although they tend to take flight, they adapt well as free-range birds or in confinement. These birds tend to be shy and not social toward people, but they are a hardy breed and can live in a variety of climates. Underneath their feathers, Lakenvelders have white skin and dark shanks.

The hens have a high production rate for laying eggs; they lay about 200 eggs a year. The eggs are small and white.

There are different versions of the Lakenvelder, including the Golden Lakenvelder and the more common Silver Lakenvelder. Bantams are the Vorwerk variety, with a black and gold combination. Lakenvelder is said to translate from Dutch to mean "shadow on a sheet."

Gingernut Ranger

The Gingernut Ranger is a cross between a Rhode Island Red and a Light Sussex. These docile, yet friendly birds are proficient egg layers with hens laying 150 to 200 large brown eggs per year. This breed of chicken has a deep breast, an upward pointing tail, and wings that give the appearance of being neatly tucked to the sides.

Their legs are clean and yellow, and each foot has four toes. The comb and wattle are both medium size. The face is smooth and red. Hens weigh 5 to 6 pounds, and roosters weigh 7 to 8 pounds.

This gentle bird is a great forager and would be happy to wander throughout your garden in search of slugs, bugs, and other treats. They manage well in confinement. Overall, Gingernut Rangers are an easy bird to start out with for new chicken owners.

Easter Eggers

Easter Eggers are, by far, the most fun variety of chicken to own. Easter Eggers are not a breed, but rather a variety of chicken that does not conform to any breed. It does not belong to a class, and therefore cannot be shown in a competition. These birds tend to be quite friendly and social. Easter Eggers lay colorful, extra-large eggs from blue to green to aqua and pink in different shades of those colors.

Easter Eggers bear confinement well and are hardy, so they can endure hot, cold, wet, or dry climates. They are docile and make for a wonderful family pet. Children will marvel at the different colored eggs — and adults will, too.

These birds have a clean leg with four toes on each foot. They are a large fowl but have a bantam counterpart. Roosters weigh 7 pounds, hens weigh about 5 to 6 pounds, and bantams are about 3 pounds. Hens lay about 200 eggs a year, but some have been known to lay 6 to 8 eggs per week. This would give you close to 400 eggs yearly. They are well worth the investment.

Easter Eggers are easy to find because they are a common mixed breed. Often, they are mistakenly labeled Araucanas or Americaunas because of the similarity of their colored eggs. Both of these breeds produce colorful eggs and are most likely crossed with the Easter Egger, but Araucanas and Americaunas are both recognized breeds.

Best Chickens for Meat

Chickens not only provide fresh eggs, but also they can provide meat for your family. Some owners become attached to their flocks and do not think they can slaughter a chicken for food, but as long as it is performed in a quick and humane manner, killing a bird for food is an honorable way to end its life.

Dorking

This British breed has been around for about 2,000 years, and its specific purpose is to be a plump, meaty bird able to feed a family. Its colors are red, silver-gray, and white. The combs of silver-gray and red birds should be single. The combs of white birds should be rose, which means they are fleshy, flat, and broad on the top. The combs are broad and solid, and the main part has a curved surface with small and round protuberances.

The rooster weighs between 10 to 14 pounds, and the hen weighs 8 to 10 pounds. Bantams weigh up to 3 pounds and are good for meat. Their legs are clean, short, and white with five toes. Their earlobes are red, and their eggs are white. Dorkings will lay about three eggs per week.

These birds are docile and easy to handle. They do not like confinement much and will be happier free-range. You need sufficient space for them to forage for insects and wander. Dorkings take up to two years to mature, and they live up to seven years. Chickens of some breeds have been known to live up to 20 years, though eight to ten years is the average life span for a chicken. Feed that is balanced and provides proper nutrients will give you a meatier bird.

Langshan

China is where the Langshan originated; it was discovered in the 1800s. The Langshan was popular in late 19th century America because of its qualities. They can tolerate all climates, are meaty, and are adequate egg producers. They also have a gentle temperament. They are blue, black, and white, with a single comb and white skin. The blue and black birds have a green or purple sheen to them in sunlight. Green is a more desirable color and represents a more prestigious bloodline. Their eyes are dark or black. Langshans have long, clean legs with four toes. Some varieties have lightly feathered legs. By today's standards, these birds are big but are not as meaty as some commercially produced chickens. These chickens stand tall, about 20 to 24 inches high and weigh 7 to 8 pounds. Their tails can be long, about 18 to 24 inches, and are erect and carried at a high angle.

These birds are medium egg producers; they provide about 140 to 150 eggs yearly. The eggs they lay are light to dark brown and, in some cases, plum-colored. These are not as common but are the most desirable color. Langshans are a good choice for new chicken owners because they are gentle and docile.

Cornish

Cornish chickens were developed primarily for meat in Cornwall, England. This breed's trademark is its muscular body and excellent carcass shape. They have yellow skin, and their feathers are short and close to the body. The feathers range in colors that are dark, white, buff, and white-laced red. Their eyes are reddish-brown, and they have a single pea comb. Their legs are clean, and they have four toes.

The roosters of this breed weigh about 10 ½ pounds, and the hens weigh 8 pounds. Bantams weigh about 3 to 5 pounds. Cornish chickens are the standard breed for grocery stores because of their meaty bodies. They have skyrocketed in the industry to become the top-selling fryer or broiler chicken.

These birds are not proficient egg layers, but they do produce brown eggs. They are not friendly poultry, so they are not the best choice for a pet. Cornish chickens tend to be noisy. They do well in confinement, but they need exercise to help them keep their muscular, meaty shape. They are also energetic birds that are always on the move.

Brahma

The name of this bird comes from the River Brahmaputra in India. Brahmas are sometimes referred to as the "King of Chickens" because of their large size. They come in an assortment of colors, including buff Colombian (meaning they have black tails or black-tipped feathers on their tail), gold, and white. Their coats can be light or dark in color. They have red eyes and a small, single pea comb. Their legs are feathered.

Brahma roosters are docile, even somewhat submissive compared with other breeds, and they weigh between 10 and 12 pounds. Hens weigh 7 to 9 pounds, and bantams weigh about 38 ounces for a male and 32 ounces for a female.

Brahmas are good egg layers and produce about 140 brown eggs yearly. Although they are large birds, they are gentle and easy to handle. They take up to two years to mature. Brahmas need a dry environment, but they can fare well in hot or cold climates. They do not fly and are content behind a 2-foot fence.

Faverolles

This chicken is a crossbreed developed originally to produce hearty, plump birds. The lineage of the Faverolle is most likely a mixture of several breeds, including Houdan, Dorking, Malines, white-skinned light Brahma, and the common five-toed fowl. The colors are black, buff, laced blue, salmon, white, and ermine (a light-colored bird). They have light red eyes and a single comb.

The weight of the male bird is 9 to 11 pounds, and the female is 7 ½ to 9 ½ pounds. Bantams are about 2 pounds. Their legs are lightly feathered, and they have five toes. They are productive egg layers and lay about 100 light brown eggs each year, even through the winter months. These active birds are always on the go and need room to roam. They are gentle and sometimes can be bullied by more aggressive breeds, such as the Cornish, old English game, or modern game chickens.

Cubalaya

This hearty bird comes in white, black, black-breasted red, or blue wheaton (having a dark blue body with a rusty coat on top). They are good egg layers; they produce cream-colored and tinted eggs but are raised primarily for their meat. They are a beautiful, ornamental bird with long tail feathers that curve downward, known as a **lobster tail**. They have bay-colored eyes, red wattles, and a pea comb. They are rare in the United States, as they originated in Cuba and are not a popular breed here.

The birds weigh 6 to 7 pounds for a male and 4 to 5 pounds for a female. Bantams are about 3 pounds. This breed is friendly and can be trained to eat out of your hand. They can endure any climate and do well in confinement.

Scots Dumpy

Scots Dumpy is known by several names, including Bakies, Crawlers, and Creepies because of their short legs. This breed was developed in the Highlands of Scotland and is now a rare breed. Their most striking trait is their short, squatty legs. The Scots Dumpy should have legs that are a mere 2 inches long from the ground. They are a heavy bird with a lot of meat on their bones. The roosters weigh in at 7 pounds, and the hens weigh 5 ½ to 6 pounds. Bantams of this breed are about 3 pounds.

This breed's legs are short, white, and have no feathers. Each foot has four toes. The eyes, comb, wattle, and earlobes of the Scots Dumpy are a bright red color, and its beaks are white. Especially in the roosters, this breed's tail is long and flowing.

Scots Dumpies are docile and gentle birds. They come in a variety of colors to include black, cuckoo, white, brown, and silver and gold. Although their legs are white in most varieties, in the black Scot Dumpy, legs are slate grey or black.

Hens of this breed are considered ideal mothers. They care for their young and are attentive to their needs. They do have a habit of going broody, though, which can make them territorial about their eggs and nests.

Best Chickens for Eggs and Meat

Some chickens can provide both meat and eggs for your family. If you want to keep your flock small or stick to one breed of chicken, you may want to begin with one of the breeds listed below. Chickens that are proficient at laying eggs and providing meat are known as dual-purpose birds.

Rhode Island Red

This bird is well known throughout North America and is one of the most popular breeds because of its gentle nature and multifunctionality.

These chickens are easy to care for, great pets, excellent egg layers, and good meat providers. They are a deep red color, with some varieties having black on their tail or wings and yellow skin. Their comb is a single or rose that is broad and solid with protuberances. The main part has a curved surface. They also have a clean leg.

These birds are proficient egg layers and produce 250 to 300 brown eggs per year. The roosters weigh about 8 ½ pounds, and the hens weigh 6 ½ pounds. The bantams of this variety weigh about 4 pounds. Roosters tend to be aggressive in this breed, but overall Rhode Island Reds are quiet and amicable. Long exposure to the sun will cause their coat colors to fade. They are content with a standard pen and coop.

Plymouth Rock

These chickens were bred for both meat and eggs, and their colors vary. The barred is a striking bird with white feathers and black, horizontal striping. They also come in white, buff, multiple penciled (a feather with several types of lines or markings), triple laced (having several layers of a contrasting color around the edge of the feather), penciled partridge (several lines or markings), multiple penciled silver partridge, Columbian (white with a black tail or black-tipped feathered

tail), buff Colombian, and blue lace (meaning the feathers have a border of a contrasting color around the edge). Their skin is yellow, and their legs are clean. The eyes are bay-colored, and they have red earlobes. A single medium-size comb sits on top of their heads.

Plymouth Rocks will lay about 200 cream- or brown-colored eggs in a year. They are a hardy bird and will lay eggs throughout the winter. Roosters weigh approximately 9 ½ pounds, hens weigh about 7 ½ pounds, and bantams are between 4 and 5 pounds.

Marans

This breed of chicken was developed in France in the 1920s around the town of Marans. This versatile bird is fleshy for meat, a good provider of eggs, friendly enough to make a pet, and suitable for breeding. Their eyes are reddish-orange, and their comb is single with up to seven serrations. Their earlobes are red, and their bodies are black, dark cuckoo, golden cuckoo, and silver cuckoo. Their legs are typically clean and are a light color, but some variations have lightly feathered legs. They have four toes.

Roosters of this breed weigh about 8 pounds, and hens weigh 7 pounds. Bantams are about 30 ounces. Marans are most noted for their eggs, which are a rich chocolate-brown color. This breed does best free-range because they are busy birds, constantly moving about. Although friendly, they do not particularly like to be handled. Consider this if they will be around small children who may want to hold them.

Wyandotte

This heavy bird is a great layer of cream- or white-colored eggs; a hen can lay 150 to 220 eggs per year. They are fast-growing and have at least 14 color variations in America, including silver laced golden, white, black, buff, Colombian, partridge, silver penciled, and barred. Their skin is yellow, and their color patterns make them a popular breed for show.

Wyandottes have rose combs, red earlobes, and red wattles. Their legs are clean with four toes. They like to take flight, so they should live in a covered run or have their wings clipped. This fowl has a good disposition and is typically calm in nature, but the males can be aggressive. They will have their own hierarchy among the flock, and more than one rooster can bring out their aggressive nature.

Roosters weigh about 8 ½ pounds, and hens weigh 6 to 7 pounds. Bantams weigh 4 pounds. Keep the pale-colored varieties away from excessive sunlight because they are sensitive to it.

Barnevelder

This chicken is not one of the most popular breeds, but they are easy to care for and great for a novice chicken owner. Their colors are black, double-laced, double-laced blue, and white. They have red single combs, wattles, and earlobes, and their eyes are orange-brown. Their legs are yellow and clean with four toes.

The roosters weigh 7 to 8 pounds, and the hens weigh 6 to 7 pounds. Bantams are about 4 pounds. A healthy hen will produce about 170 brown eggs per year. The color of the eggs will lighten as the hen gets older. The double-laced varieties are noted to be the prolific egg layers.

Barnevelders are quick growers, which means their frame and build fill out in a relatively short time compared to other breeds, making them good to raise for meat. Their temperament is docile and friendly. They are prone to bullying if living among other breeds. They do well in confinement and are not prone to flying, so a low fence will keep them corralled.

Chantecler

This is the first chicken breed to originate from Canada. Developed from crossbreeding several other types of chickens, the Chantecler was created by a Trappist monk who realized that Canada did not have a chicken to call its own. This is a large bird, with the males weighing 7 to 8 pounds and the females weighing 5 ½ to 6 ½ pounds. Bantams are about 2 pounds. They come in two colors: white and partridge. Their skin is yellow, and their legs are clean with four toes. Their wattles and pea combs are small and red. They were bred this way to help them weather harsh Canadian winters because birds with larger wattles and pea combs are more prone to frostbite. Smaller body parts are easier to keep warm and prevent from freezing. Overall, a larger bird is hardier and can survive the severe weather.

Chanteclers are a quiet and docile breed. They are proficient egg layers, with hens laying about 210 brown eggs per year. They are used for both meat and eggs. Although a hardy breed, they are somewhat rare.

Java

Java chickens thrived in the United States between 1850 and 1890. They are an ideal farm bird as the hens are ample layers, and the birds are tender and juicy table fare. Java chickens come in black and mottled colors. They were popular in New York and New Jersey in the mid to late 1800s because their black pinfeathers could easily show consumers if the birds had been plucked correctly. As the chicken industry grew, chicken entrepreneurs decided they could conceal white-feathered birds more easily if the plucking was sub-par. This practice nearly caused the Java to be driven to extinction as there was not much demand for them any longer, and larger chicken breeders stopped breeding the birds.

Despite this, the breed persevered, and small farmers raised the Java because their dual purpose suited their needs. Even today, the young cockerel makes for a good roaster, and the rich brown eggs provided by the hens are tasty and bountiful.

Java roosters weigh about 9 ½ pounds, and Java hens weigh about 6 ½ pounds. They are easy to care for, and their docile nature makes them a pleasant family pet. These birds have a clean leg, yellow skin, and dark shanks. They have a single comb and red earlobes. This bird will provide you with plenty of food and companionship.

La Fleche

Originating in France in the 1600s, the La Fleche chicken comes from the Valley of La Sarthe. This breed has been around for centuries. They come in white, cuckoo, and blue lace, but black is the most common color, and it is the color they are most known for among chicken breeds.

La Fleche is a hardy table bird. Males weigh 8 to 9 pounds, and hens weigh 6 to 7 pounds. Bantams weigh in at 3 pounds. Although their coat is a deep black color, this breed has remarkable white meat as a table bird. If you are looking for a proficient egg layer, the La Fleche hen lays 180 to 200 large eggs each year. Their eggs are white to light brown color.

As a pet, La Fleches are not people friendly. They are somewhat shy, yet docile. They are active and thrive as free-range birds because they enjoy foraging for food. La Fleches move around and like to roost in trees. You can train them to return to the coop each night by feeding them at the same time each day. They will be hungry and will learn that feeding time is in the evening. This is the easiest way to gather your flock at the end of the night.

La Fleches have a long, V-shaped wattle, and their comb has dual spikes or horns. They have even been referred to as the "Devil's Head" because of their shape. Their earlobes are white, and their legs are clean with four toes.

Ixworth

The Ixworth breed of chicken made its appearance in 1939 and originated in Suffolk, England. It is proficient at egg laying and provides sufficient meat to be considered a good table bird. These chickens were created from a mix of the white varieties of the following birds: Old English game hens, Sussex, Minorca, Orpington, and Indian game birds.

Their comb is a pea comb. They have clean, light to white legs. Their eyes are orange-red. The male weighs about 9 pounds, and the females weigh about 7 pounds. There was a bantam version of the Ixworth, but it faded out in the late 1930s to early 1940s. This is considered a rare bird. The hens tend to go broody, but they do lay about 200 eggs per year.

Vorwerk

The Vorwerk breed is a likable, docile breed of chicken that bears confinement well. This breed comes in black buff black in the United States. In Holland, though, it comes in blue buff blue, and white buff white. The breed is rare because of a small gene pool. Chicken colors can be hard to describe and the same terms may even mean different things when applied to hens and roosters or to different breeds. In the case of the Vorwerk, "black buff black" means the bird has a black head, buff or golden body, and black tail. Blue buff blue means the head is bluish in color, the body is buff or golden, and the tail is bluish. White buff white means the bird has a white head, buff or golden body, and a white tail.

The Vorwerk is similar to the Lakenvelder, but it is a different breed. Vorwerks are bulkier and have less tail. It comes in a standard and a bantam size. Male standards weigh 5 ½ to 7 ½ pounds. Female Vorwerks weigh 4 ½ to 5 ½ pounds. Bantams weigh 27 ounces. Their skin is slate gray, and their eyes are orange red. Their coat is black on the head and tail and buff on the body and the breast. Their wattles are red and medium size.

The hens are proficient egg layers. They lay 150 to 200 brown, medium-sized eggs per year. Vorwerks are suitable to live in all climates. They are good table birds and provide ample amounts of eggs. They make good pets due to their docile personality and do well as a show bird.

Buckeye

Originating in Ohio, this dual-purpose breed is thought to be the only chicken breed developed by a woman. A woman named Nettie Metcalf originally bred them in 1896 in Warren, Ohio. Metcalf bred Buff Cochins, Barred Plymouth Rocks, and some black-breasted red game birds to create the Buckeye so it could withstand cold Ohio winters. Although it was normal for women of the time to care for and manage poultry for their families, Nettie Metcalf is the only woman known to have developed a breed of chicken.

These hardy birds can withstand both cold and hot temperatures because of their pea comb and tight feathering. Hens are good layers and lay medium-sized, brown eggs throughout the year. They weigh in at 9 pounds for a rooster and 6 ½ to 7 pounds for a hen, so they make good table birds. They are known to have nice yellow skin, good thigh meat, and a large breast. The Buckeye is an active breed well suited to being free-range. They can be vocal and noisy, the roosters are known to be territorial, and hens of this breed tend to be friendly. This is an endangered breed.

Best Pet Chickens

You may want to keep chickens for a pet, as a hobby, and for companionship. Eggs are an added bonus. The following breeds are easy to raise, gentle, and attractive. They are not necessarily good egg layers or good for their meat.

Jersey Giants

This bird is large and needs lots of space to move about. They were originally bred for their meat, but their slow-growing nature deters chicken owners from this purpose. The plumage is a dark black with a dark beak and an angled tail. Some varieties are white, blue, and splash (having one solid color with a splash of a darker color on top). The single comb is red, as are the wattle and earlobes. They have a clean, dark-colored leg.

Despite their size, Jersey Giants are calm and easy to handle. They are alert and interactive, which makes them good pets. Roosters can weigh up to 13 pounds, and hens can weigh up to 10 pounds. Bantams are not typical for this breed because their main trait is their size. They produce up to 180 brown eggs per year. They also have a gentle crow, so the neighbors should not mind. Their home should be large enough to house the flock comfortably. You will know they have enough space when the birds have room to move around, perch, and sleep.

Orpingtons

This chicken makes a great choice to raise in the backyard because of its docile and cuddly nature. They have small heads on robust bodies, and they come in black, blue, buff, and white. They have a single, red, serrated comb and an elongated wattle. The earlobes are small and red, and their legs are short and clean with four toes. The dark-colored birds have darker eyes, and the lighter colors have red eyes.

Orpington roosters weigh about 8 pounds, and the hens weigh about 6 to 7 pounds. Bantams weigh about 4 pounds. They are decent egg layers and produce 160 brown eggs per year. Some varieties produce a pink-tinted egg. They do well in confinement but enjoy the chance to wander free and forage for insects. This poultry is easy to handle and makes a great family bird.

Red Star

Red Star chickens are hybrids. They make good pets because they are quiet, docile, and petite. Hens are prolific layers and produce more than 200 brown eggs yearly. They have a red buff color, single red comb, red earlobes, and clean legs with four toes. Some varieties of the Star breed come in black.

This bird is about 6 pounds for a female and 7 pounds for a male. Bantams are about 4 pounds. They are a hardy bird that can withstand colder temperatures and will lay eggs in winter months. A standard coop will make a fine home for them.

Sebright

Sir John Sebright from England developed these little birds in the 1800s. This breed of chicken is beautiful and makes for a good pet or exhibition bird. They bear confinement well. They are bantams, with the males weighing 22 ounces and the females weighing 18 ounces.

The colors of the Sebright are gold and silver with black lace. They have dark red eyes, red combs, clean legs, and four toes. They are not good egg layers and only produce about 52 tiny eggs yearly. It is difficult to raise these birds from eggs, as they have a high mortality rate, and their embryos are delicate and small. They are popular show birds because of the black lace markings on their coat.

Booted Bantam

This bird is also known as the Dutch Booted Bantam and is popular in Germany and the Netherlands. It originated in Asia and was brought to the United States in the early 20th century. They are ornamental birds with attractive coloring that can be black, porcelain, self-blue, and white. They have profuse plumage, their tail is angled upwards, and their eyes, wattles, and earlobes are red. They have a single comb with five points. Their legs are feathered, as are their feet, and they have four toes.

The Booted Bantam is one of the few breeds that is a true bantam; the males grow to about 2 pounds and the females to about 1 to 1 ½ pounds. Their nature is gentle, and they are known to follow their owner around the yard. They make great garden birds because they forage bugs but are gentle around the plants. Soft bedding is recommended for them to tread upon because of their feathered feet.

They are fair egg layers and produce two to three eggs per week. These bantams lay small cream-colored or tinted eggs and produce mostly in the summer. This docile bird is sure to be a lovable addition to your flock.

Delaware

This is a relatively new breed of chicken developed in the 1940s. The breed was originally called "Indian Rivers." They are a rare breed — a cross between barred Plymouth Rock roosters and New Hampshire Reds hens — produced to provide ample amounts of both eggs and meat. Their eggs are brown, and an average hen will produce four per week.

They are friendly and calm birds that make great pets. Male Delawares grow to 8 pounds, and the females grow to 6 pounds. Bantams are about 4 pounds. They are mostly white with some barring markings, a single comb, a clean leg, and four toes.

Seramas

Seramas are a new breed of bantam chicken that was developed in the past 15 to 20 years. It is a small, light bantam breed that does not remain true to its color or size when bred. This means that any eggs you hatch can be one of 2,500 documented color varieties. Hatch day is a treat if you are raising your flock from eggs. Eggs from Seramas are very small. It takes five Serama eggs to equal the size of one Grade A Large egg from other chickens. Their eggs usually hatch in 19 days, two days less than that of other chickens. Seramas typically produce only about 60 eggs per year. Also, the chickens can be one size bigger or smaller than the parents. Cocks weigh about 8 to 10 ounces and hens weigh about 6 to 10 ounces.

These birds are only 6 to 10 inches from the ground to the top of their comb. They are ideal pets for people with little space. A pair of Seramas can live comfortably in an 18- inch by 24-inch cage enclosure. They are "people" birds. They love attention and interaction with human beings.

Seramas come from the jungles of Malaysia and are used to temperatures of 90 to 100 degrees. They tend to be stressed if they are in climates with temperatures below 40 degrees, so it is in their best interest to keep them indoors if you live in a cold climate.

This breed has a clean leg with four toes. Its wattles typically have five points. The hens are known to be good breeders. Because this breed has a variation in size and color, no two birds look very much alike.

Campine

Campine chickens originated from Belgium but never became quite popular in the United States. They are an ornamental bird that can be used in shows as well as being a well-adapted pet. Campines can be a bit wild and prefer to be free-range as opposed to caged, but they adapt well in confinement and can be quite friendly. Chicken owners claim that Campines can be trained to eat out of their owner's hand.

These birds weigh about 5 pounds for the male and 4 pounds for the female. They have a clean leg and a large, single comb. Their skin is white and their shanks are blue. Hens lay medium sized, white eggs. They are average egg layers and produce about 150 eggs per year. They are economical eaters, which means they do not eat much.

Campines are not docile birds but can be tame. They attempt to fly and love to be on the go. The best environment for these chickens is a place with lots of space to roam and forage. Campines are active, lively, and not broody birds. They are fun to watch and care for as pets.

Miss Pepperpot

How can anyone resist this charming little hen with a name like Miss Pepperpot? Miss Pepperpots are only available in the female gender because they are Black Sex Link chickens. This means that they are the result of a hybrid cross, in this case between a Maran and a Plymouth Rock. With Black Sex Link chickens, the father is a red bird. Chicks of both sexes hatch out black but only the females will go on to have the coloring of the Miss Pepperpots. The coloring and appearance of the birds is linked to their gender. Their feathers are black with a green sheen to it. On their chest, they have red and gold feathers. They have a black beak and clean legs that are slate grey. Their thick plumage protects them from severe weather. They can survive in a hot or cold climate and in wet or dry weather, as long as they have the proper care.

Because Miss Pepperpots are hybrids, breeding males and females from similar bloodlines together will not produce Miss Pepperpot chickens. The only way to produce Miss Pepperpots is by repeating the hybrid breeding.

Miss Pepperpots are adequate layers of large brown eggs. They are more popular in Europe than in the United States. These hens are a modern hybrid with gentle and friendly personalities. They will enhance your flock with their demeanor and certainly will be a conversation starter when you mention to your friends that Miss Pepperpot moved into your home.

Sultans

Rumor has it that all Sultans can trace their family tree back years and years ago to one crate of birds that was brought to England from Istanbul. These gentle birds were a favorite among Turkish royalty. The breed is all white, with a topknot, muff, and beard. Sultans have vulture hocks and a feathered leg with five toes. They have a V-shaped comb. Outside of the United States, other variations of this breed exist, such as a blue variety.

Sultans are docile, and the standard breed for this bird weighs in at 6 pounds for the rooster and 5 pounds for the hen. Bantams weigh about 3 to 4 pounds. Hens are poor egg layers. They lay small white eggs but not very frequently. All in all, this breed is a great family pet or a beautiful ornamental breed used for show. They make great pets for children. They tend to be a delicate bird, so harsh climates and cold weather are not suitable for them. Sultans can be easy prey for predators. Take extra care if they are free-range birds. This chicken is a good forager, and they make great garden wardens.

Buying Eggs and Chicks

You can own chickens at various stages of their lives: eggs, baby chicks, pullets and cockerels, or hens and roosters; it all depends on what fits best into your lifestyle. Starting out, you may want to keep your flock around the same age to keep things simple because hatching eggs while trying to keep your pullets and cockerels from mating may require more time and attention than you initially expected. Also, bigger, stronger birds will fight the smaller, weaker birds for food. Start small, and remember that you always can add to your brood.

Beginning with Eggs

Starting with eggs can be a fun and rewarding experience, especially if you have children. A fertilized egg grows and changes each day in the shell, and after about 21 days, it will hatch. You can follow the process inside the egg with a process known as **candling**. To start your flock with eggs, you will need an incubator, which can be purchased or homemade, to keep the eggs in a constantly heated environment that resembles a mother hen. You will need to turn the eggs every day to avoid deformities. Some incubators are mechanically designed to turn the eggs, which is beneficial because it will turn them all equally at the same time each day.

However, do not count your chickens before they hatch because not all eggs will hatch. Embryos are delicate and, for a variety of reasons, may not make it to the last stage of development. If you have children, it might be best not to tell them exactly how many eggs you ordered or what day they are arriving to prevent any disappointments a cracked egg might cause. A good activity to do with kids is to have them follow the growth of the chick and predict how many eggs will hatch. This prepares them for the possibility that not all the eggs will hatch and helps them focus on the positive side of hatching the eggs. Everyone anticipates the day the baby bird chips its way through the shell and emerges into the world. Soft baby chirps are delightful, and eggs are a fun way to start on your journey of raising chickens.

CASE STUDY: PROPER HANDLING OF EGGS: FROM HEN TO CONSUMPTION

Phillip J. Clauer
Poultry Extension Specialist
Animal and Poultry Sciences

Used with permission from Virginia Cooperative Extension, Virginia Tech, and Virginia State University.

To ensure egg quality in small flocks, egg producers must learn to properly handle the eggs they produce. This article will discuss how you can ensure that your eggs will be of the highest quality and safe for consumption.

A. LAYER HOUSE MANAGEMENT

The condition of the egg that you collect is directly related to how well the flock is managed. Feeding a well-balanced ration, supplementing calcium with oyster shell, water, flock age, and health all can affect egg quality. However, since these factors are covered in other publications, this fact sheet will place emphasis on egg quality and handling after it is laid.

1. Coop and nest management

- Keep the laying flock in a fenced area so they cannot hide their eggs or nest anywhere they choose. If hens are allowed to nest wherever they choose, you will not know how old eggs are or with what they have been in contact, if you can find them at all.

- Clean environment: Keeping the layer's environment clean and dry will help keep your eggs clean. A muddy outside run, dirty or damp litter, and dirty nesting material will result in dirty, stained eggs. Clean out the nest boxes and add deep clean litter at least every two weeks.

- Clean out wet litter in coop and make sure the outside run area has good drainage and is not overgrazed.

- Nest space: Supply a minimum of four nesting boxes for flocks containing 15 hens or less. For larger flocks provide one nest for every four to five hens in the flock. This will help limit egg breakage from normal traffic and daily egg laying. Make sure nests have a deep clean layer of litter to prevent breakage and help absorb waste or broken-egg material.

2. Collect eggs early and often.

Most flocks will lay a majority of their eggs by 10 a.m. It is best to collect the eggs as soon as possible after they are laid. The longer the egg is allowed to stay in the nest, the more likely the egg will get dirty, broken, or will lose interior quality.

Collecting eggs at least twice daily is advisable, especially during extreme weather temperatures.

3. Other considerations for layer house management

- Rotate range areas often or allow enough area for birds in outside runs to prevent large dirt and mud areas from forming by overgrazing.

- Prevent eggs from being broken in order to minimize a hen learning to eat an egg and developing egg eating habits.

- Free choice oyster shells will help strengthen the eggshells.

- Keep rats, predators, and snakes away from the hen house. They often will eat eggs and contaminate the nesting boxes and other eggs.

B. PROPER EGG CLEANING AND HANDLING

1. Collect eggs in an easy-to-clean container like coated wire baskets or plastic egg flats. This will prevent stains from rusted metal and contamination from other materials that are difficult to clean and disinfect.

2. Do not stack eggs too high. If collecting in baskets, do not stack eggs more than five layers deep. If using plastic flats, do not stack more than six flats. If you stack eggs too deep, you will increase breakage.

3. Never cool eggs rapidly before they are cleaned. The eggshell will contract and pull any dirt or bacteria on the surface deep into the pores when cooled. Try to keep the temperature relatively constant until they are washed.

4. Wash eggs as soon as you collect them. This helps limit the opportunity of contamination and loss of interior quality.

5. Wash eggs with water 10 degrees warmer than the egg. This will make the egg contents swell and push the dirt away from the pores of the egg. If you have extremely dirty eggs, a mild detergent approved for washing eggs can be used. Never let eggs sit in water. Once the temperature equalizes the egg can absorb contaminants out of the water.

6. Cool and dry eggs quickly after washing. Store eggs, large end up, at 50-55 degrees and at 75 percent relative humidity. If eggs sit at room temperature (75 degrees F), they can drop as much as one grade per day. If fertile eggs are kept at a temperature above 85 degrees F for more than a few hours, the germinal disc (embryo) can start to develop. If fertile eggs are kept above 85 degrees F over two days, the blood vessels of the embryo may become visible.

If eggs are stored properly in their own carton or other stable environment, they should hold a quality of Grade A for at least four weeks.

C. SORTING AND GRADING EGGS

It is best that you sort the eggs before you store, sell, or consume them. The easiest way to sort eggs is to candle them with a bright light. This process can help you eliminate cracked eggs or eggs with foreign matter inside like blood spots.

1. How to candle eggs: Hold the egg up to the candling light in a slanting position (see figure 1). You can see the air cell, the yolk, and the white. The air cell is usually in the large end of the egg. Therefore, put the large end next to the candling light.

Hold the egg between your thumb and first two fingers. Then by turning your wrist quickly, you can cause the inside of the egg to whirl. This will tell you a great deal about the yolk and white. When you are learning to candle, you will find it helpful to break and observe any eggs you are in doubt about.

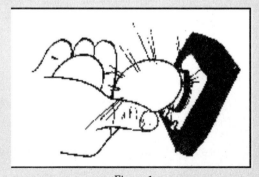

Figure 1.

2. Identifying cracks: Cracked eggs will appear to have a white line somewhere on the shell. These cracks will open if you apply slight pressure to the shell. Remove cracked eggs and consume them as soon as possible or discard.

3. USDA Grade Standard: Use the specifications given in the table below to determine the grade of an egg by candling. Consider air cell depth, yolk outline, and albumen quality.

QUALITY FACTOR	AA QUALITY	A QUALITY	B QUALITY	INEDIBLE
Air Cell	1/8" or less in depth	3/16" or less in depth	More than 3/16"	Does not apply
White	Clear, firm	Clean, may be reasonably firm	Clean, may be weak and watery	Does not apply
Yolk	Outline slightly defined	Outline may be fairly well-defined	Outline clearly visible	Does not apply
Spots (blood or meat)	None	None	Blood or meat spots aggregating not more than 1/8" in diameter	Blood or meat spots aggregating more than 1/8" in diameter

- Air cell depth: The depth of the air cell is the distance from its top to its bottom when the egg is held with the air cell up (see figure 2). In a fresh egg, the air cell is small, not more than 1/8 inch deep. As the egg ages, evaporation takes place, the air cell becomes larger, and the egg is downgraded.

- Yolk: A rather dense layer of albumen or white will surround the yolk of a fresh, high-quality egg. Therefore, it moves only slightly away from the center of the egg when it is twirled before the candler. Because of this, yolk outline is only slightly defined in the highest quality eggs. As the albumen thins, the yolk tends to move more freely and closer to the shell. A more visible yolk when candled indicates a lower quality egg.

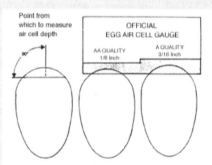

Figure 2. Measuring air cell depth

- White or albumen: The character and condition of the white or albumen is indicated largely by the behavior of the yolk of the egg when the egg is candled. If the yolk retains its position in the center when the egg is twirled, the white is usually firm and thick.

- Eggs with blood or meat spots more than 1/8 inch in diameter are classified as inedible. Eggs with small spots collectively less than 1/8 inch in diameter should be classified as Grade B. The chalaza is distinguished from a meat spot by a bright area of refracted light that accompanies its darker shadow. Blood spot eggs can be consumed without harm, however, most people find the appearance undesirable.

4. Also, remove any eggs with unusual shell shapes, textures, ridges, or thin spots on the shell if you plan to sell the eggs. These eggs are edible but break easily and are undesirable to most consumers due to appearance.

D. STORAGE OF EGGS

1. Store eggs small end down in an egg carton to keep the air cell stable.

2. Date carton so you can use or sell the oldest eggs first and rotate your extra eggs. Try to use or sell all eggs before they are three weeks old.

3. Store eggs at 50-55 degrees F and 70-75 percent relative humidity.

4. Never store eggs with materials that have an odor. Eggs will pick up the odors of apples, fish, onions, potatoes, and other food or chemicals with distinct odors.

5. Never hold eggs at or above room temperature or at low humidities more than necessary. Leaving eggs in a warm, dry environment will cause interior quality to drop quickly.

E. SALE OF EGGS

There are no laws that prevent the sale of eggs from a home-laying flock. However, you should take some basic steps to ensure that the eggs you sell have uniform quality.

1. Follow the suggestions about collection, washing, storage, and sorting above.

2. For marketing, it is usually best to size the eggs. Medium, large, and extra large eggs sell best. Egg sizes are expressed in ounces per dozen.

Small — 18 oz.
Medium — 21 oz.
Large — 24 oz.
X-Large — 27 oz.
Jumbo — 30 oz.

Egg scales can be purchased at many farm supply stores.

3. Never sell eggs in cartons with another egg producer or store name on the carton. It is illegal to do so. Only sell eggs in generic cartons or ask your customers to bring their own carton to carry the eggs home in.

4. Most small flock producers base their prices on the current store prices in the area they live. However, many producers niche market their eggs as a specialty item and receive premium prices. If you have your birds in a fenced outside run and have one male for every 10 to 15 hens in your flock, you can sell eggs at a premium as fertile, free-range eggs. Brown eggs often will bring higher prices as well.

Remember, prices also will be driven by supply and demand. If you do not have a lot of competition and have a good demand, you usually can get a higher price for the eggs you sell. It is critical that you pay attention to quality and keep a constant year-round supply for your customers. Be prepared to replace any eggs that are not satisfactory to a customer. Learn about and correct the dissatisfaction.

F. WHAT IS THE PROPER WAY TO COOK AND HANDLE EGGS?

Consumers always should keep eggs refrigerated until the eggs are used. Eggs should not be eaten raw. Pasteurized eggs should be used in recipes that call for raw eggs that are not going to be cooked (i.e. eggnog, ice cream, etc.) Eggs should not be combined and left to stand at room temperature before cooking for more than 20 minutes. Eggs should be individually cracked and immediately cooked.

Baby Chicks

If you do not have the time to dedicate to hatching, you can purchase chicks one to several days old. The following websites offer them:

- Murray McMurray Hatchery (**www.mcmurrayhatchery.com**) — This site offers baby chicks, other types of birds, equipment, and supplies.

- Estes Farm Hatchery (**www.esteshatchery.com**) — This hatchery website sells different breeds of chicks and pullets. A chick starter kit available for $55 includes everything you need to begin raising 25 to 50 chicks. It comes with a corrugated boarder, heat lamp, waterer, and vitamins among other items to start your journey.

Before ordering chicks online, do your research. Some online hatcheries require you to purchase a minimum number of chicks; often, the minimum number is about 25 so the chicks have enough body heat to survive the journey. If the minimum purchase is 25 chicks, you need to be prepared to care for that many or have a plan to share the chicks with others. Hatcheries ship chicks when they are 1 day old because at that point, they have consumed enough food to last 72 hours from the hatching process. This gives them sustenance to survive the process.

Chicks are shipped via the United States Postal Service (USPS) with Special Handling. The USPS tells customers to expect two to three days for shipment and to also ship live animals at the beginning of the week — that way animals are not stuck at a post office during the weekend with no food or water. Take into account current weather conditions as well. Many hatcheries will not ship chicks in extreme conditions, including heat and cold. Your chicks probably will be

shipped in a special, vented box, and you will need to schedule a time to pick them up at the post office. Most hatcheries will give you an estimated arrival date and will contact you when your eggs or chicks are scheduled to arrive. At the post office, open your new box of chicks to ensure they are alive. Be sure you understand the online hatchery's policy on chicks that do not survive the journey, and if needed, file a claim with the post office if you think the birds were mishandled. A good seller will have details on their policy regarding transport and what the compensation is in this event.

If you prefer to get your chicks in person, go to your local co-op, farm, farmers market, or some pet stores to get your birds. Most of these places have chicks available in the spring, especially around Easter. Be sure to examine the condition of the pen at the store. If the pen, water, and feed are dirty or if there are any dead chicks in the pen, do not purchase your chickens from that store. The chicks' health already might be compromised from a poor start in life. It is important to check the vent of the chicks. If there is any fecal buildup, the chicks might be harboring a disease.

Chicks are cute, fluffy, and ready to be a part of your family. Babies need a different blend of food and lots of water. After the first few days of life, they will need a starter mash, which provides extra nutrients as they grow. They also need a heat source such as a heat lamp. Chicks are still adjusting to temperatures outside the egg and the incubator, and they need heat to stay warm to remain healthy.

If you receive your chicks as opposed to hatching them, be sure you have a warming box ready to put them in. Traveling will have created some stress for the birds already, so it is important to make their transition to their new home as comfortable and seamless as possible. Immediately put the chicks in the warming box, which should be 90 degrees F. A small, key ring thermometer is easy to attach to the box and will provide a quick reference so you can monitor the temperature throughout the day. If you do not have a box prepared, put the birds in an open box in your oven. Keep the oven light on, and keep the temperature at 90 degrees F. You do not want to bake your birds. Set up your box with a heat lamp, bring the temperature up, and promptly transfer the chicks to their new home.

Make sure water is available at all times. Do not use a deep bowl, as chicks can drown. A heavy, shallow bowl that is not easily tipped over can be used. Or, a waterer with a chicken nipple or valve can be used. Some babies have trouble getting started. If you notice one of the chicks not drinking, lead them to the water, and dip their beak gently so they can learn how to drink.

If you do not have starter mash available right away, you can use instant oatmeal or flaked infant cereal. This can be done for the first and second day. After that, the birds should be switched to mash, as they will need the nutrition provided in the starter mash. Be sure to purchase an ample amount or write down the name of the feed so you do not have to change the mixture of the mash. You may want to write down the name of the store you purchased it from right on the bag of feed so you can reference it easily.

Chicks should not be handled too much. They are still delicate babies. You will need to pick them up to check their vent, which is the opening eggs and droppings exit the body, or to move them to a new location. To check the vent, slip one hand under the chick by its stomach with one hand and put use your other hand on top of the chick to hold the top of the chick firmly, but gently. If you see droppings stuck to the chick's vent, clean them off with a toothpick or a damp cloth; if the vent becomes clogged, the chick will not be able to release droppings and will get sick and die. It will be very tempting to want to cuddle and play with the birds because they are so cute at this age. Try to handle them only when necessary until they are a few days old and are stronger.

Pullets and Cockerels

Pullets or cockerels might be best suited for your needs. These chickens are under 1 year old and are easier to care for at this stage because they are old enough to be on their own. They can be outside without constant supervision because they have feathers to keep them warm and are old enough to fend for themselves. They also will most likely not drown in the water bowl. These birds can also be purchased from online hatcheries.

Pullets begin to lay eggs at 3 to 4 months old. Or, if you are raising them for meat, depending on the breed, you will be able to slaughter them sooner than if you decided to raise the chickens from eggs. Starting with young birds will help start the reproduction cycle of your flock.

Purchasing Your Birds

When you are ready to buy your birds, your home and neighborhood probably will dictate how many you can own. If you are hatching eggs, purchase a dozen because chances are not all of them will hatch. If more hatch than you originally planned for, you always can find homes for your extra chicks. One fun shopping tip about buying eggs is that you can purchase a mixture of bantam eggs, which is usually any mixture the breeder selects, so when the eggs hatch, you will have a surprise variety. You can specify whether you want all male or female. They are sold in groups of as little as three eggs, and for less than $10, you can start your flock. If you are buying chicks or young birds, do not start with any more than four birds. Owning one bird is fine, but it will be lonely, as chickens are social animals.

It is important to be sure you purchase your birds from a reputable source whose top priority is hatching healthy chicks. Mail-order companies and feed stores are fine, provided they can tell you the source of their chicks. Make sure the chicks were hatched in a reputable hatchery, not in a backyard with questionable sanitation standards. You can be sure a hatchery is reputable by researching if they are a part of the National Poultry Improvement Plan (NPIP) and if the breeding flock is yearly tested and certified disease-free. The NPIP is a voluntary program between federal and state governments and the poultry industry to prevent the spread of poultry disease.

Several websites offer eggs and chicks, including:

- Randall Burkey Company (**www.randallburkey.com**) — This website sells chicks as young as one day old or eggs that are ready to hatch. They offer a variety of chicken eggs and other poultry. Once you place an order, you will discuss a delivery date with the salesperson to be sure you can be there to receive your shipment.

- M&B Farmview Farm (**http://mbfarviewfarm.com**) — M&B Farmview Farm sells baby chicks and supplies, in addition to other livestock, including pigs and baby Jersey cows. They sell butchered meat and offer directions to their store in Hamburg, Pennsylvania, and their location at a local farmers market with the hours of operation. They clearly explain what is available for sale online or at their store, as well as pricing.

Another online resource to try is Craigslist because you may be able to find your poultry free or for a minimal charge. Always use common sense and take appropriate precautions when buying online. Websites such as Craigslist are not regulated, and occasionally, people may try to defraud you out of your money. Do not give credit card or bank information online unless it is a secure site. Do not be afraid to ask many questions, especially about any guarantees the seller has. Always be sure to inspect the quality of your animals.

If you prefer to go to a local hatchery to pick out your bird, most have day-old chicks available in the spring. Nothing says spring like the soft chirping of newborn chicks. If you are thinking of buying roosters, check your local ordinances first; some neighborhoods do not allow roosters because of their crowing at sunrise. Roosters are also more aggressive to each other and to people, and they can be harder to handle. Roosters do not lay eggs, but they can provide you with meat. If you consider having both males and females, the roosters are rough when mating. They claw at the chickens' backs and often scratch and peck them.

Having more than one male creates the need for dominance, so be sure you have lots of room for them. A flock of chickens has a pecking order, and if there is one male, he automatically takes the lead. If you have more than one male, the more dominant rooster will be at the top of the hierarchy. You can expect aggressiveness in most roosters, especially if you have several of them. In a flock of all hens, one hen typically will take the leadership role. If you have enough space for the chickens to roam, there is less of a chance of them pecking each other and displaying aggressive behavior.

Housing and Feeding Chickens

Chickens are easy to care for, but because of inclement weather, predators, and just for their overall well-being, chickens need a structure that will keep them safe and dry and give them a place to sleep at night. Hens also will require a safe place to lay their eggs. The coop can be almost anything that you want it to be, but any standard coop needs to meet certain requirements.

Chicken coops

Coops can be any size, shape, color, or material. The size of your flock will determine how large your coop will need to be and how much material you need to get started. You can purchase materials for your coop at lumberyards, hardware stores, online, thrift stores, and flea markets, or you can find recycled materials from Habitat for Humanity (**www.habitat.org**) stores. Habitat stores have lumber and other items such as doors and windows that you can recycle. It just takes a little creativity. To find a local Habitat store, go to the organization's website and type in your ZIP code. If you plan to use recycled lumber, do not use wood that is painted or has been chemically treated because the chickens peck at everything, and these can be hazardous to their health. Regardless of the type of coop you use to house your chickens, it needs to have the following elements:

- Sound structure
- Bedding and flooring
- Nesting boxes
- Runs
- Roosts or perches
- Feeders and waterers
- Lighting for both chicks and chickens
- Ventilation
- Insulation
- Protection from predators and weather

The rule of thumb is to allow 3 to 4 square feet of space per chicken and 2 square feet for bantams to keep from over-crowding. Find a space on your property that adheres to any zoning laws (such as keeping fowl 50 feet from your nearest neighbor) and has enough room for you to build your coop. It should be in an area that gets enough sunlight and drainage. Ideally, it should be on a gently sloping piece of land that would allow heavy rainwater to dry quickly. If this is not possible, elevate the building to avoid water problems because your coop will need to stay dry.

A solid roof will be the best protection for your flock. Aviary netting or wire will work, too, but a solid roof offers added protection from the elements. You can use metal panels, wood, or roofing shingles. Some predators, such as raccoons, can pull apart chicken wire, so use welded wire fences that you can purchase at feed stores and lumber yards.

You can make a basic coop from a shed with fencing around it. Include the other requirements, such as ventilation, perches, and bedding, and you will have a safe, simple home for your chickens in just a few hours. Check every angle of the coop to ensure it is secure from predators and the elements.

Runs

A chicken run is an enclosed area where chickens are allowed to move around. The run should have 10 square feet of space per chicken, but the bigger the run, the better it is for the chickens. If you have trouble with predators, or anticipate having trouble with them, cover your run with wire mesh. The windows and doors on your coop need locks to secure the birds at night or when unsupervised. Some predators, raccoons especially, are clever and can break into even the most secure runs and coops.

Bedding

The floor of the chicken coop can be concrete, wood, linoleum, or vinyl (the last two are easier to clean), but it should be covered with wood shavings, wood pellets, hay, or straw. Pine wood shavings are the best choice because they hold up well and smell good. Never use cedar because it can be toxic to your birds. Sawdust is not recommended because it can cause respiratory problems. Hay and straw can attract mites, lice, and rodents; you can still use it, but you will need to clean more frequently and check daily for infestation.

The **deep litter method** is the most popular bedding method because it takes little time and provides compost. This method requires layering 4 to 8 inches of wood shavings on the coop floor; you will need to rake the shavings every day to spread them evenly. Your chickens will help do this naturally, and you can throw corn on the floor to encourage the birds to scratch through the shavings, which will keep the bedding even and aerated. Raking the shavings helps aerate the wood, which will decompose on the bottom. After it mixes with the chicken manure for six months to a year, the shavings will become compost, and you can spread it in your garden or lawn for fertilizer. You need to clean out the coop only once or twice a year; if your hen house starts to smell, you will know it is time to clean.

To clean the coop, shovel out the wood shavings and remove feeders, waterers, and anything else that can be taken out. Put on some rubber gloves and mix one part bleach, one part dishwashing liquid (antibacterial), and ten parts water. Scrub the coop from top to bottom with a scrub brush, and rinse it well with a hose. Wait until the coop is completely dry before putting fresh bedding down and allowing the chickens back in. Moisture can cause mold and mildew, which can cause illness in your flock.

It is perfectly acceptable to clean your coop weekly or monthly if you do not like the thought of doing it only twice a year. If you choose to do this, only 2 or 3 inches of wood shavings or hay is necessary to use at one time. You can make the shavings thinner in the summer months and thicker in the winter. Mesh wire can cover part of the floor to catch manure, but it is not recommended for the entire floor because it is not healthy for the birds' feet, and it makes the floor too cold in the winter. Chickens also have the need to scratch, and wire does not give the same opportunity to scratch that wood shavings do. Scratching is a natural behavior chickens exhibit as they search and forage for food and explore their surroundings.

Nesting boxes

Hens need nesting boxes to lay their eggs. The standard size is 15 inches long, 15 inches wide, and 12 inches deep. Some chicken owners get creative and use baskets or something similar for the boxes. Hay and straw are best to use as filler, and these boxes should be changed monthly to prevent health problems. The number of nesting boxes depends on how many chickens you own; one box for four to five hens is adequate. Keeping the boxes at a slant will help ensure the birds do not roost on top of each other.

For laying hens, the need to nest arises 24 hours after a hormone fluctuation that is a result of ovulation. A hen — both domestic and wild — naturally will find or build a nest where she can lay an egg because of this fluctuation. As this behavior is purely biological, it is essential to provide your hens with the materials they need to nest. Hens without a way to nest may be frustrated or distressed, depending on the breed.

Lighting

Good lighting is essential in the coop because it promotes maximum egg laying and stimulates egg production, especially in the fall and winter months when the days are shorter. If the coop is not designed to let in much sunlight, even artificial light will help stimulate egg laying in hens. Using two 65-watt bulbs will be sufficient for a coop that is 8 feet by 10 feet. Lighting also can synchronize pullets to start laying at the same time. FarmTek (**www.farmtek.com**) offers a variety of lighting fixtures designed specifically for poultry, and it offers everything from solar lighting to light bulbs to infrared heat lamps.

You should regulate how much light your chicks receive. Guidelines are:

- Chicks up to seven days old should have light 24 hours a day.
- Chicks one to six weeks old should have light eight to 12 hours a day.
- Chicks six to 19 weeks old should have light 12 hours a day.
- Chicks 20 weeks or older should have light 12 to 16 hours a day.

Lighting can induce early egg laying in pullets, so it is necessary to monitor how much they are exposed to each day. Lights provide warmth for the birds, and you can use timers to regulate how much light your chickens receive each day.

Ventilation and insulation

Good ventilation may seem obvious, but it is important not to overlook this when you are preparing your coop. Ventilation allows fresh air and oxygen into your coop, as well as the release of carbon dioxide. Without it, potentially toxic carbon dioxide can build up in the coop and harm the flock. A simple way to create air passageways is to drill several holes in the top of the walls and cover them with mesh. If you prefer, you can have windows in the coop. Although windows can help keep your birds cool in the summer, you also will need a good vapor barrier and insulation to keep them warm in the winter. Be sure the ventilation and insulation work together to achieve the most comfortable environment. Keep in mind that the insulation inside your coop will need to be covered so your birds do not peck at it.

Roosts or perches

It is a natural instinct for chickens to want to perch off the ground to protect themselves from predators, especially at night. The birds sleep shoulder to shoulder on an elevated roosting bar if they have a coop or will sleep in a tree if they are free-range. The number of roosts in the coop depends on the size of your flock. If you have more than one perch, do not situate them directly on top of each other, so the birds can freely go to the bathroom without hitting another bird.

Arrange your perches in a ladder style, sloping toward the back of a wall. You can even use an old ladder for your roost. Perches should be across from the nesting boxes so you can collect eggs without having to walk through bird feces. Do not structure perches above the feeders or water containers to prevent bird droppings from contaminating them.

Wood works better than metal or piping when constructing roosts or perches, and a broom handle or dowel will work well. Perches should be 2 inches in diameter for chickens and roosters, 1 inch for bantams, and the edges need to be smooth and rounded for better gripping. Space the bars about 12 inches apart because if there is enough space for chickens to roost, it is less likely they will perch on feeders, waterers, or other places not meant for perching.

The floor beneath the roosts will collect the majority of the bird poop, and this area will need to have easy access, which you can attain by opening a window or shutter on the wall behind the coop. Some coops have manure boxes under the perches that are several inches high, filled with bedding, and covered with moveable screen lids. You can take the manure from these boxes every day or once a week and use it for composting and fertilizer. You also can clean the screen lids when you remove the manure. You should be able to move the boxes so you can do a deep cleaning from time to time. If you do not want to use the manure boxes and your coop does not have a window, you can put in an easy-to-clean floor, such as linoleum, under their roosts. If you plan to use linoleum on the entire floor, sprinkle bedding across it except under the roosts so the chickens can scratch and walk around without hurting their feet.

Pastured Poultry

A common way to raise pastured poultry involves putting 75 to 100 3- to 4-week old meat chickens in movable pens during the growing season. These floorless 10 foot by 12 foot by 2 foot pens are moved daily by sliding them along the ground, providing fresh pasture. Chickens also receive a grain-based ration. At 8 to 14 weeks, the chickens are butchered.

Feeders and waterers

You also will need to find a space for feeders and waterers in your coop. Waterers can be placed both inside and outside, but food should be kept strictly inside the coop to avoid luring outdoor critters to your chickens' home. Feeders come in different sizes, shapes, and prices, but deep feeders will prevent excess waste because chickens will not spill as much over the sides.

If you decide to use a trough feeder, fill it only one-third full to help reduce waste. Automated feeders are available at feed stores and co-ops. These feeders have a timer and will release food for your birds if you are not available to feed them yourself. You also can make homemade feeders from buckets and recycled household items. Go online to sites such as Banty Chicken Domain (**www.bantychicken.com**), and join chicken-owner forums to find other creative feeder ideas from fellow chicken fanciers. As long as the feeder is secure and holds enough food, it will work.

Chickens are messy eaters, and one way to help control the mess is to elevate the feeder so it is about the same height as the back of the chickens. This keeps their feet out of the feeder, which helps prevent some of the mess. If you would rather not purchase a feeder, you can toss seed to your birds. This requires a few extra minutes each day but will help you bond with your flock.

You also will need to purchase water containers. Remember, when you are selecting a waterer that baby chicks require special attention. If you must use an open bowl, place stones in it so if a chick falls in, the stones will prevent it from going completely underwater. A nipple-type waterer is similar to the water bottles hamsters use and is designed to keep water clean. You also can find water cups that attach to cages. Purchase a water bowl heater if necessary to prevent water from freezing in cold weather. This product is not necessary but will ensure that your birds have water available even in frigid temperatures.

Preparing for Your Coop

Once you know what your coop will need and you have the location and the equipment, you are ready for the coop. You can design your own plans or find blueprints online. Prices vary, but some are free. Select a design based on your skill level and ability to read the plans as well as your flock's needs. Here are some websites that can help:

- Green Roof Chicken Coop (**www.greenroofchickencoop.com**) — This website offers plans, precut coop kits, and assembled coops for sale.

- Build Eazy (**www.buildeazy.com**) — This website offers a variety of build-at-home projects. You can access free, step-by-step instructions on how to build a coop at home, and the instructions will include a list of materials and photos of what your project should look like.

- Brain Garage (**www.braingarage.com**) — This website provides free plans for a chicken coop, along with a variety of building plans for other projects. This website offer tips, designs, and some plans you can download free.

Because no one wants to look at a shabby building, you can paint or decorate the outside of your chickens' home. However, do not paint the inside of the coop. Chickens like to peck, and the chemicals they ingest will be passed on to the eggs they lay that your family will eat. Also, paint could be toxic to the flock.

Chickens have an innate need to scratch and dig at the sand with their claws. They love to roam in gardens and on grass to forage for bugs and worms. Bantams will be lighter and easier on your landscape. Chickens also need dirt. They do not bathe in water but instead roll around in the dust and consider this a luxury. Their coat of feathers is made up of oils that the dust helps dry out. They also preen themselves, which keeps them clean by getting rid of built-up oil. Chickens love to sunbathe, and the sun provides them with vitamin D and assists in their overall health.

CASE STUDY: INHERITED JOY

Danny Williams

Several years ago, Danny Williams inherited three bantam Silkies from a friend who was moving out of state. Named Pickle, Lil Bit, and Elvis, each has their own personality. "I never thought chickens could be so charismatic," Williams said.

Initially, Williams thought the bantams would be a hassle to care for and maintain. However, he says, "Nothing can be further from the truth. I spend maybe $40 a month on seed and hay. The building supplies cost about $80 to $100. You can sell eggs to cover these costs. Sure, it can be smelly and messy at times but definitely worth it."

The coop Williams and his wife have for their flock was made from leftover lumber that Danny used to build an addition on to his house. He also had some shingles for the coop's roof left over from the new roof he put on his own house. Williams said, "The floor is basic plywood. I stained it with water resistant polymer. This may seem extreme to some, but it is easy to clean. Just hose it off. That is what I was looking for — something easy. I was afraid the clean up would be a nightmare each week, but it really is not a problem."

Williams does not have trouble with predators, but his old Labrador retriever enjoys chasing the birds every now and then. He said, "I do not know if he tries to catch them or is just playing with them. I do not think he would know what to do if he did catch one."

For new chicken owners, Williams has this to say, "It is a joy I never thought I would have. Funny little creatures. I find the clucking noises rather serene and soothing." He adds, tongue in cheek, "Anyone want to buy some eggs?"

Tractor coops and urban coops

If your brood is small, you may want to consider a mobile coop called a **tractor coop**. These are bottomless, mobile coops, and they are designed for chickens to scratch and graze. These portable coops are on wheels, and you should push them around your yard so your birds have fresh pasture, and so your yard will have the chance to produce new grass over the used patch of land. Do not use a chemical pesticide where your chickens will be grazing because that can be toxic, and the pesticides can pass through to the eggs. Plus, your birds will nibble up any pesky insects, so you do not need chemical control.

City dwellers can purchase an urban coop such as the Eglu online from Omlet (**www.omlet.us**). A 20-foot by 30-foot space is all you need to set up an Eglu. They come in several sizes and colors and are offered in an egg shape or as a cube. The egg shape looks like half of an egg and provides shelter for your birds. One end is enclosed, and the open end has fencing that extends from it, which is the run. The fence is enclosed on all sides and on top, keeping your chickens inside and predators outside. It has a hatch to let your birds in and out. The Eglu sits directly on the ground and does not have wheels. It is designed to house two to four chickens.

The Eglu Cube sits off the ground on wheels with a ladder extended from the doorway to the ground for the chickens to enter and exit. The actual coop is rectangular, and you can order it with a rectangular run that attaches to the coop. The run is available in different sizes to fit your needs. The cube option also has a hatch to allow your chickens out.

Both the Eglu and the Eglu Cube are designed to keep your chickens warm in the winter and cool in the summer. They are easy to clean, with a removable panel underneath the coop. Nesting boxes and perches are inside, and you will have access to reach in and collect eggs. They are stylish, and prices start at $495. You also can order chicks with your Eglu on these websites:

- Omlet (**www.omlet.us**) offers coops for sale as well as chicks. This is an informative website with information about breeds and products.

- My Pet Chicken (**www.mypetchicken.com**) provides coops and products as well as chicks for sale. It also has information on caring for chickens and descriptions of different types of chicken breeds.

If you do not have the skills or time to build a coop, you can buy standard-size coops at co-ops, feed stores, supply stores, and online. Other places you can peruse are farmer's co-ops and flea markets.

Farmers' co-ops

Farmers can purchase items they need in bulk at these co-ops to save money. The products are sold at a lesser price because there is no "middle man" present. You do not need to become a member in a co-op to shop at one, but if you are, you enjoy added advantages because shopping here keeps money local and gives back to your community. Here are some ways you can locate a co-op:

- Look in your local yellow pages.

- Check online at Co-Operative Feed Dealers Inc. (**www.co-opfeed.com**). Established in 1935, this site is a distributor for independent farm, garden, or pet supplies in the Northeast.

- Check online at Local Harvest (**www.localharvest.org**). This website allows you to type in your ZIP code or city and state to help you locate farmers markets, farms, and places to go for sustainable and organic products and food in your area. The site is also a source of information on community-supported agriculture.

Supply stores

These stores are helpful because the staff is usually well educated and ready to help you make your selection. You can go in person to a location or order coops online. If they do not have a product you are looking for, they often can help you find it at another location or order it for you. To locate a supply store near you:

- Check your local yellow pages.

- Check online or at your local Tractor Supply Co. (**www.tractorsupply.com**). This website and store offers farming and agriculture supplies. The site mostly sells products but does offer information on farming.

- Visit Horizon Structures (**www.horizonstructures.com**). This website offers products for farming and agriculture, and it has a variety of coops to choose from.

Online retailers

The benefit of ordering online is it is easy to find what you need. You can peruse a website at any time of day or night, and the product will be delivered to your door. Most websites offer a phone number for a help line, but depending on the time of day you visit the site, service representatives may not be available.

- Egganic Industries (**www.henspa.com**) — This online store sells organic chicken feed, coops, and coop accessories.

- Shop the Coop (**www.shopthecoop.com**) — This website provides information on housing for your birds, and you can purchase a coop here.

Farmers markets and flea markets

These are great places to find bargains and unusual items. If you are purchasing eggs or birds here, ask several questions, especially about the age of the pullet because a hen's laying ability is directly related to her age. Buying a coop here gives you an opportunity to discuss raising chickens with someone who has experience. The downside is there are no refunds or returns on products you buy here.

Once your coop is set up, you are ready to move your chickens in. Do not get your chicks before their home is complete so you do not need to find a temporary place to keep them. If you are ordering your flock online, you may have to coordinate a pickup or delivery time with your post office. Planning everything ahead of time will make for a smooth transition.

If you plan to raise chickens from eggs, expect to devote extra time in your day to the eggs. Chickens are delicate in embryo form and require someone to check the temperature and humidity level in the incubator about once an hour, especially if the incubator is homemade or not self-regulating. Baby chicks, either in the egg or a few days old, demand a lot more attention than a full-grown chicken. If you are hatching eggs, you will need to monitor them and turn the eggs daily.

Feeding Your Chickens

Baby chicks and chickens should have a fresh supply of food throughout the day, and you do not have to worry about them overeating because chickens only eat when they are hungry and need to. Fill feeders early in the morning. Checking the feed on a regular schedule will keep your birds happy and less stressed and will prevent moldy food from being left in feeders.

As treats, chickens love watermelon, cooked eggs, seedless grapes, carrots (raw or cooked), apples, cooked grits, lettuce, kale, cooked pasta, peas, raw pomegranates, cabbage, asparagus, bananas, and the list goes on and on. Some chickens may be finickier than others. Chickens love eggs, but it is best to feed them only cooked eggs. If you give them a taste for raw eggs, they may not let you collect them in the morning, as they may beat you to it. Also, seedless grapes are better for chicken's digestive systems.

Items you should not feed chickens include salty foods, such as pretzels, potato chips, or salted French fries, as this can cause salt poisoning in small bodies. Candy of any sort, especially chocolate and sugar-filled candies, is bad for their systems, as with any pet you may have. Raw green potato peels can create a toxic substance called Salanme if you feed it to your flock. Avocado skin and pits also are not recommended for poultry, as they contain low levels of toxicity and can be harmful.

Chickens are easy to care for, and they can eat almost anything. Keep in mind, though, that if you are raising your birds for meat or eggs, you or your family and friends eventually may ingest the food you give to your birds. Be selective to keep your bird's health at an optimum. They will appreciate it, and they can be trained using food. Give them treats, but be aware of the foods you give your flock.

Before your chickens arrive, be sure to have everything you need, because good planning will help your chickens make a smooth transition. When you are planning for supplies, do not forget chicken feed. You have an array of feeds to choose from, or you may decide to make your own. Remember not to purchase too much feed at once because you should not store it over long periods; it can attract rodents, and if it gets damp, it can become moldy.

You can find chicken feed at local feed mills, supply stores, co-ops, and even some grocery stores, depending on where you live. Chickens are natural scavengers, and they will peck and hunt daily for food. But even free-range chickens will need you to supplement their diet with feed unless you have an abundance of land for them to forage. It is estimated that an acre of land can sustain 50 to 400 chickens, but that is probably not accurate in the winter months when greenery is hard to find.

You may be tempted to buy a cheaper feed for your chickens, but be aware that the product is mostly bulked up with fillers such as wheat-milling byproducts. This will fatten your birds up but has little or no nutritional value. It is like junk food for poultry and will affect its flavor. A fat chicken will lay fewer eggs than a healthy chicken.

Chicken feed comes in three forms:

- **Mash** is a mealy or powdered form of chicken feed, usually made of grains.
- **Pellet** is a harder form of chicken food.
- **Crumble** is a mixture of mash and pellet.

Chickens tend to waste more mash because it spills to the ground and dissolves into the dirt. **Chicken scratch** was a popular feed before people realized how important nutrients were to the quality of the chicken and the eggs it produced. The scratch was made up of whole grains and cracked corn. If you use chicken scratch, it should not be their only feed because it does not provide enough nutrients, such as oyster shell, to harden the chickens' eggs.

Chicken feed also comes in different mixtures. Look around the feed store, and you will see feed for different chicken ages and purpose: baby chicks, pullets, layers, broilers, and crushed oyster shell, among others. Oyster shell helps the development of the eggshell, and if a chicken does not have enough in its diet, the eggs it lays will be brittle or soft. Commercial feed mixtures will be balanced, so you do not have to add anything to them.

Make your own!

Making your own feed may save you some money, but it will require more time. You will need:

- Split peas — these have a high protein content
- Lentils — a plant from the legume family producing flattened seeds used as food and a good source of protein
- Oat groats — minimally processed oats
- Hulled barley — these help provide intestinal protection
- Sunflower seeds — benefit the heart
- Sesame seeds — rich in vitamins B and E
- Flax seeds — this provides omega-3
- Winter wheat — higher gluten protein than most wheats
- Whole corn — this provides energy for flock
- Soft white wheat — this is lower in protein and higher in carbohydrates compared to hard wheat
- Quinoa — good source of dietary fiber
- Kelp granules — gives the birds potassium, iron, and fiber
- Oyster shell — provides calcium and helps build hard egg shells
- Granite grit — helps aid digestion in birds
- Millet — most nutritious of the grains, providing proteins, carbohydrates, as well as phosphorous and other nutrients
- Kamut — this is known as a high-energy wheat

Mix equal parts of the ingredients, except corn (use two parts), soft white wheat (three parts), and hard red winter wheat (three parts). Mix, and store in an airtight bin.

Because chickens do not have teeth, they eat **grit**, which is stored in the crop area of their stomachs. Grit is little stones that break down the food so the chicken can digest it. You can find it at the same places you purchase chicken feed. You can add it to food or give it separately. Grit is not the same as oyster shells; oyster shells dissolve in the chicken's stomach, and grit does not.

After shopping for your birds and purchasing or making their feed, your chickens have all the essentials they need to be welcomed into your home. Enjoy spending time with them. If you opt to hatch eggs, you can look forward to experiencing the birth of new life. New chicks are adorable, and hatching them in your home can provide a wonderful experience for the whole family to enjoy.

Chicken Health

Poultry can carry highly contagious diseases. If your flock is diagnosed with certain illnesses, you are required by law to report it to the U.S. Department of Agriculture (USDA). Failure to do so may result in fines or punishment.

Reportable diseases include, but are not limited to, avian flu or bird flu, chronic respiratory disease, and paratyphoid.

Common diseases that affect poultry include:

Air-sac disease: This disease is similar to chronic respiratory disease, except air-sac disease is found in chicks as well as older chickens. Symptoms to look for are nasal discharge, rattled breathing and wheezing, and loss of appetite. Treat with antibiotics.

Avian influenza or **bird flu:** This spreads quickly through a flock. Symptoms associated with bird flu include sudden death, dark wattles and combs, soft eggshells or no shell, fever, sneezing, coughing, watery eyes, diarrhea, and loss of appetite. The cause is a type A influenza virus. **Bird flu is required to be reported to the USDA.**

Breast blister: This affects the keel or breastbone of the chicken. It is a large blister that becomes a callous and forms when the breast bone leans against a roost with sharp corners, wire flooring, or wet, packed bedding. To treat, open and drain the blister, and apply an antibacterial ointment. Prevention includes wrapping sharp corners of the coop in a softer material, keeping the bedding dry and clean, and not using wire flooring for the entire coop.

Bumble foot: This affects the chicken's foot pad, where an abscess will form. The chicken may be resistant to walking. To treat, you may need to take the bird to your vet for antibiotic injections. Keep the foot clean, and keep the chicken on deep, soft, bedding. This is not contagious for other birds, but it may cause impetigo or skin infection in humans.

Cage layer fatigue: Cage layer fatigue is a nutritional disease in chickens and other poultry when their legs becoming bowed or the bones become soft. This is often associated with osteoporosis and usually is observed in egg-laying hens. It is caused by a deficiency of calcium, vitamin D, or phosphorous. Prevention is the key. Providing your flock with nutrient-rich feed will help to keep them healthy.

Campylobacteriosis, also known as liver disease: This disease affects the intestines. It is chronic and spreads slowly. Symptoms include watery diarrhea; scaly, shrunken comb; weight loss; and death of apparently healthy birds. There is no known treatment at this time, so prevention will be key to keeping your flock safe. Keep the coop clean, isolate sick birds from your flock, do not mix birds from different sources, and keep rodents out because they carry disease.

Cholera, acute: This is a curious disease with no known cure. Birds die suddenly, and it spreads rapidly. Symptoms include fever, increased thirst, mucous discharge from the nose and mouth, bluish comb and wattles, and diarrhea. Prevent this disease by avoiding already mature birds that you do not know the health history of, keeping the coop clean, not mixing birds from different sources, and providing good nutrition. This can occur in birds of any age, but if you purchase a mature bird, you do not know if it may be a carrier of the disease. If you identify this disease, you still have time to save the uninfected flock. A chronic form of cholera is rare in chickens.

Chronic respiratory disease: Symptoms to identify this condition are raspy breathing, coughing, sneezing, nasal discharge, and squeaky crow. Antibiotics can be used for treatment, but survivors typically remain carriers. Prevention includes vaccination, keeping the coop clean and well ventilated, and minimizing stress. **You will need to report this disease to the USDA.**

Colibacillosis: This disease is also called E. coli infection. Symptoms include fever, swollen joints, lameness, and diarrhea. Treatment includes antibiotics, but they need to be administered in the early stages of the disease to be effective. Prevention includes good sanitation, rodent control, and hatching healthy eggs.

Conjunctivitis: This disease affects the eyes. Signs that your bird has conjunctivitis are if it is rubbing the eyes with its wing, avoiding sunlight, and cloudiness in the eyes. This condition does not spread from bird to bird. It is caused by infection, vitamin A deficiency, and ammonia fumes from excessive accumulation of bird droppings. Prevention entails keeping the coop clean, the bedding dry, and providing good nutrition. Treatment includes increased vitamin A and a visit to your vet if the symptoms persist.

Marek's disease: This disease attacks the organs, nerves, and skin. It is more common in larger breeds than in bantams. Symptoms are enlarged feather follicles or white bumps that scab over, dehydration, rapid weight loss, stilted gait, wing or leg paralysis, and death. There is no known treatment. Remove infected birds from your flock; you most likely will need to kill them. Prevention includes vaccination and good sanitation. Marek's does not affect humans.

Newcastle disease: Newcastle is also called avian distemper and domestic Newcastle. It affects the respiratory system and nervous system. The whole flock can be infected in about a week if the disease is not caught and treated. Symptoms include wheezing, gasping, and coughing followed by drooping wings or dragging legs. Help prevent Newcastle through vaccination, clean coops, and good overall care of your birds through good sanitation and a balanced diet. Treatment includes separating birds from the healthy flock and keeping them warm and well fed. Then watch for the secondary signs as in drooping wings and dragging legs. Take the birds to the vet if symptoms persist. Humans can catch an eye infection from handling sick birds, so use rubber gloves, and wash your hands to keep from spreading the virus.

Omphalitis: This disease is present at the time of hatching from an incubator. The cause is typically poor sanitation in the incubator. High humidity during incubation can prevent the chick's navel from healing properly. Also, infection could set in if contaminated droppings are on the hatching eggs or if hatching eggs are cracked. Chicks, up to 4 weeks old, will have a drooping head, mushy or scabby navel, and lack of interest in food and water. There is no cure available; the sick chicks will die or need to be killed. The best way to prevent this is to hatch clean, uncracked eggs in a clean incubator with proper temperatures.

Osteopetrosis: Osteopetrosis affects the bones. It is a retrovirus. Symptoms are thickened leg bones, stilted gait, and stunting. This condition often occurs in combination with lymphoid leukosis, a disease of the blood-forming organs. There is no treatment. Prevention includes purchasing your chicks from a reputable buyer and knowing their background, not reusing chick boxes, not raising chickens on wire, and avoiding flock-wide injections or vaccinations using one needle.

Paratyphoid: This common disease affects the digestive organs and possibly the entire body. It is caused from a salmonella virus in litter and soil. In young chicks, symptoms include dead embryos at the time of hatch, poor growth, increased thirst, huddling in around heat with ruffled feathers, increased chirping, swelling in both eyes, diarrhea, and dehydration. This disease has no treatment, and survivors will be carriers. Prevention is difficult, but keep coops, bedding, and water clean; collect hatching eggs often; and replace nesting litter often. **You will need to report this disease to the USDA.**

Pasted vent: Chicks mostly suffer from pasted vent. This occurs when feces clog the bird's vent, and the chick has blockage when trying to defecate. If the vent seals up, death can occur. Treat this by washing the infected area with warm water and carefully picking at the adhering matter with a toothpick or something similar. Although this is common in chicks, hens are affected as well. Clean droppings that stick to vent feathers as soon as you notice them.

Pox (dry): Pox affects the skin and can appear in birds of all ages, excluding newly hatched chicks. The virus is identified by wart-like bumps found on the comb and wattles that grow larger and change in color. They start out white, turn yellow, and then proceed to a reddish-brown, gray, or black. Other symptoms include a drop in egg production, weight loss, and scabs on the head and neck. Prevention is difficult, as this virus is carried through mites and mosquitoes. Vaccination is recommended. No treatment is known, so isolate infected birds. There is no harm to humans; chicken pox in humans is a different strain of virus.

Staphylococcic arthritis: This can affect the joints or the entire body. Symptoms include swollen joints, resting on hocks (the part of the leg below the thigh but above the ankle), fever, and hesitancy to move. The cause of staphylococcic arthritis is a common virus strain in the poultry environment. Treatment is obtained through antibiotics. Prevention involves keeping your chickens in uncrowded housing to prevent injuries that allow the virus to enter the body. For humans, consuming infected meat can cause food poisoning.

Sudden death syndrome: This is common in broilers. Although the cause is unknown, it is suspected that giving broilers high-carb feed to induce rapid weight growth affects the heart and lungs, causing a heart attack. Postmortem findings include feed-filled intestines and bloated, bright red lungs. It has no cure, and the best prevention is to eliminate as much stress as possible in your flock's environment.

Thrush: Thrush affects the upper digestive tract. Symptoms include diarrhea, weight loss, and slow growth caused by a Candida yeast-like substance that lives in the chickens' bowels. You can prevent this disease by practicing good nutrition and sanitation. Treatment includes isolating infected birds and cleaning and disinfecting coops, feeders, waterers, and bedding. Clean mouth sores with an antiseptic such as hydrogen peroxide. A home remedy to help cure your bird is to first do a "flush." Add 1 pint of molasses per 5 gallons of water and offer it to your bird for no more than eight hours. Or, give the bird an Epsom salt flush. Use 1 teaspoon of Epsom salt in ½ cup of water and squirt the solution down the bird's throat twice daily for two days or until recovery. You also can try using ½ teaspoon copper sulfate per gallon drinking water every other day. Do not use a metal waterer with this mixture.

Twisted leg: Twisted leg is also known as crooked legs, valgus leg deformity, or long-bone distortion because it affects the long bones of the leg. The chicken may have a pointed protrusion at the hock joint, and affected birds sometimes walk on bruised or swollen hocks. The cause may be nutritional, genetic, or possibly due to the environment they are raised in. There is no treatment. Prevention includes raising birds on litter and not wire. Also, do not feed your birds for rapid growth. This condition will not harm humans.

Ulcerative Enteritis: Ulcerative Enteritis affects poultry including chickens, ducks, turkeys, and game birds. It causes inflammation and ulcers in the intestines. This can be fatal, but 90 percent of the time is not. It appears in both acute and chronic form. It is caused by a bacteria passed on through the feces. If another chicken pecks at feces that are infected with these bacteria, it can contract it. Sometimes, flies that have fed on contaminated feces can carry the bacteria and pass it on to other birds as well. Symptoms include blood in diarrhea, listlessness, and depression. Chickens can be treated for ulcerative enteritis by antibiotics such as streptomyocin or furazolidone added to their feed.

Parasitic worms

Worms are a common problem in birds and poultry. The key to success is ridding the source or host of the parasite so you are not continually treating a recurring problem. A host is any living thing that provides an ideal environment for the parasite to survive. Treatment can become costly and frustrating, and parasites can become resistant to medications. Prevention and cleanliness of your bird's environment will be your best defense in this fight. Six common parasitic worms found in chickens are:

- Nemathelminthes, a type of roundworm
- Nematodes, a type of roundworm
- Acanthocephalans, a thorny-headed worm
- Platyhelminthes, a flatworm
- Cestodes, a tapeworm
- Trematodes, a flukeworm that has external suckers so it can attach to the host body

Chickens will develop a resistance to parasites over time. These microbes exist in the poultry world just as germs and common colds exist in the human world. When a chicken is ill or stressed, it is more susceptible to suffering from the consequences of these infestations. Parasites can make your bird lose weight, cause breathing problems, and block the respiratory organs and airway.

Parasites can be passed from chicken to chicken indirectly. An infected chicken can shed a worm's eggs in its excrement. Chickens tend to eat feces, and they may ingest contaminated chicken droppings. New worms will hatch in the chicken's intestines, making that chicken its home and beginning the cycle again.

Sometimes, there is an intermediate host body. For instance, a grasshopper may eat the chicken droppings infested with the parasite's eggs. Then, a chicken may eat that grasshopper, thereby ingesting the parasitic worm and starting a new cycle. This is why it is hard to prevent parasites entirely, and at some point in your ownership of chickens, you will encounter this problem. By keeping your chickens' home and environment clean, including their feed and water, you will be able to keep most illnesses at bay. Like children, chickens will get sick from time to time. By educating yourself and spending time with your chickens, you will be able to catch any signs of sickness in your flock. Early detection will help care for them and potentially save their lives.

Mites and lice

Parasitic worms live inside a host's body, whereas mites and lice live outside the body. Their damage can cause mild irritation, infection, and possibly death. They carry diseases from bird to bird. If not treated immediately, external parasites spread quickly. Their ability to multiply, compounded with the fact they are microscopic, makes it difficult to maintain control of these parasites.

Mites are more active at night, which is a good time to check your birds. They come in a variety of types:

- **Red mites:** These are more common in litter-raised birds than in caged birds and are predominant in warmer climates or during summer months. One female mite lays as many as 120,000 eggs. Chicks are vulnerable and can die if you have a severe red mite infestation in your flock.

- **Scaly leg mite:** These mites burrow under the unfeathered part of skin on a chicken's legs. Infestation causes the scales on the bird's legs to rise up and away from the skin. Visually check your bird to see that its legs and scales are healthy. In a severe case, these mites will move to wattles and combs. Treat them with petroleum jelly.

- **Feather mites:** These mites live in the bird's plumage and damage the chicken's coat by eating the feathers. They are not common in North America.

- **Fowl mites:** Fowl mites are common and are found in cooler climates. Symptoms of infestation include large numbers of mites on the skin during the day, scabby skin around the vent, darkened feathers around the vent, and mites crawling on eggs in the nest. Using a pesticide approved for poultry will help control infestation. The appropriate pesticide will list on the bottle that it is approved for poultry. The danger involved with the fowl mite is that it lives its entire life on a chicken, which is about a week. This means a higher rate of reproduction as it goes through its life cycle.

Lice also come in a variety of species. Some lice prefer chickens and no other type of bird or mammal. Different types of lice have different preferences for the parts of the body they feast on. These parasites feed on the feathers and skin, but some varieties eat through the skin to get to the blood.

- **Head lice:** This is the most common lice infestation. The Polish and Cochin chicken breeds are susceptible to head lice because of the amount of plumage around their faces. Spraying them lightly with poultry-approved pesticide will help prevent lice. Be careful to avoid the eyes.

- **Wing lice:** They like to hide under a chicken's wing and may infect the vent area and breast.

- **Body lice:** If a chicken is infested with body lice, you will notice scabs on the bird's skin and egg masses at the base of the feathers.

- **Fluff lice:** This is one of the least invasive forms of lice. It is predominantly common in the South. They live on the fluff and cause little irritation because they are not very active.

Again, the best prevention is honing good sanitation practices and keeping chicken bedding clean and dry. Check your birds at least once a month for mite or lice infection. Disinfectant spray is the best defense for controlling these external parasites. Make sure any chemicals you use on your flock or within their environment are safe for you and your birds.

You can find a plethora of products to help prevent or conquer mites and lice at your local pet store, co-op, or online. Poultry Protector is one product that you might choose. It is organic and can be used on your birds and in their coop. The average cost for a bottle is between $6 and $12.95. The product can be found on these websites:

- Smith Poultry & Game Bird Supply (**www.poultrysupplies.com**) — This site offers a variety of products for caring for your flock. It includes products for your birds as well as their surroundings.

- American Livestock and Pet Supply, Inc. (**www.americanlivestock.com**) — This website offers products for chickens and other farm animals.

- IPS-CareFree Enzymes, Inc. (**www.carefreeenzymes.com**) — This site offers a variety of organic and chemical-free products for chickens and other farm animals.

Another product that kills mites and lice is Orange Guard, which is a water-based pest control product found at Orange Guard (**www.orangeguard.com**) and on Amazon (**www.amazon.com**).

You can choose from a variety of shelf products when purchasing insecticides. Shop around and see which work best to fit your needs and your lifestyle. Be sure to keep you, your family, and your birds safe and healthy so you can enjoy a long and satisfying relationship.

Stress

One last key element regarding your birds' welfare is stress. Chickens are deeply affected by stress. Causes of anxiety can include loud noises, bad weather, predators, overcrowding in a coop, excessive bright light, not enough bright light, the lack of a regular routine, and living with other aggressive birds. Some stressors, such as loud noises, are common and affect most birds, but for the most part, anything can trigger a stressed reaction in a chicken. Why is stress so bad? Too much stress produces higher levels of hormones in chickens, which can be stored in their muscles. If these chickens are used for slaughter, you may be consuming unnecessary hormones. The muscles also tend to be tougher in highly stressed birds. This is why cage-free birds often are tenderer than commercial birds. But this is not the only reason to limit stress in a chicken's life. Stressed birds are much more likely to contract illnesses because of weakened immune systems, and sick birds can ruin an entire flock.

Stress also has an affect on egg layers, and they may reduce the amount of eggs they produce. The quality of the egg may decrease as well because of the excessive hormones produced in the chicken's body and passed down to the egg.

Symptoms of a bird with anxiety are loss of appetite, changes in normal behavior patterns, diarrhea, labored breathing, and sometimes death. To help prevent stressful conditions, make sure your flock has a clean, safe, and dry environment. Provide adequate ventilation and plenty of sunshine. The great part is you do not need to have years of experience to know what constitutes a happy home.

To get the most enjoyment from your birds, strive to keep them as stress free as possible. Certain types of breeds are tougher and able to endure stress and harsher environments more than other breeds.

Preventing chicken stress

You can take several steps to reduce the stress your chicks might experience:

- Provide a secure coop with adequate lighting.
- Clean their home.
- Provide enough space.
- Keep the coop warm in the winter and cool in the summer.
- Interact with your flock daily to familiarize them with people.
- Teach children to respect your birds.
- Keep other family pets away from your flock if they are aggressive or loud.
- Hold your birds upright and never upside down. It frightens the chickens.
- Have enough food and fresh water available.
- Handle them gently.
- Collect hens' eggs daily so they will continue to produce fresh eggs. Separate the roosters from the hens.
- Provide a roost for the chickens.
- Provide enough grass for your chickens to forage.
- Give your flock adequate attention.

Clipping wings

There is something so restricting when you imagine a bird with clipped wings — it seems unnatural to alter what comes naturally to birds. The truth is, though, when owning chickens, some breeds are able to fly, and if your fence or surroundings are not built to keep them secure, clipping their wings may be one solution. Because the neighbor's dog or a two-lane highway may be within their reach, clipping their wings can keep them safe and keep them alive. In some cases, clipping a bird's wings helps to keep the bird free-range because you do not have to keep it enclosed most of the time.

If this is your first time clipping a bird's wing, you may want to enlist the help of an experienced friend. If you do not know of anyone who has chickens and has done this before, find a friend or family member that can help you hold the bird during this process. Clipping your chicken's wing should not hurt the bird. It is like clipping your dog's nails. Most often, the animal is afraid of the process. For birds, the vibration from the actual clipping of their stiff feathers scares them. There should be no blood or minimal blood. If you clip your chicken's wing, and the bird starts to bleed, use your first aid kit to stop the bleeding. If the bird is bleeding heavily, call or visit your vet immediately to treat the bird.

You can clip a chicken's wings when its adult feathers are grown in. Even if a chicken has its adult feathers, it is advisable to wait until flight becomes a problem. Do not cut pinfeathers, which are the tips of new feathers on a bird's body. Clipping one wing is enough to prevent the chicken from taking flight; it throws the bird off balance and still allows it to fly, just not very high. Some chicken owners prefer to clip both wings to keep the bird balanced. The wings will grow back, just like people cut their hair and it grows. There are tutorials of how to clip wings posted on YouTube (**www. youtube.com**) by chicken owners. Go to the website and type in the search "How to Clip a Chicken's Wings."

To get started, you will need:

- An assistant
- Very, very sharp scissors
- Old towel
- Rubber gloves to protect your hands
- A first aid kit (just in case of injury)
- Treats for when the task is complete

1. First, decide who will clip the wings and who will hold the bird.
2. Gather your chicken. Be calm. If you cannot get hold of the chicken, it is not advisable to chase it around. This stresses the chicken. Try again at another time or try to gather another bird.
3. Hold the chicken by the legs. Support its body by keeping your hand underneath its body. Your palm should be open and flat. Leave either the left or right wing free.
4. Talk to it in soothing tones.
5. Spread the wing. Display it in its entirety.
6. The first 10 feathers from the outside of the wing are flight feathers; these flight feathers are usually longer than the rest and often a different color. Cut just beyond the edge of the nest layer up. This is approximately 3 to 5 inches.
7. Quickly clip the bird's wings. Use very sharp scissors. Dull blades may hurt the bird.
8. Give your bird a treat.

Chickens molt annually, so you will need to clip your chickens' wings each year with its new growth of feathers.

Breeding Chickens

Whether you already have some chickens or you are a novice chicken owner, breeding chickens can be a great way to enhance your experience. Breeding provides you with an opportunity to create the type of bird you want. These birds are designed for your purposes and to fit into your needs. Whether you are doing it for a hobby, for food, or for money, you will be able to achieve your goals with time, patience, and knowledge. Breeding chickens is not recommended for city dwellers unless you have enough space to accommodate your birds. If you end up with a large quantity of birds while you are breeding, you may find yourself with a lack of space. However, if you do have room for your coop and run, as well as an area for your incubator and chicks, you can breed chickens successfully in your urban home.

Consider what breeding a flock of chickens entails before you begin your new endeavor. This process has many components, though the rewards are worth it. Once you have the physical materials you need, it is time to get started on your plan of action. You must have a clear idea of the process because you do not want find yourself wondering what you should do next at any point. Live animals will not wait for you. Each day will be an adventure, and if you are not prepared, you might miss out.

In the beginning, it is important to start small. As a new breeder, you will want to gain some experience before you tackle large amounts of birds. Start small by owning and breeding one rooster and two hens. Do not get two roosters because they will fight for male dominance. In the future, you may want to produce more than one type of chicken, and at that point, you will need more than one rooster. But in the beginning, keep it simple. It is natural to want to take on more, but be aware that if you are successful from the beginning and your hens' eggs are fertilized, you could end up with many eggs. Those eggs will hatch baby chicks, and before you know it, your flock is more than you may be able to handle.

CASE STUDY: STARTING FROM SCRATCH

Jesse Dykes

Jesse Dykes and his wife, Jessica, live outside of Nashville, Tennessee, on five acres of property. The rural location was a prime environment for ticks and spiders. "It was so bad that we would have several ticks on us from the time it took to walk to the house from our car," Dykes said. They decided to get some chicks to help with insect control. In just a few months, the ticks were almost nonexistent. Now their flock is primarily for eggs and meat.

Dykes and his wife started out with eight chickens of mixed breed from Tractor Supply (**www.tractorsupply. com**) to help learn about them without spending much money. Now nearing a flock of 50 birds, they currently have Rhode Island Reds, buff Orpingtons, and barred Rocks, and they are in the process of getting some Jersey Giants.

Dykes recommends starting with day-old chicks, as opposed to hatching your own eggs. He said, "From my experience, it is not economical to buy an incubator, eggs, and then hatch them. Most hatcheries charge more for eggs than day-old chicks."

He continues, "We initially bought our day-old chicks from the Tractor Supply Store. We have since found a local hatchery by the name of Poultry Hollow. My wife and I also source our chicks from Mypetchicken.com and Mc-murrayhatchery.com. My Pet Chicken is excellent about shipping low number orders. In general, I would suggest new chicken owners buying from their local co-op or Tractor Supply Store for their first batch. The store clerks are very knowledgeable and willing to help customers with questions. In the end, the store route was less stress on us when we first got into raising chickens."

Living on five acres of open land has its challenges. Dykes found that hawks were the No. 1 threat to his flock. Keeping them safe was hard. He says, "We lost five chickens and three ducks in one day to four hawks. Identify your predators ahead of time and plan for them."

Dykes made the coop they use. "We actually have what most people would call a chicken tractor. I built it from mostly a mixture of scrap wood, cedar mill lumber, and store-bought lumber. The coop section of the tractor is 4 foot by 4 foot with two stories. It is about 24 inches from the ground. The run is 12 feet long and includes a section running under the coop. The run is 4 feet wide and about 5 feet high. The coop section's roof tops out at about 8 feet or so tall."

Dykes offers some tips on how to build a coop: "First, never use pressure-treated wood. The only section of our tractor that has treated wood is the runners. These are the boards that actually come in contact with the ground. We tried to use cedar as much as possible. For wood preservation, a few companies make non-toxic stains. One of them comes in powdered form. Backyardchickens.com has some amazing designs from all over the continent. Their forum is a great resource for design ideas."

Regarding feeders and waterers, Dykes offers the following advice: "You do not have to buy expensive equipment to feed and water your chickens. Look around on the Internet for lower cost solutions. If you are handy, you can save quite a bit of money with homemade solutions. For example, a 5-gallon waterer usually runs about $40. A 5-gallon bucket with a few poultry nipples can cost $20 or less. Some people even use food grade plastic barrels that can hold 50 gallons. My feeder is made from a 5-gallon bucket and a galvanized feed/water basin from Tractor Supply Company. It cost me $5 to make it. Get creative! I also built an auto feeder that we fill biweekly. Initially, we spent a few hundred dollars building a coop, buying the equipment and the chicks. It certainly does not take that much. We intended to get more serious about his adventure, so we were willing to spend more money up front."

Part of your plan will be deciding which breed of chicken to raise. Take into consideration the size of the bird and the amount of room you have to offer. Decide upon the reasons you want your birds, and consider other family members or children who will be affected by the choice to raise chickens.

Breeding egg layers

If you are seeking to breed birds for their egg-laying ability, you can choose the type of eggs you will get by the bird you intend on breeding. It is fine to inbreed for show birds, meaning that you use the same birds from the same family, but it does not work for egg layers. Crossbreeding is a successful method to create good egg layers. Crossbreeding entails taking a hen from one family of chickens and breeding it with a rooster of another bloodline.

Breeding for meat

If you are planning to breed and raise your chickens for meat then you should choose breeds that are known to be good meat chickens. Many of the chickens discussed here will be good for your table, but some chickens excel. The White Plymouth Rock and the White Cornish are outstanding birds for meat production. They make the most use of their feed and grow large in a short time. These birds can gain 4 to 5 pounds in just six weeks from the time of hatching. You can eat them or sell them as fryers or roasters.

Even if you are not raising your chickens for meat, there will come a time when you will need to cull chickens from the flock, especially if you are breeding. Often, you will find a weak or sick chick, even under the best conditions, and instead of trying to nurse it back to health, most of the time the humane choice is to kill the bird. This is not easy for some animal owners, and if you do not feel comfortable taking on this task, have a plan, so when the time arrives, you are not in a panic. If you know other chicken owners, talk with them to see what they do in these circumstances. They may know someone to refer you to for these purposes.

Breeding for show

Breeding for show requires more attention to detail when you purchase the bird. When you choose an ornamental bird, you do not want to reproduce its flaws. This is true when you make your selection for any breed, but a show bird's main purpose is its physical attributes. Do not mistakenly think certain genes will not appear in your future flock because there are no guarantees. You do not want to set yourself up to be disappointed. Pick a bird that has the ideal traits for its breed, and you can then improve one trait at a time. Part of the enjoyment of breeding for show is creating the perfect bird for you.

Once you select your breeds, you will need to find high-quality birds to get started. You can find quality breeders through other chicken owners. It is always better to get a recommendation and purchase a bird from someone you trust. When buying an adult bird, a pullet, or cockerel, it is easy to be misled on the quality of the bird you are getting. Even experienced chicken owners can be duped when buying an older bird because you really do not know its exact age or history. If you do not know anyone who can give you a reference, ask around at your local pet store or co-op. Chicken owners most likely frequent these places, and salespeople are there to help you. They usually can point you in the right direction. If this is not an option, check local classified ads. You may not know your seller, but do not be hesitant in asking questions. Inspect your bird for any physical deformities or parasite infestation. If the bird looks and sounds healthy and has the qualities you want to breed, take your bird home.

Selective breeding and crossbreeding

Selective breeding entails mating two birds of the same breed that have the desired characteristics you are looking for to produce a new bird that will hopefully have all of the qualities you want. This can help establish a new bloodline for your flock. **Crossbreeding** is taking two or more different breeds of birds and mating them together to achieve a new breed that has the most promising characteristics you want. These are known as **hybrid chicken breeds**. Creating the perfect bird is not always successful, as some genes may not be passed down to the new chick on the first try or ever. However, if you keep breeding your chickens, you should be able to get the outcome you desire.

Types of hybrid chickens:

1. Golden Comet = crossing a Leghorn and Rhode Island Red
2. Isa Brown = crossing Rhode Island Reds and Rhode Island Whites
3. Daisy Belles = crossing Rhode Island Reds and Sussex
4. Black Sex Link chickens = crossing Rhode Island Reds or New Hampshires and Barred Rock hens
5. Cream Legbar = crossing a Brown Leghorn with a Barred Rock and Aracauna

You can create your own breed. Just like dogs and other domestic animals that are crossbred, chickens can have many types of breeds in their bloodline if they are not purebred. These breed mixtures can provide beautiful and distinct birds.

Here is an example if you want to breed blue-laced red Wyandottes:

If you mate:
   Blue with blue, you will get: 50 percent blue, 25 percent black, and 25 percent splash
   Blue with a splash, you will get 50 percent blue, 50 percent splash
   Blue with black, you will get 50 percent blue, 50 percent black
   Splash with black, you will get 100 percent blue
   Black with black, you will get 100 percent black
   Splash with splash, you will get 100 percent splash

Roosters

Roosters, or cocks, are male chickens. Young roosters are called cockerels, and castrated roosters are called capons. You will need to have one rooster to fertilize your hen's eggs. Roosters can have an aggressive nature, especially if you own more than one. The chicken's innate need to fulfill the pecking order can cause them to fight, even to the death, for dominance. If you plan to have more than one rooster, you may need to separate them from each other, but keep them with several hens. Chickens are social creatures that need to interact with other birds or people for their overall well-being.

Roosters are known for their crowing. Typically, roosters crow at the crack of dawn, but they can crow at any hour, even in the middle of the night. They usually do not do this; often it is triggered by a noise that startles the bird.

Roosters are also the more colorful gender. Their markings are brighter and more intense than most of their female counterparts' markings. They also care for their hens and chicks. If a rooster finds food, he will call out to the rest of the flock and indicate by the tone in his voice that food is available. A rooster also may pick a favorite among the flock to mate with. He will save the best food for her and is gentler with her during mating. Roosters are known to guide their little chicks when walking around the yard, and they will fight to the death to protect their flock from predators. They are loyal to their families.

Taming a mean rooster

Mean roosters have turned many people off from raising chickens. With their well-developed spurs, rooters can inflict serious wounds when they see you as a threat to their flock dominance. Each time you enter the coop, you will have to remind your rooster you are the top dog of the flock by following the steps given in this section.

An alpha rooster usually dominates the pecking order of a flock by getting first dibs at food, water, and hens. The hens also have an alpha hen that is the boss. Unlike the roosters, hen social order is harder to see, but it is there. The alpha rooster asserts his dominance constantly. If another chicken attempts to eat first or another rooster tries to mate a hen, the alpha male will rush over and administer a good peck or even pummel the out-of-bounds interloper with beak, claws, and wings.

Your job is to make sure you are not the victim of such an attack. Starting when the chickens are small, take a few minutes each day to observe their behavior. When the chicks start to fight (or spar), break them apart by gently pushing them back with your fingers. Each fight you see, do the same thing. This will let the flock know that you are in charge. As they get older, you will still have to reinforce your dominance. It is fine to pick up a rooster and pet him. But a rooster should not be eager to approach you. If he does, he will think that he is the top chicken not you. It will not hurt to take an occasional swat at him if he seems too comfortable with you.

Do not let the rooster eat before the hens. Doing so will give him the cue that he is dominant in the flock, when in reality, you should be the dominant member (in his mind) of the flock. In essence, you are top rooster and need to allow the hens to eat before him, the less-dominant rooster. If he tries to come to the feeder first, push him away so the hens eat first. After the hens are eating, it is fine if the rooster begins to eat. If a rooster tries to breed a hen in your presence, push him off and chase him away. It is the same concept as eating; he has to wait until you leave to be able to breed the hens.

The main thing when it comes to roosters is that you have to be on guard at all times. If these techniques do not work, or if you are unable to be consistent in asserting your dominance, it might be safer for the rooster to be destined for the soup bowl.

Broody hens

An egg-laying hen will produce eggs every one to two days. The average egg-laying cycle takes about 25 to 26 hours to complete. Right before a hen lays an egg, her hormone levels rise. This gives the hen her "homemaking" initiative, and she seeks out a nest and lays her egg. Most of the time, the hormone level drops, and the hen leaves her nest and will return when she is ready to lay her next egg. Sometimes, though, the hormone level does not drop as quickly. This happens more frequently in winter when not as much daylight is available and makes the hen want to sit on her eggs. As each day progresses, the hen leaves the nest less and less, instead collecting her eggs and sitting on them. This is known as going broody. Hens then like to wait until they have laid about ten eggs, which can take about ten days if they lay one egg a day. Hens do this because they think they are going to hatch the eggs, and instinctively, they want their chicks to hatch at the same time, which is 21 days later.

When a hen is broody, she becomes territorial. She may make low, growling noises if she is approached or if she feels her eggs are in danger. Mother hen may even peck at you. She will leave her nest only for food and drink, and some hens do not even do that, which may be dangerous to their health. They may defecate on the eggs, which you will need to clean if you intend to hatch them or eat them. It is not unusual for eggs to be dirty when you collect them. About $^1/_3$ of the eggs you collect probably will be dirty. You can clean eggs by dry cleaning them with a loofah or a sanding sponge from a hardware store. Dry washing eggs is safer than washing them with water. As long as the eggs are dry, bacteria is less likely to get inside the eggshell.

Certain breeds of chickens tend to go broody more than others. Examples of broody chicken breeds are Australorp, Brahma, Buckeye, and Chantecler. Other breeds have been bred to remove the broody gene. Examples of non-broody birds are Rhode Island Reds, Leghorns, Minorcas, and barred Rock.

Collecting the eggs each day will help prevent a chicken from going broody. If the broodiness is a big problem, you may want to remove the nesting boxes. A hen's broodiness is a problem if your bird is no longer producing additional eggs or if she is aggressive and preventing other hens from laying eggs. A hen will find anything that resembles a nest to lay her eggs in, such as a planter or crate. Once she is on there, it will be hard to remove her because she will be feisty due to her hormones kicking in.

If you want your hen to become broody, for instance, if she is producing more eggs than you need, leave several golf balls or plastic eggs in her nest to induce the process. Chickens can be tricked into thinking they are hatching their own eggs. They will not know the difference. You can even do this to help move her cycle along. She will be broody for an average of 21 days if she sits on her eggs, and when they do not hatch, she will lose interest and go back to her normal daily routine.

Mating

You can try several different mating techniques depending on your skill level and the number of birds you have. One type of mating is flock mating, which is not recommended for the novice breeder and chicken owner because it can produce a large quantity of birds, and as a novice, you may not be ready to handle so many birds immediately. With flock mating, flocks are made up of about 14 hens and one rooster, and the rooster can mate freely with the hens. This is a good method if you want to produce many chicks. The main negative aspect is that you cannot keep an accurate record of which hens the rooster is mating with and how many eggs they are producing. Also, you have less control over the quality of the birds you are creating. This may be a method to choose once you have more experience and plan to have a large flock of chickens.

The other method of mating is in pairs or trios. One or two hens grouped with one rooster will help control the quality of the chickens you hatch. This is especially important for breeders who will be showing their birds. You can do this by putting the birds in pens or cages together. Their natural instincts will take over.

Some roosters will court their hens first. If a rooster has many hens to choose from, the courting appears to be less frequent. To court, the rooster may circle the hen, and she will bend over in front of him. He will then jump on the hen's back, holding on to her with his beak and claws. They will mate for several seconds, and the process will be over.

Some roosters are more aggressive than others when mating. Often a chicken will have feathers missing and scratches on her back from a rooster. Although most chickens are compliant when a rooster is ready to mate, some hens run away. The rooster may accept this but also may chase the chicken and forcibly mate with her. The mating ritual is initiated by chemical changes in the birds, and this usually makes the birds compatible for reproducing.

Using only two or three birds allows you to keep excellent records. You will want to do this so you know which birds produced a particular offspring. Write down the dates, the traits, and the birds that you used to create your breed. You may want to change the traits or reproduce them, and your memory may not always be accurate.

Nesting boxes

Nesting boxes, where broody hens sit on their eggs, are an essential part of the mating and breeding process. You can make them out of wood or plastic, or you can purchase premade ones. You should have one box for every two to four hens you own. Some breeds will not want to share their nesting box, such as a Cornish chicken, while breeds such as Silkies would prefer to all climb into one nesting box and hatch their eggs together. If you are unsure of whether your birds will like sharing their nest, plan to get more boxes.

Nesting boxes typically are placed in the coop and can be on one level or stacked on top of each other. If you stack them, make sure they are not higher than the roosts in your coop. Otherwise, the birds will want to sleep in them, and you may run out of room for your broody chickens. The nests should be about 12 inches wide by 12 inches long by 12 inches deep. You can customize boxes to fit your needs, but that size should work fine for your flock.

Wood shavings or straw make a comfortable bed. Sawdust is popular because it is inexpensive, and it absorbs any droppings, but it can cause the birds to develop breathing problems. Commercial chicken bedding can be purchased from a farm and feed supply store. Some of the recycled wood bedding works well because it has less moisture content than fresh wood shavings. Drier wood means less chance for mold and mites therefore keeping your chicken healthy and happy. If you prefer not to purchase commercial bedding, you always can use straw or hay. The main objective is to find filler that works for both you and your flock.

Always keep the bedding clean and dry, and use 2 to 4 inches of bedding. After all of your hard work in selecting a breed and mating your birds, you do not want to have your fertilized eggs ruined because they sat in a dirty bed. Cleaning the box once a week or more frequently as needed should be sufficient.

Hatching Eggs

Many people who raise chickens prefer to start with eggs rather than chicks or adult birds. Hatching eggs is not difficult, but you do need to pay careful attention to details. Otherwise, your first attempts at hatching eggs may not be successful. Order your eggs from a good hatchery, or buy them from a good local source. Make sure your incubator is in good condition and works properly. Temperature and humidity are critical. And follow all of the directions for incubating the eggs carefully.

Using incubators

If you choose to hatch your eggs artificially, you will need an incubator. You can find these at feed and farm supply stores. Find a location inside your home to keep the incubator, and set it up on a level surface. Follow the directions provided with the equipment, and keep the incubator away from sunlight, as that can affect the inside temperature. Following these steps provides a safe environment secure against predators and the elements.

In general, there are two types of incubators: forced air and still air. Forced air helps spread heat equally throughout the incubator, and a still-air incubator does not promote the movement of heat. The temperature of a forced-air incubator should be at 100 degrees F, while a still-air incubator should be slightly higher at about 102 degrees F.

If you decide to make an incubator yourself, be sure you have a well-designed plan, the right equipment, and the skill level necessary. The website My Pet Chicken (**www.mypetchicken.com**) offers tips and directions on how to make incubators, and it offers incubators for sale in different sizes and shapes. Some are high tech, and some are basic. You also can purchase egg turners from this site.

Turning eggs

Eggs must be turned every day, and using an automated egg turner is an easy way to ensure this is taken care of. If you decide not to purchase an egg turner, you can turn the eggs manually. Mark one side of the egg with an X and the other side with an O, and rotate the egg 180 degrees, which is a half-turn, five times a day. Be gentle; you are the egg's parent.

Rotating the eggs an odd number of times per day helps ensure the embryo is receiving the correct amount of rotation. The chick's head is in the large end of the egg so you are turning the chick when you rotate the egg. Turn eggs each day until day 18. After that, the chick is preparing to hatch and should not be moved. Chicks will begin to hatch around day 21, and it should take about 24 hours for all of the eggs to hatch.

Incubator settings

Have your incubator set up 24 hours before receiving your chicks with the temperature between 99 and 100 degrees F and humidity adjusted correctly. When you put the eggs inside for the first time, the temperature will drop because you will have let some of the warm air out by opening the incubator and because the temperature of the eggs is cooler from transport. The temperature should stabilize and remain constant before you put the eggs in, which could take up to four hours. This is a critical step in caring for your eggs; even a minor adjustment either way could kill your embryos. Humidity should be 58 percent to 60 percent on days one through 18 in the incubator. After that, gradually increase it to 65 percent. As your eggs age, they need more humidity to make the adjustment easier for the birds.

The incubator will have a water pan, or if you are using a homemade model, you can add a water-soaked sponge inside with the eggs. Humidity can vary slightly, as it is difficult to get the perfect setting. Make sure you monitor the humidity because low humidity will cause the shells to stick to the chicks or may produce small chicks or chicks with rough navels; high humidity will cause an unabsorbed yolk sac that will smear on the baby bird.

High-tech incubators are self-sufficient, which makes the process easier because it does all of the work. If you are using a basic incubator, such as one made of Styrofoam, check on the eggs all day long. These types of incubators work well but require a lot of manual monitoring. Probe thermometers will help determine the temperature.

Make sure your incubator is properly ventilated to keep fresh oxygen in and bad gases out. Vents are important because the buildup of gases can be toxic to the eggs. Vents should be located above, below, or on the side of the incubator. Gradually open them during the incubation period, so by the time the eggs hatch, the vents are fully open. This is also a critical point in the care of the embryos. If you are making your incubator, you must provide a vent. If you are purchasing an incubator, make sure it has vents.

Bad odors coming from the incubator mean that one or more of your eggs has gone bad, so remove the affected egg and discard it. If you do not remove it, it may explode because of built-up gases and contaminate the other eggs. Plus, you surely will not want to smell the foul odor for long. If an egg has not hatched around day 25 or 26, it is safe to assume it will not hatch, so discard it immediately.

After day 18, do not open the incubator except to add water to keep the humidity constant. Close the vents at this time. It will be tempting, as you have been handling your birds for three weeks, but keeping the vents shut will keep the environment stable for your chicks. Newborn chicks should not be touched too much because they are delicate and prone to illness, as their immune system is not strong at this stage. In just a few days, though, they will be bouncing around, and you can play with them.

Once they hatch

The chicks can stay in the incubator for about four hours after they hatch to dry out and stay warm. Chicks will not need food or water for the first 48 hours after they hatch because their shell will provide enough nutrients for them to survive. Put some food such as starter mash or chick feed and water in their starter box after 48 hours to get them used to it. They also will feel less stress if they eat and drink on their second day. They will not overeat, but they may need you to pick them up and take them to the feeder. Some chicks are more adventurous than others, and timid chicks may not find the food or might get pushed out of the way. Watch your brood to ensure they are getting the nourishment they need.

The **starter box** is the chicks' home after they hatch because they are too fragile and immature to be in the coop at this stage without a mother hen. Your starter box can be a large cardboard box with a heat lamp. The box should be at least 2 feet by 2 feet and about 1 foot high with a mesh cover. There is enough room in this size box for about ten chicks when they are first born, but they will need more room as they grow. The temperature needs to be kept at 90 to 95 degrees F for the first week, and you should reduce the temperature 5 degrees each week until you reach room temperature. Use a thermometer to gauge the heat inside the box. If you notice the chicks are chirping extra loudly and are standing apart with their mouths wide open, the temperature is probably too high. If the chicks are chirping in a shrill tone, they are most likely too chilly. Content chicks chirp in a soft tone, and close monitoring will help keep the babies comfortable and healthy.

Have 2 inches of bedding in the starter box. Do not use newspaper or any type of slick bedding because it is not good for the development of the chicks' feet and legs. Mesh wire can be convenient for cleaning purposes (if it is removable), but wood chips are the best option because they are soft enough for the chicks' tender toes. Some babies eat the shavings, which can cause blockage in their system and lead to death. Keep a close eye on them. Be sure they are not eating things that are not good for them, are not being smothered by the other chicks, and are not getting into the water bowl.

Chicks love water, so have plenty available. For a chick's first drink, gently dip its beak into the water, but be careful not to wet its feathers. Chicks can catch a chill easily, so keeping them dry is imperative. You also should wash feeders and waterers daily in a mild dish detergent to keep them sanitary.

Chicks poop frequently, so be sure to keep their box and bedding clean so bacteria do not grow. Also, check your chicks' behinds regularly to make sure they are clean. Occasionally, feces will stick to their backsides and block the flow of the poop, so you will need to wash them with a warm, damp washcloth and toothpick. It is not pleasant for you or the bird, but this blockage can kill the chick if not taken care of immediately. If you continue to have trouble, or do not want to handle the bird, take it to your vet. Manure also can build up around the toes, so clean this area in the same manner. If the droppings remain on the feet, other birds may peck at it, and it can cause the chick to walk on the side of its feet, resulting in a crooked gait.

Purchasing fertile eggs

If you do not want to go through the process of finding the perfect hen and rooster to start your flock, you can purchase fertile eggs to hatch at home. This will save you the time of searching for a suitable pair of birds to mate and waiting for them to produce fertile eggs.

You can find a hatchery locally or online. Many websites will let you shop for the breed of chick you want, such as Murray McMurray Hatchery (**www.mcmurrayhatchery.com**), and they will ship your eggs to you to start your cycle of breeding.

You will not be able to select the gender of your bird using this method. Instead, you must wait until the chick is old enough to determine its sex. You also will want to purchase more eggs than you actually need to increase your chances of getting both sexes in your batch. And, not all eggs will endure the shipping process, so it will be beneficial to order extra so you are not disappointed in the amount of chicks you hatch.

Eggs you receive through the mail will need some time to adjust to their new surroundings. Even though the hatchery takes the utmost care in ensuring their safe delivery, eggs can get twisted and need to be set straight. Place eggs, large side up, in a clean egg carton to allow air bubbles to stabilize and move back to their proper place. Leave the eggs stabilized for at least 12 hours, large ends up. Do not wash the eggs, as you may wash away the protective coating and expose it to disease and infection. You should start turning your eggs as soon as they are delivered to you and you place them in your incubator. Eggs are usually sent Express Mail or a comparable way. It is not necessary to turn the eggs during this rapid trip as they are generally in motion the whole way. There is minimal health risk involving the eggs at this time. The primary health risk involving your eggs comes when there is a change of temperature and cold eggs are placed in a warm incubator. If your eggs "sweat," it can make the eggshell permeable, which can allow bacteria to enter the egg. Always make sure that you allow your eggs to warm to room temperature gradually before placing them in the incubator.

Collecting and Storing Eggs

The fun part is when you can reap the rewards for all of your hard work. Each day you need to go to the chicken coop and retrieve any eggs you do not plan on hatching. If you leave eggs in the nest for too many days, the chickens may peck at them, or you may initiate broodiness in one of your hens. Also, if you plan to consume the egg, you will want to wash it off and refrigerate it.

Go to your hen house and take a basket or bowl with you to carry your eggs. The hen most likely will be out of the coop by now and about her daily business. Pick up the eggs and gently place them in your basket or bowl. If you find broken eggs or dirty nesting boxes, clean them out so they do not create a bigger mess or health problems later.

When you return from the coop, you will need to clean your eggs. Submerging them in cold water will actually push bacteria through to the egg, so it is better to dry clean your egg. To do this, sanitize a sponge or washcloth and blot and rub the outside of the egg to remove dirt and feces. If the egg is just too messy to clean in this manner, you will need to use water, preferably running water. Use warm water and rinse the egg well using your sponge or washcloth and sanitizer. Set the eggs out to dry in a wire or mesh basket, or dry them with a paper towel.

Next, put the eggs in a carton or crate (or whatever you choose to keep them in) and label with a date. Put them in your refrigerator to maintain freshness. Eggs are good for about three weeks when stored in the fridge, as they are chemical-free and do not have hormones or preservatives to extend their shelf life.

Selling eggs

You may find you have more eggs than you know what to do with, even when eating them at every meal. Selling your extra eggs may be an option. First, check with your local county extension office to see whether any laws regulate the sale of eggs in your area. Find your office by searching the National Institute of Food and Agriculture (www.nifa.usda. gov). This website has information on the laws and regulations concerning agriculture in your community. The local extension office page has a map. Just click on your state to find the branch nearest you.

You can sell your eggs at a local farmer's market or flea market. If your city allows, you also could set up a table in front of your house with a large sign promoting homegrown eggs. For an inexpensive way to advertise your eggs, put an ad in your newspaper's classified section. Craigslist (**www.craigslist.org**) is another great way to advertise free. Selling eggs from home is an easy and fun way to make some extra cash. You can even put them in decorative cartons or baskets.

Always make sure the eggs are clean and free of any chicken droppings or feces. Also, make sure the eggs are whole and not cracked. Do not sell old or questionable eggs because people can get very sick from contaminated eggs. If you are unsure of the quality of an egg, throw it out.

Spring and summer offer more opportunities to sell eggs outside the perimeters of your home. When the weather is warm, many communities get together and have multiple family yard sales. This is a great place to catch a flow of people in a shopping mood. Most people who attend yard sales are looking for a bargain, so price your eggs cheaper than a grocery store would.

The warm weather also indicates the start of fair season. County fairs and festivals provide a delightful environment to sell your eggs. Food tables typically are set up close to one another; you can network with other people in your community and connect with more potential customers. As families browse the food tables, you can strike up conversations about your flock and the eggs they just produced.

Local restaurants and caterers may be looking for wholesome food opportunities year-round, especially if they are customizing their menus to maximize the sustainable food in their region. This is a good time to have homegrown food to sell. Look up restaurants in your community and target your sales to smaller food outlets. Obviously, you would not try to sell your wares to major chains, as they have their own approved purveyors to supply food, but smaller, independently owned restaurants, grocery stores, and caterers have the freedom to purchase from whomever they wish.

Once you do find some clients, they may want to order eggs from you on a regular basis. Be sure you will be able to deliver on any promises you make to your customers. If you are inconsistent in your sales, they may not use your services. Discuss the options with your clients when you start your sales calls. Find out what their expectations are before you sell to them. Be sure you can meet their needs. Let them know what the turnaround time is between placing an order and delivery. Also, decide on a time to deliver the eggs. Communication with your customers will build your relationships. Keep records of all orders and sales, so if there are any questions or concerns, you always will have documentation to rely on.

Gifts

Fresh eggs make wonderful gifts for neighbors, coworkers, friends, and family. Buy or make little baskets or decorative cartons. Craft stores have inexpensive markers and stickers you can use to personalize egg cartons for your friend or neighbor. Include recipe cards with your basket so your friends can enjoy their eggs in different ways, too. They will be delighted at your thoughtfulness, and your excess eggs will not go to waste.

Eggs are a benefit of owning chickens. They are wholesome and are a staple in most people's diets. Regardless of whether you have a rooster, your hen will continue to produce eggs until she is too old to do so. In the meantime, you can harvest your cache and share your wealth. If you do not want to keep a hen past her egg-laying years, which is about five years, you can give her away as a pet, donate her to a farm, or butcher her for her meat. If roosters are butchered, they usually are butchered as cockerels for the young meat. Compared to roosters, hens have better meat for eating.

Chicken sexing

In new and young chicks, it is difficult — if not impossible — to determine their sex until they mature. Some breeds have markings or distinctive colors that help identify gender much earlier than with other birds. Some chicks are hard to identify, and you may not be able to identify the chicken's sex at all. Even experienced chicken owners have difficulty at times determining the sex. Do not get frustrated, and understand that this is a hard process. If you really must know the sex of your chick, and you are not able to do it on your own, consider taking it to a local hatchery or farm and asking for assistance.

When you ordered your fertile eggs, you may have specifically requested hens or roosters. Keep in mind that one rooster is all you need for a flock. If you ordered a mixture of eggs and are unsure of the sex of the chicks, you can use a process called **sexing** to tell whether your bird is a hen or rooster. The first way is called **vent sexing**; the other is called **feather sexing**. Either method can be done as early as 1 day old, but it is not an easy process because a chick's sexual organs are inside its body, and someone with little or no experience should not do sexing

Vent sexing

Vent sexing is difficult for the novice chicken owner but can be learned. The best way to start out is to purchase already-sexed chicks and practice on them. Always remember that you need to handle these are delicate babies with care. To vent sex a chick, it must be between 12 and 36 hours old. The vent is harder to open after the first 36 hours of life, and the process could hurt the chick. Use clean hands with short fingernails. Have bright lighting so you will be able to see the tiny opening.

Hold the chick in your left hand on its back with the rump away from you. The legs should be between the first and second fingers of your left hand. Place one thumb on either side of the vent and apply light pressure. You will need to roll the skin away on each side of the vent. Warning: This may cause the chick to poop. Just clean up and try again.

After you apply light pressure, inspect your chick's vent. If the chick is a male, you will see a bump about the size of a match head or smaller. This is the intermittent organ and should be in the center of the vent. The organ is usually dark, but in light pigmented birds, it will be pinkish. For female chicks, you should not see any bumps once you open the vent. A bump, no matter how small, always indicates the chick is a male. Female birds may have a dark spot inside the vent, which may look like a bump but is actually just color. You may need a magnifying glass to help see.

Do not make the process longer than it needs to be to reduce the chance of harming your bird. If you are having trouble determining the sex, put the chick back under its heating lamp and try again later. If you apply too much pressure on the chick's vent, you may expose some of its internal organs. If this happens, release pressure and make sure the bird's vent is closed with the organs back inside. Wipe the chick clean and put it back under its heat source. Do not sex this chicken further. The chick should heal properly, as its body is still developing, and the organs will move back into place. Do not sex bantam chicks because their size and body parts are very small, and even the most delicate of handlers may harm them because of their fragile nature.

Novice chicken owners or owners who are new to sexing chicks often make mistakes in determining gender. Do not feel discouraged if the rooster you thought you had begins to lay eggs or the hen you have been doting on starts to crow. Even experienced owners make mistakes because the process is very challenging.

If you decide you do not want to try vent sexing your chick, you can try feather sexing.

Feather sexing

Feather sexing, or sexing by appearance, is the second method for determining gender. Physical characteristics that appear as the chicks grow can indicate whether the bird is male or female. Feathers are the first indicator. Certain breeds of chickens, such as the Black Sex Link and the Red Sex Link, show differences between males and females through genetic traits. The Black Sex Link female is born completely black. Black Sex Link males are black with one white spot on the top of their heads. The Red Sex Link female is buff or red as a chick, and the Red Sex Link male hatches as a white chick. Although most breeds do not have this distinction, you can still use a chicken's feathers to determine its sex. Patterns and markings are usually different for the hen than for the rooster. As the chicks feather out, you can get a better view of the patterns. The colors of the feathers are another indication. Males are more colorful, and their coats are made up of more vibrant colors. The hackle feathers around the neck are pointed on a male and rounded on a female. These secondary characteristics should give you the clues you need to identify the gender.

If you still cannot tell from the feathers, look at other physical traits. Combs and wattles tend to grow faster in males. In most cases, they are larger as well. The legs and feet of roosters are typically bigger and grow more quickly, too. Lastly, if the feathers and body parts do not give away the bird's gender, its behavior can lead you to the answer. Males will have a more dominant personality and may even scuttle with other males.

Once you determine the sexes of your flock, you will want to separate them as they mature into pullets and cockerels. Males and females grow at a different rate, and separating the birds keeps them on an even keel. The cockerels frequently chase the pullets to mate with them, and separation will help control breeding. If you fail to separate your chicks, your flock can grow quickly before you are ready.

Taking your chickens outside

Your chicks can go outside at 4 or 5 weeks old if they are supervised and can go out unsupervised at 8 weeks old. If you have other chickens, the 8-week mark is a good time to introduce your chicks to your adult flock. Some breeds are quicker to mature than others, such as the leghorn, which may require you to adjust their timeline. They should be fully feathered and able to care for themselves before you take them outside. Also, take into consideration the weather conditions and the environment they will be in. You will find that roosters and breeds such as Faverolles are active and will not want to be confined for long.

Dealing with sick chicks

After several weeks, you may notice that some chicks are weaker or have health problems. Depending on the reasons you are keeping your chickens, you may have to remove sick birds from the brood because their illnesses may be contagious. If you are raising show birds, these chicks will not qualify to participate in exhibitions. Do not breed deformed or weak birds because there is a chance of reproducing that gene. As long as your birds are not sick, deformed, or weak, you can raise them for meat or as pets. Keep them in a separate pen so they do not mate with your show birds.

Vaccinations are an important part of your chickens' health. Any time after they are 8 weeks old, chicks should be inoculated for fowl pox (sorehead) and Newcastle disease. Fowl pox is a form of canker sores, and Newcastle disease is a respiratory disease. Vaccinate for only one disease at a time, and leave about three weeks between inoculations. Be sure you vaccinate all birds. Disease can spread rapidly throughout your brood, so prevention is the key.

If you need to give your birds medication that comes in the form of pills, some chickens will peck at it and gobble it up. If this is not the case, and you need to find an alternative method, crush the pill and sprinkle it in a treat for your chicken. To crush a pill, take the back of a spoon, put the pill on a plate, and press hard. Mash up any large pieces. You can take this powder, add a little water to it, put it in an eyedropper, and dispense into the bird's mouth. If you have an entire flock to dispense medication to, you may want to invest in an inexpensive coffee grinder or small mixer that you can pour the pills into to crush. Then add to treats or add water to the medication and use an eyedropper to give to the chickens individually. Chickens tend to be hungriest first thing in the morning and last thing at night, even though they can eat throughout the day. Feeding them the medication at these times will help to ensure the birds consume the entire treat with the medicine in it.

Chicks for Sale

Because of your generous care and devotion to your flock, you could end up with an abundance of happy, healthy chicks, perhaps more than you planned on, so you may consider selling your birds. You can set up a booth at a local farmers market or flea market. Newspaper ads and online sites are also a fast way to get the word out that you have chicks for sale. You may want to contact local farmers who can buy in bulk or ask your neighbors whether they would like to partake in your hobby.

Selling chicks can be a fun way to supplement your income, and you may even decide to raise them strictly for sale. You will need to research how much your breed of chick is selling for in your area. A fancier breed or rare breed will command a higher price. Chicks, pullets, and cockerels most likely will sell faster than older chickens, and though you may be tempted to exaggerate the youthfulness of your bird, be honest about the chicken's age. Because you would not want someone to mislead you if you were the buyer, do not do so to someone else.

Your Chickens' Meat

Many of the breeds discussed here make excellent chickens for the table. You can learn to butcher your own chickens or find a local butcher to do the job for you.

It is common for old layers to be butchered or sold for meat. Local butchers can cut up your birds if you choose not to do this yourself. If you do not live in an area with a neighborhood butcher, a farmer may be able to do it for you. You also can learn to butcher your own meat; it is not for everyone but is easy enough to do. Just a word of advice: Naming your birds will make it harder to slaughter them in the end.

The first thing you should do during the butchering process is to find a location to butcher your birds. If you have children or other family members in your home who would prefer not to witness the process, select a location outside your home. Ideally, a separate shed or building with ample lighting would work well. For an indoor space, you also will need a table, water access, and some type of drainage for waste. If you opt to butcher outdoors, you may want a temporary screen or fence for discretion, but the choice is yours.

The following is a checklist of items you will need before butchering your birds.

- Ax, meat cleaver, or large sharp knife. Country Horizons (**http://countryhorizons.net**) offers these for sale in addition to other poultry and farming products.

- Table with cutting board top. Butcher Block Co. (**http://butcherblockco.com**) and AWP Butcher Block, Inc. (**http://awpbutcherblock.com**) offer these. The size of the table depends on your preference. A small butcher-block table is about 28 inches wide by 24 inches deep and 33 inches tall. The AWP Butcher Block, Inc. offers this size and the next size larger, which is 48 inches wide by 24 inches deep and 36 inches tall. Find the size that meets your needs, and be sure it is treated to prevent microorganisms and germs from inhabiting the block of wood.

- Rubber gloves. You can find these at most grocery stores and department stores or online through Rubbermaid (**www.rubbermaid.com**). This website provides a place to shop for durable household items that can be cleaned and stored easily.

- Rubber apron. You can find these at a sporting goods store or in the garden department of larger department stores. Amazon (**www.amazon.com**) offers useful products such as a butcher's apron made of cloth that is 34 inches long and will protect your clothes from blood and dirt.

- Large pot to boil water. This pot should be large enough to fit your largest bird.

- Stove or propane burner large enough to fit the pot.

- Kill cone or hooks or large nails. Find kill cones at feed stores and hardware stores. The website Sure Hatch (**http://surehatch.com**) has kill cones in different sizes.

- Trash receptacle. These can be found at any home store or department store such as Walmart®, Target, or Bed, Bath and Beyond.

- Plastic tubs to ice down the birds after butchering. These tubs can be found at a local department store, party supply stores, or online at Target (**www.target.com**). Just type "plastic tub" in the search engine, and you will find a variety of sizes and shapes. An 18-gallon tub is deep enough to submerge the birds in plenty of ice.

- Sink or hose with running water

- A knife sharpener to sharpen blades can be purchased from Country Horizons (**www.countryhorizons.net**).

- Boning knife or butcher knife. These are sold at sporting goods stores, kitchen supply stores, and larger department stores. Online, a variety of boning knives can be found from Cutlery and More (**www.cutleryandmore.com**). This site has different blades and handles to suit your needs.

- Rags or paper towels. These can be purchased at your local grocery store, or you can use old cloth towels that you do not plan to use after you use them for butchering.

- Cleaning spray, soap, or disinfectant. These can be found at your local grocery store or department store.

- Freezer bags. The size will depend on the size of the bird you want to freeze. These can be found at your local grocery store.

- Freezer space to store your birds. The size of the freezer you need will depend son how many birds you want to store. You may kill and use your birds immediately. You may want to kill your flock and store them for future use. Have a plan of action and that will help you determine how much freezer space you need.

- Work table to debone and carve the carcass. Butcher Block Co. (**www.butcherblockco.com**) has a selection of worktables to choose from if you do not have one already.

Before you butcher your chicken, you will need to put on a rubber apron, gloves, and protective eyewear. This will keep you clean and safe from cuts and scratches. Next, you will need your equipment. Some people kill chickens with their hands; others prefer to use a sharp knife or ax. Always make sure the blade is sharp. The table you use will be on the receiving end of the blade, so it should have a chopping-block top or be made of wood. Use a tree stump if you are outdoors.

A piece of cone-shaped metal or plastic, known as a killing cone, can be purchased from sporting goods stores or online. The cone slides over the chicken's head and is inverted either to kill the chicken or let the blood drain from a dead chicken. If you do not have a cone, you can hang the carcass upside down from a nail or hook for the same effect. Hang them at least 3 feet off the ground over a bucket to collect the blood. You will need a trash receptacle for the waste.

Butchering is best done before daylight. The chickens will be sleeping in their hen house, and it will be easier to pick them up and bring them to the slaughter area. The dark helps keep the birds stay calm, and the quietness of the morning hours will keep them from being excessively stressed. Birds that are less stressed will taste better because they have fewer hormones running through their body. Also, they bleed cleaner, which makes the butchering less messy.

Do not feed the birds the night before, and provide little if any water. The birds will be easier to clean if their digestive tracts are empty. Also, keep their coop dark. When entering the coop in the morning, be quiet and calm as you collect your birds. Ideally, you want to have the slaughter part finished before sunrise so the bird can drain and be butchered for dinnertime.

Methods of Killing your Chickens

When it is time to kill a chicken, it is important to keep the process as humane and stress free for the bird as possible. Also, be sure to make the process as sanitary as possible, as you and your family will be eating the chicken's meat. If you have the opportunity, watch a friend or butcher kill and process a chicken before you attempt it on your own. If you do not have this option, the following steps will ensure a quick and painless end to the bird's life.

Without a knife or ax

One way to kill a chicken is to wring its neck. Pick up the chicken and hold it upside down with one hand. Slide your free hand down the chicken's neck to just below the bird's head and take hold. Grasp the neck firmly, jerk it down, and back up again with a twist to break the chicken's neck. Pull hard, but be aware that if you pull too hard, you may yank its head off.

Another way to kill a chicken without a knife is to kill it with a stick. Lift one end of a long stick, such as a broom handle, and slide the chicken's neck under the stick. Put one foot on one end of the stick, keeping it on the ground, and pull back on the other end of the stick, letting go of it quickly. It should snap back and break the bird's neck. You will need to hold on to the chicken's feet the entire time so it does not escape.

After killing the chicken, you will need to cut off its head and turn it upside down in a kill cone or hang it on a nail or hook to let the blood drain. Dispose of the blood by pouring it down the sink or drainage system and flush with lots of water. Clean and disinfect the entire area.

With a knife or ax

To kill your chicken with a knife or ax, first put on your rubber apron and make sure your knife or ax is sharp. Dull blades will only cause the animal to suffer and will not get the job done. Get your knife professionally sharpened or use a knife sharpener, found at any department store in the houseware section.

If you are using an ax, you will need a tree stump or table with a top that can handle the blade slicing into it. The surface you choose should be low and give you enough room to swing your ax up and then bring it down on the bird's neck. Also, you will need to hammer two nails into the stump or run a wire across the area. The chicken's neck will slide between the nails or under the wire to hold it in place. The nails only need to be as far apart as a chicken's neck, and the wire only has to be loose enough to slide the chicken's head underneath it.

Hold the chicken upside down, with your ax in one hand and the bird in the other. Slide the chicken's head between the nails or under the wire. Do this quickly. Pull back on the bird's legs slightly so the neck is stretched out. In one swift move, strike the ax down on the chicken's neck, making a clean, quick cut. Hold on to the feet because you do not want to let the bird go, as it will move. The body will still run off in those first few moments after the kill because of residual nervous energy. Letting the bird run will be a bloody mess and can be a traumatic sight for some people.

Kill cones make slaughtering a bird with a knife easier. Hang the cones in your slaughterhouse or somewhere you plan to do the killing. Put your bird in the cone, with the small opening on the bottom and the large opening on the top. Your bird will be upside down with its head through the small hole at the bottom. Pull to stretch its neck and make a quick cut right below its jaw. If you do not have a kill cone, tie the birds together and hang them from a nail or hook that is at least 3 feet from the ground. Kill the bird within seconds of putting it in the cone or hanging it from the nail. It is not humane to let it just hang there; plus, it may escape.

Once the bird is hanging, stretch its neck a little and then slit the throat with a sharp knife. You can either perform one clean, quick cut to remove the chicken's head, or you can make a slit to only drain the blood — if taking this approach, be sure to only cut the jugular and not the windpipe. Cutting the windpipe will cause the bird anguish. If you do not immediately take the head off, the bird may feel some distress for a few moments until it bleeds out. Once the blood is drained, then you can cut the head off. Have buckets beneath the cones to catch the blood. Let the chickens hang until all of the blood runs out of their bodies.

Whichever method you chose to use, your priority should be to provide a fast, painless death for the chicken. The first time you butcher an animal, it may be difficult for you. This is natural, especially if you raise the chickens and become attached to them. A humane death is an honorable ending for any bird. Aside from the emotions, butchering is a messy task. This is why some owners prefer to do a group slaughter, which entails killing more than one bird in your flock at the same time. The process is still the same; however, you need more kill cones to hang the birds upside down. Gather your birds one at a time. After you slit the throat or remove the head, hang your bird in the kill cone then get another bird and do the same. After you have your desired amount of birds slaughtered, proceed with the butchering.

Processing the Carcass

The next step is to pluck the chickens. To do this, put on your rubber gloves if you have not already. Have a large pot with scalding hot water ready to soak the chickens to kill germs and clean them. The water should be about 140 degrees F, which you can test with a candy thermometer or deep-fryer thermometer. Hold the chicken carcass by the feet and dip it into the pot for about ten to 15 seconds. Pull the bird out, and try pulling one of the feathers. If it comes out easily, the chicken is ready to be plucked. If the feathers do not come out easily, dip the chicken again. Keeping the bird in the water for too long or having the temperature too high will cook the skin, so monitor the process. If the chicken is partially cooked, cool it immediately, or discard it so bacteria do not grow in the meat. Warm temperatures are the perfect breeding ground for bacteria.

At this point, when the feathers are ready to come out, dip the bird into an ice bath using the plastic tubs to help prevent tears in the skin. This is not necessary, but it may make plucking easier. Now, pull out the feathers in the direction they grew. This may seem time-consuming, but it is faster than some of the automated plucking machines available commercially. Once you get the hang of it, the process will move quicker.

Featherman Plucker (**www.featherman.net**) and Schweiss Welding (**www.schweisswelding.com**) are two companies that sell automated chicken pluckers. Pluckers are also available online at Fleming Outdoors (**www.flemingoutdoors. com**). Fleming Outdoors has an expanded inventory of items that you may need. They have incubators, feeders, waterers, poultry laying nests, wooden coops and hutches, electric poultry fences and poultry catchers, along with poultry scalders and pluckers. Schweiss Welding sells several pieces of equipment. Their products are more streamlined; they offer a chicken plucker that promises to pluck your chicken in 30 seconds, including pinfeathers. It sells for $495 and arrives already assembled. The Featherman Plucker retails for $975; it holds four or five birds and plucks them in less than 20 seconds.

If automated pluckers are out of your price range, you may want to build your own. The book Anyone Can Build a Tub-Style Mechanical Chicken Plucker, written by Herrick Kimball from Cumberland Books, is a guidebook on building a machine that plucks feathers. The cost of the book is $15 to $20 and is available on the websites Cornerstone Farm Ventures (**www.cornerstone-farm.com**), Amazon (**www.amazon.com**), and Egg Cartons (**www.eggcartons. com**). The book details how to build the Whizbang plucker, and testimonials claim that the machine can pluck your chicken in 15 seconds or less, including pinfeathers. Building your own plucker is a fraction of the cost of purchasing a new, commercial plucker and scalder. The book contains plans on how to build your own plucker.

After plucking, examine your bird. Make sure the flesh does not have any sign of diseases. If you have a small flock, you should have been monitoring your birds all along. But if you own many birds, it may be hard to keep track of each one, especially if they have hidden lesions or bumps on their bodies. If you come across a chicken with abscesses or lumps filled with pus, do not eat the bird.

Other problems to look for are sores or open wounds and tumors. If you find them on a chicken, discard the carcass. These sores and wounds can be signs of something toxic for you if consumed. When in doubt, throw it out. Throw out the carcasses if the butchered birds were left for more than an hour at temperatures over 40 degrees. Do not eat birds that were found dead.

Now that you inspected your plucked bird, take the carcass to the worktable, and get your knife out. Remove the chicken's head if you have not done so already. If you want to save the neck, carefully remove the esophagus and trachea tubes. If you do not want to save the neck, slice it off near the body, and discard it.

Cut the feet off, slicing through the cartilage above the foot at the first joint. This is easier to cut through than the bone. Lift and then slam down a meat cleaver or sharp knife to make a clean cut. Discard the feet unless you like to cook with them. If you do want to keep them, put them in a storage container, and refrigerate. They can be deep-fried or made into a soup.

At the bottom of the spine, you will see a yellow spot or yellow bump near the tail. It is the oil gland. Lay the bird breast-side down. Lop off the tail at the spine and throw it away. Or, if you prefer to leave the tail on, take your knife and slice under the oil gland, down and past the tail, to cut out the gland and bypass the tail. Some people leave the oil gland in, but it gives the chicken a bitter taste if you do.

Flip the bird over onto its back, and cut into it above the vent. Your objective is to make a small hole in the carcass to remove the organs. Do not cut too wide or too deep, but the hole should be wide enough to fit your hand into. Stick your fingers in and pull apart the skin. If you find bird feces, wash them out. Take the carcass to the sink or to a running hose and, while holding your bird, flush out the feces. The water should run down the vent side, not across the whole body, so it is not contaminated. You may even want to use a mild dish detergent to wash off any affected areas. Rinse completely.

Once the bird is clean, wash any contaminated areas on your table. If you plan to cut the bird into pieces, use kitchen shears to slice through its back and remove all of the organs. Otherwise, you will need to insert your hand inside the bird. Place your hand inside the carcass and move your arm up until you reach the bird's neck. Spread out your fingers, as much as you can, and rake your hands down the inside of the carcass to pull the organs out. Do this gently. Do not grab, as you may break open some of the organs inside the bird. Once you pull the organs down to the vent, scoop them out, and toss them into the trash.

At this point, check the chicken's liver, which should be reddish-brown. If it is pale or discolored, it is probably diseased, and you should discard the chicken. If you want to save the heart, liver, and gizzards, sort through the internal mass that you just removed, and separate the organs you want to save. Once you do that, double-check to make sure the cavity is clear of debris. Take the chicken back to the sink or water source and rinse it inside and out. Refrigerate your bird as soon as possible.

Spray down the cutting area with disinfectant or bleach cleaner, and use rags or paper towels to dry the area well. Spray down the area a second time and repeat the process. Be thorough in your cleaning, as some diseases can live on countertops and surface areas. Clean the kill cones by soaking them in warm bleach water to disinfect, then rinse them well. Wash your rubber gloves and aprons by spraying them with bleach and rinsing. Clean your hands every time you come into contact with the carcass or pieces of the bird. Good sanitation is important for you and your family's safety.

Cutting your chicken

After your bird is plucked, clean, and processed, it is ready to cut. You may not have the skills of a professional butcher, but you can cut your chicken similar to the way you would find it packaged. The simplest way to cut your chicken is to begin with cutting the chicken in half lengthwise, which means down the breast, and then cutting the parts away width wise. You will need a very sharp chef's knife and a pair of very sharp kitchen shears. In just a few simple steps, you can have your chicken completely cut up.

- Step one — With your kitchen shears, cut the chicken in half along the breastbone. You need to make sure your kitchen shears are very sharp in order to accomplish this.

- Step two — Flip the chicken over, and cut along both sides of the bone to remove it from the breasts. You can either discard the bone or save it, storing it in the freezer so you can use it to make your own stock.

- Step three — Now you should be staring at two halves of the chicken. The next thing to do is flip one of the halves over so that it is laying skin side up. Then, using your sharp chef's knife, cut halfway between the wing and the leg. If you are having difficulty cutting it, then you can place the knife in the spot that you want to cut it and push down on it with your other hand. Repeat this same process with the other half of the chicken. If you want to, you can cut the remaining pieces in half a second time.

Professional Butchering

You may know right from the start that you do not want to butcher your birds. If no one in your household wants to slaughter your birds, you will need to find someone to do it for you, such as a friend or fellow chicken owner. You also could have a professional butcher handle the slaughter for you.

In the early 1900s, butcher shops were common on city streets. There was an art to butchering. In cities such as New York and Los Angeles, butchers may still have storefronts. Today, though, most grocery chains have their own meat departments inside the stores, and machines now take the place of professional butchers. So where can you find a butcher?

The website Local.com (**www.local.com**) can help you find any type of service anywhere in the United States. Type "butcher" in the search engine and your ZIP code in the "area" box. You also can type in the radius you want your search area to cover. The names, addresses, and phone numbers of all of the butchers in that area will appear on your screen. Then, start contacting them to see who can get the job done for you. The Yellow Pages online (**www.yellowpages.com**) provides a similar service. Type "butcher" and your ZIP code into the search fields, and information will pop up on all relevant businesses listed with the yellow pages.

If you still cannot find a butcher, try advertising in the local classifieds under the "wanted" section. Or go to your local grocer, and ask someone who works in the meat department whether he or she can do it for you or can recommend someone who can.

A knowledgeable butcher will know how to cut any type of meat. Chicken is a common meat, and any butcher should be able to cut it up for you. Butchers should know a healthy bird or carcass when they see it. They should not be willing to cut up poultry that is sickly or tainted. A good butcher will know how to make clean cuts and will be able to distinguish prime cuts of meat from lesser cuts. Most butchers have been an apprentice or have on-the-job training. Your butcher should be able to discuss the parts of the bird with you in detail and have a clean environment in which your bird is prepared.

State Zoning Laws Regarding Owning Chickens

Zoning laws about chickens vary from state to state and city to city. You should always find out what the law says about having chickens in your community before purchasing any chickens. You can find information about chicken laws on these sites:

Backyard Chickens (**www.backyardchickens.com**)

Handcrafted Coops (**handcraftedcoops.com**)

American Legal Publishing (**www.amlegal.com**)

The City Chicken (**www.thecitychicken.com**)

a2gov (**www.a2gov.org**)

Municipal Code Corporation (**www.municode.com**)

You can also check the websites for your state and city government.

Chicken Coop Plans

 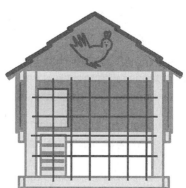

Bill of Material

Item	Qty	Description	Item	Qty	Description
1	6	2x4x3'-0"	16	1	1/2" plywood x 1'-2" x 1'-8"
2	6	2x4x4'-0"	17	4	1/2" plywood x 1'-2" x 1'-2"
3	4	2x4x8'-0"	18	1	1/2" plywood x 1'-0" x 2'-0"
4	2	2x4x2'-9"	19	2	1/2" plywood x 2'-7" x 8'-0"
5	1	2x4x3'-9"	20	4	2" hinges
6	1 box	3" deck screws	21	1	1 latch
7	1	1/2" plywood x 3'-0" x 4'-0"	22	6	1x1x8"
8	1 box	1 5/8" deck screws	23	1	2x4x2'-0"
9	1	1/2" plywood x 2'-11" x 4'-0"	24	2	2x4x4"
10	1	1/2" plywood x 2'-11" x 4'-0"	25	1 bdl	Shingles
11	1	1/2" plywood x 1'-7" x 3'-0"	26	1 box	1" Roofing Nails
12	1	1/2" plywood x 1'-7" x 3'-0"	27	1 roll	Wire Mesh
13	1	1/2" plywood x 1'-2" x 3'-1"	28	1 box	1" heavy duty staples
14	1	1/2" plywood x 1'-0" x 3'-1"	29	1 gallon	primer
15	1	1/2" plywood x 1'-4" x 3'-3"	30	1 gallon	paint

A sample chicken coop plan

Step 1: Assemble Base Frame:

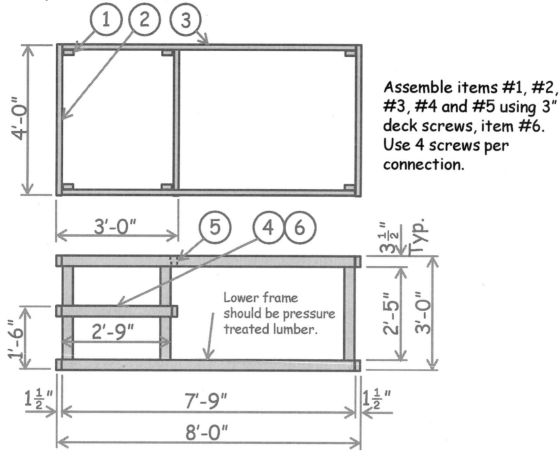

Assemble items #1, #2, #3, #4 and #5 using 3" deck screws, item #6. Use 4 screws per connection.

Lower frame should be pressure treated lumber.

Step 2: Cut Out and Install Coop Floor:

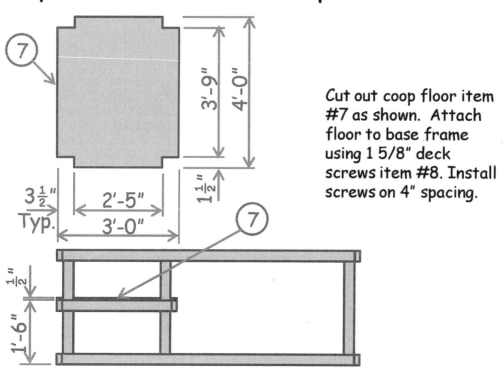

Cut out coop floor item #7 as shown. Attach floor to base frame using 1 5/8" deck screws item #8. Install screws on 4" spacing.

Step 3: Cut out Plywood Components:

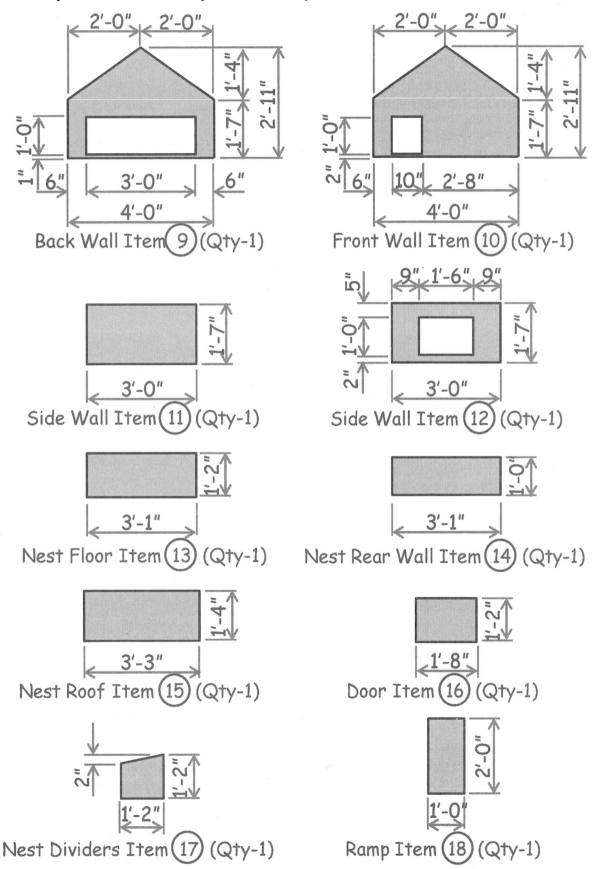

Back Wall Item ⑨ (Qty-1)

Front Wall Item ⑩ (Qty-1)

Side Wall Item ⑪ (Qty-1)

Side Wall Item ⑫ (Qty-1)

Nest Floor Item ⑬ (Qty-1)

Nest Rear Wall Item ⑭ (Qty-1)

Nest Roof Item ⑮ (Qty-1)

Door Item ⑯ (Qty-1)

Nest Dividers Item ⑰ (Qty-1)

Ramp Item ⑱ (Qty-1)

Step 4: Assemble Nest Box:

Assemble nest box items #13, #14, & #17 using 1 5/8" deck screws item #8. Install screws on 4" spacing. Space item #17 dividers equally.

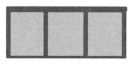

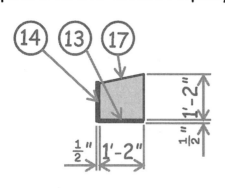

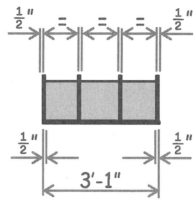

Step 5: Attach Walls and Nest to Base Frame:

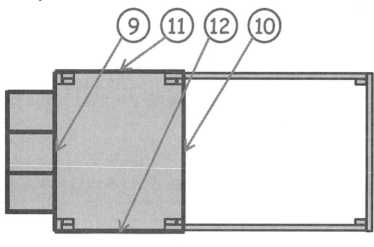

Attach coop walls to base frame using 1 5/8" deck screws item #8. Attach nest box items #13, #14, & #17 to rear wall using 1 5/8" deck screws item #8. Install screws on 4" spacing. NOTE: Nest floor should be 2" lower than coop floor.

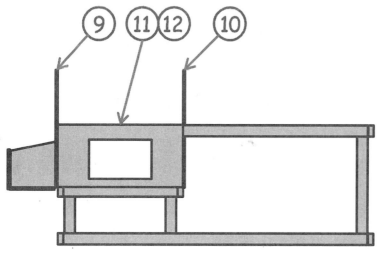

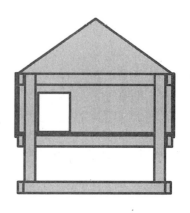

Step 6: Install Roof, Door, Nest Lid, and Ramp:

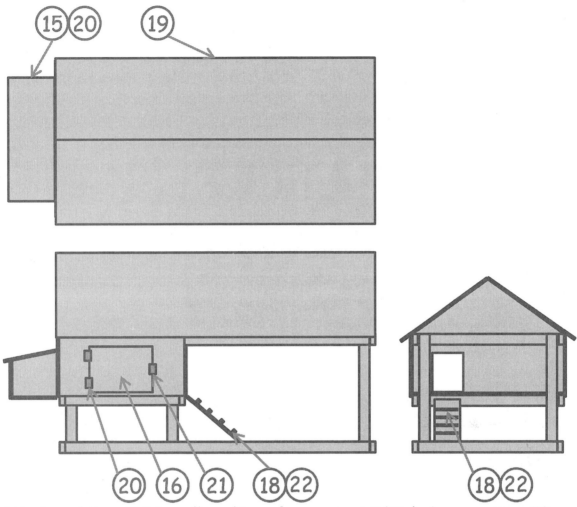

-Attach roof item #19 to walls and base frame using 1 5/8" deck screws item #8.
-Attach nest box lid item #15 to rear wall using 2 hinges item#20.
-Install access door item #16 complete with latch item #21 and hinges item #20.
-Attach ramp item #18 to base frame using 1 5/8" deck screws item #8.
-Attach cleats item #22 to ramp, equally spaced, using 1 5/8" deck screws item #8.

Step 7: Assemble Perch:

Assemble perch items #23 & #24 using 3" deck screws item #6. Use 4 screws per connection. Attach perch to coop floor using 3" deck screws item #6. Locate 6" from front wall of coop and 3" from side wall, parallel to front wall.

Step 8: Install Roofing Shingles, Wire Mesh, and Paint to suit:

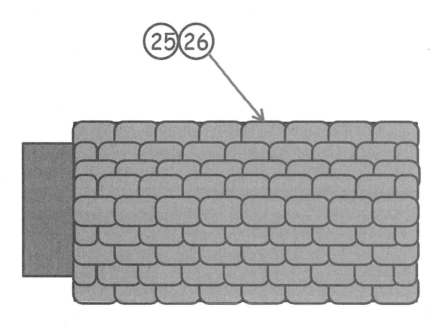

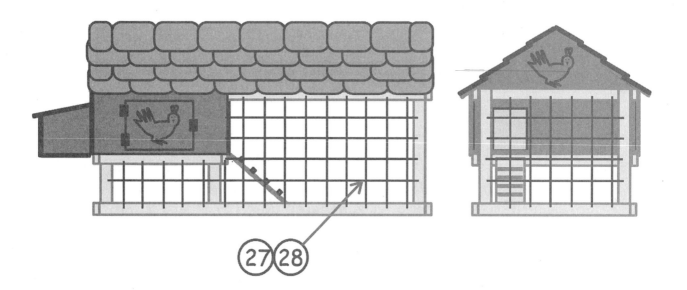

-Install roofing shingles item #25 to plywood roof using roofing nails item #26. Follow manufacturers instructions.

-Attach wire mesh to exterior of base frame using 1" heavy duty staples.

-Prime and paint to suit.

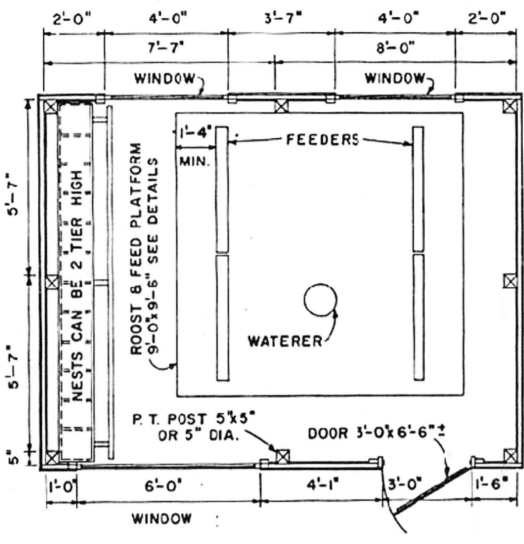

FLOOR PLAN

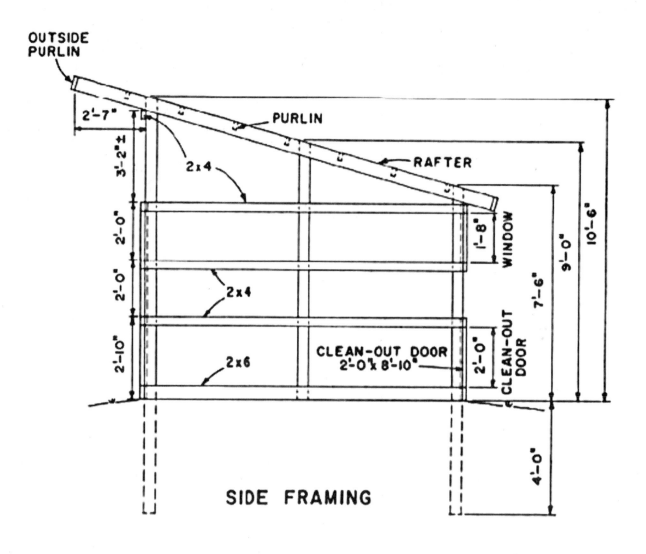

SIDE FRAMING

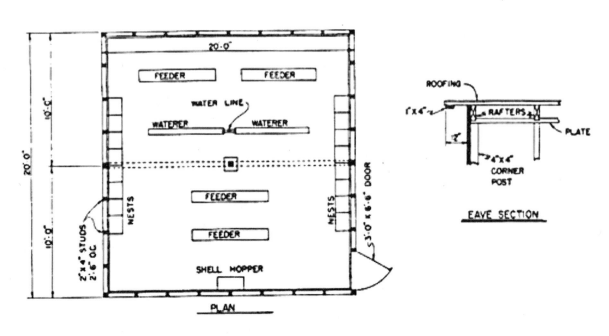

PLAN

EAVE SECTION

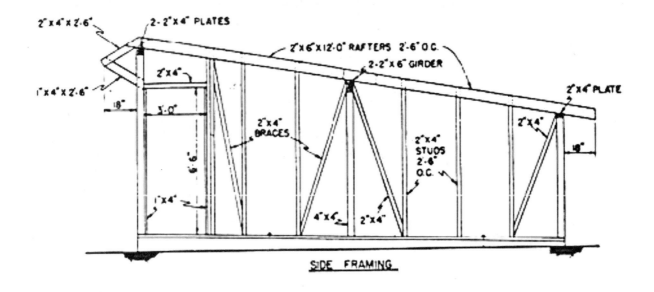

2"x4"x 2'-6"

2- 2"x 4" PLATES

2"x6"x12'-0" RAFTERS 2'-6" O.C.

2- 2"x 6" GIRDER

2"x4" PLATE

1"x 4"x 2'-6"

2"x4"

18"

5'-0"

6'-6"

2"x4" BRACES

2"x4" STUDS 2'-6" O.C.

2"x4"

1"x4"

4"x 6"

2"x4"

18"

SIDE FRAMING

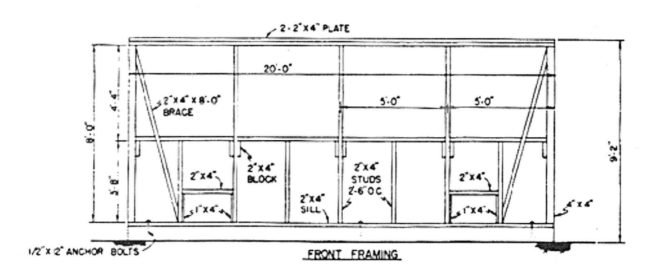

2- 2"x 4" PLATE

20'-0"

2"x4"x 8'-0" BRACE

5'-0"

5'-0"

4'-4"

8'-0"

3'-8"

2"x4" BLOCK

2"x4"

2"x4" STUDS 2'-6" O.C.

2"x4"

9'-2"

1"x4"

2"x4" SILL

1"x4"

6"x 6"

1/2"x 12" ANCHOR BOLTS

FRONT FRAMING

Plan for an 8' x 8' layer house — 15 to 20 hens

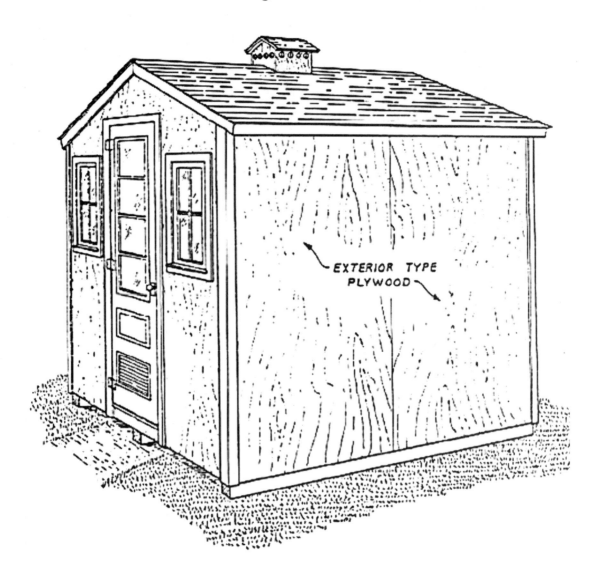

EXTERIOR TYPE
PLYWOOD

PERSPECTIVE

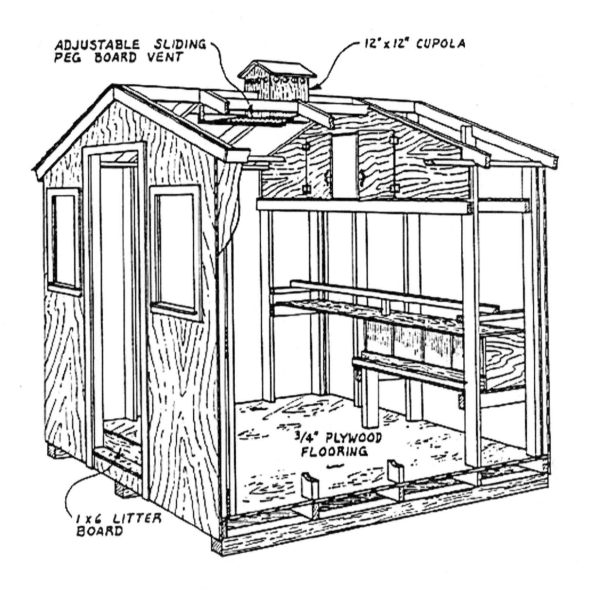

ADJUSTABLE SLIDING PEG BOARD VENT

12" x 12" CUPOLA

3/4" PLYWOOD FLOORING

1 x 6 LITTER BOARD

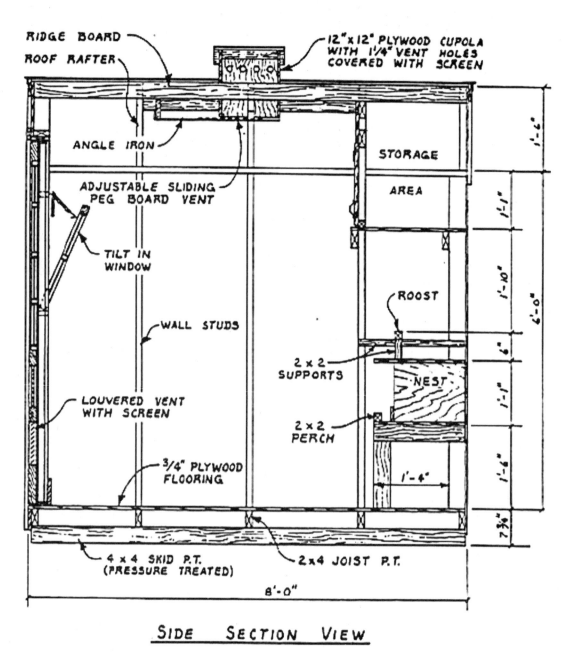

SIDE SECTION VIEW

Reviewed by Audrey McElroy, associate professor, Animal and Poultry Sciences

Chapter 4

Ducks and Geese

DUCK AND GOOSE GLOSSARY

Breed: A group with common ancestors and characteristics that distinguish the group. Often, the breeds need to be maintained through selective breeding.

Broody: Term used for hens sitting on a clutch of eggs in a nest. A broody hen will stop laying eggs to incubate the eggs and will seldom leave the nest until the eggs hatch.

Class: A smaller category of a type of birds. Often, the name will relate to the origin of a bird.

Down: Young birds are born with this fluffy hair that does not protect them like feathers. The feathers grow in during the first few weeks of life.

Drake: A male duck. Mature drakes (except for the Muscovy breed) can be differentiated from the duck by curled tail feathers.

Duck: A female duck and the general term for the species

Duckling: A young duck

Gander: A male goose

Goose: A female goose and general term for the species

Gosling: A young goose

Husbandry: The agricultural practice of breeding and raising livestock

Hybrid: The offspring of genetically dissimilar parents

Hygrometer: An instrument used to measure humidity. With birds, a hygrometer is used to measure the humidity inside an egg incubator.

Farm: Any operation that sells at least $1,000 of agricultural commodities or that would have sold that amount of produce under normal circumstances

Feed mill: A place where feed for animals is produced for commercial use

Flighty: The tendency of a particular breed of bird to be excitable and nervous

Free-range: When birds are allowed to graze rather than being raised in confinement

Grain elevator: A place where farmers store and sell their grain

Hatchery: A place where eggs are hatched

Molt: An annual process in which a bird loses its feathers and replaces them with new feathers

Nesting Box: A box in a pen where females can lay their eggs

Pen: A farm building for housing poultry, also called a coop. They can be portable as well.

Pinfeathers: Also called blood feathers, these feathers contain a blood vein and if pulled will cause a bird to bleed.

Variety: In birds, this will be a unique characteristic that occurs in a certain branch of a specific breed. An example would be different feather coloring or a plume of feathers on top of the head.

History of Ducks and Geese

Ducks are closely related to swans and geese; in fact, biologists have had difficulty classifying the three species into different categories. The three species belong to the biological family Anatidae, meaning birds that swim, float on the surface of the water, and (in some birds) dive in water for food. For the most part, the birds in this group eat plants and grains and are monogamous (one mate) breeders under natural conditions.

It is no wonder biologists have trouble classifying the three species, as there are more than 100 species of wild ducks alone. Despite the large number of wild ducks, all domestic ducks, except for the Muscovy duck, were domesticated from the wild Mallard. The Mallard belongs to a group of wild ducks called **dabblers**. This describes their feeding habit of dabbing their bill in the water to filter food particles from the water. Mallards have an appetite for grasses, insects, bugs, worms, small fish, toads, snails, frogs, and even snakes.

The Chinese are credited with first domesticating wild Mallards around 2000 B.C., but ducks also were domesticated around the same time in the Middle East. Ducks were first domesticated for meat and egg use, although later ducks were used to control pests in rice paddies. Even today, people will herd flocks of ducks to the rice paddies. In the field, the ducks feast on insects, snails, slugs, small reptiles, and waste rice; they provide great pest control without using harsh chemicals.

The Muscovy duck had a far different history. The Muscovy is actually a perching duck and will roost and nest in trees. They are a native of Central and South America. It is thought they were domesticated in pre-Inca Peru to be used as pets. The Muscovy is a carnivorous duck that eats small mammals, snakes, frogs, flies, and other insects. They can grow to be larger than most breeds of duck. In the United States, many people keep this breed as pets because they do not make much noise, and they have distinct personalities.

Geese are hardy, lively birds that practically raise themselves after they lose their down. Not much maintenance work is required for the majority of a goose's life. They are elegant birds and have a unique personality while being versatile.

The goose was domesticated both in eastern Asia and in northern Africa, Europe, and western Asia. In eastern Asia, the swan goose (Anser cygnoides) was domesticated to become the Chinese goose. These geese possess a large knob at the base of their bill. The European-type goose was domesticated from the Greylag — or wild grey — goose (Anser anser) in northern Africa, Europe, and western Asia. Both types have been used since first domesticated for their meat, down, and eggs.

Archaeological evidence in Egypt has shown that geese were kept in ancient Egypt since 300 B.C. The Romans dedicated geese to the goddess Juno. Huge flocks of geese were raised in western Europe and slowly herded to Rome to supply this great city with meat and feathers. As time advanced, large flocks were raised in southern England, Holland, and Germany and were driven to markets in large cities during the fall. Another important product of the goose was the quill, which was used for pens.

Despite being domesticated for centuries, the goose has not undergone the drastic changes seen in other domesticated livestock. The major changes include an increase in size, more fat deposition under the skin, selection for color (most

notably white), and improved fertility. The domestic goose does tend to have an upright posture than its wild brethren and generally is unable to fly.

In Asia, the goose is still an important livestock species. Markets do exist in the United States, particularly among immigrants from Asia and along the eastern seaboard. Geese often act as guards for property. For example, the company that brews Ballantine's Finest Blended Scotch Whisky has been using geese to guard their maturing products since 1959. The guards are nicknamed "The Scotch Watch." When being sold for meat, geese are usually marketed for a fall market, particularly around the Christmas season.

Duck Breeds

When deciding on which breed of duck you would like to raise, there are two main types to consider. Ornamental ducks are ducks kept for the pleasure of keeping waterfowl. Their striking plumage and amusing behavior are their primary benefits for humans, and generally, they do not make good meat or egg producers. Utility, or commercial, ducks have been bred for meat, down, or egg production. These are the primary duck breeds discussed in this chapter. Ducks come in many different feather colors, and males and females can be distinguished by feather color.

Indian Runner: This breed of duck is unique in its upright stance; it looks like a bowling pin on webbed feet. It was developed from the wild mallard in the East Indies two centuries ago. Because of their physical conformation, they run rather than waddle like the typical duck, which makes walking to the fields an easy task. They are active foragers, especially of insects, snails, and slugs, and do put on a good deal of flesh considering they are a lighter duck. Indian Runners are great egg layers, sometimes even outlaying chickens. Generally, females lay about 200 eggs each year. They are not considered good egg sitters so eggs from a female Indian Runner may need to be incubated by another hen or in an incubator. The adult male Indian Runner seldom weighs more than 5 pounds. Indian Runners are utility ducks, good for egg production and insect control.

Khaki Campbell: The Khaki Campbell is a breed developed in England by Adele Campbell in the late 1800s. Campbell crossed her Indian Runner hen with a Rouen **drake** (male duck) in order to produce ducks that would lay well and have bigger, meatier bodies. Her breeding strategy worked because the resulting breed, the Khaki Campbell, is an excellent layer. The hens more readily will sit on the eggs, unlike the Indian Runner duck. A hen will lay more than 300 eggs a year. The Khaki Campbell does have a flighty temperament and needs room to forage. They are also adaptable to variable climates and perform well in hot, dry deserts, wet, tropical environments, or cold winter weather. As an added bonus, the Khaki Campbell is an admirable insect, slug, and algae eater.

Pekin: The Pekin is the most common breed of domestic duck. These white ducks are great for meat production as they grow rapidly and pack on more pounds of meat per pound of feed than other ducks. The Pekin duck was developed in China from ducks living in the canals of Nanjing. An adult female will lay about 200 eggs a year. They are not as broody as other ducks, so they might not sit on a nest. Drakes can weigh more than 12 pounds and females more than 11 pounds.

Rouen: The Rouen breed is similar in coloring to the wild Mallard. They were originally developed in France and were imported to England where the breed was bred into the modern-day Rouen. There are two types of Rouen: the production and the standard. The production Rouen weighs between 6 and 8 pounds; the standard Rouen is much larger and weighs between 8 and 10 pounds. Females lay about 70 greenish eggs a year. They are good meat producers but take from six to eight months to mature. This slow maturation rate has lead to commercial duck growers to be reluctant to raise Rouen's on a large scale for the meat market. The meat from the Rouen is leaner than the Pekin, which makes it a popular duck for restaurants.

Muscovy: The Muscovy is unique in that it was not developed from Mallards. It is a Brazilian breed that can become quite large; males can weigh in at more than 10 pounds. They come in a variety of colors, but they all have a distinctive bright red tissue above the beak and around the eyes. They do not swim much because they have underdeveloped oil glands, which makes their feathers less water resistant than other breeds, but they do have sharp claws, which they use to roost in tree branches. The females become broody three times a year and will incubate the eggs of other ducks or poultry species. If you have eggs from another duck, the Muscovy can hatch them for you.

Cayuga: This breed was developed in New York in the 1800s from native ducks. They are considered a medium-weight duck primarily used as a meat bird. Adult males reach 8 pounds. They have unique coloring with a greenish-blue sheen over dark feathers. Eggs from the Cayuga can be variable colors depending on the season. When they first start laying eggs, the eggs may have a gray or black color. As the laying season progresses, the eggs will start to lose this dark coloring and may even become white.

Goose Breeds

Emden: The Emden was developed in Germany and the Netherlands and is the most common commercial goose breed. They are typically white with orange bills and feet and blue eyes. They grow rapidly, which makes them large meat-type geese. When mature, the **gander** (male goose) can weigh close to 30 pounds. They make excellent barnyard alarms, as they can be protective of their territory and flock. They can be aggressive, especially ganders protecting their flocks, so small children and pets should be watched when around a flock. Male Emden goslings have a lighter grey down than the female goslings. The goose can lay up to 40 eggs during the breeding season. It is also a good breed for a crossbreeding program as these geese mature early, are good foragers for food, and the females are good mothers.

Toulouse: The Toulouse is a large breed and can weigh up to 25 pounds. It is noted for its cold tolerance and is a popular breed in the Midwest, though it has its origins in France. The Toulouse breed has dark gray feathers on its back, lighter grey feathers on its breast, and white stomach feathers. It has a dewlap or flap of skin hanging under its lower jaw and a bulky body. The Toulouse was bred in France to produce foie gras. As such, it is not as good a forager as other geese breeds and does well when confined to a pen. The goslings also mature slower than other breeds. The goose lays about 35 eggs per year and is a good mother. However, they can be clumsy and break eggs if the nest is not well padded.

Chinese: This breed is the smallest of domestic geese. They have been called Swan Geese, as they carry their body upright (similar to swans). They are distinctive geese because they have a knob at the base of their beak. The knob on the male is larger than the female. Chinese geese come in two colors: brown and white. The white variety has a more attractive carcass, as their pinfeathers are not as noticeable. Another added trait is they make excellent weeders; they eat weeds from vegetable crops without causing much damage to the vegetables due to their smaller size and better agility at moving. Female Chinese geese will lay 50 to 60 eggs during the breeding season (February through June). The Chinese goose makes a good guard goose for the farmstead.

African: The African goose is related to the Chinese goose, but it is a much larger breed. It has a distinctive knob on its forehead near the bill and a dewlap. It is about the same size and weight as the Emden breed, and ganders can weigh close to 30 pounds. The colored variety of African has brown top feathers and a lighter underbelly. The White African variety has white feathers and orange bill, knob, legs, and feet. Despite its name, it does not come from Africa, but its origin is murky. A mature gander weighs 22 to 24 pounds while a mature female weighs 18 to 20 pounds. They can start breeding their first year and can produce eggs for many years. They lay around 35 to 40 eggs a year.

Pilgrim: The Pilgrim goose breed was developed in Iowa but might have had origins in colonial America. They can be easily sexed from their feather coloring; adult males have mostly white feathers while females have gray feathers. This trait is called **auto-sexing**. Even when a day old, the breed can be sexed on color: male goslings are gray-yellow with light bills and female goslings are olive-gray with dark bills. This is a medium-sized breed, with mature males weighing 14 to 15 pounds. It is also a calmer breed than most of the goose breeds but will still sound an alarm at perceived signs of danger. They are good foragers and good mothers. The female lays 35 to 40 eggs each year.

Sebastopol: This unique breed has blue eyes and curly, twisted feathers that are usually white. Due to their unique feathers, they should have bathing water available to keep their feathers clean. Because of their feather pattern, they are more susceptible to chilling. Unlike other geese, water does not roll off the feathers. They are a gentle breed of goose and are not aggressive. This makes them more susceptible to predation. Females can lay about 40 eggs a year and will brood the eggs of other geese. In fact, they may steal eggs from other nests and roll them into their own. Female goslings have darker down than the males. Ganders weigh around 14 pounds, and females average about 11 pounds.

Duck and Geese Husbandry

Having a flock of ducks or geese running around the farmstead is truly an amusing and heartening sight. These birds offer many benefits to the small-scale farmer, including meat, weed control, and — in the case of geese — even a natural alarm system. After the first few weeks of life, ducks and geese are easy keepers and make great foragers for bugs and weeds.

Ducks are much smaller than most geese. When full grown, a duck can weigh from 4 to 11 pounds and can live as long as 12 years. Geese are large birds that weigh as much as 30 pounds when mature, and they live much longer than ducks — up to 25 years. Geese are loyal family members and prefer to choose a mate for life. They are protective of their flock, which makes them great farm watchdogs.

Ducks can provide reliable source of eggs and meat. Like chickens, some breeds have been bred to be exceptional layers of eggs, while other breeds have been developed to provide substantial quantities of meat. If you plan to collect eggs from your waterfowl, ducks would be the best choice. Two breeds, the Indian Runner and Khaki Campbell, are best known for their prolific egg production. Geese do not lay as many eggs as ducks, but the Emden breed will lay around three dozen eggs during the breeding season.

Although the eggs of ducks and geese can be eaten just like chicken eggs, goose eggs generally are not consumed in the United States. Eggs from geese are large, and compared to chickens, geese lay far fewer eggs. This makes them unpopular for commercial production. Few recipes call for them. Most likely, there will not be a market for the eggs produced by your ducks or geese, but your family may enjoy eating them. Duck eggs have a higher yolk fat content and white protein content than chicken eggs, so when cooked, the whites do not become as stiff as chicken eggs. If the duck has been eating a lot of algae, worms, or grubs, the eggs may have a slightly musty taste. Eggs should be collected twice daily, washed in warm water, and promptly stored in the refrigerator.

Duck meat is higher in iron, niacin, and selenium than many other types of meat. Good duck meat breeds include Pekin, Rouen, Muscovy, and Aylesbury. The meat from both ducks and geese is all dark meat and is richer than chicken or turkey due to the higher fat content — this gives the meat a distinctive taste popular in many gourmet restaurants. Ethnic markets are particularly interested in obtaining a steady supply of quality duck and goose meat. Geese have provided a rich source of protein for centuries, with many people enjoying the meat and liver. But even more so, a roasted goose has long been a traditional Christmas dinner over the centuries. Foie gras is made from the fattened livers of force-fed geese and is especially common in French cultures. Goose meat breeds include the Emden, Toulouse, Chinese, and Africans.

Unlike other poultry species, domesticated waterfowl are mostly disease resistant. However, like the young of any animal species, ducklings and goslings need to be kept dry and warm when they are covered in down. Once the young are fully feathered, they enjoy being outdoors in all but the coldest of weather. They do keep a layer of down under their feathers, which insulates them from cold. In addition, they have an oil gland at the base of the tail. They will rub their chins and cheeks over the gland to collect the oil, which they will then rub onto their feathers. This oil makes their outer feathers waterproof. Mothers will rub some of the oil from her oil gland onto the down of her young until they are able to perform this function on their own. Ducks and geese need to keep their feathers in tip-top condition to keep them dry and warm, so these animals spend a substantial amount of time preening.

Geese will need shelter during subzero weather and protection from aggressive predators such as coyotes. Ducks and geese will also need shade during hot weather. Ducks should be brought into a shelter every night as smaller predators such as raccoons, foxes, and weasels can decimate a flock in a few hours. Geese naturally flock together and will return to a home base each night, even when they wander more than a mile away from home. Vehicles also take their toll on a flock, so if you plan to keep waterfowl, they will need to be kept away from roadways.

Geese are not as vulnerable to predators as ducks and some other poultry are because of their size, but they do enjoy having a shelter available at night.

Young geese are still susceptible to predators. As the larger breeds grow, predators become less of a threat due to the weight of the birds. Dogs and coyotes may kill smaller geese, or they may scare larger geese. When scared, geese will huddle together, and this may cause some geese to be smothered to death. A fenced area with 5-foot-tall fencing makes a good night resting spot for the geese. Be sure to provide your geese with feed and access to a water source in their resting spot. Alternatively, the geese can be locked inside a sturdy building at night to protect them from predators.

This is particularly important in geese less than 5 months old when they are still smaller. Geese younger than 8 weeks of age should not be left out at night on the pasture and should be herded inside a secure shelter for safekeeping from poor weather and predators.

Buying Ducks and Geese

Ducklings and goslings are purchased the same places as chickens: directly from the hatchery or through feed stores. They will come in a straight run (both sexes), or they can be sexed if you want to have more of one sex. Generally, a straight run will be a few cents cheaper to purchase than those segregated by sex. For the average small-scale farmer, a straight run will be satisfactory for ducks or geese raised for meat. Males generally will be heavier than females. If you want to breed ducks and geese, you may want them sexed so you can have a proper ratio of males to female. One drake will breed five to six females, and most ganders will breed only with one or two females.

When purchasing your ducklings and goslings directly from the hatchery, ask when they will be mailed. It is safe to ship newly hatched waterfowl as long as they are properly packaged in sturdy cardboard containers with plenty of air holes. They can go without food for a day or two while being shipped, as after hatching they retain part of the yolk from the egg in their body. This will give them a food source.

What to look for when buying ducks and geese

Make sure someone is home to receive the ducklings or goslings when they arrive in the mail. Open the shipping container in the presence of the mail carrier to ensure you have received the number of birds ordered and to check for any dead stock. If you received fewer birds than you had ordered, or if there are any dead birds, the postal carrier can give you a claim check to submit to the hatchery. If you chose to purchase your stock from a store, closely scrutinize their pen conditions. It should be dry, and the feed and water containers should be clean and full. The ducklings and goslings should be active if awake with no noticeable discharge from eyes or nose. Peek under their tails. The vent (anus) should be clean with no buildup of fecal material.

Ducklings and goslings should be raised separately because of the goslings' larger size. You can keep them in separate pens. However, general care is similar, so the material presented in this chapter will apply to both species.

Housing and Feeding Ducks and Geese

Prior to ordering or heading to the feed store to purchase your new additions, the pen, feeders, and waterers should be set up and ready. The pen should be in a draft-free, fully enclosed building with good ventilation and lighting. A corner of a garage or barn will work as well, provided you keep running motors out of the area so the birds are not subjected to fumes. Allow 6 inches of space per bird. Increase this to 1 foot per bird after they are 2 weeks old to add more space for the birds as they grow. For example, you would start out with 5 feet of space for ten ducklings and, after two weeks, increase the space to 10 feet.

The pen floor should be covered with an absorbent litter. Four inches of wood shavings, peat moss, or chopped straw will be sufficient. The litter will need to be maintained to eliminate wet, dirty spots. Add fresh litter as needed to maintain 4 inches of bedding. Heat and light can be provided using a heat lamp with a 250-watt bulb, or a hover brooder can be used. A hover brooder uses propane heat coupled with a metal pan (or hover) to direct and retain the heat over the young. If you want to use a heat lamp, plan to use one heat lamp per 15 goslings or 25 ducklings. Hover brooders typically come with instructions for chicks. Because ducklings and goslings are larger than chicks, brood one-half as many ducklings and one-third as many goslings as you would chicks.

The heat-source temperature should be between 85 and 90 degrees F. This temperature can be reduced 5 to 10 degrees every week until the temperature is about 70 degrees F. After the sixth week and if the weather is mild, the birds will be fully feathered and will no longer need supplemental heat. The birds should be confined near the heat, feed, and water sources during the first two to three days after arrival. Observe the birds closely to determine if the heat source needs to be raised or lowered. As with chickens, if the birds avoid the heat source and are lurking at the edges of the pen, raise the heat source a few inches. If they huddle under the heat source, lower it a few inches.

Waterers

Waterers should be full when the birds arrive. There are many types of reasonably priced waterers available. Do not use an open pan for young ducklings or goslings; they should not get wet when they are in the down stage lest they become chilled. A chilled baby bird can quickly become hypothermic and die. Instead, use a waterer with a base wide enough for the birds to dip their heads and bills without being able to fall in. Adding commercial electrolyte or vitamin powder to the water the first few days can give the young birds a healthy boost. You can use electrolyte formulas found at the grocery store, or you can purchase packets to mix from farm supply stores.

Do not let young ducks or geese have access to swimming water or leave them outside in the rain. The feathers of young ducks and geese are not fully developed to protect them from water, especially during the down stage. If they have been hatched out by a mother duck or goose, they can have access to swimming water with the adults because the mother will not let them remain in the water for too long, and she will protect them from rain. By 4 or 5 weeks, the ducklings will be feathered out and will be able to tolerate most weather conditions. Goslings can be placed on pasture at about 6 weeks of age in good weather.

Ducks enjoy water not only for quenching their thirst but also for cleaning their bodies and exercise. Ducks cannot survive without access to bathing water. They will need a deeper trough than is required for chickens to dip their bills in to drink. It is their habit to splash water onto their heads and bills to clean themselves.

If you have a few birds (fewer than ten), you can use a hose and a small kiddie pool to provide bathing water. This will need cleaning and refilling twice each day. The ground surrounding the pool will quickly become muddy with the ducks hopping in and out of the pool. You can combat the mud issue by frequently relocating the pool to a new area or placing it on sand or gravel. Alternatively, you can build a small platform using water-resistant two-by-fours and welded wire. It should be 2 to 3 feet wider than the pool to allow a place for the ducks to step on as they enter and exit the pool. The platform only needs to be about 6 inches off the ground. It should not be so tall that it is difficult for the birds to hop up. The birds also should have a waterer for drinking. They should not be able to swim in this water but only submerge their head and drink water.

If you have more than ten birds, provide separate waterers and bathing tubs for each group. The bathing tubs should be cleaned twice a day. You can use a small pond for bathing if you already have one on your property, but the banks quickly can become damaged if too many ducks use the pond. To combat bank erosion, the bank can be reinforced with large stones. Ducks can be quite damaging to the shoreline as they dig in the mud in search of food.

Ducks are susceptible to predation, especially domestic ducks that have a limited ability to fly. You should provide your ducks with a predator-proof pen. They can roam during the day, but at night put them in a pen. Predators such as dogs, weasels, coyotes, and raccoons are most active at night. Strong woven wire should be used with squares of less than ½ inch. Weasels are able to squeeze through any wire bigger than this size. The top of the pen should also be covered to prevent animals from climbing over the top.

Inspect the pen weekly. Check the pen or building for any signs of tunneling under the floor or foundation. Patch any holes with concrete, wood, or wire as soon as they are found. Make certain the doors and any windows are solid, that latches work, and that they are free from damage.

Also, you may prefer to keep your ducks penned and confined to a certain area during the day. Many types of fencing material can be used such as chicken wire, welded wire, woven wire, game bird netting, and lightweight plastic fencing material. The fencing material should be a minimum of 2 feet tall to keep the ducks inside. If you need to keep dogs out, the fence should be 5 feet tall or higher.

The spacing between the wires should be ½ to 1 inch. Any bigger and the ducks can stick their heads between the wires. This may cause them to become trapped or, even worse, a predator can bite the head of a duck that sticks its head outside the fence. The fencing material should be stretched taut and secured to posts (steel or wood) securely driven into the ground.

Keep in mind that ducks will need shade if temperatures approach 70 degrees F or above. Natural shade through trees or allowing access to a covered pen will be adequate. If the ducks are kept fenced in an opened area, you can build a simple shade for them using three 12-inch long 2-by-4 boards and a piece of ½-inch thick plywood. FarmTek (**www. farmtek.com**), an agricultural supplier, also carries lightweight livestock canopies and covers composed of tough, weather-resistant plastic, which make a simple and affordable shade cover for ducks.

Feeding Ducks and Geese

A good commercial starter feed will get your young goslings and ducklings off to a good start. They are generally disease resistant, so a medicated feed will not be necessary. In fact, certain medications found in chick starters can cause health problems in goslings and ducklings. Chicks peck at their feed while goslings and ducklings are voracious eaters. This means they can overdose on the medicated feed, causing organ damage. Look for starter feed made for ducklings and goslings, or feed them an unmedicated feed. If your feed store does not carry starter feed for ducks and geese, they may be able to order it for you. Starting the first week of life, small amounts of fresh growing grass or fresh clippings also can be fed to the birds. After four weeks, their diet can be supplemented with cracked corn, and they can be switched to a grower ration.

A plot of pasture enclosed by a 3-foot, woven-wire fence makes a great feed source for the birds when they are about 6 weeks old. As an alternative to heavy, permanent wire fencing, you can use a lightweight, portable electric fence, called **poultry netting**, made of plastic and electro-plastic strings. By using a fencer to deliver an electric charge to the fence, you can keep the geese inside and thwart predators with a stiff shock if they try to gain access to the flock. Premier fencing (**www.premier1supplies.com**) carries poultry netting, fencers, and plastic PVC posts along with valuable tips on how to use the netting for poultry flocks.

Both ducks and geese are great at foraging both bugs and plants. Geese are larger than ducks and will need more pasture, or they will quickly become defoliated and heavily soiled. They do not care for alfalfa or tough, narrow leaved grasses. Good plants for pasture are brome grass, Timothy, orchard grass, bluegrass, and clover. The pasture will need to be monitored, as it quickly can become defoliated and heavily soiled by the geese. Grass for goose pasture should be about 4 inches in height. Longer grass can become bound up in the goose's crop — the outcropping of the esophagus — and cause death.

If you are not raising your ducks for meat production or egg laying, adult ducks can forage for much of their food if they are allowed to roam. Feed should still be provided for the ducks, however, as there will be seasonal variations in food supply. To make feeding less complicated, a **gravity feeder** can be used. This type of feeder is a round-shaped container on a base that dispenses feed down as the ducks eat at the bottom.

Place the feeder(s) inside a pen to encourage your ducks to come to the pen in the evenings. It should be in a covered area so rain will not be able to destroy the feed. Nasco (www.enasco.com) carries many styles of feeders for poultry producers made from both galvanized steel and plastic. Feeders and waterers for adult ducks should be cleaned as they become soiled and disinfected once a month.

If your geese or ducks are to be slaughtered for home use or for market, they should be fed a finishing ration formulated for turkeys starting one month before slaughter. This will provide them extra nutrients allowing them to fatten before slaughter. Birds not intended for slaughter do not need to be fed a finishing ration. Finishing rations and other feeds for your birds can be found at feed supply stores.

Duck and Geese Health

Although waterfowl are disease resistant, infectious diseases can and do take toll on unlucky flocks. To keep your ducks and geese as disease free as possible, try to limit their contact with wild birds that can carry viruses and bacteria from an infected flock to yours. Another strategy to minimize disease is to keep your birds' water source, feed, and pens clean of droppings. If feeders or waterers become soiled with feces, a good scrubbing with bleach water (1 teaspoon bleach per gallon water) will help kill disease organisms. Allow the cleaned equipment to dry before refilling with feed or water.

If you plan to pasture your flock, make sure there is enough ground for the birds. Overstocking pens and pastures is an invitation for disease organisms in the feces to grow and multiply. Rotating pastures using small paddocks will be beneficial in two ways: Fecal material will get a chance to dry, and the action of sunlight can neutralize many disease organisms. It also will give the pasture plants a chance to grow back.

Here are some common diseases that can affect ducks and geese:

Avian influenza: This disease has caused much concern throughout the world. Avian influenza affects both ducks and geese. The mild form causes such symptoms as lethargy, trouble breathing, diarrhea, and loss of appetite. Death losses are rare from the mild form of avian influenza, but the more severe form can cause death of the entire flock and is characterized by the above signs plus facial swelling. There is no specific treatment for avian influenza aside from good husbandry, and there is not a vaccination. Prevention includes strict attention to rodent control, disinfection of boots and equipment, and control of wild birds. Humans also have been affected by avian influenza. If your ducks or geese have avian influenza, you need to report it to your state and local authorities, as well as to the USDA. Ducks and geese are at increased risk of contracting avian influenza and they need to be tested if you suspect they may have the illness to keep them from spreading it.

Botulism: Ducks can be affected by botulism, otherwise known as limber neck. The disease is caused by the bacterium *Clostridium botulinum*, which grows in the mud and vegetation in warm, stagnant water. The duck ingests the bacteria, and it releases a toxin. The bird may be found dead, or it may be paralyzed but conscious. Treatment is possible during the first 24 hours by force-feeding the duck water and feed. The bird should be placed in a shaded, dry nest away from predators while the toxin wears off.

Chlamydiosis: Ducks are susceptible to chlamydiosis, or parrot fever. Signs of an infected duck include nose and eye discharges, sinus infections, reddened eyes, diarrhea, weight loss, and loss of appetite. The disease is spread from infected bird to healthy bird from discharges and feces. Wild birds can spread the disease to domestic ducks. Chlamydiosis is also spread through contaminated boots, clothing, and equipment. Once an infected duck recovers, it can still be a carrier of the organism. Treatment is done using the antibiotic chlortetracycline.

Fowl cholera: This infectious disease is caused by the bacterium *Pasteurella multocida*. Both ducks and geese can contract this disease, which strikes suddenly and causes numerous deaths in the flock. Factors that can cause an outbreak include overcrowded pens or ponds, spread of the disease from wild birds, and cold and damp weather. Although sudden death is usually the first sign of the disease, some birds will have convulsions, rapid breathing, become listless, have nasal discharge, or have vents matted with droppings. Treatment for those birds in the flock not ill from fowl cholera is an antibiotic in the water. This treatment is done as a preventive measure. All sick birds should be removed from the flock and treated elsewhere. Dead carcasses should be burned.

Fowlpox: This disease can cause disease in ducks of all ages. There are two forms of fowlpox. The wet form causes canker sore-like lesions in the mouth and throat. This can cause trouble breathing due to obstruction of these respiratory passages. The dry form causes raised, bumpy growths on the legs. It can cause problems with growth and egg production. Mosquitoes carry and spread this disease. Spraying for mosquitoes can help control the spread. Vaccination is suggested if fowlpox becomes a problem in your flock.

Infectious hepatitis: This disease affects young ducklings between 2 and 3 weeks old. A virus that is either ingested or inhaled by waterfowl causes this disease. The sick duckling appears to be unable to gain its balance and will be seen lying on its side with its head drawn back toward the tail. Their legs also will make paddling motions. Most cases result in death within a day of signs. Vaccinations are available for healthy ducklings in an infected flock. Mothers can also be vaccinated two weeks before laying eggs to pass immunity on to the ducklings.

Intestinal parasites: Different types of intestinal parasites can affect geese and ducks. Coccidiosis, roundworms, flukes, and tapeworms are ingested by the birds from the ground or feed contaminated with feces. Signs of infection are varied and range from young geese with stunted growth, lethargic birds, diarrhea, or death if the birds are heavily infected. If you suspect your flock has intestinal parasites, take a sample of feces to your veterinarian to examine for parasites. Once the parasite is identified, treatment is through medication in the feed or water.

Salmonellosis: The bacterium *salmonella*, an organism that can affect a wide variety of animals and humans, causes this disease. It can quickly become a flock-wide problem due to its tendency to spread quickly. Signs of salmonellosis include lethargy, diarrhea, swollen joints, and lameness. Identification of the disease is only made through laboratory testing of feces from infected birds and examining carcasses of dead or dying birds. A bird that survives salmonellosis will remain infected for life, and it should be separated from the rest of the flock to prevent spread of the disease.

Parasitic diseases

Parasitic infections can plague your birds, especially if they have access to dirt. Check your birds daily to assess their overall health. Things to observe include feather loss, weight loss, unusual appearance, sitting huddled away from the flock, and decreased egg production. Infected birds can be more prone to developing other diseases that can quickly lead to death.

Most birds raised with access to dirt flooring will harbor a few internal parasites. These generally will not cause symptoms or problems and are not easily transmitted to humans.

Birds get parasites by eating the parasite eggs found on food, in the dirt, or in water. Insects, earthworms, or snails — all tasty treats for foraging birds — also carry the parasites or their eggs in their bodies. To control parasites, you can do some specific things:

- Do not overcrowd your shed or outside pens.
- Try to keep wild birds away from your domestic flock.
- Use insecticides, if necessary, to control insects in sheds.
- Change bedding frequently, and keep it dry.
- Remove droppings to keep birds from pecking at them.
- Keep your birds on a quality feed, formulated with plenty of vitamins.
- If you suspect internal parasites, have your local veterinarian identify the species so you can properly medicate the birds.

Coccidiosis: This disease is caused by parasites that cause decreased growth and death in birds. After ingesting the organism in feed or water contaminated with feces, it grows in the intestine and causes damage to tissues. This damage leads to decreased absorption of nutrients, decreased feed intake, blood loss, and an increased susceptibility to other infections. The primary symptoms are an outbreak of bloody diarrhea along with lethargic birds that huddle together with ruffled feathers. These outbreaks are usually related to an increased number of birds in a small space: The higher the stocking density, or number of birds in a space, the greater the number of coccidia in a smaller area. With less space per bird, the chances of infection increase because there will be a greater concentration of coccidia. Levels of coccidia in the digestive tract will not cause much damage, but higher numbers will cause serious problems. It is usually a more severe problem in young birds. Treatment includes the addition of coccidiostats — medications that kill coccidia — in the feed or water. Prevention relies on manure removal, moving birds to fresh ground, and decreasing stocking density in pens.

Internal parasites

Birds quite frequently are exposed to internal parasites by ingesting these organisms in the feed, water, or soil. Some common internal parasites include ascarids (round worms), cecal worms, capillaria worms, and tapeworms. Signs of a bird affected with internal parasites vary but can include pasting of the vent, diarrhea, poor or stunted growth, or lack of appetite. The only sign may be slightly reduced weight at marketing time. Worms can be treated using medications readily purchased at farm stores and veterinary offices.

Nutritional deficiencies

Nutritional deficiencies can be a problem in poultry, especially while they are still growing.

Angel wing

Angel wing also is known as crooked or slipped wing and affects geese. The last joint of the wing becomes twisted, causing the wing feathers to point out rather than lay flat against the body. Males develop the condition more often than females. Angel wing is caused by an improper diet while the goose is young. Too much protein or too many calories combined with low vitamin D, vitamin E, and manganese levels prevent the last joint on the wing from developing properly in relation to the rest of the wing bones. There may be a genetic predisposition to developing angel wing, and those adults affected with this disease should not be kept for breeding purposes.

The condition can affect both wings or just one wing, though if only one wing is affected, it will likely be the left wing. Feeding your geese a proper diet during the growing stage can prevent the disease. If the disease is caught early in a young, growing goose, the wing can be wrapped in wide self-adhesive wrap, called **vet wrap**, and the wing secured to the body. A diet with low protein and calories supplemented with vitamin D, vitamin E, and manganese should be fed to help the joint develop properly in the affected goose. If the condition is caught early and the wing is treated, it should grow properly and look normal.

Handling Aggressive Ganders

Ganders raised and imprinted on humans can become aggressive toward humans because they view humans as rivals for mates. This may happen at about 5 months of age. They will display dominant signs such as putting their heads down, pointing their bill up, or spreading their wings out. Sometimes humans that tease or chase geese can provoke this behavior as well. Do not allow children or immature adults to harass your geese.

If a gander does display such behavior toward you, you will need to confront it immediately before it becomes a major problem. Step toward the bird. He should back off, but if he does not, loosely grab a wing. You will need to work quickly as the gander may try to bite you when you attempt this maneuver. When he tries to back off, let go of the wing. He may try to intimidate you a few times, but it is important for you to confront the gander each time he tries to be the dominant figure. If this behavior continues unchecked, it will turn into a major problem every time you come around the flock.

If you do have an aggressive gander, you can try to get the upper hand by grabbing him and pinning him to the ground. His wings will flap (and they can pack a punch), and he may bite you. He definitely will squawk but keep him down until he submits by resting. Then let him go and repeat as necessary until he leaves you alone. Wearing heavy leather gloves, safety glasses, and a jacket will help protect you from his wings and bill.

Breeding Ducks and Geese

Ducks and geese intended for breeding should have a wing or leg band applied so you can identify them when you breed them. Banding should be done soon after hatching, and each band used on one animal should have identical numbers. Records should be kept regarding the parents of each duck, how many eggs each duck or goose lays, if she is broody and for how long, and how many eggs are hatched for each female. Poorly performing ducks and geese can be identified by their band and culled.

The tail features of ducks descended from Mallards, which is about every bird, will help you determine the sex. Drakes will have a few curled feather tips at the end of their tails while females' tails will lie flat. Geese are not so easily identified as adults. They should be purchased as sexed and banded as soon as possible so you can tell gander from goose. For those breeds that cannot be sexed on physical characteristics (for example, Pilgrims by feather color, Emden by down color, and Chinese by beak knob), vent sexing will need to be done. This is performed when the ducklings or goslings are a couple of days old.

The bird is held with the vent facing the person performing the sexing. The right thumb and first finger are placed on either side of the vent and pressed firmly over the vent. The vent is then parted slowly to expose the inner lining. The left thumb is used to gently pull back on the skin surrounding the vent. This will expose a pink colored cloaca and the penis (a small protuberance) in the male will be visible. The females have a genital eminence, or small fold of tissue. Adults are sexed in a similar manner but will struggle when caught.

Only those ducks and geese in good physical shape should be kept for breeding. Legs should be straight and free of deformities, as should the beak and wings. They should comply with breed standards for coloring, body shape, and weight. A drake can breed five to eight females. For geese, only one gander should be used for one or two females. Ducks can be bred during the first year; geese should be 1 year old when they breed. Geese prefer to mate on water, and the water should be deep enough for the geese to swim in.

Most duck eggs take 28 days to hatch, with the exception of Muscovy duck eggs, which take 35 days. If the female incubates her own eggs, make sure she has water and feed available near the nest. Pekin and Indian Runner ducks do not make good egg sitters, so you may need to have a foster mother incubate the eggs. Duck eggs can be brooded by broody chicken hens, but the eggs will need to be sprinkled with water every day to keep them slightly moist. If you plan to artificially incubate the eggs, the process is similar to chickens except for differences in humidity and temperature. Incubation requires 99.5 degrees F and 55 to 75 percent humidity. The eggs need to be turned at least twice daily but preferably four times a day. At day 25, the temperature should be lowered and the humidity slightly increased. Once the ducklings are hatched, allow them to dry in the incubator for one hour. Then, they can be moved to their prepared brooding pen.

Geese eggs take 30 days to hatch. Temperature in a forced-air incubator should be 100 degrees F, while in a still-air incubator, the temperature should be maintained at 103 degrees F. The humidity should be 50 to 55 percent for the first 27 days of incubation. Eggs should be turned 180 degrees, four to six times each day. The final three days before hatching, increase the humidity to 75 percent. When the goslings hatch, the doors to the incubator should be opened to allow the humidity to escape; this allows the goslings' down to dry. After an hour, they should be dry and can be moved to the brooding pen.

Nest boxes for geese should be a minimum of 2 square feet. Larger breeds may require more space. You can build your own boxes out of wood or purchase them from a poultry supply company, though it might be difficult to find a wooden box large enough for geese. If the female incubates her own eggs, make sure she has water and feed available near the nest. A female should not leave her eggs unattended more than once a day. Most females can successfully hatch up to a dozen eggs.

If you plan to incubate the eggs, collect them at least twice daily, but be sure to use caution. During breeding season, the geese can become ornery. You most likely will be hissed at as you collect eggs. To prevent being injured by protective mothers, situate nest boxes near an aisle in the pen, wear gloves, and protect your eyes with safety glasses. You can also create a distraction by feeding the birds as you collect their eggs.

Using Waterfowl for Weed Control, Insect Control, and as Alarms

Because of the goose's large size, excellent vision, and loud voice, and because of some breeds tend to be aggressive, they make good guard birds. Geese are intelligent and have a good memory. They remember people or animals that scare, harass, or frighten them. They also remember troublesome and scary situations. These factors make the goose a good guard bird against intruders. Geese have a preferential appetite for grasses and will avoid eating broad-leaved plants, which makes them ideal weeders for gardens or vineyards. Before chemical weed control became commonplace, specialty crop growers relied on geese to keep the grass picked in such crops as asparagus, mint, beets, beans, onions, and potatoes. To use geese for weeding gardens, the garden rows should be at least 1 foot apart, and a fence should enclose the garden.

Let the geese have access to the garden once the plants have established themselves, and the geese will eradicate the grasses and small, tender weeds. For plants that ripen above ground, such as tomatoes, do not allow the geese to weed these plants when the vegetables are ripe as they might peck at the colorful plants. Geese prefer to eat grasses (weeds) to vegetables, so remove them once the weeds have been eaten to keep them from sampling the vegetables. If snails and slugs are a garden problem, ducks can be let into the area to feast on these garden pests. Ducks are good algae and insect eaters in ornamental ponds. However, do not stock the pond too heavily or they may deposit too much feces in the water and destroy all plant life.

```
CASE STUDY:
WHY WATERFOWL?

Suzanne Peterson
Azariah Acres Farm
Foley, Minnesota
www.azariahacres.net
```

Suzanne Peterson raises geese and ducks on her farm, Azariah Acres, near Foley, Minnesota. Peterson grew up on a hobby farm where she learned that she really enjoyed caring for animals. Her love of animal husbandry led her to start farming for the joy of seeing animals grow.

Her first foray into farm birds was with chickens, but she found the market for small farm-raised chickens very competitive. In 2008, she had the opportunity to raise geese and ducks. She found a market for these two species and discovered that they are easier to raise than chickens. Peterson markets her birds as already butchered birds at a local farmers market.

Although Peterson feels ducks and geese are easier to keep than chickens, there are still many chores associated with waterfowl. She spends about an hour a day caring for her 15 geese and 80 ducks, including feeding, cleaning pens and waterers, thawing waterers in the winter, and clipping their wings to keep them contained. Recordkeeping is also an important chore. Peterson keeps records on when babies are hatched, how much feed the birds consume, each bird's weight at the butcher, and any disease or malformation issues.

Good fences are important as predators such as dogs and coyotes can decimate a flock. Cats, possums, owls, and hawks also can snatch young ducks and geese. Finding a sick or injured bird is the worst part of raising geese. However, she rarely has disease problems with her birds as she gives them ample access to water year-round and provides them plenty of pasture and pen space — the most important part of keeping disease out of a flock.

"The best aspect to raising ducks and geese is their intelligence and hardiness," Peterson said. "They are really interesting and beautiful animals." She feels raising geese and ducks could be a good family project if the birds are handled a lot. If not, she feels a child under 10 should not be around geese as they are very strong and can be aggressive. However, if the animals are handled a lot, even a young child could help with the ducks and geese. Peterson suggests a beginner waterfowl farmer start with two to four geese or 20 ducks to get a good idea of the care needed for these birds.

Ducks and Geese for Meat

Butchering ducks and geese is similar to butchering chickens. Pekin ducks can be ready to butcher at 8 weeks of age when they are 5 pounds. Rouen ducks mature much more slowly and will be ready for butchering at 5 to 6 months. Geese are usually raised for the holiday market during the late fall. They should be 5 to 6 months old and weigh 10 to 15 pounds, depending on the breed. The down from the breast area can be washed, dried, and saved for use in pillows or clothing. After butchering, geese and ducks can be dry picked, but scalding the feathers first makes them release easier and cuts down on skin tears.

Older ducks and geese provide the best quality down. Down is found only on the stomach and chest of ducks and geese. It only makes up about 12 to 15 percent of the total feathers of a bird. To remove the down from a bird, after the bird is butchered, you can pluck out the tiny pinfeathers by hand. Placing the duck or goose in a vat of scalding water for a few moments will help loosen the down feathering so the down can be hand-plucked more easily. The down is plucked by hand.

If you do not want to save the down, the goose or duck can be waxed after the large feathers are removed. This process will remove the down and smaller feathers that are more difficult to remove. Melted paraffin wax can be purchased and heated to 140 to 155 degrees F. The goose or duck should be dipped twice into the wax then dipped into cold water to set the wax. When the wax sets to a flexible form, it can be stripped off along with the down and feather. The wax can be strained of the feathers and down and reused.

Web Resources

Here is a list of Internet resources relating to ducks and geese, poultry and waterfowl. You can find more information to help you with raising your ducks and geese by visiting some of these websites.

General farm

The National Association of State Departments of Agriculture: **www.nasda.org**

The National Sustainable Agriculture Information Service: **www.attra.ncat.org**

The Sustainable Agriculture Research and Education Organization: **www.sare.org**

United States Department of Agriculture: **www.usda.gov**

United States Department of Agriculture Food Safety and Inspection Service: **www.fsis.usda.gov**

Buildings

Chicken Coop Source: **www.chickencoopsource.com**

Amish Goods: **www.myamishgoods.com**

Build Eazy: **www.buildeazy.com**

Egganic Industries: **www.henspa.com**

Feather Site: **www.feathersite.com**

Free Chicken Coop Plans: **www.freechickencoopplans.com**

Green Roof Chicken Coop: **www.greenroofchickencoop.com**

Omlet: **www.omlet.us**

PVCPlans.com: **www.pvcplans.com**

Supplies

FarmTek: **www.farmtek.com**

Horizon Structures: **www.horizonstructures.com**

Nasco: **www.enasco.com/farmandranch**

Premier Fencing: **www.premier1supplies.com**

Tractor Supply Company: **www.tractorsupply.com**

General poultry

The American Livestock Breed Conservancy: **www.albc-usa.org**

University of Minnesota Poultry U: **www.ansci.umn.edu/poultry/index.html**

Chickens

My Pet Chicken: **www.mypetchicken.com**

National Chicken Council: **www.nationalchickencouncil.com**

Guinea fowl

Frit's Farm: **www.guineafowl.com/fritsfarm/guineas**

Guinea Fowl Breeders Association: **www.gfba.org**

Peacocks

Amy's Peacock Paradise: **www.amyspeacockparadise.com**

United Peafowl Association: **www.peafowl.org**

Game birds

North American Game Bird Association: **www.mynaga.org**

Pheasants Forever: **www.pheasantsforever.org**

Feed supply companies

Nutrena® Animal Feeds: **www.nutrenaworld.com/nutrena**

Purina® Mills: **www.purina-mills.com**

Hatcheries

Cackle Hatchery: **www.cacklehatchery.com**

Dunlap Hatchery: **www.dunlaphatchery.net**

Holderread Waterfowl Farm & Preservation Center: **www.holderreadfarm.com**

Murray McMurray Hatchery: **www.mcmurrayhatchery.com**

Porter's Rare Heritage Turkeys: **www.porterturkeys.com**

Sand Hill Preservation Center: **www.sandhillpreservation.com**

Stromberg's: **www.strombergschickens.com**

Chapter 5

Pigs

PIG GLOSSARY

Barrow: A young male pig

Boar: An adult male pig

Butcher hog: A hog weighing between 220 and 260 pounds raised for slaughter

Creep: The area in a farrowing site that is off-limits to the sow, where the piglets can get feed

Crossbred: A pig that is a cross of different purebred pig breeds

Dam: Mother

Farrow: For a pig to give birth

Farrow to finish: Raising pigs from birth to being market or slaughter-ready

Feed efficiency: The amount of feed it takes for a pig to gain 1 pound

Feeder pig: A young pig, usually just weaned, that is produced by a breeder but raised by someone else; usually between 35 and 70 pounds

Finished hog: A fattened hog that is ready for market or slaughter

Gilt: A young female pig

Grower pig: A young pig being raised for market or for slaughter; usually a pig over 50 pounds

Grower to finish: Raising pigs from the weaner stage (about 8 weeks) to market or slaughter size

Hog: A pig weighing more than 120 pounds

Market hog: A pig that weighs 220 to 260 pounds and could be sold at market

Purebred: A pig that belongs to a recognized pure breed

Shoat: A pig from weaning age to 120 pounds

Sire: Father

Sow: An adult female pig

Swine: Generic term for pigs

Topline: The spine or back or the pig, especially in silhouette

Underline: The line formed along the stomach of the pig

History of Pigs and People

In the 19th century, a young girl led her father, the amateur archaeologist Marcelino Sanz de Sautuola, to a cave near the Spanish town of Santillana del Mar. There, on the cavern walls and ceilings, was an astonishing series of paintings depicting the animals known to Cro-Magnon humanity, including wild boars. Uranium-thorium dating of the pigments in these cave drawings lead some scientists to estimate that the images were 25,000 to 30,000 years old. Indeed, few animals have had longer and more extensive relationship with humans than pigs, which were among the first animals to be domesticated. The earliest domesticated pigs, which descended from Eurasian wild boars, probably occurred in Central Asia about 10,000 years ago. By 5000 B.C., the practice of keeping pigs was widespread, and Emperor Fo Hi wrote the first book on raising pigs in 3468 B.C., the same year he is thought to have also penned the traditional book of prophecy, the I-Ching. Zhou period tombs from ancient China (1121–221 B.C.) often included pigs carved from precious stones, thought to ensure the deceased prosperity in the afterlife.

In Europe, it is estimated that pigs were first domesticated around 5000 B.C., and the animal played an important role in much of the history and mythology of the continent. In the Aeneid, Virgil claimed that in the 6th century B.C. Aeneas saw a vision of a "sacred white sow," the female pig indicating the place on the Tiber River that should be the site of Rome. Pork was the favorite meat of the Romans, who considered cows to be beasts of burden and did not often eat veal or beef. In Petronius' Trimalchio's Banquet, roast boar with dates was the centerpiece of the feast, and such dishes were a central part of the wealthy Roman diet. If, as Napoleon said, "an army marches on its stomach," the Roman Empire would be built upon a foundation of bacon, as its legions were rationed with pork, grain, and wine; additionally, the boar was sacred to Mars, the Roman god of war.

Among the Celts, the boar was seen as a symbol of fertility, power, and prosperity, and the animal was sacred to the goddess of the hunt, Arduinna. The bones and joints of pigs have been discovered buried in Celtic tombs, suggesting the importance of these animals in their culture. The Druids referred to themselves as boars and emulated the animals' solitary forest existence. Throughout the Middle Ages, the importance of pigs to the developing agrarian economy grew steadily, and the boar appears in many examples of heraldry.

In 1493, Christopher Columbus arrived on the island that would come to be known as Puerto Rico with eight pigs that Queen Isabella had ordered him to bring. Almost 50 years later, Hernando de Soto landed in Florida with a small herd of pigs that would grow to many hundreds in just a few years. De Soto and other Spanish explorers offered some of these animals to the indigenous peoples as a token of goodwill, and numbers of them escaped into the wild and became the ancestors of the razorbacks and feral pigs of the southern United States.

Sir Walter Raleigh brought a number of sows to the Jamestown colony in 1607, and although the settlers endured a great deal of hardship, they were to be the first permanent English establishment in the New World. Over the course of the next century, pigs were to become a staple throughout the colonies because of their natural adaptability and utility.

As pioneers moved west, they brought pigs with them in their wagon trains, and soon large herds were to be found across the settled regions. In the War of 1812, salt pork was shipped to American troops in barrels stamped "U.S." Although the "U.S." stood for the meat packer "Uncle" Samuel Wilson, soldiers coined the term "Uncle Sam," one of America's most widely recognized patriotic symbols. Throughout the history of the United States, the importance of hogs to the nation's economy has continued to grow, along with the relationship between pigs and politics. In the 19th century, the term "pork barrel politics" was coined to describe actions undertaken by politicians to solely benefit their constituencies. The "pork barrel" was a container that held lard or salt pork, and keeping it well supplied was a matter of constant concern for the average American.

In 1961, pigs broke into the financial markets when the Chicago Mercantile Exchange began trading pork belly futures contracts as an innovative risk management device for meat packers; because frozen pork bellies can be kept in cold storage for extended periods, they can be held in inventory and sold when market prices meet the sellers' needs. Pigs are no less important elsewhere in the world; today, every continent has a pig population, except Antarctica.

Breeds

Breed selection is an important part of the decision-making process for new pig owners, whether you intend to keep them as pets, for breeding, or to raise them for the table or market. Your geographic location is important when determining which breed to raise because different breeds do better in different climates. Darker pigs are common in sunnier southern regions because their pigmentation helps protect them from sunburn. If you live in a colder state, you may wish to choose a breed with a shaggier coat that can help them stay warm in winter months.

A key factor in making this decision is which breeds are available in your area, but it is also important to consider what you plan to do with your pigs. If you are planning to establish a breeding program, you want to buy the best stock you can find. Purebred pigs are pedigreed, carefully regulated, and expensive. If you are just planning to fatten a pig or two for the table, crossbred pigs will do nicely, so long as they are produced by a knowledgeable, responsible breeder with a purposeful breeding plan.

Pet breeds

> "I am fond of pigs. Dogs look up to us. Cats look down on us. Pigs treat us as equals."
>
> — Winston Churchill

There are a number of breeds more suited to pet ownership than the larger meat breeds. Many of these pigs are still raised as food breeds, but their smaller size makes them better as pets. Because of their great similarity to humans, both in physical attributes and in their social behavior, they can fit right into a human household under the right circumstances. It is important to consider, though, whether your household will fit right in with them. Are there members of your family who would be incompatible with pigs? Do you have other pets that might behave aggressively toward them?

Because pigs are such social animals, they can form strong bonds with people and other animals. You should realize that this also means they often require companionship, so you will need to consider whether you are able to provide them the type of home they need. Do you have the space needed? Can you devote the appropriate amount of time to your pet pig?

Miniature pigs can be either midgets, which means they are much smaller, but proportionally identical to their larger counterparts, or dwarfs, which means they are smaller and proportionally different, such as potbellies.

African Pygmy/Guinea Hog

The African pygmy, or Guinea hog, is a small black pig descended from larger red hogs thought to have been imported to the Americas from Africa aboard slave ships. One reason African pygmies make good pets is that they have long life spans, sometimes reaching 25 years. An African pygmy is only 40 to 60 pounds, making this a manageable breed. They have kinked tails, straight backs, and medium, pricked ears. Their shiny black coats are hairy rather than bristly, which makes for better cuddling. Not a potbellied breed, African pygmies are grazers and prefer lush, green grasses. This friendly, adaptable breed can be a cute, cuddly companion for many years.

Juliani/Painted Miniature

Painted miniature pigs were imported to the United States from Europe. They range from 15 to 60 pounds and have a small potbelly, a slightly swayed back, and proportionally longer legs than true potbellies. They can be black, red, white, silver, or a mixture of these colors. They are among the friendliest, most playful miniature pigs and are considered extremely gentle. Also, they are so small that they integrate more easily into an average home — some are even kept in urban apartments.

Kunekune

This fine pig is a more recent addition to the family of pet pigs in the United States. Imported from New Zealand, their name comes from the Maori word "kune," which means fat and round. Their most distinctive feature is probably their wattles — tassels hanging from their lower jaw — known as pire pire in the Maori language. Their ears may be erect or semi-lopped, and they come in a wide range of colors: black and white, red, white, brown, and gold. A mid-sized pet pig, they range from 90 to 120 pounds, have attractive pug noses, and may have spotted or calico coats.

Kunekunes are efficient grazers, so during the summer months, they may sustain themselves just by keeping your lawn well trimmed. In addition, they do not usually root, so they will not spoil the appearance of your grass.

Vietnamese Potbellied

Developed from the "I" breed of Vietnam in the 1950s, potbellied pigs are among the most common pet breeds in the United States. Keith Connell, who saw their potential as zoo animals, first brought them into the United States through Canada in 1985. As the name implies, the potbellied pig has an exaggerated potbelly with a swayed back, erect ears, extremely short legs, and a straight tail. Potbellies have wrinkled faces and a short snout, which gives them a somewhat comical expression. When purchasing a potbellied pig, try to be sure the short snout is not too exaggerated because this can cause respiratory problems. Potbellies are usually black, white, or a piebald pattern of black and white.

They often are found in zoos because they have an appearance many people find appealing, and they are friendly and even-tempered. In fact, because of their docile disposition, they are a mainstay of the petting zoo; not only do children love them, but they also seem to love children. This friendly manner and sociable behavior has made them the most popular miniature breed in the world.

Potbellied pigs may be small, as little as 25 pounds, though most are between 100 and 250 pounds. If you are thinking about buying a potbelly, this is an important consideration because though the young pig is a tiny animal, it may grow to the size of a large adult human. If you are looking for a petite pig, it is a good idea to look over the breeder's adult animals. Too many have bought a tiny pig only to realize that the adult pig is more than they can handle. This is a growing problem in the United States, and as a result, it is increasingly common to find pigs in animal shelters.

Yucatan/Mexican Hairless

Originating in Central and Latin America, the Yucatan is a gentle breed of pig ranging from slate gray to black in color. Yucatans have straight backs, short snouts, and medium-sized ears that are usually erect. Their skin and body systems are probably the most similar to humans, which has made them the most common pig used in laboratory testing. Yucatans can reach 200 pounds, though some considerably smaller strains are bred.

Breeds for food production

Although all pig breeds are edible, most pig owners prefer to draw a relatively firm line between pet breeds and food breeds. Not only is this important from an emotional standpoint, but food breeds also tend to be larger and have other characteristics that are more desirable for farmers, including their breeding qualities, docility, efficiency of weight gain, and, of course, meat quality. The food breeds raised for meat are divided into three categories: meat types, bacon types, and lard types. Meat hogs tend to have large frames with leaner bodies that provide a fine grade of muscle. Bacon hogs, on the other hand, tend to have long bodies that provide larger sides of bacon with plenty of lean meat. The third type of hog, the lard hog, has more or less disappeared in recent years, as the demand for leaner pork has grown and the use of lard in cooking has decreased.

Eight breeds of pig provide most of the pork produced in North America, with commercial breeders primarily concentrating on complicated crosses of three breeds: the Duroc, Hampshire, and the Yorkshire. Crosses of these breeds in succeeding generations, along with crosses to the Landrace, the large English white, and a few other breeds, are used to produce large litters, the most efficient feed-to-gain ratios, and other measures that are important for commercial pork producers.

On the other hand, small farmers are usually better off focusing on raising purebred pigs or simpler crosses. Instead of using complicated breeding schemes to achieve super pigs, or pigs that have been created from multiple hybrid crosses such as those used by commercial pork producers, it is better to focus on one breed that produces large litters and has few losses before weaning. Look for breeds with good mothering traits that produce plenty of milk for their young. Consider hardier breeds that will thrive in a modified confinement setup instead of living in a confinement system. You may wish to consider some of the breeds that have slower weight gain, especially if you have a local restaurant market with owners interested in trying more flavorful pork.

Berkshire

Berkshires were presumably "discovered" by Oliver Cromwell's troops when they were stationed at Reading, England, during the English Civil War in the 17th century. Berkshires have such flavorful meat that they fast became the most popular breed among England's upper classes; indeed, they kept a herd at Windsor Castle within sight of the royal residence. Maintained as a distinct breed, they are widely considered "England's oldest pig."

When imported Berkshires reached the United States in 1823, they had a sandy or reddish coloring. However, they were quickly crossbred with other breeds, which led to the color pattern we see today: black with white feet, snout, and tail, identical to the Poland China pig. The Berkshire is a smaller hog, though, with boars averaging 500 to 750 pounds and sows 450 to 650 pounds. In 1875, a group of Illinois breeders and importers formed the American Berkshire Association to ensure the continuation and preservation of the breed and its conformation standards, including short, erect ears and a medium-dished face with deep sides.

Berkshires offer a good growth rate and fair reproductive efficiency, though their litter sizes tend to be relatively small. However, the quality of the Berkshire's meat has made it a favorite of gourmet cuisine, with its exceptional marbling and flavor. The meat is prized in Japan, where they are bred in the Kagoshima Prefecture.

Chester White

The Chester White is an American hog breed that originated in Pennsylvania in the early 19th century, based on a cross of the English Chester, Lincolnshire, and Yorkshire breeds. Although only a medium-sized hog, the Chester White is popular with breeders and packers because of its high quality of muscle tissue and because its lighter color has an appealing appearance to consumers. In addition, the Chester White has a high degree of cutability, meaning that a larger percentage of its mass translates into marketable cuts of meat.

The biggest advantage of the Chester White lies in its exceptional breeding abilities. A Chester sow breeds back quickly; that is to say, once she has farrowed, she may breed again more quickly than is common in other breeds. Chester White sows are known to farrow as many as three litters a year, and these litters often contain ten or more pigs that reach market size. In addition, the sow carries these strengths when bred with other types of pigs, which makes them a popular choice in crossbreeding programs.

The Chester White has a medium frame, a slightly dished face, medium-sized lop ears, and a thick white coat. In addition, the Chester White is an extremely sound animal that is able to maintain its health in different conditions, so smaller farmers with simpler facilities and outdoor pastures often find them a good choice.

Duroc

Durocs are a red hog that ranges from a tawny golden color to a deep mahogany. Durocs have large lop ears that hang over their eyes, a curly tail, and a slightly dished face. The average boar weighs about 900 pounds, and the average sow reaches 750 pounds. They are considered a good meat breed because of the high quality of their muscle tissue, large bodies, and relatively low fat content.

Considered a Northeastern breed, there is some dispute as to these hogs' origin. Some claim they descended from the pigs brought to the New World by de Soto and Columbus, while others believe their ancestors were the African Guineas that may have come along with the slave ships. As a distinct breed, they originated in the early 19th century with a farmer named Isaac Frink of Saratoga County, New York. As the story goes, Frink was visiting his neighbor Harry Kelsey's farm when he took a liking to some reddish hogs. He purchased a few of them to start his own herd, and because the breed was unnamed, he decided to call them Durocs after Kelsey's famous Thoroughbred stallion. Later, they were crossed with Jersey reds, producing a hog that has developed into one of today's most popular breeds.

The Duroc is among the most common breeds found in the United States. The boars tend to be aggressive, and they often are used in crossbreeding programs, especially with Hampshires or Yorkshires. The sows can produce large litters, and the young pigs gain weight faster than almost any other breed. This, along with their extreme hardiness, accounts for their popularity.

Hampshire

Like all breeds with names ending "-shire," Hampshires are an English breed, though the breed that is well known today was developed in Kentucky. With erect ears, they are mostly black, except for a white band across their shoulders and forelegs; because of this distinctive marking, they are also known as saddlebacks.

Hampshires are somewhat smaller than other meat hogs, with sows reaching about 650 pounds and boars reaching 800 pounds. They are low in lard, with high-quality meat and a large loin eye area. The loin eye area of a pig is the large muscle in the pig's back that provides the meat for pork chops. A large loin eye is highly desirable. In addition to their high meat quality, Hampshire sows are exceptional mothers who remain fertile longer than most. Their breeding potential and high-quality meat make them a popular pig. According to the American Swine Registry, Hampshires are the No. 4 recorded breed in the United States.

Hereford

The Hereford is the most American of hogs because they are not bred in any measurable quantity anywhere else. Their fans consider them the best-looking pigs, and they certainly are distinctive, with their flashy red and white coloration, like Hereford cattle. The Hereford has a slightly dished face, medium-sized lop ears, and a deep red back with white trim around its legs, head, and tail. John Schulte of Norway, Iowa, originated the breed in 1920 based on a cross between the Chester White, Duroc, and Poland China breeds.

With boars averaging 800 pounds and sows averaging 600 pounds, Herefords do not grow to be as large as other meat hogs, but they are quite popular for other characteristics. Herefords develop rapidly and reach maturity at 200 to 250 pounds in just five or six months, and they are able to do so on less feed. Herefords are adaptable to a variety of different climates, and because of their quiet demeanors, they are a popular choice for youngsters engaging in 4-H club and FFA projects. The sows make excellent mothers, producing and weaning large litters. This, combined with their efficient feed use and rapid maturation rates, also means Herefords can be profitable.

Poland China

Strangely, Poland China hogs are neither Polish nor Chinese. They originate in the Butler County/Miami Valley region of Southeastern Ohio. The Poland China is a large, black hog with white "points" — face, feet, and tail — and lop ears. They tend to be long-bodied, lean, and muscular, making them an ideal meat type, with average boars of about 900 pounds at maturity and sows of about 800 pounds. Big Bill, the largest hog ever recorded, was a Poland China of 2,552 pounds owned by Elias Buford Butler of Jackson, Tennessee, in the early 1930s.

Like Durocs, Poland Chinas are hardy animals that feed well. In addition, they are exceptional breeders that are well suited to transportation because of their quiet dispositions.

Spotted Poland China

Spotteds are actually so closely related to Poland Chinas that they almost could be considered the same breed — the spotted looks just like a Poland China but with spots. However, spotted breeders consider theirs a better pig, and since 1914, they have been organized under their own breeding association. As their name implies, they have a spotted coloration, either white with black spots or black with white spots, which they inherited from the Gloucestershire Old Spots side of their family.

Most feel that spotteds offer only a moderate meat quality, though the sows are known for their exceptional mothering ability. Not only do they produce a good quantity of milk for their young, but they also give birth to large litters — one of the largest of the colored breeds. Like Poland Chinas, they are good feeders; they mature early and grow rapidly.

Landrace

Landrace hogs originated in Denmark, which jealously guarded exportation of these hogs for centuries. However, in the 20th century, importing these fine animals became possible. They have a soft white coat with pink skin, long, drooping ears, and flat backs. Although their legs tend to be short, they have a long, lean body that makes them an ideal bacon type. In addition, their long bodies have 16 or 17 pairs of ribs and thus produce more cuts of meat. The typical pig has 14 pairs of ribs.

Landrace pigs tend to be quite docile, and they grow rapidly. One of their most desirable characteristics is that Landrace sows produce unusually large litters, as well as a great deal of milk with which to support their piglets. As a result, Landrace sows often are used in crossbreeding programs, particularly with Durocs.

Yorkshire

Like the Landrace, the Yorkshire pig is a bacon type with white hair and pink skin. It has a dished face with erect ears and a long, lean frame that supplies ample, high-quality bacon. They were brought into the United States in the early 1800s, though it was not until the 1950s to 1970s that the breed really flourished. Yorkshires are comparatively small, with mature boars averaging 600 to 800 pounds, and they tend to grow slowly. Nevertheless, it is a popular breed commonly found in commercial pig farms across the United States.

Yorkshires breed well, with large litters and sows producing plenty of milk. Yorkshires commonly are seen in the media — if you can think of a famous pig from TV or film, it was probably a Yorkshire. For example, Arnold Ziffel, who often upstaged Eva Gabor on TV's *Green Acres*, along with Babe from the 1995 film of the same name, were Yorkshires.

Ossabaw Island

Feral Ossabaws inhabit the island in Georgia from which they draw their name. In the 1500s, Spanish explorers often left small herds on islands in the Americas to establish future sources of food, and the pigs of Ossabaw Island are thought to be descended from one of those herds. Although some may see them as a pet breed, Ossabaws are usually prized for their dark, unusually textured meat, as it resembles that of the black Iberian pig.

Living in an isolated island environment has had some interesting effects on the breed. One consequence of their isolated existence in a sparse environment is an extremely high level of intelligence, which they require in order to exploit every possible food source. In addition, Ossabaws carry a "thrifty gene" that permits them to store fat effectively. The consequence is that domestic Ossabaws, which have ready access to ample food supplies, often develop a form of diabetes. Due to the breed's problems with diabetes, the breed is rarely ever crossbred with other pigs. Ossabaws should be between 14 to 20 inches tall and 25 to 90 pounds, which translates into an approximate maximum of 4.5 pounds per inch of height.

Ossabaws come in a wide range of colors, but unless crossed with pigs of other breeds, they never develop stripes. Generallly, they have solid or spotted coats, sometimes resembling a calico pattern. Ossabaws may be red, gray, blue, and even white, although this is quite rare.

Ossabaws today are critically endangered. They are currently found in a few zoos on the mainland, but the pigs generally are not allowed to be removed from Ossabaw Island because they are at risk of carrying porcine vesicular stomatitis and because pseudorabies is found on the island. There are fears that the pigs on the island could transmit these diseases to pigs on the mainland.

Pigs for composting

Although it would be unusual to get pigs for the sole purpose of using them to help with your composting, if you are a homesteader, or if you have a small farm, you may wish to consider adding two or three pigs to your livestock herd. Pigs are excellent at rooting and turning soil.

In order to encourage pigs to help with your composting, you can set up a small fence capable of holding two or three pigs around your large compost heap. Electric netting or Pig QuikFence™ would work well. Many people place a layer of straw over the compost so the pigs can work it into the compost as they root. The pigs will turn over the compost thoroughly, trying to find anything good to eat in it.

It is a good idea to have other uses for these pigs in addition to the composting, as the composting will not keep them busy for long. If you are not interested in raising pigs for this purpose, you may wish to consider borrowing pigs for a day or two from a neighbor who raises pigs. You will need to have a very large compost heap to keep the pigs interested and busy. Even if you add material to the compost heap every day, you would need to supplement the pig's diet with more nutritious food.

You could use any kind of pigs for composting, though it may become difficult to keep larger pigs inside a small enclosure.

Pig Husbandry

Pigs are wonderful, intelligent, sociable animals, but it is important that you seriously consider your ability to live up to the responsibilities that proper care for them entails. Although the decision to keep an animal should never be taken lightly, this is particularly true of pigs, which have very special requirements — although this is counterbalanced by the rewarding experience you can have with them. To begin with, if you are thinking of keeping a pig as a pet, you should be aware that the average lifespan of a domestic pig is ten to 15 years, and some breeds can live substantially longer.

The next important consideration is the size of animal you are able to handle. In the 1990s, it became trendy to own a "yuppy puppy," or miniature pig, but many people did not realize that "miniature" is a relative term when applied to pigs. When the full-sized animal can be 900 pounds, or even bigger, "miniature" can mean 200 pounds. As a result, many pigs ended up in animal shelters waiting their turn to be euthanized. The problem persists today, though numerous pig rescue organizations have formed in response. By working to educate others about pigs, and by working hard to ensure that your pigs are properly cared for, you can make yourself a part of the solution.

In terms of intelligence and curiosity, a pet pig is much like a toddler. If there is some trouble it can get into, it will. If there is something it should not eat within its reach, it will eat it. You can train your pet pig in the same way that you train a puppy, but if your pig is bored or left alone too much, it will eat makeup that is lying around, medicine, or just about anything else that smells remotely appetizing to it. Just as you would need to childproof your home when a toddler starts to walk, you need to pig-proof if you plan to have an indoor pig. If there is a way your cupboards can be opened, or if there is a weakness in the fence, your pig will find it.

Depending on the size and type of pig, you may need to provide only a pet bed or a nest of blankets and a pet door in your house, or you may need to establish an entire indoor/outdoor area for its use. The amount of space at your disposal for your pig's use largely determines the type of pig ownership that will be possible for you.

Another point you will find stressed throughout this book is that pigs are social animals with emotional needs. It would be cruel to raise a pig in isolation. Make certain that your pig has plenty of companionship, whether it is other pigs, different animals, or yourself. Just as a pig is comparable to a toddler in other respects, you will probably need to devote a similar amount of time to caring for your pig as you would a child. Few pet boarding facilities are set up to handle pigs; if you intend to travel, you should check to see if a boarding facility in your area has the facilities and abilities to care for swine. If you plan to maintain a herd, you probably will have to give up the idea of family vacations for a while. Raising livestock requires you be there every day to administer their needs, monitor their health, and remove manure. Even pastured pigs require too much attention to be left alone for long.

Do not be discouraged: raising pigs is fun, rewarding, and profitable. Like any undertaking, though, it is important to start with your eyes open so you know what you are getting into.

Characteristics and Behavior

Domestic pigs have changed a great deal over the last century or so. The dwindling use of lard in cooking has led pork producers to breed a leaner animal to satisfy consumer demand. The round, fat pigs of the past, called "chuffy" pigs or "cob rollers," are no longer as prevalent. Wild pigs, which are termed "leggy" or "rangy," do not quite meet the needs of the modern pig breeder either because they lack the meat quality consumers want. Instead, the contemporary swine falls somewhere in between the two, favoring a larger loin eye area.

A pig's anatomy is remarkably similar to that of a human being. Pigs have a respiratory, cardiovascular, and digestive system so much like ours that it is common for them to be used as test animals in laboratories. This is important because it helps pig owners understand these animals and how to care for them. Essentially, pigs need the same things humans do. If your diet, climate, and shelter seem comfortable to you, it is safe to assume that it is suitable for your pig as well.

Like human beings, hogs are omnivores, which is probably a big part of their success, both as a species and as a complement to humanity. Omnivores are extremely adaptable, which allows them to survive more readily in new environments and ecosystems. Like many omnivores, pigs are extremely intelligent, using their exceptional brainpower to hunt out new food sources and opportunities. According to the National Pork Producers Council, pigs are the fourth smartest animal after humans, apes, and dolphins.

Often, they are friendly, sociable creatures, but at the same time, they tend to be individualistic — each pig has a unique characteristic. Some pigs, especially boars (adult males), may exhibit aggressive or antisocial tendencies, though most are gregarious, curious, and playful. Most males are castrated when they are a few days old because they are destined to be feeder pigs instead of being used for breeding. If you are considering raising pigs, they should be raised in groups, or at least with some form of companionship. Most pigs bond readily with other animals or human beings, and you will want to be sure your pig is not lonely. Often, a badly behaved pig is a bored or lonely pig, so attend to the animal's emotional needs — not only for the pig's sake, but also because a contented pig is easier to manage. You should provide a pig with toys, because pigs are often as playful as puppies. Suggested toys include empty plastic trash cans they can push around, a bowling ball, or knotted pieces of rope or strips of cloth attached to the walls of their pen, which they like to pull.

Pigs have poor eyesight, as their small, bleary eyes seem to suggest. For this reason, they tend to be wary of new places and are easily startled. Although their wild counterparts can be nocturnal, modern domestic pigs lack the tapetum lucidum, or inner-eye reflective tissue, that allows improved night vision, so pigs are not fans of dark places. The placement of their eyes favors lateral vision, but they lack the fine musculature needed for sharp focusing. This means if you are trying to move pigs, you will need to consider the effect that darkness and their limited forward vision has on them. A pig may put up a terrible fight about moving forward into a dark building, for example, because its forward vision makes the area ahead seem frightening. However, if you use a carrier or scoot the pig forward by means of a chute with pig boards placed close behind it and in front of it, the pig will move forward without any problem.

Pigs tend to interact with each other through their excellent sense of hearing and ability to vocalize, making pigs great communicators. It has been observed that pigs can make more than 20 distinct sounds that communicate meaning to other pigs. For instance, a single grunt, short or long, seems to indicate that a pig is happy, while a pig that grunts many times in succession is hungry. When a pig grunts several short times together, it usually means the pig is angry, and when a pig squeals, it is an indication the pig is in pain or fear. Sows give instructions to their piglets at feeding time and are known to make soothing noises as their babies nurse.

For all the power of pigs' ears, their most important tool is their super-sensitive snout. A pig's snout is its fingers, eyes, and nose, all in one. The surface of a pig's snout is covered in thousands of tiny hairs that aid in capturing scents. Not only can they smell out all kinds of different foods with that powerful snout, but it also contains a structure of cartilage that they are able to use as a sort of shovel to root around, turning over clumps of earth to expose tender plants or grubs. They achieve a surprising degree of dexterity with their snouts, rivaling even the elephant's remarkable "fingers" in the tip of its trunk. Although a well-fed pig does not need to root to find food, most will do so to amuse themselves and better understand their environment, so it is best to provide them with fresh straw or hay. Sometimes rooting can be an undesirable behavior, and some farmers put a humane ring through a pig's nose in order to prevent it. If you are keeping pet pigs, be aware that most breeds will tear up lawns or flowerbeds. Rooting is an excellent way to turn the soil, but it can destroy anything planted.

Pigs have rather short legs when compared with the length of their bodies, though this does not prevent young or fit pigs from achieving surprising speeds — in some places, pigs are even raced. Their feet are made up of four toes, each with an individual hoof, though they walk only on their front two, which are larger and more solid, while the other two dewclaws at the back of the hoof rarely touch the ground, except when a pig is moving at top speed.

One unfair stereotype about pigs is that they are dirty animals. It is certainly true that pigs like to wallow, or lie about, in mud and water because they do not have sweat glands. A cool wallow allows them to regulate their body temperatures when it is hot. In addition, light-colored pigs are susceptible to sunburn and biting insects, and a coat of mud will protect them from both. However, if your pigs are given sufficient shade and a clean living area free of fecal matter to minimize insects, your pigs can wallow just as well in fresh, clean water. Most pigs are excellent swimmers, though potbellied breeds sometimes injure their bellies by kicking their back feet. You can provide your pigs with a mud wallow, a child's wading pool, or even a small, clean concrete pool. Pigs love water, and so always make certain there is an ample supply for swimming and wallowing during the summer months, as well as for drinking.

Although most farm animals will defecate or urinate wherever they happen to be when the urge takes them, pigs do not do this. In fact, they are quite fastidious about such things, designating a specific place in which to do their business that is well separated from their nesting and feeding areas. Pigs living communally also will cooperate in this, establishing one or two restroom areas respected by all. This makes housetraining a pet pig easy. Researchers at the University of Illinois also found that pigs will not play with a toy that has been soiled with feces.

Pigs often are found in dirty, muddy pens, but you should not keep your pigs this way. One reason people may do this is that it helps create emotional distance from animals intended for butchering. It is important that you, as a responsible owner, make certain your pigs spend most of their lives with clean bodies, bedding, and food, even if a mud wallow is in the mix. It can be difficult to include a clean mud wallow in a pigpen, but not impossible. Along with kiddie pools for your pigs, you could include a shallow concrete wallow filled with water. Not only will keeping your pigs clean make life better for the pigs, but it will lead to better meat and a better overall experience for you.

Anatomy and Physiology

Pigs have a cardiovascular system with a heart and lungs located in approximately the same places as a human's heart and lungs. They have a gastrointestinal tract that is similar to human's as well. As farm animals go, they are not the most efficient grazers because they have only one stomach, unlike the cow that has four stomachs.

Pigs have a long snout they can use like a digging tool when they "root." Rooting allows them to dig and turn over soil to find food or anything edible beneath the topsoil. As you might imagine, the pig also has a remarkable sense of smell that they use to sniff out anything to eat. Between their hooves and their active snouts, pigs can keep the ground dug up effectively.

The mulefoot pig, a rare old breed, has a single hoof on each foot, like a mule. They are the only pig with this trait, although this trait is sometimes passed along when these pigs are crossbred.

Many people are unaware that pigs have hair. Their hair can range from a light, soft fluff to a harsh bristle, depending on the breed and sex of the pig. The color also varies a great deal. Pigs can be black, white, **piebald** — black with white bands or spots and points (feet and ears) — red, sandy, spotted, striped, gray, and mixes of these colors. Many people believe that pigs are pink but "pink" pigs are actually white breeds. Their pink skin shows through, however.

Some breeds of pigs also have wattles. **Wattles** are long pieces of flesh that hang from their cheeks. They are not jowls, but hang behind the jowls, under the ears. There is no real purpose for wattles. They are simply a feature on some breeds.

Pigs can have either erect or flop ears. Flop ears, also called lop ears, are drooping ears. Some ears are so long that they can cover the pig's eyes. In many cases, this is a good way to identify a breed if all other characteristics are the same.

So-called "Hogzillas" that have been in the news in recent years in the United States have been found in Georgia and other Southern states. They are likely domestic pigs that have gone feral, according to DNA testing. Other specimens have been the offspring of a wild hog and a domestic pig. Pigs can revert naturally to a feral state rapidly because of a lack of interaction with humans. When this happens, their physical appearance can change, which includes a change in their skull. The dish-shaped face of the farmer's pig can change in just a few months to the straighter skull of the wild pig. This change allows the feral pig to use its snout more effectively for rooting and digging. The feral pig's teeth will continue to grow, particularly its wolf teeth that will become tusk-like. The feral pig will continue to put on weight until it weighs far more than the farmer's pig.

On the farm, feeder pigs usually are slaughtered when they reach 230 to 250 pounds. It typically takes about five or six months after weaning to reach this weight. Sows kept on the farm for breeding may reach 600 pounds, depending on the breed. Boars kept for breeding may reach 800 pounds, depending on the breed. Some of the feral hogs discovered have weighed 800 pounds or more.

Without a trip to the butcher, the lifespan of a pig is about 12 to 15 years, though some miniature pigs may live longer.

Buying Pigs

In this section, you will learn all about purchasing your first young, recently weaned pigs, or shoats. However, it is important to have their living area established before you bring them home, and you will need to conduct a little research to find the best breeders in your area. If you know anyone in the business, you have a tremendous advantage, but you can learn a good deal by talking with local feed store owners and veterinarians. Check your newspaper's classified ads, yellow pages, or Craigslist (**www.craigslist.org**), but be sure you have also consulted with your region's pork producers' associations or breed associations such as the American Berkshire Association, the United Duroc Swine Registry, or the American Livestock Breeds Conservancy. Breeders that join such associations tend to be more concerned with their reputations and work hard to ensure their stock is healthy and well bred. Finally, you need to check into your community's zoning laws to ensure they permit pig ownership.

If possible, never buy your pigs from a stockyard, auction, or other third-party seller. Buy directly from the farm of origin if you can because the more livestock is transported, the more chances there are for something to go wrong. Transport to an auction means contact with pigs from other farms, which means there is a greater likelihood of disease and injury. When you buy directly from the breeder, you have a better opportunity to assess the conditions of the place where your new pigs originate. You can learn much just by looking. If the farm is generally in disrepair and not well maintained, you can be sure the animals on it have not fared any better. Dirt and manure are a normal part of any farm, but a good farmer keeps the farm in order so it functions well. Animal enclosures should not have significant manure buildup, and bedding should appear fresh and clean.

Once you have settled on a breeder, you can begin to think about making a purchase. One of the best beginners' approaches is to purchase a couple of shoats in the spring and fatten them for fall hams, keeping one for the table and selling the other, if you so choose. There is some division about whether it is better to work with **barrows** (young, castrated male pigs) or **gilts** (young female pigs), though each has its advantages. Barrows tend to gain weight faster than gilts, but gilts can accept more nutrient-rich feed and produce leaner meat. In general, either will do, and your decision should really be based on the best-looking pigs available.

Early in the spring, contact the farms and breeders in your area to find out when they are **farrowing** — that is, when their sows will be giving birth. You will want to buy your feeder pigs when they are in the 6- to 8-week-old range. This is a good time to buy your pigs because their prices are at their lowest at this age, and they are easy to handle. As the piglets get older and the farmer invests more in feeding them, their cost will increase. Sometimes it is possible to pick them out before they are weaned and return for them later. If this is possible, you might want to do so. Good breeders castrate their young male pigs as a matter of routine, so this should be done, and the animals should be well healed before you bring any home.

What to look for when buying pigs

When you go look at the pigs, the farmer most likely will have all the young shoats for sale in a single pen. Take some time to look them over. Healthy pigs usually will move far away from visitors and then gradually approach as they grow more accustomed to the newcomers and their natural curiosity takes over. Pigs that make no movement when strangers approach should be viewed with suspicion; such listless behavior is often a sign of poor health or injury.

In general, crossbred or hybrid pigs tend to be more vigorous than purebreds, though only when the crossbreeding is part of a planned breeding program. Ask the farmer about his or her breeding approach; most will be happy to talk about their ideas about breeding because it says much about who they are as farmers. If possible, you want to look at the parent stock as well, to see what kind of animals you are buying. Look at all the pigs in the group. In your mind, separate all the largest animals first, because you want to take home the biggest in the lot. Discount any that do not seem lively or are notably lethargic. Watch out for animals that are limping noticeably, have diarrhea, or keep themselves separated from the other pigs.

A pig's snout should be straight, not twisted or malformed, and there should not be any excessive runniness from its nostrils. Watch for sniffling and shaking, signs of respiratory problems and sickness. Feel around the jaws for lumpy nodes or pustules, which can be a sign of abscesses in the jaws — these can be treated, but you do not want to buy a pig if you notice these problems. Next, look at the pig's eyes; they should be bright, free of discharge, and widely spaced, which many farmers feel is a sign the young pig will "grow into" them.

Beyond simple weight and age considerations, the relationship between weight and age is an important sign of an animal's potential for growth. Feeder pigs should weigh about 35 to 45 pounds at 8 weeks, and 60 pounds at 12 weeks. There is some variation by breed and gender, but these figures are meant to be guidelines, not fixed rules. Just make sure you do not buy a 12-week-old pig that only weighs 20 pounds, unless it is a miniature breed and you want a small one.

The USDA also has a grading system for feeder pigs based on their "logical slaughter potential" and "thriftiness." These technical terms refer to a pig's growth potential and feed-to-gain efficiency. There are six categories (grade 1 being the best), but you should not purchase a pig of worse than grade 1 or 2.

- Grade 1 pigs are long-bodied, with thick muscling throughout and full hams and shoulders that are thicker than the rounded back.

- Grade 2 pigs appear similar to grade 1 pigs, but their muscling is slightly less thick, and they are slightly shorter-bodied. It is unlikely that, as a beginner, you would be able to tell the difference between a grade 2 and a grade 1 pig, but both make good starters.

- Grade 3 starter pigs seem short in relation to the size of their heads, and the muscling of their bodies appears thin over flat backs, with narrow shoulders and hams.

- Grade 4 pigs are decidedly short, and their thinly muscled bodies appear flat and thin, particularly in their lower regions.

- Utility grade pigs are thinly muscled throughout the bodies and have an unkempt appearance with tapered legs and thin hams and shoulders.

- Cull grade pigs seem weak because of disease or poor care, and they can only make a normal market weight after an extremely difficult and costly feeding regimen.

How should a healthy piglet act?

Piglets are remarkably different in temperament and personality, but certain characteristics are seen in all healthy pigs. Curiosity is an ever-present trait. Piglets are also incredibly energetic. Unless they are still unweaned, pigs should spend plenty of time playing with littermates, food, and whatever else they are able to get hold of. Piglets that isolate themselves or seem excessively sleepy should be avoided. These signs can indicate malnutrition or illness.

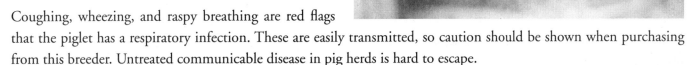

Pick the piglet up gently. Does it squeal loudly? This would be a normal reaction because pigs do not like being picked up for any reason. If one goes limp and quiet when you pick it up, there is most likely a respiratory problem present. It is best to pick a pig up by its rear legs. If you attempt to pick it up and cradle it like a baby, it most likely will squeal and squirm more.

Coughing, wheezing, and raspy breathing are red flags that the piglet has a respiratory infection. These are easily transmitted, so caution should be shown when purchasing from this breeder. Untreated communicable disease in pig herds is hard to escape.

Take plenty of time to watch how the piglets play among each other. They reveal much about their personalities in the way they play and interact. Some will appear dominant, while others seem very submissive. Return later if the piglets are not yet weaned. You will not be able to tell much about them while they are still nursing. Normally suckling piglets are either sleeping or eating.

Handling Pigs

The more time you spend with your pigs, the better. Pigs are friendly, sociable animals and if you spend time with them, it will make it easier to handle them. They enjoy being scratched and petted.

Piglets can be caught and picked up by the rear legs. They will squeal, but they are not being harmed. If you need to give your piglet a vaccination or hold a pig, you may lay the pig on its back if its small enough, or it might be a two-person job to hold the pig standing in place if the pig is larger.

Pig boards and snares

Pigs are one of the more difficult animals to move, but there will be times when you need to move them. You can carry a small shoat similar to the way you would carry a dog by holding it in your arms and supporting its stomach and chest. The piglet will squeal, so be prepared for protests. As the pig gets a little larger, use a **pig board** or hurdle. This is a tall board with cutouts or handles in the top so you can grip the board. If you place one board behind a pig and one in front of it to limit the pig's movement options, you can scoot the pig forward in the direction you want it to move. This method works well if you need to load pigs to walk up or down a ramp to go in or out of a truck, for example. You also can get a pig to go into a dark building like a barn using this method. Most pigs object to entering dark places because of their poor eyesight.

For larger pigs, such as sows, you may need to use a snare to get it to go where you want. A pig's head and snout are not really formed to accommodate a collar or halter. To overcome this problem, pig farmers use a snare. The **snare** is a flexible lead that loops around the pig's upper jaw and snout. Once the snare is in place, the farmer can lead the pig. There is no pain involved. This is often the only way to encourage an 800-pound boar to go where you want it to go.

Different methods work best with different pigs, depending on their size and degree of cooperation. You will need to practice to find out which methods work best with your pigs.

Housing and Feeding Pigs

Although the three little pigs had to face a wolf huffing and puffing at the door, your pigs should have a much easier time of things. However, you will still need to decide what kind of structure to provide for your pigs. There are many housing options for pigs today, depending on the size of your herd, your goals for raising pigs, and the kind of pigs you keep.

People have kept pigs in just about every kind of enclosure you can imagine, from nailing together old bits of wood lying around to use as fencing; to using dog kennels for a sleeping place for their pigs; to using a cleaned out oil drum lined with bedding as a sleeping spot. No matter what your situation or how much room you have, it will probably be possible for you to keep a pig or two.

Structures

The most popular way to keep pigs on a small farm is to provide them with a covered, dry place to sleep next to an outdoor enclosure. This kind of setup allows the pigs to move around, even if it is a small space. They can be fed and watered in the outdoor enclosure. And, because pigs prefer to relieve themselves in one particular area of their enclosure, this setup will allow them room to move away from their feeding station and bedding area and keep the pen cleaner. If you choose to use this kind of setup, you can convert an existing structure, such as a shed, or you can build a new structure for your pigs.

Converting existing structures

Often the easiest way to begin keeping pigs is by converting an already-existing structure on your property, such as an unused shed, a workshop, a lean-to, or an old barn. Ideally, allow a space that is 5 feet by 7 feet (35 square feet) for sleeping space for each adult sow. Sows will need more room if they have litters: plan on at least 8 feet by 8 feet (64 sq. feet) for a sow and litter. For young pigs less than 50 pounds, allow about 4 to 6 square feet per pig. For pigs that you are growing out (from 50 to 200 pounds), allow about 8 square feet per pig. This assumes the pigs will have access to a pen when they are not sleeping. You can estimate 1 acre for two sows and their litters; or 1 acre for 25 young pigs less than 50 pounds; or 1 acre for ten pigs that weigh between 50 to 200 pounds. If you have less than 1 acre of ground for your pigs, you can make adjustments in your herd to fit the room you have.

When you convert an existing structure for your pigs, it is usually wise to have it enclosed on three sides, shielded against the prevailing winds in your area. One side of the shelter should remain open so the pigs can move into the pen for their feed and water. You may have to cope with whatever flooring already exists in the structure. Pigs usually do best on a hardwood floor. Wooden floors are easier on their hooves and legs than concrete and stay cleaner than a dirt floor. Concrete can be a good choice, provided there are some grooves in the floor to keep the pigs from slipping.

Remember that floors tend to get wet and can become slippery, so you will need to provide your pigs with plenty of good, clean bedding. Change out the bedding regularly to keep your pigs healthy and happy. Pigs traditionally enjoy straw as bedding but you can also use wood chips or sawdust as a bottom layer. This is a good idea if you have a dirt floor because it will make the space a little easier to clean. Topping off the wood chips or sawdust with straw will provide your pigs with something to chew on and keep them comfortable. Soybean stalks or dusty bedding of any kind is not recommended as they can cause respiratory problems. Aim for bedding that has good absorbency and that your pigs can rearrange as they like. That way they can pile it deeper for warmth or spread it out to stay cooler.

Building a new structure

You also can build a new structure for your pigs. When building a new structure for your pigs, consider the location. You may be fond of your pigs, but you will probably not want them to be too close to your house because of their odors. You should consider factors such as your weather and how much sun will shine on their location. Some nearby shade trees will be welcome during hot weather. You should consider how much rain you get and whether your area is prone to flooding. Place the new building for your pigs on higher ground so the adjacent pen will not get soggy. You should consider access to your building because you may need to have pigs and feed delivered in large trucks and hogs hauled to the butcher.

Once you have chosen a good location for your new structure, you can begin building. Depending on how large the building will be, you may want to include some farrowing pens for your sows. It is recommended that the building be wired for electricity so you can have a heat lamp, heating pad, and other things that may be needed during farrowing or during a veterinarian's visit. A wooden structure is recommended if you are building from scratch. Metal buildings can hold in too much heat in the summer and cause your pigs to be uncomfortable. Make sure you lay a good foundation for the building that allows some air circulation beneath the structure because it is likely some wetness will seep through at times.

Walls in the building do not need to be made of wood because they can pick up dirt and be hard to clean. Pigs also may be inclined to chew on them. Instead, consider poured and reinforced concrete walls with an insulated interior. These walls will provide your pigs with more warmth in the winter and stay cooler in the summer. Ventilation is critically important in any building housing pigs, so make sure your building allows good airflow. For flooring, you can consider wooden or concrete floors. Wooden floors are believed to be warmer and easier on the hooves and legs, especially for large pigs. Concrete is easier to clean and will last a long time. If you do choose to go with wooden flooring, hardwood floors are recommended because they will last longer than other kinds of wood. Choose wood that is 2 inches thick to stand up to regular use from heavy swine.

The size and type of permanent structure you build will depend on how many pigs you plan to raise and what your focus will be. You can determine if you will need special areas for weanling pigs or if you need more room for finishing hogs. Building a new, permanent structure is an expensive proposition, but it may be worth the expense if you intend to devote a great deal of your business to raising hogs. You can obtain more specific building plans from your county extension services agent. The University of Tennessee has some excellent building plans online for many types of swine housing: **http://bioengr.ag.utk.edu/extension/extpubs/PlanList97.htm#Swine%20Plans**.

The mobile pig house

Mobile pig houses cover many different kinds of housing units. Quonset-type huts can be used successfully for raising pigs, as can hoop structures. Quonset huts are prefabricated, lightweight structures made of corrugated galvanized steel. They are all-purpose buildings that are easy to assemble, easy to move, and easy to clean. They are popular with livestock producers who often use them to house livestock, to store farm equipment, and to store hay. Hoop shelters have the added advantage that they provide good ventilation and plenty of natural light. You can keep sows or weanling pigs in these units or even use them to finish pigs before butchering.

Farmers who pasture raise their pigs typically provide mobile pig houses that can be moved as the pigs are rotated to different pastures or paddocks. For sows that farrow in the pasture, you can provide farrowing huts. Some of these huts are built of wood on an A-frame construction and slightly resemble a large doghouse. The sow can take possession of her farrow hut and deliver in a natural way. These huts are easily moved and can be cleaned and used again as needed.

Pasturing

There have been times in our history and in many parts of the world when pasture-raising pigs was common. With this approach, pigs typically are turned out in the pasture and left to grow. They grow more slowly than their confined counterparts, and they are exposed to the weather. Pigs cannot thrive on pasture grasses or forage alone, so their diet must be supplemented with feed.

There are a number of pros and cons to pasture raising pigs.

Benefits of pasture-raising pigs

- Pigs grow more slowly (meat has more flavor, distinct from commercial pork).
- Less early investment in buildings
- Lower production costs for the farmer (labor, feed)
- Permanent buildings are not needed.
- Pigs are under less stress (less cannibalism, less aggression).
- Manure is used in the pasture.
- The pigs' immune systems are stronger.

Problems with pasture-raising pigs

- Pigs grow more slowly (involves more costs to raise).
- Pigs may have an increase in internal parasites.
- Pigs can escape from fencing.

One thing that should be mentioned is that pigs that spend time in the pasture are usually happy. Although that fact by itself cannot determine whether you raise your pigs in the pasture, it is an important consideration.

If you are interested in pasture-raising your pigs, it is estimated that good pasture can provide between 30 and 50 percent of the nutritional value of grain. You will need to supplement your pigs' diets, especially if you have pregnant sows. Farmers who become seriously interested in pasture-raising pigs usually plant diverse fields of grasses and legumes so they can graze their pigs rotationally. This offers their pigs the widest range of nutrition and keeps the pastures from becoming overgrazed.

Fencing and Pens

Fencing and pens for your pigs do not have to be complicated, but they do need to be sturdy and well installed. Pens are often part of pig housing with an indoor sleeping area for pigs. In other cases, pens can be used as a **drylot**. Just as it sounds, a drylot is a large, dry lot on dirt where pigs are kept. You can plan to keep one large hog in 150 square feet of space in a drylot.

Whether you are putting up a pen for a drylot or as part of a housing setup, the pen needs to be designed for the pigs you intend to keep in it. If you use rails or planks, for instance, small shoats will wiggle their way between them. If you use woven farm wire that is not strong enough, some hogs will be able to push it over or push through it. Hog panels are a good choice to contain your pigs because they are designed with pigs in mind. **Hog panels** are all metal, woven-wire, and easy to move. They also attach easily to metal posts, which makes them easy to put up. They are 34 to 54 inches tall by 16 feet long. You can buy them new or used. Used is fine, and you will save money if you buy them secondhand. You may consider wooden-slatted fencing if the slats are close together. This kind of fencing will keep shoats inside the pen, and larger pigs cannot push through it. If you use wooden-slatted fencing, you will need to make sure that the slats are placed close to the ground so young shoats cannot crawl under the fence. You may wish to place some wire fencing at the base of the fence or run a strand of electric fencing around the bottom of the fence to keep small pigs from trying to dig their way out. Like many animals, pigs usually think the grass is greener on the other side of the fence.

You can purchase hog panels at the Tractor Supply Company store (**www.tractorsupply.com**) and at feed supply stores. You may be able to find hog panels for sale secondhand on Craigslist or in your local newspaper at a significant savings. You can check with local farmers to ask if they know anyone who may have some to sell. You might find hog panels for sale at livestock auctions. You will be able to find wooden-slatted fencing at most home supply stores, such as Home Depot, or you can go to a lumber yard and purchase the lumber to build the fence to your specifications.

You also can use electric fencing to keep your pigs in place. It is economical — a 4,000-foot coil of electric fence wire is $100, and a 5-mile AC electrical fence controller to send electricity through the wire is about $40. Electric fencing is easy to find in home supply stores and other places, but probably you will have the widest selection in a store such as Tractor Supply Company. Pigs learn quickly to stay away from the fence. If you are worried that the electric shock will hurt your pigs, you can try touching the wire yourself. The shock is unpleasant, but it is not harmful. If you put up electric fencing, put up two strands of wire. One strand should be about 4 inches off the ground to prevent young pigs from scampering under, and the second strand should be 12 to 16 inches off the ground to keep larger pigs from leaning over the wire. For additional security, you can add a third wire 30 inches off the ground. Make sure you mark the wire every few feet with caution tape to warn the pigs, as well as yourself and other visitors to your farm, where the wire is.

If you are fencing a larger area, such as a pasture where pigs will be raised, electric wire, barbed wire combined with electric wire, and electrified netting are all possibilities if you are fencing large tracts of land where pigs will be grazing. Field fencing is one of the most expensive options, and it is hard to install, but this kind of fencing can last up to 50 years. You will not need to replace this kind of fence in the near future, and it will do an excellent job of keeping pigs or any other farm animal contained. General-purpose field fencing usually starts at $159 for fence that is 47 inches tall and 330 feet long; studded "T" posts for the fence are $3.99 each at the Tractor Supply Company at the time of this writing. As usual, you may be able to find better deals if you buy secondhand. Electrified netting is also expensive, but it is versatile and can be moved from place to place. It is useful if you plan to use rotational grazing for your pigs. You can move the electrified netting wherever your pigs are grazing. Most electrified netting in the United States is sold by Premiere1Supplies.com and can be purchased online with free ground delivery. Fifty feet of Pig QuikFence is $57; 100 feet is $70.

When you are installing your fences, you will need to put up a few gates. Give some careful thought to whether gates should swing inward or outward. For instance, if you do not want your pigs to try to rush out of the pen into an open area when you enter, it is best to plan a gate to open inward. If your pen opens into a pasture for the pigs, however, it may be fine to have a gate that swings outward to allow the pigs to have easier access to the larger area. If you have a gate to a barn entrance, you may wish to control access and have a gate that opens inward so you can control how many pigs you allow to enter at one time. Consider the best locations for your gates. If you have adjoining pens, for example, you may wish to place a gate inside the pen as a shortcut instead of having to drive pigs out of one pen and into the other. These may seem like minor matters, but they can make a big difference when you are driving your pigs from one pen to another or carrying out your daily chores.

Hygiene Considerations

Your pigs' living quarters will have a direct impact on their health, the quality of meat they produce, and on you or anyone else who works around them. Good planning can make it much easier to maintain hygienic conditions around your pigs, make cleaning the pen easier, and make for a more pleasant work environment on the farm.

Pigs are naturally clean animals, and they prefer to use one area of their pen or lot as a bathroom. Once this area is established as the bathroom spot, your job of cleaning out the pen each day should be decidedly easier because you will only have one place to concentrate your cleaning efforts. You also should check the sleeping area each day and clean out any wet or dirty places. Put down fresh straw or other bedding to keep the area dry and comfortable for your pigs.

One of the chief reasons for diseases among swine is overcrowding, so try to keep the number of pigs you house together down to lower numbers. Hygiene can be affected when pigs tear up the ground with their hooves. It is likely that after it rains your pigs' pen may turn into a muddy pit. There is not much you can do about mud in your pigs' pen if you are raising them on dirt, but you can rotate your pigs to new pens from time to time if you have the space available. This will allow one pen to dry out while your pigs use the new pen. Rotating your pigs to clean pens tends to cut down on the spread of disease and parasites as long as you make sure that the new pen has been sanitized since its last use.

You can raise your pigs on concrete flooring. This can be a viable option if you have outdoor concrete pads already on your property where grain has been kept or barns have stood before. Concrete is not an ideal surface for pigs because it is hard on their hooves and legs and not comfortable if they wish to lie down outdoors. Concrete can also become hot during the summer months unless there is plenty of shade provided. However, it is easy to keep clean and not subject to disease and parasites in the same way that dirt pens are.

Sand is another option for your pens to keep them cleaner and more hygienic. Pigs enjoy sand, and it is relatively comfortable for their legs and hooves. Sand does not promote the spread of disease or parasites as much as dirt does. Sand also can provide good drainage for your pen, so water and urine do not collect.

You also can make your pigs' living situation better and cut down on slipping, sliding, and mud by placing your feeding and watering stations on concrete platforms in the pens. The platforms do not have to be high. The goal is to keep the pigs from sliding around in the mud as they spend time in these important areas.

Remember that ventilation is also important to hygiene if your pigs have an indoor sleeping area or if they are confined part of the time. Good airflow will help reduce disease. If your pigs are housed, you can solve ventilation issues by having one side of their sleeping area open to the outside, have a window in the building, or have a fan in the top of the ceiling.

Food, Water, and Shade

Your pigs have a number of basic requirements to stay happy and healthy. Without food, water, and shade, your pigs cannot grow and be happy. There is a wide variety of watering and feeding methods for you to choose from, depending on how many pigs you will be raising, your husbandry methods (the way you raise and care for your livestock), and how much money you plan to invest in your equipment. Some watering and feeding methods will mean much more work for you, but they will cost less. Others methods will cost much more, but you will have much less work to do each day. Before you purchase your feed and water equipment, it is a good idea to see if you can talk to other farmers or visit their farms and see how their equipment is set up. This is especially helpful if you find other farmers who are raising pigs with the same intentions as yourself.

Waterers

You cannot underestimate the importance of water when raising your pigs. Pigs will need free access to water at all times. You can estimate that each pig will consume about two to three times as much water as feed per day. That means that a 100-pound grower pig that eats 6 pounds of feed per day will consume about 12 to 18 pounds of water, or 1.5 to 2.2 gallons. The amount of water your pigs drink will fluctuate slightly depending on the weather and changes in their feed. However, you should continue to have fresh water available to your pigs at all times.

There are a number of different watering methods for pigs ranging from a simple water dish or tub of water for a single pig to expensive automatic heated waterers. A water dish or tub for your pigs is a perfectly fine way to start out if you are raising one or two pigs. A water dish or tub is typically made of rubber, plastic, metal, or even concrete. The important thing should be that it is durable so it can stand up to use by your pigs. Pigs will be more likely to turn over lightweight tubs, so you can try to use heavier tubs, but they may still play with them. A water trough may be a more practical choice, whether you have one or two pigs or several. You can make a water trough from an old water tank cut in half and placed on concrete blocks or wooden blocks, or you may purchase a new trough from a livestock supply store. Water troughs can be anchored in place or they may be moved from place to place if you plan to move your pigs to different lots.

You may choose to water young pigs by means of nipple drinkers. Nipple drinkers are 1-gallon containers with a metal valve that acts as a nipple on the side. These waterers are good for young pigs, and they keep out dirt and debris but they have to be anchored securely to keep pigs from dislodging them. The nipple drinkers gradually can be raised higher as the pigs become bigger. Nipple drinkers can be attached to a permanent pipe system so water is constantly available. However, this method of watering is not heated, so they are not recommended as an outdoor waterer. Nipple drinkers have to be purchased and are not homemade devices.

A hog watering tank can hold between 35 and 250 gallons of water. These tanks have a "hog drinker," or a trough cut in the side where the pigs can drink. They automatically refill themselves with water, and they can be heated for winter watering outdoors. However, these tanks are hard to keep clean if you are raising your pigs on dirt flooring. When the pig puts his head into the trough, it is washing its face in the drinking water. A hog watering tank does make it easy to give pigs medicine or supplements because you will know how many gallons are in the waterer and can mix appropriately.

The most expensive way to provide your pigs with water is with an automatic heated watering tank. This watering system is beneficial because the water flow is automatic, and this system has a flip lid that pigs learn to use. This prevents dirt and debris from entering the tank. The tanks can be drained for cleaning, which means they are less work for the farmer.

Feeders

A feeding dish or tub can work well if you are raising one or two pigs. If you are feeding several pigs, you will need to use a trough with dividers to keep pigs from being too greedy. Otherwise, a dominant pig may stand in the trough and prevent the other pigs from eating or try to claim all of the feed by pushing the other pigs away from the trough.

Some farmers prefer to feed their pigs by putting feed on the ground for them and scattering it around the pen, away from sleeping and bathroom areas. This method is most often used by small farmers who prefer a more natural approach to raising their pigs because it allows pigs to eat their food off the ground as they would if they were grazing or foraging.

Wall feeders are another option for feeding your pigs. Piglets that have not been weaned yet are frequently fed by means of wall feeders in the creep, or the part of the farrowing area where the sow cannot follow them, when they begin having their first meals. This prevents the sow from trying to get their feed and being in competition with them for food.

Hayracks, such as those used for horses, can be set at a height comfortable for your pigs to use, and filled with hay, alfalfa, or other grasses. This is a good option for your pigs when they are indoors. Hay is usually left in a bale when it is provided to pigs outdoors, or the pigs use the automatic feeders.

If you are raising a large number of pigs, the easiest way to feed your pigs is with a self-feeder, or bulk bin feeder. Self-feeders are popular, and pigs quickly learn to use them. Self-feeders can hold between 50 pounds and several tons of feed. Self-feeders are expensive — an average self-feeder for three to four pigs will usually cost $75 to $100; and a small, used bulk bin feeder capable of holding 4 tons of grain may sell for about $1,000 — so you will not want to purchase one of these systems unless you know you intend to continue raising pigs. The trough portion of the feeder has flaps the pigs open when they want to eat. The farmer can adjust how much feed is available to the pigs. A 40-bushel hog feeder (the Big "O" oscillating feeder, with 12 feeding stations) sells for around $1,400 at BarnWorld.com (**www. barnworld.com**).

What to feed your pigs

Although pigs are not too fussy about their food, feeding them the right feed can lead to better and faster weight gain, which can mean better profits for you. Every pig raiser wants to see happy, thriving pigs, which results from knowing something about feed.

Pigs do eat like pigs. That is to say, they like their food — a lot. A pig's appetite and its ability to gain weight quickly compared to other farm animals are traits that have made it dear to the hearts of farmers. At one time, pigs were known as "the mortgage lifters" because of their excellent return on investment to the farmer and their ability to help pay the mortgage. Just a little feed and some scraps tossed your pig's way for a few months, and it can present you with a freezer full of delicious pork. If you grow an extra pig, you can sell the second pig at market and more than make up your feed and other costs.

If you are like most first-time pig owners, you may be filled with some concerns about feeding and nutrition. Fortunately, pigs are efficient animals, and they can thrive on different kinds of diets. For pigs raised in pens, you can expect to provide most of their nutrition from grain in some form, along with as many table scraps as you are able to provide. Many small farmers make a habit of collecting vegetables, bread, and other things from their kitchens each night, adding some milk to the food remains, and giving this mixture to their pigs. If you have a garden on your property, your pigs will welcome anything that you wish to toss their way. Some people suggest that pigs should avoid potatoes and other plants of the nightshade family. Young potatoes often have a tint of green on them and are high in the toxin solanine, which is a glycoalkaloid that can be hard for your pigs to digest. Eating a few may not harm your pigs, but it is best not to feed them a large amount as they can cause diarrhea and other gastrointestinal problems, or in extreme cases, death. You can also check with grocery stores to see if they have leftover produce.

If you are trying to feed your pigs an organic diet, you probably will want to avoid feeding them meat scraps, unless your meat scraps are certified organic. Pigs love eggs, and it is fine to feed them eggs, shells and all. If you have hens on your farm, you will have a constant source of eggs for your pigs. However, discourage your hens from laying their eggs near the pigs. Pigs quickly will learn to follow the hens and eat their eggs if they can get to them.

If your pigs are allowed to forage, they can find many tasty things to eat on their own. Pigs that eat acorns and chestnuts will have particularly flavorful pork. However, you should try to keep your pigs away from areas where black walnuts fall because these can be toxic to your pigs. The American Society for the Prevention of Cruelty to Animals (ASPCA) has a good website with photos of more than 400 toxic plants (**www.aspca.org/pet-care/poison-control/plants**). If you have questions about the plants growing on your property, consult your county extension services agent or someone from your local university's agriculture or biology departments. They will be able to identify plants for you.

The following plants are known to be poisonous to pigs, so learn to identify them and keep pigs away from them or remove them from your property:

- Black-eyed Susans
- Jimson weed
- Lambs quarters
- Nightshade
- Pigweed
- Pokeberry
- Spotted water hemlock
- Two-leaf cockleburrs

Grains

Most of your pig's diet probably will come in the form of grain. Most grains have high concentrations of energy, so they help your pig gain weight more quickly. You can grow your own grains as crops, which is an economical way to feed your pigs, you can buy grain from a local feed mill, you can purchase commercial feeds that rely heavily on grains, or you can have custom grain mixes made up for your pigs by your local feed mill.

There are five basic grains in common use for feeding pigs: corn, wheat, milo (sorghum), barley, and oats. Corn is the most common of these grains. When the other grains are used, such as wheat or barley, they are not used as a full grain feed ration or as the sole form of grain that is fed to the pig. Instead, they only make up part of the grain ration fed to the pig. This is because they are less palatable in some cases and have fewer of the nutrients that pigs require. When you feed your pigs these grains, they will need more supplements. Corn can be fed as a full grain feed ration by itself, which explains why it is so popular as a feed for pigs.

Corn is high in carbohydrates and low in fiber. It is an especially good feed for **finishing** hogs, when you are trying to put the last pounds on a hog before going to market. However, you will need to supplement your pigs with protein and vitamins and minerals if you feed them corn.

Protein

Your pigs must have good sources of protein in order to have the amino acids they need to thrive because their bodies cannot make amino acids on their own. Amino acids are necessary to build muscle, for gestation, lactation, and growth.

Because protein is essential for growth, pigs need different levels of protein at different times in their lives.

PIG PROTEIN REQUIREMENTS	
Age	**Protein %**
Nursing/weaning	18-20
Growers (50-125 lbs)	15-16
Finishing (125-250 lbs)	13-14
Young gilts and boars	15-16
Adult sows and boars	13-14

A number of good protein supplements commonly are added to a pig's feed. Soybean meal is a popular protein supplement. Soybeans can be grown easily in case you are interested in growing your own crop. You should not allow pigs to eat raw soybeans, however. They contain trypsin inhibitors, which can prevent the young pig's body from absorbing protein properly and inhibit growth. Although soybean meal is economical, it still lacks vitamins and minerals. If you use soybean meal as your protein source, you can use alfalfa meal as a good source of vitamins and minerals for your pigs. Mix the soybean meal, alfalfa meal, and corn together for a good, nutritious feed for your pigs.

Other plant sources of protein include wheat, bran, alfalfa meal, distiller's grains, brewer's products, corn gluten meal, and hominy feed. Depending on the grain and protein supplement you choose for your pigs, you will need to find the right mixture of vitamins and minerals to add to your pigs' diet. For example, if you use alfalfa meal as a protein source, it is already a good source of vitamins and minerals, which means you will have to use fewer vitamin and mineral additives. The downside of using some of these other plant protein sources is that they are more costly than soybean meal. For example, at one feed store, a 100-pound bag of soybean meal was $19; a 50-pound bag of alfalfa meal was $12; and a 50-pound bag of corn gluten meal was $24. You will need to consider the fact that soybean meal has about 38 percent protein compared to 16 to 18 percent protein for alfalfa meal, and 40 percent protein for corn gluten meal. So, choosing the best protein supplement is not always easy.

Vitamins and minerals

Vitamins and minerals typically come in premixes to be mixed into grains or feeds, unless they are supplied in the form of a specific supplement such as alfalfa meal. However, premixes can be expensive and are usually best purchased in bulk. For one brand, a 60-pound bag of starter premix was $37.50 with a ten-bag minimum order if purchased online and delivered. Premixes can be purchased at many feed stores where livestock feed is sold.

Vitamins and minerals need to be given to your pigs in the right formulation because too much or too little of certain ingredients can lead to health problems. For example, selenium is toxic even in low amounts, though a lack of selenium can cause sudden death in rapidly growing young pigs. It must be fed at just the right amount (3 parts per million for pigs). Less salt (sodium) is good for finishing and growing pigs. The vitamins and minerals that your pigs require will fluctuate at different stages of their development. Your pigs can rely on some vitamins and minerals from the soil if they graze, and they will get some vitamin D from the sun if they are outdoors. However, pigs that are confined indoors will rely completely on vitamin and mineral supplements.

Other supplements and additives

Along with vitamins, minerals, and protein supplements, your pigs may benefit from other additives to their feed. Meat and bone meal, fish meal, and tankage are all animal-based supplements that can add high-quality protein and/or fat to your pigs' diets. Meat and bone meal and fish meal are leftover byproducts from slaughter and processing. **Tankage** is a liquid product from rendered (cooked down) animal carcasses. When it comes to palatability, pigs seem to prefer the taste of soybean meal to other protein supplements. Meat and bone meal, fish meal, and tankage are good sources of phosphorus and calcium. They can be used for up to half the necessary protein in your pigs' diets.

Pigs are fond of milk products, and these products can supply many of the nutrients missing from grains. Milk products are easy to digest, and they are especially good for young growing pigs. Dried whey and dried skim milk are typically added to the starter mix diets of young weaned pigs in order to improve growth performance. They can be fed until the pigs weigh about 30 pounds. Lactose is milk sugar and dried whey contains 70 percent lactose; dried skim milk is made up of 50 percent lactose. Whey contains lactose, lactoglobulin protein, lactalbumin, water-soluble vitamins, and minerals. Dried skim milk has a similar content but has less lactose and more milk proteins. Dried skim milk usually costs more than whey and is reserved for younger pigs. If you have a cow or two on your property, you easily may be able to spare some milk for your pigs. You still can give milk to your adult pigs though they will not benefit from the milk as much as young pigs. Molasses often is added to a pig's grain mix both to improve palatability and to help keep dust down. Molasses is high in iron, but it is also high in calcium, which prevents the pig's body from absorbing the iron.

Commercial Feeds

If you are starting to think that feeding your pigs is too complicated, there are good commercial swine feeds available at feed stores. They come in many different formulas: for starting weaning pigs, for shoats, for growers, for finishing hogs, for pregnant sows, and for breeding. Some areas of the country have more choices in feed available to them than others, but commercial swine feed is usually available wherever livestock feed is sold. If you can locate a good feed store, they likely will carry some of these brands, or they may be able to order them for you. If you do not live near a feed store, you may be able to find a distributor who sells online or over the telephone if you are willing to buy in bulk.

Organic feed

According to the latest reported figures from the National Ag Statistics Service of the USDA in 2010, for the year 2008, there were 8,940 hogs and pigs certified organic in December 2008 on 258 farms in the United States. In order to be certified organic, pigs must be raised organically from the last third of the gestation period until butchering. Antibiotics may not be used, which includes antibiotics in feed. Growth hormone stimulants may not be used, and artificial ingredients and preservatives are kept to a minimum.

You can begin an organic program with grower pigs that have not been raised organically and change over to organic, but you will not be able to sell their pork as organic. In this situation, the piglets will need to be weaned onto an organic starter feed. Continue to feed them an organic diet by feeding them organic grain and supplements raised on your own farm or purchased from a local organic farm. Sources for organic grain can be harder to find than commercial feeds, but they are available. Some feed mills offer organic grains, and you can have custom mixes made to your specifications. You can contact individual organic farmers in your area to see if they sell organic grain. Talk to your county extension services agent to find out about organic farmers near you. He or she may also be able to suggest other sources for organic grain. You can find national sources of organic grain through ATTRA, the National Sustainable Agriculture Information Service site at **http://attra.ncat.org/attra-pub/livestock_feed**. They have listings for organic livestock feed suppliers throughout the country. There are also commercial organic feeds available that do not contain antibiotics or other preservatives. You will need to check to see if these feeds contain genetically modified corn or other grains. Modesto Milling (**www.modestomilling.com**), the Buckwheat Growers Association of Minnesota (**www.buckwheatgrowers. com**), and Ranch-Way Feeds (**www.ranch-way.com**) are a few companies that create organic feeds for pig farmers.

Custom mixes

If you raise your own grain or if there are farmers in your area who raise grain, you have the option of going to your local feed mill and requesting a custom feed mix for your pigs. This can be a good choice if you are not happy with the commercial choices available to you. This approach is usually most cost effective if you have a large number of pigs and you can purchase several tons of custom mixed grain, but your local feed mill also can custom mix grain for you and sell it to you by the 50-pound bag.

If you have your grain custom mixed, you can have your protein supplements and your vitamins and minerals added at the same time the grain is milled, which means less work for you because you will not have to mix up each ration for your pigs. Custom mixes can be great labor savers if you have more than a few pigs eating the same diet. You may be able to buy your grain from local farmers, so you will know where the ingredients came from and how they were grown.

Storage

The subject of feed inevitably leads to the issue of storage. There is usually a cost savings to buying grain and supplements in bulk, but buying in bulk makes storage more difficult. Just where do you put 3 tons of grain? Bulk bins are usually the best place to store large amounts of grain, and they have self-feeders in the bottom so pigs can feed themselves. At the moment, you may not think you would need a ton of grain, but keep in mind that one pig will eat about 7 pounds of grain per day. That is about 50 pounds per week, or 200 pounds per month. Multiply that by your number of pigs. If you have five pigs, you will easily use 1,000 pounds of feed in a month. So, it is not unusual to buy 2,000 pounds or more in one purchase.

Feed mills can put grain into a large bag for you that will hold 1,000 pounds. They can place this bag in the bed of a pickup truck, and you can bring it home. A tractor can move the bag to a bulk bin, or you can dip the grain out in just a few minutes by using a 5-gallon bucket.

You do not have to purchase tons of grain at one time. Do not purchase more than a month or two worth of grain at one time to prevent the grain from becoming dusty or moldy. Store your feed where it will be dry and where vermin will not be able to get to it. Feed will always attract rodents, so take care that you use rat-proof containers. For instance, you can store a 50-pound bag of feed in a metal trash container with a lid that fits securely. Make sure you never place feed containers where your pigs can get to them, or they will help themselves.

Pig Health

With good care, good feed, and good housing practices, your pigs should stay in good health if you have purchased them from disease-free sources. However, pigs can succumb to disease if one of the following situations occurs on your farm:

- If your pigs' needs are not being met in some way

- If they are not getting the proper nutrients

- If you are overcrowding animals

- If you are not practicing good husbandry and you are failing to clean out the pigs' pen or keeping things in poor condition or

- If the pigs are being stressed in some other way

Part of your daily care of your pigs should include observing them to make sure they are in good health. You often can do this when your pigs are eating. If there is a pig that is not hungry or that stands by itself or if there is a pig that is listless or that seems different from the day before, notice it, and take it seriously. It is highly unusual for a pig to miss a meal. Pigs are social animals, and if a pig is by itself, something may be wrong. Pigs should not be listless or uninvolved in the things going on. The more you watch your herd, the more you will get a good feel for how your pigs behave when they are healthy and feeling good, and the sooner you will recognize when something is wrong with them.

Your pig supplies should include a basic first aid kit for your pigs. This kit should contain many of the same items that you would include in a first aid kit for your family, such as triple antibiotic ointment, iodine, alcohol, styptic powder, bismuth subsalicylate, and similar treatments. It should also contain a rectal thermometer. You can use a rectal thermometer to take your pig's temperature if you are concerned that the pig may have a fever. The normal temperature for a pig is 102.5 and anything over 103 degrees can be considered a fever. If your pig does have a fever, it can help you identify if your pig is ill and which disease it may have.

Diarrhea or scours is a frequent symptom of diseases in pigs. If your pig has diarrhea, it may become dangerous quickly, particularly to young animals because they can become dehydrated. You can add electrolytes to your pig's water and encourage it to drink to help it. You can purchase powdered electrolytes to mix in your pig's water, or you can purchase a substance such as Pedialyte® liquid. Try to get your pig to drink enough to replace the fluids it has lost, which may be quite a lot of fluid. In a pinch, you can use sports energy drinks with electrolytes. Try to quickly determine what is causing your pig's diarrhea, and call your veterinarian for help in case it is something serious.

Diseases

Here are some of the most common pig diseases and their symptoms:

Atrophic rhinitis: Atrophic rhinitis is an illness that infects young pigs and leads to physical deformity. The cause is presumed to be germs that enter the mucus membranes of the nose. Nose to nose contact infects one animal to another, until the entire litter is sick. Symptoms usually do not show up until piglets are 3 weeks old. There is usually no fever, but the pigs have sneezing and a discharge from the eyes, along with inflamed mucous membranes. The most noticeable symptom is an acute irritation of the nose, which makes the pigs rub their noses against anything they can find. The disease eventually will affect the bones of the snout and deform them. The face will gradually become misshapen and the bones around the face and nose may disintegrate. The snout may become very noticeably curved along the side. Young pigs are prone to pneumonia with rhinitis. Up to 30 percent of pigs with atrophic rhinitis may die. Testing is available to identify carriers of atrophic rhinitis, and it is recommended that new animals be tested before they join your herd to prevent them from passing this disease along to your pigs.

The breeding herd should be vaccinated against the disease. It may take up to four months for immunity to develop. Use sulfa drugs to medicate sows through their feed from the time they enter the farrowing site until they wean their piglets. Inject piglets with amoxycillin on days three, ten, and 15 while they are nursing, and inject them again at weaning time with a long-lasting antibiotic. Continue this method of vaccination for at least two months until all of your sows have been vaccinated. Give sows a booster vaccine two to three weeks before each subsequent farrowing.

This sickness can carry on through quite a few litters if it is left untreated. Inoculating farrowing sows will help prevent it, but rhinitis management has to be done on a continuous basis.

Brucellosis: Brucellosis manifests itself in aborted litters, arthritis in sows, and inflamed testicles in the boar. Brucellosis can be passed through feed contaminated with urine, manure, or other discharges from affected pigs. It also can be passed through shared water. Brucellosis is sexually transmitted, so if you are breeding your sow to an outside boar, you will need to ask for proof that the boar has been tested recently for brucellosis. If an infected sow does have a litter, she will pass the disease along to the nursing pigs in her milk. The only treatment for brucellosis is to remove animals from the herd and to disinfect the entire area. If the entire herd is affected, the only reliable way to prevent the spread of the disease is to destroy the herd. It is required by law in some areas because it is a matter of public health. Many states require certification that pigs are brucellosis free before allowing them to be shipped into their area. You can check with your veterinarian or your county extension service agent to see if brucellosis testing is required in your area before shipping.

Hog cholera/African swine fever: At one time hog cholera, or classical swine fever, was one of the most deadly of all swine diseases. There is no treatment for hog cholera. The symptoms include a high fever, lack of appetite, diarrhea, and coma leading to death. It is extremely contagious. However, there have been no outbreaks of hog cholera in the United States since 1976. Officials remain vigilant. African swine fever resembles hog cholera, and it is present in the United States. Any pig that displays a high fever should be isolated to prevent contagion.

African swine fever has symptoms that are very similar to hog cholera. Lab tests usually are needed to be able to distinguish African swine fever from hog cholera. Otherwise, the virus exhibits the same sudden onset. Pigs may be found suddenly dead. Pigs may have high fever, lack of appetite, and seem listless. The pig may show red or blue areas on its chest or stomach and on its extremities. There is diarrhea, problems breathing, vomiting, and miscarriage in pregnant sows. When these symptoms occur, virtually all pigs exhibiting them will die within one week. If a pig does recover, it will be a carrier for the virus throughout its life.

African swine fever is spread from one pig to another. There is no effective treatment or vaccine at this time. When African swine fever appears in a herd, it is essential to slaughter the herd immediately before the virus can spread to other farms. Otherwise, the entire pig population is at risk. Everything on the farm must be cleaned and disinfected, or discarded. A quarantine or isolation zone may be set up around the area to see if other farms may show signs of the illness.

Parvovirus: Parvovirus is believed to be widely present in pig herds. It does not have noticeable outward symptoms or cause death in mature animals. Instead, parvovirus results in reproductive problems. Parvovirus infection can lead to miscarriages in the sow between day 12 and 20 after breeding and a delay coming in season for rebreeding. Once infected, the sow can continue to lose litters and be slow to come in season, or to come in heat again for rebreeding. There is no treatment for pigs with parvovirus.

There is a vaccination against parvovirus. Buying disease-free pigs from established farmers who have no reproductive problems is another safeguard. You also can maintain a closed herd, meaning that you do not bring in new pigs that could pass along diseases to your pigs. If you do have new pigs, it is best to pen your current gilts and dry (unbred) sows near them a few weeks before breeding. This way they can be exposed to any potential viruses or germs before breeding and develop antibodies. Later, after breeding, it would be more dangerous to incubate any new virus because it would cause a loss of the embryos. The gilts and sows then will be able to pass their antibodies to parvovirus or any other viruses along to their piglets. You can then have the piglets vaccinated for parvovirus when they are a few weeks old. Keeping your gilts and sows up-to-date on their vaccinations is always recommended.

Porcine Reproductive and Respiratory Syndrome (PRRS): Porcine Reproductive and Respiratory Syndrome, or PRRS, has a host of symptoms and is sometimes confused with pseudorabies. PRRS affects the pig's lungs, which leads to reduced oxygen levels. There is a high fever, loss of appetite, coughing, and breathing problems. There also can be reproductive problems, such as late-term abortions for pregnant sows. At the moment, there is no treatment for PRRS but veterinarians may treat the pig with antibiotics to prevent or lessen secondary infections. There is a vaccine for PRRS, but it seems to be only moderately successful against the virus. There are research efforts to make a more effective vaccine.

Pseudorabies (mad itch): Pseudorabies symptoms include paralysis, fever, coma, and death. Among adult pigs, the symptoms include the telltale "mad itch," which can make the pig rub itself raw before dying. Pseudorabies is contagious and is caused by the herpes virus. Most states require testing for this disease as it is easily spread to other farm animals and causes death. When it initially shows up on a farm, the symptoms are manifested in high numbers of miscarriages and weak pigs.

There is a vaccination for pseudorabies, but it is only available in states where pseudorabies is considered widespread. The vaccine does not prevent pseudorabies; it only prevents the symptoms from manifesting. The United States declared pseudorabies eradicated from the commercial pig sector in 2004, but the disease is still found among the feral pig population. Pseudorabies is a legally reportable disease: if it appears in your herd, you must report it to your veterinarian and health officials. The disease may be transmitted to other animals, and they may display symptoms similar to rabies though pseudorabies is not related to rabies. Incinerating the carcass may be necessary after a pig dies from pseudorabies.

Swine dysentery: Swine dysentery may be identified by diarrhea, particularly bloody diarrhea. It is most common in the Midwest among larger pork producers. The disease affects the large intestine in pigs. It is acute, coming on quickly and rapidly escalating. It is also fatal. So far, there has not been much success with a vaccine for swine dysentery. The disease is usually traceable to sales barns or to people who have tracked manure from an infected farm on their shoes. It can affect any pigs, but it most often affects young growing pigs. Pigs picking up or eating manure from a sick pig or a pig carrying the disease usually spread it. If your feeder pigs contract swine dysentery, it is not unusual to lose up to 20 percent of your herd. The pigs that survive will likely have stunted growth and may do poorly. There are currently no specific cures for swine dysentery. The best way to stop it is to keep it from coming to your farm. Practice good hygiene, quarantine new pigs, and ask visitors to wear plastic over their shoes to prevent the spread of disease.

Swine erysipelas: Swine erysipelas is a bacterial disease that usually occurs in young pigs between 3 and 12 months old. Swine erysipelas can be fatal. The erysipelas bacteria live in the soil on the farm, and once the bacteria are established, they can be hard to eradicate. Infected pigs continually re-infect the soil with bacteria in their urine and manure. Symptoms of swine erysipelas can be recognized by the lesions that appear on the neck, ears, shoulder, and stomach of the pig. They are usually red and form a diamond shape, but the lesions may range from pink to purple. Once the skin lesions appear, the pig may die in two to four days. Milder forms of the disease do not cause death, but the pig's temperature may spike up to 108 degrees, which can lead to dehydration and harm to internal organs. Penicillin is used to treat swine eryisipelas. If you suspect your pigs have swine erysipelas, you should contact your veterinarian. You will need to discuss ways to eradicate the bacteria from your farm so your pigs are not re-infected.

The type of bacteria that causes swine erysipelas is always present on pig farms. It is in the soil, carried by other animals, and present in the tonsils of pigs. There is little you can do to remove it from your farm. However, there are contributing factors that may make swine erysipelas more likely to appear in your pigs. You may see a surge in swine erysipelas if you have encountered any of the following on your farm:

- You have wet and dirty pigpens.
- You give your pigs wet feed, especially if you feed milk byproducts.
- Your pig house constantly has pigs living in it without a chance to air out for a few weeks or months.
- Your waterers carry the bacteria.
- Your pigs are otherwise ill or stressed.
- There are sudden changes in temperature with a fast onset of summer weather.
- You make drastic changes in your pigs' diets.

You may not be able to do much about changes in temperature or summer weather, but you can see to it that your pens are clean, and you can control your pigs' diet, among other things. Try to take care of some of these conditions, and you may keep swine erysipelas from appearing.

Transmissible gastroenteritis (TGE): Transmissible gastroenteritis (TGE) is one of the most serious diseases found among pigs. It is found mainly in the Midwest among large pig producers. The virus acts rapidly and causes changes in the intestinal lining, which results in a large loss of fluids. All pigs can be affected, but it is most harmful to piglets younger than 2 weeks old. The fatality rate among piglets of this age may be as much as 100 percent. Symptoms in young piglets include watery diarrhea and rapid dehydration. The disease is highly contagious, and if one litter is infected, other litters might be infected quickly. Older pigs have a better chance of survival, but they will shed the virus in their manure for months after their recovery. Vaccinations may be effective, but the disease spreads so rapidly they are often too late to work. The best way to combat TGE is to practice isolating new pigs when they are brought to the farm and to insist that any visitors wear plastic over their shoes to prevent them from tracking germs from other places to your farm.

Parasites

Parasites are an ever-present fact of life on a pig farm. They live in the soil, and they are easily transmitted to your pigs when they root. Parasites are also found in bedding, passed from pig to pig, and exist in manure. Even the cleanest farms with the most well-cared-for pigs most likely will have animals with some parasites. In dealing with parasites, the trick is to keep them to a minimum, so they do not overwhelm your pig's immune system and cause it to become ill or weaken it so it becomes the target of an opportunistic disease. Parasites can be internal or external.

Internal parasites

Pigs can be subject to a number of different worms such as ascarids, round worms, whip worms, kidney worms, lung worms, muscle worms, nodular worms, pork bladder worms (also known as the human tapeworm), red stomach worms, stomach hair worms, thick stomach worms, thorny headed worms, and thread worms. Worms can exist in the lungs, the kidneys, the stomach, the liver, and even on the skin.

Being subject to so many different kinds of worms means there is no one method of worming (wormers are called **anthelmintics**) that will kill all of the worms or prevent infestation. If your pigs are carrying lots of worms, then treating them generally requires a rotational worming program.

There are four basic products used for worming: doramectin, fenbendazole, ivermectin, and levamisole. Although all of these products are good, one product used alone each time can cause the worms to build up a tolerance, and it will not effectively reduce the worms your pigs are carrying. In a rotational worming program, a different kind of wormer is used each month until the internal parasites are brought down to a lower number. Once worms are not a serious issue anymore, you can change to worming your pigs once every six months.

In most cases, you will not be able to tell that your pigs have worms unless they carry a heavy infestation of parasites, but pay attention to your pigs' physical condition. If your pigs are coughing, losing muscle tone or body weight, showing bad skin, have diarrhea, or show blood in their feces, they might have worms. With a heavy infestation, they may shed worms in their manure. At other times, your only sign may be that they are not gaining weight properly. Any time your pigs seem to be doing poorly without an obvious reason, consider whether they might have worms. It is a good idea to have your veterinarian test your herd for worms on a routine basis to see what their status is and if you need to adjust your worming protocols.

Worm medicine can be given to your pigs in various ways, including injections, topically, or in the feed and water. Topical application is usually the least effective of these methods because pigs have a tougher skin, and they do not absorb things through it easily. Taking medication orally usually works well as long as the medication is not being wasted in lost feed. You will need to determine the proper dosage to give each pig based on its age and weight.

Good pen and pasture management will also allow you to reduce the parasite load. Rotate pens and pastures when possible and allow them to sit empty for several months. This will kill off many of the parasites because they will not find a host. Sunlight will do a great deal to sterilize the soil and make it clean again. When pigs are using pens, clean them out regularly so parasites from the manure do not linger and move into the ground.

External parasites

Pigs are also subject to several external parasites, which include lice and mites (which cause mange), ticks, mosquitoes, and flies. Various insecticides are used to rid pigs of these pests, some of them made specifically for swine. You will need to read labels carefully to understand the precautions and apply them only as directed. Some insecticides have pre-slaughter intervals, which means you will not be able to use them within a certain time before slaughtering your pigs. Otherwise the chemicals in the insecticides might remain in the meat when slaughtered. Make sure you have read the label and understand this information.

Treatments for various external parasites can be applied in different ways. There are sprays, dips, pour-ons, and feed additives. Some of the treatments are aimed at treating the pigs' indoor living area. Again, make sure you read the label carefully and apply the product properly, or it will not work effectively.

Tips for disease prevention

There are many things farmers can do to prevent disease and illness on their farms and keep their pigs healthy.

Isolation

If you have an already-established herd and you are bringing in new pigs, it is in the best interests of your pigs to isolate the newcomers for two to three months when they arrive. They should be kept at least 100 yards away from where your current pigs are to ensure the new pigs will not spread any diseases to your herd. It will give your new pigs time to adjust to life in their new surroundings. If you turn them lose into the same pen as your current pigs, you will cause your pigs a great deal of stress, and it will most likely lead to aggression and fighting. Give your new pigs time to settle in while you observe them for any signs of illness.

If you are bringing sows to your farm for breeding to your boar, they should arrive several weeks before breeding so you can monitor them. They will need time to accustom themselves to their surroundings. Some sows might go out of season temporarily when they are moved to a new farm, though they probably will come back in season quickly if the boar is in a nearby pen. Allow the sows and the boar to become used to each other from a distance. If the visiting sows have a few weeks on your farm, they will have time to develop antibodies to any viruses on your farm and will build up immunity before breeding.

Finally, it is a good idea to have an isolation pen or a small pig house where you can keep a sick pig. When one of your pigs does become ill, you will need to remove it from the other pigs immediately both so you can treat it, and so it will not have a chance to keep infecting the other pigs. Whatever you use, remember that it is vital to clean the area with a good detergent before you try to disinfect it. It will do no good to disinfect an area that still has debris or fecal matter in the floor. If you are cleaning an open area, you may wish to consider using a pressure washer, especially if you have been handling pigs with viruses.

Vaccination

Vaccinations can be a good way to protect your pigs against diseases, but it is not recommended that you try to vaccinate your pigs against every possible swine disease. There are too many diseases and vaccines and most of the diseases will never occur where you live. It is not sensible to stress your pig's immune system with unnecessary vaccines. It is not cost-effective to vaccinate your pigs against diseases that do not exist where you live, either.

Hygiene

Good hygiene is one of the most important ways you can promote good health for your pigs. In addition to taking care of your pens and keeping your farm clean, it is important for you to consider how other people and farms affect your pigs.

Before you purchase a new pig, the seller should provide you with a certificate of health signed by a veterinarian. You even may wish to have your own veterinarian examine the pigs. This is recommended if you are purchasing purebred pigs or breeding stock. It is worth spending the extra money in these cases to make sure the pigs are healthy and fit for breeding. These extra steps can prevent you from bringing pigs to your farm that may spread disease.

No matter where you obtain a new pig, remember to isolate the pig or pigs for a short time when you bring them home. Pigs do not like to be alone, so it is best if you buy more than one pig at a time. However, it is better if you buy from only one source. When people come to visit, have them put plastic booties over their shoes. Alternatively, they could step in a pan of bleach to kill germs on their shoes. Or you could discourage visitors to your farm, especially if you have a young litter of piglets. You may want to take this route if you have a litter less than 2 weeks old, which is when piglets are vulnerable. Tell people they can see the piglets when they are a little older.

When to call in the vet

If you are just starting out raising pigs, it is a good idea to try to find a large animal veterinarian before you purchase animals. To find a large animal veterinarian in your area, you can look in your yellow pages, check online, or ask other farmers to recommend one to you. You can check the website for the American Veterinary Medical Association (**www.**

avma.org/statevma) for veterinarians in your area, but not all veterinarians belong to that organization. Find one, talk to him or her, and invite him or her to visit your farm.

Once you bring your pigs home, you probably will need to have your veterinarian come out to perform a few vaccinations, whether they are grower pigs or pigs that you are preparing for breeding. Most veterinarians like to visit a herd when it is healthy, so they can size it up. This gives them something to use as a baseline in case they need to visit when some of your animals are sick. They also can talk to you about preventive care and get to know you better. Having a good relationship with your veterinarian is important for both you and your vet.

If you have a sick animal, it is important that you do not wait too long to call the vet. Although there is no need to call the vet every time your pig sneezes, it is important for you to know your animals well enough to know when something is wrong. If your pig has a fever or diarrhea, it is probably a good idea for you to call the vet, especially when you are not experienced at raising pigs. If the vet says there is nothing to be worried about, you will feel better. And if it is a serious illness, the vet will know how to treat it. As you become more experienced in raising pigs, you may be able to distinguish a serious swine disease from one that is not so serious, but when you are just beginning, it is best to err on the side of caution instead of risking your herd.

Breeding Pigs

Everyone loves a happy ending, but placing a gilt and boar together is no guarantee that they will produce piglets. Environment, health, stress, and diet play as big a role in successful breeding as having a viable couple. Whether you plan to breed right away or over time, it is important to understand how the reproductive system works in order to maximize the chance of healthy piglets.

Purchasing a pregnant sow is an alternative way of starting a herd if you want to avoid the time and headache of matching a gilt and boar. This process works, but it is impossible to estimate an outcome for the litter.

Taking care of the litter begins long before a pregnancy starts. A healthy diet, stress-free atmosphere, and proper care of the sow before, during, and after pregnancy are the keys to continued healthy pig production. The better the effort you put into the overall breeding program, the better your results will be.

CASE STUDY:
KEEPING THE GIRLS HAPPY

Noni Mammatt
Australia

CLASSIFIED CASE STUDIES
directly from the experts

Noni Mammatt has been raising pigs in Australia for 16 years. She began with a sow that farrowed a month later and presented her with 15 piglets. Through many twists and turns over the years, Mammatt has come to have a current operation of 130 sows. She has had as many as 400 sows and says that she will probably have about 500 sows again soon, along with a large number of grower pigs. Mammatt's focus is selling mated or bred gilts.

Mammatt says she raises pigs for several reasons. "I like the animal immensely and the habits and their curiosity aspect. If other people like pigs the way I do, then yes, they should grow them. They are not like sheep and cattle. They come for a look instead of running away."

Mammatt suggests that others can get started raising pigs the same way she has done. "Do as I have done and get one that is mated and a few smaller gilts and a small boar and give it a go. A little reading might be a good idea beforehand. Borrow books from the library and from older members of the pig industry. You also get some verbal experience from these people on how to feed and what to add when making up your own feeds and how to keep them warm and dry and lean for market."

Mammatt prefers to keep her pigs outdoors. "I run my pigs all outdoors... I have done this for 16 years. I have them in paddocks, and they are given grain. They also have access to pasture when the paddock is locked up for the season and this is free feed so to speak. The pasture is only around knee high, so there is plenty of protein in the feed, which will last a good amount — for 25 to 30 sows around five to six weeks of feed.

"I like the idea of outdoor production as it is a healthy way to produce pigs. It is also a cheaper option than building an indoor unit."

Mammatt says she raises several breeds, along with one of her own creation. " I raise large whites, Hampshire, Berkshires, Landrace, Duroc, and red saddles, which are a little different from the norm. These are a breed of my own, which I have slowly developed, and I am now getting pure litters coming through. They are quiet, produce plenty of milk, have good numbers, do not seem to lose too much condition while they carry their young, and make great mothers as well as fosters. Are good to handle, also."

She says she feeds wheat, barley, and lupins to her sows via a selection of diets formulated by a nutritionist. "I then only have to follow what is given to me and add the grain that is on the diet. I have experimented a little with feeds as well. I give hay for bedding, and the sows consume some of this as well. The growers also eat hay, and this helps them digest the grain feed."

As for tips on raising pigs, Mammatt said, "The old timers who used to grow pigs back when I was not around would feed their pigs beer if they saw a sow with problems during labor. This quieted the old girl down."

Mammatt offers these last words about how she raises her pigs: "Being small producers, we probably do things a little differently than our indoor counterparts. I grow with huts to keep them dry and shaded and ring lock and barb and a hot wire to keep my girls in their paddocks. I use sprinkler systems around the piggery for their wallows. I use nipple drinkers for them to drink out of, and for the growers I use both a trough and a nipple drinker. I feed the girls on the ground, and I feed my growers in self-feeders. I have a lane way to move pigs around in. I weigh my pigs in a shed to keep the water out of the scales and the hot sun from beating down on the pigs and me. I have a chappy who brings his truck to my place to load pigs and take them to market."

Choosing Your Breeders

Once you have decided what your breeding goals for the future are, you will be able to choose your pigs for breeding better. If you are just starting out, and you are not yet familiar with the other pig farmers in your area, talk to your veterinarian, your feed store owner, and your county extension services agent about good local pig breeders. If you plan to purchase purebred pigs, check with your breed association for help in locating the nearest breeders. You also can visit breeder auctions and sale barns to find gilts and boars for sale.

When you start to look for your breeding stock, there are some important things to keep in mind:

- Start planning well in advance. If you have gilts or sows ready to breed, do not wait until the last minute to look for a boar for them. You will have a better selection of breeding partners if you begin searching early.

- Study pig genetics and pedigrees. Pedigrees are particularly important if you will be raising purebred hogs.

- No pig is perfect, not even yours. There is always room for improvement in each generation. Try to choose a boar for your gilt or sow with the goal of improving some things about her.

- When you visit another farmer's farm to look at gilts or sows for sale or to look over a boar for breeding, ask if you can see as many relatives as possible. It is always a good idea to see parents, offspring, siblings, and other closely related animals. You are not just buying a sow or gilt, you are buying their genetic contribution to your own herd.

- When you visit another farm with the purpose of looking at breeding stock, make sure you ask plenty of questions. Ask how the pigs are being raised, what they eat, if they have had any diseases, how they have been wormed, if they were bred naturally or by artificial insemination (AI), and anything else you think is pertinent.

- You will want to keep your eyes open and observe the farm. Is it well kept? Do the pigs seem happy? Mud and manure are normal parts of hog raising, but you will want to make sure any pig you buy for breeding comes from a farm that is not prone to disease. You will want to make sure the pigs you buy have not been stressed unduly because this could affect their fertility.

- Finally, try to obtain breeding stock that comes from a farm similar to yours. It is easier for pigs to adapt to a new place if they will be going to a farm that is operated using the same methods.

Your eyes should be able to tell you if the gilts or sows are in good flesh. As with young pigs, gilts and sows for breeding should have bright eyes and be lively, with no signs of illness. You should select the largest, most well-developed gilts available. If you are breeding purebred pigs, you will need to know more about the correct conformation for your breed but, in general, a good gilt will have a good body capacity — in other words, she will be long and wide in the middle. This will give her plenty of room to carry a large litter of piglets. She should have at least six pairs of evenly spaced mammary glands. She should have a somewhat level topline or spine along the top of her back, which will contribute to staying physically sound. Her hooves should be big and well formed. Ideally, your gilt or sow will have large hams as well.

The trend today is toward longer, leaner pigs instead of the cobby or rounded pigs often seen in the past. Pork today is about 30 percent leaner than it was in the 1950s due to selection for leaner pigs and different body types. It compares favorably with chicken and beef in terms of calories and fat.

The female reproductive system

The female pig reproductive system consists of a right and left ovary, one cervix, uterus, oviduct, vagina, and vulva. The internal sexual reproductive organs are located beneath the rectum in the abdomen. They are supported internally by a strong connective tissue that thickens during pregnancy.

The ovaries are at the center of pig reproduction. They provide the hormones and eggs, making reproduction possible. The pituitary gland in the brain stimulates the follicle stimulating hormone (FSH) and luteinizing hormone (LH) into action. These hormones are responsible for stimulating reproduction in the female pig.

The follicles, the hair-like structures that cover the surface of the ovaries, are stimulated to produce an egg with these hormones. Although there are thousands of follicles, a normal female will only produce ten to 20 eggs at one time. The eggs are released at estrus, which is the time that the female is receptive to the boar. Test this by pushing down firmly on the backside of the female. If she "stands" in a breeding position, then she is in true estrus.

Fertilization of the eggs happens in the tube that connects the uterus and ovaries. This tube is called the oviduct. It carries the sperm in one direction and the eggs the other way. They meet at the halfway point, called the ampulla. It is better to have sperm waiting for the eggs because the egg can only be fertilized within 12 hours of its release. The sperm needs to be introduced by natural or artificial means to the female once it is determined that she is in estrus.

Before breeding, make sure that your gilt or sow is current on vaccinations that are usually given in your area. It is best to consult with your veterinarian or county extension services agent to find out which vaccinations are recommended where you live. There is no need to stress a gilt or sow by giving her unnecessary vaccinations. At the same time, it is important to provide her as much immunity as possible to the diseases in your area so she can pass that immunity along to her newborns.

The male reproductive system

The boar's reproductive system is composed of the penis, the two testicles, the scrotum that covers the testicles, the urethra, and the vas deferens. Although the penis and the scrotum are the most visible parts of the male reproductive system, the vas deferens and the urethra, which are unseen, are important in moving sperm from the testes to the penis and delivering the sperm during reproduction.

The **vas deferens** is a muscular tube that lies above and behind the testes, close to the urethra. During mating, the vas deferens helps propel the sperm in the testicles up into the urethra. From the urethra, the sperm can be ejaculated out of the penis and into the sow's vagina. The testicles rest inside the scrotum or scrotal sac. The sac is a thin, muscular skin that is flexible. It has fibroelastic tissue inside. The sac keeps the testicles at a steady temperature to aid in sperm production and to provide protection for the sensitive testicles.

Male sperm production is a continuing process. As groups of sperm cells leave the testicles, new sperm cells are produced to take their place. They are stored in the scrotum to mature for up to seven weeks. A constant replacement process ensures a healthy male always has available sperm. Stress from a difficult living environment, poor diet, excessive heat, and illness will greatly reduce the sperm count in a male. Rectifying these situations in a short amount of time will help the male recover sperm count quickly. Long-term stress permanently reduces sperm counts.

The benefit of the male reproductive system is it is visible to the eye. Problems such as abnormal swellings, damaged penis, and size variance in testes are obvious. This makes shopping for a boar that much easier.

Building Your Herd

Building a herd is easily achieved through a variety of methods. You do not necessarily have to purchase a gilt and a boar and start a herd from scratch. Thoroughly researching the local market should turn up pig farmers who are willing to sell pregnant sows. The drawback to this method is in not knowing if the genetics are as stated. There is also a question of diet and stress levels on the pregnant sow. A veterinary check can suggest whether the sow is healthy overall, but it still can leave questions as to the long-term care she has received both before and after being impregnated. Ask for references when embarking on this type of herd building.

It is best to buy more than one sow from the same farmer when possible. Buying several sows from different farms will subject the sows and piglets to germs that they are not used to. Pregnancy and birth are not great times to take the chance of introducing illness to your herd. Do not transition the pregnant sow to a new type of food. Make sure you have the same type of food on hand that she is currently eating. Dietary stress will show in weight loss, poor milk production, and the possibility of miscarriage.

Avoid purchasing gilts that are first-time moms. The stress of a first pregnancy compounded by a change in residence might cause the female to become aggressive to the piglets when they are born. The survival rate for these piglets is slim without intervention. This adds to the variable mortality rate that already exists for first-time litters.

Traditional breeding is sometimes dangerous for the gilt. Overly aggressive boars can kill a young female. Mixing a little traditional breeding along with purchasing already pregnant sows will give you a chance to develop good pairs without compromising initial herd growth.

Feeding for Breeding

A good diet is a major factor in maintaining the health of your breeding hogs. Optimum breeding performance only can happen if the hogs are healthy and happy. Developing good feeding habits that your pigs can depend on will produce good results.

The healthy function of the pig's reproductive system depends on good genetics and good food. Though there is limited control over genetics, you are in the driver's seat when it comes to food. Read the ingredients of any food before feeding it to your herd. Feeds that contain nearly all fat-building ingredients are not the best to offer. There needs to be a balance of protein building blocks to promote healthy gestation.

The more litters produced annually, the higher the toll on the health of the sow. Feeding for pig breeding involves much more than daily sustenance. It is just as important to consider replenishing nutrients that are drained in producing each litter of pigs.

Gestation

The average length of gestation for sows is 114 days. During this time, the sow should be fed 4 to 6 pounds of quality mixed food per day. Weight gain is necessary at this time to prepare for feeding the piglets. Avoid commercial foods that add antimicrobials, as they are passed on to the piglets through the milk. A better solution to illness prevention is to feed the sow a healthy mixture of mixed grains, alfalfa, red clover hay, and table scraps. The added minerals and vitamins will build the immune system and create nutrient-rich milk for the piglets.

Roughly 50 percent of the diet should consist of mixed grain. Too much alfalfa or table scraps will cause loose stools. This can lead to dehydration issues and affect the milk production. Field grazing is encouraged as long as it is not close to her due date. Maintain the 7 pounds per day of food along with the grazing. The energy expended will cancel out the calories taken in.

Dietary modifications

Modifications or manipulations of the diet are made frequently in an effort to boost the number of pigs per litter. Temporary reduction in food intake four to six weeks before mating can raise the piglet number by one or two per litter. This is a remarkable number over the entire breeding career of a sow.

The normal feeding routine calls for 6 pounds of feed per day. The food intake should be brought to 7 pounds per day once pregnancy is achieved with an added pound per piglet once she is nursing. Dietary restrictions during gestation will cause harm to the litter and the sow. An increased diet after pregnancy will ensure plenty of rich milk for the new-borns to drink. The diet can return to the normal 6 pounds per day once the piglets have been weaned, provided the sow is in good shape. Make sure she is fit before breeding again.

Keeping the sow happy

A happy sow is a healthy and well-adjusted sow. Pigs enjoy clean and comfortable surroundings. Good food and a clean water source are musts when attempting to breed. All water troughs should be filled with clean water daily. The food should be placed in troughs or self-feeders that are easily accessible. The less she feels she needs to "fight" for her food, the happier she will be.

Using high-quality foods is important. This does not always mean the most expensive. There are actually brands of high quality that do not cost a fortune. Nor does it mean feeding your pigs swill or garbage. It is important for you to learn what is in the food you feed your pigs and to buy nutritious food for a fair price. It is worth the investment to grow a healthy herd. However, you may feed your pigs healthy food scraps from your own kitchen or vegetables from your garden. Your pigs will enjoy them.

Adding bran to the feed in the week leading up to the birth of a litter will help boost the comfort level of the sow. Constipation is not only bothersome, but it can cause fetal distress to the piglets at birth. It is best to avoid those problems altogether. A nutrient-rich diet during pregnancy and suckling keeps the sow healthy. Avoiding large drops in weight during this process reduces stress on her both emotionally and physically. She will be more likely to take her time when feeding piglets if she is not experiencing hunger pains herself.

Farrowing

No matter how many piglet deliveries you experience, there is always excitement in the air when a new litter is on the way. Farrowing, or giving birth, is a natural process that needs to be supervised closely. This is especially true with gilts experiencing a first litter. Problems are not a common occurrence, but when they crop up, they can be serious.

There is much you can do to prepare for a safe birth. Proper quarters and comfort will go a long way in keeping stress to a minimum. Assisting the sow with the piglets as they are born will help her focus energy on finishing the farrowing process. The female should be treated both inside and outside for parasites a week or two before the farrowing begins. Parasites can wreak havoc on the health of newborn piglets. Your veterinarian can provide internal parasite controls that are safe for pregnant pigs. If you are raising your pigs organically or trying to avoid chemicals, you will need to use something along the lines of garlic or rosemary as a wormer, though these herbs may not get rid of all of your sow's worms. If you plan to use a stronger natural wormer, consult with a holistic practitioner to make sure you do not use anything that could harm the piglets. You will need to control external parasites on and around your pigs by keeping their bedding changed, removing manure frequently, and treating for any pests bothering your pigs with either natural or chemical methods.

The human presence is vital in making sure the piglets are breathing and feeding and that the sow does not crush them due to confusion and pain. Mark the expected farrowing date on a calendar, and make plans to be around. It will be a wonderful experience you will not want to miss.

Preparing a farrowing site

Small pig raisers typically create a small pen for the farrowing female. If you plan to use a small pen, thoroughly clean and disinfect the area before use. Steam cleaning and spraying the pen down with a disinfectant spray will suffice. It needs to shine all the way down to the metal or wood. Add a 3- to 4-inch layer of straw bedding to create a comfortable place for the sow to rest while giving birth. Set aside a corner area with a heat lamp to place the pigs as they are born. The goal is to try to maintain a draft-free ambient temperature of 80 degrees. This will be comfortable for both mother and babies.

You need to place the sows in the farrowing pen about a week before the due date. This will give their system time to gain immunity against any unfamiliar germs. She will then pass these immunities on to the piglets. Grab every advantage you can get. Design the pen so you have plenty of light to see what is going on. Emergencies will require quick action on your part. Easy access to the pen is essential.

Signs of labor

Pig breeders are able to make a close estimate as to when piglets are due, but at times, the sow can deliver early or late. Here are some of the signs to look for:

- **Restless movement:** At the onset of labor, the sow becomes restless. She cannot seem to find a comfortable position. She frequently will alternate between lying down, standing, and pacing the pen.

- **Swollen teats:** The mammary glands will swell as they fill with milk to feed the piglets.

- **Nest-building behaviors:** It will seem as if she is trying to prepare the area for the piglets. This involves moving the straw, scratching at the floor, and circling.

- **Vaginal discharge:** There will be a slight amount of vaginal discharge during hard labor. If it has a strong, putrid odor, contact your veterinarian.

- **Slightly elevated temperature:** Use of a rectal thermometer will confirm if the temperature has gone up. A slight fever is normal during delivery. The normal temperature for a pig is 101.5 to 102.5 F.

- **Circling and sniffing:** Increased amounts of circling in the pen and sniffing at her backside are strong indicators that birth is imminent.

Remove and wipe down the piglets as she delivers them. Place them near the teat once she has settled down to avoid injuring the piglet. Check the temperature after farrowing. If the temperature remains elevated to 104 degrees or higher, you will need to contact the veterinarian.

Signs of trouble in labor

The normal time for delivery of piglets is one every 20 minutes. Gilts take slightly longer because they are less experienced with giving birth. Prolonged labor tires the female. All of the following problems will require some type of intervention:

1. Three or four hours of labor with no results when it has become obvious the sow is experiencing a great deal of pain or pushing. This most likely indicates there is a piglet in breech position or a dead piglet blocking the birth canal.

2. Foul-smelling or bloody vaginal discharge

3. A partially visible baby that is blue in appearance and has not exited after some time

If this is your first experience with a farrowing emergency, it is best to call the veterinarian for assistance. Self-intervention can be attempted, but you must make sure to give the sow a shot of antibiotic afterward. No matter how clean your hands and arms are, the chance of infection remains high.

•   Clean the vulva with antibacterial solution to avoid introducing germs to the birth canal.

•   Clip and clean your fingernails before assisting with the births.

•   Scrub your hands and arms with antimicrobial solution. Clean them up to the elbows.

•   Lubricate the hand and arm you will be using. Dish soap will work if nothing else is available.

•   Bring all of the fingers and thumb together to a point and insert into the vulva. Enter slowly as the sow will be in fair amount of pain. Reach all the way to the area of obstruction.

•   Grab the piglet by the head, if possible. Pull it carefully toward you. Work with the muscle contractions to avoid hurting the sow more than necessary.

•   If the piglet is in breech position, firmly grab the back legs and slowly pull the piglet out.

Post-farrowing matters

The first 12 to 24 hours after farrowing are the most critical for the sow and for the newborns. Infection and stress-related problems will make themselves apparent within this time. Monitoring the progress of the piglets and the mother several times a day is important. The earlier problems are detected, the easier they are to fix.

The sow's diet will need to be increased slowly to avoid digestive problems. The sow's appetite gradually will pick up as she continues to nurse. The larger the litter, the more food she will need. One of the important goals of post-farrowing care is retaining the health and vigor of the female to make rebreeding possible.

Caring for the sow

The sow will be relieved once farrowing is over, but you will still need to monitor her for stress, unhappiness, and signs of illness or fatigue. With a healthy delivery, she should be up and about within an hour or two. She should be made to get up and move if she seems unwilling. Listlessness and disinterest in the feeding activities of the piglets are red flags that something is wrong. Monitor for any temperature spikes, which could indicate infection. The earlier she is started on antibiotics, the more positive the outcome. Check often that her teats are releasing milk.

The sow will need to be checked often for signs of mastitis-metritis-agalactia (MMA) syndrome, which is serious and needs to be dealt with immediately. Mastitis is hardened and painful teats and can be so bad that the sow refuses to feed the babies. Metritis is an infection of the uterus. Antibiotics will be needed to clear this up before she succumbs to toxins in the blood. Agalactia is a lack of milk. A shot of oxytocin will help stimulate the milk production. Do not attempt more than two injections of 1 or 2 cubic centimeters in a day.

If the sow initially shows aggression toward the piglets, pull them out of her pen, and keep them in a warm area. Slowly reintroduce the piglets to her after she has calmed down. Her stress level and hysteria will decrease in an hour or two, and the piglets will still be able to receive the all-important colostrum feeding up to 24 hours after the birth. Consider fostering the pigs with another sow and hand-feeding colostrum if she seems unable to accept the litter. Most sows are good mothers and instinctively know what to do when their piglets are born. Any confusion or rejection is usually short term.

Some pig raisers recommend keeping the farrowing site calm and quiet before farrowing in order to soothe the sow. You may wish to play soothing music during the farrowing. Talk calmly to the sow. It also will help keep the sow calm if the person present has a good relationship with her. All of these suggestions can help sows be more relaxed during farrowing, which, in turn, makes them more accepting of their piglets. These suggestions can be particularly helpful with gilts when they are first-time mothers.

Feeding a nursing sow

Nursing sows need to increase their food intake to compensate for the nutrients lost when feeding their young. You can provide the sow with a light meal soon after farrowing. Providing the sow with 3 to 4 pounds of feed plus a can of pumpkin to induce regularity is a good idea after farrowing. You also can include any of her personal favorites, such as

vegetable scraps, to get her to eat. Then, gradually build up her diet again to her pre-farrowing meal intake — 7 pounds — plus 1 pound for each piglet she is nursing. This needs to be cut to ½ pound per piglet if it is a litter with fewer than ten piglets. Adding bran to the diet post-farrowing is a common practice to avoid strain in the groin area from constipation. Constipation can be a serious problem at this stage and might make the sow stop eating or feel otherwise ill.

The food may have to be offered three times a day for her to have the time and appetite to eat it. It also depends on the appetite of the individual female. You will have to experiment. If it is hot, the sow might eat better in the early mornings or late evenings.

Fresh water should be available to the nursing sow at all times of the day and night. Producing milk requires plenty of water. The water will help prevent the sow from becoming constipated. The ultimate goal is to maintain the sow in good condition so that she can rebreed quickly after weaning.

Characteristics of Newborns

Playful and curious tend to be the overwhelmingly common descriptions regarding young pigs. Though they start small, about 3 pounds and 8 inches long, their growth rate is phenomenal. To kick the growth spurt into full drive, it requires plenty of eating and sleeping.

The piglets' first feedings from their mother are important. These initial feedings pump in the necessary ingredients for a strong immune system, passed through the colostrum from the sow. Of course, the most natural way for young pigs to receive colostrum and the antibodies it contains is by nursing from their mother. Continued regular nursing produces a healthy pig of acceptable weight and size.

Runts of the litter are pigs that have been deprived of feedings at some level. This translates into a pig that may be more prone to illness and will never regain the growth opportunity lost. Healthy pigs are more than willing and able to nurse from the moment of birth.

The tiny stature of newborn pigs leaves them prone to injury. The most common infant fatalities are from accidental crushing by the sow. Rolling over on the newborn pigs will cause significant problems and possibly death. Maintaining an area a few feet away, complete with a heat lamp, will prevent most injuries of this type. Pig rails and **creeps**, or areas set aside by rails or bars where the sow cannot follow the piglets, are a common feature of many farrowing spaces in order to allow the newborns to roll away from their dam and avoid being crushed.

Sleeping is a necessary and favored activity of newborns. The body is using so much energy to grow that there is precious little left for other activity. After three weeks, they will begin exploring their environment. Pigs that isolate themselves and sleep more than the rest of the litter might be experiencing health problems.

Special needs of piglets

Do not be afraid to jump in the pen with them once they have weaned. The more you familiarize yourself with healthy young pigs, the more you will develop a keen eye to spot problems early on. They will squeal with delight to interact with you.

On a serious note, things can take a turn for the worse quickly with piglets. You must be diligent about watching for signs and symptoms of serious diseases and illnesses. Early and aggressive treatment could well be the thing that saves their lives. The following are things that need to be highly monitored or given special consideration when raising young pigs. There are warning signs when newborn pigs are in trouble, but there is often little time to act on these. Spending quality time with the litter will help you clue in on changes and problems before they reach a critical point.

Colostrum

The intake of colostrum is possibly the most vital way to ensure a pig's survival, second only to taking in that all-important first breath. Colostrum is the sow's first milk, produced 12 to 24 hours after giving birth. The inability of the pig to drink in this nutrient- and antibody-rich substance could spell disaster. Pigs known to not intake colostrum show rapidly declining health. Survivors are plagued by low lifetime weight and height gains. Lack of immunity to the most basic of germs and disease means the pig is susceptible to illness.

Extra colostrum can be collected and stored in frozen form. Storing it as cubes tends to be the easiest, most convenient fashion. It must be thawed before use. Boiling or microwaving colostrum will destroy the nutrients and antibodies, thus rendering it useless. If you are heating colostrum, warm it up to body temperature for the young piglets (101.5-102.5 degrees F).

You can gather or purchase alternative forms of colostrum. The best substitutes seem to be from cows and goats. The colostrum these animals produce is not quite as nutrient rich, but it will do when no other source is available. It is also possible to purchase colostrum mix from feed stores in an emergency.

Temperature

Newborns of any species enter the world with a total dependence on care. The provision of food, shelter, and a clean environment falls on the sow, as well as the pig owner. One often-overlooked ingredient for raising healthy pigs is temperature.

Temperature stress is remarkably easy to spot in young pigs but too often ignored. Piglets must be maintained in a dry, clean, comfortable environment in order to thrive. Newborns that are too hot or too cold are equally harmed. Of course, sows may be bred at any time when they come in season and have a gestation period of 114 days, which means that litters may arrive year-round. It is normal to rebreed three or four days following weaning when the sow comes in season again. This is considered an optimum time for breeding. Sows usually have two to three litters of piglets per year.

Cold pigs will pile on top of one another. A certain amount of piling is normal, but a constant bid to seek the warmth of others is a signal that the air temperature is probably too chilly. Overheated pigs will separate out from one another. This is highly unusual behavior with newborn pigs and is a red flag that there is a temperature problem. Panting and deep breathing are both indicators that they are too hot. Pigs that suffer heat stroke have a nearly 100 percent mortality rate. Touch the pigs when unsure of their comfort level. Dry, hot skin means the temperature needs to be brought down. Cold, clammy skin means the pigs are too cold and might be suffering from exposure.

Dehydration

Piglets need to suckle up to 16 times per day, so a few missed meals will quickly trigger dehydration. This leads to serious weight loss and death in the most serious cases. Providing methods of rehydration, antibiotic regimens, and temperature stabilization will save some pigs. Looking for early signs of illness can make all the difference. Dry skin, sunken eyes, watery-looking stool, and lethargic demeanor are warning signs that the pig is in trouble.

Breathing

Pigs that are struggling to breathe are involved in a life or death situation. As a pig owner, you must be proactive in ensuring you are doing all you can to resolve the issue. This book will cover the two more serious causes, but consult your veterinarian in any instance of serious medical emergency.

Long, intense labor will stress a newborn. The extent is unclear until the birthing process is complete. If the pig is not breathing, open the mouth and clear out any mucus that might be clogging the airway using your fingers. Remove any remaining sack membrane covering the baby pig, and gently pull them up by the back legs. Swing them slowly between your legs in a pendulum motion. This will drain any remaining mucous and fluid. Clear the nose and throat once again to allow air passage. Closely monitor any pigs that have a hard time breathing initially, as they are susceptible to pneumonia. Keeping them warm and dry will assist in their full recovery.

Anemia

Anemia is another condition that may affect a piglet's ability to breathe. A main ingredient of red blood cells is a protein called hemoglobin. It is charged with the duty of carrying oxygen-rich blood to the cells and bringing carbon dioxide back to the lungs to be expelled. Iron is a critical part of the composition of hemoglobin. A dietary and environmental lack of iron causes serious and potentially fatal problems.

Anemia due to acute iron deficiency is capable of causing fatal breathing difficulties in young pigs. Baby pigs grow at an astounding rate. The faster a piglet with anemia grows, the more at-risk it becomes. Labored breathing or diaphragm spasms called thumps are indicative of serious anemia in pigs.

A natural fix would seem to be to add iron to the diet of the sow. Unfortunately, this does not work. Iron deficiencies have to be resolved within the individual pigs. This is not a hard task with small farms, but it could be a real problem in larger sow operations. It will make your choice of housing and containment that much more important.

Orally administering iron can be effective, but this is time-consuming and hit-or-miss. Common methods include applying an iron paste to the sow's udders, weekly doses of iron pills, or soil added to the creep floor, though soil should be completely free of any swine parasites and eggs.

Iron injections offer more than enough protection against anemia if given in the proper form and manner. Iron-dextran or iron-dextrin complex is the best form on the market to date to treat iron deficiency anemia. The recommended dosage is one injection of 100 milligrams for pigs weaning at 3 weeks and 150 milligrams for those being weaned after 3 weeks. The shots should be given intramuscularly (in the muscle) in the ham (rear) or neck muscle. Clean the injection site well with an alcohol swab before giving the shot to avoid infection.

Health-Related Procedures

Several procedures can be done while pigs are small. These procedures should be done when the pigs are young because the younger the animal is, the less pain the pig feels during the procedure.

It cannot be stressed enough that processes such as these only should be performed by a qualified person. Use sterile equipment in good working order. Always remove the pigs from the immediate vicinity of the sow to avoid stressing her. Instinct will make her protective of her offspring.

There is no way to completely avoid stressing the pig when completing any of the procedures, but initiating them within the first 12 to 24 hours of life works best. Doing as many as possible in one session will help reduce the overall stress. Whether it is due to an immature nervous system or other factors, younger piglets seem less reactive to pain. This does not mean they do not feel pain; it means they react less to it and recuperate faster.

Many surgical procedures performed on older pigs, no matter how slight, are met with great resistance. The larger the pig, the harder they are to control. It can turn a one- or two-person activity into a multi-person challenge. It is much easier to perform these common procedures on young pigs when they are small, easy to control, and they can quickly recover.

Castration

Castration takes away the ability to produce sperm, so male pigs that are raised for breeding are naturally bypassed for this procedure. **Barrows**, or males raised for meat and show purposes, must be castrated in order to remove **boar taint**, or the foul taste of testosterone from the meat. Castrating young male pigs makes it much easier to raise them in a group until they are old enough to go to market.

Castration should always be done while the male pig is young to ensure minimal hormone output into the system. Too much hormone released into the pig's body affects both the taste and smell of the meat. It provides a pungent odor that is not well tolerated on the market. The prices for non-castrated males versus castrated are noticeably less at sale date. Older boars are sent to market later in life, but they bring much lower prices per pound.

Even though it is considered a straightforward procedure, castration never should be attempted for the first time without the presence and assistance of a veterinarian or qualified professional. Incorrect castration will cause damage and unnecessary pain to the pig. Watching the process a few times beforehand is helpful.

- Lay the young male pig down on its side on a small hay bale.

- Have someone secure the back legs to keep them from moving.

- Make a small incision over each testicle, cutting through the scrotum. Use a sterile scalpel or castration knife for this.

- Pull each testicle free of the incision along with some of the cord. The thin cord will be visible inside the incision.

- Cut the testicle loose or pull until the cord breaks.

- Spray on a generous layer of antiseptic solution. No bandage is necessary.

Keep a close eye on the site of the castration for several days. Check for swelling, fever, discharge, or any other sign that it may not be healing properly. Keep pigs in a clean, dry stall to promote healing.

Developing hernias after castration is not uncommon, but a veterinarian should be consulted if this occurs. The problem is much too serious to self-treat. Tissue protruding through the incision or bulges is a sign that the area has herniated. The tissue will have to be pushed back into place and the incisions stitched shut.

Tail docking

Docking the tail on pigs most often ends up being a procedure based on personal farmer preference. Animal rights groups tend to vilify the process as being inhumane and unnecessary and the cause of undue stress and pain. The tail does contain bone, but in young pigs, it is a soft, gristle-like, or cartilage-fibrous consistency.

Bleeding when docking pig tails is minimal and often absent altogether. The market tends to be fickle regarding the value and desire of tail docking. Feeder pigs without docked tails may not sell at market.

Pigs that have to be fed in close confines are subject to having their tails bitten. This leads to infection or worst-case scenarios of cannibalism and death. The pig with the full tail is viewed as a liability in this case, and many farmers will pass them up without hesitation.

A whole other segment of farmer values the aesthetic over practical. Smaller farms have fewer problems with overcrowding in feeding areas, and the preference is to have the tail intact. Checking into the whims of your local market will help guide you in making the best decision for your business.

Ear notching

Notches cut into the pig's ears are used as a means of identifying the litter and the number of said litter. When done during the first few hours after birth, the procedure seems to go virtually unnoticed by the pigs. A sharp, sterile cutting instrument should be used. Follow up using an antiseptic spray to prevent infection.

Check with your state on requirements for ear notching. Some states require this procedure for disease control and monitoring. Most pig breed registries also require ear notch identification before issuing pedigree certifications.

Navel care

The navel should be treated with an iodine solution after the birth of each piglet. Bear in mind that the navel will be in contact with the flooring and other pigs on a frequent basis. It presents an open door to infection.

Check often for inflammation or fever around the navel. The area should heal in approximately one week. Contact a veterinarian if problems arise. Infections can overtake young pigs quickly and cause death.

Wolf teeth

It will be important to don your dentistry cap and clip the eight wolf, or needle, teeth on each pig. Pigs are born with their teeth in place; these teeth are as sharp as needles and cause pain to the sow when the newborns are nursing. It may become so uncomfortable for her that she shoves the pigs away. These teeth can cause damage to littermates in the fight to suckle.

There are two on the left front and two on the right front, both top and bottom. Use a sharp pair of clippers to trim these down to the gum line. Have an extra person hold the pig and help keep the mouth open. You will need a good visual on these teeth as they are clipped. Be sure to avoid nicking the gums because the pigs will have a hard time eating with a sore mouth.

Weaning

Weaning pigs on a small farm can be done successfully by 8 weeks of age. You will start noticing the pigs beginning to munch on some of the sow's food by roughly 6 weeks of age. Once they begin to develop a taste for solid food, you can begin setting aside an area for weaning. To reduce stress on both pigs and the sow, pick an area where neither will be able to see, hear, or smell one another.

The initial weaning holding area should be relatively small. Something in the neighborhood of 4 feet by 6 feet is adequate space for an average size litter of ten pigs. A smaller area will be more comfortable for the pigs when first being pulled away from the sow. They will pile together seeking comfort. Ensure the holding area is secure. The pigs will spend much of their free time looking for a way to get out and find the sow. Remember that fencing materials have to be designed to contain animals as small as shoats. Standard pig containment materials will have gaps wide enough for them to crawl through.

Use shallow containers of food and water when first introducing them to their new diet. They will need to be filled frequently, but pigs will not have any problems accessing the food. Add flavored gelatin to the water to encourage them to drink regularly.

Monitor the shoats closely to see that they are all eating and drinking enough. Expect a slight drop, or at least a stabilization of their weight, during the transition to the new diet. Tie any feeders open until they learn where the food is located and how the feeder operates.

Health and safety issues

Weaning healthy pigs safely should be the priority of every pig farmer. Monitoring weight, observing behavior changes, and noticing food or water intake changes may be the only clues you have of existing problems. Keeping food and water available will not be enough to transition pigs to a new way of eating. There are numerous ways to add flavoring to both food and water. Try anything that will safely work. Be persistent because malnutrition, even over short periods, affects the overall health of the pig.

Breed Registry Agencies

When purchasing or raising a litter of purebred piglets, you will want to register them with the agency handling that particular breed within 90 days of their birth. The litter certificate will need to be filled out and sent in. Include copies of the registration for the parents.

Ear notching is the method used to identify the individual piglets. If they have not had the procedure done, you should request that the breeder have it done before you take the piglet home. Lack of ear notching will nullify any paperwork you receive for registration.

Pig registration has to be done by current members of the registry organization. If you are not a current member, you will need to acquire membership or ask the breeder to complete the registration for you. The fee for registering is usually nominal, but make sure that the breeder is able to register the pig before purchase if it is an important issue to you. For example, if you raise Duroc, Hampshire, Landrace, or Yorkshire pigs, you can register them through the National Swine Registry. The cost of registering a litter that is 90 days old and under is $12 if you are an NSR member. For litters that are over 90 days old, the cost is $24 for members. Non-members can register litters, but the costs are double. If you own a boar of one of these breeds, you can have it on file with the registry. Sows and their litters can be tracked with the sow productivity program. These programs allow the organization to follow things such as the number of piglets being produced per sow, the number of piglets being weaned, and the breed's efficiency of production as it depends on number of pigs weaned per sow.

Why is registration important?

Registering purebred swine is the only definitive method that agencies and organizations have to keep track of the pig population. It shows the current trends in pig breeding and rearing by offering true numbers regarding growth of the herd, litter sizes, and breeding successes or failures. A real picture emerges of whether advances in genetic research and development are working. The results can pinpoint problem areas that need to be worked on as an overall breed to ensure their survival.

The swine industry depends on knowledge of where pigs that enter the marketplace originate. Illness and disease can be traced easier by knowing the lineage of the hogs being sold. This helps protect both the market and the consumer. In addition, purebred pigs provide the genetic basis for commercial hybrids, which make up most of the pork production in North America, and for breed improvement. Purebred pigs also have distinct characteristics that could disappear without breeders and registries dedicated to promoting them.

Registering your purebred litter adds value to your herd. Pure bloodlines are worth much more than mixed breeds. It provides paper proof that the pigs are what you represent them to be.

Protection of rare and endangered species

There are breed registry agencies that work for the expansion of breeding rare and endangered species of swine. Many smaller farmers opt to set aside a small area to help keep some of these breeds from falling off the map. Tamworths, Berkshires, and large blacks, not to mention the Gloucester Old Spots and others, all have their fans, with good reason. These rare or heirloom breeds are maintained today mostly by small farmers who are intent on keeping the breeds going and showing the world their virtues.

Aside from assisting with the information needed to start breeding these types of pigs, breed registries are able to maintain detailed databases regarding the successes of current breeders. It is encouraged to maintain a pure line of any rare breed of pig you may decide to raise. Mixing rare types of pigs with more commonly found varieties places them at greater risk of extinction. Every litter of mixed piglets is a missed opportunity for a pure bloodline.

Heirloom breeds of swine have become popular with many chefs and aficionados of the **slow food movement** who appreciate more flavorful food. The slow food movement is an international movement that has grown as an alternative to the fast food such that people eat on the go. People who are interested in "slow food" are interested in many foods that are harder to find and that often take longer to prepare. They often prefer foods with unique flavors. Many of the rare, older pig breeds do not grow as rapidly as commercially raised pigs. They take longer to grow, and their meat is much more flavorful than most modern pork. Pork from these breeds can sell well at farmers markets and through direct marketing by farmers. Niche markets can be one of the keys to success with rare pig breeds.

The National Swine Registry

The American Yorkshire Club, the Hampshire Swine Registry, and the United Duroc Swine Registry joined forces in 1994 to form what is now known as the National Swine Registry. The American Landrace Association fell in with the NSR in 1998. As of this writing, these four breeds that make up the NSR comprise 75 percent of the purebred hog population in the United States. They represent the largest portion of the swine industry. Their genetic work is renowned worldwide.

A large concern for the NSR is in keeping the breeds genetically viable and pure. By consulting with owners regarding proper crossbreeding, they ensure strong, stable bloodlines. They help make and maintain a pool of pedigree swine by registering purebred litters.

Certified Pedigree Swine

Formed in 1997, the Certified Pedigree Swine organization is a combination of the Chester White, Poland China, and spotted swine organizations. Their goal is to maintain a registry of purebred swine to help preserve the purity of these three breeds. Genetic advancements in breeding methods are the consistent goals of the CPS.

Other registry organizations

There are numerous organizations that sponsor registration of various pig breeds. The process of registration is similar, though the fees may vary.

Pigs for Meat

The decision to butcher your pigs may not be easy for you, especially if this is your first time raising pigs. Pigs have personalities, and you may have grown fond of your pigs. However, you can try to remember that your pigs have a purpose, just like other farm animals. One way or another, most people depend on farm animals for their food, although many people today no longer realize where their food comes from. Many people choose to raise pigs for their pork because they like knowing how their food was raised. Making the decision to butcher your pigs is part of the process.

There are no regulations governing home slaughtering. If you decide to butcher your pigs yourself, you are free to kill your pigs and butcher them as you prefer. The meat must be used only for your home consumption, and you cannot sell any of the meat. However, if you intend to sell any of the pork from your pigs, your pigs must be slaughtered and processed by a licensed and inspected processing facility. Who butchers and processes your pigs will depend on how you intend to market and sell your pork. Licensing and rating for butchers ranges from custom, state-inspected, USDA-inspected, to organic. There does not seem to be one central listing for butchers in the U.S. or in each state, but you can search the Internet for butchers in your area or check your local telephone listings.

Butchering laws

- A custom butcher is only licensed to butcher and process animals that will be consumed by the person who owns the animal. The meat cannot be sold to consumers. When the pig is butchered, the meat is packaged and labeled as "Not For Sale." Custom processing facilities are inspected and required to meet sanitary conditions and some of the same labeling and storage requirements of the USDA.

- The rules for state-inspected facilities vary somewhat from state to state but, generally, meat butchered and processed by a state-inspected facility only can be packaged and sold inside that state. About half of the states in the United States have this kind of state inspection system in place. The state inspection system must be "at least equal to" the regulations and guidelines provided by the USDA.

- If you wish to have your pigs butchered and processed at a USDA-inspected facility, then the animals will need to be inspected both before and after butchering by a USDA-certified inspector. USDA inspection does cost more, but you will be able to sell your meat anywhere in the United States. There is a per-animal fee as well as any additional costs from extra package labeling, however the additional marketing opportunities often make USDA inspection worth the cost. Many restaurants and grocery stores prefer to purchase meats that have the USDA seal of approval.

Processing fees, which includes killing your pigs, can cost from around $20 to $60 per animal for large hogs. There is also a processing fee for the dressed weight of the pig. This fee is usually 30 to 45 cents per pound. There may be further fees for more processing, such as curing, boning, or smoking the pork.

There are currently few organic butchering and processing facilities in the United States. Some of them can process both organically raised and nonorganically raised pigs. However, the processing tools and all of the equipment used must be cleaned between processing the organic and nonorganic meats in order to keep the organic meat separate. Prices for processing at organic facilities can be much higher. When pork is processed to meet organic standards, it cannot contain any synthetic artificial ingredients, additives, or preservatives. There is typically minimal processing. The materials used for packaging cannot contain synthetic fungicides or preservatives. And there must be specific labeling that identifies the meat as organic according to USDA labeling requirements. According to the USDA, no claims can be made on the labeling that organic pork is in some way inherently better than pork produced by other, more traditional methods of production. If you are interested in finding an organic processor in your area, the best way to find one (other than talking to other organic growers) is to contact your state agriculture department. They should have a listing of organic processors if there are any in your state. Local Harvest (**www.LocalHarvest.org**) is a good website for more information about finding more organic meat processors.

On-farm processing is an option in a few places in the United States. On-farm processing involves using a mobile processing unit (MPU). These units typically have sprung up in areas where there is a lack of processing facilities. Most

MPUs are state-licensed, although some may be USDA-inspected. MPUs usually only are able to process a few animals, so they are not a good option if you have lots of pigs to butcher. If you have an MPU in your area and you choose to use it, be aware that they often expect the farmer to do much of the work him or herself or to help with the slaughtering, packaging, and cleanup. However, if you do not have a butcher or processing facility located near you, a mobile processing unit may be something to consider if you do not want to slaughter your own pigs.

Butchers

If you are raising just a few pigs of your own for home consumption, then autumn is the traditional time for butchering your pigs. This way you will not have to be concerned about feeding and housing your pigs over the cold winter months. You will have plenty of bacon and other pork in your freezer for the next year, and you can buy a few more weaner pigs in the spring to start the process over again if you like. This is often an economical way to raise pigs and feed your family with a minimum of expense and work.

If you have a choice of butchers, you should arrange to visit them in advance to see their facilities and talk to them. Find out how they are licensed and inspected, as well as what they charge. You will need to make sure they meet the right inspection criteria for the selling method you have in mind. For instance, if you intend to sell your pork products nationally, do not take your pigs to a state-inspected butcher.

Also, ask to purchase some samples so you can see how the butcher prepares the meats. Most butchers have their own recipes using different spices for making sausages and for curing meats. There can be a wide range in the amount of salt or smoke used in curing meats and in the kinds of spices used. You will want to make sure you like the way these pork products taste before you commit to allowing a butcher to process your pigs. Pay special attention to the ham, sausage, and bacon the butcher produces because these products will be most popular with customers. If you do not like their flavor, your customers may not like them either. Anything produced will reflect on you and not the butcher, so make sure you like what the butcher will be doing to the meat.

Some butchers may allow you to be on site while a pig is processed so you can observe the procedure, if you are comfortable being present. If you are present during the entire procedure, you can tell if there is anything you find objectionable or if the butcher's work is acceptable.

The butcher's processing normally will include cutting your pig into standard cuts of meat and curing the hams, sausage, and bacon. If you would like the meat prepared some other way, such in different cuts or leaving some of the meat uncured or "green" so you can cure it yourself at home using your own recipes, you will need to discuss this with the butcher before butchering and processing. Make sure it is fully understood and agreed upon before the butcher begins work on your pigs. You will need to pick up these fresh (uncured) meats as soon as the carcass is chilled and ready to be cut or cured. Remember, however, that you will not be able to sell these home-cured or home-smoked meats. They only can be used for home consumption because they were not completely processed by an inspected butcher.

When discussing arrangements with the butcher, also discuss packaging. Packaging can make a difference to customers, so find out what kind of packaging the butcher normally uses. White butcher paper wrapped around the meat will be fine if you are having the meat processed for home consumption. However, if you plan to market and sell your meat, it is usually best to choose clear, vacuum-wrapped packaging. Cryovac or vacuum-sealed packaging costs more to produce, but it allows the consumer to see the meat, which can make it more appealing to consumers. Being able to see the meat is also helpful when the meat is in the freezer at home.

Getting your Pigs Ready for Slaughter

Once you have chosen a butcher and made an appointment a month or so ahead of time, you will need to get your pigs ready for slaughter. The ideal weight for slaughter is usually considered about 225 pounds. Any weight that your pig adds over 225 pounds is usually deposited in the form of fat. Unless you are trying to raise pigs for their lard, it is usually a waste of feed and money to keep feeding a pig after it weighs 225 pounds.

There is an easy and generally accurate method for determining how much your pig weighs without putting it on a scale. You can measure the **heart girth** of your pig in inches (the distance around the pig just behind its elbows), then measure your pig's length, from between the ears to the base of the tail. Use the following calculation:

Heart girth x heart girth x length, divided by 400 = estimated weight

If your pig is going to weigh a little more than 225 pounds at the time of processing, there is no need to panic. Consumer tastes tend to prefer leaner meats these days, but some excess fat can be trimmed off. If the meat is good, people will appreciate it. Some breeds are known for having more fat as marbling, and the fat adds taste to the meat. The important thing is to know your breed and know what is ideal for it.

If your pigs are being given antibiotics in their feed or other supplements that should not be given to humans, you will need to discontinue feeding them to your pigs during these last several weeks. You should consult the labels on anything you are giving to your pigs and make sure you follow the label directions to discontinue use before slaughtering. There is often a withdrawal period of several weeks between the time an animal stops receiving a medication or supplement and when it is butchered. Be sure you are complying with these safety instructions for human consumption.

As the time for slaughtering and processing approaches, you will need to arrange transportation to the butcher for your pigs. Whether you have one or two pigs or a much larger number, it is important to keep your pigs calm and stress-free before, during, and after transport. Pigs that are stressed and upset before being butchered do not have tasty pork. You do not want to do anything to cause your pigs to release too much adrenaline into their bloodstream from becoming anxious.

If you have the space, you can place the pigs that are headed for slaughter in a separate pen a couple of days before their trip to the butcher. You can wash them down at this time. Most farmers also remove feed from pigs 24 hours before taking their pigs to slaughter. This reduces the chance of contamination from food being digested in the animal's digestive tract. It also makes it easier to remove the internal organs of the pig.

It is recommended that you transport pigs that already know each other together in a livestock trailer. If you attempt to transport your pigs with pigs that they do not know, you will likely have fighting and pigs that are upset. This is the last thing you want. You should also avoid transporting two unfamiliar boars at the same time, as they are likely to fight.

Keep your pigs calm overnight. Once you are ready to leave for the butcher in the morning, your pigs probably will lie down in the trailer once you begin driving. Drive slowly and carefully. Once at the facility, you should move the

{life on the} FARM

a collection of small animal photographs

including animal fun facts

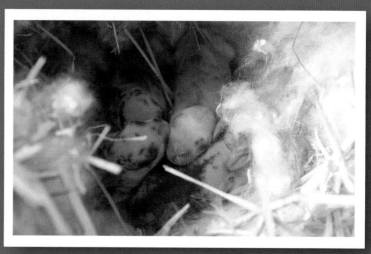

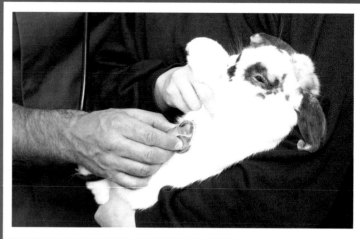

rabbits}

rabbit fun facts:

* The American Rabbit Breeders Association has 45 recognized breeds of rabbits.

* Rabbits need hay for their digestive systems and to prevent fur balls in their stomachs.

* Rabbits have 28 teeth.

duck fun facts:

* Ducks have been domesticated as pets and farm animals for more than 500 years, and all domestic ducks are descended from either the mallard or the Muscovy duck.

ducks & geese}

geese fun facts:

* Geese have a very strong instinct to return to their general area of birth to mate and nest. They either return to the exact site or to a nearby pond or body of water. Some even fly 2,000 to 3,000 miles to return to these sites.

chickens}

chicken fun facts:

* Chicken are pretty fast. The chicken can travel up to 9 miles per hour when it wants.

* There are more chickens on Earth than there are humans.

4

chicken fun facts:

* The chicken is the closest living relative of the Tyrannosaurus Rex.

* The longest recorded distance flown by any chicken is 301.5 feet.

pigs }

pig fun facts:

* Pigs have no sweat glands and, therefore, do not sweat, which means pigs are clean: They do not sweat and become greasy. They only get dirty when they roll in mud to cool themselves off.

pig fun facts:

* A pig's best sense is its smell — its long spout is very sensitive and can smell food a few feet below the Earth's surface.

goats}

goat fun facts:

* The pupil in a goat's eye is rectangular in shape instead of round like other animals'.

* Goats were one of the first animals to be tamed by humans and were first herded nearly 9,000 years ago!

goats fun facts:

* They are extremely curious creatures and will pick up things with their mouths to "investigate" them (such as tin cans, for example), but they hardly ever eat them.

sheep }

sheep fun facts:

* During World War I, Woodrow Wilson's wife grazed sheep on the White House lawn. The wool was sold to raise money for the Red Cross.

* One pound of wool can make 10 miles of spun yarn.

sheep fun facts:

* Most ewes give birth to twins.

* Sheep have poor eyesight but an excellent sense of hearing.

dairy cattle }

dairy cattle fun facts:

* Dairy cows provide 90 percent of the world's milk supply. The best cows give over 25 gallons of milk each day. That's 400 glasses of milk!

* Cows drink about a bathtub full of water and eat around 40 pounds of food a day.

dairy cattle fun facts:

* Cows are milked for an average of three to four years. A cow must have a calf in order to produce milk. Calves are fed milk until they are eight to nine weeks old.

* Cows have 32 teeth.

beef cattle }

beef cattle fun facts:

* Hamburger meat from one beef would equal 720 quarter-pound hamburgers, enough for a family of four to enjoy hamburgers each day for nearly six months.

* More than 100 medicines used by humans come from cattle.

beef cattle fun facts:

* Beef is the number one source of zinc in the human diet in the United States.

* One cowhide can produce enough leather to make 20 footballs, 18 soccer balls, 18 volleyballs, or 12 basketballs.

more farm fun facts:

* Like snowflakes, no two cows have exactly the same pattern of spots.

* Twenty-nine cuts of beef meet government guidelines for lean.

* There are 47 different breeds of sheep in the U.S.

* Contrary to popular belief, goats have sensitive stomachs and are therefore very picky eaters.

pigs slowly, without yelling at them or trying to make them move faster. Keep them calm. At the processing plant, the butcher and his or her helpers will take over.

Cuts

Whether a butcher is processing your pig for you or you are slaughtering your pig yourself, you will need to be knowledgeable about the cuts of meat that can be obtained from your pig: the shoulder, the side, the loin, and the leg. You can obtain the following meats from these cuts:

Shoulder

Shoulder butt, roast, or steak

Blade steak

Boneless blade Boston roast

Smoked arm picnic

Smoked hock

Ground pork for sausage

Side

Spare ribs/back ribs

Bacon

Loin

Boneless whole loin
     (butterfly chop)

Loin roast

Tenderloin

Sirloin roast

Country style ribs

Chops

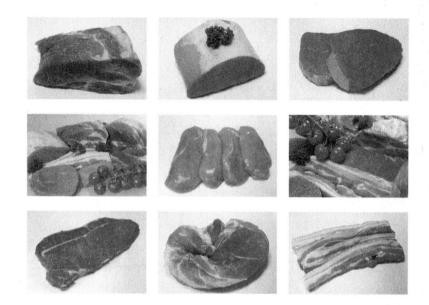

Leg

Ham/fresh, smoked, or cured

*Source United States Department of Agriculture

Other parts of the pig are also used. Pig's ears, brains, kidneys and other organs, as well as pig's feet and the pig's tail, frequently are found on the menus of chic restaurants these days. Chitlins or chitterlings are an old-time Southern favorite. They are pig intestines and can be served either as a stew or fried. Cracklins are fried pork rinds, or pig skin. The fat from your pig can be used as lard. You can use virtually everything from your pig in the kitchen.

A pig that weighs 225 pounds will usually present you with about 75 percent of its body weight as a dressing percentage, or 170 pounds of meat, bones, and fat after slaughter for the carcass or hanging weight. Plan to be able to use about 60 percent of this weight as pork you can eat or sell, or 102 pounds. The biggest part of this usable pork will be the ham, which usually accounts for about 23 percent of the carcass or about 23 pounds in this case. The side and the loin areas will each make up about 15 percent of the carcass, or about 15 pounds each. The picnic and the Boston butt from the shoulder will each account for about 10 percent of the carcass weight, or 10 pounds each; the miscellaneous parts, such as the feet, the jowls, the skin, the fat, and the **shrink**, or the amount of weight loss due to urination and defecation, will account for about 25 percent of the carcass weight, or 25 pounds in this case.

There will be some small variation in the amount of lean pork and fat from your pigs depending on whether they are gilts or barrows. Gilts usually produce more lean pork than carcasses from barrows of the same weight.

After processing

After processing, you will need to pick up your meat from the butcher within a day or two, depending on the butcher's refrigeration storage capacity. Naturally, you will need to make sure you take iced freezer chests with you to transport the pork, particularly the uncured pork such as shoulder, loin cuts, and any miscellaneous parts. You will need to have good freezer storage capabilities at home in order to store the pork, especially if you have pork from several pigs, and you intend to sell some of it.

If you will be selling some of the pork for retail sale, carefully inspect the packaging at the butcher's facility before taking it home to make sure the packaging is what you requested.

Slaughtering at Home

Slaughtering your pigs yourself at home is not for the tenderhearted, but if you wish to control every aspect of raising your pigs and producing your pork, it may be something that you want to do. However, before deciding that you want to slaughter your pigs or engage in home butchering, you should thoroughly consider the task. Killing large animals is no easy task, no matter what method you use. You will need to have the physical strength to hoist and move the heavy, dead weight of your pigs. Once you begin the job, you will need to finish it because the meat will quickly start to spoil if you delay. You will also need to work with a number of sharp knives and other special implements during butchering. If any of this gives you pause, you may wish to send your pigs to a good butcher instead of trying to do this job at home. Most people who raise pigs do use the services of butchers.

If you are still interested in the idea of slaughtering your own pigs, then it is recommended that you visit someone else's farm when they are slaughtering pigs so you can see firsthand what is involved in slaughtering and butchering pigs at home. You may be able to assist and get some experience before you attempt to do this job with your own pigs.

Planning ahead

If you will be slaughtering at home, you will be much more dependent on the weather than if you were using a butcher. You probably will not have access to the temperature-controlled environment that a butcher has. That means that you most likely will need to slaughter your pigs in the cooler months, or at least during the coolest part of the day, such as the early morning hours. Alternatively, you may be able to do the slaughtering yourself and arrange with a local butcher to chill and cut the carcass for you. If you do use a local butcher to chill and cut the carcass, you will need to make the arrangements far in advance for the same reasons that someone taking their pigs to the butcher needs to make arrangements a month ahead of time. Butchers can be in high demand at some times of the year, so book ahead of time if you would like them to chill and cut your meat, even if you intend to do the actual dispatching yourself.

If the temperature is less than 30 degrees F, you can slaughter pigs at any time because bacteria that could spoil the meat will not grow fast at these temperatures. However, if the weather is extremely cold (below the mid-20s), you should not allow the carcass to freeze right after slaughter as this will make the meat less tender than if it is chilled first before freezing. You also will need to select carefully where you are going to slaughter your pigs. Your space requirements will depend, to some extent, on the methods you intend to use. After killing your pig, for example, you will need to remove the animal's skin and hair. There are two ways to do this. You can either scald the pig by placing it in a large vat of water, or you can skin the pig. If you choose to scald the pig, you will need access to a large vat of water, some way to heat the water to boiling, as well as a way to hoist the pig up over the vat and lower it into the water. This can be accomplished by using a tree limb and swinging the pig over it using meat hooks with assistance from others, and so on. You can move the pig with help from others to lower it into the vat of scalding water and raise it several times. You will need to be able to apply chains to your pig's hind legs in order to raise it over a tree limb, for example. It is usually easiest to do this if you can attach the chains to a vehicle to help lift the pig off the ground and raise the chains over the tree limb.

You also will need to have a place to slaughter your pigs. This can be done outdoors, but it is often better if you can do it indoors to keep dust and debris away. You will need to drain blood from your pig at this time, so the site should be a place that is easy to clean up. It is often easiest to do this right on the ground, especially if you have a concrete floor or if you place a tarp on the floor. Others prefer to slaughter the pig outdoors. You can put down plenty of straw to help soak up some of the blood on the ground. Wherever you choose to slaughter your pigs, clean up the site before you begin your work. The area should be clean and sanitary. If you are working outdoors, clear the area of leaves and debris so they will not blow up on to the carcass while you work. Place a layer of straw on the ground where the pig will be suspended and the blood is to be let. If you are working indoors and the area has a wooden or concrete floor, wash the floor and all of the equipment with soap and water before you begin. Make sure you rinse the area completely because any sanitizers could discolor your meat or alter the meat's flavor.

It is important to have good, sharp tools for slaughter. You will need sticking knives for sticking the pig to let the blood, skinning knives for skinning the pig, boning knives and butcher knives for cutting meat, a steel sharpener to keep your blades sharp, meat saws to cut through large sections, and meat hooks for moving large hunks of meat. You can find these tools at a place such as HomeButcher.com (**www.homebutcher.com**), among others. Tools are not cheap. A skinning knife will be around $25. A boning knife is $16 to $19, depending on which kind you get. A manual meat saw is about $50. You can purchase an entire processing kit from HomesteadHarvest.com (**www.homesteadharvest.com**) for about $60. It contains many of the tools you will need for skinning and boning, as well as a bone saw.

Other useful implements to have on hand as you prepare the pork cuts include:

- Thermometers
- A meat grinder
- Meat needles so you can sew rolled cuts of meat
- Hair scrapers to scrape the hair off the pig
- Hand washtubs
- Clean dry towels

- Soap
- Vats for hot and cold water

A manual meat grinder can cost from $50 to $90, while electric meat grinders range from $100 to $2,800. All of your tools should be thoroughly cleaned before use with dish soap. You will need a sturdy table to hold all of your tools. You also can purchase preblended seasonings and cures at a place such as HomeButcher.com (**www.homebutcher.com**) if you do not want to use your own recipes.

If you have the proper tools for slaughter, it will make your job easier, and your work will be more efficient. You should plan on your first pig slaughter taking about two to three hours, which is much longer than it will take you after you become more proficient.

Before slaughtering day, study pig anatomy. Make sure you are familiar with where the pig's organs are and where the bones are, as well as the pig's digestive system. You will be seeing them all up close soon. Also, make sure you know where the jugular veins are, so you can make a good cut in the neck.

Before the day for slaughter, try to round up some people who can assist you. Having people on hand to help you move the carcass can be a great help. If you have people to help you who have experience with butchering, so much the better.

Killing your pig

There are several acceptable ways to kill a pig for butchering. The fastest, and perhaps the most humane way, to kill your pig is by using a sticking knife to quickly and efficiently stick your pig in the jugular vein in its throat. This is easiest to do if you have the pig raised above you with its head hanging down. You can do this if you have placed chains or straps between the pig's hocks and hooves and lifted it by raising the chains over a tree limb or over a beam in a building. The pig will be unhappy about this position, but you should be able to press your sticking knife against the point of the breast bone and make a 4-inch vertical incision in the middle of the neck. This cut should sever the jugular vein and the blood should begin to flow. You should have tubs placed below the pig to catch the blood to prevent the area from becoming too messy. If the area is too slippery, you will not be able to work properly. When pressing the sticking knife into the breast, be careful not to press too deeply, or you could cause internal bleeding that can affect the meat.

Butchers usually will use an electrical stunner to stun the pig before cutting the throat. On some farms, the farmer will use a mechanical stunner to stun the pig first. A mechanical stunner can be used anywhere, whereas an electrical stunner needs electricity to operate. Many farmers will not have access to electricity if they are killing their pigs in a field. A butcher slaughtering large numbers of animals more often uses an electrical stunner. Other people prefer to use a .22 caliber rifle to shoot the pig in the forehead between and slightly above the eyes. With any of these methods, it is essential that you are accurate and do not cause the animal any distress. The kill should be swift, and you should not allow the animal to suffer. Try to stay calm before making the kill. If you are upset or agitated, it will also upset the pig. Obviously, if you are using firearms or stunners, you should take all necessary safety precautions.

No matter which method you use for killing the pig, the next step in the process is to bleed the pig. This needs to begin within about two minutes of killing the pig so the blood will flow freely. Pigs that are hung upside down do bleed the best, but if you do not have a way to suspend the pig, you can bleed the pig with it lying on the ground on its back. If the pig is stunned, you can have someone stand over the pig on the ground and hold its front legs. Locate the edge of the breast bone, thrust your sticking knife under the bone with the sharp point aimed toward the tail, and then thrust upward to sever the carotid artery. The pig should bleed, but if it does not, you can insert the knife a little more deeply, and there should be plenty of blood. Again, have pans ready to catch the blood.

Removing hair and skin

In order to remove the hair and skin from a pig, they traditionally have been scalded in hot water and scraped, with the skin left intact. However, today many people prefer to skin the pig because it is easier and requires less equipment. It will be up to you to decide which method of removing hair and skin you prefer to use. Many chefs and food aficionados today find uses for the skin of the pig in food dishes. Whichever method you prefer, you will be able to find uses for the skin if you are interested in keeping and reusing it.

Scalding and scraping

The purpose of scalding the pig is to loosen the pig's hair and the **scurf**, or the layer of skin oil, dirt, and cells on the skin, so they can be more easily removed. It long has been believed that it was necessary to leave the skin of the pig intact on the pig in order to achieve proper curing for the ham and bacon. However, in recent years, more people tend to skin the pig and cure pigs without the skin. If the pig is skinned badly, it can ruin your bacon, however. Scalding the pig requires more work and more equipment than skinning the pig.

In order to scald the pig, you will need a heat source and a water source. Most people use 55-gallon drums or barrels. Start by heating about 50 gallons of water close to boiling while you are killing the pig and letting it bleed. This water should be heated either in the barrel you intend to use for the pig or transferred to the barrel when you are ready to place the pig in it.

You likely will need help in moving the pig into the barrel. Some people prefer to dig a shallow hole for the barrel that will contain the pig so it is easier to place the pig inside the barrel. If you dig the hole at a slight angle, you can kill and bleed out the pig next to the vat or barrel, and it will be easier to move the pig into the vat when you are ready to place the pig into it. Make sure you do not make the angle too low, or the vat will not contain enough water to cover the pig.

Another method is to build a fire beneath the vat you will be using to scald the pig. In order to use this method, you will need to dig a pit for the fire and rig a sturdy method for suspending the vat over the fire while the pig is in the vat. If you can place heavy metal legs on the vat, like a cauldron, then it could hold the weight of the pig over the fire.

You will need to use a thermometer to assess the temperature in your vat. It is best to scald the pig slowly at a temperature of about 140 degrees F. At this temperature, it will take between three and six minutes to scald the hair and scurf from the pig. The pig's hair can be very difficult to remove, especially in the fall when the pig has begun to grow thicker hair for winter. If you are scalding your pig during the fall and your pig does have this winter growth of hair, you may need to use higher temperatures, between 146 and 150 degrees or keep your pig in the scalding water for longer periods. You may wish to add ¼ cup of rosin, lime, or another alkaline mix to the scalding water to help remove the scurf. This also will make your pig's skin appear whiter.

It can be difficult to keep the water in the vat at a precise temperature. You will need to continue to check the temperature of the water in the vat by using your thermometer throughout the process. You should have more boiling water ready to add if necessary. You can also add cooler water if the water is too hot. If you begin with a water temperature between 155 and 160 degrees, the water should be at a scalding temperature when you are ready to place the pig in the vat. If it is cold weather, the cooler outside temperature will cool the water in the vat faster.

Once the pig is in the vat, you will need to keep it moving and pull it from the barrel several times in order to keep it from overscalding. If the pig begins to overscald, it will cause the skin to contract around the base of the hairs, known as "setting the hair." This effectively cooks the skin of the pig. If the skin becomes overscalded, it will make the hair difficult to remove.

When the water reaches the correct water temperature of 140 degrees, place the pig in the vat head first. Turn the pig in the vat, rotating it, and pull it in and out of the water occasionally. Check the pig's skin often for signs that the hair is easy to remove. The hair should start coming off first over the back and sides and then in the flank areas. After you can remove the hair easily from the flanks, remove the pig from the vat and place the pig rear first into the vat. Be sure to check the water temperature and raise the temperature back up to 140 degrees. The temperature will no doubt have cooled during the several minutes the pig has spent in the vat.

Once the rear of the pig is in the scalding water in the vat, you can start pulling the toenails and dewclaws from the pig's front feet. You can insert a hook into the top of the nail and pull in order to remove the nail. Start scraping as much of the hair off the head as possible, paying special attention to the hair around the ears and snout. You can use a knife or a bell scraper for this job, which is a scraper made for removing hair. Some bell scrapers have a hook on the end for removing the toenails.

Continue to turn the pig in the barrel so that it does not overscald. Lift the pig out of the barrel and test the looseness of the hair. Once all of the hair is loose and easy to remove, you can remove the pig from the barrel.

Ideally, you will have a sturdy table to place the pig on so you can continue to remove the hair. Alternatively, you may place the pig on a piece of plywood on the ground to continue working. Remove the nails and dewclaws from the pig's back feet, and remove the hair from the pig's tail. Work to remove the hair on the pig's legs by gripping and twisting the hair. Work on the difficult areas such as the head, feet, and jowl first while the pig's skin is still hot from the vat. Then you can move to the easier areas such as the pig's back and sides. You can use the bell scraper for these easy areas. Try tilting the scraper up toward the forward edge and pulling it forward, using as much pressure as possible.

You will need to work quickly because the pig's skin will set as it cools down, making it harder to remove the hair. If you find areas of hair and scurf that are hard to scrape, cover them with a piece of burlap, and pour hot water over the material to loosen them. You can make scraping the legs and head easier by moving them if they begin to set. This will keep the skin stretched and loosened.

After you have removed most of the hair, you will need to pour hot water over the pig so you can continue to scrape. Place the bell scraper against the pig's skin, and move it in a rotary motion. This will help remove the scurf and the remaining hair. If there are still patches of hair that are not removed by the bell scraper, you can use a knife. If you prefer, you can use a knife for the entire skinning process. You can use whichever tool you are more comfortable using.

At this point, you are ready to hang and suspend the carcass. You can start working on the carcass by cutting off the soles of the feet. Cut between and around the toes. You should use your knife to expose the pig's gambrel tendons. You can do this by cutting through the skin that lies on the back of the rear legs from the dewclaws to the hocks. Carefully cut along each side of the tendons. Be careful not to cut the actual tendons, otherwise, you will have no way to suspend the pig. Insert the spreader or gambrel (the instrument called the gambrel) under the tendons in each leg in order to expose them. Fasten the legs to the spreader bar, and suspend the carcass from it. The legs will need to be spread at least 14 inches apart. When your pig is suspended, make sure neither its head nor its forelegs are touching the ground to avoid contaminating the carcass with bacteria.

You can use a blowtorch or a small propane torch to singe off any remaining hair and scurf from the pig. Singeing will remove most of the remaining hair, and it will darken other small hairs so they can be seen. You will need to be careful that you do not burn the skin when using one of these torches. Burning the skin not only can make the skin unsightly, but it can also affect the flavor of the meat. You do not want to partially cook the pork at this point in your processing. You can shave off any remaining hair and wash the carcass completely.

Skinning

It takes less time to skin a pig than to go through the scalding and scraping procedure. It also takes less equipment. You will still need to be able to hoist the pig up to work on it, however. After you have stunned and bled the pig, you can place the pig on a sheet of plywood, some concrete, or in some straw. Wash the blood and any dirt or debris from the carcass. Turn the pig over onto its back, and hold it in position with blocks, such as cinder blocks, on each side.

You can begin the skinning process by cutting the skin around the pig's rear legs, just below the dewclaws. Make a cut through the hide and down the back of the leg. Continue to cut over the hocks and up to the midline at the center of the hams. Carefully skin around each side of the leg. Remove the skin to a point below the hock.

At this point, you can open the skin down the animal's midline. Cut from the point where the pig was stuck, around each side of the genitals, and move on to the anus. Make this cut by inserting the point of the knife under the skin with the blade held upward. This process is called cutting from inside out. It protects the meat from becoming contaminated from materials on the hide. Avoid cutting too deeply as this could puncture the intestines and contaminate the meat.

Next, remove the hide from the inside of the hams. You will need to be careful because it is easy to cut through the fat layers and into the lean meat. You must continue to be careful not to contaminate the meat. Continue to skin along the animal's sides toward the breast area. Grip the loosened hide in the opposite hand and pull it up and out away from the animal. By doing this, you will produce tension in the hide, which will remove any wrinkling. It will allow the knife to slide smoothly and easily. Hold the knife firmly, and place it against the hide, turning the blade slightly outward. Skin as far down the sides of the animal as possible, but do not skin around the front legs. The skin around the front legs will be removed separately.

Return to the rear part of the carcass, and remove the hide that is left on the rear of the hams. Do not skin the outer portions of the hams at this point. Wait until you have raised the carcass to a better working height. You can remove the pig's rear feet by sawing through the bone. Cut about 2 inches above the hock. Insert the spreader or gambrel under the large tendons on the rear legs, and attach the legs to the spreader securely.

You can hoist the carcass to a convenient working height to remove the skin from the outside of the hams. This is usually about waist high. Start skinning around the outer parts of the hams, but leave as much fat as possible on the carcass. Next, remove the hide from around the anus and cut through the tail at the joint closest to the body. The tail is edible, and some people like to save it. Continue and pull the animal's hide down over its hips. You should be able to pull the hide from the hips and back off and slide it over the hips. This will leave layers of fat on these sections of the carcass. You may need to use a knife to cut between the skin and the fat in some cases if large sections of fat are coming off when you remove the hide. Some fat needs to remain on the pig to protect the meat inside, to give the pork flavor later when it is cooked, and for curing some of the cuts. You will be able to decide during the meat cutting process how much fat you want to leave on each cut.

Hoist the carcass to its fully raised position. Cut open the hide down the back of the forelegs, and remove the hide on each side of the forelegs. Proceed to skin along the inside of the forelegs and the neck. Move to the shoulders and jowls and then to a halfway point to the back of the carcass, skinning as you move along. You can pull down and out on the hide slowly and remove it from the animal's back. The skin should come off easily, leaving the fat beneath it intact, but if the fat does begin to tear, you can use a knife to pat it back into place. Continue pulling the hide as far down the back as possible. When it become difficult to remove the hide around the animal's neck, you can complete the removal with your knife.

If you intend to save the pig's head, you will need to skin over the animal's head and down the face, cutting at the snout. Remove the front feet by sawing just below the knee joint.

Evisceration

Evisceration refers to removing the pig's organs and intestines. During the evisceration process, you will need to be careful not to allow the contents of the stomach, the intestines, or the other organs to come in contact with the carcass and meat. Some of these organs contain bacteria and fermenting food that can harm your meat and cause it to spoil. You will be removing the **leaf fat**, or the fat around the pig's kidneys, used for making lard. The pig's head also will be removed. By the time you are finished with this part of the slaughter process, only the meat sections of the carcass will remain.

Your pig should be hanging, head down, from the gambrel. It is a good idea to have a large tub positioned under the pig in order to catch the intestines and other organs as they come out.

You will begin the evisceration process by removing the pig's anus. You do this by cutting around the anus and making a cut deep into the pelvic canal. Pull the anus outward and cut any remaining attachments to it. Be careful not to cut the large intestine, as its contents could contaminant the carcass. Once the anus is loosened, tie it off with a piece of string so it will not cause any contamination.

When slaughtering a barrow, you will need to remove the penis or "pizzle." Cut through the skin and the fatty tissue that lies along each side of the penis and around the opening. Lift the penis upward and make a cut beneath it along the midline. Cut along the penis and between the hams, then pull the penis upward and remove it where it attaches at the base of the ham. There is a natural separation between the hams. You can continue the cut you made between the hams and expose the white connective tissue. Cut through this connective tissue to the pelvic bone or aitchbone. Continue to cut through the cartilage between the pelvic bone and separate the two hams. You should be able to do this in young pigs; however, you may need to use a handsaw to split the pelvic bone in older pigs.

Next, you can proceed to open up the pig's chest cavity. You can make a cut from the place where the pig was stuck to the upper end of the sternum or breastbone. Insert your knife at the top edge of the sternum and make a downward cut. It is best to cut slightly off-center. Proceed to open up the chest cavity.

Then, open the animal's midline. Begin at the opening you made to split the pelvic bone. Insert the handle of the knife in the opening and point the blade outward, away from the inside of the pig, in order to avoid cutting the intestines. Open the midline all the way up to the breast opening. Let the intestines and the stomach roll out and hang. Do not let them fall out because they are still connected to the esophagus. If they tear at this point, they will spill their contents into the carcass and contaminate the meat. Proceed to pull the loosened large intestine past the kidneys. Cut the connections to the liver, and remove it by pulling outward on it and cutting the connective tissue. Next, you can remove the gall bladder from the liver. Cut beneath it and pull. Do not allow the contents of the gall bladder to spill onto the liver.

Carefully pull the stomach and intestines out, and cut through the diaphragm. The diaphragm is a thin sheet of muscle and white connective tissue. It separates the stomach and the intestines from the lungs and heart. Next, pull outward on the lungs and the heart, and cut down along the sides of the windpipe to cut its attachment at the head. You also will need to separate the heart from the lungs. You can do this by cutting across the top of the heart. Split the heart open, so it can be thoroughly washed. Clean the heart and liver thoroughly, and put them in ice or ice water so they can be prepared later. Many delicious food dishes can be made from the heart and the liver of the pig.

Splitting and head removal

Once the pig's organs are removed, wash the inside of the carcass before splitting it. With your handsaw, start splitting the carcass from the interior between the hams. Try to keep the split as close to the center of the backbone as possible. Saw through the tail area to a point halfway through the loin. Move around to the back of the pig, and keep sawing through the shoulder and neck to the base of the head. If the split goes off center, continue to saw through to the next vertebra, and then get back to the center.

You will need to remove the pig's head at the **atlas joint**. This is the joint closest to the head. If you have properly split the carcass, this joint should be exposed. After you have cut through this joint, continue to cut downward along the jawbone. Leave the jowls attached to the carcass. You can remove the tongue if you like, wash it completely, and place it with the liver and heart to be used later.

Next, remove the kidneys and the leaf fat. You can remove the leaf fat by loosening it from the diaphragm muscle and lifting up on it. You may have to scoop some of the leaf fat out with your hands. Leaf fat is used to make lard and is highly prized by many people.

Once you have finished splitting the carcass and removing the parts, examine the carcass and the organs to make sure everything looks satisfactory. This is normally a meat inspector's job, but as you are slaughtering your pig at home, you will have to perform this duty yourself. Look for bruises, injuries, parasites, abscesses, and tumors. Is there any congestion or inflammation in the lungs? Do the intestines, kidneys, and other organs look all right? Does the interior of the carcass look normal? Check the carcass thoroughly for any signs of problems. If you do find something, it could affect the meat you intend to eat, or it could indicate a possible sickness that could affect your other pigs. If you find something that concerns you, contact a meat inspector or a qualified veterinarian to look at the carcass.

The carcass will need to be thoroughly washed and chilled for 24 to 48 hours before meat can be cut.

Chilling the carcass

Bacteria already have contaminated slaughtered hog carcasses during the slaughter process. These bacteria can spoil the meat unless their growth is stopped as soon as the slaughter process is finished. Immediately chilling the carcass and keeping it at low temperatures can drastically slow this bacterial growth. If you are slaughtering your pig during cold weather and the temperature is between 28 and 35 degrees, it is possible to wrap the carcass in a sheet, hang it, and chill it in a well-aired shed, as long as it is safe from any cats, dogs, or other predators looking for free meat. However, you must not allow the carcass to freeze. Freezing the carcass within a day following death can cause the meat to become tough.

If the weather is warm and you cannot cool the meat to less than 40 degrees, you will need to arrange to transport the carcass to a local market or butcher so it can be chilled for 24 to 48 hours. The carcass must be chilled for this length of time before making any cuts on the meat. Otherwise, bacterial growth cannot be prevented. No cuts of meat can be made on carcasses that have not been properly chilled because it is not safe to eat meat from carcasses that have not been properly chilled.

Where to Sell Your Pork

As already discussed, you will not be able to sell any meat you slaughter on your own farm yourself. If you have meat butchered by a licensed butcher for resale, you will be able to sell your meat to your chosen market.

Labeling

We have already discussed the kind of packaging that the butcher can provide. You will also need to consider the labels that will go on your packages. Are you artistic? Is someone in your family artistic? Can you come up with a nice logo for your farm? You will need an image or something so people can identify a label with your products and your farm. It should be simple but easy to recognize. If you have a word or a catchy phrase, people may associate it with your products. Try to think of something simple that will stay in people's minds. Your phrase or logo does not have to come from an expensive ad agency. You and your family can think of a good idea for your products.

Who is your customer?

It always helps to ask yourself who your customer is. Who will be buying your products? Are you selling to other people like yourself? Are you selling to chefs? To food lovers? Are you selling to suburban families? To local people? To people far away? The better you can picture and identify the person you are selling your pork products to, the easier it will be for you to understand how to market your products to them. If you know to whom you are selling, you will know what they want. For example, you could sell your cuts of meats locally at farmers markets, or you could sell to someone who lives in the suburbs. They might like to buy a half hog, already dressed and ready to go in their freezer. The suburban family may not have the room or the time to raise their own pigs, but they enjoy pork products, and they have a large freezer to store the pork. Or, you could have your own Internet site to sell your products to people interested in purchasing home-raised pork. It is possible for you to sell your pork in all of these ways. You have to know how to market your products. Local buyers might care more about buying pork that has been raised locally. A suburban family might care more about your prices. Someone buying on the Internet might be more interested in the kind of pigs you have and how they are raised (pasture raised, organic practices, and so on). Learn to emphasize what your customers are looking for.

Where are you selling?

Are you selling at farmers markets? Local, independent grocery stores? A chain of grocery stores? Online markets? Gourmet or organic stores? Your own website? Are you selling directly to restaurants? To ethnic markets? How are you selling your products? How are other people selling their products? You may wish to consider all these when you look for outlets for selling your meats. As a small pork producer, you may not be able to compete with large producers in terms of lower costs or large volume, but you can find niche markets where your pork will be appreciated for its special qualities. Emphasize those points, and you can be highly successful.

Chapter 6

Goats

GOAT GLOSSARY

Abomasum: The last of the four compartments in a goat's digestive system, where true digestion occurs

ADGA: American Dairy Goat Association

Advanced registry: A doe documented to have given a set amount of milk over the course of a year (high-yield)

Alcilli: Another name for alveoli

Alveoli: Tiny sack-like structures containing cells that secrete milk in a mammary gland

American: A doe that is seven-eighths pure of one breed or a buck that is fifteen-sixteenths pure

Anthelmintics: Medications that eliminate worms

Artificial insemination (AI): The impregnation of a doe using frozen sperm from a donor buck

Blind teat: A nonfunctional teat

Broken-mouthed: A term for a goat missing some of its front incisors

Buck: A male goat

Buckling: An uncastrated male kid

Burdizzo®: A tool used to neuter young bucks

CAE: Caprine arthritic encephalitis, a viral rheumatic joint inflammation passed from mother to kid

Castrate: To render a buck sterile

Chamois: A deep, reddish-brown color found in the Oberhasli breed

Chevon: Goat meat

Chevre: A type of goat cheese originating in France

Colostrum: The first nourishment a mother provides to her kid

Concentrate: Feed that contains a high proportion of nutrients and is low in crude fiber content (less than 18 percent of dry matter)

Confinement feeding: Feeding goats a controlled diet inside a shelter or yard

Conformation: The degree to which an individual goat matches the ideal standard for its breed

Cud: Soft masses of undigested plant fiber that return from the rumen to the mouth for additional chewing

Deep littering: Allowing a mattress of bedding to accumulate on the floor of the stable by adding fresh hay on top every day

Dental palate: A hard, tough pad of tissue that takes the place of teeth in a goat's upper jaw

Disbudding: The process of cauterizing a kid's horn buds

Doe: A female goat

Doeling: A young doe that has not mated for the first time

Dual-purpose breed: A breed of goat that can belong to more than one of the three usage categories: milk, meat, or fiber producing

ENE: Estimated net energy, provided by carbohydrates and fats

Elastrator: A device used to castrate a kid using a tight rubber ring

Elf ear: The short, 2-inch ear of a LaMancha goat

Estrone sulfate: A hormone produced by a living fetus about 35 days after conception

Estrus: The state in which a goat's ovary contains a fertile egg and her uterus is ready to establish it

Experimental: A goat resulting from an accidental breeding between purebred goats of different breeds

Flehmen: The raising of the head and drawing up of the upper lip by a buck ready to mate

Floppy kid syndrome (FKS): A disease that affects kids between three and ten days old; symptoms are muscular weakness and depression, progressing to flaccid paralysis and often death

Foot rot: A bacterial infection that causes liquification of tissue in and around the hoof

Foot scald: A red, moist bacterial infection of the tissue between the toes

Freshening: The commencement of milk production after kidding

Furstenberg's rosette: A many-folded mucus membrane that prevents leakage of milk from an udder and acts as a barrier to bacteria

Gopher ear: The almost nonexistent ear of a LaMancha goat

Gummer: A goat that has lost all its teeth

Hardware disease: Life-threatening damage to the wall of the reticulum, caused when a goat swallows sharp or pointed objects

Hermaphroditism: The presence of both male and female reproductive organs

Hybrid vigor: The tendency of a mixed-breed animal to be healthier and stronger than a purebred

Ketosis: A disease of pregnant goats occurring when the body breaks down its own reserves of fat

Kid: Newborn or immature goat

Kidding: The process of giving birth

Lactation: The production of milk

Let down: The release of milk within the udder prior to milking

Linebreeding: The breeding of closely related goats to intensify their genetic traits

Loose stable: A stable in which the goats are housed together in an open area instead of in individual stalls

Lungworm: A parasite that infests the lungs and respiratory passages

Mammary gland: The part of the udder that secretes milk

Mastitis: A common inflammation of the udder generally caused by poor sanitation practices, insect bites becoming infected, or injury to low hanging udders

Meconium: The first feces passed by a newborn kid

Monkey mouth: A condition in which the lower front teeth protrude beyond the edge of the upper dental palate

NASS: USDA's National Agricultural Statistics Service

National Animal Identification System (NAIS): A program to assign identification to each farm and its livestock so diseased livestock can be quickly tracked

Native on appearance (NOA): A goat that appears to be of a specific breed but is undocumented

Omasum: The third of the four compartments in a goat's digestive system; its function is to absorb nutrients

Oxytocin: A hormone that controls milk let down

Pannier: A basket worn by a pack goat

Papered: Registered with a breed association

Parrot mouth: A condition in which the lower incisors fall behind the leading edge of the upper dental palate

Pasteurization: The process of heating milk to a specific temperature and maintaining it for a specific length of time, in order to kill harmful bacteria

Pedigree: A document or chart with the recorded ancestry of a goat, its parents, grandparents, and so on

Placenta: Afterbirth

Polled: A goat that is naturally hornless

Purebred: Goats that, according to ancestry, fall into a breed group defined by national and often international breed standards

Recorded grades: Goats that meet a list of requirements regarding appearance and quality of milk

Registered purebred: A goat that has been registered with an official registry organization and is listed in the herd book

Registration: Documents verifying that an animal is registered in the official herd book of a recognized registry organization for that breed

Reticulum: The second of the four compartments in a goat's digestive system, which serves as a fluid pump

Roughage: Highly fibrous plant material, feed with a fiber content higher than 18 percent

Rumen: The largest of the four compartments in a goat's digestive system, where fiber is broken down

Ruminant: An animal whose digestive system consists of multiple stomachs

Sausage teats: Teats that are exceptionally wide

Scurs: Misshapen horns that can twist down into the goat's face

Settle: To become pregnant

Soiling: Confinement feeding

Sow mouth: A condition in which the lower front teeth protrude beyond the edge of the upper dental palate

Stanchion: A head restraint used to hold a goat during milking, hoof trimming, and inspections

Star milker: A system exists whereby a goat is given a star rating depending upon her consistent yield (measured day by day) and the percent of butterfat her milk contains. A star milker generally must give 10 to 11 pounds of milk in a day.

Stays: The horizontal wires on a wire fence that hold the vertical wires in place.

Step-in fence posts: Posts made of metal, plastic, or fiberglass that can be inserted into the ground using body weight

TDN: Total digestible nutrients, provided by carbohydrates and fats in a goat's diet

T-posts: Metal fence posts used to fill in the spaces between wooden corner posts

Teat dip: A disinfectant applied to teats after each milking to prevent mastitis

Wattle: A fold of skin under the face on the side of the neck

Wether: A castrated buck

Teat: The opening through which milk comes out of the udder

Topline: The line of a goat's spine

Udder: The part of the goat containing the mammary glands that produce milk

Udder attachments: The ligaments that attach the udder to the goat's abdominal wall

Udder supports: Another name for udder attachments

Urinary calculi: Bladder stones

The History of Goats and People

Goats have been companions to man almost since the beginning of human civilization. The goat was one of the earliest animals to be domesticated. (Both goats and sheep lay claim to being the earliest herd animals.) Early hunter-gatherers drank goat's milk and soon learned to make cheese. Archaeologists have found evidence that goats were being kept, rather than hunted, about 10,000 B.C. at Ganj Dareh, a Neolithic village in western Iran. Mounds of domestic goat bones unearthed at Jericho have been carbon-dated to 7000 to 6000 B.C.

DNA findings released in 2001 suggest goats may have been domesticated in other regions of the world as well. Gordon Luikart of the Université Joseph Fourier in Grenoble, France, and his colleagues speculate that another goat strain found in the Indian subcontinent, Mongolia, and Southeast Asia is descended from a she-goat tamed about 9,000 years ago in an area of Pakistan called Baluchistan, in the Indus Valley. Archaeological evidence suggests that Baluchistan was a major center of domestication. A third unrelated strain, of as a yet-undetermined origin, is believed to have been the ancestor of today's Swiss, Mongolian, and Slovenian breeds.

Domestic goats are thought to have shaped the development of human civilization by providing a portable supply of meat and milk that allowed hunter-gatherers to become agricultural nomads. Goats were small, easy to handle, and able to thrive in arid, semi-tropical and mountainous areas where horses, cattle, and other larger herbivores could not survive. Their skins supplied leather and pelts for robes and rugs. The woolly fur of goats was woven into the earliest cloth, and goat horns were made into drinking vessels, ornaments, and musical instruments. Goats carried their owners' belongings on their backs or pulled them on sledges as they traveled from region to region. Young kids were used as sacrificial animals for religious rites. Goats achieved mythical stature as fertility gods; the Greek god of forests and flocks, Pan, was born with the legs, tail, and horns of a goat; and the Teutons believed that the chariot of Thor, the thunder god, was pulled through the heavens by two he-goats.

Domesticated goats spread west from the Fertile Crescent across Europe and eventually into Great Britain, sometimes escaping and establishing feral populations in remote areas where they can still be found. Today, goats are the third most plentiful animals in the world. The estimated world population of goats today is about 460 million, the majority of them in developing countries where goat products are common and widely valued.

More than half of the world's population drinks goat milk, although in the United States goat's milk is only slowly gaining in popularity. Europeans have appreciated the special attributes of goat's milk for generations, and products such as chèvre (goat's milk cheese), butter, yogurt, and ice cream made from goat's milk are popular in European nations. Until about 400 years ago, goats surpassed cattle in Europe as the preferred milking animal, and in much of the world, they still do. The reasons are simple: Goats are less expensive to purchase than larger animals, and the amount of feed a goat requires per gallon of milk output is less than that needed for cattle. Goats are hardy, smaller, and more manageable. Goats multiply rapidly. Three or four goats are a much safer investment than a single cow because if one goat fails to produce or becomes sick, the others can replace it. These qualities make goats ideal for small dairy operations or for household use. Cow's milk only began to predominate when modern dairies became a large, organized industry because larger animals could give greater quantities of milk.

Dairy goats in the United States

Goats were brought to the Americas in the 1500s by Spanish seafarers who carried them on their ships to provide milk and meat and often released them on small islands where they multiplied and could be caught and slaughtered for fresh meat by future voyagers.

A visitor to Plymouth Colony in September 1623 noted that the colony possessed six goats. In 1849, North America's first purebred goats, seven Angora does and two bucks, were imported to South Carolina. In 1904, the first North American dairy goat exhibition was held at the St. Louis World's Fair, and in the same year, the American Milk Goat Record, now the American Dairy Goat Association (ADGA), was established. During the early 1900s, several breeds of dairy goats were imported. The first officially documented Pygmy goats were imported to the U.S. during the 1950s as zoo animals.

During the first half of the 1900s, goat's milk in the United States primarily was marketed through pharmacies as an alternative for people who were allergic to cow's milk. In the 1970s, a movement toward self-sufficiency and sustainable agriculture revived an interest in raising dairy goats. Small, adaptable and consuming relatively few resources, one or two goats could supply all the milk a family needed. During the 1980s, Americans became increasingly interested in healthful and natural foods, and during the 1990s, the rising popularity of specialty cheeses and ethnic cuisines contributed to a growth in demand for goat milk and goat milk products.

Before the late 20th century, travelers in rural America occasionally spotted a few goats mixed in with a farmer's livestock in the fields, a nostalgic reminder of the "old world" of European ancestors. During the last few decades, there has been an upsurge in the number of Americans raising goats for meat and milk and a steady annual increase in the number of dairy goats.

According to the USDA's National Agricultural Statistics Service (NASS), 360,000 milk goats were listed in the United States in January 2011, an increase of 4,000 since the previous year. Dairy goats are found in every state in the United States, but the largest numbers live in Wisconsin (50,000 head), California (38,000 head), Iowa (31,000 head), and Texas (20,000 head). Because these statistics are based on dairy operations large enough to be licensed and regulated as working dairy businesses by the U.S. government, they do not include goats raised on hobby farms or kept in backyards. The population of producing dairy goats in the United States could be 400,000 or more if these smaller operations were taken into account.

The main dairy goat breeds in the U.S. are Alpine, LaMancha, Nubian, Oberhasli, Saanen, and Toggenburg. Each of these breeds is capable of producing more than 2,000 pounds of milk per year, but the U.S. imports more than 50 percent of the dairy goat cheese products it consumes, mostly from France.

CASE STUDY: MEYENBERG GOAT MILK PRODUCTS

Harold Jackson
Meyenburg Goat Milk Products
www.meyenberg.com

In 1934, Harold Jackson bought Meyenberg Goat Milk Products because his infant son, Robert, suffered from cow's milk allergies and digestive problems. Initially, Jackson Mitchell's Meyenberg Goat Milk Products produced only evaporated goat's milk, sold exclusively in pharmacies as an alternative for infants sensitive to cow milk. Robert D. Jackson assumed ownership of the company in 1954, and he and his wife of 43 years,

Carol, turned the small evaporated milk company into the largest manufacturer of goat's milk products in the U.S. and the preeminent global manufacturer of goat's milk products. Recognizing competition from the proliferation of new infant formulas, Jackson began marketing goat's milk to a larger population, focusing special attention on health conscious consumers, seniors, and children.

During the 1980s, a growing national awareness of health and nutrition issues renewed consumer interest in unique natural products. To meet demand, Meyenberg opened plants in Arkansas and California and doubled his goat milk production and annual sales within a year. A unique ultra-pasteurization process allowed for a wider distribution of fresh goat's milk products to markets across the country, including Meyenberg ultra-pasteurized fresh whole goat milk and 1 percent low-fat pasteurized milk, evaporated, and powdered goat milk. In 2004, the company introduced European style goat milk butter and goat milk cheddar, and in 2008, goat cream cheese.

Recent trends have fueled yet another boom in goat milk consumption: consumer desire to avoid foods containing additives and bovine growth hormones (BGH), a mushrooming demand for foods that are 100 percent natural, and a growing appreciation by gourmet chefs, who use goat milk to enhance recipes. Meyenberg products are currently available in 90 percent of U.S. supermarket chains, as well as through leading health-food distributors and stores. Its farms and facilities produce more than 20 million pounds of goat milk annually, and its lines of distribution stretch around the world.

Goats are an easy-to-keep species because they have minimal housing needs. They eat little grain, but they do need good quality hay and pasture. One big advantage of owning goats is that they will eat many weeds and brush that cattle will not consume. However, contrary to popular belief, goats will not eat tin cans or garbage. Such items may actually prove to be a health hazard to goats, and they should not be given access to these non-food items.

Goats are curious animals, and they love to explore their environment with their lips and tongues. They are very smart and will search fences, gates, gate latches, and their living quarters for an escape route from confinement. Because of their nimbleness and good sense of balance, they are high climbers and can even climb over fences. Low tree limbs surrounding pens or pastures also provide another escape route for goats.

Goats are a versatile animal in terms of providing humans with food and fiber. Their meat is popular around the world, and the Boer goat is a popular meat goat. Dairy goats provide milk, which can be substituted for cow's milk for people with allergies. Goat's milk is made into cheese, butter, yogurt, and ice cream. Unlike cow's milk, goat's milk is naturally homogenized, and the fat stays suspended in the fluid. Goat milk has a slightly sweet taste. In terms of fiber, Angora goats give plenty of mohair, up to 15 pounds yearly, to be woven into fine clothing articles. Likewise, each mature Cashmere goat yields about 9 ounces of soft cashmere wool each year.

Breeds

Before you decide on a breed of goat, you will want to determine what you want to achieve with your goats. Are you primarily interested in goats for milk? Do you want to raise goats for meat? Some breeds of goats are more suited for meat production, and others are high-milk-producing goats. Goat breeds vary with weight and size. This is important when considering your pasture availability. Smaller goats will take less pasture to maintain weight. However, you might sacrifice on meat quantities with a smaller goat. Smaller dairy goats might give less milk, but if the goat milk is strictly for family consumption, this might be a good option for you. There are more than 300 different breeds of goats in the world. To get you started, here is a brief introduction to the breeds and types of goats commonly raised in North

America. Some breeds may not be available in your area, so you will need to do some sleuthing to find out if the specific breeders are near you — not all breeds are raised in every country. Your local county extension agent can help you locate goat farms in your area.

Dairy goats

Alpine: The Alpine goat was developed in Switzerland. Its ears are upright and the face is dished or scooped. The Alpine is usually brown and white or black and white, though other colors are seen. It is primarily used as a dairy goat. Females weigh about 135 pounds and males weigh about 170 pounds.

LaMancha: The LaMancha is quickly recognized by its small ears. It was developed in the United States from crossing Spanish goats with Swiss and Nubian bucks. It is an excellent dairy goat, giving milk with high butterfat. The LaMancha goat can come in a variety of colors and has a calm and gentle temperament.

Nubian: The Nubian goat is a large animal with a convex nose and long, pendulous ears. It is the most common breed and makes a good dairy goat. It produces milk that is high in butterfat, but it does produce less milk per day than other dairy goat breeds. It also produces a fair amount of meat and is considered a dual-purpose goat breed. Does generally weigh at least 135 pounds when mature, and bucks weigh at least 175 pounds at maturity. The Nubian is usually brown.

Oberhasli: This breed is typically a deep reddish brown with black stripes on the face. The breed was developed in Switzerland and was formerly known as the Swiss Alpine. This breed is slightly smaller than other standard-sized goat breeds but is a good dairy goat breed that produces up to 1 ½ gallons of milk per day. The breed is considered a rare breed but is growing in popularity.

Saanen: This breed is usually all white. The Saanen was developed in Switzerland but quickly spread throughout Europe. The does are heavy milkers and weigh about 145 pounds. They are also the largest of the dairy goat breeds.

Toggenburg: Another Swiss breed, the Toggenburg is mid-sized and rich brown with white highlights. The hair is short to medium in length, and they are a solid color from light fawn to dark brown. They have white markings on the legs and two white stripes down the face. They are a dairy goat breed, and does give up to 1 ½ gallons of milk per day.

Fiber goats

Angora: The Angora goat is used as a fiber goat for its mohair fleece. On average, more than 10 pounds of mohair is sheared from the average Angora goat. Mohair is similar in chemical composition to wool but has a smoother surface giving it a silky texture. Angora goats of both sexes have horns and droopy ears. Does usually weigh 80 pounds as adults. Bucks average 200 pounds. As an added bonus, Angora goats are fantastic browsers, controlling weeds and brush in areas inaccessible to mowers.

Cashmere: Cashmere goats are technically a type of goat and not an official breed. Most breeds of goat, with the exception of the Angora, can produce cashmere down in various amounts. Cashmere fleece is a fine, crimped down. Goats with cashmere fleece usually have long, straight, coarse guard hairs on the outer part of their bodies. The cashmere fleece underneath the guard hair keeps them warm. Most of the best cashmere has traditionally come from the Middle East, but unrest in that region of the world in recent years has caused a disruption in the supply. New Zealand and Australia now supply much of the best cashmere in the world. U.S. farmers have imported goats from Australia and New Zealand to build on their cashmere breeding programs and to breed with American goats.

Pygora: The Pygora goat is a cross between the Angora and the Pygmy goat. It was first bred in Oregon in 1987. Pygoras are multiuse and popular for their different types of fleece, as milk goats, and also are kept as pets. They can have cashmere-type fleece, mohair-like fleece, or a combination of these two fleeces. Pygoras are popular as pets because they have the smaller size of Pygmy goats. Pygora goats may not be more than 75 percent Angora goat, nor more than 75 percent Pygmy goat. They can live to be 12 to 14 years.

Meat goats

Boer: The Boer goat has pendulous ears. It was developed in South Africa as a meat goat and gains about a quarter pound of weight daily until it reaches full maturity. It is the best-performing goat in terms of weight gain among the meat-type goats, which means the Boer goat reaches market weigh quickly. The doe commonly will have twins. Males weigh about 260 pounds when mature, while females weigh about 215 pounds.

Kiko: Kiko goats were developed in New Zealand as meat goats. They were created by crossing feral does with Nubian, Toggenberg, and Saanen bucks. Kikos are usually white and are generally a hardy breed. According to one recent study, the Kiko may be more resistant to parasites than other goats. They also may have fewer problems with foot rot. According to the same study, Kikos weaned kids that weighed more per doe compared with Boer goats. On the other hand, Boers are still preferred at sale barns. Many goat breeders like to breed a Boer buck with a Kiko doe.

Myotonic: The Myotonic, or Tennessee Fainting Goat, is another meat breed. They are also known as the Wooden Leg or "stiff leg" goat. They have a recessive gene that causes their muscles to freeze up when they are alarmed. This makes them temporarily fall over. They are one of the only breeds native to the United States. The Myotonic goat is heavily muscled through the rump and deep in the chest. However, they are smaller than the other major goat meat breeds. These goats are particularly good for crossbreeding purposes. Numbers of Myotonic goats are low compared to other meat goats, which means they might cost more. With their fainting characteristic, they are easier to contain inside fences, but they are also at greater risk from predators.

Savannah: The Savannah is a new breed in the U.S. and were only imported in the late 1990s. They have a large frame and are well muscled. They are white with some black pigment on the ears. They have the same body characteristics as the Boer goat.

Spanish: The Spanish goat was first brought to Texas in the early 1540s by Spanish explorers. Only the fittest goats survived, and they became a very hardy breed, good at foraging. They lived mainly in the wild, and this provided an advantage to smaller goats that needed less food. They are also good mothers. Some goat breeders have been able to breed for bigger size, more muscle, more milk, and other desirable traits. Spanish goats are one of the main meat goats in the United States. These goats come in many different colors and color patterns.

Pet goats

Pygmy: The Pygmy goat comes from Africa and is kept primarily as a pet. The Pygmy goat has a straight, medium-long hair coat, and it may be of any color. It has a small, blocky body. Does should measure less than 22 $^3/_8$ inches at the withers, while bucks should measure less than 23 $^3/_8$ at the top of the shoulders.

Buying Goats

There are many different kinds of goats for different purposes. Start by reading up on the different breeds so you will know what kind of goats you are looking for. Do you want goats for meat? For milk or cheese? For fiber? For weed control? It always helps to know what you have in mind. Next, make sure you are prepared for your new animals before you bring any goats home. Have shelter, feed, waterers, buckets, and other things you will need in place. You need to be prepared to care for your goats before you bring them home.

Where to buy kids and adults

As with other kinds of livestock, you usually can buy goats from many different sources, including auctions and sales barns. However, these are not always the best places to get your goats. It is generally best to buy your kids and adult goats directly from another farmer who breeds them. Visit farms to see where the goats are raised. You can tell a lot by visiting a farm. This often will give you a good overview of the goat's health and hygiene. Healthy goats come from healthy farms. Goats that come from auctions and sales barns have been exposed to animals from many farms, which means they could have picked up diseases. In addition, sellers want to get rid of the animals for some reason. You are much better off going directly to a breeder's farm and asking to see breeding-quality goats.

What to look for when buying goats

- **Pedigree:** A document or chart with the recorded ancestry of a goat, its parents, grandparents, and so on

- **Registration:** Documents verifying an animal is registered in the official herd book of a recognized registry organization for that breed. When it is said that an animal has "papers," it means that the animal is registered.

- **Registered purebred:** A goat whose papers are readily available; it has been registered with an official registry organization, it is listed in the herd book, and there is a document to prove it.

- **Purebred:** Goats that, according to their ancestry, fall into a breed group defined by national and often international breed standards. Purebreds may or may not have papers documenting their ancestry. For example, a breeder who keeps a small herd of purebreds but does not want the expense and trouble of acquiring papers for each one he or she owns might sell you a goat that is not officially registered. You have to take the breeder's word that the goat is purebred. Breeders are generally honest and reliable, but if you want to register your animal in the future, proving pedigree may be difficult.

- **Grades:** Goats of mixed breeding

- **Recorded grades:** Goats that meet a list of requirements regarding appearance and quality of milk. Buying a recorded grade is good way to obtain a high-milk-producing goat that is less expensive than a purebred.

- **Americans:** A doe that is seven-eighths pure of one breed, or a buck that is fifteen-sixteenths pure. This is determined by tracing ancestry from a point at which two different breeds were bred and the offspring were then bred back into a pure line, until offspring are nearly pure but not quite. Americans offer you the opportunity to know something from their pedigree about how the goat will grow and produce, as you would with a purebred, but they are often less expensive.

- **Native on appearance (NOA):** Appears to be of a specific breed

- **Experimental:** A term that denotes an accidental breeding between purebred goats of different breeds

Two terms refer specifically to milking quality rather than ancestry. A doe that falls under one of these categories might be attractive. Both of these classifications are based upon a point system and are determined by someone independent of the owner.

- **Advanced registry:** A doe documented to have given a set amount of milk over the course of a year (high-yield)

- **Star milker:** A system whereby a goat is given a star rating depending upon her consistent yield (measured day by day) and the percent of butterfat her milk contains. A star milker generally must give 10 to 11 pounds of milk in a day.

Purebred or mixed breed?

There are various considerations and reasons for why a goat farmer would want purebred goats, but there are equal reasons for why one would not. The choice depends upon your goals, your finances, and your immediate priorities.

Having a purebred allows you to make predictions about the goat based on years of knowledge about the breed's behavior and milk production. Each individual is unique, and being purebred is not a guarantee, but purchasing a purebred goat provides some certainty that the goat will perform as expected. You can make predictions regarding adult size, temperament, reproduction, health, and vigor of a purebred goat. Some breeds are more prone to specific illnesses or physical flaws. Some breeds are can be bred year-round, such as the Nigerian Dwarf, and others breed seasonally. If your goats are all of one breed, you will be able to predict the adult size of any offspring.

In many cases, you will be able to get a better price for a purebred goat if you decide to sell it or its purebred offspring. If you want to show your goats, they must be purebred and have papers to prove it. Showing your goats advertises your farm and the quality of your goats, and this can be profitable when other goat keepers seek to purchase them for their own herds. If you want to make money from stud fees by keeping a buck or two for breeding, a purebred buck will bring higher fees, and one with some success in the show ring will bring even more.

On the other hand, starting your herd with purebred goats will be more expensive than starting with goats that are not purebred. If your immediate goal is providing milk for your family and learning to keep and milk goats, a goat of mixed breed will serve your purpose well. These goats are generally referred to as grades. A grade can give great milk, be highly productive, and make a wonderful pet. Many dairy herds are made up of mixed-breed goats, and sometimes this is deliberate. As with many species, mixed breed animals often display "hybrid vigor" — they are healthier and stronger on average than purebred animals.

Selecting and buying your goats

After you have learned something about each breed's strengths and weaknesses, milk and meat production, milk composition, fiber, size, appearance, and temperament, you can begin looking for your own goats. You probably will recognize some breeds, such as the Saanen, the Nigerian Dwarf, and the LaMancha, on sight because of their distinct physical traits. Begin by seeking out goat herds living and breeding in your immediate area. Visit several of them, and get to know the ranchers and breeders who may later become part of your support network. As you explore resources and interact with breeders and sellers, keep a notebook handy and take notes. Question goat keepers about their experiences with their goats, and ask them why they prefer one breed to another.

When you are ready to purchase a goat, there are several places to look:

- **The Internet:** You can find goats advertised for sale on the Internet on classified ad sites such as Craigslist (**www.craigslist.org**) and on state Department of Agriculture websites. Try an Internet search with keywords such as "goat for sale" or "LaMancha."

- **Magazines and journals:** Many publications list breeders and have classified ad sections. Some of these are *Goat Biz*® *Magazine* (**www.goatmagazine.info/goatbiz**), *Goat Rancher* (**www.goatrancher.com**), *Dairy Goat Journal* (**www.dairygoatjournal.com**), and *The Goat Magazine*™ (**www.goatmagazine.com**).

- **Shows and events:** Livestock shows and events take place year-round. You will find goat owners and breeders — even goats for sale — at any of these. Visit the online sites or call various goat breed associations to find out when and where shows and events are taking place. These events, even when you are not quite ready to buy, are a good place to learn about breeds, see them up close, and question the experts. Visit the goat barn at a county or state fair. You can see some of the best breed specimens there, learn a bit about showing, and chat with owners.

- **Breeders:** Find breeders by contacting goat associations and by doing an Internet search.

- **Auctions:** Be wary of buying a goat at a livestock auction. The animals being auctioned off are probably being sold for a reason. A goat may be an inferior milker, have a difficult temperament, or carry some undesirable genetic trait. Worse, the animal may come from a herd infected with foot rot or some other contagious disease that can spread to your healthy goats. Even if the goat is healthy, simply being in the auction pen is likely to expose it to disease. Occasionally, a good bargain can be found at an auction, but reserve this method of goat acquisition until you know goats better.

- **County extension office:** Your local agricultural extension office can refer you to farmers who raise and sell goats in your immediate area. The staff often can give valuable advice, including current pricing in your area and what to expect once you start negotiating with a seller.

Pricing — not black and white

The price of a dairy goat can range from around $50 to hundreds of dollars. Many variables determine the price of a goat: the popularity of the specific breed; whether the goat is purebred, grade, or not registered at all; the goat's sex, age, and milk production; the individual's health and breeding history; and its conformation, or how closely an individual goat matches the ideal standard for the breed. Price can vary depending on the time of year, whether a goat has won a ribbon in a show, and whether a doe is pregnant. Finally, price varies according to geographical region.

You will not know exactly how much you can expect to pay for goats until you start shopping around, but you can learn about the factors that go into pricing a goat and be able to judge whether you are being offered a fair price. If you are genuinely interested in a particular goat, do not hesitate to negotiate and see if you can work out a price that is satisfactory to both you and the seller. Many who are experienced in buying and selling goats will tell you, you can always find a purebred goat at a bargain price and a mixed breed offered for an unfairly high price. The more you educate yourself about the realities of pricing in your region, the less likely you are to lose money in a bad deal or unwise investment.

Evaluating a dairy goat

Browsing through the breed prices in your region will give you a general idea of what you will pay for a goat of a particular breed and what you will pay for a mixed breed.

When you evaluate a dairy goat, look for these three key physical characteristics:

- Milking: Is the shape and condition of the udder good, and are suspensory ligaments intact?

- Body shape and structure: Is the animal sturdy, with the bones supporting the musculature of the body, and is the body of the correct shape and size?

- Overall health: Does the animal show any sign of disease?

When you are examining a specific dairy goat, you will first want to know what sort of milker she is. A goat may be sweet, affectionate, and attractive, but if she does not produce milk, she does not suit your purpose. Ask for permission to milk each goat you consider. If you do not yet know how to milk, ask to observe the milking. Observe what sort of temperament the goat displays during milking. Note the type of restraint used during milking because this is what the goat is accustomed to. A reputable goat seller will not object to your touching the goats and observing or performing milking.

A second major consideration is the goat's conformation — how closely it matches the ideal physical specifications for its breed. Conformation is important whether the goat is of a given breed or a mix. An animal's quality is judged by specific standards of appearance because these physical characteristics affect the animal's overall health and potential to produce milk. For example, the internal milking apparatus may not be formed correctly in a goat with double teats. This will make milking difficult, and output may be far less than that of a better example of the breed. Physical flaws can shorten the milking life of a doe and reduce its lifetime milk production, even if she is a good milker now. If you plan to sell purebred registered kids for profit, conformation defects in the adult may pass to its kids and lower their market value, along with your reputation as a breeder. No individual goat has perfect conformation, but good conformation contributes to the overall health of your herd, lower veterinary expenses, and the future milking productivity of your dairy.

Overall body type and condition

Start by getting a general idea of the goat's health and physical condition. Ask to see the goat's papers. If the goat is purebred, ask to see the registration and any show cards. A show card will contain notes from the judges on the goat's conformation. If the animal is not a purebred, it may be registered with another type of registry. Ask to see those records.

The goat's owner should keep barn records that will tell you what kind of milk producer the goat has been. If the herd is registered, an independent party may keep records of the production for the herd and individual goats. Remember that the yearly output for a goat is far more significant than its daily output because output fluctuates throughout the year. Finally, ask to see health maintenance records, which will supply information regarding any illnesses in the individual or the herd, evidence of testing for common caprine (goat) diseases, and vaccination records. If the seller does not have these records and expects you to take his or her word that health has been maintained and vaccines are up to date, be wary of buying. Do not let good rapport with a seller lead you into trusting too easily and buying carelessly.

Skin and fur

Take a close look at the goat's fur and the skin. Check for dullness, excessive flakiness, or any abscesses in the skin. Skin should be thin, soft and a little loose over the middle section of the goat. Look for evidence of lice or mites, as this indicates the goat has not been well cared for. Skin problems can be an indication of internal health issues. Internal parasites affect the appearance of the skin.

Check that the fur is thick and consistent. Except for the Nubian, most goats do not have excessively shiny fur. It is usually coarse to the touch. As you become more familiar with goats, you will know how a goat's fur should look and will be able to spot abnormalities more easily. Make certain there are no bare patches and that the goat's skin generally looks clean and healthy.

Head, nose, and mouth

A healthy goat's eyes are bright and clear (Note: Goats' eyes have a rectangular pupil). Dull eyes are a sign of illness in an animal, and there should never be any mucous discharge from the eyes. The goat's muzzle should be broad with large, well-distended nostrils, indicating adequate nasal passages for breathing. The lips should be muscular because goats use them to browse for food. The jaws should be strong, and the wear of the teeth should be in keeping with the age the seller has reported.

The windpipe should be large and well developed. You can feel it through the neck, and you should observe no breathing difficulty. If you plan to show a purebred, look for a broad forehead and a jaw that is neither overshot nor undershot. Ears should be of correct shape and size. The neck should be slight and feminine in the doe and heavier and more masculine in a buck, with the length proportionate to the size of the animal. It should blend into the shoulders and widen toward the base.

Forelegs and chest

The forelegs should be set squarely under the goat to support the chest, not too narrowly or too far apart, as both positions will result in eventual undue strain on the shoulders and knees. Look for a broad chest, which will probably contain a well-developed respiratory system.

Barrel

The barrel, or body of the goat, should be broad, and deep — large in every way. This is where the digestive system resides, and a well-developed digestive system requires plenty of space to function properly.

Hipbones and rump

The shape of the hipbones and rump is important because this part of the goat's body carries the weight of the udder. The distance between the hipbones and pin bones should not be too narrow but should appear to support the animal sturdily. The rump should be broad, and the slope slight. A broad rump supports an udder well, and a broad shape also indicates the suspensory ligaments are well attached.

Udder and teats

The udder should be firm, with strong suspension. Large size is not important: udders that are too large or too pendulous eventually can hang low and risk being injured or stepped on. A large udder has less to do with milking ability than with fleshiness. You should not see any growths, rashes, or abnormalities on the skin of the udder.

The teats should be well formed — long enough to milk and not too wide. Sometimes called sausage teats, wide teats can interfere with the function of the milking apparatus. Keep in mind that short teats often lengthen over time with milking. If a goat has short teats, allowing her kids to nurse may stretch them and make them longer. There should not be double teats or teats with two orifices (openings).

Wattles and horns

Some goats have them; some do not. Wattles are folds of skin under the face on the side of the neck. Usually these are cut away with a clean pair of scissors shortly after birth. They are purely ornamental and, in fact, can be a problem because kids and other goats sometimes bite at or suck at them and cause sores. Horns are also ornamental. Most dairy breeders remove horns because they can be used as weapons, and a goat can accidentally hurt another goat or a human with them. Some breeders prefer the decorative nature of the horns or want the goats to be as natural as possible, so they leave them intact and learn to be cautious around them.

If you plan to show your goat, horns are not permitted and should have been removed. Horns that are not removed when the kid is young (disbudding) are difficult to remove later (dehorning), and this must be done with a surgical operation performed by a veterinarian.

A word about weight

Excess weight puts stress on joints and ligaments and causes serious complications during pregnancy. If you wish your goat to be healthy and stay that way, it should not be overweight. A veterinarian can teach you to judge when your goats are gaining weight, in which case, cut down on feed. If you purchase a goat that is obviously overweight, ask about any current and former health issues, and get the weight off as soon as you can.

Look at the seller's environment

Look around the goats' home for signs that the seller is responsible and cares about the goats. Goats that have been valued and well maintained are more likely to be healthy. Check for signs of cleanliness in the barn. Is it well swept and is there good air circulation? Are the goats tied? Do they have plenty of room for exercise and good shelter from the elements? Are feeders and stalls clean? Is the water clean and fresh? If the seller's barn records are incomplete and poorly kept, chances are his or her goats have been equally neglected.

Buying your goats

When you purchase a goat, it is important to have a written contract between you and the seller that specifies who is responsible for what, how payment will be made, who will transport the goat, what kind of health testing will be done, and what will happen if the goat dies after the deposit is paid. Many breeders use standard contracts; if your seller does not have a contract, prepare one yourself. Read the terms of the contract carefully before you sign it.

Here are some general guidelines for the purchase of your new goat:

- **Communicate clearly.** Tell the seller upfront what you are looking for, and do not waste the seller's time. If you think a seller might be waiting to hear from you and you are not interested, say so as soon as possible so the seller can show the goats to another buyer.

- **Settle any outstanding health concerns.** If there has been a problem with disease in the herd, or you suspect a problem, request a blood test. You may be required to pay for this, but it may save you hundreds of dollars in veterinary expenses later on. Be firm about health concerns — a responsible seller will not mind your diligence.

- **When negotiating a price, be polite.** You may want to buy from this seller again, so do not burn your bridges by being pushy or rude. If you decide against the sale and walk away, doing so politely can preserve the relationship, and because gossip travels, it can protect you in encounters with other sellers.

- **Expect to pay a deposit.** This will not be returned if you back out of the sale, because the seller has spent time on you and has perhaps kept other interested buyers away for you. If the animal dies unexpectedly or if kids are miscarried, the deposit should be refunded.

- **Keep your word and be on time.** Do what you say you will. Do not be late on the day you pick up the goat. Do not be late with payment. Old-fashioned manners are important when dealing with ranchers and farmers.

- **Arrange transportation for the goats.** It should be clear ahead of time whether the goats are to be picked up by you or are to be delivered. If you arrange to pick them up, arrive at the promised time. Once the goats are home and settled, contact the seller to say a final thank you and to notify him or her that the goats arrived safely. This will also give you the opportunity to ask any final questions you may have.

Begin Keeping Records Right Away

Besides beginning your barn (milk production) record, keep your other records accurate and organized from the first day when you bring your goats home. Obtain vaccination and worming records, along with any medical records from the seller, as well as registration records for your purebred goats. File these in folders as soon as you receive them — do not leave them in a pile on the corner of your desk. If you are paying for your goats on the day you receive them, remember to file those receipts. Keep receipts for any rental vehicles or transport fees. Also, make sure you file copies of licensing and regulatory paperwork.

Anatomy of a Goat

There are about 100 documented breeds and varieties of domestic goat. All goats share similar characteristics, breeding traits, and flocking instincts. Goats are small ruminants, meaning their digestive systems consist of multiple stomachs.

Domestic goats are typically categorized according to their usage as dairy, meat, or fiber-producing goats. The term "dual purpose" refers to a breed or individual goat that belongs to more than one of these categories. For example, you might have a milk-producing goat with lovely long hair that can be sheared and spun into yarn.

Goats are herbivores. Their bodies process grains, plants, and their own mothers' milk to supply all the nutrients they need. All herbivores share some common traits. For example, if you look at the head of a goat, sheep, horse, or cow, you will notice the eyes are set on the side of the head, not at the front like human eyes or those of your dog or your cat. This is because in the animal world, herbivores are most often the prey of carnivores. Carnivores have eyes that see ahead for tracking and hunting. Herbivores are stalked and set upon as they graze, and eyes in the sides of their heads allow them to see danger approaching from the side or behind. Herbivores feel safer in numbers (herds) and are usually in a paranoid state of mind, ready to fight or flee from danger. This is the way your goats view the world.

When you speak to a veterinarian, another goat owner, or perhaps to a judge at a livestock show, they will use anatomical terms specific to a goat. The illustration below shows the main parts of a female goat's anatomy:

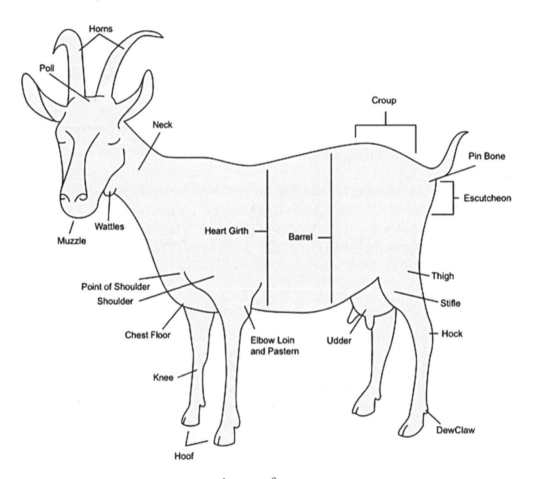

Anatomy of a goat

Digestive system

A goat is a ruminant, an animal that chews its cud. Like cattle and sheep, goats have four stomach-like compartments in their digestive systems. Each of the four — the reticulum, rumen, omasum, and abomasum — plays a unique part in digesting food matter. It is important to understand how the digestive system of a goat works so you can avoid digestive problems caused by improper feeding.

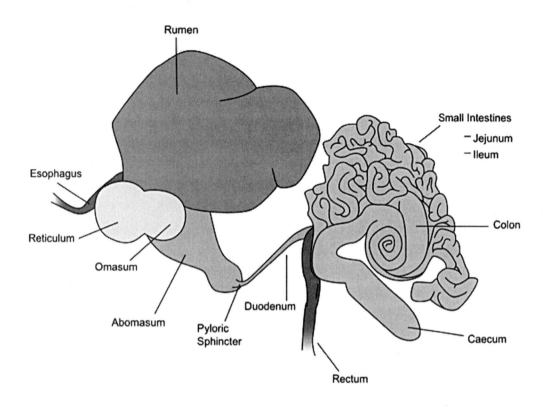

Digestive system of a goat

- Rumen: This is the largest compartment, comprising about 80 percent of the whole stomach. It is sometimes called the fermentation vat because this is where most of the fermentation takes place. The rumen is most important for the digestion of fiber, and fiber makes up a large part of the goat's diet.

- Reticulum: This is separated from the rumen only by a partial wall. When dissected, the inside is made up of many little cups that look like a honeycomb, so it is often called the "honeycomb" compartment. It functions as a fluid pump.

- Omasum: Also called many ply, this compartment has many folds, similar to a cabbage. Its function is to absorb nutrients.

- Abomasum: This is the second largest of the four stomachs and is referred to as the "true stomach" because it is where real digestion occurs. The abomasum contains pepsin enzymes and hydrochloric acid that break down proteins into easily digested simple compounds.

When a ruminant eats, the partly chewed food enters the rumen and reticulum, where it ferments with the acidic saliva. A well-developed rumen can hold 4 to 5 gallons of liquid and fermenting fiber. What cannot be broken down is sent back to the mouth as soft masses (cud) to be rechewed before entering the rumen and reticulum again. The walls of the rumen and reticulum absorb fatty acids and vitamins. After the plant matter is thoroughly broken down, it enters the second two chambers, the omasum and abomasum, where nutrients are extracted and final digestion takes place.

The digestive systems of kids (baby goats) do not function in the way those of adult goats do. Newborn kids use only the abomasum (true stomach) to digest liquid food. As the kid begins to experiment with eating roughage, its rumen begins to develop, and then the other chambers. Once you notice a kid chewing its cud, the four stomach chambers are likely fully formed and functional.

In order to maintain the rumen in good working order, a goat requires the right proportion of roughage to grain. Feeding too much grain to a goat is not only expensive, but also it impairs the muscle tone of the rumen. The digestive systems of adult goats that are not fed enough fiber begin to function more like those of single-stomached animals, and the contractions of the rumen almost cease. On the other hand, when the goats have too much fiber without enough grain to provide energy for digestion, the rumen becomes so full that food cannot pass into the omasum, which results in bloating and death.

Udders

Proper care of a goat's udder is essential to milk production and the health of the doe. The udder of a goat has two halves, each containing a single mammary gland; it has two teats where a cow's has four. The two sides of the udder should be the same size and separated by a cleft. The mammary glands contain tiny sacks of cells called alveoli (or alcilli) that secrete milk, surrounded by muscular cells that allow the milk to exit, also called "letting down" the milk, when the udder is stimulated by milking or a kid sucking.

The udder is suspended from the abdominal wall by a series of ligaments called udder attachments or udder supports. If these become abnormally stretched or weakened for any reason, the udder hangs too low and is prone to injury, such as being stepped on by the doe or by other goats.

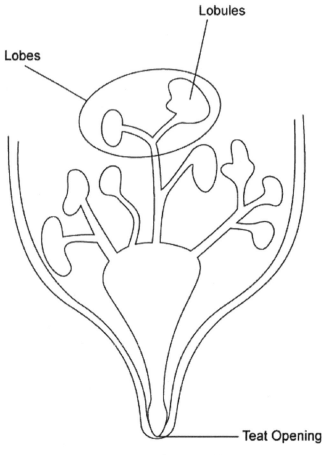

Diagram of a goat's udder

Here is an overview of the visible parts of the udder and their respective functions:

- Udder cistern: The area above the teat that holds the milk; also called the gland cistern. This is the part of the udder that appears full. Each cistern holds about 1 pound of milk at a time.

- Teat cistern: The reservoir between the streak canal and the udder cistern, through which the milk passes on its way down and out of the udder

- Streak canal: The final passageway for milk out of the teat

- Furstenberg's rosette: A many-folded mucus membrane that works as a plug to prevent leakage. It also keeps bacteria from entering the streak canal and traveling up into the udder.

These parts of the udder are invisible to the naked eye:

- Alveoli (plural): Tiny sack-like structures containing cells that secrete milk when hormonal conditions are appropriate. These cells are surrounded by muscle cells that contract during milk let down.

- Lobules: Bunches of alveoli bound together

- Lobes: Bunches of lobules

- Myoepithelial cells: These cells surround the alveoli and release a hormone called oxytocin that stimulates the udder to let down the milk.

- Milk canals: A series of tubes that carry milk from the alveoli to the udder

The alveoli secrete milk, which then travels down the milk canals to the udder cistern, where it accumulates. At the time of milking, the myoepithelial cells release oxytocin, which causes the milk to travel from the udder cistern through the teat canal to the streak canal and out into your milk bucket or jug. After milking, the Furstenberg's rosette closes, effectively plugging the entrance to keep out bacteria and prevent leakage.

The health of the udder is maintained by milking at regular 12-hour intervals, massaging and washing the udder before milking, and using teat dip and an udder balm.

Horns

Goats are horned animals, for the most part, though a few breeds are naturally polled, or born without horns. Both the male and female of the species carry horns. The length and size vary with the breed. Certain breeds, such as the Saanen, are purposely bred to be hornless, but this has some consequences. The gene for hornlessness is linked to a gene for the development of hermaphroditism (the presence of both male and female reproductive organs). Female goats that received a hornless gene from both parents (homozygous) will be barren, and bucks may suffer from blocked semen. Horned goats and polled goats that received the hornless gene from only one parent do not have these problems. To avoid producing sterile offspring, a hornless female should always be bred with a horned buck.

Some goat owners elect to remove the horns from their animals for safety and convenience. Others like to leave things in a natural state. Goats use their horns to scratch themselves, which helps to control lice and keep their skin healthy, and on occasion to defend themselves against attacking dogs or other predators. Goats rarely wound people intentionally with their horns, but they can use them to damage fences, shelters, and equipment. If polled goats and goats with horns are kept together in the same herd, they should be watched carefully. A dominant or aggressive goat may use its horns to injure others.

Dairy goats and goats used for shows routinely have their horns removed because it makes them much easier to handle and removes a possible source of injury. Goats with horns cannot fit their heads easily into milking stands or through feeding racks fitted with keyholes, slots with an opening at the top to allow the head to enter, to control feeding behavior. They are more likely to get their heads caught in a fence or a hole in an enclosure or building wall.

Horns are removed with a relatively simple procedure called disbudding when goats are young and the horns are still buds. This is the safest horn removal option. Removing larger horns as the goat ages is a surgical procedure that should only be performed by a vet and is painful and traumatic for the animal. It requires removing skin from the goat's forehead and leaves holes that take time to heal.

Teeth

A goat has front teeth only in its lower jaw; the upper jaw has a hard, tough pad called a dental palate.

When a kid is born, it often has its first two front milk teeth and sometimes the first four have already broken through. By its third month, all the milk teeth have broken through. At about 15 months, the adult teeth begin to appear, and by the time the goat is 3 ½ to 4 years old, it has all its adult teeth. An adult goat has 12 molars in the upper and lower jaws and eight front teeth in the lower jaw. A goat with all its adult teeth is "aged." When the goat is 5 years old, the front incisors begin to spread apart and wear down, and eventually they break off and fall out. A goat with missing front teeth is "broken mouthed." When all the teeth are gone, the goat is a "gummer." It is possible to tell the age of a young goat by looking at its teeth, but once it is more than 5 years old, the wear and condition of the teeth may vary according to its diet and the location in which it lives. A coarse diet wears teeth down faster than a soft diet.

Development of Goat Teeth

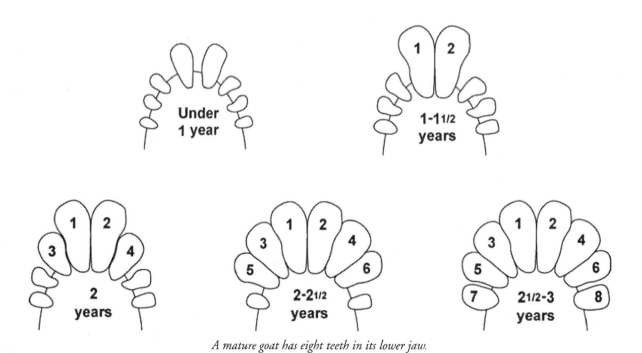

A mature goat has eight teeth in its lower jaw.

Handling Goats

Goats are one of the trickiest animals to handle. You should handle kids often from a young age to get them used to it. You will need to handle your goats regularly for things such as worming, vaccinations, hoof trimming, and other routine matters. These events will go much more smoothly if your goats are used to being handled.

Goats are different from some other livestock. When they are upset they may lie down or cram themselves into a corner. They sometimes become aggressive toward each other. Unlike some animals, goats are led by their females and stay in family groups. And, if you have any weak spots in your fences, your goats will find them.

Goats can wear halters or collars, which helps in leading them. They can be led by offering them a bucket of feed. It is usually easiest to handle a goat if you lead it to the corner of a small pen and block its escape. In this situation, you can trim a goat's hooves or give the animal vaccinations. You can restrain the goat against a wall or place it on a milking stand to work on its hooves.

Be calm and patient when you work with goats. Keep your voice low, and try to minimize stress.

Safety and goats

Goats are friendly and generally nonaggressive; however, they can knock you down. Also, if they are horned, you can accidentally injure yourself simply by turning too quickly and running into a goat. If you are small in stature, or if you have children who plan to help with the goats, you must keep safety in mind when selecting animals for your herd. Goat breeds vary greatly in size; some goats weigh 150 pounds. The temperament of an individual goat is also a consideration; a particularly rambunctious or malicious older goat may be too much for a child to handle.

The more familiar you are with an animal, the safer you are. Many barnyard injuries occur because someone does not know how the livestock will move or how they will react. The more you understand your goats, the more confidence you will have in handling them, and the more pleasant your experience will be.

Goats are normally friendly and enjoy the company of humans, but a goat that is injured, frightened, or nervous might not be as friendly. A buck that is eager to mate will be more assertive than usual. Males should be handled and trained while they are small; if they are not, they grow into big teenage goats that want to play with you and may deliver a powerful head-butt. A goat will rear up high on its hind legs before butting anything, so you have a few moments' warning. A goat that does not want to be milked might use its horns or its bare head to toss a pail across the room, toss a passing cat, or kick out at you while in the milking enclosure. These occurrences are uncommon, but keep them in mind, and be aware of what could happen.

Do not treat a kid like a puppy

When kids are small and cute, it is tempting for children to play with them like puppies, pushing against their heads. This can inadvertently teach them to butt people when they become adults. Play with kids by running with them and chasing them, petting and scratching them, teaching them to walk on a leash, and obey commands or hand signals.

Housing Goats

The goat shelter should protect the goat from wind, predators, and wet weather. Your geographical location will drive your housing scheme for goats. In dry, arid regions, little will be needed other than a wind and shade protection.

Colder, harsher climates will require a sturdier structure to protect the goats from winter wind chill and wet snow. If you plan to have dairy goats, your housing plans will need to be a bit more elaborate. The barn should be a sturdy structure devoted to your dairy herd and should not house other goats or animals. Pens do not need to be cemented but should be maintained in a clean and dry manner. The does can be kept in a loose housing situation, which provides one or two large pens for the goats, or the does can be confined to their own individual pen or tie-stall.

Structures

Each type of housing presents its own benefits and problems. A loose house situation, in which the goats are kept in one or two large pens inside a barn and allowed to move around freely, gives the does exercise and social contact. The manure pack can provide extra warmth in the winter as it emits some heat and insulates from the ground. A manure pack is essentially what it sounds like: a layer of composting manure, along with bedding, where the goats are housed. Although it may sound unappealing and unsanitary, a manure pack is often an excellent natural source of heat when housing farm animals. The big disadvantage of a loose housing situation is it is hard to maintain the manure pack with a dry upper layer. Hay must be fed off the ground to lessen the transmission of parasites. The individual pen housing option, in which eat goat has its own pen, will have higher initial costs due to pen or stall construction and can deprive the does of exercise and social contact. With the loose housing option, the does also can be provided with outside access to a pen or pasture during good weather. This is also the most popular option for young stock and meat-type goats. Bucks also should be given their own shelter with the same standard as the housing for the does and young stock.

Dairy goats have more requirements than goats raised for meat or fiber or kept as pets. In addition to shelter and feeding areas, you will need space for milking, for processing milk and storing equipment, and for taking care of kids and pregnant does. Everything has to be kept as clean as possible to protect the purity of the milk and the health of the does.

Milk production and quality is closely linked to stress levels in your goats, so you want to make their environment as pleasant as possible by providing the most comfortable accommodations you can afford. Goats need places where they can stay warm (in cold weather) or out of the sun (in hot weather) and sleep safely; pens or enclosures where they can be separated from other goats from time to time; an outdoor run or exercise yard; pastures or fields where they can forage; and objects to climb on. Feeding and watering stations should be accessible and easy to keep clean. You will want to provide stall areas that can be easily cleaned and pens that are safely separated from storage areas. How  many pens and pastures, and how much space you need, depends mostly upon the nature of your region's climate, the goals you have in mind for your operation, and of course, the size of your herd.

If you are starting with just two or three goats, keep the arrangements simple. You can expand your facilities later when you decide to increase your herd. Before constructing any special buildings or investing in expensive dairy equipment, consult your local agricultural officials and zoning department to make sure any improvements you make comply with zoning laws, building codes, and regulations. Local agricultural bureaus will have information and advice specific to goat keeping in your region, including recommendations for housing, building plans, and warnings about disease.

To determine how much land you need for your goats, first check local government zoning regulations. Besides being zoned for livestock, you might have to comply with regulations specifying the amount of land required per animal housed. A minimum amount of space probably is required to house any livestock at all. In most rural areas, the rules governing goat keeping will not be too restrictive for your purposes. Some urban areas do not allow livestock to be kept at all, while others are friendly to community gardens and small farm enterprises. In some areas, goats are defined as livestock while in others they are defined as companion animals. This definition can affect the success of a dairy-farming operation.

Most people are surprised to learn that, when well managed, five acres can support 100 dairy goats. You can keep a dozen goats on one or two acres, including land for your stable. Within this space, specific areas and enclosures should be allotted for various purposes.

Yards and fences

No animal can escape like a goat. Goats are clever and like to work at solving problems. A small flaw in a fence presents an irresistible challenge to a goat brain. Prepare an escape-proof enclosure before you bring home your first goats. Goats love to eat shrubs, vegetables, garden plants, and tender rose bushes (which contain a lot of vitamin C). They also love to jump on top of cars. A reliable, well-made fence is essential to everyone's well-being and peace of mind.

A well-built fence remains strong for as long as it is needed, prevents goats from going where they do not belong, and protects them from dogs, coyotes, and other predators. Good fences also protect goats from demolishing your trees and shrubs. For keeping goats, you will need three types of fencing: boundary or perimeter fences, interior fences, and barn lot fences.

- Fences around the perimeters of your pastures are the longest fences and are usually permanent; they should be constructed of quality materials that do not require much maintenance.

- The interior fences used to divide pastures up into sections for rotation, or to separate goats, can be either permanent or temporary and movable. These do not need to be as durable and strong because even if the goats escape, the perimeter fences will still keep them in the enclosure.

- The fences that enclose your barn lot or goat yard must be able to withstand a lot of wear and tear and abuse from the goats.

Goats like to put their feet up

Whatever facility you are constructing for goats, remember that they like to stand on their back legs and rest their front feet on any available object or projection. This means your wire fences eventually will begin to sag, dirt will get into watering pans, and hay will be dragged down from feeders. Horizontal elements of wooden fences and gates should be on the outside of the goat enclosure, not inside where the goats can climb on them.

A small, fenced-in exercise yard adjacent to your goat enclosure is ideal, even if you have a large pasture for your goats. This should be in a sunny, dry spot, preferably on the southern side where it will get the most exposure to sunlight. A slight slope will help to keep it drained and dry. If the yard tends to be muddy or damp, at least part of it should be paved with concrete or pavers for easy cleaning. Walking on this hard surface will help to keep hooves trimmed. The fencing around this enclosure must be particularly goat-resistant because it will take more of a beating — confined goats will entertain themselves by attempting to destroy the fence.

Several types of fencing are appropriate for goats, including wire fencing, wooden, and electric fences. Your selection should be based on your budget and how you intend to manage your goats.

Woven wire fencing

Wire fencing is widely used by goat keepers. It consists of smooth, vertical wires held in place by horizontal wires called stays. The vertical wires are spaced 6 to 12 inches apart. The horizontal wires are generally closer together at the bottom and wider apart at the top. Wire fencing is available in galvanized, high-tensile (able to resist stretching), and polymer-coated, high-tensile varieties. The numbers on the packaging tell you the size and spacing of the fence; for example, 8/32/9 fencing is 32 inches tall, has  eight horizontal wires, and vertical wires every 9 inches. Wire fencing and other fencing components can be found at stores such as Tractor Supply Company (**www.tractorsupply.com**), feed stores, and home supply stores.

Typically, wire fencing 4 to 5 feet high is used and is attached to 7-foot posts spaced 12 feet apart. A strand of electric wire 12 inches from the ground and another strand at about the shoulder-level of an adult goat should discourage the goats from leaning on the fence or rubbing against it. Many goat keepers use wire fence 32 inches high and augment the height with several strands of electrified or barbed wire above it.

The disadvantages of wire fencing are its cost and the time and expertise needed to install it properly. Once installed, a woven wire fence is more or less permanent. It is durable but needs to be checked regularly and repaired if it starts to bend or sag. Horned goats enjoy tugging at the wire with their horns and sometimes get their heads stuck in the wire squares. Using wire with 12-inch spacing between the vertical wires can mitigate this problem.

Strong wooden fence posts must be used for corners and gates, but in between them, you can use T-posts, which are metal posts, often made from recycled railroad tracks, that are pounded into the ground with a handheld post pounder.

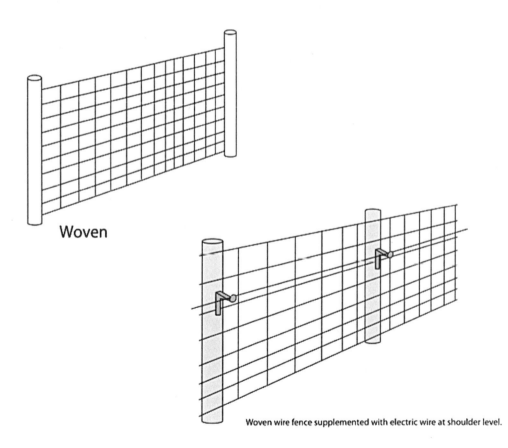

Woven

Woven wire fence supplemented with electric wire at shoulder level.

Choose fence posts carefully

Fence posts are treated to make them durable and resistant to rot and insects. Because dairy goats might gnaw on them, pay careful attention to the chemicals used to treat the wood. Pentachlorophenol is effective in preventing decay and insect damage but contains carcinogenic compounds called dioxins. Posts treated with creosote may damage the hides of sensitive livestock.

High-tensile wire fencing

High-tensile fencing, developed in New Zealand, uses several strands of smooth wires held along posts, or combinations of posts and spacers called battens, stays, or droppers. This fencing system uses smooth 12 ½-gauge wire with yield strength of 1,600 pounds. (A conventional 12 ½-gauge wire will yield at tensile force of less than 500 pounds and break at less than 550 pounds.) Each wire is stretched with 250 pounds of tension, maintained by permanent in-line stretchers or tension springs. The higher tension in the wire reduces sagging but requires using strong end- and corner-brace assemblies. High-tensile fencing is less expensive than barbed or woven wire fences, requires less time to erect, to repair, requires fewer posts, is easier to handle, lasts longer, and is easily electrified.

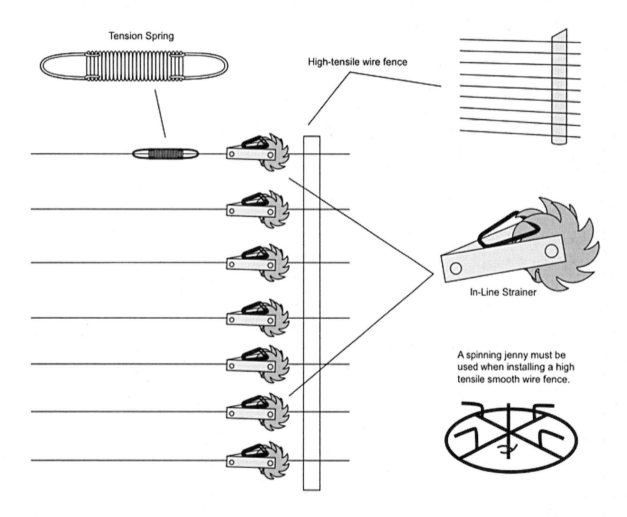

Example of a high tensile wire fence

Non-electrified steel wire fences must be grounded

All non-electric fences using steel wires on nonconductive posts must be grounded to protect humans and livestock from electric shock due to lightning and fallen electrical wires. Grounding electrodes should be a standard galvanized steel post or a ¾-inch galvanized steel pipe driven in firm earth to a minimum depth of 3 feet. A ground should be installed every 300 feet in moist or damp soils. Grounds should be used every 150 feet in dry, sandy, or rocky soils. All fence wires should be connected to the ground rod. Wire fences should be broken up at maximum intervals of 1,000 feet by means of a wooden gate, wooden panel section, or insulating material.

Wooden fences

A fence made of vertical wooden palings 47 inches high, with the bottom no more than 2 inches off the ground and no more than 2 inches of space between the palings, is largely goat-proof. Goats can squeeze through small spaces, so the fence should be regularly inspected to ensure all the palings are sound and firmly attached. A wooden fence can be reinforced with wire fencing to make it escape-proof. Wooden fencing is usually too expensive to be used for large enclosures.

Electric fences

Some goat keepers swear by electric fencing, but goats occasionally can escape through it. It is better used to reinforce a wire or wooden fence, or for interior partitions within a larger enclosure or pasture. Electric wire of various types and

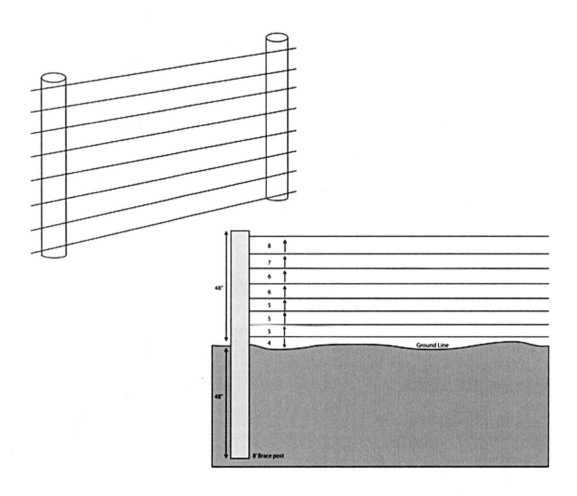

Example of an electric fence

sizes is available at farm stores, as well as electrified string net, polywire, polytape, and rope fences. These fences are easy to move and rearrange and are ideal for temporary fencing, such as when you are moving your goats around different areas of a pasture. They are designed to work with step-in fence posts, made of metal, plastic, or fiberglass that can be inserted into the ground using your body weight. Electric fence chargers cost between $60 and $300, depending on the length and sophistication of your fence system. Fi-Shock™ (**www.fishock.com**) and Parmak (**www.parmak.com/ Fencers/FencerMain.htm**) sell solar-powered electric fence chargers that are convenient for remote locations.

Goats can be trained to fear an electric fence by luring them toward it with grain until they experience the electric shock.

Barbed wire

Barbed wire can be used to goat-proof existing farm fences, but it is not recommended for dairy goats because it can injure their coats and udders. To contain goats, a barbed wire fence should be built of eight to ten strands of tight, evenly spaced 15-gauge wire.

Livestock panels

Livestock panels made of welded steel rods are excellent for temporary enclosures such as paddocks and pens, but as with wooden panels, they are usually too expensive for fencing. They are easy to install and move around. Sharp edges and snipped wires should be smoothed with a file to avoid torn clothes and injury to your goats. Sheep stock panels have smaller spaces between the welded wires so small animals will not get their heads caught, but these are even more expensive.

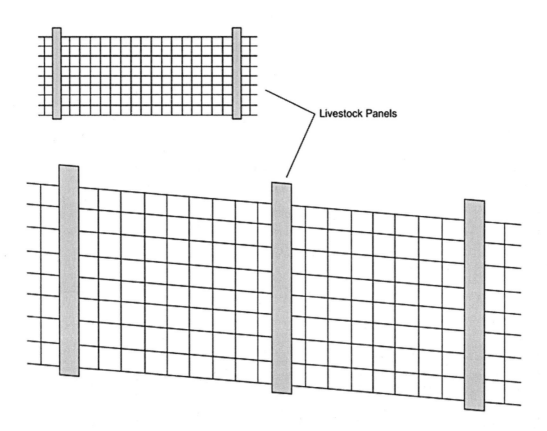

Example of livestock panels

Gates

Fences as well as gates and doors must be made escape-proof. Gates should open inward so goats cannot push their way out. Some goat keepers install strong springs that snap the gates shut. Place latches low on the outside of the gate where goats cannot lean over and reach them. Goats are notorious for opening latches on doors and gates; make certain yours are durable and lock firmly into place so your goats cannot escape the enclosure or let themselves into the room where hay or feed is stored. It is a good idea to put a goat-proof latch on any refrigerator door or any cupboards that hold medicines. Crossties and frames should be on the outside of a gate where the goats cannot use them to get a foothold. Gates and fences should never be topped with sharp pickets because goats can get their heads and hooves stuck between them.

Sheds, stables, and barns

You can keep goats in sheds, old chicken coops, barns, and garages made of wood, stone, concrete, cement block, corrugated iron, and even cement half-pipes. The type of shelter you use will depend upon several variables, the first of which will be your climate. In a mild climate, you will need to keep your goats from overheating during hot summer months. Some goats are sensitive to heat, particularly if humidity is high. If your farm experiences snow, harsh wind, and frozen ground for several months out of the year, your shelter will need insulation and protection from the cold.

Dairy goats should be kept happy and comfortable because stress can harm milk production. If your goats are fortunate enough to have a large pasture area, a three-sided field shelter should be located in the part of the pasture farthest from the barn so they can easily find refuge from hot sun, rain, and cold wind. In a cold climate, a low shelter no more than 5 feet high in the front and 3 to 4 feet high in the back will hold the goats' body heat in around their bodies.

Photo courtesy of Soggy Bottom Farms

In addition to field shelters, you will need a permanent building for long-term shelter, storage, possibly office space, and a milking area. A barn is ideal, but this could be a smaller structure, such as a stable or garage. If you are able to store feed, bedding, and medical equipment in a separate building away from the area where goats are, you may be able to manage with just a large shed for milking and permanent shelter.

The recommended size for a goat shelter ranges from 12 square feet per animal in a situation where the goats will be outdoors much of the year and have a lot of space for outdoor exercise to 24 square feet per animal in a climate with long, severe winters or hot and humid summers. The more time the goats must spend inside, the more space you will need to allot per animal to keep them comfortable and healthy. If you are planning to breed your does, you need extra space for birthing pens and housing kids. In addition to the living space where goats will spend most of their time, you will need to add extra square footage for storage and milking areas.

Housing Requirements for Dairy Goats

	LARGE AND MEDIUM GOATS	PYGMY GOATS
DOES		
Open housing	16 sq. ft.	10 sq. ft.
If goats are to be kept indoors year-round	21.5 - 27 sq. ft.	18 - 25 sq. ft.
Yard	200 sq. ft.	130 sq. ft.

	LARGE AND MEDIUM GOATS	PYGMY GOATS
Minimum exercise area	50 sq. ft.	40 sq. ft.
Stalls	6X6 ft	5X5 ft
Stall partition height	3.5 ft	3 ft.
Milk parlor	5X8 ft	5X8 ft
Fence height	5 ft.	4 ft.
Feeding shelf	15.5 inches wide	15.5 inches wide
If kids are being raised, space per kid	5.5 sq. ft.	
Water	2 to 10.5 quarts daily	2 to 10 quarts daily
Storage — bedding for one year	4 cubic yds.	
BUCKS		
Housing	40 sq. ft.	30 sq. ft.
Stall partition	5 ft.	4 ft.
Yard	100 sq. ft.	70 sq. ft.
Fence height	6 ft.	5 ft.

Your permanent shelter should keep out moisture, wind, and drafts, but, at the same time, it needs to be airy and well ventilated, with adequate air circulation. Clean, well-circulated air is a priority because goats are particularly prone to pneumonia, asthma, and other respiratory illnesses, some of which can prove fatal. Condensation on the inside walls of the shelter and an increasingly intense and pungent smell of ammonia are signs that air circulation is poor and more ventilation is needed. If you build individual stalls for your goats, use wire mesh, welded pipes, or wooden palings with spaces between them so the goats can see each other and interact. You will need a place where you can isolate a domineering or sick goat, and places where young kids can find refuge from adult goats, such as inside dog crates or barrels.

In addition to a resting area, the goats need a feeding area where they can line up to eat. It must be long enough to accommodate all the goats at the same time. A sill, such as a wooden beam or a raised ledge, should separate the feeding area from the resting area. The area where the goats stand when they are eating should be only lightly littered with straw and swept out daily.

As you assemble your shelter, keep in mind that you will be wheeling a wheelbarrow down aisles and in and out of stalls anytime you transport bedding, refuse, or feed, and leave yourself enough space to maneuver comfortably. Access to electricity and fresh running water will make your work much easier. Without running water, you will have to carry water to your goats twice a day. You will need a sink area for preparing feed and washing equipment and feed utensils.

Temperature

The climate in which you live will determine how much you need to control the temperature and humidity inside your barn or stable. Goats are healthiest and happiest when the air temperature is between 46 degrees and 70 degrees F. Goats are fine in temperatures down to 0 F, as the herd produces its own heat. When the temperature drops below that, you will need to provide some kind of artificial heating. Goats begin to suffer when the temperature rises above 80 F and need access to shade and cooling breezes.

Artificial heating and cooling should be used only when necessary. If you live in a climate where you can sustain comfortable temperatures inside the goats' permanent shelter area without artificial heat or air conditioning, you still should have some large ventilation fans hung or installed up high, away from the goats (any electrical cords must be secured away from the herd's reach as well). These will help with air circulation in warm weather, keep the urine smell down, keep stalls dryer, and maintain indoor air quality at an acceptable level for goats and humans.

If you live in a climate where you can maintain a good barn temperature year-round without artificial heating and cooling, you probably do not need to insulate the goat shelter. Insulation helps keep the shelter comfortable in extreme temperatures. It should be installed behind a sturdy wall away from your goats, which happily will eat it if they can reach it. A moisture barrier never should be used in a goat shelter because it will result in condensation and unwanted moisture inside the shelter.

Ventilation

Poor ventilation in a goat shelter can be detrimental to the goats' health and milk production. Excess moisture and harmful gases and dust can cause respiratory problems, while temperature extremes reduce productivity and make goats and humans uncomfortable. A good ventilation system distributes fresh air without drafts to all parts of a shelter, helps maintain desired temperatures, and reduces ammonia levels.

Construction materials

Goats are just as happy in a simple shelter as they are in a state-of-the-art goat palace. A shelter can be made of stone, cement, wood, or metal. Metal is the least desirable because it is less stable, and it will be cold in the winter and hot in the summer. Do not use soft materials such as plasterboard or plywood where goats are kept because they inevitably will destroy it. All materials need to be sturdy and resistant to gnawing.

There should be no gaps, holes, or openings anywhere wider than 2 inches as noses, hooves, and even small heads could be caught when curious goats investigate. Check for open spaces between the wall and floor. Interior partitions should have openings no wider than 2 inches between slats. Make certain the floor is free of holes. The roof of a goat shelter should be designed to keep goats from climbing on top of it.

Wooden Shelters

There are a few points to keep in mind when selecting wood for your goat shelter. Some woods splinter more easily than others. Goats also gnaw at certain types of wood, particularly if they are bored or if they are lacking in minerals. Be very careful about using treated wood and selecting paints or stains — some of them contain ingredients that can poison or sicken your goats. When building partitions of wood, do not leave more than 2 inches of space between slats because a horn or leg, or even a kid's nose, may be caught. Use screws for construction instead of nails, which will make it much easier to disassemble the structure if you decide to remodel later on.

Lighting

Windows and natural light inside the goat shelter encourage milk production and help with ventilation during warm weather. However, you will need to be able to close windows in bad weather. Electric lighting inside the shelter is helpful when you are milking or doing chores on winter evenings or if there is an emergency during the night.

During some times of the year, lighting in the goat shelter can be used to increase milk production and stimulate earlier breeding. Goats normally breed in the fall, when days begin to get shorter, so they are pregnant through the winter months (about 150 days on average) and give birth in spring. If all your goats are kidding at the same time, they will lactate at the same time and be drying off within weeks of one another. This leaves you without consistent milk production throughout the year. You may wish to influence the breeding cycles of some of your does so they give birth in fall; this way lactation cycles, lactation curves, and drying off periods are staggered, and your milk production is steady. Decreasing available barn light in early spring will simulate the naturally occurring shortening of days in fall and encourage estrus in does and breeding behavior in bucks.

Flooring

Most goat keepers prefer concrete flooring because it is easy to keep clean. It can easily be mopped with bleach. Concrete does not absorb urine, so moisture will accumulate on its surface. If you design the floor so there is a central gutter (outside the stalls of course), or if the floor slopes slightly so urine and wash water will run toward a gutter in the side of the stall or pen, it will not be difficult to keep your stalls dry and urine free. A concrete floor is cold and hard, so you will have to be diligent about providing adequate bedding material for insulation.

Wood or hard dirt floors are softer and stay warmer than concrete. However, wood will tend to absorb moisture (and urine) and will be susceptible to rot and mold. It will be more difficult to keep clean. Dirt floors have a similar problem: urine will soak into the floor and make mud, on which your goats will lie. It will be difficult to disinfect the floor with a bleach wash or other detergent because it will soak into the dirt. You will not be able to disinfect a dirt floor because it is impossible to wash away detergents safely. Keep these factors in mind when deciding on flooring for your goat shelter.

Sleeping platforms

Goats like sleeping platforms — simple wooden platforms raised a few inches off the floor in their resting area. These keep goats up off a cold, hard floor and away from rodents or insects that might be active in their bedding at night. They are also cooler in summer because air circulates underneath. Make these platforms movable or with removable slats so you can clean underneath. They should be lightly covered with bedding.

Bedding

Regardless of what sort of floor you have, you must provide bedding in the stalls and rest areas so goats can find warmth and so they do not develop pressure sores from lying on hard surfaces. Straw makes the best litter, but you can use sawdust or peat. About 1 pound of straw per goat should be added to the bedding per day. Urine and fecal matter will accumulate at the bottom of your goats' bedding, creating a damp area underneath. As long as you have enough thickness on top of this to keep your goats dry, the damp area is acceptable and, in fact, unavoidable. Fresh dry hay can be spread on top of the bedding every day, a method called deep littering. In some conditions, the layers underneath will begin to compost, creating extra warmth for your goats. The deep mattress of straw bedding needs to be cleaned out about once every three months and replaced with fresh bedding to control odor and insects. Do not forget that as the straw bedding grows deeper, it raises the height of the floor, and the goats will find it easier to get over partitions and enclosure walls.

Do not let the used bedding accumulate: remove it immediately to the fields or garden, compost it, or sell it as fertilizer. Remember to use a wheelbarrow designated only for manure and bedding, not one used for hay and feed. If you are unable to dispose of used bedding immediately, you will need a manure storage area.

Feeding Area

Goats are fussy eaters. They yank out selected morsels and step backward, scattering hay on the floor of the feeding area. They will not eat soiled feed or hay off the floor. Goats should not eat off the ground because they can ingest parasites from fecal matter.

Ordinary livestock feeding racks and troughs are wasteful because so much of the hay falls on the ground and because goats often soil their food by putting their front feet in the racks or jumping up into them. Goat farmers have developed many devices for feeding goats. Not only are goats messy when eating, but they also can be pushy and bossy at mealtime; they do not like to share. An ideal feeding station is designed to minimize pushing, minimize waste, and keep food off the ground. It should have enough openings to allow all your goats to feed comfortably, and the openings should be narrow enough so that curious kids cannot jump in and soil the hay with their dirty little hooves.

Wire feeders

Many goat owners buy commercial heavy wire feeders designed to hold hay. The best of these are sturdy and take a lot of abuse without sustaining serious damage. Some owners will not use wire feeders because goats easily can hook a hoof in them, or horned goats can become tangled and stuck. Because they are wire cages, they are not appropriate for holding anything but hay. A common type fits firmly over the side of a stall; it is relatively inexpensive, and several of these can be purchased to place in various locations. A wire feeder can be moved easily from place to place as long as there is a sturdy bar or low wall to hang it on. This is useful when you need to separate mothers and kids from the rest of the herd or isolate a sick goat. A variation of this type of feeder can be placed on a common low wall or bar between pens, where hungry goats can access it from either side.

You frequently will see a fence-line feeder on a goat farm. This is a feeder made of heavy wire mesh that hangs on the fence or is made up of a loose section of fence. These are frequently homemade rather than purchased commercially.

Bag feeders

At livestock shows, you will notice that some people carry portable hay bags, which can be filled with hay and hung on a bar as a temporary feeder. These bags have large openings in the sides through which the goats can access the hay and pull it out to eat. Some are made entirely of netting. Although these commonly are used for horses, many goat owners point out that these bags can be safety hazards for goats that tend to climb up on feeders. A goat could become tangled in the bag feeder and break a leg — or a neck — trying to free itself.

Wooden mangers

A popular type of manger is the keyhole manger, a wooden structure that allows each goat a slot through which to place its head while eating. This design is useful because it discourages competition and makes it more difficult for goats to toss the hay out of the manger. Some of these feature a latch that comes down to restrain the goats in the slots.

Another type of feeder holds the hay in a rack slightly above the goats with slats sloping outward at an angle of 63 degrees. The space between the slats is narrow enough that the goats have to tilt their heads sideways to get them into the rack to eat. If the goat steps backwards, the slats trap its ears. Goats soon learn to keep their heads inside the rack while they eat.

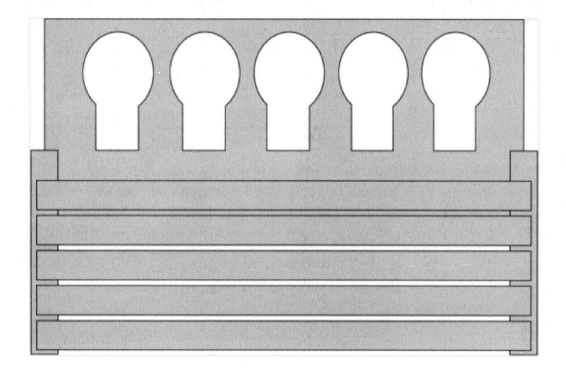

Examples of keyhole feeders

Feeding shelves

The best solution is a feeding shelf protected by a feeding gate through which the goats stick their heads to eat. A feeding station that keeps goats separated while they eat prevents the bigger animals and dominant does from depriving the smaller goats of the grain and high protein feed they need to produce milk.

The feeding shelf should be at least 19 ½ inches wide and long enough to accommodate all the goats. For large, fully grown goats, the shelf should be mounted at a height of 15 ½ to 19 ½ inches above the floor. Kids and smaller goats can be accommodated by building the shelf so its height can be adjusted as they grow or by placing a narrow step or shelf in front of the feeding gate about 10 inches above the floor, on which they can place their front feet while feeding. Nail a raised edge or board along the front of the feeding shelf to keep the food from sliding off.

A feeding gate in front of the feeding shelf acts as a barrier that prevents goats from jumping onto the shelf. Goats thrust their heads through openings in the feeding gate and sort through the food on the shelf, picking out what they want to eat. The feeding gate forces the goats to spread out while feeding and ensures each goat has equal access to the feeding shelf. In addition to the feeding shelf, you can place a hayrack on the wall in the resting area and fill it with inferior hay. Anytime they want, the goats can eat hay from the rack, and whatever falls on the floor becomes part of their bedding. Also, you could suspend a hook from the ceiling to hold bunches of fresh forage. Mount mineral licks on a wall or a stand up off the floor to keep them from being stepped on and soiled.

Plans for building goat feeding stations are widely available online or from county agricultural extension offices. Many goat farmers build their own, and some are willing to build them for other goat owners. Dairy suppliers and goat supply catalogs sell ready-made feeding stations. Regardless of which types of feeders you choose, always have safety in mind. Try to imagine all the ways that a goat can be injured before you invest in any feeder.

Watering

Goats always need a supply of fresh, clean drinking water, especially when they are lactating. For a small herd of a few goats, you can supply water in buckets or tubs. Several small containers are preferable to a single large one because they are easier to clean, and if one is soiled or spilled, there is still clean water in another container. Because goats tend to knock these over or step in water containers and soil their water, it should be changed twice a day. For larger herds, automatic drinking troughs designed especially for goats are available. In winter, special heaters can be placed in water containers to keep the drinking water from freezing.

Buck Stables

If you are keeping bucks for mating, they will have to be separated from the does. Several bucks can be kept together in an open area. Their enclosure must be fortified to withstand their strength, and partition walls should be at least 5 feet high to prevent goats from escaping. Bucks need about 33 square feet of resting space and 54 square feet of yard, preferably outside. Bucks should be kept at least 50 feet downwind from the does to prevent their odors from affecting the does' milk.

Accommodations for Kids and Mothers

If you plan to keep kids together with their mothers for several days after birth or to raise some of your kids to add to your herd, arrange an area in your shelter where the mothers and newborn kids can be separated from the other goats. Any spaces in the stall partitions must be small enough that tiny kids cannot slip through under the partitions or between slats, so make sure you address these spaces. Arrange provisions for feeding and watering the doe and her kid(s) in the stall. To give young kids access to water and feed, watering pans and feeding shelves will have to be placed lower or made so their height can be adjusted.

Kids of the same age can be raised together successfully in a group, but do not mix kids of different ages because older kids can transmit disease and bacteria to the younger ones. To avoid the spread of disease and to ensure they are getting the proper amount of nutrition, kids should be fed separately from adult goats in their own area through a feeding gate that prevents them from spilling and soiling their food. Allow 5 ½ square feet of floor space and about 8 inches along a feeding shelf for each kid. After the kids stop nursing, you can move them to a young goat area where they have more space (10 ¾ square feet). The amount of space you need to allot for kids and young goats depends on how you plan to operate your dairy business and how large your herd will be.

Pastures and Outdoor Enclosures

Most goats are kept outside during daylight hours for at least part of the year, where they can freely forage for vegetation and obtain adequate exercise, sunshine, and fresh air. Goats can be pastured together with horses, cattle, or sheep because they browse vegetation other livestock will not touch. Owners of meat and fiber goats often turn them loose into wooded areas to browse. This is not advised for dairy goats because they can injure their udders on rough undergrowth and because the quality and type of forage they eat affects the flavor of their milk.

Dairy goats typically are confined in open pasture and kept closer to the stable or barn where they are milked. Goats like to hang around close to the shed or barn — they are less apt than sheep or cattle to wander for long distances. They also like to be close to where people are.

The amount of forage your goats can access will affect your budget — if they are grazing on pasture, they are not eating as much feed out of your barn. In winter months, you will be providing almost all of their food, but you can lighten the financial burden in warmer months by providing access to areas for foraging and browsing.

The ideal solution is to establish at least one extra enclosure that can be left empty for weeks at a time to recover while the goats are in another pen. The size of these enclosures is up to you. A larger area will stay cleaner and give your goats more exercise. It will be necessary to maintain some control over what grows within the enclosures, such as toxic weeds. If you enjoy walking, wander over a large pasture periodically to check the quality of forage. The presence of a few poisonous plants will not necessarily harm your goats; if they have enough other forage to eat, they are not likely to consume more than a tiny amount of a harmful plant.

If you do not have enough land to fence two larger enclosures, you will need to have at least one. In addition, you will need at least one small pen to separate livestock when weaning kids or isolating a sick or overly aggressive animal from the herd. If you decide you want to keep a buck for breeding, you must be able to accommodate him separately from your does.

To move a small herd of goats from one pen to another, or from pasture to barn, all you need is a bucket of grain. Simply walk out into the field and rattle it, and the goats will follow you anywhere. However, a larger herd of a dozen goats, even fewer if you are physically small and have a large breed, will soon have you on the ground in their goat-like enthusiasm to get at the grain.

Feeding Your Goats

Proper nutrition is crucial to successful goat farming. Milk production and pregnancy put heavy demands on a goat's body that must be met with good nutrition. There are various schools of thought regarding the feeding of goats, from complete control of the diet to allowing free pasture grazing. Goats naturally prefer foraging, but climate and the shortage of sufficient pasture usually make it necessary to feed the goats at least some additional hay and grain. Most small-scale goat farmers settle on a combination of the two. Because no two farms and no two pastures are exactly alike, working out the best feeding program for your goats takes trial and error, as well as practice.

The challenge for a goat farmer is providing the necessary nutrition for each goat with the least expense. The availability of good natural forage changes with the seasons and the weather. If natural forage or hay do not provide adequate amounts of protein, carbohydrates, minerals, and vitamins, purchase grain rations and supplements to compensate for the lack of nutrients. Good quality hay means less expensive grain rations. Pregnant and lactating does have greater nutritional needs than dry does or bucks. It is wasteful to provide more nutrition than a goat needs, but inadequate nutrition results in lower milk production and poor health.

Goats are more like gazelles and antelopes: they eat less food but select the most nourishing parts of a plant, such as young shoots, tender leaves, and small blossoms from among grasses, shrubs, and trees. When goats are consuming large amounts of lush green grass, they are not necessarily acquiring all the nutrients they need for optimum health and milk production. Goats that graze freely in pastures may still require grain and nutritional supplements to keep them in good health.

Calculating your goats' nutritional needs

Goats need energy — referred to as TDN (total digestible nutrients) or ENE (estimated net energy) — protein, minerals, vitamins, and water. Energy needs vary with a goat's size, age, and maturity; whether it is pregnant or lactating; weather conditions; the amount of stress it is subjected to; and the nutritional elements in the rest of the goat's diet. Milkers need a sufficient quantity of energy to continue producing large quantities of milk and maintain their body weight. A doe that receives insufficient nutritional energy may go into heat late, and her newborn kids may be weak. Overfeeding nutritional energy causes the accumulation of body fat, may inhibit fertility, and endangers the health of a doe during kidding.

A doe with a high milk yield needs extra energy in the first three months after she gives birth to a kid. If she does not receive adequate nutrition, her body tries to compensate by breaking down its own reserves, already depleted by pregnancy.

Planning a feeding program

Calculating your individual goat's nutritional needs and formulating your own feed mixtures is a science. Langston University offers a free goat ration calculator (**www.luresext.edu/goats/research/rationbalancer.htm**) that allows you to enter information about your goats and recommends optimum ration mixtures. Unless you grow your own grain, want to feed your goats only organic feed, or have a large herd, it is easier to use commercially prepared goat feed.

When starting out, you can avoid mistakes by buying goat feed from your local feed store and closely following the directions on the package. You also can consult a local farmer who raises goats successfully and follow his or her feeding program. Your program will vary according to the amount and type of land you have, the number of goats, and your geographical location, which will determine seasonal availability of plants for browsing. Your feeding program will change with the seasons as different growth appears and disappears in your pastures, new hay is harvested, and your goats are subjected to different weather conditions.

Roughage composed of live plants and hay will make up the major part of your goat's diet because it is an important element for keeping the rumen working and healthy. Too little or too much roughage can be detrimental to goat digestion: Too little roughage decreases muscle tone in the rumen, which causes it to work less efficiently, and too much roughage can disturb the balance of organisms in the rumen that work to break down fiber. In a young, milk-fed kid, the rumen and reticulum take up only 30 percent of its stomach space. In a mature doe, the rumen takes up 80 percent of the stomach space, and the reticulum takes up another 5 percent. The rumen of a young goat will not increase in size without proper stretching and development. Your kids must begin eating roughage even before they are weaned from their mothers' milk so their rumens develop well.

Water

Your goats' water needs to be fresh and clean. Milk production relies on water consumption, and milk quality relies upon the water's cleanliness. Bacteria living in unclean water are ingested by the goats and eventually end up in their milk, where they affect its taste and quality. Bacteria in the water can make the goat sick if ingested. Make a habit of keeping drinking water fresh and clean.

Water helps goats control their body temperature, aids in waste elimination, and improves their digestion. The amount of water an individual goat needs is determined by temperature, the moisture content of their forage, dietary salt, the amount of exercise it gets, and whether it is lactating. A lactating doe needs to consume more water than the amount of milk she produces.

Design a way to fill water containers frequently and easily. Hoses or faucets should be adequate and within easy reach of containers (remember that hoses must be wound up and taken away from chewing goats after filling water containers). Place plenty of water sources around in several locations where the goats regularly spend time. Elevate smaller containers, such as pails and small tubs, off the ground where they will not be stepped in and turned over, or contaminated by feed, feces, or dirt from the ground. Wash water containers regularly with a solution of a disinfectant such as Nolvasan, chlorhexidine, or bleach, scrubbing with a hard-bristle brush, and always rinse thoroughly. These disinfectants will kill bacteria clinging to the sides of the container.

Water in outdoor containers should be prevented from freezing. Do not force your goats to eat snow because their water is frozen. Goats like their water slightly tepid. In winter, special heaters can be placed in water containers to keep the water at an ideal temperature. Does that are not lactating and bucks can be watered once a day in winter if they are given enough warm water to drink their fill.

When does drink more water, their milk production increases. Adding some molasses to the water encourages does to drink more. Warming the water in winter and cooling it during hot weather also encourages drinking. Lactating goats that have free access to water whenever they want it produce 10 percent more milk than if they are only watered twice a day. You can install automatic watering devices that supply clean water through a nozzle whenever a goat tries to drink from it.

Water makes up more than 60 percent of the soft tissue of your goat's body and about 87 percent of goat's milk. All of the fluid lost through milking, urination, and expiration (breathing) needs to be replaced daily. A goat dies when it loses more than 20 percent of its water content.

Roughage

Roughage is highly fibrous plant material. It provides energy for milkers and young goats and gives added energy to female goats in late stages of pregnancy. When broken down, roughage provides a goat with important nutrients. Goats get this needed roughage when they browse the brush and bushes in a pasture, gobble up weeds, or eat green twigs and bark from the trees. They may get it from grass clippings, dry cornstalks (called corn stover) or turnips, parsnips, and carrots. You usually can obtain beet pulp or citrus pulp, also good roughage, from the feed store. Goats can get roughage from silage (corn and hay plants allowed to ferment in a silo). Many goats get daily roughage in the form of quality hay.

Green pasture

An exclusively lush pasture (green forage) can be healthy for your goats, with some limitations. Green forage generally consists of grass and succulent plants containing a lot of water; this means it contains fewer minerals than dry food. In order to get enough minerals, your goat has to eat an abundance of green forage but becomes satiated long before it has consumed enough nutrients and minerals. For this reason, green forage does not provide all the requirements of a healthy goat diet, and it is not desirable to raise goats on green pasture alone. A lush pasture diet can cause bloat if your goats consume enough of it.

One solution is to restrict the time your goats remain in the green pasture. However, it will be difficult to assess how much they are eating or how much green forage they are getting as a percentage of their diet. Another way to give green forage is to do it by confinement feeding, sometimes called soiling. The goat keeper cuts roughage from the pasture and brings it into a confined space to feed the goats. This way, the amount fed to the goats can be monitored.

A word of caution about grass clippings

If you are feeding your goats grass clippings from your lawn, consider the fertilizer and weed killer content in the grass. Fertilizer is never a good thing to feed to goats, and weed killers are toxic. If you do not use fertilizers and weed killers, you can feed grass clippings to the goats.

Mixed pasture

Pasture filled with a variety of grasses, weeds, brush, and woody plants is ideal for your goats. This is the type of pasture referred to when goat owners talk about natural, or free-range, feeding. Many goat owners maintain a few fenced pastures. Goats benefit from the exercise and the mental stimulation of exploring a pasture.

Ideal pastures are soil-tested, fertilized to compensate for deficiencies, planted with specific desirable grasses and plants, and managed to prevent overgrazing. Weeds that are particularly suitable for goat pasture include yarrow, daisy, chicory, dandelion, plantain, nettle, thistle, and wild roses, such as multiflora.

Goats can clear a pasture of all growth in an amazingly short time (sometimes a day or two per acre). They eat their preferred forage first before moving on to less appealing plants, and they can end up eradicating their favorite plants entirely. The solution is to limit their time in the pasture or rotate the goats through several enclosures, or paddocks, to give plants time to regrow. This is best done using movable fences within a large pasture enclosure with a secure, permanent fence. Because fewer of their favorite plants are available inside the smaller area, the goats finish them off and move on to other, less desirable plants. Goats also can be tethered and moved from one area to another. Tethered goats should be kept under close observation because their grazing habits make it easy for them to become tangled up in the tether and even hung on tree branches.

Pasture land must be monitored closely and frequently for the presence of toxic weeds. Toxic weeds can make your goats ill, do permanent damage to their nervous systems, and even can be deadly. Goats tend to avoid many poisonous weeds, and they nibble here and there, never eating a whole lot of anything at one time, so a few toxic weeds in a pasture should not be a problem. It is not true, however, that goats avoid eating toxic plants. They browse the best of what is available; if the good stuff is scarce or gone, they will turn to the toxic options. They accidentally may ingest toxic weeds while eating something else, such as new spring grass in a low-lying area.

Poisonous Plants

Countless plants contain material toxic to goats if enough of it is eaten. Some of these plants are well known, some are rare, some are poisonous only under certain circumstances or only if specific parts of them are eaten, and some are common garden ornamentals. You can find numerous lists of plants toxic to goats on the Internet (see the list maintained on the Fias Co Farm website: **http://fiascofarm.com/goats/poisonousplants.htm** and the U.S. Department of Agriculture website: **www.ars. usda.gov/Main/docs.htm?docid=10086**.

Some common pasture plants that are toxic to goats include the following:

- Amaryllis
- Avocado (leaves and fruit)
- Bracken fern (grows in shade)
- Dock weed
- Hemlock
- Locoweed
- Milkweed
- Mountain laurel
- Oak leaves (some types only)
- Sorrel
- Rhubarb
- White clover
- Wild cherry (wilted)

Be aware of the possibility of nitrate poisoning. Many plants good for goats provide nitrates, which is a necessary nutrient. However, under certain conditions these healthy plants can come to contain toxic levels of nitrates. Unusually high levels of nitrates accumulate in some plants, including oats, corn, alfalfa, pigweed, lamb's quarters, and Johnson and Sudan grasses, when they undergo a growth spurt after a dry spell. Another common source of nitrate poisoning is when goats consume animal waste or fertilizer. This usually happens when runoff from a nearby, contaminated field waters the plants they eat, or the goats drink it.

Hay

Hay is made from a variety of plants cut when still green and then allowed to dry (cure) before they are baled for storage. When these plants are cut at the right stage of growth and cured using the right methods, they retain nutrients that are valuable for your goat in addition to providing the fibrous material to keep its digestive system working well. Hay is more or less bright green color and is different from straw, which is the golden-colored dry leaves and stems left after the harvesting of grains such as wheat, oats, and barley. Hay is used as feed while straw is used as bedding.

The average goat eats at least 4 ½ pounds of hay per 100 pounds of body weight every day. A well-built Swiss milker will eat about 5 pounds of hay every day, and more during pregnancy. Hay that is fresher and composed of high-quality grasses and plants is more expensive. Some people make the mistake of feeding a poorer-quality hay, reasoning that it saves money, but feeding high-quality hay means you will be feeding less grain and other supplements; you do not save money by using cheaper hay. Like grain, high-quality hay is high in protein, so if your goats are getting the protein from the hay, they will not need as much in the form of grain.

Hay falls into two basic categories:

1 **Legume hay** is made of plants such as clover or alfalfa. It is higher in protein and calcium — important nutrients for all goats but especially for lactating does. Alfalfa is considered ideal hay for dairy goats because it is rich in calcium, and its protein content is around 13 percent, compared to 5 percent for some grass hays.

2 **Grass hay** is made of grass such as timothy, Johnson, brome, or orchard grass. If your goats are eating grass hay, provide supplemental protein and calcium with grain.

Experiment with various types of hay and with supplementing high-protein grain. Hay — or comparable roughage — should make up the major part of the goats' diet, and their diet must contain adequate protein. Lower quality hay can be fed to adult bucks or to does that are drying off between lactations.

Hay pellets can be purchased from feed stores in various sizes. These are ideal for goats because goats tend to be messy eaters. They will rummage through a big pile of hay, strewing it all over the floor, just to find a little piece of leafy stem. If you feed pellets, there is far less mess and more hay ends up in the goat. The only disadvantage is that pellets are more expensive.

Grain: a good thing in small quantities

The amount of energy provided to the goat per unit of feed is measured in therms. Alfalfa hay, the hay probably highest in nutrients, contains about 40 therms per 100 pounds of hay. The grains corn and barley contain almost twice this amount of therms. Goats need many of the nutrients present in a good grain ration that are not present in a roughage diet.

Grain ration contains added nutrients, such as salt (needed in lactating animals), protein, fats, and added vitamins and minerals such as iron. It also contains molasses, which acts as a binding material, cuts down on dust, and provides some additional minerals. Grain ration has as its foundation an assortment of grains such as corn, barley, rye, wheat bran, oats, sunflower seeds, and soybeans. It might contain soybean or linseed oils as added fat sources. It might contain dried vegetable matter, such as tomatoes, kale, carrots, turnips, beets, and parsnips.

Grain ration for goats can be obtained by the bag at a feed store. When you buy it premixed, you are assured that your goats are getting the necessary nutrients, premeasured in the best proportions. You will find that your goats are fond of their grain ration. Feeding too much of it is detrimental to their health, but they might not agree with you. You usually can use grain to lure a goat into a truck, into a stanchion, or anywhere else you need it to go. Grain must be stored securely where the goats cannot access it.

Important vitamins

If your goats are being fed a combination of forage and grain ration, they probably are getting the vitamins they need. Sometimes lactating or pregnant animals need more, especially if they are stall-fed and do not have the opportunity to consume a wide variety of plants through foraging.

- **Vitamins C, K, and the B:** These vitamins are all manufactured within the goat's body and do not need to be supplemented. Lactating animals may need supplementary vitamins A, D, and E.

- **Vitamin A:** Vitamin A helps goats resist various diseases. It is closely associated with reproductive health; it keeps udder cells healthy and helps the udder resist infection. It also contributes to eye health. To some extent, a goat manufactures vitamin A itself when it consumes foods that contain carotene such as carrots, yellow corn, and some green forage plants. However, vitamin A deficiency is not uncommon.

Kids deficient in vitamin A are prone to respiratory illnesses, often exhibiting watery eyes and mucous nasal discharge, coughing, and diarrhea. Because goats as a species are particularly susceptible to pneumonia, these kids can end up with pneumonia. In adult goats with vitamin A deficiency, you might observe susceptibility to infections, or night blindness (they will panic and flee if you approach them in the dark). It is believed that vitamin A deficiency is a cause of infertility in bucks.

- **Vitamin D:** Goats produce vitamin D when exposed to sunlight, as do other mammals, and so goats need plenty of sunshine to be healthy. Vitamin D is necessary to absorb essential minerals such as calcium and phosphorus.

- **Vitamin E:** Vitamin E is particularly important to the quality of milk. Vitamin E deficiency in a milk goat can cause her to produce milk that tends to spoil rapidly.

Mineral supplements

Novice livestock owners often are confused about whether and how to supplement minerals. Oversupplying some minerals can cause severe health issues that are just as dangerous as mineral deficiencies. Most goat owners provide supplemental minerals in loose form (available at a feed store), and make them available to the goats at all times. You will find that individuals who need supplementation to their diets tend to take just what they need.

Mineral deficiencies are often due to the composition of the soil in the region. If soil does not contain enough phosphorus, for example, there will not be phosphorus in the plant life. Or there might not be enough iron in the water. It helps to be aware of any major mineral deficiency in your area, so you can troubleshoot possible health problems when they begin to appear.

Salt blocks with added minerals are generally not favored for goat owners for several reasons. Chief among these is the tendency for the goats to overdose on salt (salty milk taste) and the tendency of goats to climb all over the blocks and contaminate them. It is better to provide loose minerals in an indoor feeder. Goats need relatively large quantities of calcium, phosphorous, magnesium, sodium, chlorine, potassium, and sulfur and small amounts of many trace minerals, most of which occur naturally in their feed.

You might want to consider providing a few minerals individually. Many goat owners claim that baking soda keeps the rumen functioning well and prevents indigestion. This can be added into the loose minerals you provide or offered separately to the goats, which will take it when they need it. Probiotics made of yeast or yeast mixtures are believed to aid digestion and improve rumen function. They can be purchased in dry or wet form. Some goat owners add them routinely to the grain ration, while others only provide it to goats suffering from digestive problems or under stress.

Some supplements can be given as a bolus (a large round mass fed orally all at once) or by injection. These are given when there is a known deficiency of a given mineral in your region of the country. Your veterinarian or agricultural extension officer can advise you if you should be giving any supplement routinely in this manner.

Bucks are prone to developing urinary calculi (bladder stones), the usually unavoidable result of an accumulation of salts. This can be quite painful, and if the stones are big enough to cause urinary obstruction, the condition is life threatening. Adding a little ammonium chloride to the buck's feed will help prevent this condition by acidifying the urine and preventing the stones from forming so easily. Take care though not to overdose; 1 teaspoon daily per 150 pounds of weight is plenty.

The very young and the very old

It makes sense to ensure that kids are getting enough food when the herd rushes to eat, jostling each other to get at the hay. Often, feeders are designed so the little ones can eat at a lower level while the taller goats lean over them to get hay higher up. Or the kids may enjoy picking up the hay that has fallen to the ground as the older goats eat. Some goats will be more assertive than others at feeding time; the more docile animals are shoved aside and may remain hungry. Observe your smaller kids carefully, and note whether they are putting on weight and growing at the rate they should.

An elderly goat also may have trouble getting adequate feed. Aged goats are weaker than the younger ones and are pushed aside or bullied away from feeders. Sometimes, stiff older joints make moving fast enough to the feeding station a difficult task. To ensure your older goats are getting enough nutrition, you might want to feed them in a place protected from the others, where there is not such stiff competition at mealtimes. The teeth of an older goat are well worn, which makes chewing more difficult. Special feed supplements may be necessary to ensure malnutrition does not become a problem. Your veterinarian can help you monitor your elderly goats for nutrition deficiencies.

Goat Health

Goats have a reputation for hardiness and endurance, but they are susceptible to illness if they are not fed or cared for properly or if they are subjected to undue stress either because of the weather or harassment by other goats, predators, or humans. Stress particularly weakens the immune system of a goat, and a traumatic experience can result in pneumonia.

You can do a lot toward keeping your goats healthy by:

- Providing the right amounts and proportions of food and a steady supply of drinking water

- Keeping their surroundings clean: clean stable, clean feed, and clean water. Many goat diseases are transmitted when goats come into contact with parasite eggs, bacteria, or viruses that have fallen on the ground from other goats.

- Providing an airy but draft-free, dry stable

- Parasite prevention through regular testing and worming

- Making sure goats have enough exercise

- Regular skin and hoof care

- Consistent washing of udders, dipping of teats, and observation of hygiene during milking

- Proper vaccination program

- Preventing injury

- Daily observation of your goats and quick response when symptoms appear

Consult your veterinarian or agricultural extension office to learn what particular diseases and parasites, if any, are problems in your area. They may recommend parasite testing or a vaccination program to prevent the spread of diseases that have affected local goat populations. The soils in your area may be deficient in one or more essential minerals, which make supplements crucial to the health of your goats.

Goats' curiosity and their habit of putting their forelegs up on trees and fences to eat make them susceptible to injury from damaged fences, wires, and sharp edges. Limit the grazing areas of dairy goats so their soft, low-hanging udders are not scratched and cut by underbrush. Bucks and meat goats do not have this problem. Goats also can be injured when vying for dominance in the herd or when horned goats are kept with hornless goats. Keep an eye out for excessive aggressive behavior or horseplay, and isolate either the victim or the troublemaker until she can be reintegrated with the herd.

Isolate new goats from your herd for 30 to 60 days

Goats easily can pick up infectious diseases and parasites at livestock auctions and fairs. Even when you buy a goat from a reputable farm, it might carry a disease. Infectious diseases have an incubation period, and symptoms may not appear right away. Once an infection or parasite spreads to your herd, it is hard to bring it under control. To keep your herd healthy and safe, quarantine new goats, and do not allow them to interact with your other goats through fences for 30 to 60 days.

During the quarantine period, vaccinate the new goats for tetanus and enterotoxemia unless the seller has provided you with reliable vaccination records. Treat them for external parasites and worm them, and watch for signs of respiratory illness and pinkeye. Observe them carefully, and if you have any doubts about their health, call your veterinarian to come and examine them.

Goats should be quarantined after they have been boarded with a veterinarian, visited another farm for stud service, or have been taken to a fair or showground.

Treating sick goats

You can perform some medical treatments yourself, such as first aid for cuts and scratches, administering worm medicine, some vaccinations, and even the lancing of abscesses. For most sick goats, however, you will need a veterinarian to diagnose the disease and prescribe the correct medication. The veterinarian can show you how to continue routine treatment on your own.

Get to know your veterinarian before you have a goat emergency or illness, perhaps by asking him or her to examine your herd and stable and make recommendations about local health problems. Post the veterinarian's telephone number where it is easily visible. If possible, get the number of a second veterinarian to call in emergencies when the first one is unavailable. Establish relationships with experienced goat keepers in your area who can act as mentors and whom you can call for advice when you have problems with your goats.

As soon as you detect symptoms of disease, isolate the sick goat in a clean, quiet stall away from the herd and provide her with her own supply of feed and water. Because separation from the herd can cause stress in a goat, locate a companion goat somewhere nearby where she can be seen and heard but will not come into contact with the sick goat. Goats appear to become discouraged quickly when they are seriously ill. Give your sick goats lots of attention, stroke them, talk to them, and hand-feed them treats. This kind of sympathetic support is an important factor in its recovery.

Vaccinating your goats

A whole range of vaccines is available for goats, but some are expensive and not all of them are necessary. Follow the recommendations of your veterinarian, local agricultural extension office, and other local goat owners regarding vaccinations against diseases that are threats in your area.

Goats everywhere should be vaccinated against tetanus and enterotoxemia (overeating disease) once a year. These vaccinations are available as a combination in a single vaccine. All your goats should receive an initial vaccination followed by a booster three to four weeks later and an annual vaccination after that. Pregnant goats should receive their annual vaccination one month before they give birth. Kids should be given their initial vaccination when they are one to two months old, followed by the booster three to four weeks later. Goats that are fed large amounts of concentrated feed may need to be vaccinated every six months because they are more susceptible to enterotoxemia.

How to give an injection to a goat

You quickly can learn to administer routine vaccinations yourself. Use a clean, new syringe for each session and a clean needle for each goat. Use sharp 16- and 18-gauge needles in ½-, ⅝-, or ¾-inch lengths. Shorter needles are used for subcutaneous injections.

Swirl (do not shake) the vaccine bottle to mix the contents. Pull back the plunger of the syringe a little further than the dose you plan to inject. Holding the vaccine bottle upside down, poke the needle through the rubber. Depress the plunger to inject air into the bottle. Pull the plunger back a little farther than the required dose, and then gently squeeze the excess back into the bottle to get rid of air bubbles. Always use a new needle to draw vaccine from a bottle to avoid contaminating its contents.

Subcutaneous (under the skin) injections: Most vaccines are given subcutaneously in the neck, over the ribs or in the hairless area of the armpit. Choose an area of clean, dry skin, and swab it with alcohol. Pinch the skin and lift up a little "tent" then slide the needle in, and slowly depress the plunger. Withdraw the needle and rub the area to distribute the vaccine.

> **Intramuscular injections:** Some antibiotics are given as intramuscular injections, usually into the muscle at the side of the neck. Have someone restrain the goat, and quickly and smoothly plunge the needle deep into the muscle. Pull back on the plunger about ¼ inch. If you see blood, you have penetrated a vein and must withdraw the needle and try again. Depress the plunger slowly and withdraw the needle.

First aid for wounds

Wounds should be disinfected with tincture of iodine or a coating of pine tar. To stop excessive bleeding, apply pressure with a clean, folded towel. If a wound is inflamed, wash it or bathe it with chamomile tea. Scratches on the udder can be treated with antibiotic ointment. For abscesses, apply a dressing or icthyol ointment. A veterinarian should stitch deep or gaping wounds. Dust with a fly-repellent powder or spread a fly-repellent ointment around the wound to keep flies off.

Goat Diseases

Contagious Ecthyma (Sore Mouth): A resistant virus that produces scabs about the lips and gums causes sore mouth. The virus is transmitted in the scabby material, which may remain viable in the soil for a long period. This disease is more serious in kids because the soreness prevents them from eating normally and because the infection may spread to their mothers' teats when they nurse. Immunity develops after the initial infection. A vaccination program can prevent the disease.

The purpose of treatment is to prevent a secondary bacterial infection. Gently remove the scabby material using gauze soaked in hydrogen peroxide, and then cover the area with zinc oxide or similar ointment. Wear plastic gloves because it is transmissible to humans.

Haemonchus contortus (barber pole worm): This is a blood-sucking stomach worm, which causes severe anemia and death in goats and sheep. It can become a severe problem in warm, humid weather. The larva live on pasture grasses. Once it is eaten, it develops into adult worms in the stomach. The female worm can lay thousands of eggs a day and sucks blood from the stomach lining. The eggs pass through the feces and contaminate the goat's environment. Treatment is through use of dewormers. Prevention revolves around not overstocking pastures and rotational grazing of pastureland.

Mastitis: Mastitis is an inflammation of the udder. It may be acute or chronic. Streptococcus or staphylococcus organisms cause most cases. The udder may appear hot, painful, tense, and hard. A wide-spectrum antibiotic may be needed or simple penicillin may be effective. The disease can be cured if treated early.

Meningeal deerworm: The white-tailed deer spreads this parasite. It usually does not cause problems in the deer, but when goats or sheep inadvertently ingest the worm larva, it damages the brain and spinal cord frequently causing death. Some infected animals will have mild signs such as limping or leg weakness while others become paralyzed. The disease cannot be diagnosed definitively in a live animal because the eggs do not show up in the feces nor can the parasite be detected in a blood sample. Direct examination of the brain and spinal cord is necessary for a diagnosis. Diagnosis is based upon signs and health history. Treatment is through use of high doses of dewormer along with supportive treatments such as steroids to reduce brain or spinal cord inflammation. Treatment will not reduce the damage done to the brain or spinal cord. To prevent, put up fencing to keep deer away.

Caseous lymphadenitis: This is a chronic bacterial infection of goats and sheep caused by *Corynebacterium pseudotuberculosis*. This bacterium enters the body through wounds causing abscesses. Once the disease is in the herd, it can quickly spread to other animals. Treatment involves lancing the abscess, draining the abscess material into a bag or container, and cleaning out the abscess with a disinfecting solution. The abscess material should not be allowed to contaminate the pens, building, or soil and should be burned.

Pinkeye: Pinkeye is a rapidly progressing eye infection caused by bacteria. Tall grasses, flies, and dry, dusty conditions seem to contribute to its spread. The goat begins closing its eye. Increased tearing, inflammation, and cloudiness and ulceration of the cornea that can cause temporary blindness follow this.

Infected goats should be separated from the herd and treated with topical ointment, or in some cases, with antibiotic injections administered by a veterinarian. Quarantining new goats can prevent the spread of pinkeye because it does not always appear right away.

Polioencephalomalacia (PEM): PEM is a thiamine deficiency most commonly occurring in kids 2 to 6 months old who are fed concentrate or feed that contains a high proportion of nutrients and is low in crude fiber content (less than 18 percent of dry matter). Feed high in grain and low in forage can suppress the normal production of thiamine by the digestive system. Feeding moldy hay, feed high in molasses, or sudden changes in feed can trigger PEM. The goat exhibits blindness, depression, lack of coordination, pressing the head against walls and fences, and convulsions. In severe cases, the goat falls into a fatal coma. Thiamine injections should be given as soon as the disease is detected, and the diet should be adjusted to include more forage and less grain.

Swollen joints: Various rheumatic illnesses affect goats in damp, cold environments, and they are not well understood. A virus that is apparently passed from mother to kid through colostrum causes one type, caprine arthritic encephalitis (CAE). In the early 1990s, researchers at the Washington State University found that 80 percent of the dairy goats they tested carried antibodies for CAE. An effort has been made since to eradicate it.

The disease progresses slowly and eventually manifests as severe swelling in the joints and apparent inflammation of the udder. There is no cure for CAE. Applying salves and heat to increase circulation in the affected areas can ease pain. Some goat keepers prevent carriers of CAE from further breeding. Kids can be separated from the mother at birth and fed with colostrum from a healthy goat or cow. Colostrum can be milked from the infected mother and cleared of the CAE virus by heating it to 131 F (55 C) for 60 minutes.

Udder Edema: Udder edema and congestion commonly is observed in high-producing dairy goats during the late dry period and after parturition (giving birth). Although the problem cannot be controlled totally, limiting the use of sodium (salt) and potassium (good sources are alfalfa hay and cane molasses) as well as high-energy feedstuffs, such as corn meal in the dry period, is helpful. Corn meal should be limited to about 20 percent of the ration. The total ration dry matter should contain about 0.2- to 0.3-percent sodium and 0.7-percent potassium. Although a lower energy and higher fiber ration is needed for the dry does, lactating does need higher energy feedstuffs in their rations with adequate amounts of good quality forages.

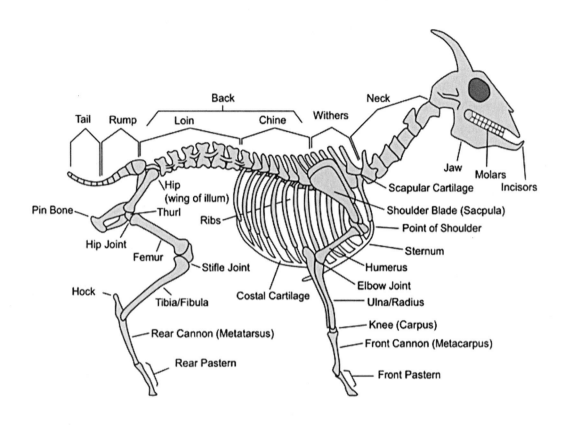

Example of a goat skeleton

Digestive diseases

Diarrhea (Scours): Diarrhea is often a response to mistakes in feeding, such as an over-high albumin content, an abrupt change in feed, too much concentrated feed, or feed that is rotten, fermented, or frozen. It also can be caused by infectious diseases and by internal parasites. Feed-related diarrhea is typically brothy and liquid, with a powerful smell. Watery stool mixed with blood indicates an infection of some kind. Intermittent diarrhea is a sign of worms.

The treatment for feed-related diarrhea is to withdraw concentrated feed and give plenty of water and branches of fir, spruce, and pine. If the goat has a fever or other symptoms, or if you suspect infection, consult a veterinarian. If diarrhea persists, check fecal samples for worms. Prolonged diarrhea leads to dehydration and a rough coat. Kids should be treated immediately because diarrhea can be fatal to them.

Enterotoxemia (Overeating Disease): *Clostridium perfringens* (type C and type D) cause this disease. Type C is seen primarily in young goats and causes a bloody diarrhea or sudden death. Type D (also known as overeating disease) affects weaned goats that are being fed high amounts of grains or that have an abrupt switch from a no- or low-grain diet to a high-grain diet. Affected goats usually are found dead without other signs. Others will appear to have a severe case of painful diarrhea. Treatment is with an antitoxin and supportive care. Prevention is through vaccinating pregnant does before breeding and three to four weeks before delivery. In adult animals, the symptoms are depression, intoxication, and poor coordination; in kids, it often just manifests as sudden death.

Bloating: Bloating occurs when a foreign object blocks the esophagus, and the goat cannot burp up the digestive gases in its rumen or when rapid eating or overeating of concentrated feed or damp green clover produces fermented foam in the rumen. Bloating in a kid is caused by faulty milk digestion. The left side of the goat bulges out, and the goat is obviously in pain. The expanding rumen restricts lung function and can cause respiratory failure. Bloat is potentially fatal.

To treat for bloating, remove the blockage from the esophagus by locating it from the outside and massaging it downwards. If the bloat appears to be the result of fermenting foam, instill a foam-destroying preparation such as vegetable oil or silicone from the vet. You also can stimulate the goat to produce and swallow more saliva by running a string gently back and forth through its mouth. Saliva breaks down the foam. As a last resort, you can release pressure by puncturing a hole in the rumen with a tool called a trochar or with a pen knife. However, this will bring only minor relief for bloat caused by fermenting foam in the rumen. This only should be done in emergencies when you cannot reach a veterinarian and the goat appears to be in dire straits, as it can result in an infection.

Acid rumen: Acid rumen occurs if a goat rapidly ingests a large quantity of sugar-rich food, such as bread, sugar beets, or concentrated food. The goat seems apathetic, hangs its head, and looks as though it is drunk. Bloating also can occur. To treat acid rumen, supply the goat with plenty of water. If the goat cannot stand up, call the veterinarian immediately.

Store concentrated food where it is secure from goats, and feed sugar-rich foods to them in gradually increasing quantities so they can become accustomed to it.

Foot scald: Foot scald is a moist, raw infection of the tissue between the toes. It is caused when *Fusobacterium necrophorum*, a bacterium that thrives in soil and manure, invades a scratch or lesion in a hoof constantly immersed in mud or warm muck. Foot scald typically occurs in only one of the front feet.

Foot rot: The germ that causes foot rot, *Bacteroides nodusus,* also thrives in wet, muddy areas where air is poorly circulated, and it multiplies in the presence of *F. necrophorum. B. nodusus* penetrates the deeper layers of the skin and releases an enzyme that causes surrounding tissue to liquefy.

A goat with foot rot limps noticeably. Symptoms include a grayish, cheesy discharge and foul odor with lameness and intense pain. Treat by carefully trimming away the rotten area and treating the infected area with 10 to 30 percent copper sulfate solution, a suitable ointment, or other treatment as prescribed by your veterinarian.

Once your herd is infected with foot rot, treating and eradicating it is a lengthy process. You can prevent foot rot by housing your goats in a dry area and by maintaining their properly trimmed hooves. Trim the hooves of new goats and isolate them for three weeks before integrating them in your herd. Similarly, isolate any goat that leaves your farm and returns, including goats that have been to shows, fairgrounds, or boarded at a veterinary facility.

Pregnancy-related health problems

Ketosis: After a kid is born, the doe's milk production sometimes increases so rapidly that it cannot eat enough feed to keep up, which causes the body to break down its own body fat. The breakdown of fat releases ketones that can be toxic in large quantities. The goat's feeding slows down, its milk production falls off, and its breath and urine have a sweetish odor. The goat is apathetic and has a rough coat. In severe cases, the goat can become comatose and die.

A veterinarian can treat ketosis. To prevent it, begin gradually increasing a pregnant goat's portion of concentrated food about two weeks before her kid is born. Start with small handfuls and gradually increase it to 1.1 pounds per day by the time the kid is born. Feed the goat high-quality feed so she gets the maximum amount of nourishment.

Toxemia during pregnancy: Toxemia can arise near the end of a pregnancy, particularly when a goat is carrying twins or triplets. The cause is similar to ketosis. The growing babies require more energy while the expanding uterus occupies more space, pushing on the rumen and forcing the goat to eat less. As the goat's body breaks down fat reserves, toxic quantities of ketones are released, and the goat may appear blind, stop eating, and fall into a fatal coma. In this case, a veterinarian can do little to save the goat.

Toxemia is more likely to occur in a fat goat, so it is best to keep milk goats slightly thin and not feed them concentrated food during their dry periods before they are bred. Goats are less prone to toxemia when they get ample exercise. Feed them the best possible roughage during the last few weeks of their pregnancies, but do not start increasing their ration of concentrated food until the last two weeks of pregnancy.

Milk fever: Milk fever is caused by a calcium deficiency brought on by milk production right after the birth of kids. The goat's body fails to draw on calcium reserves in its bones, especially if the goat has been fed calcium-rich alfalfa or concentrate during the final weeks of pregnancy. The goat exhibits a weak, limping gait before the birth and may sink into a coma and die after the birth. A veterinarian can rescue a goat even in acute circumstances by giving a calcium infusion. Avoid overfeeding calcium in late pregnancy, and compensate for calcium-rich food with increased amounts of phosphate in the diet.

Johne's Disease: Johne's (Yoh-neez) disease is an incurable, contagious, antibiotic-resistant bacterial disease that infects the intestinal tracts of ruminants. Afflicted goats are dull, depressed, and thin, and they eventually die.

Poisoning

Eating or licking lead-based paints, ingesting pesticides and fertilizers, or eating poisonous plants inadvertently mixed in with chopped feed, can poison goats. They may eat toxic ornamental plants along fences or wilted leaves of trees in which toxins are concentrated during the fall. Symptoms of poisoning are vomiting, frothing, staggering, rapid or labored breathing, changes in pulse rate, labored breathing, cries for help, and sudden death. If you realize early enough that a goat has been poisoned, you may be able to induce vomiting with a drink of warm salt water or with 2 table-spoons of salt placed on the back of the tongue. A veterinarian may be able to administer an antidote to the poison if it can be identified.

Respiratory illness

Poor air quality, especially with a high content of ammonia fumes from urine, and cold, damp living quarters can bring on inflammations of the respiratory system. Goats lose their appetite, run a fever, breathe hard, have a nasal discharge, and sneeze or cough.

It is easier to prevent respiratory illness than to treat it. Maintain a well-ventilated but draft-free stable and dry, warm sleeping quarters. In winter, a cold, dry stable is preferable to a warm, damp one. Avoid stressing your goats during cold weather by changing their stables or feed unnecessarily.

Skin problems

Goats are plagued by fungal infections, lice, and mites, particularly if they are kept in a stable where they are not able to groom themselves, scratch against fence posts, rub, and lick themselves. The goat constantly tries to scratch itself, hair falls out, and scales, scabs, and bald patches appear.

Goats have healthier skin if they spend time outdoors. If kept in a stable, they should be brushed regularly with a stiff brush.

Lice

Goats that are twitchy, fidgety, and have dull coats are probably infested with lice. Small amounts of lice do not cause problems for healthy goats, but a goat with a serious infestation will rub itself against every available object, lose hair, and have dandruff and dry skin. Dusting, spraying, or dipping can control lice. Your veterinarian can recommend a louse powder suitable for dairy animals. The entire herd must be treated at once. An old remedy is two parts lard to one part kerosene rubbed on the goat. Fresh air, rain, and sunlight prevent lice from becoming a serious problem.

Mange

Tiny mites that burrow into the skin cause mange. Symptoms of mange are irritated, flaky skin followed by hairlessness and thick, hard patches of skin. Demodectic and psoroptic ear mange are specific to goats, while sarcoptic mange affects all species of animals. Mange can be treated with medications available from a veterinarian.

Screwworms

Screwworms are present in the South and Southwest United States despite eradication programs. Screwworm flies lay eggs on open wounds, and the eggs hatch into hundreds of larvae that feed on the living flesh for five to seven days. If a goat has a foul-smelling wound with larvae in it, contact your veterinarian immediately.

Ringworm

Fungal skin infections such as ringworm require treatment. Treatment includes using a solution of glycerine or tincture of iodine. Apply daily treatment of a mixture of equal parts tincture of iodine and glycerin or a 20-percent solution of sodium caprylate to the lesion until it disappears. The antifungal activity of thiabendazole may provide a useful treatment.

Internal parasites

Nearly all goats, even those that are healthy, harbor various kinds of worms that inhabit the stomach, intestine, liver, or lungs. Eggs are excreted and develop into infectious larvae either on the ground or in an intermediate host. These larvae are ingested by feeding goats and grow into worms inside the goats' bodies. Goats are susceptible to illness caused by these parasites whenever their resistance is diminished by stress, heat, poor nutrition, or another health problem. Goats also harbor coccidia, single-celled parasites that do not harm adult goats but can cause fatal intestinal illness in kids.

Symptoms of internal parasites are weight loss, rough coat, paleness of the mucous membranes of the eye and mouth, repeated diarrhea, and decline in milk production. Goats suffering from internal parasites often arch their backs, and there may be swelling under the jaw. Lungworms can cause coughing and a nasal discharge. The condition can be diagnosed by examining the feces of the goat under a microscope to determine what type of eggs are being excreted.

The best way to prevent illness is to maintain the goats' resistance by providing a good diet with a high content of minerals and vitamins. Good hygiene and pasture management help control the numbers of parasite larvae ingested by goats. Implement the following recommendations to decrease the chance internal parasites will harm your goats:

- Keep water and feed from being dirtied by goat droppings.

- Clean the feeding shelves and water containers often.

- Try to provide fodder, such as hay and leafy branches, free of parasite larvae.

- Replace litter straw often and construct floors and yards so they are easy to clean.

- Collect green feed from fields that have not been used as goat pastures or been fertilized with goat manure in the past year.

- When rotating goats from one area of pasture to another, leave the grazed areas to rest for three to six months. Large numbers of larvae may survive even longer in humid climates. Ideally, the goat pasture should be used as a hay field in between grazings, or used to pasture cattle or horses because they do not carry the same parasites as goats. If possible, there should be a two-year interval before an area is used again to pasture goats.

- Drain or avoid swampy pastures. The large liver fluke thrives in host snails that live only in swampy areas.

- Limit the number of goats in a pasture to six or seven per acre.

Worming your goats

Commercial worming preparations such as Moxidectin, Ivermectin, Levamasole, Fenbendazole, and Albendazole have proven effective in controlling internal parasites. Before worming, do a fecal analysis to identify which parasites are present and in what numbers. Your veterinarian can suggest the most effective wormer and recommend the right dosages.

Worming preparations (anthelmintics) come as boluses (large pills), liquids, pastes, gels, powders, and crumbles. Boluses are popular, but many goats balk at swallowing them. They can be hidden in a wad of peanut butter or administered with a balling gun. Some goat keepers refuse to use boluses because they can choke a goat.

If using a paste, make sure the goat's mouth is completely empty. Put the paste in the back corner of the mouth on the left side. Gently hold the goat's muzzle closed and massage the throat until the paste has been swallowed. Drenching is administering a liquid using a bottle. It can be tricky but is a necessary skill for a goat keeper. Squirt the liquid in the left-hand corner of the mouth, stopping at regular intervals to allow the goat to swallow. To avoid getting liquid in the lungs, keep the muzzle level and never raise the head.

Goats in rotating pastures should be wormed just before they are moved to a new pasture so they drop their eggs before the move. The most effective times to worm your goats are in the last month of pregnancy, a day after kids are born, at the beginning of the spring or summer, and just before the goats are returned to the stable for the winter. Goats that remain in the same pasture year-round should be regularly checked and wormed. It is difficult to control parasite larvae without resting pasture. If possible, goats should be confined in the stable for two days after they are wormed so they drop the eggs there. Goats kept in a stable all the time do not need worming if their feed and water is kept clean.

Humans should not consume milk from newly dewormed goats. Read the label, ask your vet, or look online to see how long you must wait before using the milk again.

Diseases that can spread from goats to humans

- **Toxoplasmosis:** A disease of cats, caused by a protozoa, can result in miscarriage in goats and humans. The symptoms are so mild in adult goats that they often are not noticed, but the microbes can be excreted in milk and can injure fetuses and infants who drink raw milk. You can prevent this disease from spreading by pasteurizing or boiling goat's milk before human consumption.

- **Tuberculosis:** Tuberculosis arises in various organs of goats and can be transmitted in milk. Tuberculosis has been all but eliminated in the domestic animals of most countries.

- **Brucellosis:** Brucellosis is still widespread in the Mediterranean and in tropical and subtropical countries. It causes undulant fever in humans and miscarriage in goats. Goats can carry the disease without exhibiting symptoms. Pasteurizing goat milk prevents transmission.

- **Chlamydia:** A common cause of miscarriage in goats in the United States, chlamydia can spread to humans and cause miscarriages. Pregnant women should avoid contact with goats during kidding time and should wear masks and gloves when handling goats.

- **Q Fever:** A cause of miscarriage in goats and sheep, the disease can spread from cows to goats. Humans can contract it by inhaling contaminated dust, consuming unpasteurized milk, and coming into contact with miscarriage material. Human beings experience flu-like symptoms.

- **Rabies:** Pastured goats can get rabies if a rabid animal, such as a rat, raccoon, or vampire bat, bites them. Goats with rabies exhibit abnormal behavior but are not necessarily aggressive. Transmission to humans can only occur if the rabid goat's saliva enters an open wound. Contact your veterinarian if you suspect a goat has rabies or has been bitten by a rabid animal. Like humans, goats can undergo a series of injections to prevent rabies.

Breeding Goats

Goats have a breeding season during which they come into heat (estrus) every few weeks for a day or two. The breeding patterns of goats are related to the survival of their ancestors in the wild; wild goats bred during fall and early winter so their kids would be born in the spring when plenty of food was available. The Swiss breeds, which originated far from the equator, have their breeding season in winter when daylight hours are the shortest. Nubian and Pygmy goats, which have their origins closer to the equator, can breed year-round. Bucks have a breeding season similar to the does.

Does usually stop lactating and are dried off for the last two months of their pregnancies to give them time to rest before their kids are born and they start lactating again. Some dry off sooner. That means each doe is producing milk for only 305 days out of the year, sometimes as few as 275. If all your does come into heat and are bred around the same time, they also will stop producing milk around the same time. This presents a challenge for dairy goat farmers, who ideally need a regular supply of goat's milk year-round. A family that relies on one or two goats to provide milk will have to do without for several weeks. The commercial demand for goat's milk is greater in the winter than in the summer, yet summer is when the goats reach their peak production. To keep the milk coming year-round, dairy goat farmers often try to stagger the breeding of their goats so some of them always will be lactating.

Does generally first come into heat in late August or September, when the days begin to shorten. If a doe is not bred during her first cycle, she will continue to go into heat at regular intervals until late in December. To ensure some of their goats always will be lactating, goat breeders try to stagger the breedings so some goats get pregnant in September and others at the end of December. This can be risky; if the doe is not pregnant by the end of her breeding cycles, she will not go into heat again for another nine months.

When to breed your does

Bucks and doelings (does that have not mated for the first time) reach sexual maturity at the age of 4 or 5 months, but sometimes, bucks reach puberty earlier. For this reason, buck kids should be separated from does at the age of 2 ½ months. A normal young doe that has been properly fed can be bred successfully at 7 to 9 months, when she has reached 65 to 75 percent of her adult body weight (about 85 pounds). Breeding will help her udder to mature.

A doe should be prepared for breeding by flushing, increasing the energy in her diet to stimulate ovulation and conception. She should gain weight for two or three weeks before breeding and for about three weeks afterwards. This can be accomplished either by feeding her high-quality forage or increasing her ration of grain. A doe bred during the first heat of her breeding cycle tends to have better milk production, and her kids will be old enough to breed by next season. You might want to postpone breeding until the second or third heat so the kid is not born during bitter cold winter weather or to stagger kidding so that your does are lactating at different times.

Recognizing estrus in your does

Estrus is the state in which a goat's ovary contains a fertile egg, and her uterus is ready to establish it. A doe in estrus exhibits a number of external signs:

- Restlessness
- Constant bleating
- Attempts to mount other does
- Swelling and redness of the vulva
- Appearance of mucus on the vulva, which turns yellowish and cloudy toward the end of estrus

Estrus is easy to detect in a goat that has already kidded once but may be difficult to confirm in young doelings. Scratch the doe and press her at the base of the tail. If she stops and lifts her tail, she is probably in heat. A goat that is not in heat would tuck her tail under and dodge your hand.

If you own a buck, a doe in heat will be attracted and want to hang around the buck's pen. Bucks follow a similar breeding cycle to does. When a buck is ready to mate, he rubs himself with fluids from scent glands on its forehead and urinates on himself so he gives off a strong odor. You can test whether a doe is in estrus by rubbing a cloth (known as a "buck rag") over the buck to absorb its scent. Put this cloth in a jar or sealed container. If the doe is in estrus, she will respond dramatically when you open the jar and let her smell the buck's aroma.

Estrus can be induced by the presence or smell of a buck or by exposure to the presence of other does in estrus. Warm temperatures sometimes inhibit estrus while cold temperatures stimulate it.

Estrus lasts for about 36 hours. The ovary does not release the egg until just near the end of the outward signs of estrus, so the best time for mating is about one day after estrus begins. It is safe to take the doe to the buck as soon as you notice she is in heat; if possible, breed her again 12 hours later to ensure conception.

Mating

Once your doe is in estrus, she must be brought together with the buck within 24 hours. Many goat owners do not keep a buck but instead pay a fee for stud service. You also can lease a buck from a local breeder and keep him with your does for several days. If you do not observe the breeding, the buck should remain with the does for at least three weeks, a complete breeding cycle. Occasionally, a breeder will accommodate your does to stay with the buck for the breeding period.

Stud service is carried out in several ways. You can transport your doe to the buck and drive her home again after a brief encounter, arrange to board her at the farm with the buck for a few days, or have the buck brought to your farm (this is called driveway service). Make arrangements with the buck's owner well in advance to be sure the buck is available when you need him during the busy breeding season. If you plan to register the offspring, be sure to ask for a service memo, a document signed by the buck owner verifying the buck bred the doe and the date. Most breeders will give a second breeding free if the doe does not get pregnant the first time.

When a doe in heat is brought to a buck, he greets her and begins smelling her from all sides. If she urinates, he smells or tastes it and makes a grimace, called a flehmen, holding his head high and drawing up his upper lip. Then he strikes his forefeet on the ground, lays them on top of the doe, and attempts to mount her. If she is at the peak of estrus, she tolerates the mounting and cooperates by lifting her tail. The copulation is complete when the buck raises himself high with a powerful thrust and throws his head back. If the doe is still in heat 24 hours after the first mating, a second mating should take place. A healthy mature buck can mate about ten to 20 times a day.

Choosing a buck

Some goat keepers breed their does solely to stimulate lactation (freshening) of does in their dairy herd and quickly sell the kids. Others breed their does with an eye to improving their herd with offspring that produce more milk, are stronger and healthier, and are productive longer. They select the best kids from each generation and sell their inferior goats. Whether you are breeding to freshen your does or to increase your herd, always seek out the best possible buck to impregnate your does. You may be tempted to use a buck from a neighboring farm just because it is convenient, but remember that the buck's genes influence not only the quality of its offspring, but the health of the mother and kid during pregnancy. A buck could carry a genetic flaw that results in abnormal fetuses or miscarriages. By selecting high-quality bucks, you will produce superior kids that can be sold at higher prices to other farmers.

Every year you make a considerable financial investment in feed, medications, and veterinary fees for your goats, to say nothing of all the time and effort you put into their care. Naturally, you want the maximum return on your investment: as much milk or meat as possible, the best fiber, and a healthy herd made up of goats that continue to be productive for eight or nine years or longer. If you are raising dairy goats, you will want to find a buck whose offspring are high-yield milkers with firm, well-supported udders. If you are raising meat goats, you will look for a well-muscled buck of good conformation that can improve your herd.

You can find a registered buck for breeding in your area by looking online at goat registries for various breed associations or searching the American Dairy Goat Association (ADGA) genetics website (**www.adgagenetics.org**). There are similar state organizations for meat goat growers such as the California Meat Goat Association, which has good information about meat goats and a link to Langston University Goat & Research Extension **www.luresext.edu/goats/training/ general.html#intro**. Your agricultural extension office or veterinarian may be able to tell you about local goat breeders who offer stud service.

When considering a buck, first look at his pedigree, if he has one, and the production records of his forebears. An undocumented buck or a grade can produce wonderful offspring, but a pedigree and official records are a sort of insurance that the buck will produce good offspring.

Next, look at the physical characteristics of your does and of the buck and his forebears. If possible, examine the buck's mother and granddam. If your does have a weakness such as poor udder attachment, the genetic background of the buck should counteract that flaw. Look for a buck descended from a family of does with strong, well-attached udders. To improve your herd, always breed your does with a buck from a family of even better does. That way the offspring will be better milk producers than their mothers. If you are interested in fiber production, pay attention to the buck's coat and the fiber produced from his herd.

Artificial insemination

In artificial insemination (AI), frozen sperm from a donor buck is thawed and inserted into a doe in heat. If you are aiming to improve your herd, artificial insemination allows you to select from a wide range of bucks with documented backgrounds. You can select a different buck for each of your does. A veterinarian or another goat breeder who has experience can perform this procedure, or you can learn to do it yourself. Defrosted semen is viable for only a few hours and should be inserted just at the end of the doe's heat cycle. Success depends on knowing exactly when a doe went into heat and how long her normal heat cycle is.

A "straw" of frozen semen costs as little as $5 to $25, but the equipment for storing the frozen semen requires an initial investment. Frozen semen is stored in a liquid nitrogen tank at -320 degrees F. A used liquid nitrogen tank costs $100 to $300 ($600 new), and it costs about $35 to $50 to refill the nitrogen tank every two months or so because the nitrogen evaporates. A single tank can hold 300 to 1,000 straws, so it is possible to share a tank with other goat keepers. You can purchase frozen semen online from suppliers such as Superior Semen Works (**www.superiorsemenworks.com**) and BIO-Genics, Ltd. (**www.biogenicsltd.com/index.html**) and sometimes directly from a buck's owner.

The advantages of AI are that you have access to a wide selection of bucks instead of being limited to those within driving distance of your farm, and you do not have to worry about transporting goats or possibly carrying disease from one farm to another. Sires are screened for sexually transmitted diseases before semen is collected.

Conception rates with AI vary from 50 to 70 percent and are affected by a number of circumstances, such as the sensitivity of the goat keeper to the goat's estrus and the amount of stress the doe experiences during the procedure. Does should be handled gently and reassured. Sometimes being transported to a veterinarian can upset the doe; if you have several does in estrus at the same time, you may be able to have the AI practitioner come to your farm.

If you use AI, be sure to obtain a Record of Artificial Insemination stating the doe, the buck, the source of the semen, and the date of insemination.

Keeping a buck

It might seem logical for a goat keeper who wants to be self-sufficient to keep a buck to service the does. Whether this is feasible depends on a number of factors, including the size of your property and facilities, the size of your herd, and whether you will be able to earn some income by offering stud service or selling superior kids to other goat keepers.

It costs as much to feed and care for a buck as for a doe; if you are keeping only two or three does, keeping a buck will double the cost of your milk. A buck often is kept together with a herd of meat goats because natural mating behavior results in a higher rate of pregnancy. Bucks cannot be kept together with a herd of dairy goats when they are in late pregnancy or after the kids are born. The presence of a buck in the herd can cause a strong "goaty" flavor in their milk due to the extra hormones in the herd. A buck can be aggressive toward kids and may impregnate the does again too soon after the births. The buck needs a separate pen and enclosure, preferably at least 50 yards away from the does. Bucks are particularly strong and aggressive, so this pen and enclosure must be exceptionally well built and reinforced to prevent the buck from escaping and rejoining the ladies. Because goats prefer company, you probably will need to keep another buck or a wether, a castrated male goat, as a friend for the buck.

A buck kid is cute and playful, but when he matures, he becomes aggressive and dominating and may be difficult to handle, especially for a child. During breeding season, bucks cover themselves with scent and urine and give off a powerful aroma that seems to permeate everything. Neighbors may find this odor offensive, and many residential areas that allow the keeping of female goats prohibit the ownership of bucks.

After the first breeding, you would be mating your buck with his daughters. Sometimes this kind of inbreeding strengthens desirable qualities such as milk production and udder strength in the offspring, but it can exaggerate flaws and weaknesses. Most bucks are sold as kids before they have been bred to show the kind of offspring they produce. An older buck that has demonstrated its superiority is expensive if it is still in its prime. A buck that is a good mate for one of your does might produce kids with undesirable traits from another of your does. This is not a problem if you are only using the buck to "freshen" your does and selling all the kids soon after birth. If your goal is to increase or improve your herd, after one or two generations you will need genetic input from another buck.

Kidding

Most does experience normal pregnancies. Depending on the age, breed, and previous pregnancies, 145 to 155 days after the last breeding date your doe will deliver one to five kids. Multiple births usually occur a little earlier; an older or poorly nourished doe may give birth later.

It can be difficult to tell whether your doe is pregnant during the first three months. The first sign of pregnancy is that the doe does not go back into heat after her last cycle. Watch the doe closely three weeks after she has been bred. Pregnancy tests can be done by a diagnostic lab or through a veterinarian or a mail-in service. Typically, a sample of urine or milk is tested for the presence of estrone sulfate, a hormone produced by a living fetus about 35 days after conception. If the doe is not pregnant and you are still in the breeding season, it may be possible to breed her again. You can continue milking a doe that is not pregnant right through to the next breeding season, though her milk production will not be as high as a goat that has given birth.

Later in pregnancy, you will be able to feel the presence of the kids through the goat's abdomen. Some veterinarians perform ultrasounds on livestock, but this is not necessary unless you are overly concerned about a doe.

Miscarriage

A goat that was bred and then comes back into heat may have miscarried a fetus. Miscarriage is not uncommon among goats. There are a number of causes: disease, poor nutrition, poisoning, death of the fetus, or the natural rejection of an abnormal fetus. Diseases that cause miscarriage include leptospirosis and vibriosis; your veterinarian or local agricultural extension office can tell you if goats in your region need to be vaccinated against these. Injury is a common cause of miscarriage. Injury can result from does butting each other to establish dominance or by climbing or jumping off elevated objects. A pregnant goat that is new to your herd or one that is overactive should probably be put in a private stall where she will be more sedate.

You may not always be able to detect miscarriage in the early stages of pregnancy. Signs of miscarriage include bloody discharge and changes in behavior such as loss of appetite, a dazed appearance, or reluctance to mingle with the herd. If you suspect a miscarriage has occurred, watch for the expulsion of the placenta. Do not rebreed a doe that has suffered a miscarriage until the next season.

Record dates and causes of miscarriage on the individual health record that you keep for each doe. If several goats in your herd miscarry or give premature birth, they may be infected with chlamydia or another disease, and you should consult your veterinarian.

Caring for a pregnant doe

Milk-producing (lactating) goats should be dried off two to three months before the kids are due to allow their bodies to nourish their kids and build up reserves. Five or six weeks before the kids are expected, boost your goats' C/DT vaccinations, trim their hoofs, and worm them if necessary. Read labels on worming preparations carefully, or consult your veterinarian, because some can cause miscarriage.

Around this time, begin supplementing your does' diet with concentrate or high-quality forage. Consult your agricultural extension office or a local goat keeper for advice on local conditions. In areas where soils are selenium-deficient, pregnant does should receive a Bo-SE (selenium/vitamin E) injection. Ensure that your goats get enough exercise. Pregnant dairy goats should be well nourished but not fat. Excess fat can lead to serious complications before and after giving birth.

About ten days before you expect your first kid, assemble your kidding supplies. If your goats will kid indoors, clean and disinfect the pens where does and kids will be kept, or construct new ones in a draft-free but well-ventilated area. Allow 25 to 35 square feet of space for each doe and her kids. Litter the floor with dust-free bedding (sawdust is not good bedding for newborn kids because it can trigger respiratory problems) and arrange for watering and feeding. Remember that a tiny kid can drown in a standing bucket of water, so use small or elevated watering containers.

A week before the kids are due, clip the hair around the does' udders and escutcheons (the area between the udder and tail), vulvas, and tails.

Drying off

Drying off is the process of stopping lactation in a dairy goat. In late pregnancy, the milk production of many does stops naturally. If this does not occur two to three months before the kids are due, stop milking to allow the goat's body to build up reserves for lactation after the birth. Some goat keepers recommend drying off gradually by reducing milking to once a day and then, every other day. Other farmers believe it is better to stop milking the doe altogether and let the pressure in her udder naturally put a stop to milk production. When milking ceases, the udder forms a mucus plug to prevent bacteria from entering through the teat. Each time you milk the goat, this plug must be re-formed, which increases the chances of infection, and the goat's udder receives another signal to produce milk. Gradual cessation of milking can result in fibrosis of the udder and lower milk production in the future.

To dry off your goat:

1. Stop milking. After the last milking, some goat keepers recommend using a dry-cow antibiotic infusion to reduce the possibility of mastitis. This is done by injecting antibiotics into the teat canal. Use a teat dip.

2. Stop feeding the goat high-nutrient foods that encourage milk production. Switch to a dry doe ration with lower concentrate and protein content.

3. Continue dipping the teats twice daily for the next four to five days.

4. If substantial pressure still exists in the udder after four days, milk out the doe, give another antibiotic infusion, and start over.

Just before she gives birth, a doe's udder will begin to "bag up" with milk in preparation for her kids. A high-yield milker may need to be milked once or twice at this time if her udder becomes too full.

Signs a doe is ready to give birth

A doe almost ready to give birth becomes nervous and restless. She may lose her appetite; turn around, lie down, and get up again repeatedly; bleat; and turn her head toward her tail. The vulva becomes red and swollen and may trail a long string of clear mucus. The mucus becomes opaque and yellow when the birth is imminent. The goat may withdraw from the herd, sometimes taking another doe along with her. Other does in the herd will show exaggerated interest in a doe that is about to kid. If they come too close, she will reject them. Do not isolate a doe from the herd immediately before she gives birth, as this can upset her; wait until after the kids are born to move her to her own stall.

A veteran doe usually begins to bag up — her udder fills with milk — about ten days before birth. Some does, however, do not bag up until later. A doe experiencing her first pregnancy will begin to build an udder four to six weeks before birth.

About 140 days after the doe was bred, start watching for signs that she is about to give birth. Make a note of pre-kidding signals on the goat's health record. No two does behave in exactly the same way, but a doe is likely to repeat the same kidding signals every time she gives birth. If you take good notes the first time, you will be better prepared the next year. You should be able to feel the kids on the right side of the doe until about 12 hours before birth. Then the uterus begins to tense, and one of the kids will be forced into the neck of the womb. At this point, the slope of the doe's rump becomes more horizontal, and birth can be expected in about two hours.

Birth

Most births take place naturally without any assistance. It is better not to interfere unless absolutely necessary; just observe the birth calmly, and be ready to step in if there is an emergency.

A goat can give birth standing and lying down. The first thing you will see is a translucent bubble, the water sac, which can burst at any time. You will see one hoof and then another, and then a little nose, wrapped in the amniotic sac. Eventually, this sac breaks. The birth slows, giving the birth canal time to dilate a little more for the head to pass. Once the shoulders are delivered, the rest of the kid plops out. Most kids are born with the front feet forward and the head lying on them; less often, the hind feet come out first.

The kid lies motionless for a short while, then lifts its head and tears the amniotic sac. Except in a case where the kid is frail, it does not need help removing the amniotic sac. The umbilical cord will break by itself. Disinfect the end of the umbilical cord by dipping it in a small container, such as a shot glass, containing 7 percent iodine for several seconds. Use a fresh container of iodine for each kid. Do not omit this step. An umbilical cord longer than 2 inches needs to be trimmed. If the umbilical cord continues to bleed, use a navel clamp about 1 inch below the kid's belly, or tie it off with clean dental floss.

The mother immediately begins licking the kid to remove mucus and stimulate its breathing. If a kid is frail and weak, you can draw off the mucus and rub gently with a towel to stimulate breathing, then place it in front of its mother to be licked. If there is more than one kid, the mother will stop licking to turn her attention to the next delivery. Move the first kid to the side so it will not be stepped on. Do not leave the doe and kids unattended until you are sure all of them have been born. A doe can have from one to as many as five kids; multiple births are more common in some breeds.

Soon, the kid will try to stand up. It will begin to suckle about half an hour after birth. Milk one stream from each teat to remove the mucus plug. If the udder is swollen, the kid may need some assistance with the teat. The first milk, known as beastmilk or colostrum, is important for the kid. It contains antibodies that disappear from the doe's milk after the first 24 hours. A newborn kid should ingest its first meal of colostrum within half an hour to two hours after birth. If the kid does not nurse, milk the doe and bottle-feed it colostrum.

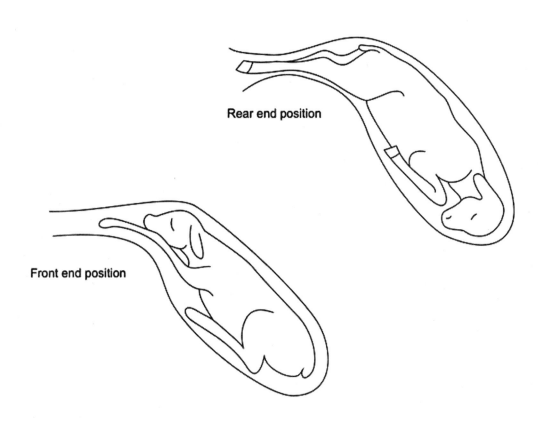

Position of a kid during birth

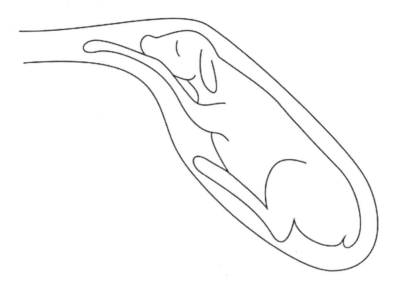

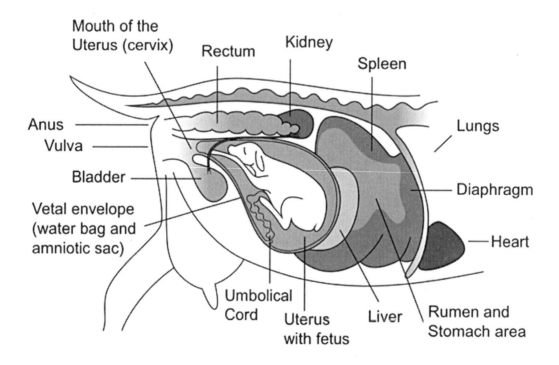

Position of kid during normal birth

Using a stomach tube

A kid that is too weak to nurse must be fed with a stomach tube. A stomach tube is a length of small, flexible plastic tubing such as that used for catheters. You can purchase stomach tubes from a goat supplier. The tube is attached to a 60 ml syringe.

Slowly and gently, push the tube down the kid's throat. The kid often will swallow as you push the tube down.

When the tube has reached the kid's stomach, attach the syringe and depress the plunger slowly to deliver milk or colostrum directly into the kid's stomach.

Make sure the tube is in the kid's stomach before beginning to push the plunger; otherwise, you might force fluid into the lungs.

The kid's suckling will assist the mother with expulsion of the afterbirth. Some does eat the afterbirth; this is completely natural. If the doe does not eat it, dispose of the afterbirth as soon as possible. You can dispose of it in a dumpster or bury it. If the afterbirth is not expelled within a few hours after delivery, call your veterinarian. If the placenta is visible but not fully expelled, do not attempt to pull it out because you could cause the goat to hemorrhage.

Most births do not require assistance. If a large kid is stuck passing through its mother's hips, give a gentle tug on the front legs. A kid born hind legs first (the bottoms of the hoofs are turned upwards) should be helped with a gentle tug because it could drown in amniotic fluid if it remains too long in this position. If a kid presents itself in any other position, you can try to reposition it. Wash your hands, and wash and dry the doe's vulva with mild dish soap. Lubricate your hand with Vaseline® or dishwashing soap and insert it gently into the vagina between contractions to press the kid back into the uterus and manipulate it into a correct birth position. As you move a tiny hoof into the birth canal, cup your hand over it to protect the uterus from being torn or injured. This should be done by someone with knows what he or she is doing; call your veterinarian or an experienced local goat keeper. If the goat has been in hard labor for 45 minutes and you have been trying unsuccessfully to help her for 15 minutes, it is time to call for help.

After the birth, offer the doe a bucket of lukewarm water with a little molasses or cider vinegar in it and a feed of hay if she wants it. Move the kids into a draft-free box or pen where they will be reasonably warm. Remove any wet bedding from around the doe. For the next two weeks, she may continue to have a slight discharge. If the weather is warm, she may shed quantities of hair. Brush her regularly. Over the two weeks following the birth, gradually increase the doe's grain ration until she is back on her regular milking diet.

Colostrum

Colostrum, the thick yellow substance secreted by a doe's udder after birth, is essential to a newborn's well-being. It contains antibodies that strengthen the kid's immune system against disease and helps to clear and condition the newborn's digestive system. Does produce colostrum for one to four days after the birth. Kids should be fed exclusively on colostrum for the first two days of life. If you are hand feeding your kids, milk the colostrum, and give it to them in bottles.

The viruses that cause Caprine Arthritis Encephalitis Syndrome (CAE) and Johne's disease pass from mother to newborn in the doe's colostrum. Heating the colostrum to 131 degrees F (55 degrees C) for one hour destroys these viruses. Do not heat it above 140 degrees F (60 degrees C) because all the antibodies will be destroyed. Bottle-feed kids colostrum that has been heated and then cooled to body temperature. Extra colostrum can be fed back to the mother or frozen for future use.

To avoid scorching the colostrum, heat it in a double boiler or slow cooker for an hour, or heat it to 135 degrees F (57.2 degrees C), and keep it in a thermos for one hour. If a newborn kid nurses from its infected mother even once, all of your efforts will have been wasted. When you are not able to be present at the birth, buy special tape from a goat supplier to seal the goat's teats so the newborn cannot nurse.

If you cannot obtain colostrum from the mother, you may be able to get frozen colostrum from another goat breeder. If fresh or frozen goat colostrum is not available, you can substitute cow or sheep colostrum. You also can purchase colostrum replacements from a goat supplier.

Keeping kids warm

Occasionally, a kid is born unexpectedly when you are not there to supervise. You may arrive at the barn to find a cold, shivering newborn. Place it in a draft-free box or pen lined with a blanket, and if necessary, use a heat lamp to warm it up. Do not let it get too hot; overheating is just as harmful as being too cold. Kids are generally comfortable at temperatures 50 degrees F (10 degrees C) or higher.

A kid that is severely chilled, still wet, and almost lifeless can be revived by placing it up to its nose in a bath of water at 104 degrees F, the temperature of the womb it just exited. When it has recovered, dry it well, wrap it in a blanket or towel, place it in a sheltered place, and watch it closely. A newborn that appears to be very cold also can be suffering from low blood sugar (hypoglycemia) — shivering, ruffling its fur, and arching its back. Warm the kid and use a stomach tube to administer at least 25 mg of 5 percent glucose solution. When it appears to be reviving, feed it 2 ounces of colostrum, using the stomach tube again if necessary. As soon as it is active, take it back to the barn. If you end up nursing a weak kid in your warm kitchen, it will probably stay there for the rest of the winter because it will not be able to adapt to the cold easily when you return it outside.

What to do with the kids

If you kept all the kids born to your does every year, goats would soon overrun you. Roughly half of all kids are bucks; because one buck can impregnate 50 to 100 does in a season, there is no need to keep more than one or two adult bucks for your herd. You might want to raise a few of your best doelings to increase your herd, to sell as dairy stock to other farmers, or raise your unwanted kids for meat. Inspect your kids after birth. Look for extra teats on the doelings. Double  teats or extra teats that are too close to the real teats can interfere with milking. Bucks that have extra teats should not be used for breeding because they could pass this trait to their offspring. A doeling that has a small pea-like growth on its vulva is a hermaphrodite and will be infertile; avoid breeding her mother with the same buck again.

Raising kids is a lot of work and requires extra space and special facilities. Kids are usually not left with their mothers in a dairy-goat herd because the priority is milk production. If the kid is left to nurse whenever it wants all day long, there might be no milk for you at milking time, and there is no way to measure the doe's milk production or even to know if the kid is getting enough nourishment. The doe needs to become accustomed to the milking routine, and the kid must become accustomed to being handled. Kids that remain with their mothers might adamantly resist separation later on and might continue to nurse long after they should have been weaned. Some goat keepers believe that nursing ruins a milk goat's teats. For this reason, kids in a dairy herd are kept with other kids of the same approximate age and fed from pans or bottles.

In some cases, kids should be allowed to nurse. If a doe has a tight or congested udder after giving birth, bring her kid(s) to nurse every few hours for several days to relieve the condition. Nursing also stretches and enlarges the teats of a first-year doe if they are too small for the hands of the person milking them.

Raising Kids

Kids, unlike sheep, do not maintain a lasting relationship with their mothers. If left to grow up in the herd, they spend much of their time with other kids, returning to their mothers only to suckle, and becoming independent when the milk dries up. After they have had their early colostrum, dairy kids can be taken from their mothers and raised together in a separate nursery area. They will sleep a lot during the first two weeks of life, then become increasingly active. Change their litter often, and give them plenty of opportunities to exercise. Kids love to play on an upturned box, a platform, or a barrel laid on its side.

The nutrition and care kids receive during their first year determines how healthy and productive they will be later in life. Kids need to spend as much time as possible outdoors. Because their young bodies are susceptible to worms and parasites, they should be separated from adult goats in a pasture that has not been grazed for six months or more. If this is not possible, a paved run that can easily be cleaned is the next best alternative. Many goat keepers use portable hutches as kid shelters that can be moved to new pasture for each new group of kids.

Keep a health record for each kid, beginning with its birth weight, height at the withers, and heart girth. Weigh the kids every two weeks. An easy way to weigh a kid is to step on a bathroom scale without the kid, then step on it again holding the kid, and subtract the first weight from the second.

Spend at least ten minutes a day with your kids and handle them often so they get used to cooperating with people. Talk to them and use their names so they learn to come when called. Put a collar on each one, and use it to move the kid where you want it to go. When you need to inspect a kid or perform a procedure, sit down and hold the kid on your lap or between your legs.

Feeding kids

Goat keepers swear by a whole range of feeding programs and schedules, most of which seem to work well. The most important thing is to be consistent and stick to the same method and feeding schedule every day. Most kids begin eating their first hay after one week and can be weaned from milk entirely at 8 weeks.

Bottle or pan feeding

Kids can be fed milk using either pans or bottles. Once a kid has learned one method, it is difficult to get it accustomed to the other. Pans are easier to wash, sterilize, and fill than bottles, but many goat breeders do not recommend pan feeding because the kid must lower its head to drink, and this may allow milk to get into its rumen. When a kid nurses from its mother, its neck is raised at an angle that closes off the passage to the rumen and allows the milk to go straight into its abomasum. Kids also tend to step in the pans or knock them over in the excitement of feeding. To accustom a kid to pan feeding, let it suckle on your finger a little, then lead it to the pan and gently hold its nose in the milk until it starts to drink. You may have to repeat this process several times. Always wash and sterilize the pans after each feeding.

Many types of bottles and nipples are used for bottle-feeding. The simplest (and cheapest) is a nipple that fits over an ordinary soda bottle. Bottles and nipples especially designed for feeding goats can be purchased from goat supply catalogs for $6 to $8. Once you have taught a kid to drink from the bottle, the bottles can be placed in a holder or rack placed just high enough that the kid has to raise its head to drink. Raise the height as the kid grows. If you are feeding multiple kids, you can also a commercial feeding device, usually referred to as a lamb bar — a large container with several nipples sticking out around its sides. Each nipple is connected to a tube that goes down to the bottom of the container so the kids suck up all the milk as they drink. You also can purchase the nipples and tubes and make your own device out of a bucket.

Teaching a newborn kid to drink from a bottle may be a challenge because it does not know what a bottle is and wants to drink from its mother. Nipples should be warm and soft, and the milk should be warmed to about 104 degrees F, the normal body temperature of a goat. Hold the kid in your lap and gently but persistently dribble milk from the nipple into its mouth until hunger takes over. After the first few days, the milk can be fed warm or cold, but most goat keepers continue to feed warm milk. The important thing is to be consistent.

What milk to use

Fresh or frozen goat's milk is the easiest and most natural milk to give a kid. If this is not available, you can use fresh raw cow's milk or regular whole cow's milk from the grocery store. Do not use canned goat's milk. You can add 3 tablespoons of corn syrup, which adds nourishment for the kid, to each gallon of whole milk or make up one of these mixtures:

- Five parts whole milk to one part dairy half-and-half
- One cup of buttermilk and one 12-ounce can of evaporated milk to every gallon of whole milk

If you are planning to sell your kids or do not want to buy cow's milk, you can use a powdered milk replacer, available from feed stores or dairy suppliers. Use only a milk replacer formulated specifically for kids and follow the instructions on the label carefully each time you mix up a batch. Do not use soy-based milk replacers or those intended for young of other species. Mix up only enough milk replacer for one day at a time, and do not pour what is left over after feeding back into the container. Do not abruptly switch brands or products. Powdered milk replacers can cause diarrhea, bloat, digestive problems, and floppy kid syndrome if used improperly. *Floppy kid syndrome is discussed later in this chapter.*

Feeding schedule

Newborn kids should be fed at regular intervals every six or eight hours for the first three days, every eight hours for the first week, and two or three times a day afterwards. Some goat keepers feed only twice a day after the first week. The feeding schedule should be consistent every day. If you must be absent at a regular feeding time, you can leave a feeding bucket where the kids can access it, cooled with ice or mixed with a buttermilk culture to keep it from spoiling.

After one week, start giving the kids fresh, leafy hay in an easily accessible manger or feeding rack so they can start developing their rumens. Cut back a little on the amount of milk, so they will feel hungry enough to be interested in the hay. After three weeks, start offering the kids small amounts of grain; if you are pan feeding, sprinkle the grain in their milk.

Suggested Feeding Schedule for Kids

	FEED	AMOUNT PER DAY	FREQUENCY
Birth–3 days	Colostrum	12–16 oz	½ cup, 4–5 times per day
4–7 days	Goat's milk	12–24 oz	1 cup, 3–4 times per day
1 week	Milk	36 oz	1 cup, 2–4 times per day

	FEED	AMOUNT PER DAY	FREQUENCY
2 weeks	Milk	32 oz	1 ½–2 cups, 3 times per day
	Good hay	Freely available	
	Water	Freely available	
3–8 weeks	Milk	32 oz	2 times per day
	Good hay	Freely available	
	18% starter grain	As much as the kid can eat in 15 minutes	2 times per day
	Water	Freely available	

After 8 weeks, gradually start decreasing the amount of milk. Kids weigh about 7 ½ pounds at birth and gain about 10 pounds per month. They should be weaned when they reach about 40 pounds, which is typically at 3 months of age. After that, feed kids about 1 pound of grain per day. The amount of grain a kid needs varies depending on the quality of the hay it is receiving and how much weight it is gaining. Cut back on grain if the kid is gaining weight too rapidly or if you cannot feel its ribs through the skin. By the time a doe is 6 months old, it can be put on a milking ration, and at 7 months, it can be bred for the first time.

Disbudding and Castration

Both male and female goats have horns; a goat that is born hornless (polled) is often infertile. Most dairy goats have their horns removed because they cannot easily fit their heads into feeding racks and milk stands and because the horns can cause injury to their human handlers or to other goats. This is usually done by disbudding, the cauterization of a kid's horn buds, when it is 3 to 14 days old. If a kid has tight skin and curly hair over its horn buds, it has still horns and must be disbudded.

An electric disbudding iron with a ¾- to 1-inch tip can be purchased from a goat supplier. Here are the steps you should follow to disbud a goat:

- Heat the iron until it is hot enough to leave a burn mark on wood.

- Hold the kid on your lap, or place it in a restraining box, and trim the hair around the horn button with a small pair of scissors.

- Grasp the kid by the muzzle, and press the hot iron on the horn button for a count of 15. The kid will scream and struggle, and you will smell burning hair. There should be a copper-colored ring around the horn bud.

- Comfort the kid and allow the iron to heat up again. Then do the other horn bud.

- Spray the area with an antiseptic spray, taking care not to get the spray in the kid's eyes.

- Give the kid a bottle of milk to console it.

Some goat keepers give the kid a painkiller, such as aspirin, 30 minutes before disbudding. Disbudding can be done without an anesthetic until the kid is 1 month old. After that, it is better to let a veterinarian do the job. A local goat breeder might disbud your goats for a small fee. If the horn bud is not completely removed or thin, misshapen horns called scurs start to grow, you will have to repeat the disbudding.

Disbudding can also be done using a caustic dehorning paste something like a wart remover, available from farm supply stores. Clip the hair around the horn buttons, then cover each horn button with a disk of adhesive tape. Cover the surrounding area with petroleum jelly to protect the skin. Remove the adhesive tape and apply caustic paste to the horn buds. Hold the kid still for half an hour to prevent it from licking the caustic or smearing it on something. Be careful that the kid does not rub the caustic paste on itself or on another goat. It can cause burns and blindness.

Castration

Bucks that are going to be slaughtered before they reach maturity do not need to be castrated. A buck that is going to be kept as a wether should be castrated as soon as its testicles descend into the scrotum, when it is between 1 week and 3 weeks old. Kids should be vaccinated for tetanus before castration. A veterinarian should perform surgical castration. Bucks can also be neutered using a small Burdizzo emasculator, a tool that crushes the testicle cords. Goat keepers often castrate kids using an elastrator, a device that stretches a rubber ring so that it can be slipped over the scrotum above the testes. The rubber band cuts off circulation, and the scrotum withers and drops off.

Tattooing or Microchipping

As soon as a kid is born, place a neckband on it with the name of its mother and its date of birth. Note the birth in your reproduction records along with the name of the sire. One to four weeks after birth, kids can be tattooed with a permanent ID number. Tattoos are preferable to ear tags or neck chain IDs, which goats are likely to chew or pull off. If you plan to register a kid with the ADGA, it must be tattooed. Tattoos help identify a goat long after you have sold it and may aid in the recovery of a lost or stolen animal.

Tattoo sets are available from farm supply stores and goat suppliers. Get one with a ¼- or $5/16$-inch die and green ink. Most goats are tattooed on the ear, except for LaManchas, which are tattooed in the tail web.

Supplies for tattooing:

- Tattoo tongs with numbers and letters
- Ink, paste or roll-on, preferably green
- Rubbing alcohol
- Toothbrush

Stand behind your goat facing the goat's rear end. The ear on your right side is the goat's right ear; the ear on your left side is the left ear. The right ear is tattooed with a unique tattoo sequence, a series of letters and numbers identifying your farm. This sequence is assigned by the ADGA when you become a member. The tattoo in the left ear identifies the specific goat. The year of the goat's birth is indicated by a letter of the alphabet designated by the ADGA: 2007 –X; 2008 – Y; 2009 – Z; 2010 – A; 2011 – B. A herd identification number showing the order in which the kid was born follow this. For example, the 22nd kid born in 2010 would be tattooed with "A22."

Fit the correct letters and numbers into the tattoo tongs and test them by punching a piece of paper. Clean an area on the inside of the ear with rubbing alcohol — avoid veins or freckles. Rub the ink over this area. Placing the smooth rubber side of the tongs against the outside of the ear, puncture the ear firmly. Tattoos should be placed so they read right way up. Using the toothbrush, rub more ink over the punctured numbers with the toothbrush for about 20 seconds. Tattooing is done quickly and is usually painless.

Microchips inserted under the skin are becoming a popular way to identify goats because they are less vulnerable to tampering. Some goat breed associations require microchipping. The microchip is usually inserted in the head near the ear or in the tail. A microchip must be read with a scanner and can sometimes migrate under the skin.

Wattles

Wattles are one or two long, thin bags of skin that hang down from the neck and can appear in any breed. No useful function has ever been identified for them. They typically are removed to give the dairy goat a cleaner neckline. Wattles can cause problems when they are caught on fences and torn or are sucked and chewed on by other goats. Wattles can be snipped off young kids with a pair of sharp, clean scissors. The wound heals without a scar.

Health Problems of Kids

Kids that are fed colostrum, kept in a clean dry environment out of drafts, given outdoor exercise, and fed carefully usually will grow up with few health problems. The most common health problems are diarrhea and constipation. Ordinary diarrhea can be caused by eating too fast, consuming too much milk or milk that is too cold, or changing feeds too quickly. Reduce feed and offer it at more frequent intervals. If the diarrhea continues, try replacing half of the kid's milk with water for 48 hours. In cases of severe diarrhea, or scours, withdraw all milk and feed for 24 hours, and give the kid warm chamomile or black tea with charcoal or oak bark powder mixed in it. Kaopectate also can be administered to stop the diarrhea. When the diarrhea stops, resume the kid's regular feeding program gradually. Continued severe or bloody diarrhea may indicate a bacterial infection requiring veterinary attention.

A kid with diarrhea can become dehydrated quickly. If the kid's skin sticks together when pinched, give it an electrolyte immediately to replace lost body fluids.

Electrolyte mix

- 1 quart purified water
- ¼ teaspoon baking soda
- ½ teaspoon salt
- 2 tablespoons honey or white Karo syrup

Mix well. Make up a new batch daily and feed in place of milk, doubling the usual quantity. Return to regular milk after one and a half to two days.

Signs of constipation are difficulty passing feces, straining, and hard, dry pellets. It is usually caused by overfeeding, ration that is too coarse or lack of water. Exercise and plenty of water help, as does a laxative such as bran. In extreme cases, give an enema of warm, soapy water.

Kids overly infested with worms will become anemic, exhibiting pale mucous membranes and poorly conditioned coats, lack of appetite, and diminished growth. Kids generally are wormed for the first time at 6 to 8 weeks old. For younger kids, consult your veterinarian.

Weakness and a staggering gait, together with diarrhea, are signs of enterotoxemia, caused when Clostridium bacteria in the digestive system multiply rapidly and release toxins. Enterotoxemia occurs in particularly well-nourished kids.

Floppy kid syndrome (FKS) affects kids between 3 and 10 days old. Symptoms are muscular weakness and depression, progressing to flaccid paralysis and often death. The abdomen is distended and may "slosh" if the kid is gently shaken. The cause is still unknown, but it is thought that overconsuming rich milk triggers the development of certain microorganisms in the digestive tract, resulting in acidosis. If detected early, it can be treated by oral administration of sodium bicarbonate and/or the tube feeding of electrolytes. More severe cases can be treated with isotonic intravenous 1.3 percent sodium bicarbonate solution.

CASE STUDY: DOWN ON THE GOAT FARM

Jason and Karlia Dahl
coyotepass@tnics.com
605-880-1354
Strandburg, South Dakota

Jason and Karlia Dahl's Boer goat farm on the South Dakota prairie is an ideal place to raise goats — and kids. They and their children have a farm well off the beaten path on a maze of gravel roads crisscrossing the gently rolling grassy plains. The Dahls decided to raise goats to help control the weeds on their new homestead, which had been allowed to revert to nature after the former owners moved out.

They did their research and decided to purchase four goats — three does and a buck started their herd, which now numbers more than 70 brown and white Boer meat goats. They suggest that anyone interested in small-scale meat goat farming do their homework first, paying special attention to how to keep your goats healthy. The best advice they have is to talk to others in the business before purchasing any goats.

Raising goats is definitely a family project. The kids pitch in to help with the chores, as cleaning pens, trimming hooves, and vaccinations are big projects. Kidding season is the most time-consuming chore. Starting in late spring, they check the goats every two hours, day and night, to catch any does that might be having trouble giving birth. Their hard work pays off during the grazing season when they watch the young goats frolic on the grassy hills, which is the best part of goat farming in their opinion.

They have invested quite a bit of money and time into their goat operation. Fences are the biggest project. They need to be goat proof, as goats are masters at escaping from even the best-planned fence. The Dahls use two strands of smooth, electric wire in the pasture, and in the barnyard, they use woven wire topped with barbed wire to keep escapes to a minimum. Housing needs for the goats are met using the existing buildings on the farm. The biggest need for housing is for small pens for the does when kidding; otherwise, the goats spend most of their time outside.

The Dahls market their goats both directly off the farm and through a sales barn. They sell both breeding goats and goats for meat. The children show goats at the county Achievement Days, and they hope to expand to other shows as well. The market for meat goats is steady and is expected to grow somewhat in the future. In the meantime, the Dahls keep busy with their playful goats and take time to enjoy them each day.

Using Goats for Weed Control

As stated earlier, goats can and are used to control weeds. This type of use is called managed defoliation in an attempt to reduce unwanted shrubs and weeds in an area while increasing the numbers of wanted grasses. Results are evident after one year of grazing but it typically takes up to four years to get good brush control. Grazing while brush and weeds are rapidly growing, typically in the spring and summer, is more effective than trying to start a brush control program after the weeds are mature, as the goats will not consume as much of the mature plants as the young plants.

Photo provided by Jason and Karlia Dahl

Goats for Milk

In many parts of the world, people drink goat milk instead of cow milk. It has a sweet taste, sometimes with a salty base. Goat milk is gaining in popularity in the U.S. and might be found in grocery stores as well as health food stores. Goat milk does not have to be homogenized. This means that there is no need to break up the fat in goat milk. The fat in cow milk tends to separate into globules but the fat in goat milk is spread evenly throughout the milk and stays suspended throughout the milk. Many times, if someone is sensitive to cow milk, they are able to drink goat milk. Goat milk is also an excellent source of calcium and other minerals.

Milk for personal use

You will milk each lactating goat twice daily. Folk wisdom has long dictated that milking be done religiously at 12-hour intervals, but recent research in France has shown that dairy goats produce just as well if there is an eight-hour and a 14-hour interval between milking each day. Apparently, the length of the interval between milking is not as important as keeping a consistent schedule. Having a full udder is uncomfortable for a goat; do not make your goats wait so long to be milked that it causes them to suffer. They will let you know with loud cries if they have waited too long. Always allow at least eight hours between milking sessions, and commit yourself to milking at about the same times every day. Irregular milking will adversely affect your milk yield and cause stress to your animals, which can affect milk quality.

It is difficult to say exactly how much milk a goat will produce because of the variance between breeds and within a breed, and between individuals. Age, climate, weather, illness, and stress can greatly influence an individual goat's milk production. It is safe to assume that a dairy goat will give, on average, about 1,500 pounds of milk per year. Note that goat's milk is measured in pounds weight, rather than in volume. Eight pounds of milk is about a gallon, but milk is measured in pounds weight rather than volume because volume measurement is far less reliable. Fresh milk tends to foam, and a gallon jar of foamy milk contains less than a gallon jar of milk that has settled. Weighing the milk gives a more accurate indication of how much milk is in a given container.

Changes in diet and climate cause seasonal changes in milk production. In order to have a consistent, year-round milk supply, it is necessary to maintain a herd and manage the does so that at least some are always lactating.

Basic Milking Supplies

Milking equipment can be as simple as a halter, a tether, a stainless steel bowl from your kitchen cupboard, and some plastic funnels, but because you will be milking your goats twice a day, every day, your life will be easier if you purchase specialized milking equipment. The cost of specific items needed for milking and processing varies considerably depending on whether you milk by hand or with a machine, the current demand for these supplies, and your geographical location. When you first establish a small dairy herd, you probably will milk by hand. If you decide to increase your herd, you may want to invest in mechanical milking equipment that allows you to milk many animals quickly.

Before bringing your first goats home, acquire the following supplies for milking:

- A milk stand or a stanchion, also called a head gate. You will use this restraint device for milking and occasionally for feeding, trimming hooves, or during veterinary procedures. The stand is often elevated to hold the goat at a comfortable height for milking. A milking stand can be purchased from a dairy supply outlet or a goat catalog, or you can build one yourself. Plans for building milking stands are available online and from agricultural extension offices.

- A milking stool. You will need more than one if several people will be milking at the same time.

- Glass containers for milk storage. Large jars are made for this purpose.

- A stainless steel milk strainer, with extra disposable filters

- At least one seamless stainless steel pail for milking

- A second stainless steel pail to be used exclusively for washing udders

- Towels and sponges for cleaning udders. These must be kept separately from barn cleaning supplies.

- Udder wash, also called "dairy soap." This is a sort of disinfectant soap made specifically for safely and efficiently washing the udders of milking animals.

- Teat dip

- A strip cup to test for mastitis, which you will be using regularly from the first time you milk

- A supply of mastitis testing kits such as the California Mastitis Test (CMT)

In order to better understand and predict the outputs of individual does, keep a chart of production. After milking, carefully weigh and record the yield of each goat by pounds weight to $^1/_{10}$ pound. This practice eventually reveals the daily pattern and lactation curve of each goat. It also provides steady documentation of the quality of each animal as a milker, if you need the information later when selling the goat or applying for special recognition or status. The output of an individual doe will vary from year to year as the animal matures and ages. Over time, you will learn how to stagger the pregnancies, kidding, and drying off your goats, so they are not all drying off at the same time. The goal always is to have a steady milk supply available.

If a goat fails to dry off naturally after ten months, and you want to give her a rest and breed her again, help her dry off by decreasing milking to once a day for a week, then every other day for a week, then stopping at the third week. Some swelling of the udder probably will continue. This pressure actually helps stop the milk flow. If the doe does not seem to be drying off or is uncomfortable, milk her out a week after the last milking.

Abruptly stopping the milking cycle of a doe may damage the udder. Be patient and help her dry off gradually. In addition to decreasing frequency of milking, decreasing her grain ration will encourage drying off. Many goat owners also decrease water, but there is a risk of stressing the kidneys any time you deny an animal free access to plentiful fresh water. Time, patience, and giving lower rations of protein-rich feed, such as grain, will allow the doe to dry off naturally.

Udder care

Healthy udders are essential to the success of your dairy. A healthy goat has a healthy udder, and a healthy udder functions optimally to produce high-quality milk. The udder of a goat has two sides, divided by a cleft in the middle. There should be one teat on either side. The udder ideally is set high and is wide rather than being low and pendulous. It is supported by a series of internal ligaments attached to the abdominal wall. In older goats or goats that are heavy milkers, these ligaments can become stretched, allowing the udder to hang low. A low, pendulous udder is more prone to being kicked or stepped on by the goat, or injured by underbrush or other objects on the ground. In severe cases, an udder support can be put on the goat to make her more comfortable, protect the udder from injury, and prevent ligaments from further stretching.

Monitor the condition and appearance of your goats' udders each day. Check frequently for scratches, cuts, and other wounds, and watch them closely for signs of infection. A sizeable cut on the udder often will bleed profusely. Apply pressure to the cut with a clean towel until blood clots, bleeding stops, and you can better see the wound to examine it. Apply iodine immediately to discourage bacterial contamination of the wound. You also may want to apply a triple antibiotic ointment. A deep wound may require suturing, which should be done by a veterinarian or a veterinary technician to avoid infection.

Mastitis

When you milk, examine the udder of your goat closely for signs of abnormality. Look for wounds, redness, lumps, discharge, unusual swelling or heat, and any sign that something is not as it should be. Mastitis is a common inflammation of the udder generally caused by poor sanitation practices, insect bites becoming infected, or injury to low-hanging udders. Mastitis is the result of infection by any of several bacteria, and a simple test of the milk reveals the specific cause of mastitis in your goat so it can be treated. Prompt and aggressive veterinary treatment is important; neglected mastitis can scar the narrow passageways within the udder, do permanent damage to the teat duct, and create pockets where bacteria remain after treatment, ready to start up another infection. In the worst cases, the teat becomes gangrenous, and the disease turns fatal.

Some goats with mastitis will display obvious signs of illness. They may develop a fever, appear listless or lethargic, avoid being milked, or display an udder that is swollen, red, and hot to the touch. More often, the first sign of mastitis is bad milk — milk that is lumpy, stringy, blood-tinged, or has a bad odor.

Goats should be tested frequently and routinely for mastitis using a test such as the California Mastitis Test. Recent research suggests that, due to the chemical makeup of the goat's milk, the CMT may not be as useful in goats as it is in cows for indicating the presence of mastitis. However, it is still useful for eliminating mastitis as the cause of a problem with the milk.

Milking Your Goats

When you start milking goats, you probably will be milking by hand. Milking is not difficult, but it does require some practice. In a short time, you will become efficient and able to do it quickly. Each lactating goat must be milked twice daily, at roughly 12-hour intervals. Some dairy operators milk three times to encourage increased production, but twice daily is the norm.

Milking by hand

Step 1: Prepare your equipment.

Place your clean milk bucket (start each separate milking with a clean pail), clean cloths, and a pail of warm, soapy water in the milking area. Place your disinfectant and teat dip within easy reach. If you wish to test for problems, place your strip cup with the rest of your materials, so you do not forget to use it.

Step 2: Restrain your goat.

Before you milk a goat, restrain her in a stanchion or with a rope tie. It is always dangerous to leave a goat tied and unsupervised because the goat can quickly get tangled up, chew through the rope, or even strangle itself. However, a stanchion allows the milker to safely walk away from the goat for several minutes. Stanchions often have a raised platform on which the goat stands so the person milking does not have to bend over.

Training a goat to stand in the headgate is usually easy. Use a tasty treat or a little grain in a bucket to lure her head into the head holder and fasten her in. Reward her with the treat.

Step 3: Wash the udder.

Brush the doe before milking to remove any loose hair or dirt that might fall into the milk pail. Using warm, soapy water and a clean cloth, wash any debris, manure, or dirt from the udder. After you have removed visible dirt, spray the udder and teats with a disinfectant. Dispense your disinfectant from a spray bottle, rather than using a communal container; it is too easy to pass bacteria between goats. You also may wish to wipe the flank clean along with the udder.

Step 4: Wash your hands thoroughly.

Wash your hands before milking each individual goat so bacteria are not transferred from one goat to another. Invest in a good hand lotion. Udder balm works wonders overnight on chapped hands. You can also use disposable gloves when milking.

Step 5: Use teat dip.

Dip each teat in your teat dip and wipe away excess with a disposable paper towel. Excess dip can taint the taste of the milk. The disinfecting properties take effect as soon as it touches skin, and it has served its purpose. Wipe it away religiously. It is a good idea to put the teat dip in disposable 3-ounce paper cups and use a new cup for each doe.

Step 6: Milk your goat.

Many goat owners enjoy the process of milking by hand. It is peaceful, quiet time with your goat. Goats enjoy attention, and when accustomed to being handled, enjoy being milked. It is easier to learn with an experienced doe rather than one unaccustomed to milking. Always milk the goat on the same side. If your goat is accustomed to being milked from one side, it may take time for her to get used to being milked from the other. Provide some feed or the doe's grain ration for her to eat as you milk. Giving her something else to think about will increase her level of patience with you. Talking to her or singing to her also will calm her.

Place your milk pail under the udder. Begin by lightly grasping each teat in one hand and pulling down firmly, but slightly. This allows the goat to let down her milk. Next, squeeze each teat firmly in a steady, smooth downward motion without pulling it. As each squeeze of your hand begins, first use pressure from your thumb and forefinger to prevent downward flowing milk from moving back up again into the canal. Keep that pressure steady while closing the third finger into the grip, then the fourth, and finally the entire hand. This is done in one smooth downward rhythm.

The first few squirts from each teat should be discarded. (The resident barn cat often is waiting nearby with an open mouth to receive these.) Milk each teat until the udder is emptied and soft. Be careful not to over-strip the teat empty of milk, or you may damage it. Just stop milking when no more milk comes out of the teat during a normal squeeze.

Use a strip cup to check the milk for signs of mastitis or other problems. A strip cup is a metal cup with a permanent filter built into the top. Squirt the first squirt from each teat into the cup, and look for lumps, flakes, or any other ab-normality that could indicate a possible problem. If you find something unusual in the strip cup, break out the CMT kit and check for mastitis. You can purchase a CMT kit, or a California Mastitis Test kit, from a feed store or online from a livestock store such as Homesteader Supply (**www.homesteadersupply.com**). Kits cost about $20 to $25.

Step 7: Redip the teats.

This is important to seal the ducts with disinfectant so bacteria cannot travel up into the streak canal (passageway) and encourage mastitis. The teat opening is surrounded by sphincter muscles that relax to let the milk flow while you are milking. These remain relaxed and the opening loose for up to half an hour after you finish milking. During this period, the streak canal is most vulnerable to the entry of stray bacteria, and the final teat dip helps prevent this. Dispose of the dip; if you have another doe to milk, prepare new solution in a clean container. Never reuse the same dip because bacteria may be passed from doe to doe in contaminated teat dip.

Always begin the milking of each doe with clean materials: clean milk pail, clean soapy water, clean towels and cloths, clean dip, and clean hands. If you learn to think about preventing the spread of bacteria, you will have fewer veterinary bills and avoid many problems.

Processing milk

Good sanitation greatly reduces the amount of bacteria but cannot eliminate contamination altogether. It is important to create an artificial environment where the milk remains free of spoilage as soon as possible after milking. Milk must be cooled to 40 degrees F (4.5 degrees C) or below within an hour of milking. Refrigeration will not cool it fast enough, so most people immerse the containers of milk into buckets of ice water or into vats of continuously circulating cold water. If you must cool more than 6 gallons per milking, you may want to acquire a dairy cooler. A dairy cooler provides a steady supply of ice-cold water in which to place containers of fresh milk, which then cools the milk to the required temperature within minutes. In order to be certified as a Grade A dairy, you may be required to have a room designated exclusively for cooling and storing milk and a mandatory cooling machine.

Pasteurization

Milk that is not handled carefully and becomes contaminated can make anyone who consumes it sick. Pasteurization is the process of heating milk to a specific temperature and maintaining it for a specific length of time to kill harmful bacteria. In the 20th century, U.S. law began requiring that all milk sold for human consumption be pasteurized. How-ever, many people believe that pasteurization makes milk less nutritious and detracts from its flavor, and pasteurization is not necessary if the milk is handled properly.

The term raw milk refers to milk that has not been pasteurized. Many dairy goat owners keep their milk raw specifically because they appreciate the taste and nutritional value of raw milk, and they want it for themselves and their families.

Advocates of raw milk point out that pasteurization gives milk a "cooked" flavor. Milk was consumed raw for many centuries. People who routinely drink raw milk develop immunity to common bacterial infections. American tourists traveling in Europe sometimes become ill after eating yogurt, ice cream, or cheese because they do not have the same built-up resistance to dairy-borne bacteria as Europeans.

To pasteurize milk, heat it to 165 degrees F, or heat it to between 159.8 degrees F and 165.2 degrees F, for 15 seconds.

Milk for private consumption does not need to be pasteurized. If you sell goat's milk or an edible product made from your milk such as yogurt, butter, or cheese for human consumption, you will need to pasteurize by law. If you run a large-scale operation, your milk will need to be transported to a local plant for processing that includes pasteurization within hours of your animals being milked. Infectious agents in milk are killed when hard cheeses are ripened for a long time, but these agents are not killed in fresh cheeses.

Dairy farmers who know their own sanitation practices and the condition of their animals feel confident their milk is quite safe for their families to drink, as long as it is consumed while fresh (within a few days of milking). Enjoying raw milk is one of the benefits of dairy goat farming, but be aware of the danger, so you can avoid potential milk-borne illnesses. Pasteurization keeps milk tasting fresh by destroying bacteria that proliferate and alter its flavor. Goat milk contains a unique enzyme called caproic acid that gives the milk a "goaty" flavor as it ages, usually after two or three days. If you choose to use your milk raw, both for safety and for the best quality and flavor, keep it chilled, and drink it fresh.

When you transport milk, keep it in an airtight container that can be kept cool at all times, either by immersing it in ice water or by transporting it in a refrigerated vehicle. No sunlight from windows should fall on the container. If you are running a Grade A dairy, your local processing plant may provide safe transport of your milk to its facilities.

Off-flavors in goat's milk

There are many reasons why your milk may have an unpleasant taste. The majority of those causes can be controlled if you are aware of them.

Causes of off-flavors in goat's milk

FLAVOR	CAUSE
Barny	Milking in a smelly barn
	Not moving fresh milk from the barn quickly enough
	Doe living continuously in a poorly ventilated barn even if she is milked in a place where air is fresh
Bitter/soapy	The goat was consuming strong weeds before milking.
	The goat was consuming strong feed before milking.
	Biological makeup of milk in late lactation
	Temperature of milk was altered too quickly, such as when warm milk is suddenly chilled
Coarse, acidic/malty	Unclean equipment
	Failure to cool milk to 40 degrees F or below
	Milk cooled too slowly, which gave bacteria time to proliferate
Disinfectant	Residue of chlorine bleach or other soap or disinfectant on equipment that was not thoroughly rinsed after cleaning
Feed/feedy/sweet	Goats have consumed or have smelled plants, such as wild onions, garlic, silage, turnips, very green grass, ragweed, grape leaves, cabbage, honeysuckle, and others.

FLAVOR	CAUSE
Foreign	Goats have breathed fumes from paint, gasoline, or spray insecticides.
Metallic/oxidized	Milk has made contact with corroded or rusted metal.
	Containers made of copper, tin, or nickel
	Goat's drinking water is high in iron or copper.
	Milk exposed to sunlight
Musty	Unclean hay or feed, unclean or stagnant water
Rancid	Foaming resulting from vigorous milking, in which too much air is mixing with the fresh milk
	Sun penetrating a glass container for even a short period
Salty	Mastitis
Utensil	Goats drinking dirty water
	Milk has made contact with unclean containers.
	Milk has made contact with equipment that is not clean.

Some factors such as dietary changes and lactation cycles affect the composition and quality of goat's milk:

- Decreasing forage-to-feed concentrate ratio decreased milk fat and increased protein.
- Feeding of sodium bicarbonate buffer improved the percentages of fat and total solids.
- Later stages of lactation are associated with an increase in the content of fat, protein, and many minerals, and with a decrease in lactose, potassium, and citrate.

Selling milk

Laws regarding the selling of raw milk vary from state to state. Some states have delegated these decisions to cities and counties. This means there are many different regulations regarding the sale of raw milk in the United States. If you are a farmer who wishes to sell goat milk directly from your goats to the public, you should check your state and local laws. You can start by checking the Real Milk website (**www.realmilk.com/milk-laws-1.html**).

If you live in an area where the sale of raw milk is allowed, or if you are able to pasteurize your own milk, then you can sell your milk directly to buyers who come to your farm. You may be able to sell milk at farmers markets. Be sure to check with your local officials to find out if you need any special permits to sell. You may need to check other laws regarding other dairy products such as cheese and yogurt, as they are not covered under laws regarding milk.

If you plan to sell goat's milk, you need to find a reliable buyer. In many areas of the United States, there are no companies that process goat's milk for commercial sale. Even where a processor does exist, it may not need additional milk producers. If you are unable to sell your goat's milk to a processor, it may be feasible to sell it to individuals raising baby animals or as pet milk at local farmers markets. Most states have prohibitive restrictions on the sale of milk or milk products directly to individuals for human consumption. Contact the agency responsible for dairy regulations in your state. The American Dairy Goat Association (ADGA) website lists the contact information for state agencies (**www. adga.org**).

Any dairy selling raw milk to be processed into Grade A milk or milk products must meet a number of requirements to receive a Grade A dairy permit. The permitting process is carried out by state regulatory agencies that send out inspectors and regularly test the milk for bacteria and drug residues. State agents typically work with a new dairy farmer during the design and building of the dairy facility to ensure requirements are fulfilled. Requirements vary from state to state but, typically, include the building of a separate room for milking and milk storage. The additional cost of building these facilities, application fees, and the time it takes to complete the application and inspection process must be factored into your business plan.

Individuals who want to purchase raw milk for their families sometimes circumvent legal restrictions by purchasing part ownership in a goat. The goat stays on the farm, but the family regularly receives its share of the milk and pays for part of the goat's upkeep. Information on goat share contracts can be found on the website for the Campaign for Real Milk (**www.realmilk.com**). Raw milk also can be sold if it is to be fed to pets or livestock. Locating individuals who want to purchase your raw milk takes a lot more effort and time than signing a contract with a milk processor who sends a truck to pick up your milk twice a week.

You may be able to develop a regular market for your raw milk by selling it to farms that raise calves or pigs or by using it to raise your own livestock for sale as meat. It will take time to establish yourself in the local farming community and find enough customers to be able to sell your milk consistently.

Processing your own milk

Rather than selling your milk, you can process it yourself and sell your own pasteurized milk, cheese, yogurt, fudge, or nonedible products such as soaps or lotions. Raw milk can be used to make cheese if the cheese is aged 60 days or more. Pasteurized milk must be used to make fresh cheeses.

To sell edible products, you will need a Grade A dairy, a commercial kitchen, and other permits or licenses. Contact your state agricultural or consumer affairs agency to learn what is required. Producing your own products involves additional labor and equipment to manufacture, package, market, and ship them. Study the products you want to produce, and make a detailed list of all the expenses involved. You will have to spend some time experimenting, practicing, and perfecting recipes and processes before you have a marketable product. Attend cheese-making classes or learn from another producer. Once you are making your products, you may be able to sell them at local grocery stores, restaurants, specialty stores, farmers markets, or online.

Requirements for a Grade A Dairy

The U.S. Grade A Pasteurized Milk Ordinance (PMO), drafted by the U.S. Food and Drug Administration, states that only pasteurized milk can be sold as Grade A. Enforcement of this ordinance is under the jurisdiction of state departments of health or agriculture (Zeng and Escobar, 1995), and local requirements may vary.

Requirements for a Grade A dairy include a milking barn or parlor with a floor made of concrete or other impervious material that can be easily cleaned, and smooth, painted, or finished walls and ceilings that are sealed against dust. There must be enough ventilation to eliminate condensation, minimize odor, and provide a comfortable environment for the milker. Lighting must be adequate, and medications must be kept in a storage cabinet. Milking stands cannot be made of wood.

A separate milk room is required for cooling and storing goat milk to minimize the risk of contamination from the milking barn. The structure must be in good repair and easy to clean. The floor should slope evenly to a drain, and wash-sinks, hot water, and on-site toilets are required. Milking lines and other equipment should be of stainless steel or other smooth, nonabsorbent material. Milk storage tanks must have an efficient cooling system. Fresh, warm milk coming out of pipelines or milking buckets must be cooled to 45 degrees F within two hours. The water supply must comply with the Clean Water Act requirements, as enforced by the EPA, and a dairy waste management system must be in place. Grade A dairies are inspected at least twice a year, and milk samples are collected periodically. (Grade A Dairy Goat Farm Requirements, a publication by Langston University is available at **www.luresext.edu/goats/library/fact_sheets/d04.htm**.)

Goats for Meat

According to the USDA, kids often are slaughtered at 3 to 5 months old and when they weigh between 25 and 50 pounds. Kids do not store much body fat until they are about a year old. Many goats are older than a year and heavier when marketed, but most, except aged cull goats, are slaughtered when less than a year old. The meat of older goats is darker and less tender, but juicier and more flavorful than kid. The meat from male goats is a lighter color and lower in fat. The meat from female goats is more desirable for steaks and chops because it is tenderer.

There is an increasing demand for chevon, cabrito, or goat's meat in the U.S. Goat's meat has been a favorite meat in many cultures for thousands of years. Today, it is gaining favor in this country. Currently, much of the goat meat sold in the U.S. is imported from Australia and New Zealand, which means there is room for American breeders to breed more goats for meat.

Raising goats for personal consumption is often rewarding. Goat meat is low in fat and excellent meat for health-conscious individuals. You can learn to harvest goats yourself or find an outside butcher. For personal consumption, meat does not need to be processed by a professional butcher.

How to slaughter and clean

Butchering a goat will take some preparation and assistance. Many people prefer to have a local butcher shop do the job, as it is not an easy task. But if you prefer to butcher the goat for your own use, it is possible to perform the task at home. Goats should be butchered when the outside daytime temperature is 40 degrees F or cooler. This temperature is ideal refrigerator temperature and will allow the carcass to cool to prevent spoilage. Goats usually are butchered when they are less than 9 months old.

You should withhold feed, but not water, from the goat you intend to harvest for about 12 hours before slaughter. The animal to be butchered should be removed from its herd mates and killed out of sight and hearing of the rest of the herd to keep from upsetting the other animals. It is best to handle the goat as calmly as possible. As with other animals, if the goat is stressed, it can cause the goat to release hormones that will alter the taste of the meat. Having a front-end load tractor will help you hang the animal so its blood can drain from the body. A pulley system consisting of a rope and block and tackle also can be used. Lead or drive the animal close to the area where you plan to hang the animal. You also should have a source of clean, running water in place near the butchering area.

Goats should be shot in the back of the head. As soon as the animal is shot, sturdy ropes or chains should be placed on its rear legs, and it should be hung upside down. The jugular vein and carotid artery on the side of the throat should be slit to allow the blood to drain. The testicles on an uncastrated male animal should be removed next by cutting the attachments against the body. Following that, the head of the animal should be removed. Remove goat heads by cutting around the neck with a knife and then severing the tendons and ligaments holding the head to the neck. Remove the front feet by cutting through the first joint on the leg.

The hide or skin will be removed next. Use a pointed knife to make a circular cut in the hide around the rear legs. From each leg, make a cut through the hide down the leg to the body. Join these cuts at the midline of the pelvis and extend the cut through the hide all the way down the abdomen to the neck. Skin the hide away from the body by removing the hide at the rear legs and working your way down the body. Pulling the loose skin as you make your cut will help peel the hide away.

After the skin has been removed, you will begin to remove the intestines. Use a pointed knife to cut around the anus to free the end of the colon from the attachment to the body. Give it a slight yank to completely free it, then tie it closed with a piece of clean string or twine. Use your knife to make a cut into the lower abdomen, being very careful not to puncture any internal organs. Extend the incision to the tip of the breastbone. Remove the penis in male animals at this point. Use a tub or a wheelbarrow to catch the intestines. Cut through the fat and tissue attachment holding the intestines inside the abdomen. Pull the anus out through the abdomen and gently, yet firmly, pull the intestines and bladder from the body. At this point, you can save the liver and kidneys for cooking if you desire. Once the intestines are out, you will need to sever the esophagus. This tube runs from the mouth to the stomach. Try to cut it as far away from where it enters the stomach as possible. Once this is cut, the intestines should be out of the carcass and in your container.

Next, cut through the diaphragm to remove the heart and lungs. Cut through the tissues attaching heart and lungs (the pluck) to the body, and sever the windpipe at the top of the lungs. The heart can be saved while the lung and windpipe usually are discarded along with the intestines. The heart is another organ from the goat that can be used for special dishes, especially in some ethnic cuisines. You will need to remove the rest of the windpipe by cutting through the neck to remove this structure. Once the internal organs are removed, wash the entire carcass inside and out with water, preferably from a running hose, to remove blood, hair, and debris. Allow the water to drain, and then cover the carcass loosely with clean plastic.

Allow the goat carcass to hang for a week or more to age the meat, which makes it tenderer. Carcasses should be allowed to hang outside only if the temperature remains between 25 and 40 degrees F — this is why it is best to butcher animals during the winter. If the temperature does not remain between this range, you will need to cut up the meat and freeze it or have an alternative refrigeration means available, such as a refrigerator at a local butcher shop.

Finding an outside butcher

If you would like to have an outside butcher harvest and process your goats, you can contact your state meat inspection agency. They inspect processors and slaughterhouses where animals are processed and maintain a listing of licensed butchers in each state. They should be able to help you find a local butcher. Or, you can check online or in the yellow pages for a butcher in your area.

Goats are covered under the U.S. Federal Meat Inspection Act of 1906 and must be slaughtered under federal or state inspection. Any carcasses slaughtered for sale must be inspected. In 2007, (the latest year numbers were reported), 837,300 goats were federally inspected for slaughter.

Retail cuts of goat are similar to those for lamb or mutton. Goat should have light pink to bright red, firm, fine-grained flesh with well-distributed white fat. In some breeds of goat, there can be color variation between males and females; in other breeds, there is no difference.

Where to sell meat

Because goat meat must be federally inspected, you can sell it anywhere meat can be sold. You can sell it to grocery stores, restaurants, ethnic markets, farmers markets, online, or directly to buyers at your farm. Ethnic markets are often one of the best outlets for goat meat because goat meat is popular in many immigrant communities, especially during holidays and religious festivals.

Arrange with butchers to process your goats well in advance of the time you want to have them harvested. Butchers often get busy, and they may be booked if you wait too long to contact them. Be sure to talk to your butcher ahead of time about how you would like your animals processed, especially if you have any special instructions. Talk to your butcher about packaging, especially if you are selling your cuts of meat to grocers or markets where it is important that the meat be packaged in clear packages so customers can see it more easily.

Laws

There are few state or federal laws regarding goats. Most laws relating to goats exist at the local level and concern zoning, or whether you can keep livestock in certain areas. You will need to check with your local authorities to find out if goats are allowed where you live.

You can also check the SmallFarmGoat.com website called Ruminations **www.smallfarmgoat.com/goatvotes.htm** to find out more about laws relating to goats.

Goats for Fiber

Goats have been producing fiber for humans for thousands of years. Mohair and cashmere are famous and highly desired for sweaters and scarves. You may be able to increase the income from your goats by shearing them when appropriate.

Mohair

Mohair is the fiber that comes from Angora goats. It usually is cut off the goats about every six months, such as March and September, or just before kidding and just before breeding. In order to bring a top price, the hair must be completely clean and of top quality. Raw mohair usually sells for $3 to $12 for a pound of white hair. It may sell for $10 to $25 per pound for colored hair. The hair from younger goats is a finer quality, so it is more valuable.

Pygora

Pygora goats range from white to chocolate brown, to black, salt and pepper, silver-blue, to shades of caramel. This means that the fiber from these goats naturally come in these colors. Pygora goat fleece can be sheared, plucked, or combed from the goat. Type B and C fleeces usually shed in the spring. Type A fleeces should be sheared twice a year, as they will not shed. Type A fleece is wavy from the base to the tip. It is silky, lustrous, and shiny with characteristics like mohair. Type B is lustrous with curls at the tip. It has characteristics of both A and C fleece blended together. Type C fleece has distinct guard hairs with a soft, downy undercoat. It is warm with a low sheen and has characteristics like cashmere.

Cashmere

Cashmere from the Cashmere goat is soft, durable, lightweight, and warm. Cashmere is, in fact, the soft down undercoat of the goat. The amount of cashmere a goat produces depends on the goat's breeding and genetics. The cashmere is actually the goat's winter coat. It starts to grow around the middle of summer and stops in the middle of winter, when the days are shortest. Goats are sheared from December to March, when goats normally begin to shed their winter coats. Cashmere can be harvested by either combing or shearing.

How to shear

In order to shear your goats, use a 20-tooth mohair comb and sheep shears. You can store the cut hair in a paper bag. Keep your goats dry during the 24 hours before shearing. Shear the youngest goats first and the oldest ones last. This way you can keep the finer hair from mixing with the coarser hair. Keep the shearing area clean, and sweep it between cutting different colors of goats. It is all right to cut slowly. Treat the animals well. Try to avoid having to make second cuts as second cuts mean shorter hairs that are less valuable. Remove stained or soiled areas from the hair before storing it.

Wash the hair several times with detergent before spinning it. Rinse completely several times. In the last rinse, you can add vinegar or denatured alcohol to bring out the hair's natural luster. Dry the hair on towels or allow a fan to blow on it when it is hanging on a towel rack.

Selling goat fiber

Goat fiber is another growing market in the United States. If you have goat fiber to sell, hands pinners who spin yarns will probably be interested in your fiber if it is high quality. You may need to learn how to spin your own yarn and market it yourself to find niche markets. You can sell the yarn at farmers markets and online with other goat products. Mohair, cashmere, and pygora are in high demand. It is simply a question of reaching consumers for your yarns.

Chapter 7

Sheep

SHEEP GLOSSARY

Bag: The ewe's udder or mammary glands

Band: A group of sheep larger than a flock; usually referring to thousands of sheep kept on range land

Black wool: Refers to dark wool; any wool containing black or dark fibers

Blood grading: The degree of fineness of wool. The term was originally used to refer to the amount of Merino blood (a breed of sheep) in an animal.

Bright wool: Light, clean wool

Broken mouth: An old ram or ewe that has lost teeth. The condition usually begins when an animal is around four years old.

Bummer: A lamb that has to be bottle-fed. Usually an orphan, but it can be a lamb that is being ignored by its mother if there are multiple births.

Burdizzo: Tool used to castrate lambs by breaking the cord without breaking the skin

Carding: Converts loose, clean wool into longer, continuous strands. Carding may be done by hand or by machine.

Carpet wool: Coarse, strong wool suitable for making carpets

Clean wool: May refer to scoured wool; hand spinners may use the term to refer to a grease wool with little or no contamination from vegetable sources.

Clip: The total annual wool production taken from a flock

Closed face: A sheep that has lots of wool around its face and eyes

Club lamb: A lamb that is raised as a club project for 4-H or FFA

Combing: Removing the short fibers and leaving the long fibers laid out straight and parallel on a sheep

Count: A yarn's fineness when spinning; system of grading wool based on how fine it can be spun

Crimp: The wave seen in wool fibers

Degreased wool: Wool that has been chemically cleaned to remove all "grease" or lanolin

Density: The number of wool fibers present per unit of an area on a sheep's body. The fine wool breeds have a greater density, and more wool fibers per unit, than the coarse wool breeds.

Elasticity: The ability of wool fibers to return to their original length after they are stretched. Better quality wool has more elasticity.

Elastrator: A device to apply a heavy rubber band around a male lamb's testicles for castration. An elastrator may also be used for docking a lamb's tail.

Ewe: Female sheep

Facing: Trimming extra wool from around the face of a closed-face sheep

Fleece: The wool from one sheep

Flock: A group of sheep

Graft: Having a ewe accept and nurse a lamb that is not her own

Grease wool: Wool just as it comes off the sheep

Hot house lamb: A lamb born in fall or early winter and harvested when it is 9 to 16 weeks old

Jug: A small pen just large enough for one ewe and her lamb; usually used for only a few days after birth

Lamb: Young sheep, usually under a year old

Lanolin: The naturally occurring grease that coats wool

Long wool: Wool that is 12 to 15 inches long. It comes from certain breeds, such as the Cotswold, Lincoln, and Leicester breeds.

Luster: The natural gloss or sheen seen on a fleece.

Meconium: The first fecal material passed by a lamb

Mutton: Meat from a mature sheep

Open face: A sheep that does not have much wool around its face

Ovis aries: Scientific nomenclature for sheep

Polled: Having no horns; usually naturally hornless

Ram: Male sheep

Ruminant: One of a category of animals, such as sheep, goats, and cattle, which have a stomach with four compartments

Second cuts: Short pieces of wool that result from cutting the same areas twice when shearing sheep

Shearing: The process of clipping wool from a sheep

Wether: Castrated or neutered male

Wigging: Removing extra wool from around the face of a closed-face sheep; also known as facing

S heep were one of the earliest domesticated animals. They were probably the first herd animal domesticated by humans, being domesticated some 10,000 years ago. Since that time, they have provided people with wool for warmth, meat, and milk for cheese and other dairy products. The gentle sheep is one of the most beneficial of all domestic animals.

The History of Sheep and People

A pasture full of white, wooly sheep with lambs bounding at their sides is a soothing image most people envision when trying to drift off to sleep. It is hard to imagine a more serene lifestyle than that of a shepherd tending to his flock, idling the day away while the sheep graze. Modern-day sheep farming is far removed from the idealized shepherd's lifestyle. In fact, most sheep farmers in the United States are part-time shepherds holding another full-time job.

In the United States today, sheep are raised for both meat (lamb or mutton) and wool. The U.S. sheep and wool industries have seen significant change since the mid-1970s. There are fewer people involved in producing wool and meat from sheep today than there once were, and operations are smaller. Historically, lamb and mutton were viewed as byproducts of wool production, even though wool sales accounted for a smaller share of revenue. As money from wool has declined, producers have turned their attention to lamb and mutton production and the possibility of other byproducts, such as sheep leather.

Breeds

According to the American Sheep Industry Association, there are more than 47 different sheep breeds in the United States. Worldwide, there are hundreds of sheep breeds, each specially adapted to their own particular geographical area. In the U.S., the breeds are divided into six categories according to purpose: meat, fine wool, long wool, dual purpose, hair, and minor breeds. For the most part, the breeds primarily are divided according to meat type or wool type sheep.

Meat breeds

Cheviot: The Cheviot is a small-framed sheep with a white face and bare face and legs. It is hornless and has long wool. A mature ram weighs 160 to 200 pounds. A mature ewe weighs 120 to 160 pounds. Ewes will average 5 to 10 pounds of fleece.

Dorset: The Dorset can either be horned or polled. They have a medium-sized frame with white faces. Mature rams weigh 225 to 275 pounds, while a mature ewe weighs 150 to 200 pounds. The fleece from a Dorset ewe weighs between 5 and 9 pounds.

Hampshire: The Hampshire breed are black-faced, black-legged, large-framed sheep. They are widely used in the United States in crossbreeding programs when larger offspring is desired. A mature ram weighs more than 275 pounds, while the mature ewe can weigh more than 200 pounds. A fleece from a mature ewe will average 6 to 10 pounds.

Southdown: This small-framed breed has a light brown face and matures early into muscular carcasses. A mature Southdown ram weighs about 200 pounds, while a mature ewe is much smaller, averaging 150 pounds. The ewe will have a fleece between 5 and 8 pounds.

Suffolk: This is the largest framed sheep breed in the United States. It has a rapid growth rate, which makes it an excellent meat breed sheep. The Suffolk has a black bare face and legs. A mature ram will weigh 250 to 350 pounds, while the mature ewe will weigh 180 to 250 pounds. The ewe's fleece will weigh between 5 and 8 pounds.

Milk breeds

Sheep milk is not popular in any modern culture. However, milk from sheep is used to produce yogurt and other cultured products. Sheep produce much less milk than dairy cows, but their milk is much richer in terms of fat, minerals, and solids. This makes sheep milk excellent for making cheese. Three sheep breeds have been bred selectively to produce more milk than other sheep.

Awassi: The Awassi is a native sheep in the Middle East and Southwest Asia. They are usually white with a brown head and legs. They have a tail where fat is stored, and they can rely on this fat for nutrition when conditions are harsh. They are a very hardy breed, able to live with nomadic shepherds and as a settled flock. They have been used to produce meat, milk, and wool, but they are most notable for their milk production, especially in extreme conditions. They are disease-resistant and able to stand extreme temperatures. They are adaptable, and the ewes make excellent mothers.

East Friesian: The East Friesian is from East Friesia in Germany. They are considered one of the best sheep in terms of milk production. In addition to an exceptionally high milk yield (300-600 liters of milk during a 300-day lactation period), East Friesian ewes also produce a greater number of lambs than normal. When crossed with other breeds, they increase milk production and the number of lambs produced. They do best in small flocks. East Friesians are not hardy and are often used as crossbreds to improve Awassis and Lacaunes. The East Friesian has a pink nose, and they have no wool on their heads or legs. They are hornless. Their hooves are pale, and they have a "rat tail" or a tail that is thin and without any wool. Their bodies are covered in white wool.

Lacaune: The Lacaune is from southern France, where it is very popular. Their milk is used to produce Roquefort cheese. Government support for the breed, starting in the 1960s, helped with selective breeding, and today, the breed is one of the most prolific of all sheep used for milk products.

Fine-wool breeds

Merino: The Merino breed is known for its fine wool, which makes great wool for clothing. Some strains of the breed can produce more than 30 pounds of fleece a year. Mature rams weigh 175 to 235 pounds. Mature ewes weigh 125 to 180 pounds.

Rambouillet: This is a white-faced, white-fleeced sheep known for its fine wool. It is descended from the Merino sheep raised in Spain. Mature rams weigh 250 to 300 pounds. Mature ewes weigh 150 to 200 pounds. Ewe fleeces can weigh up to 18 pounds.

Long-wool breeds

Lincoln: The Lincoln sheep is the world's largest breed of sheep with mature rams weighing 250 to 350 pounds, while mature ewes weigh 200 to 250 pounds. When fully grown, their fleece spirals down in heavy locks and is coarse. The ewe's fleece weighs 12 to 20 pounds.

Romney: Although classified with the long-wool sheep, the Romney is also a good meat sheep. Mature rams weigh 225 to 275 pounds, and mature ewes weigh 150 to 200 pounds. A fleece from a mature ewe will weigh 8 to 12 pounds.

Dual-purpose breeds

Columbia: The United States Department of Agriculture developed the Columbia breed through crossing Rambouillet ewes with long-wool breed rams. Mature Columbia rams weigh 225 to 300 pounds, while mature ewes weigh 150 to 225 pounds. The fleece from a Columbia ewe weighs 10 to 16 pounds.

Corriedale: This white-faced sheep has a large frame with an ample wool coat. A mature ewe's fleece weighs 10 to 17 pounds. A mature Corriedale ram weighs 175 to 275 pounds, while a mature ewe weighs 130 to 180 pounds.

Other sheep breeds

The minor sheep breeds and the haired sheep breeds are not too common in the United States.

Finn: The Finn sheep is an example of a minor breed of sheep. It is native to Finland and is a smaller sheep. A mature ram weighs less than 200 pounds, and a mature female weighs around 140 pounds. Ewes of this breed have been known to have up to four lambs at one time.

Katahadin: The Katahadin is an example of a haired sheep breed. Although all sheep have both hair and wool, wool is the predominant fiber in most sheep. As the name suggests, the haired sheep has more hair than wool. The Katahadin was developed in the United States during the 1950s. Because they do not have a fleece, they are not sheared. Instead, they are used primarily for meat. Mature rams weigh between 180 to 250 pounds, and mature ewes weigh between 120 to 160 pounds.

Buying Sheep

Before you buy any sheep, it is a good idea to study breeds of sheep and decide exactly what your goals are. Are you interested in producing wool? Are you more interested in producing meat? Are you interested in producing dairy products? Making these decisions will help you know what kind of sheep you want to buy.

When buying sheep, it is a good idea to go to an established breeder. Try to visit a number of sheep farms if possible. Talk to experienced breeders. Not only will you get better lambs and sheep from good breeders, but you also will make valuable contacts that can help you as you raise your own sheep.

Where to buy lambs and sheep

Sheep make a wonderful addition to the farmstead and can be a valuable tool for weed control. They provide fiber and meat, both potential side sources of income to an off-farm job. In a small-scale farm enterprise, sheep fit well into a low-input farming system because they need minimal housing if lambing coincides with warm spring weather. Starting out with a small group of ewes (ten to 20) and a ram is an

excellent way to enter into sheep farming. It is not advisable to purchase your breeding stock from an auction or sales barns. Ewes at these places are usually old, diseased, or crippled and will bring heartache to the farm family.

It is best to purchase registered sheep so you can have some guarantee that the ewe or ram you are getting has been born when the breeder states it was born, and so you will know who its mother and father are. You can purchase registered sheep at their association's state, regional, or national herd shows. Check your local feed store for fliers and posted information about upcoming shows; and check with sheep breed associations to find out if they will have upcoming shows in your area. You can find links to sheep breed associations on the Hobby Farms website: **www.hobbyfarms.com/ farm-resources/livestock-resources/Sheep-Breed-Associations.asp**x. Another option is to purchase sheep to replace old or culled ewes from a commercial sheep grower who raises ewes for his or her own flock. Sometimes these growers raise more than they can use and offer them for sale. You can locate these growers by contacting your county extension agent, a local veterinarian, or through local farm newspapers.

What to look for when buying sheep

When buying sheep, examine the lambs and sheep to make sure they are healthy individuals. Their eyes and noses should be clear and free of discharge. Their ears should be clean inside with no signs of parasites. Their skin and coat should look healthy. Check the sheep's teeth. Do the teeth look in good shape? Do they appear to coincide with the proper age of the animal? Check the sheep's feces. There should be no trace of diarrhea. The feces should look small and firm. The animal's hooves should look healthy with no signs of swelling or redness. If you are buying a ewe, check the animal's udder and teats to be sure she will be able to give milk. The seller should be able to provide you with records for the sheep that list all medications and vaccinations that have been given. Ideally, the seller will be honest with you about why they are selling the sheep.

Handling Sheep

Handling sheep is usually easier than handling other livestock animals such as goats or pigs. Sheep are flock animals and if you can get them heading in one direction, they all usually will follow. However, there are times when you will need to separate individual sheep to do routine animal husbandry such as trimming hooves, worming, giving vaccinations, doing pregnancy checks, and so on. When you need to work with an individual sheep, you may need to tip the sheep. In order to tip a sheep, you should stand to the side of the sheep, hold the sheep under the front legs, lift them up, and use your knee to help place them in a sitting position. The sheep should be leaning back against your legs. If you are handling a large sheep then you will probably need someone to help you. This sitting position is very comfortable for the sheep, and they are usually quiet and placid while you trim hooves or check them.

If you do not feel up to tipping a sheep, you can try using a chute to hold a sheep while you do some of these routine chores. A chute is a very tight-fitting, fenced-in area that holds the sheep in place so you can do your work. It is a very confined area, but it does not harm the sheep.

Housing and Feeding Sheep

Sheep are housed similar to goats, but goats and sheep should not be kept together in a confinement situation, as the goat will most likely bully the more docile sheep. Sheep will do well on pasture but should be provided a shelter in inclement weather. Pregnant sheep should be monitored closely, and when nearing the end of their pregnancy, they should be placed into well-bedded (straw) lambing pens to lamb.

Pasture

Sheep will get a large portion of their nutrition from pasture and hay. Ewes in late pregnancy or that are lactating and rapidly growing lambs will need to be supplemented with grain. Sheep do not require soda like goats, but they will need salt and minerals. The mineral copper is toxic to sheep so read the label closely on your salt/mineral supplement to make sure it is nontoxic to sheep.

Feeding Lambs and Sheep

Most people who raise sheep raise them on pasture and forage, along with salt and mineral supplements. Some people feed hay. But commercial sheep feeds are available. Sheep should be fed concentrated feed in the form of grain before and during breeding season and at times of peak production.

Sheep cannot tolerate very much copper in their diet, but they do need some. It is a mistake to leave out all copper from their diet.

It is normal to begin feeding lambs still in the pen with their mother a creep ration that includes supplemental concentrates, along with hay. A creep ration is feed that is sometimes fed to lambs that are about 3 weeks old, when they are starting to become interested in adult food. You can begin feeding them this ration as early as 21 days old. The "creep" is an area in the pen where the lambs can reach food but the ewe is too large to go, so she cannot get to their feed.

Sheep Health

There is a saying in the veterinary field, "sick sheep seldom survive," which sadly holds true in far too many cases. Sheep are notorious for hiding sickness, most likely because they are prey animals and often must hide illness from predators as not to appear weak. A sick sheep will give few, if any, signs at being sick until it is obvious it is ill. By then, it may be unable to stand.

Lamb care

Lambs should have their tails docked to prevent fly strike, a condition where flies deposit eggs in the skin of the lamb, which will hatch into maggots. Docking consists of using a stout, rubber ring (elastrator) to remove the tail. The specially compounded elastrator ring is put in place around the tail with a pair of elastrator pliers and cuts off circulation to the tail, producing a feeling of numbness. The feeling quickly passes, and the tail falls off after a few days. It should be done when the lamb is 7 weeks old. The ring is applied about 1.5 inches from the base of the tail. Male lambs not intended for breeding should be castrated by using the same type of rubber rings used in tail docking. The ring is applied just above the testicles; make sure both testicles are in the scrotum. Ask for a demonstration from an experienced shepherd or veterinarian before you perform this task for the first time. The rubber ring is simply a thick, strong ring made of a special rubber compound. Leave the ring on until the testicles come off.

Lambs should have access to fresh water and hay or pasture starting at 1 week old. Weaning can be started at 6 weeks for orphan lambs. Provide plenty of fresh water and good quality pasture to the lambs being weaned. At the time the lamb is weaned, it should be given a dewormer. Dewormers kill worms and parasites, which compete with the lamb for vital nutrients and can lead to poor lamb growth. Lambs should be vaccinated against tetanus and pulpy kidney. If the mother had been vaccinated against these diseases and if adequate colostrum was fed to the lamb, these vaccines can be given to lambs at 3 months old. If not, the lamb should be vaccinated when the tail is docked. Three to four weeks after the first vaccine, the lamb will need a second injection of the same vaccine.

If you find a weak lamb, the most important steps to take are to dry the lamb thoroughly using warm towels to bring its body temperature up. Most shepherds will bring the lamb into the house and place it in a cardboard box or large plastic tub lined with disposable bedding. Fill hot water bottles or a used, plastic soda bottle with hot water and wrap it in towels. Place the wrapped bottle up against the lamb. A heat lamp can be used to provide warmth. When the lamb warms up, it will start to bleat and want to be fed.

The lamb should be fed colostrum, preferably from its mother. Cow colostrum can be fed if the mother does not have sufficient colostrum. Return the lamb to its mother as soon as possible. An orphan lamb should be placed in a warm, dry pen with a supplemental heat source. Many people will let the orphan bunk in a box in the house or a warm basement until it is a week old. Then, it will be put into its own pen in the lambing barn.

Ewe health

Viruses and bacteria causing miscarriages in ewes can be a big problem, and these bacteria and viruses are considered zoonotic as they also can cause symptoms in humans. Pregnant women should never handle dead lambs or fetuses, placentas, or placental fluids. Miscarriages can be reduced by strict sanitation of the lambing areas and by keeping other animals out of the lambing pens. Any ewe that has aborted a lamb should be isolated from the flock to help decrease the transmission of the disease organism. The aborted fetus and placenta should be placed in a plastic garbage bag, tied shut, and brought to a veterinary clinic to be examined. Usually the tissues will need to be sent to a university diagnostic lab to determine the cause of the abortion. Some common causes of abortion include:

- **Chlamydia** causes enzootic abortions of ewes (EAE). Abortions occur during the final month of pregnancy along with stillbirths and weak lambs. Infected sheep spread it to others through uterine discharges, placentas, or fetal tissues. If there is an epidemic, the entire flock can be treated with tetracycline.

- **Q fever** is caused by the bacteria *Coxiella burnetii*. Many sheep may not show any signs of having the Q fever organism. It can cause late-term miscarriage along with infertility problems. If your sheep is diagnosed with Q fever, it will need to be reported to federal authorities, as it is an organism that can be used in bioterrorism. Treatment is through use of tetracycline.

- **Vibriosis** is the disease caused by *Campylobacter* and causes late-term miscarriages, stillbirths, and weak lambs. Treatment of an abortion outbreak is with tetracycline. A vaccination is available that will prevent the disease in sheep flocks. The first year, the ewes are vaccinated twice in early gestation then once again half way through the gestation period. After this initial series, the ewes are vaccinated once yearly after the breeding season.

- **Toxoplasmosis** causes abortions during the last month of pregnancy, stillbirths, and weak lambs. The organism is spread by cats defecating in feed or by contamination of water or the environment by cat feces. Cats should be kept away from sheep feed sources and away from pregnant ewes.

Two diseases, in addition to the diseases that are responsible for causing miscarriages, can threaten the health and life of an ewe:

Pregnancy toxemia: Pregnancy toxemia occurs late in the pregnancy. It is more common in ewes that are overly fat or thin or in older ewes carrying multiple fetuses. The cause is a metabolic disorder where the ewe does not take in adequate nutrition during late pregnancy when the lamb(s) are growing rapidly. An ewe with pregnancy toxemia will appear bright and alert but will be unable to stand. Treatment consists of giving the ewe glucose orally and via the vein. Giving ½ to 1 pound of grain to ewes in the late stages of pregnancy can prevent toxemia. Keeping your ewes in good body condition (not too fat or thin) will also help prevent this disease.

Mastitis: Ewes can suffer from mastitis, which is an infection of the mammary glands. Similar to dairy cattle, bacteria can cause acute or chronic forms of mastitis. In acute mastitis, the mammary glands will be swollen, warm, and red. The ewe may act painful and might not let her lambs nurse. Acute mastitis is treated much like cattle mastitis with antibiotics, frequent milking, and using anti-inflammatory medicines. Chronic mastitis is also treated with antibiotics.

Other diseases affecting sheep

Where the previous section focused on diseases that only affect ewes, several diseases can affect rams and ewes alike. A thin and sickly ewe may be detected at shearing time as the thick wool hides the signs of a thin or malnourished sheep. Some of these illnesses are chronic wasting diseases, which can become a flock-wide problem. These diseases can also affect goats as well.

Border disease: Border disease is a virus that causes disease in lamb fetuses. Other names of this disease are hairy shaker disease or fuzzy lamb syndrome. It causes abortions, mummification, or weak lambs. Lambs with border disease that survive birth are persistently infected and spread the virus via secretions. The disease is first suspected when the flock begins to lamb; fewer lambs than expected are born, the lambs that are born are small and hairy, and some lambs have tremors. There is no treatment or vaccination available. Sick lambs should not be used for breeding, but it is helpful to expose unbred ewes to these lambs so they can develop immunity. The ewe will be able to kick the virus out of her system and will pass her immunity on to her offspring.

Ovine Progressive Pleuropneumonia (OPP): Ovine Progressive Pleuropneumonia is a chronic, debilitating disease in sheep. Other disease conditions associated with this virus are polyarthritis, neurological problems, and mastitis. The primary route of transmission is via lambs ingesting colostrum infected with the virus, but the disease may be passed between adult animals as well. A less efficient way the virus is spread is through ingestion of contaminated food or water or by inhalation of aerosolized virus. Clinical signs are seen in sheep more than 2 years old. The signs of OPP include chronic pneumonia, rapid or difficulty breathing, lack of a fever, and a loss of body condition despite good appetite. Pregnant ewes may have lambs that are weak or small if infected with OPP. There is no treatment for OPP and no vaccine to prevent it from occurring. Control is based upon testing flocks, culling affected animals, removing lambs from affected ewes before colostrum is consumed, or else feeding lambs pasteurized colostrum and milk from affected ewes. Pasteurization inactivates the virus that causes OPP, so it will not cause infection in lambs consuming this type of colostrum.

Bluetongue: Bluetongue is indistinguishable from foot and mouth disease and is therefore a reportable disease. Foot and mouth disease is a serious illness in sheep and cattle. It is important to differentiate bluetongue from foot and mouth disease, as currently foot and mouth disease is not present in the United States. If it is discovered in the United States, all exports of livestock from the country will cease, and all affected animals will be slaughtered. All sheep exhibiting the signs of bluetongue/foot and mouth disease need to be reported. Testing will be performed on the sheep to determine which disease is affecting the sheep.

Biting insects transmit the bluetongue virus from sheep to sheep. There are two clinical diseases of sheep: reproductive disorders and a vasculitis disease of several different organ systems. The vasculitis disease causes fever, facial edema, salivation, nasal discharge, oral ulcers, reddened nose or mouth, pneumonia, lameness and stiffness, and death. Reproductive disease can manifest as dummy lamb births, miscarriages, or stillbirths. A dummy lamb is a lamb that does not suckle, seems slow, is weak at birth, and may not have a good chance of survival. Prevention revolves around controlling the vectors (insects) of the disease. Using insecticides around the barn, prompt removal and proper disposal of manure, draining of stagnant water, and using insecticides on sheep will help to reduce the number of biting insects.

Pizzle rot: Pizzle rot, or balanoposthitis, is a common condition in wethers (castrated male sheep) and less so in rams. High protein levels, especially when caused by feeding on rich pastures, produce a urine rich in urea, a waste product the body produces from protein metabolism. The alkalinity of the urine makes an ideal growth medium for bacteria, such as *Corynebacterium renale*, which is the primary culprit in pizzle rot although other bacteria can cause the condition as well. The bacteria interact with the urea in the urine to produce ammonia. Strong ammonia can scald the prepuce and surrounding area, leading to necrosis of the tissue. Scarring and stricture formation can block the urine flow and lead to retention of urine. Keeping the belly and prepuce closely shorn will help urine dry quickly. If the condition is caught early, removing the rich feed sources is successful at resolving the condition. Later stage treatment is rarely successful as there will be extensive damage to the urinary tract that will be impossible to correct or reverse.

Orf: A virus causes contagious ecthyma (Orf). The most common sign is shallow ulcers that appear in the lip, nostril, and feet areas. Lambs are most commonly infected and may be reluctant to nurse due to mouth and nose lesions. Lambs might spread the disease to unvaccinated or unexposed older animals.

In the male, lesions also appear on the penis and prepuce while in the female lesions will appear on the vulva and teats. It is a zoonotic disease that can be transmitted to humans. Orf is spread by direct contact, including breeding. Animals might be reluctant to mate due to the pain of the lesions. The disease typically runs its course in three to four weeks. Secondary bacterial infections can happen that lead to more debilitating conditions such as damage to the reproductive tract or deep tissue infections.

Scrapie: Scrapie is a degenerative disease of the sheep's nervous system. The disease has a long incubation period before signs are noticed. It is similar to other diseases that affect the nervous system such as bovine spongiform encephalopathy (BSE) of cattle, chronic wasting disease of deer and elk, and Creutzfeldt-Jakob disease of humans. Scrapie is caused by a tiny piece of protein (prion) that is very resistant to heat or disinfectants. It is spread from infected sheep to other infected sheep, most commonly from an infected mother to her lambs. Lambs during their first few months of life are most susceptible to contracting scrapie. It is believed that some sheep are more genetically susceptible to scrapie. The disease is found worldwide and was first diagnosed in the United States in 1947 in Michigan.

A prion enters the body through the mouth. For the first two years, it remains in the body in low levels in the lymph nodes. Then it spreads to the nervous system and multiplies rapidly, causing damage to the nerve cells. Sheep will show signs such as tremors, lack of coordination, behavioral changes, and a manner of walking that looks like a bunny hop. Some sheep may be intensely itchy, rubbing against objects until their wool is worn off (hence the name scrapie). The affected sheep will die one to six months after signs occur. Sheep do not develop immunity to scrapie, so there is no vaccine or cure. There is no simple diagnostic test that can be performed on live animals and no treatment. If the disease is found in a flock, all infected ewes, rams, and their offspring are killed by the authorities, the premises will need to be rigorously cleaned, and the federal government will monitor the flock to tract the progression of the disease. There is currently a nationwide scrapie tagging program but it is administered at the state level with different requirements from state to state. Talk to your local extension service agent to find out what the requirements are in your state.

Breeding Sheep

A female lamb will reach puberty when she is between 5 and 12 months old. Weight, breed, genetics, and her nutritional status influence when she will come into estrus and is ready to stand for mating. Single-born lambs, larger lambs, heavy-fed lambs, and lambs born early in the lambing season tend to come into estrus sooner because of reaching puberty sooner than twin-born lambs, lambs that are not fed for fast growth, or younger lambs.

When to breed

Before you breed your ewes, they should be in the best health condition possible. A sick ewe will have difficulty carrying a pregnancy to term, may give birth to sickly lambs, or may not be able to properly care for her lambs. Vaccinations should be finished before breeding to ensure the mother can fight diseases and pass on some of her immunity to her lambs. The herd should be treated with a dewormer and have their hooves trimmed as a matter of routine maintenance. Intestinal worms are highly contagious; so all sheep in the herd should be treated at the same time to lessen the chance of having an infected sheep in the herd. Any sheep with abscesses, those in poor body condition, those with poor teeth, or sheep with any chronic health condition should be treated aggressively or culled.

The sheep's estrous cycle averages around 16 days. Standing estrous — when the sheep will show interest in the ram and stand to be mounted by the ram — is influenced by the presence of the ram and lasts for around 30 hours. Most sheep show estrous when the days are shortest. The daylight enters the eye and stimulates the brain, which in turn regulates the release of hormones that stimulate estrous. In the Northern Hemisphere, the most natural time to breed sheep is October through November. This seasonal estrous (polyestrous) is normal for most sheep although some sheep breeds will mate all year. An ewe in estrous will be hard to detect unless a ram is present. Then she will show the ram attention (such as nuzzling him) and standing still for him to mount her. One ram can service 30 females.

Lambing

The average length of gestation is 148 days. Around ten days before lambing (giving birth), the ewe's udder and vulva will swell. The teats become firm and fill with colostrum, which is the vital first milk the lamb needs to develop its immune system. An ewe close to lambing should be moved to a lambing pen or "jug." This is typically a 5-foot by 5-foot pen that is isolated from the rest of the flock. It should be kept scrupulously clean and deeply bedded with clean, dry straw.

As lambing approaches, a thick white mucus will discharge from the vulva. Uterine contractions will cause the ewe to become uneasy and swish her tail. She might bleat and get up and down. The ewe might start to strain as the cervix continues to dilate in preparation for the lamb to pass through. The placenta (commonly called the water bag) will appear at the vulva and burst, releasing fluids to help lubricate the birth canal. The ewe will strain in earnest to expel the lamb, which will come out front feet first with the head not far behind. The entire delivery process from rupture of the water bag until the lamb is on the ground takes about one hour for a single birth and two to three hours if twins or triplets are delivered. The placenta should pass out of the birth canal about two to three hours after lambing. There should be one for each lamb delivered.

The ewe will do her motherly tasks after the lamb is born. She will dry the lamb, and after the lamb stands, she will nudge the baby to her teats to nurse. Lambs need colostrum in order to build their immune system. It is vital that lambs receive this milk, which is rich in antibodies and immunoglobulins (both components of the immune system), in the first six hours after birth. The lamb's intestinal system is designed to allow these substances to pass from the colostrum directly into the blood stream. After 24 hours, the intestinal wall changes, stopping this process. Each lamb should receive a minimum of 4 ounces of colostrum as soon as possible after birth. Some ewes are unable to let down their milk at first. You may need to gently massage the udder for a minute and milk a stream of colostrum from the teats. Check each lamb and ewe every six hours after birth to make certain the lamb is nursing and that the ewe has not rejected her lamb(s). Record the weight of each lamb at birth. This way, you can tell if a lamb is not gaining weight or nursing. Keep the lamb and ewe quietly together for three days to ensure a strong maternal bond and that the lamb is nursing well before releasing it to be with the rest of the flock.

Orphan lambs

An ewe may reject a lamb, particularly if she gives birth to twins or triplets or if she becomes ill. Some ewes reject lambs for no known reason. In this case, you will have to be its mother. Make sure the orphan receives its colostrum. You will have to teach the lamb to drink from a bottle. Prepare a bottle using any of the commercial milk replacements available. If it is the lamb's first feeding, use warmed colostrum. Place the nipple in the lamb's mouth, and use your hand to move the jaws together. The lamb should soon get the idea that milk comes from the nipple and start to suckle.

If the lamb is weak or has a poor suckle reflex, it will need to be tube fed. If you have never attempted this, ask an experienced person or a veterinarian to show you how to tube feed the lamb, or you may risk placing the tube into the respiratory tract and unintentionally kill the lamb. Do not over-feed lambs. They can contract scours (diarrhea) or even die from too much milk in one feeding. Lambs need about 500 milliliters of milk a day, spread over four or five feedings, for the first week. After the first week, follow the directions on the milk replacer bag to determine how frequently and how much milk replacer should be fed. In cold weather, a little extra warm milk will compensate for the extra energy the lamb will need to keep warm.

Orphaned lambs should be kept in a warm, dry, and deeply bedded pen, preferably within eye and earshot of the rest of the flock. The pen should be constructed so the lambs will stay in it, and the rest of the flock will keep out. This way the orphans will not be bullied by larger lambs or even by the ewes. After they are weaned, they can rejoin the rest of the flock.

CASE STUDY:
NOT A SINGLE BLACK SHEEP

Ingrid Bey and Dave Plunkett
Belle Acres
belleacres@earthlink.net
10960 W. 260th St.
Belle Plaine, Minnesota

Dave Plunkett and Ingrid Bey raise between 14 and 22 ewes on their 10 acres near Belle Plaine, Minnesota. Bey, a veterinarian, joked they needed lawn mowers for their pastures, and sheep fit the bill. They also enjoy the fact that sheep are docile animals and are relatively easy to handle. A friend of theirs raised sheep, so they were able to ask questions and observe how much work is involved in raising sheep. They started sheep farming by purchasing three ewes, each of which had twin lambs. Four of the lambs were female, so they kept those four and grew their flock. They rented a ram for the first few years before they purchased a ram of their own.

They highly recommend finding a good sheep producer to act as a mentor before deciding to raise sheep. Sheep are living animals that require care and cannot be treated like machines. They recommend starting with a small flock and learning how to care for and keep sheep before getting a large number of sheep. They have found limiting factors to raising sheep to include: labor at lambing time, feed costs, and a lack of market opportunities.

They have found the most enjoyable and the least enjoyable part of sheep farming is the lambing season. It is a very stressful time with nightly checks of ewes ready to lamb. Despite the best of care, some lambs will die, and there will be complications with labor and delivery. But the lambs that do thrive are fun to watch as they run and jump around the pasture with reckless abandonment. They also derive extreme satisfaction that their lamb meat is delicious and wholesome. They are very proud when a customer tells them that their lamb is the best lamb they have ever eaten.

They direct market their lamb meat to individual customers primarily found through word-of-mouth. They are members of the Minnesota Lamb and Wool Producers and the Sustainable Farming Association of Minnesota. Through these organizations, they are able to list their lamb. One novel way they were able to connect with customers was through donating a lamb to an annual charity auction, which was a good source of new customers for them. Any lambs not sold to customers are then sold at the live auction barn, but they get about half the price there as they do through direct marketing.

They spend about 30 to 60 minutes a day caring for their lambs. During lambing season, the time commitment greatly increases. Baling hay and cleaning pens are two tasks that require sizable amounts of time. They have their sheep on a deworming schedule because parasitism is a big concern. One difficult aspect of sheep farming is, it is hard to find a shearer to shear a small flock. They ended up doing the task themselves this year and may have to continue to do so in the future.

Sheep for Milk

Sheep milk is not very popular in the United States. However, sheep milk, usually from the milk breeds listed above, is used to make cheese and yogurt. Feta, Roquefort, and ricotta cheeses all are made from sheep's milk. Sheep produce less milk than cows, but sheep's milk is richer in fat, solids, and minerals. This makes it perfect for making cheese. Sheep's milk has even more lactose than cow milk, so it is not a good alternative for lactose-intolerant people. If you are interested in raising sheep for their milk, choose a breed such as the Awassi or the Lacaune, or an East Friesian crossbred.

As with goat's milk, you can do anything you like with sheep's milk for your own personal use. You can drink it straight from the sheep, make cheese or yogurt with it, or use it for other purposes.

Selling milk

If you intend to sell sheep's milk, you will need to check the laws in your state regarding raw milk versus pasteurized milk. You can check them on the Real Milk site: **www.realmilk.com/milk-laws-1.html**. Laws regarding other dairy products, such as cheese and yogurt, are separate from laws regarding milk. Check those laws to see if you can sell cheese and other dairy products made from your sheep's milk.

Sheep for Meat

Mutton and lamb have been popular meats throughout history. The Cheviot, Dorset, and the Suffolk are popular breeds to raise for their meat. In the United States, the following cuts of meat are usually available:

- Square cut shoulder — shoulder roast, shoulder chops, and arm chops
- Rack — rib chops and riblets, rib roast
- Loin — loin chops or roast
- Leg — sirloin chops, leg roast (leg of lamb)
- Neck
- Breast
- Shanks (fore or hind)
- Flank

If you are raising sheep and lambs for personal consumption, there are no laws about how you harvest your lambs. You may butcher your own sheep and lambs on your property or take them to a processor to have a butcher do the work for you. You can use a custom butcher. He or she does not need to be state or USDA-licensed because you are not selling the meat.

How to slaughter and clean

Butchering a sheep will take some preparation and assistance. Many people prefer to have a local butcher shop do the job, as it is not an easy task. But if you prefer to butcher the sheep for your own use, it is possible to perform the task at home. Sheep should be butchered when the outside daytime temperature is 40 degrees F or cooler. This temperature is ideal refrigerator temperature and will allow the carcass to cool to prevent spoilage. Sheep usually are butchered when they are less than 9 months old.

Withhold feed, but not water, from the sheep you intend to harvest for about 12 hours before slaughter. The animal to be butchered should be removed from its herd mates and killed out of sight and hearing to keep from upsetting the other animals. It is best to handle the sheep as calmly as possible. As with other animals, if the sheep is stressed it will release hormones that will alter the taste of the meat. Having a front-end load tractor will help you hang the animal so its blood can drain from the body. A pulley system consisting of a rope and block and tackle also can be used. Lead or drive the animal close to the area where you plan to hang it. You should also have a source of clean, running water in place near the butchering area.

Sheep should be shot in the back of the head. As soon as the animal is shot, sturdy ropes or chains should be placed on its rear legs, and it should be hung upside down. The jugular vein and carotid artery on the side of the throat should be slit to allow the blood to drain. The testicles on an uncastrated male animal should be removed next by cutting the attachments against the body. Next, the head of the animal should be removed. Remove sheep heads by cutting around the neck with a knife and then severing the tendons and ligaments holding the head to the neck. Remove the front feet by cutting through the first joint on the leg.

Remove the hide or skin next. Use a pointed knife to make a circular cut in the hide around the rear legs. From each leg, make a cut through the hide down the leg to the body. Join these cuts at the midline of the pelvis, and extend the cut through the hide all the way down the abdomen to the neck. Skin the hide away from the body by removing the hide at the rear legs and working your way down the body. Pulling the loose skin as you make your cut will help peel the hide away.

After the skin has been removed, begin to remove the intestines. Use a pointed knife to cut around the anus to free the end of the colon from the attachment to the body. Give it a slight yank to completely free it, then tie it closed with a piece of clean string or twine. Use your knife to make a cut into the lower abdomen, but be careful not to puncture any internal organs. Extend the incision to the tip of the breastbone. Remove the penis in male animals at this point. Use a tub or a wheelbarrow to catch the intestines. Cut through the fat and tissue attachment holding the intestines inside the abdomen. Pull the anus out through the abdomen, and gently, yet firmly, pull the intestines and bladder from the body. At this point, you can save the liver and kidneys for your use. They can be used for cooking. Once the intestines are out, you will need to sever the esophagus. This tube that runs from the mouth to the stomach. Try to cut it as far away from where it enters the stomach as possible. Once this is cut, the intestines should now be out of the carcass and in your container.

Next, cut through the diaphragm to remove the heart and lungs. Cut through the tissues attaching heart and lungs (the pluck) to the body, and sever the windpipe at the top of the lungs. The heart can be saved, while the lung and windpipe usually are discarded along with the intestines. The heart is another organ from the sheep that can be used for special dishes, especially in some ethnic cuisines. You will need to remove the rest of the windpipe by cutting through the neck to remove this structure. Once the internal organs are removed, wash the entire carcass inside and out with water, preferably from a running hose, to remove blood, hair, and debris. Allow the water to drain, and then cover the carcass loosely with clean plastic.

Allow the sheep carcass to hang for a week or more to age the meat, which makes it tenderer. Carcasses should only be allowed to hang outside if the temperature remains between 25 and 40 degrees F — this is why it is best to butcher animals during the winter. If the temperature does not remain between this range, you will need to cut up the meat and freeze it or have an alternative refrigeration means available, such as a refrigerator at a local butcher shop.

Finding an outside butcher

You can find an outside butcher by contacting your state meat inspection agency. This agency inspects processors and slaughterhouses in each state. They maintain a listing of butchers, which they should be able to share with you. Or you can check online or in your yellow pages for butchers. Be sure to contact a butcher in advance. They are often in demand and their appointments fill up.

Selling your sheep's meat

If you intend to raise sheep for profit, you will need to have your sheep and lambs processed by a butcher that is either state-licensed or USDA-licensed so you can sell your meat to the public. If a state-licensed butcher processes your meat, you can sell it within the state, although, in some cases, state inspection is more stringent than USDA inspection. If USDA-licensed butcher processes your meat, you will be able to sell your meat across state lines. This means that you can sell online and ship meat products to customers in other states. Clearly, these options open up more markets for you.

All lamb found in retail stores is either USDA-inspected for wholesomeness or inspected by state systems that have standards equal to the federal government. Each lamb and its internal organs are inspected for signs of disease. The "Passed and Inspected by USDA" seal ensures the lamb is wholesome and free from disease.

Inspection is mandatory; grading is voluntary, and you must pay to have your meat graded. Inspection is necessary to make sure your meat passes minimum standards. Grading the meat will tell the consumer how the meat is rated, with higher ratings commanding higher prices. USDA-graded lamb sold at the retail level is Prime, Choice, and Good. Lower grades (Utility and Cull) are mainly ground or used in processed meat products. Retail stores may use other terms that must be different from USDA grades.

USDA Prime lamb has more fat marbling, so it is the tenderest and most flavorful grade. However, it is higher in fat content. Most of the graded lamb sold in supermarkets is USDA Choice or USDA Good. The protein, vitamin, and mineral content of lamb are similar in all grades.

Where to sell meat

If your meat has been state-inspected, you can sell to local grocery stores and restaurants. If your meat has been USDA-inspected, you are free to sell to anyone across the country. You also can sell to buyers who visit your farm. You can sell as much lamb or mutton as you can to anyone who wants to buy it. You also can sell your meat at farmers markets and online. Specialty markets and ethnic grocery stores are other good outlets.

Be sure to talk to your butcher in advance about how you want your lambs and sheep processed, especially if you have any special requests. You may have customers who want lambs cut a certain way or who intend to pick up their meat at the processor's facility. Arrange with the butcher to have the meat picked up or to be delivered.

Handling and Cooking Lamb

From the USDA:

How to handle lamb safely

Raw lamb. Select lamb just before checking out at the register. Put packages of raw lamb in disposable plastic bags (if available) to contain any leakage which could cross-contaminate cooked foods or produce that will be eaten raw, such as salad.

Take lamb home immediately and refrigerate it at 40 degrees F or below. Use ground lamb or stew meat within one to two days; lamb chops, roasts, and steaks within three to five days or freeze at 0 degrees F or below. If kept frozen continuously, it will be safe indefinitely.

It is safe to freeze lamb in its original packaging or repackage it. However, for long-term freezing, overwrap the porous store plastic with storage wraps or bags to prevent "freezer burn," which appears as grayish-brown leathery spots and is caused by air reaching the surface of food. Cut freezer-burned portions away either before or after cooking the lamb. Heavily freezer-burned products may have to be discarded for quality reasons. For best quality, use frozen lamb roasts, steaks, and chops within six to nine months; ground lamb, three to four months.

Ready-prepared lamb. For fully cooked, take-out lamb dishes such as kabobs, gyros, or Chinese food, be sure they are hot at pickup. Use cooked lamb within two hours (one hour if the air temperature is above 90 degrees F), or refrigerate it at 40 degrees F or below in shallow, covered containers. Eat it within three to four days, either cold or reheated to 165 degrees F. It is safe to freeze ready-prepared lamb dishes. For best quality, use within two to three months.

Safe thawing

There are three safe ways to thaw lamb: in the refrigerator, in cold water, and in the microwave. It is best to plan for slow, safe thawing in the refrigerator. Ground lamb, stew meat, and steaks may defrost within a day. Bone-in parts and whole roasts may take two days or longer.

Once the raw product thaws, it will be safe in the refrigerator before cooking three to five days (for roasts, steaks, and chops) and one to two days for ground lamb. During this time, if you decide not to use the lamb, you can safely refreeze it without cooking it first.

To thaw lamb in cold water, do not remove the packaging. Be sure the package is airtight or put it into a leakproof bag. Submerge the lamb in cold water, and change the water every 30 minutes so it continues to thaw. Small packages of lamb may defrost in an hour or less; a 3- to 4-pound roast may take two to three hours.

When thawing lamb in cold water or in the microwave, plan to cook it immediately after thawing. Never thaw on the counter or any other location at room temperature. Leaving food out too long at room temperature can cause bacteria (such as *Staphylococcus aureus*, *Salmonella* Enteritidis, *Escherichia coli* O157:H7, and *Campylobacter*) to grow to dangerous levels that can cause illness.

Foods defrosted in the microwave or by the cold-water method should be cooked before refreezing because they potentially might have been held at temperatures above 40 degrees F, where bacteria multiply rapidly.

It is safe to cook frozen lamb in the oven, on the stove, or grill without defrosting it first; the cooking time may be about 50 percent longer. Do not cook frozen lamb in a slow cooker.

Marinating

Marinate lamb roasts, steaks, or chops in the refrigerator up to five days. Lamb cubes or stew meat can be marinated up to two days. Boil used marinade before brushing on cooked lamb. Discard any uncooked leftover marinade.

Storage times

Because product dates are not a guide for safe use of a product, how long can the consumer store the food and still use it at top quality? Follow these tips:

- Purchase the product before the date expires.

- Follow handling recommendations on product.

- Keep lamb in its package until ready to use.

- Refrigerate lamb roasts, steaks, and chops three to five days (ground lamb or stew meat, one to two days); and three to four days after cooking.

- If product has a "use-by" date, follow that date.

- If product has a "sell-by" date or no date, cook or freeze the product by the times recommended above.

- Once a perishable product is frozen, it does not matter if the date expires because foods kept frozen continuously are safe indefinitely.

- For best quality, use frozen lamb roasts, steaks, and chops within six to nine months; ground lamb, three to four months.

Safe cooking

For safety, the USDA recommends cooking lamb patties and ground lamb mixtures, such as meat loaf, to a safe minimum internal temperature of 160 degrees F as measured by a food thermometer. However, whole muscle meats such as roasts, steaks, and chops may be cooked to 145 degrees F. For approximate cooking times for use in meal planning, see the following chart.

Times are based on lamb held at refrigerator temperature (40 degrees F). Remember that appliances and outdoor grills can vary in heat. Use a food thermometer to check for safe cooking and doneness of lamb.

APPROXIMATE LAMB COOKING TIMES °F				
CUT OF LAMB	**SIZE**	**COOKING METHOD**	**COOKING TIME**	**INTERNAL TEMPERATURE**
Lamb Leg, bone in	5 to 7 lbs.	Roast 325°	20 to 25 min./lb.	Medium rare 145° F
	7 to 9 lbs.	Roast 325°	15 to 20 min./lb.	Medium rare 145° F
Lamb Leg, boneless, rolled	4 to 7 lbs.	Roast 325°	25 to 30 min./lb.	Medium rare 145° F
Shoulder roast or shank leg half	3 to 4 lbs.	Roast 325°	30 to 35 min./lb.	Medium rare 145° F
Cubes, for kabobs	1 to 1 ½"	Broil/grill	8 to 12 minutes	Medium 160° F
Ground lamb patties	2" thick	Broil/grill	5 to 8 minutes	Medium 160° F
Chops, rib, or loin	1 to 1 ½" thick	Broil/grill	7 to 11 minutes	Medium rare 145° F
Leg steaks	¾" thick	Broil/grill 4" from heat	14 to 18 minutes	Medium rare 145° F
Stew meat, pieces	1 to 1 ½"	Cover with liquid; simmer	1 ½ to 2 hours	Medium 160° F
Shanks	¾ to 1 lb.			
Breast, rolled	1 ½ to 2 lb.	*Braise 325°	1 ½ to 2 hours	Medium 160° F

Braising is roasting or simmering less tender meats with a small amount of liquid in a tightly covered pan.

Microwaving. Refer to the microwave's oven manual for microwaving lamb, and check it with a food thermometer.

Partial Cooking. Never brown or partially cook lamb to refrigerate and finish cooking later because any bacteria present would not have been destroyed. It is safe to partially cook or microwave lamb immediately before transferring it to a hot grill or conventional oven to finish cooking.

What is the yield of cooked lamb?

After cooking bone-in lamb leg or roast, one pound of raw weight will yield 8 to 9 ounces of edible meat. Ground lamb or boneless cuts will yield about 10.5 ounces of edible meat.

Sheep for Fiber

Humans have used wool fibers since ancient or even prehistoric times. However, today much less wool is used than in the past because of the use of synthetic fabrics. There is less wool production today, and sheep more often are raised for meat than fiber. There is still a great interest in good fiber though. In 2004, a bale of the world's finest wool sold for $3,000 per kilogram in Australia. The final price was $279,000 in Australian dollars for the bale, or about $300,000 in U.S. dollars.

Shearing

In order to shear your sheep, use a 20-tooth mohair comb and sheep shears. Hold your sheep on the ground, between your legs. Use firm, slow strokes with the electric clippers to remove swaths of the sheep's wool down to the skin. You can store the cut fleece in a paper bag. Keep your sheep dry during the 24 hours before shearing. Shear the youngest sheep first and the oldest ones last. This way you can keep the finer fleece from mixing with the coarser fleece. Keep the shearing area clean and sweep it between cutting different colors of sheep. It is all right to cut slowly. Treat the animals well. Try to avoid having to make second cuts as second cuts mean shorter fleece that is less valuable. Remove stained or soiled areas from the wool before storing it.

Wash the wool several times with detergent before spinning it. Rinse completely several times. Dry the hair on towels or allow a fan to blow on it when it is hanging on a towel rack.

About wool

Wool is the textile fiber that comes from sheep. It is crimped and elastic, and it grows in clumps or clusters called staples. With its natural crimp, wool fabrics have more bulk than other textiles, which allows them to retain more heat. Wool also provides insulation that keeps heat out in hot conditions. The finer the wool, the more crimps it will have. Merino wool, which is fine, may have up to 100 crimps per inch.

Wool easily absorbs moisture, which makes it hygroscopic. The wool fibers are hollow, and they can absorb up to one-third of their weight in moisture. Wool also absorbs sound. Most wool is naturally a creamy white color, but it may vary depending on the color of the sheep. Wool burns at a higher temperature than cotton and some other fabrics. It is nearly self-extinguishing. It has many qualities that make it excellent for carpets and is often used by firefighters, soldiers, and others who may be in situations where they face fires. Wool is resistant to static electricity, and it is considered hypoallergenic.

Selling wool

Hand spinners often are interested in buying wool directly from sheep breeders. There is an increasing demand for wool from sheep that have been raised organically. You also may wish to sell the wool directly to the public at farmers markets or online if you are selling other products from your farm. If you have specialty sheep with a particularly desirable kind of wool, you can market those qualities.

Laws

There are relatively few laws concerning sheep at the state and federal level in the U.S. You will need to check your local laws to be certain there are no zoning or animal issues where you live that would interfere with you keeping or raising sheep.

Chapter 8

Cattle

CATTLE GLOSSARY

Aging: Allowing the sides or quarters of beef to hang in the freezer for several days so natural enzymes can break down the connective tissues that make the meat tough

Beef pooling: A shareholder system in which one customer is in charge of coordinating orders for a group of people who buy beef in bulk; also called "cow pooling"

Biosecurity: A plan for bringing in new animals to your farm and keeping them quarantined to avoid exposing your current animals to illness, parasites, or infections

Breeder auctions: Auctions for animals of particular breeds or held to disperse a breeder's stock

Bucket system: A dairy milking system in which vacuum tubes connected to the cow pump milk into a small bucket. The milk is then poured from the bucket into a holding container.

Bulk tank: In dairy farming, a bulk tank is a stainless steel refrigeration unit that keeps milk collected from multiple cows cool until it is collected. Tanks range in size from 600 gallons to 8,000 gallons.

Bull: Male cattle

California Mastitis Test: The CMT is a test kit for determining if a cow has mastitis. They are especially useful for dairy cows.

Carrying capacity: The stocking rate your pasture can support

Co-packer: A company that packages products to your specifications

Community supported agriculture: A system in which community members pay for "shares" of food a farmer is expected to produce in the upcoming year. The money covers the cost of farming expenses, and shareholders get first choice of the kinds of food they want. For beef and dairy products, shareholders might be buying a stake in a particular animal.

Cooperatives: Cooperatives are groups of farmers who share resources and who market their collective products under one brand name.

Cow: Adult female that has had a calf

Cud: A normal process in ruminant animals, which is regurgitated stomach content cattle chew on to aid digestion

Cull animals: Cull animals are animals that are no longer needed on the farm. They may be older, unhealthy, or infertile, or the farmer may be upgrading his stocker. Beware of buying a farmer's cull animals unless you know their history.

Culling: Selling animals you do not want to raise anymore

Custom-exempt plants: Processing plants where only the facilities are inspected by state inspectors. The meat does not have to be inspected because you are having your cattle custom processed for your own consumption, and you are not selling any of it.

Fenceline weaning: Calves are separated from their mothers by a fence so they cannot nurse, but they can still see, hear, and smell their mothers.

Grafting: Uniting calves with a nurse cow

Group housing: Raising calves for veal in small groups in pens instead of in crates

Heifer: A female calf that has not had a calf

Herd sire: The bull that contributes the most to the genetics on a farm or the bull in residence

Heteosis: Another term for hybrid vigor

Homogenized: Milk that has been placed in a machine and the machine has broken up the fat globules into small pieces so the cream will not rise to the top. The fat is dispersed throughout the milk.

Hybrid vigor: The mating of two unrelated, or distantly related animals, usually in the hope of increasing desirable traits, such as milk yield, meat qualities, size, or other traits

Milk shares: An arrangement that allows people to buy raw milk in some states. This practice is legal in some states and illegal in other states. Check your state and local laws to see if it is legal where you live.

Mob feeding: Groups of young calves are kept in their own paddock separate from their mothers. Instead of nursing, they are fed from a mob feeder or large barrel with nipples that contains milk from the herd.

Nurse cows: Cows that nurse their own calf and the calves of other cows

On the hoof: Selling your animal, or shares of your animal, while it is still alive

Open cows: Non-pregnant cows

Open heifer: A heifer that failed to conceive when bred

Organic plan: A plan for an organic farm that lays out how the farm will be run, what types of feed and fertilizers will be used, and where those substances will come from. The plan must include details on recordkeeping. An organic plan is necessary if you wish to become certified organic.

Pasteurization: Heating milk to kill bacteria

Plate cooler: On large dairy farms, a plate cooler is a common type of cooling equipment. It precools the milk before it goes to the storage tank.

Polled: Typically meaning when cattle are born without horns (a genetic trait) but can be used as a general term for hornless

Progeny: Offspring

Riding: A female cow mounts other female cows, usually because she is in heat.

Salvage value: The price you receive for selling an older or unproductive animal

Silage: Silage is fermented, moist forage made from almost any green, growing plant. It is stored in either silos or concrete bunkers with airtight tarps. If not stored properly, dangerous bacteria can grow which can sicken or kill your animals.

Standing heat: A reliable sign that a cow is in heat, when she allows other cows to mount her.

Steer: Castrated male

Stocking rates: The number of animal unit equivalents you can keep on your pasture. This number will relate to your maximum herd size. Stocking rate is the pounds of dry matter in your field each year divided by the pounds of dry matter per year eaten by each cow.

The History of Cattle and People

Humans domesticated cattle in the early Neolithic period, and they have been one of the most useful of all animals. They have been worshipped in religious ceremonies and are still sacred to Hindus. They have been raised for their beef, for milk and dairy products, for their leather hides, used as draft animals, or animals used to pull things such as wagons or plows, and used in sports such as bullfighting. The Minoans on the island of Crete used them in games, dating around the 14th century B.C., where young men would leap over bulls. Cattle were one of the earliest forms of human wealth. Today, cattle are raised primarily for beef and dairy products in the U.S.

There were originally three distinct species of cattle: Bos taurus, found in Europe, with similar bovine types in Africa and Asia; Bos indicus, or the zebu; and Bos primigenius, or the aurochs. The aurochs is the bovine ancestor of both the Bos taurus and the Bos indicus. Today, cattle are recognized as one species, and these animals are considered subspecies.

Raising Cattle

Some people are satisfied growing just enough meat or milk to provide for themselves and their families. They enjoy the process of working with nature and like the idea of knowing where their food comes from. If this is you, then you will not need much to get your operation going: a few acres, a small number of animals, fencing, and some key herd management equipment.

However, most farmers want to sell to other people for profit. Many depend on farm income for their livelihood or for supplemental income. Depending on the type of animal you buy and its age and condition at the time of sale, buying an animal for your herd will cost a few hundred dollars and maybe as much as a couple thousand dollars. It can take a couple of years to ready a beef animal for slaughter or for a cow to produce enough milk to pay for your investment.

If you want to make money, you need to have an idea whom you are going to sell to. Decide on your target market, and develop a plan for getting your product in their hands. Do you know where to make the connections necessary to sell directly to customers? Are there farmers markets or other groups in place to help farmers find customers? Is there a restaurant or grocery in town that might buy your products?

What Kind of Farm Will You Have?

The goals of all cattle farms are not the same. Some beef farmers are proud to say their animals are born on their farm and live there until time for slaughter. Other farmers focus on specific phases of cattle development and buy or sell animals at points between birth and death. For example, stocker-cattle farmers handle animals in the phase between weaning and the finishing stage. Some dairy farmers will hire contractors to raise their heifers — females that have not given birth — so they can concentrate on their lactating animals. All of these systems have their merits. Here are some cattle-raising strategies you should be aware of:

- **Cow-calf:** Cow-calf farmers raise cows and bulls with the goal of producing calves. These calves are sold later to other farmers who will continue raising them for beef, sold to farmers who will use them as breeding stock, or kept on the farm until they are ready to be slaughtered for beef. If you wanted to start a cow-calf operation, you could purchase pregnant cows or cows with young calves. Calves can be sold after weaning when they are a few months old. Some farmers sell all their calves at weaning. Others keep them until they are yearlings, which means they are between 1 and 2 years old and have had time to put on more weight. This can increase the amount you make on each animal, but only if you have enough grasses to feed them cheaply during winter. There are also farmers who breed purebred animals and sell the calves as breeding stock.

- **Stocker cattle:** Some farmers concentrate on stocker cattle that are beef cattle between the weaning and finishing stages, when they add an extra 200 to 400 pounds to reach their mature weight and are ready for slaughter. Finished weight depends on breed; most grass-fed cattle breeds are finished at about 1,000 to 1,200 pounds. Stocker cattle typically weigh between 400 and 600 pounds when they are purchased after weaning. These farmers buy calves from cow-calf farms. The calves can be grown on pasture and then sold as feeder cattle, which are cattle ready for the finishing phase. Stocker operations have more flexibility than cow-calf operations because they do not have to wait out their cattle's natural breeding and nursing cycles to buy or sell animals. They can buy and sell animals at different times of the year, including selling their entire herd in the fall; so they do not have the expense of winter feeding that breeding herds must deal with.

- **Grass finishing:** You can grass finish calves that are born on your farm or bought from someone else. Grass-finished beef is a niche product that provides extra value per pound for your meat because customers appreciate the health benefits of animals raised in more natural environments than those of conventional beef. The main challenge of grass finishing is to keep animals gaining weight their whole lives with no periods of loss. This can be especially tough when grass stops growing in winter. It usually takes longer to grass finish animals than grain-fed cattle.

- **Farmstead dairy processing:** Although many dairy farmers sell their milk to other companies, many grass-fed farmers find that they can make more money by processing their milk into other foods and selling packages of their own brand. You can use milk to produce cheese, yogurt, or other products and sell them in stores, on the farm, or other local outlets.

- **Dairy beef:** Dairy steer calves, which are castrated male calves, can be raised on your dairy farm or bought cheaply from other dairy farmers and raised for beef to produce extra income.

- **Dairy replacement heifers:** Dairy farmers who want to focus on their lactating animals sometimes contract with someone else to raise their replacement heifers. Heifers are young females that have not given birth. Replacement heifers are females that will be used for breeding, and on dairies, they will be milked after giving birth. Farmers use replacement heifers to step in when they dispose of cows that are no longer suitable for breeding, such as a cow that is too old to breed anymore. Sometimes these heifers are raised by a contractor who will return them to the owner shortly before birth. Some cow-calf farmers also make money by selling replacement heifers to other farmers. Caring for replacement heifers might not be a job for a beginning farmer because the other farmers might not trust a novice to take care of their valuable heifers.

You should consider if you want to be certified by a particular organization because you will have to prove to certifiers that farm decisions, both big and small, comply with these standards. Many certifying agencies, including the American Grassfed Association and the National Organic Program, require documentation, such as receipts or tags from medicines and feed supplements you use on your farm. The AGA designed its recordkeeping system not to require much time.

Farmers that choose to be certified, either under the National Organic Program, by the American Grassfed Association, or by other organizations, do so because these third-party certifications serve as assurances to customers that the farmers adhered to certain standards. Many customers will pay more these products; for example, customers who buy from

AGA-certified farmers want products from animals that were allowed to live as naturally as possible — outdoors eating grass. Customers who buy organic-certified products want to know that their foods were created without the use of potentially harmful synthetic chemicals.

Under the National Organic Program, a field is not considered organic until three years after the last use of synthetic chemicals. Still, many farmers do not mind the additional challenges of finding organic fertilizers, pesticides, and feeds because they believe it will pay off in the long run and because they believe it is the right thing to do. Learn more about organic certification at the USDA National Organic Program website at **www.ams.usda.gov/NOP**. One note of caution: It takes considerable skill to run a completely organic farm. If you are a first-time farmer, it is probably better to concentrate on building your farm management skills, such as keeping your animals healthy naturally and building your soil and plant health before seeking organic certification.

To be certified under the National Organic Program, you must keep records of the substances you use on your farm and submit to inspections from accredited certifying agencies. At the beginning of the process, you have to fill out a farm plan detailing these steps and carefully examine each step of your production process. Everything, including seeds, fertilizers, and pesticides, has to be organic. You will have to work with certified organic processors, which takes extra time and commitment. Forty percent of organic dairy producers say the most challenging aspect of organic milk production is the certification paperwork and compliance costs, according to the USDA.

To actually use the word "organic" on the label, you must be certified under the National Organic Program. However, there are other certifying agencies that strive for principles similar to those of the NOP but aim to be simpler so small farmers are able to achieve these standards. One example is Certified Naturally Grown (**www.naturallygrown.org**), which seeks to reduce much of the government paperwork that makes becoming certified under the NOP prohibitive to many small farmers.

Determining your ideal herd size

When first establishing your herd, it is better to start out small and grow into an operation than to start big and get in over your head. One important thing for a first-time cattle farmer to learn is how to handle animals and to learn the skills of rotational grazing to improve your pasture. Some people only want to raise enough animals to provide milk or meat for their families. These farmers only need a minimal number of animals. For milk, you might only need a cow or two. For beef, you might be able to buy two or three weaned calves every year.

If you want a few cows but do not want the expense of a bull, you could start with weaned calves that you raise as stocker cattle. You could let them grow larger on your pasture, then sell them to another buyer who will finish them, or you could grass finish them yourself. If you start your cattle operation with cows that were recently impregnated, you would not need a bull for another year. If you start with new cow-calf pairs and you plan to rebreed the cows the next year, you will need a bull within about three months. You do not need a bull if you plan to use artificial insemination.

If you are serious about starting a cow-calf beef operation, you can use one bull for every 20 to 30 cows as a rule of thumb — if you have the land and skills to support it. If you feel that might be too much to handle at first, you could start with ten cows and perhaps share a bull with a neighbor. For example, if you plan to calve in the spring, you could share a bull with someone who plans to calve in the fall. Plan to keep two to four calves for your beef business and sell the rest on at sales barn, where large producers usually buy them as part of the commodities market. Large numbers of buyers and sellers congregate at sale barns for auctions. Buyers usually include feedlot operators who finish their purchases for beef, or backgrounders who fatten up the calves more before selling them again.

If you start small, you may have more land than your cows can keep up with, so you should just give them a section of your pasture that you can subdivide into smaller sections. Then rotate your herd through these subdivided sections. You could take the sections of pasture that you do not use for grazing and cut them for hay, which you could sell or use for your own reserves.

If you want a larger operation, your herd size ultimately will depend on your land, as your pasture only can support a certain amount of animals. Knowing your financial goals will give you an idea of what you want your farm to look like in a few years. If you already own a farm, a big part of the equation is filled in for you: Your maximum herd size will be determined by how many animals your land can support. The term "animal unit equivalent" (AUE) comes into play here. This measurement is calculated based on the nutritional requirements of an animal relative to a 1,000-pound cow that is with or without a nursing calf. The calculation assumes that 1 animal unit will consume 26 pounds of dry matter per day. Dry matter is the feed in plant material after moisture is removed. As you can see from the following table, not every animal will count the same, and the same animal will not count the same at various points of its life. A calf is worth .50 an animal unit, but when it grows to 1,000 pounds, it will be worth a whole animal unit. A mature bull is worth more than 1 animal unit.

ANIMAL	WEIGHT (IN POUNDS)	ANIMAL UNIT EQUIVALENT (AUE)
Young cattle	500	.50
Cow	1,000	1.0
Bull	<2,000	1.5

Stocking rates are the number of AUE per acre you keep on your pasture. **Carrying capacity** is the stocking rate your pasture can support. The easiest way to figure these is to ask a local farming expert such as a county extension agent who can give you an idea of what pastures in your area that are similar to yours can carry. The average available dry matter per year depends on the area of the country and the quality of the pasture. Not every acre of your farm will be good pasture; for example, heavily wooded areas do not produce much grazing grass. The amount of dry matter available per acre per year can be as little as 2 tons to more than 5 tons. So, if your field yields 3 tons per acre per year and you have a 50-acre farm, that is 150 tons per acre, which equals 300,000 pounds per acre. Deciding how many cows to keep is an inexact science — varying weather conditions from year to year will cause fluctuations in your pasture growth. But if you want to read more about making your own estimates, try "Forage Production and Carrying Capacity" from the University of Idaho (**www.cnr.uidaho.edu/what-is-range/Curriculum/Contents/MOD3/Stocking-rate-guidelines. pdf**) or "Stocking Rate: The Key to Successful Livestock Production" from Oklahoma State University (**http://pods. dasnr.okstate.edu/docushare/dsweb/Get/Document-2050/PSS-2871web.pdf**).

A formula you can use to figure stocking rate is the estimated amount of available dry matter in your field per year divided by the amount of dry matter a cow eats a year, or

(Pounds of dry matter per year) ÷ (pounds of dry matter per year per cow) = stocking rate

So, if each cow needs 26 pounds of dry matter per day, that is 780 pounds per month, or 9,490 pounds per year. If your field yields an estimated 300,000 pounds per year, and each head of cattle needs 9,490 pounds per year, your field could support 31.6 head of cattle.

It is probably a good idea to estimate a bit low on stocking rate to provide a cushion for when your pasture growth is below average. In times when growth is above average, you can buy extra stocker cattle or keep a few cattle you had planned to sell.

As you get better at managing your herd's rotation patterns, you will be able to provide more nutrition from grazing and rely less on stored forage and supplements. You also may be able to increase your stocking rates because your pasture yield will improve.

The Differences in Raising Cattle for Milk and For Meat

Dairy farms and beef farms can both succeed, but each type of operation poses its own challenges. Beef production and dairy production depend on different breeds of animals. You can buy beef and dairy animals from similar sources, such as public auctions or private sellers, but you will base your purchases on different sets of criteria. Different breeds often are used for beef rather than for dairies, and each type of operation provides differing management challenges.

With cows you intend to raise for beef, consider the following points:

- Your goal is to get the animals to fatten to a weight that will produce the best meat before slaughter. Grass-fed beef cattle may need 20 months or even two years or more to reach finishing weight, compared to a typical 16 to 18 months for grain-finished cattle.

- Beef calves are left with their mothers for between six and nine months. Then, they can be sold to other farmers or kept on the farm to continue to grow.

- Beef animals usually are killed at slaughterhouses and then cut up by butchers. Depending on whom you plan to sell your beef to and the laws in your state, the facilities and the carcasses may need to be inspected by state or federal officials.

If you plan to raise cattle for dairy products, here are some points you should consider:

- Your goal is to get them to produce as much high-quality milk as possible. Dairy cattle usually are milked twice a day, every day — once in the morning and once in the evening — for much of the year. Many dairies are seasonal, meaning they breed their cows at the same time and have a dry period where they do not milk cows, which is usually during the last two months before cows calve again. At this stage of pregnancy, cows use less of the nutrients they take in for milk production and put them toward their developing fetuses.

  - Dairies depend on new mothers to provide milk to sell. On conventional dairies, calves are fed milk replacer solutions. Because grass-fed dairies aim to give cattle as natural a feed as possible, these dairies must find other ways to provide milk for their calves. These methods include letting mothers nurse their own calves, diverting milk from the herd into barrel feeders for the calves, or using **nurse cows** that nurse their own calf and the calves of others.

- Dairy farms also require extra equipment, such as milking machines and coolers.

- It is especially important to know your state's laws about selling raw milk, which is one of the most hotly debated issues in agriculture. Eleven states allow licensed dairies to sell milk to retail outlets, according to the National Conference of State Legislatures. Twenty states allow people to buy raw milk off the farm or get milk if they buy ownership shares of an animal.

- Each state has different laws governing milk sales. It is important that you speak to state agricultural officials to familiarize yourself with the laws in your state. You probably will need a license to sell milk to processors or milk companies. If you sell milk, government officials will have to inspect your dairy facilities.

Building Your Herd

You need the right animals for your farm. You want animals suited to your climate that can grow strong, stay healthy, and that produce good quality meat or milk. You have many options when it comes to breeds. There are dozens of breeds in all shapes, sizes, and colors. Each breed has characteristics that make it desirable to certain farmers — for example, the Angus breed has a reputation for producing high-quality meat.

If you are starting a herd from scratch, you can choose what breeds you want to work with. Although certain breeds are used more often than others, many farmers say breed is not as important as choosing the best individuals from within a breed. Cattle used most often in grazing systems are smaller with wide bodies, because it is easier to pasture-finish a 1,100-pound animal than one that needs to grow to 1,500 pounds. Dual-purpose breeds used for both milk and meat often are used in pasture-based systems because of the flexibility they provide in the types of products you can sell. On most dairies, male calves are not desirable because they cannot be milked, but if you use a dual-purpose breed, the male calves born on dairy farms can grow into acceptable beef animals.

If you are buying animals, you also have flexibility in the ages of animals you buy. You can buy cows with newborn calves, weaned calves that have been taken off milk, or yearlings, which are between 1 and 2 years old. You can keep these animals just through the growing season and then sell them, or you can keep them until they reach their ideal weight for slaughter.

Appearance of a healthy animal

Farmers always are looking for certain traits when purchasing cattle. You want a masculine-looking bull with large, rounded shoulders and a big scrotum; these features signify appropriate testosterone levels and virility. He also needs to have no injuries or problems with his legs so he can safely mount females. You also want fertile cows with feminine traits, such as wide, calf-bearing hips. You want your breeding stock to produce calves that can grow quickly and mature early but are not born so heavy that birth is difficult on the mother. These traits can be predicted based on the animal's own growth statistics and the statistics of all the calves fathered by its parent. After you have farmed for a while, you also will be able to see which mothers produce the best or fastest-growing calves.

At an even more basic level, you want animals that look healthy. A healthy cow has clear eyes, erect ears, a healthy coat, clean muzzle and nostrils, and a good appetite. Consider having a veterinarian check out animals before you buy them from a private seller. You or a vet can take an animal's temperature with a rectal thermometer; its temperature should be around 101.5 degrees F. Animals should be able to move effortlessly and without pain. If they favor a leg or seem to have pain when they move, they could have injuries or illnesses you do not want to deal with. If you are buying animals, stay away from the sick ones because you do not want to bring illnesses onto your farm. Look for reputable sellers who vaccinate their animals. They should be able to show you records of what they vaccinated for and when the vaccinations were given.

Where to find animals

Before you buy cattle, get an idea of the fair market value of the animals you are planning to purchase by checking prices in newspapers or online or by talking to experts that you trust. The USDA has a website (**http://marketnews. usda.gov**) dedicated to market reports that shows up-to-date prices farmers are getting for their cattle. This will vary by breed and by current market conditions. If you have a fair price in mind before you purchase your cow, it is less likely someone will take advantage of you. As you get more experience raising cattle, you probably will develop more ideas of when you might be able to find a bargain. For example, prices for calves are usually lower in the fall than they are in the spring, because this is when most farmers sell newly weaned calves. You should buy from farmers who raise their animals in conditions similar to yours. These farmers also should raise their animals to your standards.

Private sales

Private sales might be the safest bet for a first-time farmer. Breeders selling bulls usually advertise in the classified sections of local newspapers or in breed association newsletters, which can be ordered directly from the associations. If you buy a bull, associations often are notified by the breeder and will begin mailing you their literature. You can also find breeders through Internet searches for breed associations; for example, the American Angus Association is **www.angus.org**. You may also receive suggestions by asking knowledgeable people in your area, such as the staff at your local feed mill.

If you are looking for a specific breed, most of them have national or state associations that help link sellers with buyers. These can usually be found with quick online searches for a specific breed and its association. For example, the North American Limousin Foundation (**www.nalf.org**) includes links to state associations. If you target a popular breed, you may be able to find a neighbor nearby who has animals for sale. This would be good because you will be able to tell what conditions the animals are raised in and if they would do well in your system.

Public auctions

One place to buy and sell cattle is sales barns, also called stockyards, where farmers gather for regular public auctions. These auctions include hundreds of animals from dozens of sellers. Most stockyards have sales about once a week. Before you go to an auction to buy an animal, it would be a good idea to go to an auction and observe. This will allow you to see the process first and know what to expect. You will be able to get an idea of how your judgment of animals compares to that of other buyers.

Sales barns may not be the best place for a new farmer to build a herd because these auctions often include many **cull animals**, animals that farmers decide to get rid of for various reasons, such as infertility or susceptibility to illness or parasites. You will not know from whom you are buying, and you may not have a way to verify if the animals are illness-free or if they are pregnant or ready to be bred. Sales barns also carry some risk because animals are exposed to so many other animals that could potentially transfer illnesses. Exceptions to this would be when stockyards sponsor breeder auctions or auctions from other certified programs.

Breeder auctions are held for animals with certain genetics, such as a Hereford breeders' auction. These can be held at stockyards or at another site. Sometimes, auctions are held for estate sales or for farms going out of business.

Online auctions

Online auctions are popular because animal sellers can show off their sale animals without taking them off the farm, which reduces stress and potential exposure to illness. Similarly, buyers like these forms of auctions because they do not have to attend an auction physically, and they can make their choices and hire someone to haul the animals to them. These auctions also expose sale animals to a wide range of potential customers. Breeders' auctions often are held online or via satellite.

Most people involved with online auctions will be honest, but there are risks. You can protect yourself by getting all the terms of your deal in writing and making sure you know all the details of the deal. For example, will the seller ship animals to you or hire a third party to do this, or are you responsible for picking them up? Sometimes you can provide a down payment (sometimes by overnight check or wired funds) and will not have to pay the total amount until the animals arrive at your farm. After you buy animals, it may be a good idea to inspect them visually before they are shipped or make it clear under the terms of the sale that you will return any unacceptable animals at the seller's expense. Good auction sites want to ensure their buyers and sellers are protected, and you can contact these companies to see what protective measures they recommend.

Beef Cattle

You may be contemplating a small herd for your own farm, or you may just want a raise a steer or two to fill your freezer with quality beef. First, decide what type of cattle operation you want. Do you want to start with young calves and raise them to harvest for yourself, or do you want to sell them as fed and finished cattle? Do you want to purchase pregnant cows or cows that already have calves? Do you want to purchase a group of cows that are not pregnant, breed them, and then wait for a calf crop?

Calves can be purchased as newborns all the way up to feeder calf size, which is about 600 pounds. A feeder calf is weaned from its mother and ready to be placed on feed — hay and grain — to be finished, which means putting flesh and fat on a calf until it meets slaughter weights, generally about 1,200 to 1,400 pounds. Your top priority when purchasing a newborn calf or a calf up to 2 months old is to make sure the calf has received its colostrum. Calves are born with an incomplete immune system and absolutely need to get more than 1 gallon of high-quality colostrum in their bellies within the first 24 hours of life — preferably within the first 12 hours. Scours, or diarrhea, are the main cause of death of young calves, and many cases are traced back to a poor immune system due to lack of sufficient colostrum.

Calves can be purchased directly off the farm or through auction barns. It is not recommended that you purchase very young calves from an auction barn because the stress of being among all kinds of cattle along with their fragile immune system equals a strong potential for a health disaster. Dairy breed steer and bull calves are especially notorious for not receiving the colostrum they require. Older calves and cows can be purchased directly from the breeder or through auction barns as well. Always ask about vaccination history, parasitical use, and calving history before purchasing. Any time you bring a new livestock purchase to your farm, quarantine it in a pen, corral, pasture, or barn for a minimum of two weeks before introducing it to the rest of the herd. This will minimize the chance of introducing new diseases into your established herd.

Beef breeds

Breed selection is important in the beef industry. Branded beef, such as Hereford or Angus, is increasingly common in grocery stores in order to build customer loyalty to a particular breed. If you plan to sell your cattle commercially, buyers look for a typical beefy type of steer or heifer as opposed to narrow-bodied steer or heifer. Here is a small sampling of the beef breeds:

Angus: Angus cattle are solid black cattle that are naturally polled. They are one of the premier carcass breeds and yield a high-quality carcass with nice marbling meat. They are widely used in crossbreeding programs to improve carcasses. It is a hardy breed able to withstand harsh winter weather. The breed was developed in Scotland.

Hereford: Hereford cattle are white-faced cattle with red bodies. The white extends from the head to between the front legs. The end of the tail (switch) is also white. Most Herefords have thick, curved horns, but there is a naturally polled strain. They yield a good quality carcass, and like the Angus breed, they are another premier carcass breeds. The Hereford breed was developed in England.

Charolais: Charolais cattle are white- to cream-colored cattle. The breed is used in crossbreeding programs as they are heavily muscled with great carcass quality. This breed matures later than other breeds of cattle and is typically fattened to larger weights. The Charolais breed was developed in France.

Belgian Blue: The Belgian Blue was developed in Belgium. This breed is unique as it is one of the few double-muscled breeds (increased muscle mass compared to other cattle). Because of the double muscling, they have a high-yielding carcass, but the mothers have difficulty delivering their calves. Frequently, a cesarean section will be needed to successfully deliver a live calf. They are generally bluish white.

Brahman: The Brahman is distinctly different from other breeds of cattle as they have a hump on the back and long floppy ears. The breed comes from India and is adaptable to hot weather and insects. They do not yield as much meat as the other breeds, but because of the ability to withstand heat, they are sometimes used in Southern states. The Brahman is usually red or gray colored.

Galloway: The Galloway is typically a black animal with long, thick, wavy hair. They also can be light brown to yellow-gray. They are a polled breed of cattle and have good-quality meat that is well marbled with fat between the muscles. Because of their thick coat, they can withstand harsh winter weather.

Gelbvieh: The Gelbvieh has the distinction of producing more pounds of weaned calf per cow among cattle. This breed is usually one of three colors: red, black, or yellow. It was developed in Bavaria and is a recent import to the United States; they arrived in the country in the early 1970s. It has a good carcass yield and grows quickly in the feedlot.

Limousin: The Limousin breed is an ancient French breed. They have high carcass yields and efficiently convert feed to muscle. They are not as heavily marbled as other breeds, so they have less fat interlaced throughout the meat. They are generally red or yellow.

Shorthorn: As the name suggests, the Shorthorn breed was named because of their short horns. This breed was developed in England. They are typically red, white, or roan (a mixture of red of white). They have a good carcass yield and produce good-quality meat.

Simmental: The Simmental breed are known as docile cattle. This breed was developed in Switzerland, and they have a heavily muscled back and loins. Simmental body hair ranges from yellow to gold to dark red. The head and lower legs are usually white. They have an excellent yielding carcass.

Housing

In general, adult beef cattle in good condition can live outside provided they have a wind block to protect from winter wind chills. A covered shed will give them protection from chilling rain or wet, heavy snow. Pregnant cows near delivery date and young calves should be provided with a shed or a barn to escape bad weather. The barn should be ventilated to eliminate ammonia fume buildup and to provide fresh air. Bedding material, such as straw or corn stalks, should be maintained so there is always a dry layer on top. It can be allowed to build up until you are able to clean the pen more thoroughly, provided there are no wet areas. Broken fence panels, bent steel posts, and rusted feeders should be removed from pens, corrals, and pastures. Cows can become impaled or entangled in these items. Fences should be maintained in good repair to prevent a curious cow from walking through a down fence line.

Housing very young beef calves

If you purchase a very young calf under the age of 1 month without its mother, it should be housed in its own separate enclosure to minimize spreading disease from suckling on its pen mates until it is weaned from milk — usually at 2 months old. These enclosures can be as simple as partitioning off a pen with cattle panels to using calf huts — plastic oval or rectangular shells — designed for the dairy calf. Regardless of what you use, make sure it is clean of dirt and manure and thoroughly disinfected. Calves being raised without a mother can be bedded with shavings, sawdust, ground corncobs, or straw. Maintain the bedding on a regular basis so the calf always stays dry. The calf will suck on any exposed surface, so make sure there are no sharp edges in the pen. As the calf moves off the bottle and when he or she is eating grain and drinking independently, you can start to group the calves in small pens, or better yet, introduce them to an outside corral for fresh air and exercise.

If you use an electric fence as an outside pen, the calves will need to be trained to the fence; otherwise, they may just run right through it when they are frolicking or playing a game with the other calves. Tie bright strips of cloth or plastic to the wire between the supporting posts. This will let the calves see where the wire is located. They may investigate and get a shock, but it is doubtful they will try to cross the fence again.

Handling

There is an inherent danger working around cattle, the largest farm livestock. Cows and calves can be tamed, but even a tame cow can knock you over or stomp on your toes if you enter the pen with a feed bucket. Always remain on your guard around bulls. Never try to tame a bull or make a pet of one. They will lose their natural fear of people and can attack when you least expect it. Farmers are injured or killed by bulls every year. If a bull charges you, run to a fence or some farm equipment to use as a barrier between you and the bull. Never turn your back on a bull. Cows can be aggressive when it comes to protecting their calves. All duties involving a newborn calf should be overseen with extreme caution. Always keep the calf between yourself and the mom — if you get between them, the mother might try to knock you out of the way. As an added safety measure, remove the calf from cow and put it in a safe place such as a pen or even inside a hay ring, but make sure the cow can see you and the baby. Minimize the time away from the cow and return the calf as soon as you are done with it.

Beef cattle are strong herd animals. If you need to separate a cow from the herd and it is unwilling to go, try separating it with another cow to keep it company. Try not to yell or strike the cow. It takes about 30 minutes for an excited animal to calm down. Move slowly and deliberately when working with cattle. Using an electric cattle prod to force an animal to move by giving it a shock is not recommended because of potential for abuse; if you do use one, only give a brief shock, and only shock it on well-muscled parts of the body. A rattle paddle — a fiberglass pole topped with a large paddle with small balls inside — is a good way to move cattle. They will move away from the noisy paddle when it is shaken, and its large size makes it easy for the cattle to see.

Cattle want to be with their herd. Usually, it is easiest to move the entire herd into your holding pen, and then separate out a sick animal and a companion. After you get the animals in quarantine, you can move the rest of the herd back into the pasture. The best way to move animals is to move slowly and deliberately and to use their natural instincts to your advantage. An important part of moving livestock is learning an animal's flight zone. This is the animal's safety zone, and you should respect this area when working with your cattle. Only work on the edge of the flight zone. If a person moves into the animal's flight zone, the animal will turn away from the person in preparation to flee. If the animal turns to face the person, the person is outside the flight zone.

If you find yourself in the animal's flight zone, step backward until the animal stops moving. To move an animal forward, take a step into the flight zone. Nervous or agitated animals will have larger flight zones. A nervous cow bobs its head up and down to watch you. It may lower its head and paw the ground, or it may try to flee from you. Calm or tame cattle are comfortable around you, stand and chew their cud when you are around, and do not move when you approach. These cattle will have smaller flight zones. If your animal is very tame, it might not even have a flight zone, and it may be difficult to move the animal at all. Cattle have a blind spot immediately behind them about the width of their hips. Try to avoid standing in this spot, as it may startle cattle, causing them to kick or flee. Another important concept in cattle handling is learning the point of balance. This is generally at the shoulder. Moving behind the point of balance will cause the cow to move forward. Moving in front of the point of balance will cause the cow to back up.

To make handling easier, you easily can tame and train your herd. Frequently walk among your cattle herd when feeding. Speak to them gently and in a low voice so they become familiar with your voice. When you move cattle, call them. Examples of cow calls are "Here, cow" or "Come, cow." Old farmers like to use the phrase "come, boss," which is an ancient term to call cattle. Do not yell or strike the animals; getting them excited will only make them more difficult to handle.

You can also use treats such as alfalfa pellets to encourage the animals to follow you at first. After a while, the promise of fresh grass will be enough to motivate cows to follow you. They will recognize you as a source of fresh food and will be excited to see you. This makes other herd management tasks easier too, because they will not be as reluctant to follow you into a new situation.

Pasturing

The majority of beef cattle are placed on pasture during the summer months. Historically, pastureland has been land unsuitable for crops. Even today, given the price of grain and the expense of hay, it is cheaper to graze pasture during the grass-growing season. Many pastures can be better managed using rotational grazing techniques, which can extend the grazing season and give you more grass yield per acre of pasture. Cattle farmers primarily perform rotational grazing.

Setting up a rotational grazing plan will take some planning. To start, grab a pen and a notebook, and sketch out an outline of your available pastureland. Divide the pasture into at least six, 3-acre paddocks. A moderately intensive rotational grazing plan — depending on your rainfall amount — can support one cow and calf pair on 1 to 3 acres. You will have to decide on the number of acres needed for your geographical region and on the number of animal units (cow/calf pair) you plan to place in each paddock. Once you have your paddocks planned, you will need to plan your fences. A three-strand electrical fence or a woven-wire fence with a top line of electric wire will hold your cattle in the appropriate paddocks. Be sure to include gates or alleyways to allow the cattle to move from paddock to paddock.

To be successful, each paddock will need a water source. You can use natural sources such as ponds, but using simple irrigation pipe will provide a more reliable and fresher source of water. This pipe can be purchased at general farm supply stores in 50-foot spools of black plastic pipe. It is connected together with simple plastic fittings to make an inexpensive water supply. Remember to drain the pipe before freezing weather sets in so your pipe does not split due to ice expansion. Generally, paddocks can share pipes to save on expense, so try a few sketches to make sure you do not use excessive pipes. A portable stock tank should be sufficient to hold the water, and many sizes can be found at general farm stores.

The fencing should be placed the fall before you plan to rotational graze. This will give the end posts time to settle in the ground to prevent premature upheaval of the posts. The watering system can be placed the spring before implementing the practice. It does not need to be buried, except at gates or where cattle may trample it or cut it with their hooves.

The principle behind rotational grazing is simple. Cattle should be placed on a paddock and allowed to graze until the grass is eaten down until 4 to 6 inches is left. Then, the cattle should be placed in the next paddock, allowed to eat that grass down to 4 to 6 inches, and then switched again. This continues until the final paddock is grazed. Then, they should be returned to the first paddock, which should be regrown with fresh grass. By not allowing the grass to be grazed too short, the pasture will recover faster. By forcing the cattle to graze in only one paddock, they will be forced to eat all the vegetation, instead of picking and choosing certain grasses or legumes over others.

Feeding

The biggest cost of a beef cow — aside from the initial investment — is the yearly feed bill. A beef cow near the end of her pregnancy can cost $1,000 or more, if she is a purebred cow with exceptional breeding. Cattle are ruminant animals; they rechew their food before digesting. This is why cattle can eat grass or woody material and turn it into meat and milk. The cow's stomach is divided into four parts: the rumen, the reticulum, the omasum, and the abomasum. A cow's stomach can be compared to a 55-gallon drum in weight and volume. Digestion begins in the cow's mouth. A cow only has lower incisors (front teeth) and a hard pad in place of upper incisors. Cows use their tongues to grab grass, shear it off with the incisors, give a quick chew with their molars, and swallow the wad. The grass travels to the rumen via the esophagus. The real action takes place in the rumen.

The rumen is a huge vat teeming with microorganisms (fauna), which work on the grass to digest it into volatile fatty acids and other useful nutrients. To help the microbes, the cow regurgitates frequently to bring wads of food back to its mouth to chew it into smaller pieces; in other words, she chews her cud. A cow's diet cannot change quickly — such as going from strictly grass to a large amount of grain, or the sudden food change will change the chemistry of the rumen, killing off the microbes. If this happens, the cow can get terribly sick with bloat, diarrhea, fungal overgrowth, or a twisted abomasum. Many cows have been killed when this has happened. From the rumen, the food travels through the reticulum to the omasum, which absorbs some of the products from the rumen and finally to the abomasum. The abomasum is considered a true stomach, functioning much like the stomach of a pig. The abomasum further digests and absorbs nutrients before passing the food onto the intestinal tract.

A newborn calf does not have a functioning rumen. It takes about four months for the rumen to develop to a fully functioning rumen. When a calf drinks milk, folds of tissue make a groove from the esophagus to the abomasums, bypassing the rumen. Introducing grain and some roughage at an early age helps the calf develop its rumen.

Grain

Grain can be a supplement feed to cattle and is used to add finish (extra fat) to a steer or cow to be butchered. Introduce grain gradually to cattle that are used to eating strictly grass or hay, as a large influx of starches can change the rumen environment and lead to serious injury or death. If you want to start cattle on grain, give them only ½ pound the first day and add in ½-pound increments daily until they reach full feed. Premixed bags of formulated feeds also can be purchased. Good grain choices are corn, oats, wheat, or barley. Never feed cows raw soybean as it can upset their stomachs. Soybeans need to be processed (heat treated) before you are able to feed them to cattle. During harsh winter weather, grain can be fed to cattle to give them more energy. Grain is rarely needed by mature beef cattle unless hay or pasture is in short supply. Rapidly growing, good-quality pasture with a mix of legumes and grass will provide all cows with the energy, protein, vitamins, and minerals they need.

Hay

Hay is essentially any dried, palatable forage. Alfalfa, clover, oats, millet, grass, and Timothy are common plants used to make hay. Note: Not all hay is equal. Hay is classified according to relative feed value (RFV). RFV is calculated by the amount of energy and protein present in the hay. Forage needs to be harvested at optimal maturity — this varies depending on plant — in order to maximize the RFV. Stem hay, alfalfa in full bloom, or plants that have been seeded out all have a low RFV. Dairy cattle, cows in late-term pregnancy, heavily lactating beef cattle, pregnant heifers, and cattle in poor condition need hay of higher RFV than stock cows. Stock cows (pregnant, non-lactating cows) and well-fleshed bulls can be maintained on rather low-quality hay because they are not growing, but they might eat more of it in harsh winter weather, stretching their rumens into a "hay belly." This will not hurt them, but some cattle can get impactions in their omasum from poor quality hay.

Other food sources

Beef cattle can be fed other types of plant forage. Cornstalks in the field or in bales make good forage for beef cattle. With permission, a neighboring farmer's cornfield can be grazed if you are able to fence it in and run your herd on the stubble. Cornstalks also can be baled and fed to cattle during the winter. The stalks have a small amount of nutritional value, but many times, corncobs or the leaves will still be intact, providing good nutrition.

Soybean bales are another option. Generally, stalks still will have some bean pods, which are high in protein, and the few raw soybean pods found in soybean bales will not hurt the cow. However, they are not palatable, and your cows may refuse to eat the bales. You must be careful not to feed supplements with urea in them, as the urea can combine with the soybean pods and make your cattle sick. Silage also can be fed. Silage can be made from almost any green, growing plant, but corn silage is the most common form. Due to its high moisture content, silage typically is used only on the farm where it is made. If you do have a close source, it makes a nutritious, highly palatable food for beef cattle. It must be fermented and stored properly or *Listeria*, a dangerous bacterium that can sicken and kill cattle, can become a problem.

Cattle will need supplemental salt and mineral at all times in order to replace salt lost by the body, help produce milk and develop fetuses, and help with general body functions. These generally are given in a premixed ration, either loose granules or in the form of a block. During summer pasture grazing, only salt may be needed unless the soil in your area is deficient in certain minerals — primarily selenium. In the winter, many farmers supplement lower-quality hay or corn stalks with an energy lick. These licks consist of a protein source, an energy source, and usually molasses. They can be formulated into 40-pound blocks up to 200-plus-pound tubs.

Reproduction

Dairies and cow-calf beef operations depend on the breeding process to make money. Cow-calf beef operations need a new supply of animals each year that will grow on the farm until they are sold later. Dairies need cows to reproduce so they can be milked. When you breed cows, plan to breed them when they are 14 to 15 months old so they give birth around the time they are 2 years old. When they are bred, they should be about 65 to 70 percent of their mature weight. For example, if a cow's expected mature weight is 1,000 pounds, she should weigh at least 650 pounds when bred. You can estimate an animal's mature weight based on breed and frame size — animals with larger frames will be heavier than smaller-framed animals.

You have to be careful about exposing cows to bulls until they are more mature. Heifers that breed much earlier than 14 months often have calving problems, including calves that are not in the correct position at birth. If you breed your own heifers and want to keep some for breeding to replace your older or less fertile cows, you should select the ones that are heaviest at weaning because these are the ones that were born first, indicating high fertility, and grew the fastest.

When choosing which females to breed, you also can check pelvic measurements to determine how easy the birthing process will be. A good cattle breeder that is selling breeding stock would have those measurements, which indicate if the birth canal will be wide enough for an easy birth. If you want to find out about a heifer born on your farm, the best time to measure the canal is three weeks to a month before breeding. A veterinarian can do this for you by measuring the height and width to determine how many square centimeters the birth canal is. For a heifer about 600 pounds that is expected to grow to 1,100 pounds or so, an average measurement is 140 centimeters squared.

If your farm operation includes breeding cattle, you can either use a bull to do it naturally, or you can use artificial insemination (AI). Bulls are expensive and high maintenance, and even if they seem tame, there is always a chance they could attack humans. If you plan to calve seasonally, you must separate the bull from cows that are able to rebreed or from heifers that are able to breed because the bull could impregnate your animals outside of your desired breeding window. You also can share or lease a bull from a farmer who uses a different calving season than you.

Natural breeding

You can find bull sellers the same way you find other cattle: in trade publications, classified advertisements, online, or through mutual connections. If you use a bull, you need to get a veterinarian to examine him before you purchase him, and you need your vet to examine him on an annual basis. The vet will measure his scrotal circumference — usually, the larger the scrotum, the higher the sperm count. Just to be sure, a sperm sample will be collected.

A good bull will have a high libido and be eager to mate, but keep in mind a high libido does not guarantee fertility. A simple way to test libido includes putting a bull in a pen with a female that is ready to breed. If he successfully mates within five minutes, he probably has a good libido. If he shows no interest, this is probably not a good sign. Mature bulls can service more cows in a breeding season than young bulls — ten to 20 cows for yearlings, about 30 cows for a mature bull, and sometimes many more for the best bulls. A yearling also will not have been used yet for breeding, so you will not be able to see how successful he has been in a breeding program, and there will no data about calves he has produced.

Disposition is important when choosing a bull. If you walk up to the fence to look at him, he should stay calm. He can show signs of being on alert, such as ears standing to attention, but he should not bolt away. He also should not move toward you as if to attack. If he runs away, or runs at you, you do not want him. If you have a large herd, you may need more than one bull. If you decide to use more than one bull, you need one bull to be the dominant bull that will sire most of the calves in the herd. The animals will have to sort out their place in the hierarchy themselves, so keep your bulls together in a paddock away from the females for about 30 days so they can establish which one is dominant. If they do not establish their order before the breeding season, some of them could attack and injure the other bulls while they are trying to mate. But if they establish their place, the other bulls can step in and do the breeding at the times when the dominant bull is tired. When using two or more bulls, those that are about the same size and breed and are raised together seem to do the best.

Artificial insemination

Artificial insemination (AI) is a common choice for people who do not want to add a bull to their herd or who want to use genes from top quality bulls. AI may be a cheaper alternative than caring for and feeding a live bull — semen comes in containers called straws that often sell for $20 or less, though semen from the most in-demand bulls can cost more. AI may be more affordable if you are looking for traits from an expensive breed or rare breed; in the case of some breeds where bulls are not available for purchase, AI may be your only option.

The downside of AI is that it is more labor intensive because you have to be sure your cows and heifers are in heat so you can inseminate them at the right time. They must be observed for at least 30 minutes twice a day to detect heat. This usually means watching them at morning and at night. If you notice signs of heat in a cow, breed her within 12 hours. Artificially inseminating a cow takes some training and practice, and many farmers prefer to pay an AI technician to perform the breeding.

The most reliable sign of heat is called **standing heat**, which means she allows other cattle, including other females, to mount her as she stands. Secondary signs of heat include pacing or restlessness. Cows in heat may group together, follow other cows, and sniff, nuzzle, or lick the rear ends of other cows. A female that mounts other females may be in heat; this is called **riding**. Rough or rubbed-off hair on the base of the tail can indicate a cow has been ridden. Another possible sign of heat is a string of clear mucus hanging from the vulva or smeared on the hind legs or tail. Bloody mucus can appear two to four days after a cow was in heat; if you see this, watch her for her next heat cycle in 15 to 21 days.

You can perform pregnancy tests shortly after attempted breeding. A veterinarian tests for pregnancy by performing a rectal palpation of the cow's uterus and ovaries. Dairy cattle generally are checked for pregnancy between 28 and 35 days after being bred; cows that are not pregnant can be rebred. Pregnancy testing also helps you learn an expected due date. Other indications of pregnancy are failure to return to heat when a cow's next heat cycle is due. Nonpregnant cows are called **open cows**. Some farmers also use what is known as a clean-up bull, whose job is to naturally impregnate cows that did not conceive with AI.

Heredity and crossbreeding

Many farmers turn to the practice of crossbreeding to improve their herd performance. For example, you might mate a cow from a high-yielding breed with a bull that is known for its fertility or for its resistance to disease. Many farmers in the South use Brahman genes so their herds can tolerate the heat. Farmers in the North may prefer breeding the Galloways for their thick coat. Farmers who try to produce both milk and meat have success breeding traditional dairy breeds with traditional beef breeds; for example, you could cross an Angus bull with a Jersey cow. In crossbreeding programs, the best traits of each breed often surface in the offspring. A weakness in one breed can be offset by mating it to a breed that is strong in that trait.

Mating two purebred animals can result in healthy, high-performing offspring by bringing out the best from both breeds. Bringing out the best in both breeds is called **heterosis**, also known as **hybrid vigor**. It is worth noting that purebred livestock does not mean registered purebred livestock. Registered purebreds are bred for reasons other than performance on the farm, such as lineage or because they look good in a show ring.

Should you decide to crossbreed your cattle, there are several strategies you can implement.

- **Crossbreeding using two breeds**: For example, you could cross two breeds and then mate the resulting heifers with a purebred bull of one of the two original breeds.

- **Crossbreeding with three breeds**: You could cross two purebred breeds and then mate the resulting heifers with a third breed. Some experts say combining three breeds can bring out the best traits in all three breeds. For example, animals sired by Holstein bulls would always be bred to Jersey bulls, and then those mixed offspring would be bred to a Guernsey. The University of Kentucky recommends using colored ear tags to identify the offspring of each sire — using one color for the Holstein's offspring, another color for the Guernsey's, and another for the Jersey's.

- **Terminal crosses**: A terminal cross is the offspring of two purebreds that will be used for beef but will not be rebred. The reason for terminal crosses is that the offspring of crossbred animals can be unpredictable. If you breed two crossbred animals, the calves could come out looking like purebreds of either breed, or some kind of mixture — there will be no way to know beforehand.

- **Buying off-farm replacement heifers:** Though many farmers use heifers born on their farm for breeding stock, you could give yourself genetic flexibility by buying replacement heifers from someone else's farm. This allows you to introduce traits from breeds not found on your farm. For example, you could buy crossbred replacement heifers to breed with your purebred bull. Or, if you only keep one bull, you could use him for three or four years and then switch to a sire of a different breed. AI also gives you flexibility in switching sire breeds.

EPD – Expected Progeny Differences

Genetics play a large part in the development of each animal and its usefulness in a beef or dairy production system. This is why selecting the right bull is critical, because genetics are big determinants in growth potential and meat tenderness. If you use only one bull, his traits will be passed on to all the calves born on your farm; if you choose your bull poorly, such as one that is not fertile or one that produces substandard offspring, it can be crippling to your farm's earning potential.

One tool many farmers use to select their **herd sire** — the bull that contributes most of the genetics to the calves born on a farm — is called Expected Progeny Differences (EPDs). EPDs are scores based on individual traits that give you an idea of how future offspring, or **progeny**, are expected to perform compared to the offspring of other animals. EPD scores are based on the performance of the animal's parents and on the performance of the individual animal. Breeders from around the country report this data to breed associations that maintain a database so buyers can make comparisons of potential bulls. For example, farmers would weigh a particular bull at birth, at weaning, and at 1 year old and report these scores to the association, which would then calculate the bull's EPD scores against the expected performance of other bulls in the breed.

These scores are useful in comparing animals within a specific breed. Breeders will provide you the scores for their bulls, which are shown as comparisons to the breed average. For example, if an animal's birth weight score is +10, that means its offspring are expected to weigh 10 pounds more than the breed average. For an animal whose offspring perform at the breed average, its birth weight score would be 0.0. You can look at the scores for one or more bulls and decide which one is most likely to produce the types of calves you want.

Common categories EPDs predict include growth, maternal, carcass, and ultrasound. Each is discussed below.

- **Growth:** The growth category predicts the growth potential of a bull's calves. Traits measured include:

Calving ease direct (CED) predicts the likelihood a bull's calves will be born without difficulties if he is bred to a first-calf heifer. A CED score is a percentage of unassisted births cows are likely to have when delivering a particular bull's calf. An unassisted birth is one in which a farmer does not have to help pull the calf out. A higher value means first-calf heifers are more likely to deliver a bull's calf without trouble. **Birth weight (BW)** predicts the pounds the bull's calves will weigh at birth. **Weaning weight (WW)** predicts how big a bull's calf will grow before it is weaned. **Yearling weight (YW)** predicts how heavy a calf will be at 1 year old. **Yearling height (YH)** predicts how tall, in inches, a calf will be at 1 year old compared to calves of other sires. **Scrotal circumference (SC)** is measured in centimeters; bigger scrotums mean better bulls.

You do not necessarily want a larger birth weight score because high birth weights often make it difficult for mothers to give birth. You most likely do want higher scores for weaning weight and yearling weight because high scores indicate the bull produces fast-growing calves. You have to weigh these scores based on your goals — if you want to sell calves at weaning, the most important score for you would be weaning weight. If you want to keep animals longer, the yearling weight score is more important.

- **Maternal:** This category predicts how a bull's daughters will perform if used for breeding. Traits measured in this area include:

Calving ease maternal (CEM) predicts how easily a bull's daughters will give birth as first-calf heifers compared to other bulls' daughters. A high score means the daughters are more likely to deliver cows without difficulty.

Maternal milk (Milk) predicts the mothering ability of a sire's daughters, specifically how her milk and mothering ability will translate to calf growth before weaning.

Mature Weight (MW) predicts how much a bull's daughters will weigh (in pounds) at maturity compared to other bulls' daughters.

Mature Height (MH) predicts how tall a bull's daughters will be (in inches) compared to the daughters of other bulls.

Cow energy value ($EN). Not all cows require the same amount of feed to meet their energy requirements. Cow energy value predicts how much a cow's energy requirements could save you in feed costs compared to the daughters of other bulls. $EN is expressed in dollars savings per cow, so a higher value in this category is preferable.

- **Carcass:** Carcass measurements are an indication of the yield from the final beef product. These include:

Carcass weight (CW) predicts the hot carcass weight of a bull's offspring compared to other bulls. Hot carcass weight is a measure in pounds after an animal is slaughtered and its head, organs, intestinal tract, and hide are removed, but before the carcass is chilled. Hot carcass weight is usually about 60 to 65 percent of the animal's live weight.

Marbling (marb) is a fractional difference in USDA marbling scores. USDA assigns beef grades based on the level of marbling, or fat within the muscles. The marbling EPD compares the projected fractional difference in marbling scores from one bull's offspring to another's. It is expressed as a percent of one-third of a marbling score. Higher marbling EPD scores are usually desirable.

Fat thickness (FAT) is calculated as 60 percent from the measurement at the 12th rib and 40 percent of fat at the rump. It is used to predict the overall fatness of an animal. Individual farmers will have to decide if they want this measurement to be higher or lower. Although fat is an indication of tenderness, fat can reduce the percentage of edible meat from the animal.

Ribeye area (REA) is a square-inches prediction of ribeye area for a bull's offspring. The ribeye area is where the most desirable steak cuts come from. The ideal ribeye area range is 12 to 14 inches, according to research from the University of Georgia that was published in the *Journal of Animal Science*. Anything larger than this may be hard to sell.

- **Ultrasound:** Like the carcass scores, ultrasound scores predict the finished beef product. Ultrasound scores, however, are based on the results of an ultrasound image so the data comes from the live animal, rather than a carcass. Traits measured include:

Intramuscular fat (%IMF) predicts the difference in intramuscular fat in the ribeye muscle compared to calves of other bulls.

Beef cattle are bred when they reach around 650 to 750 pounds or around the age of 14 months. A heifer must be well developed before breeding, or she may experience a difficult delivery. Heifers should be fed carefully during pregnancy, as they still will be growing; you do not want them to gain too much fat, because that can lead to pregnancy problems. The cow's estrous cycle is 21 days, and the pregnancy lasts about 280 days — or about nine months.

Most cows have single calf births, which is a desired trait because it lessens chances for birthing difficulties. Twin pregnancies occur in up to 5 percent of cattle and increases as the age of the mother increases. A female calf with a male twin has a good chance of becoming a freemartin due to the effect of male hormones on the female. This happens if during the pregnancy, the male hormones negatively influence the reproductive organ development of the female calf, causing them to be deformed. Freemartin heifers are generally sterile.

Generally, beef cows are bred to coincide to deliver their calves during the late winter or spring. Late winter — February or March — calving has the advantage of having a heavy calf (about 600 pounds) during the fall market period. Most people plan to market calves soon after the summer grazing season ends, so they do not have to feed the calves the more expensive grain and hay. The big disadvantage in breeding is having a calf born during poor weather such as snow or — even worse — mud. Calves with good mothers that dry them with their tongues and get them to stand and nurse can withstand snow and cold weather. A muddy or wet calf quickly become can chilled and die. Spring calving on clean pastures helps eliminate the chilling and disease problems associated with mud and snow. Timing the breeding to coincide with your particular geographic area's warmer spring weather can save you time and the heartbreak of a calf dying.

Calving

As a cow nears her delivery date, some changes will occur. About ten days before calving, her udder may start to become firm and full. The vulva and tail head may "spring," or become swollen and loose, jiggling when she walks. She may isolate herself from the rest of the herd, and she may stand with her tail raised. It is a good idea to place a cow ready to give birth into a clean, dry pen deeply bedded with straw so the calf is born into a clean environment. If the weather is warm and your cattle are on pasture, she also can be moved to a clean pasture.

Immediately before labor — or during stage one of labor — contractions of the uterus will make the cow restless. She may kick at her sides, swish her tail, and get up and down frequently. Cows will remain in stage one labor for as little as three hours to up to three days. During this stage, ligaments relax, and the cervix, vagina, and vulva are dilating to allow for the passage of the calf.

Stage two of labor begins when the water bag appears at the vulva. The cow will start to strain and push as the calf has moved into the birth canal. The cow may get up and down or stop pushing at times. Check her every 30 minutes to see if labor has progressed to stage three. Normally, stage two of labor lasts from 30 minutes in a cow to up to three hours in a heifer. If it is taking longer for the calf to appear at the vulva, your cow may be having a difficult delivery. You will want to check the cervix in this case. Occasionally, the cervix will fail to dilate. To check for this condition, you will need to use soap and water to wash the vulva with your hand and arm. Use a rubber glove or obstetrical sleeve and gently insert your hand into the vagina. If the cervix is only dilated the width two or three of your fingers, the cervix may not be dilating properly, or the uterus may be twisted. Call your veterinarian immediately if you suspect this is the case.

If the cervix is fully dilated, and you can feel the three essential structures on the calf (two front feet and a head or two rear feet and the tail) at the opening of the cervix or in the vagina, the cow might have uterine inertia or poor uterine contractions. You can use two clean pieces of soft, nylon rope to make a slipknot above the lower joint (fetlock) of the legs and a half hitch loop below the fetlock. Apply moderate traction to assist in the delivery. Do not use excessive force or a tractor to apply traction. Time your pulls with the cow's attempts to push. If you are unsuccessful after two or three attempts, call your veterinarian.

Stage three occurs when the calf appears at the vulva. Normal delivery position of a calf is front feet first with the head resting between the legs. Occasionally, a calf will deliver hind feet first. This is a normal variation and should not be cause for concern as long as both back feet are coming at the same time. Dystocia occurs when the calf is presented in strange positions. Sometimes a foot will be flexed back, but it can easily be corrected by pulling the foot into the normal position. Other calves can have legs bent back, a head twisted to the side, rear end coming first, or the calf can lay across the birth canal. These types of presentations will need to be corrected by a veterinarian to protect the uterus from tears and to minimize damage to the calf.

Stage four is the passing of the placenta. Many cows will consume the placenta, and it usually does not cause any problems. One of the important last points to do in a birth is to check the uterus for a second calf by slipping a clean, gloved hand into the birth canal. Many times, twins can cause birthing difficulties a cow may be having. If the labor was difficult, the uterus and vagina should be checked for tears or excessive bleeding. If there are tears in the wall of the uterus or large amounts of blood coming out of the vagina, call your veterinarian for treatment.

Check the calf after delivery. Make sure all mucus is removed from the mouth and nostrils. The calf should be blinking and attempting to lift its head immediately after delivery. If the calf is not breathing, use a piece of straw to tickle its nose. If that fails to stimulate a breath, you can try chest compressions or even mouth-to-snout breathing. When the calf takes a breath, stop rescue breathing. If a calf is gurgling fluid, drape the lower half of the body over the side of a pen or two bales of hay or straw so the head hangs down below the upper body. This will let fluid escape from the respiratory tract. Chest compressions while the calf is draped can also help with breathing. Get the cow up or gently drag the calf to the cow's head, so she can begin cleaning and drying the calf off. You should dip the calf's umbilical cord stump in a tincture of 2.5 percent iodine.

Problems associated with calving

Uterine prolapse: A uterine prolapse occurs when the cow strains and pushes her uterus out of her body. It is unmistakable when this occurs, as a large muscular sac will protrude or hang down from the vulva. When this happens, call your veterinarian immediately; it is an emergency. Pen the cow up to prevent her from injuring this fragile organ and prepare for the veterinarian's arrival by removing soiled bedding and laying down a deep layer of fresh bedding. The veterinarian will attempt to replace the uterus. The majority of uterine prolapses can be successfully replaced provided medical attention is promptly received. The cow can bleed to death if the uterine artery was torn when the prolapse occurred. Occasionally, after replacement the cow will continue to strain and push the uterus back out. The veterinarian may stitch the vulva shut and give the cow medicine to contract the uterus to prevent this from happening.

Hypocalcemia: Hypocalcemia, or milk fever, can occur soon after calving, especially in older dairy cattle. The udder can make such huge demands for calcium that it depletes the calcium in the cow's blood stream to the point that she becomes weak or is unable to stand. Calcium is needed for muscle contractions. A cow with milk fever is weak, wobbly, and will have cold ears. Some cattle will be restless, may pace, and bellow. Milk fever is treated with calcium given in the vein and possibly, supplemental oral calcium gel. Calcium can be purchased at local veterinarian offices or at farm supply stores.

Calving paralysis: Calving paralysis occurs when nerves in the cow's pelvis are injured during delivery. Heifers are more prone to calving paralysis due to their smaller pelvic opening. Signs can range from a weak leg or not using a leg to an inability to stand. If you suspect calving paralysis, call your veterinarian for treatment. Treatment consists of injections of steroids and non-steroidal, anti-inflammatory drugs to reduce inflammation of the affected nerves. Another important component of treatment is excellent nursing care. If large cows lie on one side for more than four hours, the muscles on the down side can die because of the extreme pressure exerted by the cow's weight. This damage can be prevented by a deep layer of straw bedding — greater than 12 inches should suffice — and turning the cow from side to side every four hours. Straw bales can be used to prop the cow on her side as well. The cow should have access to water and hay while down. She should be goaded to stand as well. You can assist her attempts to stand by grasping the tail at the base and lifting as she tries to rise.

Retained placenta: A cow normally will pass her placenta within six hours after the birth. If she has not expelled the tissue after 12 hours, it is considered retained. As long as the cow is healthy, eating, and does not have a fever, it is best to trim off any placenta protruding from the vulva. It should be expelled within a week after calving. If the cow with a retained placenta stops eating, ceases milk production, or runs a fever, call your veterinarian for treatment. Removal of a retained placenta is not recommended. Instead, the veterinarian may use drugs to try to get the uterus to release the retained bits of placenta. The also cow will be placed on antibiotics and anti-inflammatory drugs to combat infection.

Dairy Cow Nursing

In conventional dairies, young calves are separated from their mothers and bottle-fed a milk replacer substance, which often contains antibiotics and other substances. Whole milk from other cows on the farm sometimes is used instead. One option for feeding your calves is mob feeding. **Mob feeding** involves keeping groups of four to ten calves in their own paddock, separate from their mothers. Instead of nursing, the calves are allowed to eat from a mob feeder, which is a big barrel with nipples on it. The mob feeder will contain milk diverted from the milking herd. This is better than milk replacer, but some farmers feel that mob-fed calves do not grow as well as calves that are allowed to nurse.

Using nurse cows is another option farmers have used for feeding dairy calves. **Nurse cows** are cows that will not only nurse their own calves, but also the calves of other cows at the same time. You might be able to get a nurse cow to feed three or four calves at a time. At the Yegerlehner farm in Clay City, Indiana, potential nurse cows were initially selected because the family did not want to milk them with the rest of the herd — the first candidates had mastitis or were cranky during milking. Alan Yegerlehner, who owns the farm with his wife, Mary, said a good nurse cow must be willing to accept other cows' calves. Even if she kicks at them during the initial feeding, with persistence she can be trained to accept them. If she keeps kicking after two or three days, it is better to try another cow. The Yegerlehners use some cows as nurses every year because the cows show an instinct for that role. A nurse cow also must have enough body fat reserved to support the intensity of milking several calves. You can tell by looking at cows if they are fat enough.

Uniting calves with a nurse cow is called **grafting**. Before grafting, calves can be left on their mothers for at least a day or more so the calf gets a good start on its mother's colostrum. You should graft all the new calves onto a nurse at the same time. These calves are separated from their mothers and kept together so they can be introduced to the nurse cow together; a good place to keep them would be your holding pen. Letting the calves fast for about 24 hours will ensure they will be especially hungry once they are introduced to the nurse cow.

During the grafting process, a potential nurse cow is caught in a head gate so she cannot try to avoid the calves that are not hers. After the first feeding, calves are separated from the nurse cow and put into their pen until the next feeding. It usually takes four to eight feedings over the course of at least a couple of days to complete the grafting process. After a couple of feedings, you can try one feeding without restraining the nurse cow in a head gate. If everything goes OK, the calves and the nurse cow are left together to bond for a couple of days before they are returned to the pasture. From then on, each grafted calf must be responsible for its own feeding because the nurse cow will not find them to make sure they eat. Nurse cows and calves usually are kept as a separate group from the milking herd because if both groups were kept together, calves would return to nurse from their birth mothers.

The nurse cow system is not perfect. The energy required to nurse multiple calves takes a toll on a cow, and a potential side effect of this is that nurse cows can have trouble conceiving a new calf the next year.

Weaning

Calves can be weaned as early as 2 or 3 months old or left to nurse as long as 9 months old. Ideally, wait to wean the calves until they are at least 4 months old to give their rumens time to develop. If you wean before it is developed, you will have to give the calves a protein source. Most often, calves are weaned at about 7 months old.

Weaning can be a stressful time for both mothers and calves. At weaning, calves are separated from their mothers so they can no longer nurse. Traditionally, calves have been totally separated from their mothers or nurse cows into areas where they cannot see each other. These calves become stressed and spend their time bawling for their mothers instead of eating. The mothers also will bawl for their calves. Mothers will slack on eating for a while, but they will eat when they are hungry.

One way to reduce stress is fenceline weaning. In **fenceline weaning**, calves are separated by a fence into an adjoining pasture where they can still see, hear, and smell their mothers. For animals that are accustomed to an electric fence, three strands of wire should be enough to keep them separated. The separation is accomplished by moving the mothers into the adjacent pasture, and leaving the calves where they are. Be careful when separating the calves and mothers. Keep in mind the principles of blind spots and point of balance.

If you plan to sell calves soon after weaning, make sure you wean them a few weeks before the sale date. Ensure the calves have access to water. Some farmers let their water troughs overflow for the first couple of days to attract the calves' attention and ensure they know where the water is. Check in on the calves to make sure they are eating and are not depressed.

Dairies that use nurse cows can keep their calves nursing for the same amount of time as beef producers, roughly six months or so. If you are still milking your other dairy cows, you can milk your nurse cows in the barn after weaning.

Veal

Veal was developed as a way to make use of the many dairy bull calves that will not be used for breeding. These calves were considered almost useless in a dairy system, so farmers began slaughtering these calves at a few months old, resulting in small, lean, tender cuts of meat.

You may have heard the horror stories about conventionally raised veal, about how the male calves are taken from their mothers shortly after birth and stuck in dark crates so small they cannot even turn around. These calves also are fed a milk substitute that keeps them anemic and keeps their meat white. Like many conventionally raised cattle, they are given growth hormones to speed growth and antibiotics to fight the infections that are likely in this type of environment. The backlash against these practices was so strong that many Americans refused to eat veal. In recent years, even many of the largest veal producers have moved away from crates and have begun raising small groups of veal calves in pens, a practice known as **group housing**. In 2007, the American Veal Association passed a resolution calling for all veal calves to be raised in group housing by the end of 2017.

Many dairy cattle farmers go further than that to humanely raise veal and instead raise pasture-raised veal. Pasture-raised veal calves are left on their mothers, or on nurse cows, and allowed to live naturally until time for harvest at 5 to 6 months old. To soothe people who are still saddened that even pasture-raised veal calves have to die so young, grass-fed cattle farmers point out that these calves are slaughtered at the same age as lambs. You can tell how veal was raised just by looking at it — pasture-raised veal will be pink or rose colored, which is why pasture-raised veal is sometimes called rose veal.

After Weaning

Newly weaned calves are still growing after weaning, and you want to make sure they still gain weight in this phase. A good forage base will take care of this, although forage's winter or summer dormant periods can slow down weight gain. If you fear your cattle are going to lose weight, you can use hay or other supplements to keep them gaining weight. The more they can gain in this phase, the easier it will be to finish them when grass growth picks up again.

Throughout the stocker phase, a good average rate of daily gain is 1 ½ pounds. You may be able to surpass this during times of peak grass growth. Daily gains will slow when grass goes dormant, but farmers have reported good-quality beef even if their animals gained as little as ½ pound a day during December or January or July and August. For optimum beef quality, researchers of a joint project called "Economic Pasture Based Beef Systems for Appalachia" from the USDA-ARS Appalachian Farming Systems Research Center, in Beaver, West Virginia, Clemson University, Virginia Poly-

technic Institute & State University, and West Virginia University, recommended about 1 pound per day during the winter months. Aim for about 2 pounds per day in the finishing phase. Many of the farmers interviewed for this book said they are not able to weigh their animals to monitor precise average daily gains. But as you develop an eye for animals, you will be able to tell if they are losing, gaining, or maintaining weight. They said they try to feed their animals well enough to keep them gaining in winter and to avoid any periods where the animals are losing weight.

General Cow Health

Cattle are vulnerable to many diseases. Vaccinations, good nutrition, cleanliness, and parasite control will give you good health assurance for your herd. However, you will need to know a little about various diseases that can strike a cow or calf and how to recognize a sick animal.

Vaccinations

This section will give common viral diseases and vaccinations recommended for all cattle. Viral diseases are difficult to treat, as antibiotics do not kill viruses. Treatment is primarily supportive by keeping feed and water available, separating sick animals from healthy animals, and using medications to reduce fevers and inflammation. Many times, antibiotics are used to treat secondary bacterial infections. Vaccinations are available to prevent many viral diseases from causing problems in your herd.

A good time to schedule vaccinations is in the fall when cows can be checked to see how their pregnancies are progressing. This way, you can schedule the help you will need to catch the cattle and restrain them for vaccination. A strong vaccination program is well worth the time, effort, and small outlay of money. Vaccinations are the cheapest health insurance you can give your cattle. In addition, when excess calves are sold at auction, having them vaccinated will bring a dividend to you at sale time. Buyers will have more confidence that your cattle will remain healthy when brought into their feedlots or herds if they are vaccinated.

Before weaning, calves should be vaccinated with a seven-way blackleg vaccine, a five-way leptospirosis vaccine, and with a combination vaccine for IBR-BVD-PI3. Heifers should be vaccinated against Brucellosis when they are between 4 and 12 months old. If pinkeye is a problem in your area, calves should be vaccinated against this before the start of the grazing season. Blackleg is a disease caused by spore-forming *Clostridium bacteria*. The spores can lie dormant in the soil for years and infect a calf when it eats feed or soil contaminated by the spores. The spores lodge in various organs and muscles in the calf, and they multiply when an injury occurs. The injury does not have to be severe, as even slight bruising can cause the spores to become active and multiply. Many times there are no signs of infection, and an infected calf may just be found dead.

Brucellosis is a contagious disease caused by the bacteria *Brucella abortus*. It can also infect humans where it causes a condition called undulant fever characterized by fevers, fatigue, joint pain, headaches, and psychotic behavior. Before the eradication program started in the 1950s, up to 10 percent of the cattle in the United States were infected with the disease. Calf vaccination of heifers and pasteurization of milk has dropped the infection rate to the point that there are no known infected cattle at this point. It does remain a sporadic disease in the wild herds of bison and elk in Montana and Wyoming.

Common cow diseases

Leptospirosis: There are many strains of leptospirosis, but only five types cause the majority of illness in cattle. In adult cattle, the disease primarily affects the cows' reproductive organs, causing miscarriages, infertility, and stillbirths. Calves may get ill with fever and blood problems.

Infectious bovine rhinotracheitis (IBR), Bovine Viral Diarrhea (BVD), Bovine Respiratory Syncytial Virus (BRSV) and Parainfluenza 3 (PI3) are viral respiratory and intestinal diseases that commonly affect stressed cattle, such as calves being weaned or sold at auction.

IBR: Infectious bovine rhinotracheitis (red nose) spreads rapidly through unvaccinated herds. Cattle show signs of a respiratory illness such as nasal discharge, a red muzzle, mouth ulcers, and a high temperature (106 degrees F or higher.)

BVD: Bovine viral diarrhea (BVD) is common in all ages of cattle, but young cattle (8 to 24 months) are the most susceptible. The primary sign of BVD is diarrhea. Other signs include dehydration, mouth sores, increased breathing, and fever.

PI-3: Parainfluenza 3 causes signs of the flu in the cow. The cow will cough, have a fever, refuse feed, and have eye and nasal discharge. Most cases are mild, but some cattle can get secondary bacteria infections leading to pneumonia.

Eye diseases

Pinkeye: The bacterium *Moraxella bovis* causes infectious bovine keratoconjunctivitis (IBK), better known as pinkeye. It is a rapidly contagious disease in some herds and affects calves more often than adults. Hereford cattle and their crosses seem more susceptible to the disease than other cattle breeds due their light colored faces. Factors that contribute to the development of pinkeye include exposure to sunlight, lots of flies around the face, dust, and being infected with infectious bovine rhinotracheitis (IBR), a respiratory virus. Controlling pinkeye entails controlling face flies through use of pesticide-laced ear tags, insecticide dust bags, and fly-control lick blocks. Treatment is with eye patches or injections of antibiotics.

Cancer eye: Squamous cell carcinoma, or cancer eye, is the most common cancer in cattle. Cattle with white faces, such as Herefords, are more susceptible to this cancer. Sunlight, dust, and aging are all factors leading to the development of cancer eye. The cancer may first appear as a smooth, white lesion around or on the eye. As the cancer advances, there may be a growth of rough, bumpy tissue. The tissue can quickly erode and die. If caught at an early stage, your veterinarian can attempt removal, but recurrence is common.

Neurological diseases

Rabies: Cattle are susceptible to rabies, just like any warm-blooded mammal. Due to spending a lot of time on pasture and their curious nature, cattle tend to investigate any stray animal wandering onto their stomping ground. A rabid skunk will bite any cow that tries to sniff it, and many times this is how a cow becomes infected with the rabies virus. Rabies is fatal, there is no treatment available, and it can be transmitted to cattle caretakers by infected saliva. Rabies in cattle takes two forms: a furious form and a dumb form. Cattle with the furious form may charge people or objects, bellow frequently, and may run around frantically. The dumb form of rabies causes the affected cow to act depressed, drool, and become paralyzed.

Grass tetany: Grass tetany affects mainly lactating beef cattle on pasture that is low in magnesium. Young, greening grass pastures seem to be the main cause of grass tetany. A cow with this disorder will have many signs associated with the nervous system. These include hyperexcitability, staggering, muscle tremors, eyelids that snap open and closed, and convulsions; affected cows frequently die. Grass tetany can be a herd-wide problem and needs to be treated early and promptly. Treatment involves moving the cattle off the pasture, keeping them quiet, and giving either subcutaneous or intravenous magnesium.

Diarrhea-causing diseases

Winter dysentery: Winter dysentery in cattle is a contagious diarrhea in cattle that runs through a herd in less than two weeks. It typically occurs during the colder time of the year. Signs include watery, explosive dark diarrhea, colic, cough, decreased milk production, and anorexia. Treatment is usually not needed, as the disease is typically self-limiting, although owners should make sure cattle have adequate water, feed, and possibly mineral supplementation due to ongoing losses from diarrhea. There is no vaccination against this disease as the cause of winter dysentery is not entirely certain.

Johne's disease: Johne's disease is a costly disease caused by *Mycobacterium paratuberculosis.* Most frequently, young adult cattle show clinical signs of Johne's disease, though many cattle in affected herds have subclinical disease. *M. paratuberculosis* causes a condition called granulomatous disease of the ileum, cecum, and related lymph nodes. This change in the intestine causes a malabsorption of protein (losing enteropathy) and diarrhea. The transmission of *M. paratuberculosis* is through the fecal-oral route, but it also can be transmitted intrauterine and through the milk. Signs of Johne's disease can mimic other diarrheal or weight-loss diseases. These signs can include diarrhea, muscle wasting (due to protein loss), weight loss, anorexia, dehydration, and eventually death. There is no treatment at this time for Johne's disease.

CASE STUDY: DAIRY CATTLE ON THE SIDE

Duane Spielman
Dr. Carmen Odegaard
Evansville, Minnesota

Duane Spielman and Carmen Odegaard moved to their small farm about 12 years ago after attending college in St. Paul, Minnesota. Spielman took a job at a large dairy farm that milks 300 to 400 cows, while Odegaard works as a veterinarian at local veterinary clinics. They decided they wanted a little extra income, so Spielman purchased some Holstein bull calves from his employer. This started a long-term side business of raising dairy beef.

Spielman and Odegaard are very diligent about maintaining the health of their calves. The calves are brought to their farm when they are 1 to 2 days old. Spielman makes certain the calves get at least 1 gallon of colostrum within the first 24 hours of life. This is the most important factor in having a healthy calf. Another important factor in raising healthy calves is cleanliness of anything the calf might touch with its mouth. This includes bottles, nipples, pails, and pens.

They prefer to keep their calves in calf huts made of molded plastic. These huts are easy to move and can be bleached between calf litters. Each calf has its own hut, which cuts down on disease transmission. When the calves are weaned, they are moved into a group of eight to ten calves in a well-ventilated pen with access to the outside. Dry air, light, and dry straw are a must in the pens.

They do not recommend purchasing baby calves from a sales barn; rather, try to find a local producer and buy calves directly from the farm. They also recommend talking with a local veterinarian to find out what reputable farms sell dairy calves. Plus, it is good to establish a working relationship with a veterinarian clinic in case medical advice and treatment is needed.

The most time-consuming period when raising dairy calves is the first week when calves have to be trained to drink. The calves are fed 3 quarts of milk twice a day — or more if the weather is very cold. They will place homemade calf jackets on the calves as well to help them retain body heat. They will closely monitor their health, as scours (diarrhea) is a big killer of young calves. Any calf that appears ill gets prompt, aggressive medical treatment. The calves will be weaned by 4 to 6 weeks of age; after this, the daily time commitment decreases greatly.

They enjoy raising dairy calves as it gives them an enjoyable part-time job with a short commute — just a few steps from the house. It also gives them a family project they hope to enjoy with their young twins, and they do not have to pay a babysitter when they go to work at this job. The cattle market is a tricky beast though. Right now, prices for Holstein beef feeder calves (400- to 500-pound cattle) are low, and this is out of the producer's control. Spielman believes they can weather the market, and it will improve as the economy improves.

Dairy Cattle

The dairy cow is the stereotypical livestock mother. The modern dairy cow has been selectively bred to give large amounts of milk: so much so there is frequently a large surplus of milk, which drives milk prices down to below the cost of production. Modern dairy farming — at least most commercial dairy farming — is a highly capitalized business run on razor-thin margins. Dairy pricing is a complicated process, dictated not merely on supply and demand but also on federal government manipulation in terms of price supports. Becoming a small-scale dairy farmer will take hard physical work and dedication as cows need to be milked twice daily, seven days a week, when they are in production.

You also will need to be a savvy business owner to keep production costs down while making sure your cattle produce enough milk to cover your costs.

Dairy breeds

There are five main breeds of dairy cattle, each having particular desirable traits, which you will want to consider carefully when deciding which breed to purchase.

Holstein: The Holstein is the most familiar breed. These large, black and white (or red and white) cows are virtually milk-producing factories. Also known as the Friesian, this breed was developed in the Netherlands. It was in the United States that the breed was developed into the high milk-producing cow. The world record holder for milk production is the Holstein. Top producing Holstein cows produce more than 65,000 pounds of milk — roughly 8,000 gallons — a year. But an average herd cow produces about 22,000 pounds of milk a year and 836 pounds of butterfat. At maturity, the average Holstein cow weighs about 1,500 pounds. At birth, a calf can weigh more than 90 pounds. Because of high-yields of milk and modern management strategies, the average productive life of a Holstein cow is about four years. They can live longer, but many Holstein encounter health problems that shorten their life spans. This is due to being confined to cement-floored buildings that are damaging to the feet and legs or being fed high-concentrate diets, which leads to foot and stomach problems.

Jersey: The Jersey cow is the smallest breed of dairy cow that is commercially milked. Jerseys are generally brown, ranging from copper to dark brown with rich, chocolate eyes. Although they are small in stature, their milk is high in butterfat. A mature Jersey will weigh about 1,000 pounds or less. The Jersey was developed in the British channel on the island of Jersey. They have small calves, weigh about 40 pounds when born, and have the added advantage of being known as a docile breed. Many Holstein herds will have a Jersey cow or two in them to increase the butterfat content in the milk bulk tank.

Guernsey: The Guernsey breed is another island breed. The cow was developed on the Isle of Guernsey, which is off the coast of France. They are a medium-sized, fawn and white  dairy cows, and an adult female will weigh around 1,100 pounds. The milk from a Guernsey is high in butterfat and protein. It is also a rich golden color rather than white due to the higher concentration of beta-carotene, a precursor to vitamin A.

Brown Swiss: The Brown Swiss breed originated in the mountains of Switzerland. It is a large, brown breed that is second to Holsteins in milk production. A mature Brown Swiss cow weighs 1,500 pounds. They produce milk rich in butterfat and protein, which makes their milk prized for cheese production. A Brown Swiss herd will average more than 21,000 pounds of milk per year. They are easy to take care of, do well in all weather conditions, and they have a laid-back temperament.

Ayrshire: The red and white Ayrshire was developed in Scotland. On average, a mature cow will weigh about 1,200 pounds. The breed is easy to keep and is not plagued by feet and udder breakdown like other dairy breeds. There is also little difficulty when birthing calves, and the calves are generally strong and healthy. Ayrshire cows are good for pasture grazing.

CASE STUDY: THE MAKING OF AN ORGANIC DAIRY FARM

Dr. Dennis Johnson
West Central Research and Outreach Center
Morris, Minnesota
320-589-1711

Dennis Johnson wanted to be a dairy farmer when he was young. He attended college, obtained his Ph.D., and became a dairy researcher. He currently is a professor of dairy production systems at the University of Minnesota. As part of his research, he has been conducting a long-term study on organic dairy farming.

Beginning farmers have a number of hurdles when they start farming. Johnson lists the three biggest hurdles to starting a dairy farm as: access to affordable, appropriate property; financial funding; and mastering the skills and knowledge associated with dairy farming. These factors should be scrutinized carefully and realistically before one cow sets one hoof in a beginning dairy farmer's barn.

At the research station where Johnson conducts his studies, part of the dairy herd is being transitioned to an organic herd. This group of cattle is in a crossbreeding program using Holstein, Montbéliarde, and Swedish Red dairy cattle genetics. The goal of this crossbreeding is to introduce ruggedness in terms of health and foraging ability into the herd. The organic herd spends more time outside on pasture and is fed less grain and supplements than the conventional Holstein herd. This helps meet the organic standard for cattle to be fed a higher forage diet than a typical dairy herd.

According to Johnson, dairy cattle can do well spending the majority of their time outside, even in inclement weather. They do need a safe, clean indoor place to be milked, but as long as they have a windbreak, a dry and clean area to lie down, and protection from sleet, they do not necessary need to be housed in a barn. Frozen teats are not an issue as long as they are thoroughly dried before being let outside. An important aspect to organic dairy farming is keeping records. An organic farm needs to be certified as organic — this includes pastures, cropland, feed, and supplements. No antibiotics or growth promoters can be used on the cattle.

Johnson is optimistic about the five-year outlook for dairy farming, particularly in the Midwest, as he feels this geographical area has the most appropriate natural resources for dairy farming. Areas of rapid dairy herd expansion in the Western United States are limited by water issues and encroaching human population. As long as a farmer is willing to take the time and learn the necessary skills, Johnson believes organic dairy farming is a viable production system.

Housing

Dairy cattle typically have been housed in barns instead of pastures as beef cattle are raised. They are animals that thrive on routine and usually will have a favorite spot in the barn. Most small-scale dairy farmers will use stanchions (devices that latch around the cows neck) or a tie-stall (where the cattle are chained to the stall via a neck chain) to hold the cows while milking. Grain usually is fed to the cattle while they are in their stalls and being milked. This also helps them associate being milked with a good thing, encouraging them to come into the barn at milking time.

Photo provided by Daryl Johnson

Some farmers choose to leave their cattle in the barn continuously, occasionally letting them out if they have stopped milking during their dry period or for just a few hours a day while the barn is being cleaned. However, it is healthier for the cow to be able to spend time exercising, and they can be maintained well in a group setting or on pasture. The main requirements for dairy cattle are to have dry teats and a clean place to lie down. The udder needs to remain clean and can be quickly contaminated with manure if a clean top layer of bedding is not provided. A dirty udder can contaminate the milk with fecal matter and bacteria. Dairy cattle allowed access to a pasture should not be able to walk into standing water or a river as some waters carry microorganisms that can cause serious udder infections.

Drying off dairy cows

You need to stop milking dairy cows the last two to four months before calving. Milk production slows greatly in this period as dairy cattle shift their energy intake toward their developing fetuses. If you have a seasonal dairy — meaning all your cows give birth at the same time — you will not milk any cows for at least two months a year. Dairies that use staggered calving seasons can keep milking some animals while drying off those that near calving. After the last milking, farmers who have conventional dairy cows will infuse all four teats with antibiotics to heal any cases of mastitis. You can use organic teat sealant solutions to avoid antibiotics that achieve the same goals as conventional sealants. Drying off is a stressful time for cattle, and you want to monitor them to ensure they are all adapting to the change. Cows' immune systems are weak a few days after drying off and two or three weeks before and after calving. Mineral or other nutritional supplements may be necessary to boost the health of the stressed animals. Cows that get sick during pregnancy can threaten the lives of the fetuses. You need to keep dry cows in good physical condition — not too fat but not too thin. After drying off, the teats form a keratin plug that prevents new infection. The plug disappears a couple of weeks before calving.

Handling and Feeding

Dairy cattle have some special handling considerations because they usually spend more time in close proximity to humans when they are milked. Dairy cattle in a herd become accustomed to a routine, and the routine should be adhered to in order to keep the cattle calm. In every herd, there is a leader cow. It is important when bringing cows into a barn or area where they are to be milked to give them enough space to follow one another and to maintain visual contact with the leader cow.

Photo provided by Daryl Johnson

Cattle rely on their vision; in fact, they have almost panoramic vision. They will hesitate to enter into a dimly lit barn or if made to walk up steps unless they are allowed time to investigate these conditions. Bright lights, shiny reflections, and shadows also will alarm cattle.

Calm cattle will be able to put their energy into producing milk and will not be nervous and jumpy when being milked. Because the act of milking places human and cow in such close contact, a dairy cow that kicks or swings her rear from side to side can injure the person doing the milking. Always speak in a low, calm voice and move slowly and deliberately around cattle. In addition to the physical danger posed by an agitated cow, a nervous or scared cow will not be as easy to milk. This will decrease milk yield and may contribute to mastitis due to milk retention in the udder. The process of releasing milk into the udder is called milk letdown. It is brought about through the release of a hormone, oxytocin, at the base of the cow's brain. In most milking herds, handling the teats by gently massaging the udder for 15 seconds is practiced to stimulate the release of oxytocin. Oxytocin affects the muscle cells surrounding the udder's milk, which produces cells, causing them to contract. This squeezes the milk out of the cells into the milk ducts that drain to the teat. Within one to one and a half minutes after this action, the teats will be full of milk. If a cow is fearful, it will disrupt the oxytocin release. They also will release another hormone, adrenaline, which will block the action of oxytocin for up to 30 minutes.

Dairy cattle are fed similar to beef cattle and have the same general requirements. However, because they are producing a lot of milk, they will need to have more high-energy grain (such as corn and soybean meal) to convert into milk. Most dairy cattle produce 6 to 7 gallons of milk a day, and they will eat about 100 pounds of feed (hay, grass, silage, and grain) a day. You will want to feed a dairy cow a high RFV value hay or good quality pasture. They should have free-choice access to hay or pasture. For every pound of milk your cow gives, you should supplement her with 1 pound of grain. They always should have water available at all times. Larger dairies will have a machine to mix a total mixed ration (TMR). All feed (hay, silage, and grain) are placed in this machine and it is ground into a product. This way the cow will consume all feeds and not be able to pick out the feed she finds tastiest. For a person with only a few cows, the cost of a TMR mixer will prove too costly. A used TMR mixer sells for a few thousand dollars.

Dairy Cattle Health

Some diseases and health concerns are specific to dairy cows. Here is some information about how to care for your dairy cows to keep them disease-free and in the best of health.

Udder anatomy

The udder of a dairy cow is an amazing thing. It is more than four teats and an udder (commonly called a bag); it is a rich factory, producing milk, butterfat, and protein with a generous blood supply. Because it is the primary focus of the dairy cow, it is important for the dairy farmer to understand how the udder works. The udder is divided into two fore and rear quarters. Looking from behind, it is divided into two halves by the mammary groove.

The teats are at the ends of each quarter. They function as a valve for the release of milk and to provide for the suckling of a calf. They are smooth and hairless. The streak canal is the duct through which milk exits the gland and is the major defense against the introduction of mastitis-causing organisms. During milking, the sphincter muscle of the streak canal relaxes to allow milk release. It remains open for about an hour after milking. Using a post-milking germicidal solution on the teat will protect the streak canal from being invaded by bacteria.

The vascular system of the udder is vast. The large mammary arteries are easily seen on the side of the udders. They are susceptible to injury from overgrown feet and dewclaws, the claws located at the side of the foot above the hooves. Ducts and cisterns drain the milk from the secretory tissues, which make up the majority of the udder.

Hoof health

Large commercial dairy farms have many problems with cattle hooves due to nutritional problems, a life spent on concrete, and wet conditions in the barns. With a small-scale farm, hoof health problems can be just as severe if you do not pay attention to the hoof. Cattle with sore feet will not eat as well, will be in pain, and are susceptible to other leg problems. A normal cow's hoof should be rounded at the tip — not overgrown on the sides — and the skin between the toes should be a healthy pink-white. An unhealthy hoof will be overgrown at the tip and sides. The skin between the toes might ooze fluid from infection, might have reddened tissues, or might have a foul odor.

Photo provided by Daryl Johnson

If a cow is allowed to exercise, foot problems should be minimal. If a cow does become lame or its hoof overgrows, plan a foot trimming session. You can attempt to trim the hoof yourself, or you can hire a professional to do the job. A large-animal veterinarian should be able to examine your cow's hoof. Another option is to hire a hoof trimmer who has the tools to come to your farm to restrain and examine your cow's feet. Either professional will check for such things as sole ulcers, injuries, warts, or infections. They can instruct you as to the best treatment strategy for your cow and likely will trim the cow's hooves.

Mastitis

Mastitis in dairy cattle causes considerable economic loss to the dairy farmer. Bacterial infection is the main cause of mastitis. Many factors contribute to mastitis in dairy cattle, including poor milking techniques, teat injury or sores, faulty milking machines, and high exposures to bacteria. Signs of mastitis include swelling, heat, and pain in the udder. Severely sick cattle will lack an appetite, be weak, and may not be able to stand. The milk from the affected quarter(s) may be watery, chunky, or have flakes. Other cases of mastitis will be a subclinical, chronic form, which will not make the cow sick but will cause increased somatic cell counts in the bulk tank.

A California Mastitis Test (CMT) kit will help you determine if your cow has mastitis. This kit comes with a paddle with four shallow wells. Milk from each quarter is stripped into each well, and a solution is squirted into the milk. The paddle is swirled. Milk with mastitis will react with the solution and cause gelling. These kits can be purchased at livestock veterinarian offices, at farm supply stores, or through online farm supply companies.

Staphylococcus aureus causes a large amount of mastitis cases, both acute and chronic, in dairy herds. It is a hard bacterium to eradicate from the quarters. *Streptococcus* bacteria also cause mastitis and are spread from cow to cow or through dirty living environments. Coliform mastitis can cause a cow to become extremely ill through the release of toxins. The cow will become weak and may not be able to stand. It will stop eating and cease to have rumen contractions. A veterinarian should promptly treat this type of mastitis in order to save the cow's life.

Preventing and controlling mastitis

Good milking procedure, fine-tuned milking machines, and a clean environment should eliminate most cases of mastitis. All people who milk and care for the dairy cow should be trained to properly prepare the milking cow for milking and how to spot signs of mastitis. Mastitis is the biggest health problem of the dairy cow because it decreases milk production and can make the milk undrinkable or unsalable.

Before milking, the udder should be cleaned with a soft, disposable cloth to remove any dirt and debris. If there is any dirt present on the teats, they should be cleaned carefully and lightly disinfected. Dry the teats well before milking by hand or placing the milking unit on the teat.

After milking, each teat should be dipped in a post-milking dip solution. This solution is usually an iodine-based liquid and can be found readily in any dairy supply store. Cows should be fed or allowed access to pasture or hay after milking. They should be encouraged to stand for at least an hour after milking to allow time for the teat sphincter muscle to close. This will prevent any bacteria from the ground from traveling into the teat if the cow lies down.

The barn, feedlot, or holding pens where cattle congregate should be scraped or cleaned of manure at least twice daily. Manure should not be allowed to accumulate where dairy cattle are held. Bedding should be changed frequently to keep the cattle on a clean, dry layer of bedding. Fly and insect control is another means to stop the spread of mastitis. Flies can harbor some of the organisms that cause mastitis.

If your dairy cow is allowed pasture access, do not let it have access to ponds or streams. Wading in ponds or standing in water can expose the udder and teats to water borne organisms, which can cause hard-to-treat cases of mastitis. A dairy cow's feet should be regularly trimmed. This includes the dewclaw. Sharp edges on a hoof can damage teat ends or the udder, especially in cattle with low-slung udders when they walk, lie down, or attempt to stand. Using a handheld propane torch, some farmers will singe the hair on the udder to keep dirt and manure from accumulating. If you use a milking machine, all parts of the machine should be serviced regularly and checked daily for any faults. Rubber parts showing signs of wear should be replaced. The vacuum setting both on the compression unit and at the teat end should be calibrated carefully. All equipment should be washed, sterilized, and properly stored immediately after milking has ended.

Treating mastitis

Mastitis is treated with prepackaged mastitis tubes widely available at veterinarian office or general farm supply stores. The tubes contain antibiotics and have a special tapered end, which inserts into the canal of the teat. It is imperative that the teat and the end of the teat be washed free of dirt, manure, and other foreign matter and the end of the teat repeatedly swabbed with alcohol before inserting the tube into the teat canal. The cow will need to be restrained in a stanchion, with a halter, or in a cattle chute. If the cow is not used to humans handling her teats, it is wise to have a second person perform tail restraint on the cow while you clean the teat and insert the tube end into the teat opening. After inserting the tube, the plunger on the end of the tube is pushed in slowly, allowing the medicine to enter the teat canal.

CASE STUDY: THE COW SENSE

Daryl Johnson
Evansville, Minnesota

Daryl Johnson got started in dairy farming at an early age. His parents were dairy farmers and when he was ready, he took over the family farm. Johnson milks about 60 Holstein cows twice a day, 365 days a year. He has been through many financial cycles during his years of dairy farming; right now, the dairy industry is in a downward cycle with low milk prices, making dairy farming a shaky prospect.

However, Johnson feels that this downward cycle might be a good time for a beginning dairy farmer to start up a small-scale dairy. Unlike just a few years ago, prices of dairy heifers and cows are reasonable and feed prices are going down as well. Both these items are among the biggest expenses of dairy farming. Another big expense is land, which is needed to spread cattle manure on, to make hay for the cattle, and to grow crops.

Dairy farming is a capital-intensive business. The majority of dairy farmers will need a close working relationship with their banker or financial institute to make sure they have enough money for needed equipment, grain, and cattle. In addition to cattle, land, and capital, there are other necessary items to make it as a small-scale dairy farmer. A barn with tie stalls is sufficient for a small dairy herd like Johnson's. A parlor barn with free stalls is another option, but it is more costly to construct. A manure-handling system will greatly reduce the labor-intensive part of manure removal from the barn. Although a stave silo is almost iconic on a dairy farm, using bags or a bunker system is a cheaper way to store silage. One item that will pay off in the end is a TMR (total mixed ration) mixer. Johnson definitely recommends this piece of equipment.

Johnson attests that the best part about dairy farming is the lifestyle and working with the cattle. Johnson spends about 14 hours a day working on his farm along with a full-time hired hand. His top three time-consuming chores are heat detection, feeding the cattle, and putting up feed. This is in addition to the milking chores and calf-feeding duties. A dairy farmer has to be fully committed to the farm in order for it to work successfully.

Having "cow sense" is a must as well, as a healthy and comfortable cow gives more milk. In Johnson's opinion, the worst aspect about dairy farming is having a cow develop feet and leg problems and not knowing why this occurs. He uses artificial insemination (AI) to breed his cows. He tries to pick sires that will improve the feet and legs of the calves, but despite this, he still has cows that have feet and leg problems.

Structures

The best advice for someone who is about to invest in the infrastructure for a cattle operation is to keep it simple. All the neat machinery and products that are advertised as making life easier might tempt you, and most of them work the way they say, but their price tag could put your farm in jeopardy. Many farmers fall into the trap of having to expand continually to survive. You must consider each purchase carefully to be sure it is necessary. You might be surprised with how few facilities you can get by with.

If there is not a barn on your property already, you probably can get by without one. One of the key principles of cattle farming is that cattle should be left outdoors, as they would live in nature. Many dairies also are being built without winter housing. The best approach probably is to start small and give the minimalist approach a chance to work. You always can add more equipment and facilities down the line if you decide you cannot do without them.

Your cows probably will need fences to keep them from getting hurt on the highway and to prevent them from eating your neighbors' yards. There are places in western states with open-range laws that permit cattle to be unfenced, but the majority of cattle farmers use electric fencing. Laws vary by location, so start with county zoning officials, or your local extension agent, to see what the rules are for you. You will have to be sure your cattle have access to water in your managed grazing plan.

It is important to design your facilities so your animals are comfortable. Here are some tips to follow so your cattle are happy in their new facilities.

- When you bring them into a holding area, give them enough space to follow one another and maintain visual contact with the leader cow.

- They do not like to go around corners unless they feel like they can see where they are going. Make sure turns are gentle and rounded rather than sharp and angular.

- Bright lights, shiny reflections, and shadows alarm cattle, as do loud noises such as clanging gates. Inspect your facilities to eliminate these distractions.

- Be sure that your fences and pens are well maintained. Animals can hurt themselves on nails, sharp corners, or broken boards.

- Provide sufficient lighting because they will not want to enter a dimly lit milking facility and will hesitate to walk up steps until they are allowed time to investigate.

If you do have to house an animal for an extended period, it is important to have a well-ventilated facility and to provide clean bedding. Bedding materials include sawdust, ground corncobs, straw, or wood shavings. The depth of bedding should be 10 to 12 inches or more. Be sure the bedding stays clean and dry by removing soiled areas and recovering those areas with new bedding.

Holding pen

If you are starting a farm from scratch, plan your holding-pen area first. You need a holding pen for routine herd management tasks, for treating sick animals, or to receive new animals. A holding area is a pen where groups of animals stand while they wait to be moved into another area, such as a loading chute or health care area. The ideal holding pen is round with enough space for each confined animal to turn around. This holding area is usually attached to an alleyway or chute, which is a panel on either side of the cow, leading to a head gate that restrains the animal's head during health care procedures. The holding area also could lead to a loading chute for cattle that are leaving the farm. You need an entrance gate that leads from the pasture, a gate leading into the chute to the head gate, and a gate to release the animal back into the pasture after treatment.

The walls of your holding pen should be at least 60 inches tall, and it should be made of boards, plywood, or some type of solid, non-transparent material such as steel. When the cattle are in the pen, or in alleys or chutes, they should be able to see where they are going, but they should have minimal visibility to what is going on outside their area. Cattle traffic should flow easily both ways between your holding pen and your pasture. The pen should be accessible in all weather by truck. You also need a power source for water or for light to take care of sick animals at night.

Your chute leading to the head gate can be short or long — a short one works if you bring animals in one at a time, and a long one allows more than one animal to wait in the alley. The holding pen and the chute should be round because cattle naturally like to circle back and corners will cause them to bunch up. Mississippi State University has a page of facility design ideas at the following address: **http://msucares.com/pubs/plans/books/beef.html**. Dr. Temple Grandin, a professor at Colorado State University, also has a great site for pen designs at **www.grandin.com**.

If you do not want to build these facilities, you can buy pens, chutes, and head gates at most farm supply stores; a couple of well-known chains are Southern States (**www.southernstates.com**) and Tractor Supply Co (**www.tractorsupply. com**). The alleys can be simple, narrowly-placed fencing, or they can be squeeze chutes that close in to hold an animal's sides so it cannot move while the farmer does what is necessary. A manual head gate will cost a few hundred dollars; a squeeze chute system with a gate that moves with a hydraulic mechanism can cost a few thousand dollars. A hydraulically working chute with all the options could cost as much as $10,000.

You may also use fencing to create a pen to receive new animals if you routinely buy them. This is a good option if your farm focuses on stocker cattle. This receiving paddock may need a sturdier fencing type than simple electric fence, such as mesh or barbed wire, because these new animals may not be accustomed to electric fencing. They also will be stressed from the move and may naturally have a wild temperament. This quarantine area allows you to watch them for signs of illness before bringing them in with the rest of your animals. You also will be able to process new arrivals with vaccinations. Another use for fencing is to create a separate area to isolate sick animals. These areas also need a water source and shade.

CASE STUDY: ROCKY MOUNTAIN ORGANIC MEATS

Rod Morrison
Chief operating officer and president
Rocky Mountain Organic Meats
Powell, Wyoming
www.rockymtncuts.com
info@rockymtncuts.com

For Rod Morrison, raising grass-fed organic beef is not just a business; it is a crusade. Morrison always has believed in farming the old-fashioned way, as organically as possible. He is part of a farmer-owned meat company that raises cattle without hormones, antibiotics, or synthetic fertilizers. The land ranched for the company includes 600,000 acres of the Arapaho reservation near Yellowstone National Park in Wyoming. Morrison is a follower of Wendell Berry, the writer who champions sustainable agriculture, stewardship of the land, and the value of rural communities.

Morrison hopes that more producers and customers realize the benefits of organically raised grass-fed cattle. He argues that conventional agriculture uses energy at an unsustainable rate. Morrison's goal is to use no more energy each day on his farm than what reaches the Earth as sunlight.

"Honestly, it is the only way we are going to be able to sustain ourselves in the long run," Morrison said. "You cannot go halfway. That is like being half married. If you are half married, then good luck."

He is the president and chief operating officer of Rocky Mountain Organic Meats, a producer-owned company of between ten and 15 farmers that raise grass-fed organic beef and lamb near the Rocky Mountains in Wyoming. All the producers are certified organic according to National Organic Program standards. This certification is important to the company's producers because they want their customers to be confident of what they are buying and of where it came from.

He ships boxes of meat to customers all over the country. But he does not just take orders; he wants to communicate with his customers and ensure they understand why he raises his beef organically and why it is important that they choose such food. Most of his boxes go out weighing 20 to 30 pounds, but he also offers a package that equals a side of beef — roughly 175 pounds of steaks, roasts, burger, and specialty slices — for $1,400. He charges about $7 a pound, a price that most customers will not pay, but which is worth it to customers who understand the benefits of raising cattle organically on pasture.

"A few are [discovering the benefits] every day," Morrison said. "And as they figure it out, they are understanding now they have a relationship with someone who produces food, and they are very happy about that."

Morrison's farm is nestled in the Big Horn Basin at the base of Heart Mountain. His fields used to be raised for sugar beets and malt barley. He planted everything with a mixture of alfalfa and cold- and warm-season grass seeds. He let these plants establish themselves for a year and a half before he began using these fields for grazing. Morrison raises 45 mother cows that produce calves each year. He also buys about 40 or so calves each year from another farmer who raises his cattle organically but does not want to finish them. Those calves arrive at about 600 pounds and are grown to between 900 and 1,100 pounds. His cattle usually finish in about 18 to 20 months.

Storage

If your farm already has a barn or other storage facility, this is a safe place to store hay. Or, you can build three-sided facilities to protect your hay. If you use a facility, make sure you can keep the bottoms of your bales dry; one way to do this is to set bales on wooden pallets to keep them off the floor. Again, you do not necessarily need a barn to store these materials. If you do not have a barn or shed, you can store hay outside if you cover it with plastic or a tarp. You also may use silage pits to store a certain type of food for periods of low forage quality, such as in winter. **Silage** is fermented, moist forage that is made from almost any green, growing plant. It is stored either in silos or in concrete bunkers that are covered with airtight tarps. If it is not stored properly, a dangerous bacterium called *Listeria monocytogenes* could sicken or kill your animals.

Shelter

Cattle have lived outdoors for thousands of years, and they can survive outdoors in even the most brutal climate extremes, but they do need some form of relief from both cold winds and the sun's rays. Overheated livestock feel malaise, and they will not eat. High winds stress animals, and they need more energy to keep warm in the cold. Barns or other existing structures could provide shade or relief from wind. Your geography also may provide some natural relief for your cattle. Tall hills or trees already on your property can slow the wind and block the sun. Some farmers also plant rows of trees as windbreaks, but it could be a few years until they grow tall enough to provide any shelter or protection.

Windbreaks

Many farmers construct artificial shades or windbreaks out of aluminum, steel, or other sturdy materials. These structures can be one-sided, meaning they have one wall and an overhanging roof held up with two posts, but some farms use simple open-sided sheds to protect animals from the harshest weather conditions. Portable units with wheels are especially useful in a rotational grazing system. You can move these units around to encourage the animals to distribute their manure and urine around the pasture. Where you place your shades or wind breaks depends on where you live and the direction from which cold weather rolls in.

Fences

Fencing can be one of the most costly expenditures for a new farm. For a rotational grazing program, you need both permanent and temporary fencing. The type of permanent fencing you use is a matter of personal choice. A common choice in rotational grazing systems is electrified, high-tensile wire as a permanent fence and portable electric wire for temporary paddock divisions. You also can use different fencing types for different sections of your farm: for example, high-tensile wire on one section of the farm and barbed wire in another section. The most common types of fencing material are:

- **Barbed wire:** Barbed wire fencing has sharp barbs to discourage animals from trying to cross through the fence. These fences, which usually consist of three to six strands, are strong and require little maintenance, because once they are up, they will last a while and are not as prone to sagging as electric wire fencing. However, barbed wire is unmerciful to wildlife that becomes tangled in the fence. It should never be electrified because animals — or people — could be hung on the barbs, which could be lethal.

- **Electric wire:** Use two or three strands of electrified wire stretched across posts that can be 50 or more feet apart. This is the cheapest and easiest fence to put up. It can be used as permanent fencing. Electric wire is not a physical barrier but a psychological one. Cattle easily can go through electric fencing, but if they are shocked, they will not want to. Electric wire fences can be hard for cattle to see, but if you turn them loose in a field, they will stumble upon it. After this, they will be able to sense the current when they are near one.

- **High-tensile wire:** High-tensile wire fences are easy to install and are stout, meaning they can withstand impact from large animals without snapping. Farmers usually use two to four lines of high-tensile wire, and usually two of these wires are electrified. This type of fencing requires regular maintenance to ensure wires do not sag and that weeds or tall grasses do not make contact with a line and drain its current.

- **Wood rail:** Wood rail fences are a highly visible barrier for cattle. These fences are expensive and require a lot of maintenance, as you have to keep the wood treated and painted.

- **Woven wire:** This type of wire is mesh fencing that is high strength and low maintenance. It is the most expensive fencing type. Many farmers also add a top strand of barbed or electric wire to prevent cattle from rubbing against the fence.

You can purchase wire fences in rolls of a couple hundred to a couple thousand feet. Check with your local building officials to ensure you install a legal fence. There may be height or post spacing requirements, restrictions near roadways, or other rules you must follow. Be sure to install fences on your side of the property line and not your neighbor's.

Generally, permanent cattle fences are 48 to 54 inches tall. Fencing systems also need end posts, line posts, brace posts, and gates.

- **End posts** are the cornerstones of your fence line. They usually are made of sturdy wood or steel. They must be buried deeply, about one-third to half of their total height below the ground, to withstand the pressure of being pulled by taut fencing. You also can pour cement in the hole around them for more support.

- **Brace posts** provide support for end posts. They usually are placed 6 to 8 feet away from the post being braced. An H-brace is two parallel posts with a horizontal post placed in between. Use a brace wire from the top of the brace post to the bottom of the post being braced. You could also use a diagonal brace, which is wedged between the ground and the end post and requires a brace wire. Another option for lower-tension fences is a bed log brace, which is a log buried on the tension side of the post that prevents the post from being pulled over. The University of Wisconsin-Riverside has a good guide to bracing posts at **www.uwrf. edu/grazing/bracing.pdf.**

- **Line posts** are needed to support fencing during long, straight stretches. You can buy line posts made out of wood, steel, fiberglass, or plastic.

- **Gates** need to be as wide as the animals or the machinery you plan to move through them. You can get gates as small as 4 feet, which are good for people, or as wide as 16 feet for large machines. One that is 12 to 14 feet wide will work for most tractors. Gates come in light, medium, and heavy weights. The heaviest gates are called bull gates. You would need a heavy bull gate in the sorting and handling areas near your chutes. Lighter gates should be fine if used in areas that use lightweight electric fencing.

It is also important to note that under the National Organic Program, treated wood is not allowed for fence posts or for any structures that come in contact with animals or crops. Alternatives for fence posts include naturally sturdy wood such as black locust that resists rot, or you can use alternative finishing products to treat your wood. Your organic certifier will be able to tell you what you can and cannot use. ATTRA, the common name for the National Sustainable Agriculture Information Service, provides information about sustainable agriculture.

Tools you may need to install a fence

The following represents some of the tools you need to build your own fence. Note that your needs may change depending on the type of fence you plan on building.

- Posts can be put in the ground manually with a **post-hole digger,** which is a clamshell-shaped tool used to dig, or with an **auger**, which is a drill-type tool that you attach to a tractor or a small farming vehicle called a skid steer.

- Stapler and staples that are 1 to 1 ½ inches long to attach fencing to wooden posts

- Wire stretcher or fence puller to tighten fences

- Hammer to tap smaller posts or rods into the ground

- Spinner or reel that allows you to roll or unroll wire easily

- Round crimper, which is a tool for making good electrical wire connections

- Digital voltmeter that tests grounding systems and helps you ensure that each section of line has sufficient charge throughout the system

Installing your fence

You can design the layout of your permanent fencing system by using an aerial map of your farm as a guide. These aerial photographic maps are available free at the local office of the Farm Service Agency, a division of the USDA that helps administer farm programs. This aerial photomap allows you mark your property lines and plan around existing buildings, water sources, and shaded areas.

You can install a fence yourself or hire a contractor to do it. Here are some tips for putting up fence yourself:

- If you put fence posts up by hand, wear thick gloves and eye goggles.

- Call your local utility companies to check for buried lines before you dig.

- Dig deep enough that the post will not lean; this is usually about one-third the height of the fence. Virginia Tech has a good guide to installing high-tensile wire fences that also includes good instructions for end posts and brace posts at **http://pubs.ext.vt.edu/442/442-132/442-132.html**.

When installing a fence, put up end posts first. Run a temporary wire from post to post to help keep line posts straight. The spacing between line posts will depend on the slope of the land and the type of fencing you use. (For example, you can space posts further apart on flat land, and the heavier the fence type, the closer together the posts need to be.) Posts between woven wire need to be closer than the posts for other fencing types because woven wire is heavier and needs more support; posts for woven wire should be about 10 to 14 feet apart. Line posts for barbed wire should be 14 to 16 feet apart. Posts for high-tensile wire, which is lighter than barbed wire, can be 15 to 20 feet apart, and posts for lighter electric fences can be spaced at least 40 feet apart on flat land.

Gates always should go in corners because it is easier to funnel cattle toward corners than toward a gate in the middle of the fence line. Avoid low spots because cattle like to walk uphill. Gates should be wide enough to provide access for farm equipment or trucks. Add a smaller gate to allow access so people do not climb the fence or the large gate.

Components of an electric fence system

Here are terms you may encounter as you develop an electrical fencing system:

- **Wires:** For permanent fences, use a thick wire because they carry current farther than thin wire. The USDA recommends 12.5 gauge or higher. Temporary fences can use lighter, six-strand polywire or polytape.

- **Posts:** Your fence will need end posts, which can be wood or fiberglass. Line posts can be T-posts, which must be pounded into the ground. Step-in posts, which feature a flange you can step on to push them down, are much easier to put in the ground and are a good option for temporary fencing for paddocks.

- **Insulators:** These let you attach electric wires to posts without actually touching the posts, so the current does not travel through the post into the ground. Good plastic insulators work just fine.

- **Crimping Sleeves:** These help you join two wires together. You put both lines inside the sleeve and use a crimping tool to squeeze the two lines together.

- **Line tap:** Line taps connect live wires to existing wires. They come in two styles, crimping and split bolt. Crimping-type line taps make permanent connections by splicing lines. Split bolt taps work for gates or other sections where you may not want a permanent connection.

- **Line switches:** These switches allow you to turn off current flowing through sections of fence instead of the entire line.

- **Gates:** Gates have handles that latch onto an anchor connected to a post. When they are unhooked to allow passage, these cause the wire to go dead. Instead of gates, some farmers with smaller herds carry a PVC pipe with a notch on the end, and they use the pipe to lift or lower the fence to allow passage.

- **Insulated wire**: Bury insulated wires under your gates so you do not have to turn off your fence every time you use the gate. The USDA recommends 12.5-gauge wire. For added protection, put the insulated wire in a PVC pipe. Dig a trench at least 12 inches deep then cover up the line.

- **Chargers**: Also called energizers, chargers send the current through the system. The USDA recommends a low-impedance energizer with a minimum 5,000-volt output. Low impedance means low resistance to electrical current. Another important measurement is joules, which measure the strength of the shock. The higher the joule, the greater the shock. Chargers can be powered by alternating current (AC), battery or solar energy, or dual battery/AC.

- **Ground rods**: These rods collect the energizer's electric circuit, providing the shock when something touches the fence. Ground rods should be installed near the charger, and they should be at least 6 feet long. Use as many ground rods as recommended by the energizer manufacturer.

- **Lightning arrestors and surge protectors:** These prevent the charger from electricity damage. Surge protectors keep the charger safe from common current surges. Lightning arrestors divert lightning strikes away from the charger.

Electric fencing is either used as the sole component in many fencing systems or combined with other fencing types for added protection. It is ideal as a movable interior barrier in rotational grazing systems. Electric fencing is fine to hold cattle as long as they are not crowded or spooked. Cattle are curious and will probably discover the fence on their own; when they do, they will leave it alone because the bite of an electric fence hurts. Another strategy is to introduce cattle to the electric fence. The best way to do this is to stretch a live wire across a small paddock, such as your receiving paddock, and entice the cattle to contact it. Placing the line between the cattle and a water source, or the cattle and hay, is another effective strategy for introducing your cattle to electric fencing.

Installing electric fencing is something you probably can figure out yourself. To stay safe while putting up your fence, wait until the whole system is up before you plug in your fence charger. Check your area's laws about posting warning signs on electric boundary fences and warn neighbors, children, or visitors about the fence. If you have never installed an electric fencing system before, you may want to seek advice from a trusted expert, such as an experienced farmer or a local extension agent.

Electric fences work as an incomplete circuit from the charger through the fence system — the circuit is complete when an animal, person, or anything else touching the ground contacts it. You have to check your fence frequently to make sure the current is flowing through each section and that no wires have come down. A visual inspection will detect downed lines, or lines in contact with tall weeds. This saps the current, so you will have to be sure the areas under the fence are grazed or mowed down. A digital volt meter will further help you check your line for problems.

Dairy Farm Facilities

Dairy farms can be as small as one cow, or as big as herds with more than 1,000 animals. There are several different kinds of equipment and methods used to milk these animals, from hand milking and simple bucket systems to complex mechanized milkers. If you do not have much equity, it may be better to get experience by working on someone else's land while you build your herd, to lease someone else's farm, or to purchase an old dairy farm so you can get your milking equipment when you purchase your land. The dairy market has been depressed, so it is possible to buy good used equipment at big sales when a dairy goes out of production.

Milking parlor types

If you are milking a small number of cows, you may be able to start out with a couple of homemade stalls and a portable milking machine. If you are buying an existing dairy barn, you could use the existing equipment or install new, more efficient equipment in old areas. Old dairy barns often use stanchions, or tie-stalls, to hold animals during milking. In a **bucket system**, vacuum tubes pump milk into a small bucket, and the milk is poured from the bucket into a holding container. In these systems, the operator is on level ground with the cows, so you have to bend to attach the teat cups of the milking machine. If you use a bucket system, you must also bend and lift to carry the bucket to the holding tank, or you can pour the milk through a filter directly into bottles. Pipeline systems pump milk from the milker to a holding area, eliminating the buckets and the need to carry them, but the farmer must still bend to attach the teat cups to the cow. These systems are labor-intensive but can be effective for small-scale farmers. Some stores specialize in equipment for small dairies, such as Family Milk Cow Dairy Supply Store (**www.familymilkcow.com**), which offers such equipment as milking machines and cheesemaking tools.

Newer dairy systems rely on milking parlors to reduce bending and lifting by elevating the cows above the milker, who stands in an area called the operator pit. This also cuts milking time and leaves time for other management tasks. The smallest dairies may not find these systems cost effective — just 22 percent of small organic dairies that had 50 cows or fewer use them, according to the USDA. But nearly all organic dairies with 200 cows or more use them. Many farmers will update existing barns with newer parlors. Some parlors are more basic than others. In most milking systems, the herd, or a portion of the herd, is walked to the parlor and held in a holding pen before each milking. Cattle wait behind a crowd gate for a stall to open.

Here is a list of milk parlor types:

- **Herringbone parlor**: Cows stand side-by-side, angled toward the operator pit. Milking clusters can be attached to the teats from the side of the cow, which makes it easier to see and clean front udders.

- **Parallel parlors**: Similar to herringbone parlors; cows are milked from the rear between their hind legs, which provides less udder visibility than the herringbone design. The walking distance between cows is shorter than in the herringbone design.

- **Side opening parlors**: Cows stand head to tail in these stalls. The walking distance in this system limits the number of stalls you can use in this design, but some farmers prefer this type of milking system because the entire cow is visible and can be checked for health.

- **Rotary parlor:** In this system, the milker stands in one spot while cows are rotated around as if on a carousel. This system is efficient, but labor intensive, because cows are rotated by in a matter of seconds. It probably is cost effective only on very large dairies.

- **Swing parlor**: In this system, two groups of cows stand in the parlor, one on each side of the operator, and one side is milked before the operator swings the hoses to the animals on the other side. When not in use, the milking hoses hang in the operator area. Cows are milked from the rear between their hind legs. Swing parlors are a popular option now because they are cheaper to install than other parlor types, but still increase the number of cows that can be milked in an hour.

- **Walkthrough parlors**: Cows enter from the rear, are milked on a platform, and exit forward through a gate.

You want the entire process for each milking to take less than two and a half hours because you want your cattle to be out in the pasture where they can eat and rest. In hot weather, many farmers delay the day's second milking until the evening when it is cooler. You also can use fans to cool cattle. Some dairy farmers invest in mist cooling systems to keep cows comfortable because heat-stressed cattle produce less milk per day than cows that are comfortable. Milk production can drop about 2 pounds per cow on days when temperatures top 90 degrees, according to University of Nebraska-Lincoln researchers.

Milk cooling equipment

If you plan to have a small operation, your cooling system may not be much more complicated than bottles and refrigerators. Many dairies use pipelines to transport milk from the parlor into the milk house, where the refrigerated storage tanks are kept. The temperature of milk is about 101 degrees when it leaves the udder and must be cooled to 38 to 45 degrees within two hours of milking to keep it fresh. A farmer with a small herd that sells raw milk off the farm could pour milk through a filter straight into bottles that customers take home. Most small farmers probably just need to store their milk in a **bulk tank**, which is a stainless steel refrigeration unit that keeps milk cool until collection. These tanks come in sizes from about 600 gallons to about 8,000 gallons. A common type of cooling equipment on large dairies is a **plate cooler**, which precools milk before it gets to the storage tank. The warm, fresh milk flows on opposite sides of steel plates from cool water, transferring its heat to the water. This saves electricity that would have been used to cool the milk in the holding tank.

Permanent lanes

Permanent travel lanes take on extra importance on grazing dairies because cattle are moved from the field to the barn once or twice a day for much of the year. These lanes are necessary because the cow procession is tough on the land and leads to compacted, muddy lanes. You want your travel lanes to be wide enough to move the whole herd, but there is no set formula for this. Some farmers march their animals single file like ants down 2-foot-wide lanes. Often, farmers go with 24-foot-wide lanes to allow access for tractors or other equipment.

Cows do not like walking around sharp corners, so you need gentle, looping corners. A good travel lane will be made of firm, flattened material such as clay, which is crowned in the middle like a road. It should be covered with a soft, safe, natural material such as lime so the animals' hooves are not injured during the walk. You should find materials with these general qualities that are native to your area because it is expensive to truck in materials from other areas of the country. When designing the lanes, use an aerial map, but also walk the farm to be sure there are no unexpected hills or other challenges. Match the topography so your lane does not impede the natural flow of water; otherwise, you will have to add culverts to allow water passage. Try to plan the lanes so there is natural shade so the animals do not have to make the trek in the heat.

Handling manure

Manure collects in milking areas and must be removed. If you have a small number of animals, you can just shovel the manure into a wheelbarrow and take it to a compost pile. Larger dairy barns have slots in the floors behind the animals so manure will fall into a pit beneath the floor of the barn where it can be collected later. Some dairies flush the floor with water. You also can scrape the manure with an attachment for a skid steer. This manure later can be used on your field, either as compost or sprayed directly on pasture.

Other Equipment You May Need

The equipment you invest in depends on what chores you want to handle yourself. It is best to keep your investment in equipment low, but there are many chores on the farm that you will be unable to do without machinery. You can probably get by with renting some of this equipment, or using a contract laborer who has this equipment and will do the work for you. Keep in mind that contract labor can cost about $30 to $60 per hour.

You probably could use a vehicle to get around your farm because you occasionally will need to haul heavy loads or pull other machinery. You could purchase a tractor, but they are costly and their value depreciates quickly. You can rent a small tractor from a machine rental business. If you do not own a tractor and do not want to buy a pickup truck, small-scale farmers can get by with an all-terrain vehicle that can pull small trailers, manure spreaders, and harrows. You can also get front-end attachments to plow snow or rent a skid steer, which is a versatile machine that comes with attachments for many farm chores. These attachments include augers for fence postholes and hay bale spears. You also can use one of these attachments to scrape manure from dairy floors.

Many farmers have invested in the equipment needed to make hay. However, making hay is an expensive process that requires cutting, raking, and baling. When you are first starting your farm operation, it might be better to buy hay, share equipment with a neighbor, or arrange for a contractor to make your hay for you.

Another chore you must consider is hauling animals to and from your farm. If you will need to transport animals frequently throughout the year, it may be worthwhile to own a stock trailer, which is a trailer used for hauling cattle. You also would need a truck to pull this trailer. If you will be making a limited number of trips, it may be more cost effective to hire a custom livestock hauler who will haul your cattle for you for a small fee.

When choosing to invest in facilities or equipment, it is smart to look around for cheap alternatives. The less money you tie up in equipment or buildings, the more flexibility you have in your budget, and the better your chances are of making it in the long run.

CASE STUDY: FULL CIRCLE FARMS

Dennis and Alicia Stoltzfoos
Owners, Full Circle Farms
Live Oak, Florida
thisisdennis@juno.com

Eight years ago, Dennis and Alicia Stoltzfoos started their farm with one cow and her 6-month-old calf. Back then, they were not sure anyone would be interested in their products — and Dennis Stoltzfoos was not thrilled that milking was an everyday chore. Today, Full Circle Farms is a beef, dairy, poultry, and pork operation that grosses $200,000 per year. The business succeeds for the same reason Dennis Stoltzfoos was willing to do the work — customers could not find more nutritious products anywhere else.

Dennis Stoltzfoos, the youngest of 11 children, was raised Amish/Mennonite on his father's conventional farm. He flirted with various jobs and spent 15 years in the alternative health field. In his early 20s, he was constantly bothered with various aches and pains, low energy, and allergies, and grew frustrated after a battery of tests revealed nothing wrong. His doctor told him his problems were in his head. So he started doing his own research and became a disciple of Weston A. Price, whose 1939 book *Nutrition and Physical Degeneration* demonstrated the benefits of animal fats and other natural foods versus processed modern diets.

"Your body makes 300 million new cells every minute," Stoltzfoos said. "You determine if those cells are healthy, medium, or weak by what you put in your mouth. Our goal is to make the most nutrient-dense products possible. We were not sure in the beginning if people would pay for food produced like this. The most surprising thing is that people cannot get enough. You cannot make it fast enough."

When Stoltzfoos recommitted to the year-round job of farming, he committed to the idea of sparing no expense to have the healthiest grasses for the healthiest cattle, and the healthiest products you can get. Their milk is in such demand that they charge $13 for a gallon of raw, unpasteurized milk. The prices other farmers charge varies, but $10 or less is common. They have about 100 head of cattle, including 30 Jersey milk cows. The family owns about 60 acres and leases a couple hundred more. Stoltzfoos uses creativity in his management decisions, borrowing principles from Joel Salatin, the famed Virginia farmer who preaches the benefits of using every animal as a tool for the good of the whole. For example, the farm's chickens move into paddocks when cattle move out so the chickens can scratch for fly larvae in the manure, aiding in soil fertility.

Stoltzfoos built his own milking stall for $100 with some 2-by-4 and 4-by-4 wooden boards. In the winter, he entices the cows in with alfalfa pellets or molasses in a trough; in summer, he removes the trough. He never feeds his cattle grain. He uses a milking unit from an Amish company called E-Z Milking Equipment. It is a vacuum pump with two buckets and two milkers. He empties the bucket through a strainer into a 5-gallon container with a tap, and his 8-year-old daughter uses the tap to fill 1-gallon jugs for customers. They spend about one hour per day milking.

They bought their first cow and her calf before they had land and held her at a friend's farm. They leased land for a couple of years before buying their own farm. As their farm grows, Dennis Stoltzfoos is always thinking of ways to make the farm more efficient. He wants to compost manure that collects near the barn, and make his milk parlor portable, which would eliminate the need to bring his cows into the barn from a half mile away. Portable parlors are not a new idea — other farmers use variations — but his version would be unique. He would model it after a poultry schooner, which is a chicken house that can be moved across pasture.

"I want to take what we have and put it in a hoop structure, like a 14-by-28 poultry schooner, and scoot it around on the pasture every day. Or move the whole thing once a week and never have to bring the cows into the barn.

Our portable milking parlor would be very small. That is what I am attracted to: Instead of getting peanuts for your milk, get a good price and have fewer cows. Small is beautiful, and life cannot get any better than on a small family farm."

Water Troughs

Water troughs are a good way to ensure clean drinking water for your animals and to prevent pollution in streams and ponds. Portable water troughs are an inexpensive way to ensure your animals can quench their thirst from any paddock. You can get portable tanks at farm stores in various sizes, from 15 gallons to more than 900 gallons. You might pay between $100 and $300 a tank. Two companies that ship plastic troughs are Go-To-Tanks (**www.gototanks.com**) and Plastic-Mart (**www.plastic-mart.com**). Some farmers do not like portable water tanks because they must be moved each time you rotate your herd, but this should not be a problem if you rotate your troughs the same time you rotate your paddock. Each has a drain plug that you can pull to empty the tank before you move it. You can buy insulated troughs or heaters to prevent them from freezing in winter. The water to fill these tanks can come from many sources, including wells, streams, ponds, or public water systems. Using public water systems provides a reliable source of clean water, but this could be expensive, depending on your local rates.

You can be creative and save money on troughs; for example, you could cut a plastic drum in half to make two troughs. You can supply water to these tanks with a simple irrigation pipe, which is available at farm supply stores. You can plan your paddocks so that several paddocks can share pipes. Leave slack in the pipes when you lay them across pasture to give the joints flexibility during freezing and thawing. Treat these pipes the same as you would water pipes or garden hoses around your house to protect from freezing — drain the pipe before freezing so it does not split when ice expands, or leave your water source on a slow drip. You can bury these pipes if you want, but for a novice farmer, it is probably better to leave them above ground to give you flexibility to make adjustments in your grazing scheme.

There are also different ways to pump water into these systems. Water pumps can be powered by electricity, gas, wind, solar energy, or gravity, if the water source is above or below the tank. There are also pumps powered by the cattle's noses — as the animals reach for water, they hit a lever that pumps water into the tank. You can buy full-flow valves, which monitor water levels and automatically refill the tank, for less than $30.

How to Introduce New Animals

You should have a plan for bringing new animals, such as new bulls, replacement heifers, or stockers, onto your farm. A term for this type of plan is **biosecurity**, which means preventive steps you take to keep new illnesses from infecting your animals. When you purchase new animals, make sure they are transported to your farm in a clean vehicle and kept in a designated training pen. You should keep the new animals in the training pen, or quarantine pen, for at least two weeks — 30 days is optimal — before letting them in with the rest of your herd. If you notice that some of your new animals are sick, you can further isolate them in a sick pen. It is permissible for the new animals to be visible to the animals that are not quarantined, but they should not be able to touch or to even get within a few feet of each other so potentially sick animals do not infect the animals that have been on your farm a while. These pens should have their own feeders or water troughs to prevent contamination of the food and water of the rest of your herd.

You should move any animals showing signs of sickness into the sick area. If they show signs of sickness, take their temperature, and if any of them develop a fever or other illnesses, have your veterinarian check the animal. While these animals are quarantined, you should vaccinate them, treat them for parasites, or worm them.

Other strategies for preventing new animals from potentially infecting your herd include milking new animals last and sanitizing the equipment afterward, which you would do anyway. You also can choose to wear different boots and clothing when working with animals in the quarantine pen. You can graze your animals near the sick corral, but you should not introduce quarantined animals to the entire herd until a month passes to be sure none of the new animals are sick.

When to Cull

One way to improve your herd over time is to cull the underachievers so your breeding stock will consist only of the best performers. **Culling** means selling animals you do not want to raise anymore; these are animals that you do not want to use for breeding or to continue to grow for beef or milk. Here are some criteria to consider when culling:

- **Temperament**: Temperament is an important factor to consider. A high-strung or nervous animal will be high maintenance and, in the end, their meat probably will not be good quality. Animals that are frequently stressed produce hormones, including adrenaline, that make their meat tough. It is normal for animals to be wary of you at first, but it is not normal for them to try to jump the fence every time they see you. If they are this nervous, you must get rid of them. You do not want aggressive animals, but you also do not want shy animals because they often get crowded out of feed or water and will not get all the nutrition or water they need, which will keep them from growing as fast or producing as much milk as they should.

- **Fertility**: If your cow shows signs of infertility or other reproductive issues, she should be culled. If you put a cow with a healthy bull for 60 days and she is not pregnant, there is something wrong with her. Those that breed late also can be culled. Occasionally, if a heifer fails to breed — known as an **open heifer** — some farmers will keep her around for another season just because buying a replacement would be expensive. Usually, because it is expensive to feed a heifer that may have trouble breeding the following year, open heifers are culled.

- **Prone to disease**: If an animal gets sick and you cannot get it healthy, you should sell it at an auction; it likely will be bought by a large-scale beef producer and will probably end up as fast-food hamburger. If you cannot get rid of worms in two treatments, get rid of the affected cow. If it has chronic eye problems, or shows early signs of cancer eye, it should be culled.

- **Performance**: Calves with low weaning weights should be candidates for early sale. If a cow's first couple of calves have low weaning weights, it might be best to sell her at auction, too.

It takes time to build a good herd. Good farmers continuously monitor their animals to identify their best producers, and the ones that are not suited for success. As you gain experience buying, selling, and breeding animals, the quality of your herd will continue to improve.

Necessary Nutrition

A cow needs about 26 pounds of dry matter intake (DMI) each day. Cattle also need this daily dry matter intake to obtain the necessary amounts of various nutrients. The biggest of these necessities is protein. Cattle usually require about 7 to 14 percent crude protein in their dry matter intake, according to the ATTRA publication "Cattle Production: Consideration for Pasture-Based Beef and Dairy Producers." Dairy cattle, cows in late-term pregnancy, lactating beef cattle, and pregnant heifers have higher nutritional needs than animals such as stocker cattle. Cattle that are not growing, such as early-term pregnant cows that reach maturity or healthy bulls, have lower nutritional requirements.

You can have cut pasture grasses, hay, or silage analyzed to learn the nutritional content of your herd's food supply. The National Forage Testing Association certifies labs to ensure the accuracy of forage tests. You can see a list of these labs on its website (**www.foragetesting.org**). If you get your forage analyzed, the key measurements are total digestible nutrients (TDN) and crude protein (CP). Forage with 10 to 13 percent CP and 55 to 60 percent TDN should provide adequate nutrition for all members of your cattle herd, according to ATTRA. Typical pastures in the vegetative stage, and even the boot stage, meet these benchmarks. Legumes in the vegetative state can contain more than 20 percent crude protein.

On high-quality pastures, cattle may need to be supplemented with fiber such as soybean hulls to help them more efficiently use protein. If pasture is lower quality, cattle may need to be supplemented with protein such as cottonseed meal. You can feed these supplements by either leaving them in the pasture or by using portable feeders such as troughs you can move around the pasture.

Cattle can get most of their nutritional needs straight from pasture grasses. But you also will have to provide your cattle with mineral supplements to replace salt lost in urine, help produce milk, develop fetuses, and help with general body functions. These generally are given in a premixed ration, either as loose granules or in block form, which are placed in mineral feeders. You may need different mixes at different seasons. For example, in spring when grass is growing quickly, cattle often do not get all the magnesium they need, and they need a higher percentage of magnesium in their mix. Selenium also is commonly deficient in soils. Local universities or feed stores can recommend a mineral mix for you.

In winter, many farmers use energy licks to supplement hay and dormant pastures. These licks, which can be put in the pasture so animals are free to eat from them, consist of a protein source, an energy source, and usually molasses. They can be formulated into 40-pound blocks up to 200-plus-pound tubs, and they are left in the pasture for cattle to lick. You can purchase these licks at farm feed stores. You have to be careful and read about the ingredients in these licks because sometimes they use animal byproducts, which are often avoided by grass-fed and organic farmers since they are not a natural diet for cattle.

Body Condition Score

Beef farmers can gauge the health of their animals by using a body condition score system. This score is used as a guideline to help you identify healthy, overweight, and undernourished animals. Monitoring the body condition score will allow you to spot animals that are in danger of slipping to unhealthy levels, which reduces fertility. If a heifer is in danger of losing her body condition, you could supplement her feed or even wean her calf early. You may also wish to cull cows that have difficulty maintaining a desirable score. Some farmers have the whole system memorized; others learn to recognize a fat or undernourished animal and adjust its feed accordingly.

There are separate scoring systems for beef and dairy cattle. Beef cattle are measured on a system from 1 to 9. A score of 1 means the animal is nearly starving; a score of 9 means the animal is obese; and scores between 5 and 7 are optimal. Ohio State University has pictures of animals in each condition at **http://ohioline.osu.edu/l292/index.html** in its fact sheet "Scoring Animals Can Improve Profits."

Here is an overview of each number in a typical beef body condition scoring system:

1 is emaciated, with no fat left and very little muscle left. The animal may barely be able to stand. An animal in this condition is probably suffering from a disease or parasites.

2 is very thin. You can see the bones of the animal, and there is quite a bit of muscle loss.

3 is thin. You can see the animal's foreribs, which are roughly in the center of the animal. You can feel each point of the spine.

4 is still thin but closer to being a healthier weight. There is some fat on the animal and the spine is not obvious to the touch.

5 is not fat or thin. The animal is starting to flesh out around the ribs, shoulder, and tail.

6 is good. There is some fat on the back, the hips, and the brisket, which is the front area below the neck.

7 is the best condition. The animal has fat on its back and the base of its tail. This fat can be used as a stored reserve in winter.

8 is fat. The bone structure is no longer visible.

9 is extremely obese.

Heifers at calving should be at about 6. Heifers with more fat than this are more likely to have reproductive difficulties or problems calving. Make sure they maintain a score around 5 or 6 after calving until it is time to breed them again. Mature cows are not growing and can calve successfully with a score of 5.

You do not want a fat bull because this lowers fertility, especially if fat collects in the scrotum. You can keep him within a range of 5 to 7. Bulls have high nutrition requirements during the breeding system. You have to watch them to make sure they do not lose weight. Bulls expend more energy than they take in while they concentrate on breeding. You can give them nutritional or energy supplements during this period.

There is a similar scoring system for dairy cattle, with 1 being thin and 5 being obese. Dairy cattle usually should be between 2.5 and 4. Judging a dairy cow's score under this system depends more on the appearance of the flesh around the pin and hook bones and tailhead, which are visible on the back of the cow. Hook bones are at the corner of the top of the rump, and pin bones are at the bottom of the pelvic area, near the midway point of the tail. The tailhead is the base of the tail. The University of Arkansas published a guide, "Body Condition Scoring With Dairy Cattle," that has pictures of cows in each condition score. (You can view it at **www.uaex.edu/other_Areas/Publications/PDF/FSA-4008.pdf**.) Here is an overview of each point in a typical dairy body condition scoring system:

1 is a very undernourished animal. The pin and hook bones are visible, and there is a cavity around the tail head. You can see individual ribs.

2 is also undernourished. The ribs, pin and hook bones, and cavity around the tail head are not as visible, but you can easily feel these bones if you touch the animal.

3 is good condition. The area around the pin and hook bones is smooth.

4 is a fat animal. All bones are covered with fat, and the area around the pin and hook bones is flat. Cows or heifers that score above 4 could have calving difficulties.

5 is obese. There are fat folds covering all bones and the tail head.

Knowing When an Animal Is Ready for Slaughter

Determining when an animal is finished can be tricky. Producers with scales can set an ideal target weight and use a portable scale to weigh their animals occasionally to see how they are progressing. If you do not have a scale, you might be able to determine visually when an animal is finished. Smaller-framed animals that gain weight quickly might not need to be very heavy, but experienced farmers get good at telling which animals are ready for slaughter. Look at areas of the body where fat is especially visible, such as the rump, sides, and back. For example, a fat, fully finished animal will have a rounded rump around the base of the tail head, flat, smooth sides with no indentations, and a flat back. Also, check out the brisket area between the front legs — if these sections are getting fat, the animal is probably getting close to finishing.

Completing the Life Cycle

A healthy beef cow can stay productive at least 12 years and often 15, 18 or even more. Some experts would recommend selling after age 12 because after this, the odds go up that the cow will die on the farm, and you might not be able to butcher it for hamburger or sell it to someone else who will turn it into hamburger (the price you receive for selling an older or unproductive animal is called salvage value).

Most bulls are used for about four or five years before they are sold. After this, the chances of reduced fertility increase. If you have a bull that you really like, you may feel it is worth the risk of decreased fertility to keep him longer than four or five years. This will depend mostly on if he is still impregnating a high percentage of cows. If he still seems viable, you can try to keep him another year. If conception rates seem to be dropping, or if it seems as though his libido is decreasing, it may be time to get rid of him. You can also have a vet give him a soundness exam a couple of months before the breeding season to make sure he is still up to the job.

It is normal for farmers to feel sadness when taking their cattle to slaughter. Farmers spend lots of time with their herd, and they often form a bond with their animals, which come to trust and depend on the farmer for food. Many farmers often become affectionate toward animals that have been especially good to them, such as a good bull or a cow that delivered many good calves. So naturally, it can be tough to send them off to slaughter. But farmers can take comfort in knowing that this is the life cycle for their animals, and that their animals are dying for a worthy purpose. They also can take comfort in knowing that they gave their cattle a good, healthy life that was as close to natural as possible.

Beef and Dairy Processing

The goal of beef and dairy cattle farming is to harvest meat and milk that can be sold as products customers want. In beef production, "processing" usually refers to harvesting (a term often used instead of slaughtering) the animals and cutting and packaging the meat. For dairy production, milk processing involves pasteurization or turning milk into other packaged products. In some states, it is also legal to sell bottled raw fluid milk. Many farmers have found they can get the most value from their products by making processing arrangements that allow them to sell their meat or milk directly to their customers. This is a better option than selling their animals to feedlots or selling their milk on the commodities market where quantity can be more important than quality.

Dairies must decide what kinds of products they want to sell. Do they want to bottle it and sell it as raw or as pasteurized grass-fed milk, or do they want to convert the milk into cheeses, yogurts, or other products that may also have added value to customers? Either way, they must either find the best processor to fit their goals or learn how to do these tasks themselves. A growing number of small dairies are processing their milk themselves, either by bottling on the farm or by making their own products, such as cheeses and yogurts. Dairy producers who do not process their milk on their farms must pay someone to process and package their products for them, participate in a cooperative that has a processing arrangement, or sell to a processing company that buys milk to make its own products.

Some farmers butcher their animals themselves, but most must take their animals off-farm to be killed and butchered. Usually, they load the animals into a cattle trailer and ship them to a slaughterhouse. When the animals arrive at these processing facilities, they usually are stunned unconscious, then hung up and cut so they bleed to death. Then they are skinned, their heads and organs are removed, and the remaining meat is split in half (these halves are called sides). These sides can be cut further into familiar retail cuts.

Knowing the Laws

Farmers must follow many laws at the federal, state, and local level. Because lawmakers are concerned about the safety of the food people eat, this is especially true in regards to processing. There are laws about how to clean equipment in slaughterhouses and dairy barns and how to store meat in butchers' freezers. These laws are intended to keep people safe, and many of the guidelines are necessary and effective. But many laws also are intended for large-scale productions, and the fine print or strict requirements can cause headaches for smaller farmers and processors. It is important to know your state's laws about selling your products. The best way to find out what you can and cannot do is to ask someone who works at your state Department of Agriculture or a local extension office.

Beef

Where beef is slaughtered and butchered and where and how dairy products are processed affect where and to whom you can sell. Government officials must inspect beef-slaughtering facilities. If you want to sell individual cuts to people, restaurants, or retail outlets, the carcass must be inspected. State and federally inspected processing plants have the same requirements to ensure that meat is safe to eat. To sell your meat across state lines, you must slaughter your animals at a plant that is federally inspected — which means, among other things, a federal inspector will check each animal. Individual states may have other laws regarding the sale of meat that is processed in state-inspected plants. For example, in Kentucky, you only can sell individual cuts of beef if the carcass is federally inspected, but in Indiana, you can sell individual cuts if it is state or federally inspected. If you have questions, the people you work with along the way — at the slaughterhouse, butcher, and retail outlets — will have a good idea of the laws in your state. Government officials and extension agents also can be reached for help.

Another option you have is to use facilities that are called **custom-exempt plants**. At these plants, only the facilities (not the cattle) are inspected by state inspectors. Often, these smaller, low-volume plants cannot justify the cost of the plant upgrades required under federal regulations. These plants only are allowed to slaughter and process animals for the use of the owner and nonpaying guests. Federal and state inspectors these facilities, but they cannot afford to keep regular inspectors around the way larger plants do. If you are raising cattle to supply beef only for your family, or if you reach a deal with customers to buy a percentage (usually one quarter or one half) of one of your animals while it is alive, you can slaughter the animal at a custom-exempt facility. Usually, the cattle farmer keeps the animal until it is time to transport it to the slaughtering facility. The percentage of the animal owned is sometimes referred to as a share.

Theoretically, a large number of families can own shares in a beef animal, but some states limit the number of people who can own shares in a single animal on the grounds that if more than a small number of people own shares, you are just skirting the laws about selling individual cuts from an animal that was inspected at a facility with an on-site inspector.

Dairies

You may need permits or licenses to sell milk off your farm or to process milk on your farm. Check with your state Department of Agriculture to see which rules apply to you.

One of the most hotly debated legal issues for grass-fed dairies is selling raw milk. Though some dairies prefer to sell pasteurized milk and dairy products, others are passionate about raw, unpasteurized milk. Most milk sold in the United States is pasteurized — heated up enough that it will kill bacteria. This practice was started decades ago when unsanitary conditions on farms encouraged the spread of disease such as brucellosis. But supporters of raw milk sales say sanitary conditions on modern-day family farms have improved greatly, making pasteurization unnecessary. They say pasteurization kills beneficial bacteria, enzymes, and minerals. One organization that advocates for raw milk is the Weston A. Price Foundation (**www.westonaprice.org**). Many health experts disagree and say drinking raw milk is risky because there is a chance this milk could carry E. coli bacteria or salmonella.

Because of these health concerns, many states do not allow the sale of raw milk. It is legal to drink raw milk from your own animals, so in some states, farmers get around these restrictions by selling milk shares. Owning a milk share means you actually own a percentage of the animal. Some farmers who sell shares also charge a housing fee to shareowners. Shareowners can then come to the farm at prearranged times to pick up milk from their cow. However, some states specifically outlaw these shares. Again, it is important to check with your state Department of Agriculture to determine which rules you must follow.

To get an idea of the national picture involving raw milk sells, the Farm-to-Consumer Legal Defense Fund, a nonprofit group that pools resources to fight for the rights of family farms and consumers, has an interactive map that provides an overview of raw milk laws around the country on its website (**www.farmtoconsumer.org**). It is legal to sell raw milk in Pennsylvania, Connecticut, Maine, New Hampshire, Idaho, Washington, California, Arizona, South Carolina, and New Mexico. It is illegal in Montana, Nevada, Louisiana, Iowa, Wisconsin, West Virginia, Maryland, Delaware, Rhode Island, Washington, D.C., and New Jersey. This interactive map can give you a look at the big picture regarding raw milk sales in the United States, but — this cannot be stressed enough — you should contact your state department of agriculture to be sure you know what laws you must follow.

How to Choose a Slaughterhouse

Another big issue for beef farmers is finding a place to have their animals slaughtered. There are not that many facilities, and many of them cater to large producers. The challenges for beef farmers are finding a facility within a reasonable distance from their farm that can do all the necessary work. Being loaded into cattle trailers and hauled many miles down the road is stressful to animals. The shorter the trip, the better, but some farmers have no choice but to truck their animals hundreds of miles away. Once you find a facility to harvest your animals, you usually need an appointment because even small- and medium-size facilities often have waiting lists. These appointments may need to be made many weeks in advance.

Some slaughterhouses also have a meat cutter on site, but some only kill. If you find a facility that only kills, your cattle may have to be taken by refrigerated truck to a place where they can be cut and packaged. You can find these facilities through your state Department of Agriculture, which keeps a list of processors, including whether they only kill, only cut, or both.

Be sure to visit slaughterhouses when you are choosing the facility you want to sell your cattle to. When you visit, call ahead and let them know you are coming because they may be more accommodating if they were expecting you than if you drop in unannounced. When you visit, talk to people, and see what kind of feeling you get from the employees. You want to work with people who respect the animals and take pride in the job they do. Slaughterhouses are noisy places, but watch the way people work — they should seem calm and in control. Look for facilities that adhere to the same principles as you did when designing your handling facilities — rounded walkways aimed at working with the animals' natural instincts.

Organic slaughter and butchering

Producers who want the organic label also must be careful in choosing processors. Organic-labeled products must be processed and handled by organic-certified operators — that means slaughterers, milk processors, and packers. These facilities also often produce conventionally raised beef, so they must take extra precautions to ensure that organically raised beef is kept separate throughout the process. One of the key attractions to organic food is that it is pure of the chemicals found in conventional agriculture, and this must continue through slaughter and processing. Such precautions to ensure this purity during the slaughtering stage include handling the organic animals first before the facilities have been exposed to conventionally raised animals that day and keeping the different types of animals in separate holding areas.

Mobile processors

Mobile processors have been growing in popularity because they offer an alternative to the long wait times at larger facilities and because they eliminate the stress of transport on live animals. These are often mobile trailers where animals can be killed, cut into sides and quarters, and chilled. Sometimes the carcasses have to be taken to a butcher off-premise for final cutting and wrapping, and these trucks can do this for you. Some are USDA inspected and some are organic. Local farming experts will know if a mobile processor could be available to you.

Meat Cutting

A meat cutter — also called a butcher — cuts your beef into retail cuts. This section provides an overview of how this is accomplished. Here are some beef processing terms you should know:

- **Hanging weight:** The weight of a side of beef as it hangs on the rail in a meat cooler. This is after excess fat and bones have been removed. Most beef is priced based on the hanging weight. Hanging weight is also sometimes called "dress weight" or "dress percentage."

- **Carcass yield:** Slaughtered animals will yield between 55 and 68 percent of their live weight for meat (the rest of the animal were blood, guts, bones, hide, and other material). The exact percentage will vary depending on breed, sex, and body condition of the animal.

- **Trim:** Meat left over after the butcher removes the best cuts. Trim is used for ground beef, roasts, or other lower-cost cuts.

Aging

When choosing a butcher, you want to make sure he or she has room to hang your beef for as long as you need. Meat needs to be aged after slaughter and before it is cut. **Aging** means letting the sides or quarters hang in the freezer for several days so that natural enzymes can break down connective tissues that make meat tough.

There are two ways to do this:

- Wet aged meat is stored in vacuum packaging and allowed to age in its own juices, usually for about seven days. Most mass-produced beef is wet aged. It is a cheaper and quicker process than dry aging. Unlike in the dry-aging process, you do not lose meat volume to shrinkage. Some niche producers also prefer wet aging because it preserves many of the meat's juices.

- Dry aging is the preferred method of most small farmers because those who do it consider this process to produce a more intense flavor. Dry-aged beef is hung in the open air. Tough muscle tissues are allowed to break down, producing tenderer meat. Dry-aged beef usually hangs for ten to 14 days. Fat on the carcass determines how long it hangs. If there is not much fat, it cannot hang as long. Beef shrinks about 15 percent in the dry-aging process.

Many grass-fed beef farmers complain about laws they must follow to cool their meat. Laws require meat to be hung in the freezer within an hour of slaughter. But for a couple of hours after cattle are slaughtered, their muscle tissues release an enzyme that keeps their tissues from tightening up, which essentially tenderizes the meat. Meat that cools down soon after slaughter does not reap the benefits of this enzyme. This is not as big an issue for grain-fed meat because these carcasses contain more fat, which insulates the meat and prevents it from cooling so fast the enzyme does not work. Grass-finished beef does not have this protective layer of fat, so the enzyme is rendered ineffective, and the meat becomes tough.

USDA grades

You can pay the USDA to assign each animal's beef a grade that indicates the tenderness and flavor of the meat. The grading system is based on age (younger beef is tenderer) and marbling (fat that grows between muscle fibers, which is a factor in flavor and juiciness). Under this system, the greater amount of marbling and the younger the beef, the better the grade. Grass-fed beef shows less marbling than grain-fed beef, even between two products that are comparable in tenderness. The grading system usually favors grain-finishing, so many grass-fed producers choose not to get their meat graded, and many producers explain this decision on their websites.

Here is a look at the USDA grades. The three main grades of beef are Prime (considered the best grade), Choice, and Select. There are also degrees of grades — high, medium, and low. Medium grades are rarely included, and high and low grades are given most often.

- **Prime:** Considered the best-quality meat. It has the most marbling and comes from animals that are finished at younger ages. Prime cuts are the rarest cuts and are usually only found at top-quality restaurants. These cuts are also the most expensive.

- **Choice**: Usually considered a notch below prime and has less marbling. Choice cuts are considered very good quality, but more affordable than prime cuts.

- **Select**: This cut is leaner than choice or prime, which is common for grass-finished animals. Even though grass-fed beef often grades lower than grain-finished meat, the products can be comparable in quality.

There are other grades — standard, commercial, utility, cutter, and canner — but meat of these levels of quality are not sold retail. Lower grades are used in low quality products, such as canned meats.

Know your cuts of meat

Customers can buy the whole animal, sides (half the animal cut lengthwise), or quarters. You also can sell your animal on the hoof, which means you sell the animal or shares of the animal when it is still alive. Beef from animals sold on the hoof is sold in bulk, usually in halves or quarters. You also can sell quarters of the animal, such as a forequarter or a hindquarter. Selling in quarters can be difficult because the best cuts come from the middle and back of the animal and it can be hard to get rid of cuts that come only from the front of the animal. Selling split sides is a way to sell a quarter of the animal and mix up the cuts — a split side is half the meat from a side of beef including cuts from the front and back.

Not every beef animal is cut the same way. You need to be able to tell your butcher some basic things about the cuts you want. If you are unsure, the cutter will be able to offer advice and suggestions. As you get used to the process, and as you get feedback from your customers, you will start to get a feel for what customers want and what they do not. Individual customers also may want different things — some want a small number of thick steak cuts, others may want more steaks with thinner cuts. If you sell a whole side of beef, it can be cut exactly the way the customer wants it. If you sell split sides, it is difficult to do custom cuts unless both customers want the same thing.

A beef carcass is automatically split into sides, but you also can think of it as being divided into quarters, two forequarters in the front and two hindquarters in the back. In general, the best, tenderest steak cuts come from the rear quarter of the animal, except for the ribeye, which comes from the front part of the middle section and is included with the forequarter. The less tender cuts come from the heavily exercised areas, including the shoulders and rump areas.

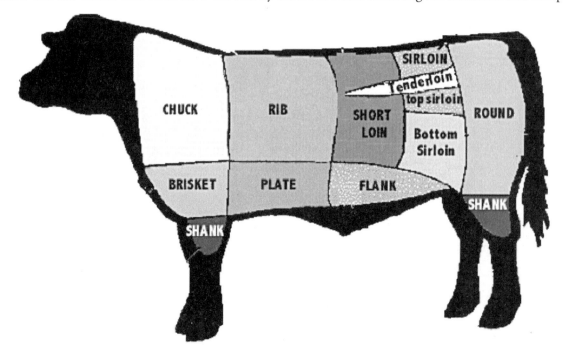

Courtesy of the California Department of Food and Agriculture

From the chuck area at the top of the forequarters, you can get several roasts (chuck eye, seven-bone, boneless chuck pot roast, cross rib pot roast, under blade pot roast, blade roast), top blade steak, flat iron steak, and short rib steak. This is where a lot of ground beef and stew beef come from.

From the ribs, you can get rib roasts, rib steak, rib eye roast, rib eye roast, and back ribs.

From the lower forequarter, you can get briskets (whole or half), or a shank cross cut. This is also where ground beef type cuts come from.

From the lower midsection of the underside, you can get flank steak, flank steak rolls, or fajita meat.

From the top middle (short loin and sirloin), you get most of the expensive cuts: T-bone steak, sirloin steak, porterhouse steak, filet mignon (tenderloin steak and tenderloin roast), top loin steak.

From the rump/round area: rump roast, top round steak, tip steak, tip roast, kabob cubes, eye round steak, bottom round roast.

Wrapping

You also should consider how butchers wrap their products. Some wrap them in plastic and cover them with white paper. If you are selling individual cuts, you may want a butcher who uses transparent vacuum wrapping to allow customers to see the meat inside the package before they buy.

Pricing

You will base your price on the desired profit you want to make; take into account your expenses per pound. You should put a monetary value on your time and labor. You can set your prices by the pound — either by live weight, hanging weight, or dress percentage — or you can just decide on a number you think is fair, if customers will pay it.

You can determine a range to charge for your meat by checking prices farmers in your region with similar operations will charge. This will depend, in part, on what customers in your area will pay. For example, you will be more likely to find high-paying customers in New York City or Los Angeles than in Metropolis, Illinois. Like any business, you will need to sell for more than what you pay in expenses. So, figure what you spent during the year on seeds, fertilizers, vaccines, gasoline for farm equipment, and anything else you needed to keep your farm going, and use that to determine how much you need to make from each animal to be profitable.

People who sell shares or in bulk usually price by the pound according to live weight, but you also can sell by dress weight because you probably will get differing amounts of meat from two live animals that weigh the same. People who sell individual cuts often also sell by the pound, but each pound is not created equally. You would need to sell your steaks for high enough per pound to balance out the lower price per pound of hamburger.

Dairy Processing

When you produce milk, you can drink it yourself, sell it, or turn it into other products to eat or sell. Milk must be cooled quickly, or it will spoil. Raw milk has a shelf life of a week or a little more. The shelf life of pasteurized milk is two to three weeks. Milk can be processed into other products to help preserve it. Farmers selling milk conventionally often contract to market their milk through a milk marketing cooperative. More than 85 percent of milk in the United

States is marketed through milk marketing cooperatives, which may bottle or process the milk themselves under a farmer-owned brand (one you may know is Land-O-Lakes butter) or sell the bulk milk to private processing companies that will package it as fluid milk or other products and sell it around the country. These farmers pump their milk into a bulk tank. Contracted milk haulers collect from these bulk tanks at least every other day.

Conventionally sold milk is always pasteurized. **Pasteurization** is the process of heating milk to kill bacteria. There are three main methods of pasteurization:

- **Batch pasteurization:** This old-school method of pasteurization involves heating milk in a vat to 145 degrees F and maintaining the heat for 30 minutes. Batch pasteurization is used on milk that will be made into cheese, yogurt, and other value-added products.

- **High Temperature/Short Time (HTST) pasteurization:** Milk is heated to least 161 degrees F for at least 15 seconds. This is the most common method used in the United States.

- **Ultrapasteurization (UHT):** Milk is heated to 280 degrees F for two seconds.

If milk is kept unopened after UHT, it does not have to be refrigerated for up to three months and can be shipped warm.

Many on-farm bottling dairies pasteurize their milk because many states require it by law. These dairies can pasteurize their products on the farm using a pasteurizing machine. The HTST method usually is preferred because it is quicker than batch pasteurizing but does not kill all bacteria — harmful or beneficial — the way ultrapasteurization does. You can buy pasteurizers from specialty dairy suppliers, as small as 2 gallons or as big as 300 gallons. You also could pasteurize milk on your stove if you cook it at the right time and temperature.

Conventionally sold milk also is **homogenized**, which means a machine is used to break up fat globules into small pieces so the cream will not rise to the top. Many dairy farmers choose not to homogenize their dairy products because they prefer the more natural product with cream at the top. However, some creameries do offer customers the option of getting homogenized milk.

Whole milk is milk that has not had fat removed. Whole milk has at least 3.25 percent butterfat; the milk from Jerseys can contain 5 percent milkfat or more. This fat can also be used to make other products such as butter or cheese. Not all grass-fed dairies sell raw milk or just whole milk. Some farmers make grass-fed skim milk or reduced-fat milk such as 2 percent milk, 1 percent milk, and fat-free milk. Some grass-fed dairies also sell chocolate milk.

You can make many other products from milk. Making these products requires extra equipment and considerable skill, so you should take time to study each product, and take time to learn how to make them from someone offering classes or farm internships. ATTRA has a list of farm internships at **http://attra.ncat.org/attra-pub/internships**.

The following are some of the dairy items you can create using milk from your cattle:

- **Cheese:** This is usually made from whole milk, but you also can make it from skim milk or cream. Cheese is made by using enzymes or cultures to separate the solids, called curds, from liquids, called whey. The solids are pressed into a cheese shape and, depending on the type of cheese you hope to create, some are allowed to age for many months or even years. Cheeses made from unpasteurized milk must age for 60 days. Cheese can be cut into smaller pieces for sale or sold in big wheels.

- **Whey:** A byproduct of cheesemaking. It can be sold as a health product or used to feed hogs, which can also be sold later for meat.

- **Cream:** A dairy product made from butterfat. Cream from grass-fed cattle usually has a more yellow color than cream from a grain-fed cow; this is a reflection of the extra beta-carotene from the all-forage diet.

- **Butter:** A product made from milkfat. Under federal law, it must be at least 80 percent milkfat. Some dairies sell unpasteurized butter. Butter can be frozen and sold year-round.

- **Whipped butter:** The same as regular butter, but it is whipped so it is easier to spread.

- **Yogurt:** Fermented with live bacteria cultures. These cultures make them easier to digest and boost the immune system.

- **Ice cream:** Ice cream made from grass-fed milk, especially without artificial colors and flavors, is a healthier option than mass-produced ice cream.

- **Sour cream:** Made by adding bacteria that sour the cream

Selling to other companies

You will not have to worry about processing if you sell to other companies because these companies will process your milk into whatever products they sell. Selling to other companies usually involves a contract, and you must produce your milk to their standards. Often, you also are not allowed to use your milk for any other sales purpose, and you must give it all to the company you are contracting with.

Cooperatives

You may also be able to join a milk-marketing cooperative. **Cooperatives** are groups of farmers who share resources and market their collective products under one brand name. An existing dairy cooperative probably already has an arrangement with a processing company. An example of a cooperative is PastureLand, a group of grass-fed organic farmers based in Minnesota. Beef farmers also can form cooperatives. An example is the brand Wisconsin Meadows, a group of Wisconsin farmers.

Farmstead processing

As mentioned earlier, many farmers who target niche markets find that they can get the best price for their products by producing it and marketing it themselves. If you want to make a living selling dairy products, on-farm processing is a big undertaking that will require an additional investment in equipment and training; some dairies also employ an additional person to do the actual processing. You will have to weigh the costs of these undertakings against the goals of your farm. It easily could cost a few thousand dollars to buy equipment such as a cheese vat, a cream separator, and packaging equipment. If you just want to make products yourself, there are companies that specialize in less costly, kitchen-size equipment, such as New England Cheesemaking Supply Company (**www.cheesemaking.com**) and Glengarry Cheesemaking and Dairy Supply (**www.glengarrycheesemaking.on.ca**). You may be able to find deals on used dairy equipment at auctions or online. You also will need packaging equipment and coolers or freezers to store your products.

If you process on your farm, it would be a good idea to take classes to learn these skills. Farmers or extension offices in your area may know of classes offered, or they may offer on-farm apprenticeships. Many dairy farms that process on site have a full-time employee to run the processing side of the business; you might even find this to be a good income for another family member. It would take time to learn these processes, so you would need to be comfortable in your livestock management skills before you took on this second endeavor.

Co-packing

If you wanted to market your own line of dairy products but you do not have the know-how or the desire to make your own dairy products, you could pay a local cheese plant to do this for you. A company that packages products to your specifications is called a **co-packer**. You would send these companies your milk, and they would turn it into cheese (or whatever dairy product you choose to make) and put your label on it. You would then be responsible for marketing the product yourself. *You will learn more about marketing strategies at the end of this chapter.*

CASE STUDY: WHITE OAK PASTURES

Will Harris, owner
White Oak Pastures
Bluffton, Georgia
http://whiteoakpastures.com

Will Harris used to take his beef cattle to a slaughtering facility nine miles from his farm in Bluffton, Georgia. When the facility closed, his next-best option was 90 miles away. Though many beef producers truck their animals to slaughterhouses even greater distances, Harris decided this plant was just too far away from his farm. So, Harris, whose grass-fed meats can be found in several states in the Eastern United States, did what only a handful of producers have done. He built his own processing plant.

The 5,300-square-foot plant, which cost $2.2 million dollars, opened in 2008. It is USDA inspected, which allows him to sell individual cuts and to sell his products in other states. The plant employs about 25 people and harvests about 18 animals per day, including many from farms in the surrounding area. Harris built it with sustainable features so nothing is wasted. Solar panels provide the energy to heat water, which is then recycled for irrigation; waste products such as bones and internal organs are used as fertilizer; hides are sold for leather.

His processing facility adheres to principles Harris himself searched for when choosing facilities in the past. His farm is certified by the Certified Humane Raised and Handled program, which means his animals were given the space and environment to engage in natural behaviors from birth to slaughter and were not given antibiotics or hormones. He did not like hauling his animals 100 miles away. He knows not everyone will have a choice in this because of the limited availability of USDA-inspected facilities, but he did not like putting his animals through the stressful trek to a slaughterhouse. He said there is no set mileage limit for hauling animals, but "the closer the better." His facilities are designed to keep the animals calm.

"The animals are never excited in the process of being dispatched," Harris said. "First of all, it is the right thing to do. We human beings assume dominion over these animals, and that makes us responsible for the stewardship of the animals. Not getting them excited and panicked is the right thing to do. Further, when you panic an animal and it goes into that fight-or-flight mode, it releases adrenaline into the system, and it literally changes the pH in the muscle tissue. And that changes the eating quality of the beef.

"We do it one at a time, the old-fashioned way: a man with a knife. It is just a professional man with a knife generating a quality product for which a sophisticated customer will pay a premium. We are professional cowboys, and we know how to work cattle. It is a full-time job for everybody who works in my plant. It is what they do for a living.

"For every farmer who does not own his or her own plant, it is incumbent upon them to go and be there to see that the processor does it correctly."

Harris runs about 650 cattle on 2,000 acres, which gives him the largest certified organic farm in Georgia. He also has a handful of associate producers raising grass-fed cattle for him. He weans calves at about 8 months old, and fattens to between 1,000 and 1,100 pounds when they are about 22 months old.

He takes advantage of the South's warm climate to provide beef year-round with a calving season that lasts from September to April. His grazing system depends on warm-season perennials including Bermuda grass, Johnson grass, and Bahia grass. In winter, he overseeds cool-season annuals, including rye grass and clover. He also uses a sheep herd to graze down undesirable plants.

He sells much of his meat to the grocery chains Whole Foods and Publix and to upscale Atlanta restaurants, which charge a premium for grass-fed beef. Having his own processing facility gives him even more control over the final product, which ultimately depends on quality. If you are targeting your product to an upscale market, the final product must be as good as it can be.

There a few terms you can use to describe your products according to USDA standards. Here are some examples:

- **No hormones administered**: This lets consumers know that you did not use the growth hormones often given to cattle in industrial operations. (Hormones are not approved for use in poultry, pork, veal calves, or exotic species such as bison and goats, and there are additional requirements if you say "no hormones administered" on products from these species.) You cannot say "no hormones" because animals naturally produce their own hormones.

- **No antibiotics administered**: This lets consumers know that you did not use growth hormones, including a type called ionophores, that often are given to cattle in industrial operations.

- **Natural**: A broad term for "minimally processed and containing no artificial ingredients." Minimally processed means that processing does not fundamentally alter the raw product, which means no chemicals, preservatives, or artificial coloring were added to the meat during or after processing; the label must clarify this. The USDA does not perform additional inspections for meat that is labeled "natural."

Getting Certified

Some customers need the assurance of third-party certifiers before they will pay the premiums prices for organic or grass-fed products. These certifications are most important for customers who do not buy directly from farmers but at specialty grocery stores or restaurants.

It is not required, but you can have your production claims certified by a third-party agency. AMS' Audit, Review, and Compliance branch (**www.ams.usda.gov/ARCaudits**) has a link to a list of accredited agencies at **www.ams.usda.gov/AMSv1.0/ams.fetchTemplateData.do?template=TemplateD&navID=GradingCertificationandVerfication&leftNav=GradingCertificationandVerfication&page=LSISO65Program**.

You must send in your certification papers when you apply for your label application.

The American Grassfed Association offers certification to assure customers that animals were kept outside, raised on pasture-based diets, and were not given growth hormones or antibiotics. To be certified by the AGA, you must be a member. You can find membership info, a list of steps required for certification, and a link to the application on the AGA's website at **www.americangrassfed.org**. If you apply for certification, your farm will be audited to determine if you qualify. If you do not qualify, the AGA will send you a list of adjustments, so you can meet compliance.

Organic certification

Products labeled as organic must not include any hormones or synthetic chemicals, including fertilizers, pesticides, or medicines such as antibiotics. To use this label, you must follow the rules of the National Organic Program and be certified by an accredited agency. There is a complete list of certifiers on the NOP website (**www.ams.usda.gov/AMSv1.0/NOP**).

To become certified, you must submit information to a certifying agent including a list of substances applied to your land over the previous three years, the ways you plan to use the land you want certified, and an official organic plan. An **organic plan** lays out how you will run the organic farm, including what types of feed and fertilizers will be used and where these substances will come from. The plan must include details on the recordkeeping system you plan to use. You must hang on to records about production, harvesting, and handling your organic products.

When you apply for organic certification, an inspector will visit your farm, observe how you do things, and write a report about this inspection. The certifying agency will review your application and the report and determine if you should be certified. If you are certified, you will be inspected once a year and will have to provide updated information about your organic management practices, such as the substances you have applied to your field. Your certifying agent is authorized to conduct unannounced inspections.

Farmers who sell less than $5,000 worth of products per year are not required to obtain certification, but they must keep records of their production practices just in case.

Other certifications

You can use other agencies for your products whose certification may make them more appealing to customers.

- American Humane Certified (**www.americanhumane.org**) is an independent verifier of humane treatment of farm animals.

- Certified Naturally Grown (**www.naturallygrown.org**) is an organization that adheres to principles similar to those of the National Organic Program but seeks to reduce much of the government paperwork and production costs that discourage many small farmers from seeking certification.

Selling Options

You have two options for selling your products: You can sell directly to the customers who will eat them, or you can sell to restaurants, retail outlets, or distributors who will sell to these customers. Selling directly to customers is called direct marketing. The advantages of **direct marketing** are that you can talk to your customers about your product and answer questions for them. Beef farmers who direct market can sell either individual cuts of meat or in bulk.

Bulk sales

If you are starting small and finishing just a handful of animals, you should probably start with bulk sales. **Bulk sales** allow you to get rid of the whole animal. You can sell:

- The whole animal
- A side of beef (half the animal)
- Quarters (either the half the front or half the back of the animal)
- Split sides or split quarters

You can also sell variety packages that include a few steaks and a few pounds of ground beef and stew meat. If you decide to do this, you should still offer small enough packages that households can afford it and have room in the freezer to store it. An empty freezer in a typical refrigerator can hold about 50 pounds of meat. Obviously, families keep more than meat in their freezer. Some farmers sell bulk packages of 30 pounds or less, but many customers who buy in bulk will need a stand-alone chest or freezer.

Individual cuts

You may be able to find outlets to sell individual cuts. Individual cuts are like what you would buy at a grocery or supermarket or restaurant — for example, one steak. Places where you could sell individual cuts include restaurants, which often are eager to buy the best cuts of locally produced beef. You may be able to sell individual cuts to groceries or to retail outlets that specialize in locally produced farm products. For experienced farmers that have a quality product, a food service business is a good outlet. The downside of selling is that it is often hard to get rid of the lower-quality cuts because the most expensive cuts will sell out quickest. Many small farmers find it hard to justify selling individual cuts because customers want the steaks but may not be interested in the stew meat or the tougher cuts. Customers may not appreciate the difference in the quality of your hamburger, which will probably cost more per pound than hamburger at a chain grocery. If you have trouble getting rid of your hamburger, try giving out samples to customers who purchase your more expensive cuts. If you are doing a good job raising your animals, they will notice the difference compared to the cheaper options.

Where to Sell

Most grass-fed cattle farmers will sell their products directly to customers. A small number have been able to get their products into chain supermarkets.

Bulk sales are most common. Locally owned restaurants and groceries are more likely than chains to buy grass-fed products. It is better to call for an appointment than to show up unannounced.

Farmers markets

Farmers markets are places where groups of farmers gather to sell their products. They usually are held outdoors on weekends in public places. Most vendors at farmers markets sell produce, but beef and dairy farmers sometimes set up. Farmers markets usually are held from spring through the fall.

Farmers markets are valuable tools for building a customer base. You can meet potential customers and answer any questions they may have. To entice customers, you could offer information sheets about the nutritional benefits of your products. You also could hand out free samples to people, so they can see for themselves how tasty your products are. Be sure to check with someone at your market to see if you need an extra state license to give out samples.

To sell at a farmers market, you usually need to apply to the person who runs it. You also may have to interview with someone or pay an application fee. Many markets only take applications early in the spring before they open. It might be a good idea to apply to multiple markets because you may not be accepted to your first choice. You could find options on the USDA National Farmers Market Directory (**www.ams.usda.gov/AMSv1.0/FARMERSMARKETS**), which offers an annual count of operational farmers markets across the country. There are about 5,000 farmers markets in the United States. If you are accepted, you will probably have to pay membership dues. These can be between $75 and $150 up front, plus fees of $5 or so per day you set up.

A small-scale beginner who does not have enough products to sell to justify the time spent at a farmers market could find a vendor there to sell your beef for you, said A. Lee Meyer, an extension professor for sustainable agriculture of the University of Kentucky Department of Agricultural Economics. This partnership could work because the vendor will have another product to offer customers, and you will benefit from an experienced seller's skills.

Community Supported Agriculture (CSAs)

Community Supported Agriculture is a system in which community members pay for "shares" of the food a farmer is expected to produce in the upcoming year. The money paid for these shares covers the cost of the farming expenses up front and allows farmers to do much of their marketing work during slow times of year. It ensures that shareholders get first choice of the types of food they want. For beef or dairy products, these shareholders may be buying a stake in a particular animal. The downside to this for customers is that they also share in the risks associated with farming, so if something goes wrong, such as the death of their animal, they may feel like they did not get their money's worth.

The concept of beef pooling, a variation on CSAs, has also been catching on. **Beef pooling**, also called "cow pooling," is another shareholder system in which one customer is in charge of coordinating orders for a group of people who buy in bulk. This person is the go-between for customers and producers, and it is his or her job to make sure all the customers in the pool get what they want. The beef pool coordinator can either ask everyone what cuts they want or take the initiative to divvy everything up so that everyone gets a relatively equal share. These pools also ensure that producers have an outlet for selling their meat.

Milk shares

Milk shares, also called herd shares, is an arrangement that allows people to buy raw milk in some states. (These shares are explicitly illegal in other states; you will have to check with state agriculture officials.) The terms of these shares can vary by farm and could depend on the laws in your state. Often, customers pay a one-time fee for a share and pay farmers a monthly boarding fee for the animal they own a share in. Customers also often pay a deposit on the bottles that hold their milk. Herd shares entitle the owners to a set amount of milk, such as 1 gallon per week for the months cows are milked. Milk usually has to be picked up at the farm; sometimes it can be picked up at a prearranged off-farm site. Sometimes, one person can pick up milk for a group of shareholders. Some farmers will buy back shares from customers who no longer want to participate; others allow shareholders to sell their share to another family. The terms of these shares vary by farm. There may be times of year when your animals are not producing milk; you need to make this clear to the customers.

CASE STUDY: ONLINE MARKETING

Ulla Kjarval
Co-founder: Sheepdog Print and Design
http://sheepdogpd.com

Many farmers have discovered that the Internet is a powerful marketing tool that allows them to reach a broad number of people while spending little money. These farmers are using social media sites as a way to connect with customers and to spread the word about their products. These sites are free and usually only require an e-mail address to join. Ulla Kjarval is a social media consultant who grew up on a grass-fed cattle farm in Meredith, New York, at the foothills of the Catskill Mountains. Her passion is not just the production of healthy food, but the preparation. She writes a food blog, **http://goldilocksfindsmanhattan.blogspot.com**, and with her sister Melkorka, cofounded Sheepdog Print and Design (**http://sheepdogpd.com**), which offers Web design and photography and often works with farmers. Kjarval said these online marketing tools are cheap in that they do not cost money, but they do require a considerable time commitment. The benefit is each farmer can connect to potential customers and tell them about the parts of farming that are important to them.

"Everyone got into farming for different reasons, and everyone farms slightly differently," Kjarval said. "Talking about how you raise the animals, what kind of breed you have, all these things that seem really inane to a farmer are fascinating to someone who is not a farmer and a potential customer."

Kjarval provided the following ways you can use social media to promote your farm's products.

BLOGS

A blog is a kind of online journal (the term blog is a shortened form of the words "Web log"). Writers of blogs write short entries as frequently as several times a day or once every few months. A blog would feature a series of articles, displayed in order from newest to oldest. Two popular blog sites you can choose to host your blog are Blogger (**www.blogger.com**) and Blog.com (**www.blog.com**). Each farmer could tailor a blog to talk about his or her own interests. For example, if your passion is treating animals humanely, you can talk about that; or if you are more interested in the environmental benefits, that could be your focus. Some blogs are dedicated to cooking grass-fed products, rather than the growing. Or, you even could provide updates on your day-to-day activities; for example, one day you could let people know you are calving, and another day you could let people know you have new products available for sale. You also could use a blog as a feature on your own website.

"I think people should start out blogging," Kjarval said. "It is a great way to build confidence and understand what your narrative is. I think it is important to tell a story."

TWITTER

Twitter (**www.twitter.com**) is a free site that lets users broadcast text messages called "tweets" that are 140 characters or fewer. Twitter might be a good choice for farmers who are not comfortable with their writing skills or who do not have the time to write whole blogs. You can set up your Twitter account so you can broadcast tweets from your phone; this would enable you to let people know when, for example, you were out in the field and about to move your cows to a fresh pasture. Users can decide if they want everyone to be able to see their tweets or if they only want certain users to view their tweets. Users who sign up for your tweets are called followers. Twitter also allows you to share links to websites, news stories, photos, and videos. The addresses to these sites, called URLs, are often longer than 140 characters, but you can convert them to a smaller number of characters at the site **http://tiny.cc**.

FACEBOOK

Users of this free site (**www.facebook.com**) create their own profile pages that can highlight their personal information. Once you have a profile, you can become "friends" with other users and share information with each other by broadcasting updates to a news feed. This news feed is a list of all your friends' updates, usually shown with the newest updates first. In their news feed, users only see information posted by their friends. Farmers can use Facebook by starting pages devoted to their farms and potential customers can link up to them by either becoming a friend or becoming a fan. One way you could use Facebook is to update your status to let people know, for example, when you have fresh beef for sale.

"It's like subliminal messaging in a way," Kjarval said. "It is kind of like having an advertisement in people's lives."

YOUTUBE

YouTube is a site that lets you upload and view videos. It is now inexpensive to film videos — handheld Flip video cameras cost less than $150. And the audience is huge — millions of people watch videos on this site. To upload content, you must register with the site. YouTube videos must be less than ten minutes, and the file size must be no more than 2 gigabytes.

FLICKR®

Flickr is a site that lets people upload images and videos so they can be shared with other people. These images can be viewed on albums on the Flickr site or posted on other Web pages. You can upload images to Flickr from your computer or from your cell phone. Once they are uploaded, you can post them on other sites or e-mail them. Flickr asks you to categorize your photos so that they can be found if users are searching for a particular topic, such as "cows" or "grass-fed cows." Yahoo! owns Flickr, so to create an account for the site you also need a Yahoo! account. Farmers could use it to post pictures from their farm or even provide slideshows that serve as a tour of the farm.

E-MAIL

Another simple way to increase sales is to collect e-mail addresses from everyone who buys from you. By doing this, you can reach out to potential customers the next time you have goods for sale. You might even let customers reserve what they want before it is ready.

New farmers could benefit from maintaining an online presence in ways other than marketing, Kjarval said. You will be able to stay in touch with farmers all over the country, and many of these farmers will be willing to share advice and support. YouTube has videos demonstrating many farming tasks that you may not be familiar with. As an example, Kjarval said she knows a new goat farmer who watched video of a goat birth before his own animals delivered. There is even a nonprofit group, the AgChat Foundation, which helps farmers use social media to reach customers and other farmers. You can use Twitter to participate or see this conversation by searching for #AgChat.

Conclusion

Keys to Success in Raising Small Animals

Now that you have read *The Complete Beginner's Guide to Raising Small Animals: Everything You Need to Know About Raising Cows, Sheep, Chickens, Ducks, Rabbits, and More*, you should have a good idea of what kind of animals you want to raise and how to raise them. You should know that you need to be prepared before you buy. That means planning. Being a farmer also means you need to assess how you are doing periodically.

Keys To Success

Know your goals. Are you raising animals for personal consumption or so you can sell the products?

Know your budget. Knowing your budget will help you determine how much land to buy, how many animals to invest in, and how much you can afford to spend on equipment.

Know the needs of the animals. Some animals require a much greater time investment than others. Some breeds are much easier to keep than others. There is a greater learning curve in some cases than others.

Set small, realistic goals. Setting small goals increases your odds of reaching them each season. Making the goals realistic means you are less likely to get discouraged and give up.

Assess your farming achievements at the end of each season. Be honest with yourself. There is always room for improvement.

Do not be discouraged if you make mistakes when you start out. It is a normal part of farming to make mistakes. The important thing is to learn from them.

Keeping Animals Happy and Healthy

Whether you are raising animals as a fun hobby, for personal consumption, as pets, or as your livelihood, if you are keeping animals, then it is up to you to make sure they are happy and healthy. Happy, healthy animals will be easier to care for, cause you less worry, and grow better. They will produce more milk and fiber. In every way, it is in your best interests to take the best possible care of your animals. In addition, when you take good care of your animals you will have the pleasure of knowing you are providing the kind of care for them that they deserve.

Humans have been raising and caring for domestic farm animals for more than 10,000 years. When you keep your animals happy and healthy, you become part of a tradition that goes back millennia. You and your animals share a special bond. Your animals can make you happy and healthy, too.

References

Chapter 2: Rabbits

Bennett, Bob. *Storey's Guide To Raising Rabbits.* North Adams, Massachusetts: Storey, 2009.

Isbell, Connie, and Audrey Pavia. *Rabbits For Dummies.* Hoboken, New Jersey: Wiley, 2009.

"Rabbit: From Farm To Table." United States Department of Agriculture. Washington, D.C. January 12, 2006.

U.S. Rabbit Industry Profile. United States Department of Agriculture. Washington, D.C. June 2002.

Chapter 5: Pigs

Hasheider, Philip. *How To Raise Pigs.* Minneapolis, Minnesota: Voyageur, 2008.

Klober, Kelly. *Storey's Guide To Raising Pigs.* North Adams, Massachusetts: Storey, 2009.

McFarlen, Arie B., PhD. *Pigs.* Laguna Hills, California: BowTie, 2008.

Van Loon, Dirk. *Small-Scale Pig Raising.* Pownal, Vermont: Storey, 1995.

Pig breed associations

American Berkshire Association
P.O. Box 2436
W. Lafayette, IN 47906
765-497-3618
www.americanberkshire.com

American Landrace Association
Member of the National Swine Registry
P.O. Box 2417
W. Lafayette, IN 47996
765-463-3594
www.nationalswine.com

American Mulefoot Hog Association and Registry
18995 V Drive
Tekonsha, MI 49092
517-767-4729

American Yorkshire Club
Member of the National Swine Registry
P.O. Box 2417
W. Lafayette, IN 47996
765-463-3594
www.nationalswine.com

Chester White Registry
Member of Certified Pedigreed Swine (CPS)
P.O. Box 9758
Peoria, IL 61612
309-691-0151
www.cpsswine.com

Hampshire Swine Registry
Member of the National Swine Registry
P.O. Box 2417
W. Lafayette, IN 47996
765-463-3594
www.nationalswine.com

Large Black Pig Registry
c/o Ted Smith
Stillmeadow Farm
740 Lower Myrick Road
Laurel, MS 39440
601-426-2264
stillmeadow@c-gate.net

National Hereford Hog Record Association
c/o Ruby Schrecengost, Secretary
22405 480th Street
Flandreau, SD 57028
605-997-2116

National Spotted Swine Record, Inc.
Member of Certified Pedigreed Swine (CPS)
P.O. Box 9758
Peoria, IL 61612
309-691-0151
www.cpsswine.com

Poland China Record Association
Member of Certified Pedigreed Swine (CPS)
P.O. Box 9758
Peoria, IL 61612
309-691-0151
www.cpsswine.com

Red Wattle Association
c/o Josh Wendland, President
21901 Mayday Road
Barnes, KS 66933
785-944-3574
wendland@twinvalley.net

Tamworth Swine Association
c/o Shirley Brattain
621 N CR 850 W
Greencastle, IN 46135
765-794-0203
brattainfarms@webtv.net

United Duroc Swine Registry
Member of the National Swine Registry
P.O. Box 2417
W. Lafayette, IN 47996
765-463-3594
www.nationalswine.com

Additional organizations

American Livestock Breeds Conservancy
P.O. Box 477
Pittsboro, NC 27312
919-542-5704
www.albc-usa.org

FFA
6060 FFA Drive
Indianapolis, IN 46282
317-802-6060
www.ffa.org

4-H Club
1400 Independence Avenue SW, Stop 2225
Washington, D.C. 20250
202-720-2908
222.4husa.org

National Association of Animal Breeders (NAAB)
P.O. Box 1033
Columbia, MO 65205
573-445-4406
www.naab-css.org

National Pork Producers Council
10664 Justin Drive
Urbandale, IL 50322
515-278-8012
www.nppc.org

Chapter 6: Goats

Feeding goats

Goat Ration Calculator. Langston University. **www.luresext.edu/goats/research/rationbalancer.htm**.

List of Plants Poisonous to Goats. **http://fiascofarm.com/goats/poisonousplants.htm**.

List of Plants Poisonous to Goats. **www.ars.usda.gov/Main/docs.htm?docid=10086**.

List of Plants Poisonous to Goats. **http://netvet.wustl.edu/species/goats/goatpois.txt**.

Rhododendron poisoning antidote. **www.goatworld.com/health/plants/antidotes.shtml**.

Rumen Physiology and Rumination, University of Colorado. **www.vivo.colostate.edu/hbooks/pathphys/digestion/herbivores/rumination.html**.

The Small Ruminant Nutrition System. **http://nutritionmodels.tamu.edu/srns.htm**.

Goat milk

Cheesemaking recipes. **www.agmrc.org/media/cms/zeng04_A2E10C94923B2.pdf**.

Composition of goat milk, courtesy of the USDA. **www.everything-goat-milk.com/goat-milk-table.html**.

Composition of goat milk. **www.dairyforall.com/goatmilk-composition.php**.

Federal requirements for processing milk. **www.federalregister.gov/articles/2010/10/05/2010-24985/milk-for-manufacturing-purposes-and-its-production-and-processing-requirements-recommended-for#p-3**.

Goat Milk Versus Cow Milk. **www.goatworld.com/articles/goatmilk/goatmilk.shtml**.

Information about milking dairy goats. **http://fiascofarm.com/goats/milking.htm**.

Raw milk laws by state. **www.realmilk.com/happening.html**.

The World's Healthiest Foods: Goat milk. **www.whfoods.com/genpage.php?tname=foodspice&dbid=131**.

Goat business references

Coffey, Linda, Margo Hale, and Paul Williams, NCAT Agriculture Specialists. *Dairy Goats: Sustainable Production. Livestock Production Guide.* August 2004. ATTRA Publication #IP258. **http://attra.ncat.org/attra-pub/dairygoats.html**.

General information about goats

American Goat Society, Beginners Guide to Dairy Goats.
www.americangoatsociety.com/registration/pdf/BeginnersGuidetoDairyGoats.pdf.

Best Management Practices for Dairy Goat Farmers, Wisconsin Dairy Goat Association.
www.wdga.org/resources/bmp8.pdf.

Barnet Harris, Jr., and Frederick Springer. *Dairy Goat Production Guide*. University of Florida IFAS Extension, 2009.
http://edis.ifas.ufl.edu/ds134.

Goat anatomy diagrams. **www.dpi.nsw.gov.au/__data/assets/pdf_file/0010/178336/goat-anatomy.pdf**.

Ireland Agricultural and Food Development Authority. **www.teagasc.ie/ruraldev/progs/goats**.

USDA Cooperative Extension System Offices. **www.nifa.usda.gov/Extension/index.html**.

Breeding and raising kids

American Dairy Goat Association (ADGA) genetics. **www.adgagenetics.org**.

Goat Identification Used by Registries. Goat ID. NAIS Working Group. **http://usanimalid.com/registryID.htm**.

National Animal Identification System (NAIS). **www.dhia.org/06%20Feb%20AIN_Admin.pdf**.

Video on bottle-feeding a kid. **www.righthealth.com/topic/bottle_feeding/Anatomy**.

Organizations

Alpines International Breed Club. **www.alpinesinternationalclub.com**.

American Dairy Goat Association. **www.adga.org**.

American Goat Federation. **www.americangoatfederation.org**.

American Goat Society. **www.americangoatsociety.com**.

American LaMancha Club. **www.lamanchas.com**.

International Nubian Breeders Association. **www.i-n-b-a.org**.

Kinder Goat Breeders Association. **www.kindergoatbreeders.com/resources.html**.

Maryland Small Ruminant Page. **www.sheepandgoat.com**.

National Association of Dairy Regulatory Officials (NADRO). **www.nadro.org**.

National Institute of Animal Agriculture (NIAA). **www.animalagriculture.org**.

National Pygmy Goat Association. **www.npga-pygmy.com**.

National Saanen Breeders Association. **http://nationalsaanenbreeders.com**.

National Toggenburg Club. **http://nationaltoggclub.org**.

Nigerian Dwarf Goat Association (NDGA). **www.ndga.org**.

Oberhasli Breeders of America. **http://oberhasli.net**.

USDA Animal and Plant Inspection Services Animal ID. **http://www.aphis.usda.gov/traceability/downloads/NAIS-UserGuide.pdf**.

Plans

Buck goat yard. **http://bioengr.ag.utk.edu/extension/extpubs/Plans/6300.pdf**.

Bucklin, R. A., W. E. Kunkle, and R. S. Sand. "Construction of High Tensile Wire Fences." Document CIR851 of the Agricultural and Biological Engineering Department, Florida Cooperative Extension Service, Institute of Food and Agricultural Sciences, University of Florida. **http://edis.ifas.ufl.edu/ae017**.Goat shelters (**www.goatworld.com/articles/shelters_gwmf.shtml**)

Cadwallader, Tom, and Dennis Cosgrove. "Grounding Electric Fences." University of Wisconsin-Extension. **www2.uwrf.edu/grazing/ground.pdf**.

Metal goat milking stand. **http://bioengr.ag.utk.edu/extension/extpubs/Plans/6399.pdf**.

Mineral feeder. **http://bioengr.ag.utk.edu/extension/extpubs/Plans/5916.pdf**.

Plans for a milking barn and milk house for ten dairy goats. **http://bioengr.ag.utk.edu/extension/extpubs/Plans/6255.pdf**. **http://bioengr.ag.utk.edu/extension/extpubs/Plans/6256.pdf**.

Standalone Hay and Grain Feeder. **http://bioengr.ag.utk.edu/extension/extpubs/Plans/5910.pdf**.

Supplies

Fly predators. **www.spalding-labs.com/Dairy/Default.aspx**.

Hamby Dairy Supply. **http://hambydairysupply.com**.

Hartford Livestock Insurance. **www.hartfordlivestock.com**.

Information on a commercial dairy goat business

Agricultural Alternatives: Dairy Goat Production. Penn State University, 2008. **http://agalternatives.aers.psu.edu/Publications/dairy_goat.pdf**.

Sullivan, Rona. Dairy Goats and a Sustainable Future. **www.dairygoatjournal.com/issues/83/83-6/Rona_Sullivan.html**.

Rutgers University, Table 79: Costs and Returns for Dairy Goat, 1500 lbs Milk/Doe, 100 Doe Herd. **http://aesop.rutgers.edu/~farmmgmt/ne-budgets/organic/DAIRY-GOAT-1500LB-MILK.HTML**.

University of California Cooperative Extension, "2005 Sample Costs for a 500 Dairy Goat Operation." **http://coststudies.ucdavis.edu/files/dairygoatsnc05r.pdf**.)

Bibliography

Belanger, Jerome D. *Storey's Guide to Raising Dairy Goats*. Pownal, Vermont: Storey Books, 2001.

Coffey, Linda, Margo Hale, and Paul Williams, NCAT Agriculture Specialists. "Dairy Goats: Sustainable Production." Livestock Production Guide, August 2004. Accessed March 16, 2011. **http://attra.ncat.org/attra-pub/dairygoats.html#resources**.

Coffey, Linda, NCAT/ATTRA, Langston University Goat & Research Extension. "General Overview: Do You Want To Be A Goat Producer?" Accessed March 23, 2011. **www.luresext.edu/goats/training/general.html#intro**.

Jaudas, Ulrich, Fritz W. Kohler, and Matthew M. Vriends. _The Goat Handbook_. New York: Barron's, 2006.

Luttmann, Gail. _Raising Milk Goats Successfully_. Charlotte, Vermont: Williamson Pub., 1986.

North, Robert. "Anatomy and Physiology of the Goat." NSW Department of Primary Industries. Agfact A7.0.3, second edition 2004. **www.dpi.nsw.gov.au/__data/assets/pdf_file/0010/178336/goat-anatomy.pdf**.

Smith, Cheryl K. _Raising Goats for Dummies_. Hoboken, New Jersey: Wiley, 2010.

USDA–NASS Wisconsin Field Office. _Sheep and Goat Review_. Volume 1, Issue 1, February 2010.

Weaver, Sue. _Goats: Small-scale Herding for Pleasure and Profit_. Hobby Farm Press/BowTie Press, 2006.

Chapter 7: Sheep

"Lamb: From Farm To Table." United States Department of Agriculture. Washington D.C. April 18, 2011.

Simmons, Paula, and Carol Ekarius. _Storey's Guide To Raising Sheep_. North Adams, Massachusetts: Storey, 2009.

Wooster, Chuck. _Living With Sheep: Everything You Need To Know To Raise Your Own Flock_. Guildford, Connecticut: Lyons, 2005.

Chapter 8: Cattle

General information

American Grassfed Association

This organization has the most comprehensive standards about grass-fed cattle. The AGA website is **www.americangrassfed.org**.

Beginning Farmers

The Beginning Farmers website (**http://beginningfarmers.org**) has many resources for new farmers, including a list of land-link programs.

Business Planning

U.S. Small Business Administration (**www.sba.gov**) and county extension offices have checklists and guidelines for creating business plans.

The University of Kentucky College of Agriculture has budgeting examples and decision aid tools at **www.ca.uky.edu/agecon/index.php?p=565**.

The Oklahoma State University Department of Agricultural Economics (**http://agecon.okstate.edu/Quicken**) sells add-on software to use with the budgeting software Quicken® to keep track of farm expenses and income.

Cooperative extension offices

Extension offices are nationwide educational services staffed by experts called extension agents who provide information to farmers, children, small business owners, and others in rural and urban communities. Search a map of the United States for offices in your area at **www.csrees.usda.gov/Extension/index.html**.

Eatwild

Eatwild (**http://eatwild.com**) offers a comprehensive site about the benefits of grass-fed farming. Features research, advice, and lists of grass-fed farmers by state.

Land link programs

There are various online resources for land link programs, which help farmers find land. One of the organizations you can reference is the International Farm Transition Network (**www.farmtransition.org**). The Farm Service Agency advertises properties for sale and gives beginning farmers first priority at **www.resales.usda.gov**.

Legal Info

The website for the U.S. House of Representatives (**www.house.gov**) features a link to U.S. laws. The "government resources" section also links to state government sites where you can find more information about the state laws you must follow.

LocalHarvest

LocalHarvest (**www.localharvest.org**) offers a directory of small and organic farms and farmers markets.

National Sustainable Agriculture Information Service

ATTRA, the common name for the National Sustainable Agriculture Information Service, provides information about sustainable agriculture at **http://attra.ncat.org**.

The Stockman Grass Farmer

This is a respected trade publication with tips for success for farmers who want to make money using management-intensive grazing.

United States Department of Agriculture

This federal agency oversees agriculture production and trade. Offers information and assistance, and makes and enforces laws. Visit its website at **www.usda.gov**.

USDA agencies include:

- Farm Service Agency (FSA) (**www.fsa.usda.gov**)
- USDA Service Center. You can search by state at its website, **http://offices.sc.egov.usda.gov/locator/app**
- To find Natural Resource Conservation Service offices, search at **http://offices.sc.egov.usda.gov/locator/app?agency=nrcs**

Weather Planning

The National Climactic Data Center website (**http://cdo.ncdc.noaa.gov/cgi-bin/climatenormals/climatenormals.pl**) has a searchable database of temperature and precipitation data, including charts that break down the probable dates of first and last freezes in each state, and in different areas of each state.

Marketing Help

California State University Chico has a website for grass-fed cattle farmers that is a good resource for labeling info, including example labels, a guide to creating your own label, links to marketing research. Visit their website at **www.csuchico.edu/agr/grassfedbeef**.

Author Biography

Carlotta Cooper was born and raised in Tennessee. Her grandparents were farmers, and she grew up with horses, dogs, and other animals. Her family raised chickens, ducks, geese, and other poultry, rabbits, and pigs. She attended the University of the South in Sewanee where she graduated with a B.A. in English as class salutatorian. She attended graduate school at the University of Virginia, studied English literature, and did graduate work in writing and rhetoric at the University of Tennessee at Chattanooga.

Professionally, Carlotta is a freelance writer, specializing in writing about animals. She has been breeding and showing dogs for more than 20 years and is a contributing editor for the dog show magazine *Dog News*. She lives in the middle of farm country in Tennessee now and writes about veterinary issues, animal reproduction, genetics, and raising and caring for animals.

Index